TABLE OF CONTENTS

 BASEBALLHQ.COM'S **2020**

MINOR LEAGUE
BASEBALL
ANALYST

PRESENTED BY BASEBALLHQ.COM | BRENT HERSHEY, EDITOR | 15TH EDITION

TRIUMPH
BOOKS

Triumph Books and colophon are registered trademarks of Random House, Inc.

This book is available in quantity at special discounts for your group or organization. For further information, contact:

Triumph Books LLC
814 North Franklin Street
Chicago, Illinois 60610
(312) 337-0747
www.triumphbooks.com

Printed in U.S.A.
ISBN: 978-1-62937-783-4

Data provided by TheBaseballCube.com and Baseball Info Solutions

Cover design by Brent Hershey
Front cover photograph by Kim Klement/USA TODAY Sports

Fifteen Years of 10s: A Revisionist History

by Brent Hershey

We're 15!

Now, that's not much to celebrate in human terms—heck, you can't even drive yet in most states. But in the public baseball prospecting stratosphere, 15 years means we're basically one of the wily veterans. When you've been in it that long, reflection comes with the territory, and we're interested in the perspective that 15 years gives us. As a publication geared toward seeing the future, it seems only natural to look back and evaluate. How did we do? And how can we get better?

Several of the articles in the "Insights" section that follow tap into different parts of this (ahem, "2020") hindsight, and we'll take that general tack here. If you've read us for long, either in these pages, in *Ron Shandler's Baseball Forecaster*, or online at BaseballHQ.com, you know that getting better at our craft is a constant goal.

For this piece, we're going to examine a portion of our player grading scale. The shorthand version of how the scale works: The grades come in two parts. First is a number rating from 1-10, which represents a player's realistic upside upon MLB maturity. A 10 represents a Hall of Fame-level player; down to 1 (minor league roster filler). The second portion is a probability rating, or how likely a player is to reach that upside. That scale runs from A (90% confidence) down to E (10%). For additional info, see our Player Grade Primer on page 5. The grades first appeared in the book's second edition, in 2007, and have continued every year since.

Each year, our *Minor League Baseball Analyst* (MLBA) evaluators/writers to assign this two-part grade for the players they evaluate. It's a challenging process. Many players are still teenagers, or in their early 20s. Their bodies may or may not have filled out. Over time, they may still bulk up, become stronger, but run slower. Arm trouble or other injuries could impede their progress. Or, they may learn how to better identify and lay off an upper-level breaking ball. There's a lot we don't know. But our writers gather information, talk to others, observe players ourselves … and then assign a grade. It becomes one reference point for you, as you build your fantasy teams. It also lives in ink.

Know your 10s

As mentioned above, a "10" grade is the top of the scale. Though the scale's definitions are laid out in terms of real-life MLB outcomes, we use these as a proxy for fantasy utility. In other words, in almost no cases would a "10" player *not* be an elite fantasy option—a first-round pick in a draft, or a $30+ investment in an auction league. A 10 grade is a way of saying that player has the ceiling to be one of most elite players in all of baseball history. And obviously, rostering these consistent, elite players give our fantasy teams a great foundation from which to build.

In one sense, rostering a 10 is the holy grail of prospecting. To be a Hall-of-Famer, a player must present both excellence and longevity. Having a 10-level player on your roster, especially in keeper/dynasty formats, is a distinct advantage. Even for 10-level players with a lower probability letter grade, the fact that such upside exists is undoubtedly important.

Another important point: 10s can be quick movers; so quick that they fly through the minors before we feel comfortable slapping that two-digit grade on their ceiling. Because they are often so talented—something their MLB teams are aware of—they might not spend much time in the minors. Clubs want to get these players into the games that count. So there's a bit of backwards survivor bias here—we may only get one or two offseasons by which to grade them. Once players outgrow their MLB rookie status (50 IP or 130 AB), they no longer qualify for this book.

An additional bit of grading background: For the past handful of seasons, writers have agreed that potential "10" players will be brought up to the group of writers to discuss before the grades are finalized. So that in a sense, recent 10s are more of a mutual decision—though often there is little debate. Prior to this practice, writers were on their own in assigning these grades—which may reflect some minor inconsistencies of approach. But such is the case in any collaborative system such as this.

Given the snapshot of our grading system and a brief look at characteristics of a 10-level player, we thought it could be fun to perform some revisionist history for every player who has been tagged with a 10 grade in the MLBA. For each, we'll examine issues such as: What was the case for giving the player a 10 at that time? Knowing some of how the player's career has developed, what grade has the player earned so far? And given the 10, what are the chances that the player will be an actual Hall of Famer?

We've included all editions since 2007. For the five most recent years, we'll suspend the actual revisionist grading task, since most of those candidates are still in the infant stage of their careers.

Top-of-the-scale talents, 15 years of the *Minor League Baseball Analyst*, and revisionist history. Who's in for a fun trip? We start our journey with the 2020 edition and work our way backwards...

2020: *Wander Franco (10C)*

Franco's amazing hit tool, bat speed, and developing power at such a young age is a great example of attributes we look for in a hitter that is 10-worthy. His tools should age well, and Franco has not really been challenged yet in the minors. He's a quick-mover who might not be eligible for the book next year. For reference, Franco was a 9C in the 2019 edition.

2019: *Vladimir Guerrero, Jr. (10C)*

Different type of player than Franco, but similar hit tool advancement and good plate approach. Prestigious power and exit velocities, and same youthful prodigy (he was entering his age-20 season). Plus, he officially has Hall of Fame bloodlines.

2018: *Ronald Acuña (10D)*

This one is holding up well after one full and one partial season. Unlike Franco/Guerrero, Acuña has considerable SB impact that will likely continue to make him a five-category contributor (and high pick) at least in the near-term. He also was entering his age-20 season after breaking out over three levels (ending in Triple-A) in 2017. Did someone say "Fast-riser"?

2017: *Lucas Giolito (10C); Alex Reyes (10D)*

With successful mechanical tweaks in 2019, Giolito finally gave a whiff of why we gave him a 10, and at his current age of 25, he's got many years ahead of him. Grade here was based on dominating AA/AAA split after a tough start to 2016, in addition to his growing legend of having a top-level arsenal. For Reyes, his elite velocity, hammer curve and success in 46 late-season MLB innings in 2016 also served to justify his 10. While injury risk dinged him down to a D, few outlets had Reyes outside the Top 10 overall given the success of his MLB transition and his killer stuff.

2016: *Lucas Giolito (10C); Alex Reyes (10D); Kolby Allard (10D)*

It's the only time we've had three 10-grade players in one book, but does come with an asterisk. Giolito and Reyes were a year younger of course, but one can see that the hype machine was building for both. These were not one-year wonders. Allard was probably the one 10-grade player in all of these whose performance (as a prep player, he was drafted in 2015) likely didn't warrant the lofty grade in retrospect—something first-year evaluator Chris Blessing readily admits. See Blessing's Tracking Prospect Progression essay on page 7 for more perspective.

Beyond the five most recent years, we should have enough MLB experience to do some revisionist grading of those prospects we once held in the highest regard.

2015 and 2014: *None*

In both years, there were no 10s given out. It's actually good to know that it happens—our evaluators don't feel there *has* to be at least one 10 in every year. However, let's examine a couple significant high grades from those editions and give them a pseudo-regrade treatment.

In 2015, both Byron Buxton and Kris Bryant received 9A grades. Those are players with elite ceilings, and an 90% chance of reaching that upside. If we were to re-grade on a player's career so far, Bryant would likely be straddling the line between an 8 and a 9 player. Certainly, his MVP season in 2016 is elite, and his roto earnings have been $25+ three of the past five years. Some injuries have played a part recently—but overall a very good start to his career.

Buxton, on the other hand, has been a grave disappointment. Like Bryant—even moreso—he's struggled with health, and his contact rate has capped his impact tools. Given how he's performed so far—and yes, injuries are folded in, as it affects experience, performance, everything—he would probably grade out as a 7 (MLB regular) so far.

In 2014, Buxton was our #1 overall prospect, also with a 9A grade. He had just flown through his first full pro season, demolishing two levels of A-ball with a .334/.424/.520 slash to go along with 12 HR and 55 SB. Amazingly, given Buxton's contact problems at the MLB level, his contact rate for 2013 was 79%. By contrast, 2019 was his first MLB season with a contact rate above 69%. There was very, very good reason prospect lists had Buxton at #1 overall starting this season. For us, the three straight years of a 9A rating—he was also 9A in 2016—is likely the only time that has happened in the book's 15-year history.

2013: *Dylan Bundy (10C)*

Bundy had just completed his first full season after being a first-round selection in 2011 (he didn't pitch in the pros that year). Talk about a quick mover: As a 19-year-old, he had blown through two levels of A-ball, 17 innings at Double-A, and finished with two short outings in the majors. His year-long totals were 105.1 IP, 68 H, 119 K, 29 BB, 2.05 ERA and 0.921 WHIP. With a high-90s fastball and two swing-and-miss secondaries, performances that matched the lofty scouting reports, and doing this all as a teenager, this grade was absolutely warranted. Obviously, he's not lived up to the billing; injuries dogged him early on, he now can't crack 92 with his heater, and he's earned more than $5 just once. It happens.

Revisionist: 7. His current profile is the epitome of an MLB regular starting pitcher. He's a rotation mainstay, but has had precious few stints of extended success. There's been lots of ups and downs, but he's never been able to overcome the inconsistency that earmarks a back-end innings eater. Likely health has been a major factor … but boy, what he was in 2012.

2012: *Bryce Harper (10D)*

Like Bundy in 2013 (and many other 10s, as we have and will see), Harper in 2012 had just finished his first full pro season and ended in Double-A at age 18. It wasn't a monster year statistically, but by this time he was the consensus #1 prospect in baseball with top-of-the-scale power (+ + + + + in our terms) and almost as good of a BA bet (+ + + +); a rare combination that other hitters with 10 grades since (Franco, Guerrero, Acuña) have to some degree. So far, Harper's career has been inconsistent from the long view—some injuries early, an MVP season in 2015 in which he earned $41. But his power is not as outstanding in today's game as it was eight years ago, and his eroding strikeout rate now gives him no better expectation than a league-average BA. But he's still on the cusp of the "elite" tier and at 27 years old, is still in the midst of his physical prime.

Revisionist: 9, but just barely—without his MVP season, he's likely more firmly an 8, as he's settled in as a high-K slugger the past three seasons ($25 each year). With at least 12 years of MLB contract ahead of him, he has the early-career base to end up among the all-time greats in Cooperstown. But he'll need to improve and string together some more elite seasons before he hangs 'em up.

2011: *Bryce Harper (10D)*

Gotta hand it to the grader here; it takes guts to make this 10D call on a player without any pro experience. This was the offseason after Harper was selected #1 overall by the Nationals. Even with the most talented player we get reports on, but who have not had a pro AB yet—think Jasson Dominguez of the Yankees as a current rough comparison—our "standard" grade is a 9E; elite potential, but a 10% chance of getting there, largely because we have no data or reports of this player against pro-level pitching. This 10D is something different: the ceiling *and* the probability are higher than a 9E. Even as a revisionist "low 9/high 8" player, there's something to be said for "hitting" on Harper here before he stepped into a pro game.

2010: *Stephen Strasburg (10C)*

See the "guts" comment above; Strasburg followed a similar pattern on his way to this ranking in 2010: first overall pick in 2009 draft, but did not log any pro experience that year. In this case, however, Strasburg had three full seasons at San Diego State, where he dominated college competition while refining his arsenal. His physicality (a developed 6-5, 225 at that point), elite fastball and plus-plus slider are rarer than we might realize. But with a pitcher, and knowing how arm/shoulder injuries can alter a career, a "10C" grade is a sticking-out-of-one's-neck move. But it mostly paid off.

Revisionist: 9. Yes, he's had Tommy John surgery, and other ailments that have landed him on the IL seven times in 10 seasons. But it rarely has affected his performance, and at least right now, he's among the game's elite starting pitchers. The Hall is probably a long shot, given that Strasburg is 31 years old already. Even if his health held up over the next 8-9 years, he would need quite the run of success in his 30s to be considered.

2009: *Matt Wieters (10C)*

The 2008 season was Wieters' first pro year, and he split it almost equally between High-A and Double-A. The combined results were convincing, to say the least: a .355/.454/.600 slash line with 27 HR in 437 AB along with athleticism and arm strength to stay behind the plate. Some of his metrics even improved (contact rate and OPS among them) once he hit Double-A. As a switch-hitter from a major college program (Georgia Tech), it sure seemed like Wieters had the ingredients to put himself among the all-timers.

Revisionist: 7. Much like his eventual teammate Bundy, Wieters' career has been marred by inconsistency and injuries—he struggled to recover much value at all after his Tommy John surgery in 2014. Amazingly, he has yet to have even a double-digit R$ season. He was in starting lineups consistently for most of his career when healthy, and so thus ends up as an MLB regular on the scale. But there's no chance for the Hall for Wieters.

2008: *Jay Bruce (10C)*

Bruce took a different track than most of the other 10s we've examined so far. When he got this rating, he was 21 years old and on the cusp of his MLB debut, having been drafted out of high school in 2005. But the sustained minors excellence as he rose through the ranks in the Reds system was undeniable: he was an established .300 hitter at the full-season level with "an impact bat that produces power and BA" (from his 2008 MLBA commentary). Similar to Harper and others, Bruce's power and BA grades pointed to this dual threat. He was ranked #1 overall on our 2008 top prospects list.

Revisionist: 8, given his five 30-HR seasons to date and a 2010-2013 run where his R$ was in the low-$20s. Bruce's hit tool in the majors never matched his minors promise, as his current MLB career BA mark is .245. In 2008, he was a centerfield prospect, but has only one appearance there outside of 35 games in center in 2008. He will not be in serious consideration for the Hall of Fame.

2008: *Clayton Kershaw (10D)*

Stop me if you've heard this before—but Kershaw's 10 grade was after he blew through two levels of the minors in his first full season. In his case, he dominated both Low-A Midwest League and then continued it in a short Double-A stint (skipping over High-A). At this point, his fastball/change-up combination were both graded higher than his curveball, which was noted for its "good depth." By the end of May 2008, he was making his MLB debut at age 20 and though he earned -$9 that season, he soon hit his stride and then reeled off seven straight seasons of $30+, including three Cy Young Awards and an MVP.

Revisionist: 10. Ahhh, to get one exactly right. Actually, at 32, he's still got some career ahead of him. But even very good performances for the next 5 or so years (and granted, he'll need health, which have slowed him in the past couple seasons) should secure his place in Cooperstown. But probably out of all the 10s we've given out so far—this one is what a mid-career 10 looks like.

2007: *Delmon Young (10D)*

The first year of the grading system, perhaps we can chalk this one up to "learning curve." However, there were lots of things to like about Young at this point in his career. He had performed well in 122 late-season ABs in Tampa in 2006; his commentary noted his "plus bat speed and above average power;" and he had three seasons of 20+ SB. But he also had a bat-throwing suspension on his record (remember that?), and the power and speed portion never materialized at the MLB level. He last appeared in an MLB game in 2015 … at 29 years old.

Revisionist: 7, though with only four seasons of 130+ games played (out of 10 MLB years total), you could also reasonably argue that he should be a 6 (part-timer). Hall of What Did You Say?

2007: *Justin Upton (10E)*

This is an interesting one on several levels. First, it's the only 10E grade we've ever given out, and kind of goes against the idea of providing the most realistic outcome. In other words, if there's a 10% chance that a player will be an impact monster (Hall of Fame material), it's probably conceivable that dropping his number grade back to a 9 raises the probability of him reaching that ceiling. But, a 10E is what Upton was given.

The second note is that although Upton follows the first-full-pro-season-after-being-drafted template (as the #1 overall selection in 2005), he did not have a breakout season statistically in the season prior. He stayed all year at Low-A South Bend, and finished with a .263/.341/.413 slash with 12 HR and 15 SB in 438 AB. But his tool grades were outstanding: a (+ + + +) grade in Power, BA and Defense, and a (+ + + + +; or highest score) in Speed. And his commentary glowed, "Plus athlete with the power, speed and defense necessary to be an impact player." It was truly a grading of tools over results.

Revisionist: Now 32 years old, Upton grades out as an 8. Though he had a couple 20-SB seasons early on, his SB totals have not reflected his top-tier speed grade from 2007. And while he has stayed healthy and hit almost 300 HR in his career so far, only twice did he break the $25 barrier. With four All-Star appearances in 13 seasons, he fits snugly in that category of better than just average MLBer, but not good enough to be considered among the game's elite. It's difficult to imagine a scenario where Upton can put up the numbers in his mid-30s to justify Hall of Fame consideration.

Conclusions

Given the fluctuations of the grading process—different evaluators, changing MLB contexts, the ever-present issue of whether to choose that higher grade/lower probability or lower grade/higher probability—a look back to understand the context of each 10 grade in our history comes out looking pretty good. Even though we now shake our heads at the Bundy or Wieters or even Young grades, almost all of these 10s were justified, given the prospect's previous performance, skills and a likely projection to MLB competition.

Remember that by an evaluator giving the 10D or 10C ranking, they still are saying that the players have no more than a 50% probability of reaching this "best ever" status. So yes, these 10s signify upside, and you want to gather as many of those players on your fantasy roster as possible. But manage your expectations: ultimately getting a "9" or even "8" outcome for those players can be a win for your roster.

In the end, baseball is a hard game. Baseball prospect grading can be just as difficult. But onward we march.

•

Long-time readers of the *Minor League Baseball Analyst* will no doubt recognize most of the elements of the pages that follow in this 15th Edition. For both new and old, let's quickly run through the features and structure.

The Insights section provides some narrative details and tools you can use as you prepare for getting the most out of your farm system and the rookies that will emerge during the 2020 baseball season. All the essays are designed to help you assemble your teams, as well as give you some food for thought on the prospect landscape.

This year, several of the essays (including, we assume, the one you just completed) address our unique grading system and some perspectives on how we've used it in the past. This year, the first Insights essay is a "Primer" on the subject, where we explain in more detail the grading process, and give some real-life examples of what we mean when we give a player an "8C" grade, for instance.

Additional topics in this edition include the further looks at our prospect ranking system, including a primer and deep

dive into the 9E prospect; how the game-wide power surge has affected scouting; reviews of the 2019 Arizona Fall League and the First Year Player Draft; and a preview of the 2020 college baseball season. If the past is any indication, no doubt many of these players mentioned in the essays will soon be fantasy cornerstones. For keeper leagues, the time to get on board is now.

Up next is the HQ100—our signature list of the top 100 fantasy baseball prospects for 2020. The HQ100 is a compilation of seven individual lists (MLBA authors Chris Blessing, Rob Gordon, Alec Dopp, Brent Hershey, Jeremy Deloney, as well as BaseballHQ.com prospect-savvy writers Nick Richards and Matthew St-Germain). This list is ranked by overall fantasy value, in an attempt to balance raw skill level, level of polish/refinement, risk in terms of age/level, and overall potential impact value. And then Dopp suggests 10 more "Sleepers" just outside the HQ100, players who just missed in 2020 or who could make the jump to the list in 2021.

While the HQ100 is a collaborative exercise, the player profiles—including the skills grades, commentaries and player ratings—are the primary work of one analyst. Assignments are divided up by organization, so that our analysts get to know an MLB team's system from top to bottom. Authors and assignments are:

- Chris Blessing (responsible for ATL, MIA, NYM, CIN, TAM, BAL, NYY, CHW, CLE, MIN, KC and SEA)
- Alec Dopp (MIL, CHC, SD, ARI, COL, OAK and LAA)
- Jeremy Deloney (PIT, SF, BOS, TOR, HOU)
- Brent Hershey (PHI, WAS and TEX)
- Rob Gordon (STL and LA)
- Emily Waldon (DET)

Given our emphasis on seeing players in person—and the daunting task when the book covers 900+ players—we did share information and insights with each other, tapping the strength of our team. In addition, each writer filled in the gaps with various scouting and front-office contacts.

Though the player profiles make up the bulk of the book, don't miss the tools that follow: the Major League Equivalencies; the Organization Grades; the Top Prospects by organization, by position, and by specific skills; the Top 75 prospects for 2020 only; an archive of our Top 100 lists; the glossary and a list of minor league affiliates. Whew … there's a lot of information in these pages.

But for now—if you have a suggestion to share, email us at support@baseballhq.com. Otherwise, grab a shovel and dig in. A better fantasy farm system awaits.

Player Grade Primer

by Brent Hershey

What follows is a quick primer on our background and grading system that we hope gives you the proper context to consume the player grades you find in each player box, and referenced in some of the essays. Feel free to refer to this repeatedly as you work your way through this book. Our hope is that the context provides a clear sense of making the most out of our evaluations.

Background

Yes, these are prospect reports, and in one sense they are like the many other quality prospect lists and discussions you'll find in pre-season books and websites that aim to prepare you for the 2020 season. There is one specific characteristic, however, about the *Minor League Baseball Analyst* evaluations that we feel makes them stand out: They are compiled, evaluated and ranked *specifically with fantasy baseball in mind*. We know that you're not just looking for the best prospects; you want the best *fantasy* prospects. As a fantasy baseball-specific publication, we feel it's our task to do that "translation" for you. Our writers write and editors edit with the goal of how much a player will contribute to a fantasy baseball roster. Among a few of their considerations that may help you:

Position(s) matters. For instance, almost all fantasy leagues require a catcher. Given the lower bar offensively for that position, we attempt to adjust when we evaluate backstops. Finding a catcher who consistently contributes on offense can be a challenging endeavor. Given how much emphasis is put on a rookie catcher's defense, and learning to manage a big-league staff upon his promotion, it often takes time for the bat to "catch up." We attempt to account for that, because finding a reliable catcher who can contribute to your fantasy squad is a huge built-in advantage. And knowing who to stay away from can be just as valuable.

Speed matters. Given the recent MLB downturn in stolen bases and SB attempts overall, those players who are successfully able to compile stolen bases continue to increase in value. Of course, SB totals in the minors are not always the best proxy for MLB SB success—pitchers and catchers are better equipped at the majors, for one thing, and there's always the question of whether the player can either hit or get on base enough. And we haven't even broached the subject of having a manager who uses that weapon in today's launch angle environment. All that's to say we take special care in evaluating speed-first players, because if they make it and can become reliable SB sources at the MLB level, they will have a unique skill set for impacting our fantasy baseball teams.

Defense matters. This point has long been touted on the opposite side: Defense doesn't matter when evaluating MLB prospects for fantasy utility; we only worry about the bat. But given the growing importance in the real-life game on position flexibility and players able to play multiple positions, it's past time to consider defensive flexibility as an important part of prospect evaluation. Prospects who are able to play MLB-quality defense at several positions are many times more likely to get opportunities

to play (which equals more AB) than, say, a player who is merely adequate defensively at just one position. The MLB game's shift to carrying more pitchers on the active roster almost means that bench players especially *have* to be capable at several positions. And it's even better if some of a teams' starting eight position players can "double up" on positions. So while no, it doesn't matter how many errors in the field a certain top-hitting shortstop makes for fantasy baseball purposes, it may matter just how many positions a player can adequately man that will be the difference between a big-league roster spot and one at Triple-A.

A pitcher's "stuff" matters. With strikeouts in the game continuing to rise, and with some multi-inning relievers knocking on the 100-K door each year, pitchers who can get whiffs continue to garner attention. Now, it's obviously only one tool: As Kyle Crick or Robert Stephenson shows, having some baseline of control, command, secondary pitches still matter—and a lack of such will eventually force a pitcher to the bullpen. But in general, we'll rate a high-K, wild pitcher higher than a Low-A change-up artist with a 2.00 ERA. Yes, a pitcher's stuff can improve, but showing the raw skills of pitch movement and getting swings-and-misses seems to project better to fantasy success than pitchers cruising on average velocity and overall arsenal but pinpoint control.

There are more elements to this complex process, of course, but those are just some examples of elements that this volume's writers take into account that may differ from other "baseball-only value" lists.

Lastly, with the above, it may seem curious that we still break up our writing assignments by MLB team—after all, beyond -only leagues, which MLB team a player is on has very little bearing as to a player's future value. The answer, for now … is that it's just the easiest way to produce this material. In our case—like other outlets—we have one analyst solely responsible for each individual organization (see specific assignments in the introductory essay). It helps with our workload of attempting to see with live looks as many of these players as we can throughout the season. And it helps because each of the evaluators fills in the gaps with information from contacts who have see the players in person.

The Grade

Minor League Baseball Analyst and BaseballHQ.com's unique grading system was developed by Deric McKamey, a former prospect writer and current scout for the St. Louis Cardinals. The system debuted in the 2007 edition of this book, and we've been using it in subsequent MLBAs and on our site ever since. While the scale is listed on the introductory Batters and Pitchers pages, sometimes there's some confusion for both new and old readers on the specifics of the system. So we'll take some time here to explain how we best intend to use it along with some examples of current MLB players.

The system is a two-part scale: A number grade comes first, which represents a player's upside—at full MLB maturity—not at the present day. And then a letter grade follows, which attaches some probability that the player reaches that upside. Let's break these elements down even further.

Upside

Upside, of course, is what we're all chasing in this prospecting endeavor. We want to get the highest performing players onto our fantasy rosters, even if we have to wait a bit for the production to materialize. And that's exactly why we use this measure—we want to help identify which players have the highest upside, regardless of other factors.

As analysts, our goal is to be realistic as possible with this number grade. This is why not everyone is a 10—even though, in the purest technical sense, there's still the infinitesimal chance that you or I would be a Hall of Fame-caliber player. Each analyst brings their own perspective and experience to providing these number grades. It comes from years of scouting players, seeing comps, realizing who worked out, who improved, who didn't—and understanding to the best of their ability the "whys" behind those examples.

Let's run through the top five levels of number grades here with the "key"—but also with several corresponding established MLB players at their current level to help level-set our expectations. And of course, some of these players can still move up or down a tier as their careers develop. This is just a snapshot of who they are now:

Gr	Description	Current Example Player
10	Potential Hall of Famer	Mike Trout, Nolan Arenado Justin Verlander, Clayton Kershaw
9	Potential Elite Player	Mookie Betts, Christian Yelich, Aaron Judge Gerrit Cole, Stephen Strasburg, Aroldis Chapman
8	Potential Solid Regular	Carlos Santana, Elvis Andrus, Justin Turner Masahio Tanaka, Robbie Ray, Sonny Gray, Raisel Iglesias
7	Potential Average Regular	Nomar Mazara, Caesar Hernandez JA Happ, Jake Odorizzi, Julio Teheran
6	Potential Platoon Player	Raimel Tapia, Freddy Galvis Daniel Norris, Matt Strahm, Jordan Lyles

So as you consume these number grades, you may find the examples above helpful given some of their real-life production levels.

Probability/risk

The second part of the Grade is a letter, given in the A-E academic scale. The letter portion is best thought of as a proxy for risk: Essentially, it is the probability that the evaluator thinks the player will reach his upside grade. We break it down into percentages, like this:

A: 90% probability of reaching potential
B: 70% probability of reaching potential
C: 50% probability of reaching potential
D: 30% probability of reaching potential
E: 10% probability of reaching potential

It's best to remember that this is *not* how close a player is to the majors—though that is one small aspect of the letter grade— as in, proven production at higher levels of the minors usually increases a player's probability grade. For instance, a player who has performed well against AA competition has some aspect of a smaller risk than a Low-A teenager.

Other things that can affect a players' letter grade:

Quality makeup. Here are two examples of makeup that could affect a player's letter grade positively: A drivenness to put in the work to improve, and/or the ability to block out other distractions and keenly focus on his craft.

A sense of conquering foundational skills that can "set the table" for further overall improvement. Think of a Low-A pitcher with impeccable ability to throw strikes, or a Double-A hitter who can just put the bat on the ball. Even if there are other aspects of these players' skill sets that are deficient—say, the pitcher can't command his fastball and the hitter has not yet developed in-game power—sometimes the foundational skills are building blocks for skills that come later. Recognizing these different tools and knowing how to express them in the letter grade is one of the things we ask our evaluators to consider.

Note that a lower letter grade that indicates more risk may include:

Concerns about a player staying healthy. If he has trouble in the minors, how likely is that to continue as he climbs the ladder?

Lack of fundamental baseball skills. This is the flip side of the above. We see this in toolsy but undisciplined players, sometimes pure athletes who have come to baseball later in their youth and have to refine their hitting mechanics or strike zone judgment. A pitcher might throw hard and have a nasty offspeed swing and miss pitch, but can't find the plate.

Makeup that might hold a player back from improving. Of course, judging and grading makeup is one of the toughest calls. But that still goes into our thought process.

One essential takeaway: not all players with the same grade are created equal. That's why it's so important to not just look at the grade; the real work our crew does is in the written comments, where we break down a player's tools/skills and attempt to give a snapshot of the player's future. Related, don't obsess over the differences in the grade. Yes, for sure, an 8B and a 9C are very close and there is some merit to saying that every 8B could easily also be graded a 9C. But we ask our evaluators to make a call, and provide them space in the comments to give their understanding of this player's potential future. In the end, *you* make the call for *your* team. Some fantasy owners don't mind the risk, and just want to shoot for upside. It is likely those owners will have more 9Ds on their roster. Others may want more sure things, and are going to lean towards the 8As and 8Bs, or even 7As, who are meant to have lower risk in their profiles. It's just how this works.

Conclusion

We do all of this knowing that there will instances when we will be wrong; and those when we'll be right—such as our early-career reports on Juan Soto (9C) and Walker Buehler (9B) and Rafael Devers (9C). Fantasy or not, both hits and misses are the nature of this business. But we hope you will find value in our work to help guide your decisions for your teams.

Tracking Prospect Progression

by Chris Blessing

In the *Minor League Baseball Analyst*, we make it easy to track prospect performance with player stats and sabermetrics in more than three dozen categories. A large part of the player box shows past prospect performance as well (the five most recent affiliate stops). What we fail to show you is our rating of a prospect in past editions of the book. Why?

Simply, it shouldn't matter. Our evaluation is based on a snapshot, which takes place after the season is completed.

What is a snapshot?

The snapshot occurs when the author assigned to the MLB team sits down in front of the computer and files a report—the player capsule. By then, authors have already compiled both quantitative and qualitative data—and in many cases, likely over-analyzed the information we collected. Some prospects are easy to write up—mostly the top 25% and the lower 25% of the prospects we cover. The more difficult writeups, the ones we spend the most time on, are those 50% in the middle. Some are solid regular players with less than 30% probability of reaching the projected role. Some are the players who grade out to average. The exceptions are the ones we project at a 90% probability of reaching their role.

Any sort of evaluation method—both inside and outside of baseball—is a snapshot. The evaluation is based on past performance, accurate comparable and sound data, whether quantitative or qualitative. Take real estate appraising, for instance. If you were buying or refinancing a house, a bank appraiser would aim to look at similar properties in similar neighborhoods that have sold during the past six months to arrive at the property's expected fair market value. An appraiser's snapshot isn't projecting anticipated growth in the future; it is projecting a fair market value for a property in a moment of time. If you were to go sell the house eight months after your appraisal, the bank would require the buyer to get a new appraisal done, because the data compiled about the market in the previous appraisal would be out of date.

It's the same for prospect evaluations. Every year, our snapshot occurs at a moment of time. Instead of appraising inanimate objects like houses, we're projecting human beings. When prospects are younger, they may have immense tool sheds, like 2020 Yankees top prospect Jasson Dominguez. Dominguez, who signed as a 16-year-old this past July out of the Dominican Republic, has been compared athletically to guys like Yasiel Puig and Bo Jackson. Obviously, my snapshot of Dominguez—a 9E player rating—doesn't include much certainty. My evaluation tells you he could potentially be elite but I have no idea how he takes to coaching, develops his body (and baseball IQ), avoids major injuries, adjusts to pro pitching, recognizes spin or any other attribute needed to reach his elite ceiling.

Then, take a prospect like the Diamondbacks' Seth Beer. We know he's a 1B/DH only prospect, has performed well in the upper minors and has an MLB skillset. In ranking him a 7A prospect, Alec Dopp, the MLBA writer assigned to the Diamondbacks organization, evaluates Beer to be an average contributor at a 90%

certainty. In other words, Beer's an MLB asset but isn't expected to be a top performer.

The snapshots in this book are intended for fantasy owners to make roster decisions based on the best available evaluations from our prospect team. Often, fantasy owners get caught up in making decisions based on past evaluations. For good reason, I call this the Kolby Allard effect.

The Kolby Allard Effect

The Kolby Allard Effect is the phenomenon of fantasy owners placing an importance on past evaluations as justification to hold onto declining investments. It's like saying that an NL dynasty owner should pick up Mets prospect Stephen Gonsalves because several outlets, including this one, had Gonsalves as a Top 100 prospect once upon a time. Waived by the Twins in 2019 and picked up by the Mets, Gonsalves right now projects to be a #5 starter/swingman (a 6B rating in the pages that follow).

There are so many prospects I could name this after, like Stephen Gonsalves. But I chose Kolby Allard for two reasons. First, Allard graduated from prospect coverage in 2019 and, although he struggled in his debut, looks to be a serviceable MLB arm. It's easier to name something after a prospect who made it. The second reason I picked Allard is I had made a splash with Allard in the 2016 MLBA by grading him with a lofty 10D. I blame a little bit of my rating on being a first-timer with the potential rating system. While I didn't see Allard pitch in 2015, I had two glowing reports from reputable contacts I continue to go to for pre-draft scouting reports on prospects. The 17-year-old Allard had present pitchability as a prep LHP, solid mechanics, physical projection, athleticism and three pitches that all flashed plus. But calling him a "Hall of Fame" contributor (our "10" rating) was a bit much, and a lesson I continue to go back to whenever feeling too high on a prospect.

However, in the next two MLBAs (2017 and 2018), I ranked Allard a 9D and 9C, even while other evaluators were cautioning his stuff wasn't up to par for a frontline starter. I kept seeing Allard on his best days and ignoring obvious warning signs, like inconsistent velocity between starts and Allard's history of back injuries. By MLBA 2019, Allard had dropped to a 7B prospect, a rating I spent more time dissecting than any other rating in that off-season. From this perspective, it seems like the 2019 rating was an accurate depiction of what Allard's MLB career could be.

Let's track the grades of a few current prospects who have multiple MLBA appearances to see if we've given our readers further confirmation of a prospect's skill set, or reasons to drop specific prospects.

Rays LHP/DH Brendan McKay

Most prospects, even the top ones, will be downgraded by a number grade in development. In November 2019, after the Tampa Bay Organization Report published at BaseballHQ.com, a reader of BaseballHQ.com's subscriber forums asked for an explanation on why McKay saw his rating drop from a 9C in 2019 to an 8A this season. While the subscriber was only referencing McKay's pitcher rating, his hitter rating dropped from an 8D to a 7C as well (McKay, the hitter, did not make the Tampa Top 15).

McKay has had a unique path in our book since being drafted in 2017. In the 2018 MLBA, Jeremy Deloney wrote up McKay's player box in the hitter's section only and rated him an 8C. In the 2019 MLBA and this year's book, I've written him up as both a hitter and a pitcher. As a hitter in 2019, McKay was an 8D prospect; this year, he's a 7C. Without improvement, he's likely just a pitcher with an interesting power bat.

There were things we all loved about McKay's offensive ability in his draft year and first full professional season. I loved his stroke and the power display he put together in batting practice without breaking a sweat. However, neither Jeremy nor I ever ranked him as an elite hitter. I never bought into his history of production. Sure, he slashed .341/.457/.659 his junior year at Louisville. However, much of his damage was against mid-week SPs (college #4/#5/swingmen); he never faced a team's top starter because he pitched on those days and his production against #2s and #3s was not impressive.

I don't see McKay's pitching potential rating drop between this season and last as a downgrade. My 9C rating from 2019 gave him a 50/50 chance of being elite. I relied heavily on two scouting contacts, both organization scouts, and my own video and analytic analysis for McKay's 9C rating in 2019. One contact put potential plus-or-better grades on three of McKay's five pitches and had the other two potentially average-or-better offerings. My second contact wasn't as high on McKay's curve or slider as the first scout was. However, he felt the whole package was above-average-or-better stuff and projected him as a #2 starter.

Fast forward to this season and my 8A grade. Again, I relied on two scouting contact looks like last year. This year, I had MLB. tv looks, Baseball Savant Statcast data from MLB action and even some spin rate reports from the minor leagues. None of his pitches appeared to take a step forward in development. I now project an average-to-above-average arsenal across the board for McKay, which is the skillset of a solid fantasy contributor or #3/#4 starter.

While these skills didn't show up consistently in his MLB sample, they were still evident in the minor leagues. We've entered more of a present projection for McKay than a future projection. 8A works because I believe in improved pitchability from last year's debut combined with the current stuff playing like a mid-rotation SP at times already. To me, the Dom and Ctl potential is still there from the 9C rating. However, the projection for low H/9 and HR/FB rates is in the rearview mirror with the stuff backing up from my previous expectations.

There have been no signs in MLBA to drop McKay as a pitcher or dual performer. However, the commentary in McKay's hitters box this year is enough reason to likely sell McKay if rostered as a hitter only.

Phillies OF Cornelius Randolph

Cornelius Randolph has been a fixture in these pages for the last 5 seasons. Brent Hershey, who handles the Phillies organization for the book and website, has written each one of Randolph's player boxes. In the 2016 MLBA, just after the Phillies took Randolph in the first round, Hershey rated Randolph a 9D and wrote the following commentary:

Best pure hitter in the 2015 high school class. Has an enviable combination of elite bat speed, balanced approach and excellent plate discipline. Already uses entire field has good pitch recognition skills; home-run power is expected develop as he matures. Doesn't run well, and average arm limits him to LF, but the bat will carry him.

Obviously, the Philadelphia amateur scouting department really liked Randolph and thought he'd adjust to pro ball, even though he was 17 years old when he was drafted. The 9D rating appears justifiable. Then, the reports kept skewing downward. In 2017, Randolph, rated an 8D prospect, dealt with shoulder/back injuries, was showing patience and a balanced approach but was struggling to find power in his game. Brent's commentary was still positive because Randolph still had time to hone his skills. By the 2018 version of the book, the tone in Brent's commentary began to change and so did Randolph's player rating, which dropped to 7D.

Still young but progressing slower than expected. Sprays singles to all fields, but extra-base pop is mainly restricted to his pull side, though did adjust swing for more power in 2017. Has sufficient bat speed but expands the zone often and struggles with LHP. Arm and questionable route-running limits him to LF.

MLBA 2018 should have been the jumping-off point for Randolph owners. We use a scouting term for prospects like Randolph called "tweener". A tweener is a profile in between roles. Sometimes it's not enough power for a corner outfielder but not enough speed/defense for a center fielder, but in this case, he's between a usable OF role and an unusable OF role. With Randolph relegated to LF, he would need his bat, specifically his power tool, to carry his player profile. Without it, he was primed to end up in the unusable pile. Since the 2018 MLBA, Randolph's potential rating has continued to drop and has bottomed out as a 6B in this year's edition. And MLB teams obviously agree, as Randolph was not protected for the Rule 5 draft in December, and ultimately not selected.

Reds RHP Vladimir Gutierrez

Vladimir Gutierrez has spent one less season than Randolph in these pages, but the outcome is becoming practically the same. Now, Gutierrez was never a top prospect. The highest rating placed on him (8D) was when he debuted in the 2017 MLBA after signing with Cincinnati as a teenager. However, he was a 7A in 2018 after it looked as though the Reds had bought into Gutierrez as a two-pitch reliever. Here is my writeup from that year:

Converted RH starter made US debut after defecting from Cuba. Throws two variants of FB, a 91-93 mph two-seam FB with solid arm-side run and drop and a 94-95 mph 4-seam FB with tailing action. Features power 11-5 power CB with solid depth and violent break. CU very much a project. Gives pitch away by slowing delivery. Solid build.

The Reds tried Gutierrez as a starter the next season. In 2019, I downgraded Gutierrez's grade to a 7C, even though his secondary pitches continued to refine. Although, the break of his CB was missing, which took away Gutierrez's only true out pitch.

Slim, athletic hurler's underlying metrics were better than his 2018 outcome. A three-pitch pitcher, he lacks a plus offering. Relies on command and consistent plane to achieve swing and misses with FB. Two-seamer hits spots, and not afraid to elevate, especially against RHH. 12-6 CB is refined and his CU flashes average.

This profile is a very generic profile. Unless your format values #4/#5 types like this, this was probably a good jumping-off point for Gutierrez owners. It got worse in the 2019 season, with command woes entering the picture in Triple-A, causing Gutierrez's potential rating to drop to 6B in this year's book.

Conclusion

It usually does not pay to hold onto past scouting evaluations when evaluating present prospect profiles. While scanning past reports can be helpful to see how a player has or has not developed, once you identify aspects that are not improving, you can get caught holding onto a declining prospect. Resist the temptation to justify a roster spot for a player an evaluator was high on 3 or 4 seasons ago but isn't high on now. Seeing the warning signs—often as lack of development—in the prospect examples posted above will help you make roster decisions this year and into the future. Happy prospecting!

The Evolving Scouting Environment: Power Evaluations

by Chris Blessing

Throughout 2019 on BaseballHQ.com, I explored how technology and analytics continue to change baseball. I explored how the industry has evolved in certain areas through data, video, biometric science & physical science, including how scouting departments find players and how player development departments develop prospects. One area where the scouting community is adjusting to changing trends is with power projection.

BaseballHQ.com doesn't use the future role/future value 20-80 scale to project prospect roles like team-based scouts do. Rather, we use a Potential Rating system. You can find our Potential and Probability rating chart for prospects on pages 25 and 71, as well as a Primer essay on page 5. Our evaluator/writer assigns a number rating to the player for upside potential and a letter rating to the player for probability of reaching the potential grade. But for scouting a specific tool, like power, we use the 20-80 scouting scale. The chart below is the 20-80 scouting skill chart with grades and ranges of expected MLB outcomes (Power/Hit) as well as run times (from bat/ball contact to touching first base).

Scout Grade	Power (HR)	Hit (BA)	Speed (LHH)	Speed (RHH)
80	39+	.320+	3.9 Secs	4.0 Secs
70	32-38	.300-.319	4.0 Secs	4.1 Secs
60	25-31	.286-.299	4.1 Secs	4.2 Secs
50	17-24	.270-.285	4.2 Secs	4.3 Secs
40	11-16	.250-.269	4.3 Secs	4.4 Secs
30	6-10	.220-.249	4.4 Secs	4.5 Secs
20	0-5	.219-	4.5 Secs	4.6 Secs

MLB Power Update

To understand how to project power in the Statcast age, let's first look at how power plays today. In 2019, 44 hitters hit enough HR to "qualify" as double-plus power (32+ HR; 70-grade or higher), up from 22 hitters in the same range in 2018. From 2016-2018, on average 25 hitters hit for 32+ HR, which was up significantly from the previous six years (2010-2015) when 14 hitters on average hit for 32+ HR. The increase from 14 to 25 double-plus HR hitters is the effect of technology and new coaching techniques for hitters.

Hitters are adjusting their swing trajectory to maximize loft. Radar systems and high-speed cameras—like Rapsodo and Edgertronic—allow hitters and coaches to track impact points and spin rates to determine the proper amount of backspin needed to generate productive loft. K-vests help hitters and coaches find biometric weaknesses in swings. These technological advances have led to better coaching techniques and have created better power hitters as a result. However, the bump from 25 double-plus power hitters to 44 double-plus power hitters in 2019 isn't only technology or coaching techniques. It also has to do with the juiced baseball.

We know the altered ball existed in 2019; we'd be fools to speculate on whether it will return for 2020. But certainly it has affected our overall research. But in the end, home runs are up no matter what, mostly a derivative of the change in coaching techniques brought on by technological advancement and analytical analysis. Juiced ball or no juiced ball, front offices, the scouting community, prospect media and fantasy owners can't deny the need to increase power expectations for prospect hitters.

Scouting Power

How scouts evaluate power hasn't changed much. Sure, there are a lot more hitters selling out for pull power and/or more vertical swing trajectory for over-the-fence power than ever before. Yet bat speed stirs the overall hitting package, which reflects strongly on the power tool. It doesn't matter if a scout is laying their eyes on a high school sophomore for the first time, Arizona State University's Spencer Torkelson or White Sox prospect Luis Robert, bat speed will determine whether the prospect should be followed or not. Combine bat speed with attributes such as physical strength, swing trajectory, barrel feel, hitting approach and the spin of the baseball coming off the bat (backspin over topspin for power) and you've got all the things scouts look for to project power.

Let's pick two vastly different prospects with similar bat quickness but little else in common: Jo Adell (Angels) and Nick Madrigal (White Sox). Looking at their size and physical projection, Adell overwhelmingly has more physical power projection, and a swing trajectory advantage as well. He uses lower-half leverage and an upper-cut swing to elevate the ball. Meanwhile, Madrigal has a flatter swing, which doesn't lend itself to creating loft and is more likely to result in line-drive, topspin-heavy contact. Both hitters have a feel for the barrel. However, Adell has much more control of the barrel, which helps Adell drive balls out to all fields in batting practice and, sometimes, in the game. Adell also has the approach for power edge over Madrigal, by a lot. With the eyes, Adell is an 80-raw, 70-game power prospect while Madrigal is a 30-raw, 30-game power prospect.

Projecting Power

For so long, we've relied on the traditional scouting scale to project out power. Using the power chart above and plugging in the grades, Jo Adell projects to hit 32-38 bombs while Nick Madrigal tops out between 6-10 HR. In today's game, I believe Adell would absolutely destroy the 32-38 HR range, especially given recent trends.

Because the power ranges on the scouting scale can't quite be trusted anymore, we need to find a better way. It might be reworking the HR scouting scale or using another metric scale altogether to grade out power projection. Or, perhaps, a combination of both. One metric is well-suited for just this: Isolated Power (ISO).

Isolated Power

We've been so consumed by projecting HR totals, we forget that power encompasses all types of extra-base hits (XBH). We can call Edwin Encarnacion a HR hitter or project Nick Madrigal as a doubles hitter but what does it mean if a single type of hit is making up most of one's power grade? On the other hand, ISO gives credit to all forms of power.

There are three formulas to calculate ISO

- 2B + 2*3B + 3*HR over AB = ISO
- Extra Bases over AB = ISO
- SLG – AVG = ISO

Researching this article, a scouting contact suggested I look into ISO as a projection tool, citing a handful of teams are already using this metric in their grading scales. The more I researched ISO, the more it made sense for projection. However, the juiced ball has wrecked the ISO scale, much the same as our HR scouting scale. Here is the ISO scale I've always used, courtesy of FanGraphs, and the number of hitters over .250 ISO since 2010.

Rating	ISO
Excellent	.250
Great	.200
Above Average	.170
Average	.140
Below Average	.120
Poor	.100
Awful	.080

Year	Batters >.250 ISO
2010	11
2011	9
2012	9
2013	5
2014	7
2015	12
2016	16
2017	22
2018	14
2019	34

The explosion in ISO has corresponded with the Statcast era and other technological and analytical advances. However, with the juiced baseball, ISO values absolutely exploded. 7 hitters had an ISO .300 or better in 2019. From 2010-2018, we had 13 hitters total with .300 or better ISO.

The trend shows power is up across the board due to the new coaching techniques brought on by new technology, and analytics. 2019 could be the outlier, especially if the juiced ball doesn't come back. However, the trend has been established in the majors. What about in the minor leagues?

Minor Leagues

Is power up in the upper minors (Double-A & Triple-A)? It's difficult to say for several reasons. First including 2019 Triple-A stats, yes—but they also used the same ball as big leaguers did. Second, overall HR and ISO numbers haven't seen the same upward trends we've seen in MLB. Third, the data set is tainted because most top performers don't end up staying at a level for an entire season—they graduate to the majors, for instance.

Because so many hitters move between levels, I used home run to fly ball ratio (HR/FB) to gauge HR power and used ISO, just like I've done with big leaguers, to gauge overall power. There were absolutely no trends visible in Double-A looking at either measure. Big power guys in Double-A often haven't really amounted to much in MLB, and these players dominated the sample. There was no spike in power production between 2015-2019. In fact, top power is down from the previous 5-year period.

In Triple-A, the MLB juiced ball has absolutely wrecked the 2019 sample. Thirty-seven hitters hit for an ISO greater than .250. From 2015-2018, 30 hitters hit for an ISO greater than .250. Looking at HR/FB, 17 hitters had a HR/FB greater than 25% in 2019. From 2010-2018, 14 hitters combined had a HR/FB greater than 25%. I believe a 2019 increase would have existed regardless of what MLB ball showed up in Triple-A. The minor league ball is cheaper and much easier for pitchers to manipulate due to the size, feel and height of the seams. However, the juiced ball made the increase in power numbers look ridiculous.

Scouting adjusts to MLB trends—the outcomes on the field, which drive our fantasy games—not minor league trends. MLB trends dictate it's time to adjust both the traditional power scale and the ISO scale to better depict power in today's game.

Modernizing Traditional & ISO Scales

First, we must determine what average production is on either scale. Looking at our old scouting scale, 17-24 HR is considered average production—which works out to 21.5 as a mean of the two values. The new HR mean, looking at qualified hitters, is the high end of our average chart: 24 HR. The new average range should be 21-27 HR. Here is the old traditional power scale next to the new traditional power scale below.

Old Power Scale (HR)	Scout Grade	Revised Power Scale (HR)
39+	80	42+
32-38	70	35-41
25-31	60	28-33
17-24	50	21-27
11-16	40	15-20
6-10	30	8-14
0-5	20	0-7

For our ISO scale, .140 was considered average before this era of production. The new mean, looking at qualified hitters, is .50 points higher at .190. To guard against possible regression due to potential ball changes, I've set the new ISO average at .180. Here's our old ISO scale next to the new ISO scale.

Old ISO Scale	Rating	Revised ISO Scale
.250	Excellent	.300
.200	Great	.240
.170	Above Average	.210
.140	Average	.180
.120	Below Average	.160
.100	Poor	.140
.080	Awful	.120

Adapting ISO to 20-80 Scouting Scale

The language between the 20-80 scouting scale and ISO scouting scale is similar yet different. An 80-grade tool is considered elite, 70-grade is double-plus, 60-grade is plus, 50-grade is average and so-on. The ISO charts, though, use different language for the upper levels. To use the ISO scale in scouting, we must conform to scouting language and grades. I've also provided 2019 examples and current prospects I would project out for each of the given power grades.

Gr	Tool Name	ISO	2019 Example	Prospect (Projected)
80	Elite	.340	Christian Yelich	Never do this to a kid
70	Plus-plus	.300	Cody Bellinger	Jo Adell
60	Plus	.240	Nolan Arenado	Luis Robert
55	Above-average	.210	Francisco Lindor	Ronny Mauricio
50	Average	.180	Starling Marte	Evan White
45	Below-Average	.160	Eric Hosmer	Greg Jones
40	40	.140	Adam Eaton	Kyle Isbel
30	30	.120	Brandon Crawford	Nick Madrigal
20	20	.119-	David Fletcher	Alfredo Rodriguez

Using Scouting Scales to Project Future Power Output

Now that we've determined the scouting projection scale to use, how do we utilize them? If your league only has HR as a power category, it's a no-brainer which scale you'll rely heavily on: the HR scouting scale. However, don't sleep on the ISO scouting scale, since it likely determines who has a better chance of producing in other categories like OPS. As your league gets deeper in analytical categories, the more important the ISO scouting scale becomes.

From 2011-2014, Alex Gordon was a perfect example of a hitter who the ISO scale favored over the HR scale. In a standard stat league, the average HR output was on the low end of the average on the traditional power chart. However, in a points league, Gordon was an undervalued commodity given his ability to hit doubles and triples, which was reflected in his ISO. He averaged .170 ISO over the time span and peaked at .200 ISO in 2011. In other words, Gordon was an above-average ISO power hitter over the time span and a plus ISO power hitter in 2011, hitting 23 HR (average power on the traditional scale) and 72 total XBH. There are always guys outperforming traditional power grades with ISO, like Brandon Lowe and Austin Meadows. Prospects who should outperform their traditional power grades with ISO include Nico Hoerner and Evan White.

We'd be doing our readers a disservice by not adjusting to power trends. As you use this book as your resource for building your fantasy farm system, realize the new power charts correspond with our PWR skills projections in each hitter's player box (left-hand side, below their name. A "+ + +" power skill rating equals average power, which corresponds with 21-27 HR and a .180 ISO.

Here's to finding the next power prospect in your farm system!

A Look at the 9E Player

by Chris Blessing

At First Pitch Arizona 2018, several BaseballHQ.com writers participated in a discussion about the grading scale we use for evaluating prospects on the BaseballHQ.com website and in the *Minor League Baseball Analyst*. Our grading scale, developed by Deric McKamey, former lead BHQ prospect writer and current St. Louis Cardinals scout, is different from the traditional 20-80 grading scale that scouts and other media outlets use.

Our Potential Ratings grading scale is a two-part system in which a player is assigned a number rating based on his upside (1-10) and a letter based on the probability of reaching that potential (A-E). (Find the complete scale on pages 25 and 71). Those ratings are assigned each offseason by the writer responsible for that player's MLB team. So if a player is handed an 8A rating, the player's potential is of a solid regular, with a 90% probability of reaching that potential.

For instance, this year writer Alec Dopp, responsible for the Oakland Athletics, assigned an 8A to prospect and likely Opening Day catcher Sean Murphy. Having scouted Murphy myself, I agree with Alec. Murphy has strong underlying metrics (ct%, bb%, and Eye) throughout his development, maintained those levels in his MLB debut at the end of 2019 and has added over-the-fence power without compromising his plate skills. This profile is the definition of a future solid regular contributor, even with the threat of wear and tear from catching.

Our discussion at First Pitch turned towards a specific rating on the scale and what it tells us about the player: the 9E prospect. Using our Potential Ratings grading system, a 9E prospect has Elite Player ability, but only a 10% probability of reaching that ceiling.

I've never been the biggest proponent of the 9E prospect. I learned my craft on the 20-80 scale, which doesn't account for separate probability ratings, except within the report. In a sense, the 20-80 grade one assigns is cut and dried. It is the role the evaluator envisions the prospect filling in the big leagues. If I slap a 60 OFP (Overall Future Potential) or a Role 6 grade (the equivalent of a 60 OFP) on a pitcher, I project the pitcher as either a #2 or #3 starter or a solid closer in major-league terms. If the player was a hitter, I'd project an everyday performer at the position, like Alec's Sean Murphy's projection at catcher.

Especially after listening to the spirited conversation on the 9E grade, I understand better why some of our writers and subscribers like the 9E grade, and even target 9E prospects deep in drafts. In the 2019 edition of this book, the collective group placed 9E grades on 21 hitters and 17 pitchers. I graded almost half of our 9E prospects, which seems awfully high for someone who doesn't really like using the rating.

I went searching for guidance and some historical perspective to better identify future 9E prospects in this year's edition.

Guidance

I've never met Deric McKamey, but after reading his methodology on the Potential Ratings, I believe my grasp for the rating system is fairly close to his intended focus. Here's a quote from

Deric in the *2007 Minor League Baseball Analyst* (MLBA) after the Potential Ratings System was introduced during the 2006 season:

> *"I try to stress upside when using the potential ratings, but am realistic and factor in the role I believe the player will have at the Major League level. The probability component to the rating is based on the chance that the player would achieve his upside potential."*

My overall feel for Deric's intended use of the Potential Ratings System is solid. However, after reading this explanation, I realized that my rating of some of the 18 prospects I called 9E prospects in last year's MLBA was short-sighted. In retrospect, were outfielders Monte Harrison of the Marlins or Seuly Matias of the Royals elite prospects going into 2019? If you squint your eyes hard enough, possibly, but I project it's a very minute chance either guy ends up as elite. Realistically, Harrison and Matias would have been better graded as 8D prospects. At best, Harrison is a high-strikeout, low-average run-and-power-tool guy, and Matias is likely a plus-plus power-only guy. This year, I would have upgraded Harrison to an 8C rating after he showed improvement across-the-board. However, due to health concerns, mid-season wrist surgery, I brought his grade back down to an 8D. Matias regressed significantly with his bat; I downgraded his rating to a 7E.

Historical Perspective

Since I believe I'm over-evaluating some 9E prospects, let's look back at some 9E prospects from the past. We'll scan these players for 2014 level, 2019 outcomes and if they are still in the 2020 book. First, from the 2015 MLBA, which was the year before I contributed to the book.

2015 MLBA 9E Hitters

Name	2014 Org/Level	2019 Org/Level	Status	2020 MLBA
OF Angel Moreno	TAM/Rookie	Unknown	Intact	Not incl
1B Dominic Smith	NYM/Single-A	NYM/MLB	Graduated	Not elig
3B Ti'Quan Forbes	TEX/Rookie	CHW/Double-A	Intact	Not incl
1B Bobby Bradley	CLE/Rookie	CLE/Triple-A	Intact	7C
OF Eloy Jimenez	CHC/Rookie	CHW/MLB	Graduated	Not elig
OF Jose Pujols	PHI/Low-A	PHI/Double-A	Intact	Not incl
SS Jorge Mateo	NYY/Rookie	OAK/Triple-A	Intact	7A
OF Phillip Ervin	CIN/Single-A	CIN/MLB	Graduated	Not elig

Every one of these position players was accurately portrayed with the 9E prospect rating, as each had a plus-plus player ceiling with a low percentage of reaching their ceiling. As we look back at 2015 hitters, only Angel Moreno, who played for the Cardinals' Low-A affiliate State College in 2018, is unaccounted for in affiliated ball. The best of the 2015 9E class is Eloy Jimenez, who is on the verge of superstardom with the White Sox. Other notable players included Dominic Smith, Bobby Bradley, and Jorge Mateo. Also, notice every position prospect rated 9E in 2015 were lower minor prospects. No one was above Single-A.

Now on to the pitchers:

2015 MLBA 9E Pitchers

Name	2014 Org/Level	2019 Org/Level	Status	2020 MLBA
RHP Franklyn Kilome	PHI/Rookie	NYM/Double-A	Intact	7D
LHP Matthew Smoral	TOR/Low-A	N/A/N/A	Intact	Not incl
LHP Kodi Medeiros	MIL/Rookie	CHW/Double-A	Intact	Not incl
RHP Touki Toussaint	ARI/Rookie	ATL/MLB	Graduated	Not elig
LHP Trey Ball	BOS/Single-A	BOS/Double-A	Intact	Not incl
RHP Erick Fedde	WAS/DNP	WAS/Double-A	Graduated	Not elig
RHP Michael Kopech	BOS/Rookie	CHW/MLB	Intact	9C

Another accurately depicted group of 9E prospects. Only Matthew Smoral, who was a high-upside LHP riddled with injuries throughout his career, is out of baseball. The big fish in this grouping is Michael Kopech, who was just a high-octane thrower in 2014. The rest of the group has been relatively underwhelming except Touki Toussaint, who will likely fill an RP role due to poor fastball command. Like the position prospects, no 2015 9E pitching prospect was above Single-A.

Verdict

The common thread of all 9E prospects is a high volatility of outcomes. Both hitters and pitchers fit into a range of outcomes. For hitters, the scale is from Eloy Jimenez to Angel Moreno; for pitchers, the scale, which appears to be volatile, is from Michael Kopech to Matthew Smoral.

Though each year is different, it does seem that I may have overvalued 9E prospects in MLBA 2019. In 2019, I covered 11 organizations (SF, CIN, NYM, MIA, ATL, SEA, MIN, CHW, KC, BAL, NYY, TB). The chart that follows re-examines prospects I rated as 9E from the 2019 MLBA.

In looking back, I disqualified six prospects to whom I originally have an 9E rating. Earlier, I spoke about the reasons for changing Harrison's and Matias' ratings. For others, I would have changed ratings for Marlins OF Connor Scott (amended to 8E), Marlins RHP Sandy Alcantara (amended to 8B), White Sox RHP Zack Burdi (amended to 8E) and White Sox RHP Dylan Cease (amended to 9D). These changes aren't based on 2019 performance, but rather the blueprint McKamey left for us in MLBA 2007 and the levels/ages/performances of 2015 MLBA 9E prospects. Here's an amended list of last year's revised 9E prospects from those 11 organizations I covered, with 2020 MLBA Potential Rating included.

Chris' 9E 2019 MLBA Prospects (Amended)

Name	Org	Reason for 9E Grade	2020 MLBA
OF Antonio Cabello	NYY	Five-tool potential with baseball feel	8E
C M.J. Melendez	KC	Elite fantasy power tools, present ct% issues	7E
OF Luis Robert	CHW	Elite tool shed, needs finish	9C
OF Mariel Bautista	CIN	Older lower level prospect who finds barrel	7D
OF Everson Pereira	NYY	Very unrefined 5-tool prospect	8E
OF Julio Rodriguez	SEA	Top DSL prospect making jump to Single-A	9C
SS Wander Javier	MIN	Plus hit/run tool; missed 2018 w/ injury	8E
OF Heliot Ramos	SF	Extremely raw approach w/ plus-plus barrel rate	8B
LHP Matt Liberatore	TAM	Pitchability with stuff; some durability concerns	8C
RHP Gr. Rodriguez	BAL	Big FB/CB combo, raw skills	9D
RHP Shane Baz	TAM	Big stuff, repeated rookie ball	8D
LHP Daniel Lynch	KC	Added velo to pitchability profile in 2019	9C

Pairing down from 18 to 12 has mostly defined the 9E prospect as a lower-level prospect with multiple plus or plus-plus tools, but little finish. Most 9E prospects should also be teenagers. There are few exceptions, like 21-year-old Mariel Bautista, who looked to have put things together in Rookie Ball, and 22-year-old Daniel Lynch, who added 5 mph to his pitches before being drafted, which turned pedestrian stuff into potentially plus pitches. There's also 21-year-old Luis Robert, who struggled with injury and pitch recognition despite ending 2018 in High-A.

Being able to see our rating scale in action from year-to-year shows you how we're able to nail down the most accurate outcomes for these prospects. In this year's book, Jeremy Deloney, assigned the Giants coverage, zeroed in on Heliot Ramos' rating by taking a full season of refinement and performance under consideration, which resulted in a lower upside grade but much more certainty in rating (8B). On the other hand, my evaluation dropped substantially for Royals catcher M.J. Melendez. His ct% in High-A careened off the side of a steep hill. He went from a potential elite upside prospect to an average upside prospect with the same level of uncertainty (7E).

Putting 9E Principles in Practice (2020)

Let's take a look at 9E hitters in the pages that follow in this year's book. Four of our six MLBA player box writers, Alec Dopp (AD), Brent Hershey (BH), Jeremy Deloney (JD) and yours truly (CB), rated at least one hitting prospect a 9E prospect. We have 10 hitters total; all were teenage prospects during the 2019 season. Included are quick notes from the writers on the "why" of each player/ranking.

Name	Org/Level	Reason for 9E grade	Evaluator
SS Antoni Flores	BOS/Low-A	5-tool athlete lacking baseball finish	JD
OF Bayron Lora	TEX/DNP	Man-child body at 18; huge pwr potential	BH
OF Brennen Davis	CHC/Single-A	Tooled up, uber-athletic OF with raw skills	AD
OF Erick Pena	KC/DNP	Lightning quick hands; lacks refinement	CB
SS Ger. Perdomo	ARI/High-A	Adv feel; questionable power potential	AD
OF Jass. Dominguez	NYY/DNP	Built-like NFL athlete; 5-tool potential	CB
SS Maximo Acosta	TEX/DNP	5-tool potential MIF; intangibles	BH
SS Noevi Marte	SEA/Rookie	Toolsy, powerful SS; yet make U.S. debut	CB
SS Orelvis Martinez	TOR/Rookie	Adv hitter; yet to face advanced levels	JD
SS Robert Puason	OAK/DNP	5-tool skills with feel for hitting	AD

Interesting to note that five of our 9E hitters are international prospects signed in the summer of 2019. The state of international scouting has changed drastically, as most Latin American prospects agree to contracts two to four years before their signings are announced (though the practice is technically against the rules). As such, they are no longer appearing at showcase events and many evaluators are going off old data. On the other hand, coverage of the organization-based fall instructional leagues, in which many of these teenagers participate, is improving. So more and more video has come out to show us how incredibly raw these 16- and 17-year-olds are. In many cases, that coverage just further justifies the 9E ranking—incredibly athletic players in deep need of baseball reps and polish.

For example, sure, Erick Pena (OF, KC) has unbelievable bat speed. However, all parts of his swing are extremely raw. The talent is there for a 9 rating, but no one in their right mind is staking the claim at this point that an "elite" rating is a likely outcome. Thus, the 9E fits Pena perfectly: high upside, extreme risk for him to get there. Once we have more data, statistics, video and in-person reports on Pena's pro games, then our grades will shift, hopefully to a more certain outcome. As we move towards covering international prospects in our MLBA player boxes, you'll see more 9E and 8E grades being applied.

Conclusion

Our goal with the 9E ranking is to identify the rawest lower-level prospects quickly and promptly. Prospect evaluation is a hype-driven subset of the player pool. For all of our ratings, ultimate fantasy utility is our goal; we as a prospect team and MLBA authors gain nothing on pinning unrealistic expectations on prospects. The 9E rating will continue to be the most speculative rating we place on prospects because we're evaluating the rawest, most elite prospects. Proper identification on our end at all the various points of evaluation will go a long way towards helping you have prolonged dynasty success.

2019 Arizona Fall League Risers and Fallers

by Alec Dopp

Evaluating prospects at the Arizona Fall League can be tricky. On one hand, a large percentage of players are sent there to make up for lost time due to injury during the regular season, and in some instances may still not be completely healthy at any point during league play. On the other hand, some prospects are sent to see how they can handle uber-advanced competition they wouldn't normally be exposed to. Similarly, other prospects are just there to accrue additional playing time. It's a mixed bag.

That being said, there always seems to be a handful of players who stand out more than others, and also those who trended in the opposite direction over the course of six weeks. As we do every year in this book, let's try to identify those players right now.

Risers

Greg Deichmann (OF, OAK): Deichmann was arguably the poster child of the 2019 AFL, as the 24-year-old OF tattooed 9 HR *en route* to a league-best .634 SLG. The former 2nd round pick missed time in AA due to a shoulder injury in 2019, but seems to be back to full strength and possibly ready for a PCL breakout in 2020. He has average ct% ability and can struggle vs. LHP at times, but he owns plus-plus raw power that should materialize in HR/RBI value, and he could get a cup of coffee with the major-league club in 2020

Vidal Brujan (2B/SS, TAM): Brujan was not necessarily a household name coming into 2019, but had a terrific AFL campaign in which he slashed .256/.380/.463 with 9 XBH and 4 SB in just 22 G could change that rather quickly. A middle infielder from the Dominican Republic, Brujan stole 24 bases in 55 G as a mere 21-year-old in AA last season and projects to have elite SB upside with his plus-plus speed. A bit undersized, he also shows good feel for the strike zone as a LHB, possesses high-volume gap power, and has potentially big upside in OBP formats.

Spencer Howard (RHP, PHI): Philadelphia's top prospect heading into 2020, Howard spent extended time on the IL in 2019 due to a shoulder strain, but returned strong from it in the desert, posting a 0.94 WHIP and 27 strikeouts in 21.1 IP with Scottsdale. Howard can touch 99 mph with his fastball and sustain his velocity deep into games, and he blends in an advanced changeup and solid slider/curveball combo to go along with it. His strong Dom track record dates back to his days at Cal Poly, and he projects to be at least a quality mid-rotation SP.

Bubba Thompson (OF, TEX): The 27th overall pick from 2017, Thompson made two trips to the High-A IL in 2019 due to hamate bone and foot injuries and that presumably played a role in his .573 OPS in 57 G. He looked much better in the AFL, hitting .254 with 3 HR and 5 SB in 21 G for Surprise. When healthy, Thompson flashes elite speed that could lead to 40+ SB and a projectable body that could hold at least average HR output. His approach and feel for hitting aren't spectacular, but with some added contact, he has upside as an everyday CF.

Kyle Isbel (OF, KC): Isbel spent extended time on the IL in 2019 with a wrist injury, after which he hit just .176/.236/.277 with 3 HR in 39 games in High-A. He was one of the more impressive bats in the AFL, though, posting a .315 BA, 15% walk rate, and 6-for-7 success rate on SB attempts. The former third-rounder has a chance for solid tools across the board. He employs a line-drive stroke conducive to solid ct% and is a plus runner with some SB upside. His swing doesn't produce a ton of loft and he may be a HR burden, but he could have BA/R/SB value.

Fallers

Jeren Kendall (OF, LA): A former power-speed threat at Vanderbilt, Kendall hit a career-high 19 HR with good underlying power metrics in High-A in 2019, but a .210/.279/.323 slash with a 50% ct% in the AFL did not help his stock. Though he still possesses plus-plus speed for SB value and is a dynamic glove defensively, Kendall's bat-to-ball skills are highly questionable and he continues to witness a steep upward trend in both his fly-ball rate and pull-rate, which means he comes with major BA downside. He's more of a deep-league target in OBP formats.

Dakota Chalmers (RHP, MIN): Oakland's third-round pick back in 2016, Chalmers sat out almost all of 2018 and 2019 after undergoing Tommy John surgery nearly two years ago. His 2019 AFL campaign yielded mixed results with Salt River, posting a 1.64 WHIP and 14% walk rate across 17.2 IP. The 23-year-old righty has the ability to miss bats with a solid three-pitch mix, including a fastball that can hit 98 mph, and a changeup and curve that both have good shape and action. However, his clear lack of command at this stage of his development is worrisome.

Jonathan India (INF, CIN): India was the fifth overall pick in the 2018 draft from the Florida Gators and posted solid numbers in A+/AA in 2019, including a .259/.365/.402 line with 11 HR and 11 SB in 121 G. His production with Glendale curtailed a bit, however, as he hit just .133 over 18 G with a 65% ct% in that span. India was among the most disciplined hitters in the SEC, but his BB/K ratio dwindled in full-season ball and in the AFL, and while it may just be the effect of a long first pro season, it's enough to raise an eyebrow and could be a concern moving forward.

Bryan Mata (RHP, BOS): Boston's sixth-ranked prospect heading into 2020, Mata displayed palpable Ctl gains as one of the youngest arms in AA in 2019. His time spent with Peoria as a late-inning RP this fall saw some regression (5.23 ERA, 11 BB, 10 K in 10.1 IP), though. Mata is still very young, has plus velocity on his fastball, and has some feel for spinning his curve and hard slider. His changeup currently lags behind his other offerings. He'll need to work on being more consistent with his control and command to reach his mid-rotation ceiling.

2019 First-Year Player Draft Recap
by Jeremy Deloney (AL) and Rob Gordon (NL)

AMERICAN LEAGUE

BALTIMORE ORIOLES
With the second-largest bonus pool available, the Orioles had a chance to inject their system with a lot of talent. They identified offense as an area of opportunity. The highlight, of course, is C Adley Rutschman (1) who immediately becomes their top prospect and among the best prospects in the entire sport. He could ascend the minor league ladder quickly. High school SS Gunnar Henderson (2) was signed to a $2.3M bonus and fared well in his pro debut. OF Kyle Stowers (S-2) doesn't stand out in any one facet of the game, but has all-around skills that could benefit the big league club within 2-3 years.
Sleeper: RHP Dan Hammer (13) showed in his pro debut that his stats matched his quality underlying stuff. With three solid average offerings in his repertoire, the college righty posted a 1.29 ERA, 3.3 Ctl and 10.5 Dom in 35 short-season innings.
Grade: A-

BOSTON RED SOX
The Red Sox did not have a first-round pick and were saddled with the lowest bonus pool of any team. Given that, they drafted extremely well. Boston selected shortstops – one college (Cameron Cannon) and one prep (Matthew Lugo) – with their first two picks before opting for two solid college RHP in rounds 3 and 4 (Ryan Zeferjahn and Noah Song, though Song will need to serve a two-year military commitment). They were able to allocate their bonus pool wisely with four draftees getting at least $500k, including 13th rounder RHP Blake Loubier, a high school RHP. Outside of Lugo, a highly projectable hitter, the Red Sox selected college players with 9 of their first 10 picks.
Sleeper: OF Dean Miller (24) was only signed to a $5,000 bonus, but he has already exceeded expectations in his first pro experience. He offers above-average power and a keen understanding of the strike zone.
Grade: B

CHICAGO WHITE SOX
This was a top-heavy draft; the White Sox spent $2M+ on each of their top three picks before inking the players selected in rounds 5 through 10 to $10k each. They had the fifth-highest draft pool and clearly focused on their top picks. 1B Andrew Vaughn (1) is a proven hitter who can hit for both BA and power. He finished the season with 107 AB with High-A Winston-Salem. The next three picks were all high schoolers. RHPs Matthew Thompson (2) and Andrew Dalquist (3) give Chicago some upside and both were signed to $2M bonuses. They were very limited in their pro debuts and may spend another year in short-season ball. The success of this draft will depend entirely on their top three picks.
Sleeper: 3B Damon Gladney (16) has legitimate swing-and-miss concerns, but he can inject a ton of power with the ability to hit for BA. He is also very crude defensively, but the White Sox hope that professional coaching will help.
Grade: B

CLEVELAND INDIANS
The first four picks were all from the high school ranks, including two shortstops—Yordys Valdes (2) and Christian Cairo (4). The top pick, RHP Daniel Espinio (1), has incredible raw stuff with a fastball that can reach triple digits. Add in two quality breaking balls and you have a legitimate high-upside prospect. Valdes is a defensive-oriented infielder who will likely be at shortstop long-term. The bat is a serious question, however. Cairo, on the other hand, isn't as polished defensively but can swing the bat, albeit with little pop. The Indians signed their first 25 selections and were able to effectively spread out their bonus pool. While the majority of their draftees are long-term projects, the haul does offer upside.
Sleeper: 1B Will Bartlett (9) has a big, strong frame that should withstand the rigors of the pro grind. He has above-average power potential to go along with a strong arm. He saw time as a backstop in high school, but 1B is the likely long-term spot.
Grade: B-

DETROIT TIGERS
Given the influx of premium arms in the system, the Tigers switched gears and put the focus on bats for this draft. They selected hitters with their first six picks, including OF Riley Greene (1) with the fifth overall selection. Greene's upside is huge and he earned 96 AB in Low-A as an 18-year-old. After Greene, the Tigers went the college route for the remainder of the draft with the exception of an unsigned 39th rounder. College infielders—3B Nick Quintana (2), 3B Andre Lipcius (3) and SS Ryan Kreidler (4)—were the next three selections and offer a variety of skills, though none can match the upside of Greene. The Tigers hope that RHP Zack Hess (7) can reach the majors quickly as a hard-throwing reliever.
Sleeper: LF Corey Packard (5) is a big, strong hitter who feasted on pro pitching in his debut, batting .297/.391/.420 with 3 HR in 138 AB between short-season and High-A ball. His secondary skills lack, but he is a professional hitter.
Grade: B-

HOUSTON ASTROS
The Astros had the third-lowest pool from which to sign draftees, which may have been a factor in their surprise selection of C Korey Lee (1) with the 32nd overall pick. While he performed admirably, he lacks the premium upside and talent of other first-round picks. Houston spent the vast majority of their picks from the college ranks with only one high school selection in the first 17 rounds. Additionally, five of the first six were hitters. OF Jordan Brewer (3) may have the most upside of any in the Astros draft class while SS Grae Kessinger (2) is a fairly polished college infielder who could tap into his power with a modified approach. RHP Hunter Brown (5) is a small college draftee who could end up being the best selection for Houston in this draft.
Sleeper: RHP Peyton Battenfield (9) has a big, durable frame and could be used as either a starter or reliever. He throws harder in short stints, but he has three average offerings from which to work. He posted a 1.60 ERA and 10.5 Dom in his pro debut.
Grade: C-

KANSAS CITY ROYALS

With the second overall pick, the Royals may have landed their future cornerstone, franchise player in SS Bobby Witt, Jr. (1). Signed to a $7.8M bonus, he offers all five tools with the hit tool being the only potential question. Kansas City then opted for another shortstop, Brady McConnell (2) from Florida, with their next selection. The top two picks totaled $10M in bonuses, but that was no concern given the Royals had the third-highest pool. College RHPs were next with Alec Marsh (S-2) and Grant Gambrell (3). Both weren't standouts in their respective pro debuts, but will likely try their hands in Low-A for 2020. This was a college-heavy draft and some pitchers—LHP Dante Biasi (6), in particular—could move quickly.

Sleeper: OF Burle Dixon (18) has good size (6'5" 185 lbs) and athleticism and could become a solid big league contributor with professional coaching. He struck out far too often upon signing but has power, speed, and defensive ability.

Grade: B-

LOS ANGELES ANGELS

In an early move, the Angels have already traded their first pick, SS Will Wilson (1), to the Giants in an effort to clear salary for the signing of Anthony Rendon. That leaves the next three picks all from high school. SS Kyren Paris (2), RHP Jack Kochanowicz (3) and OF Erik Rivera (4) all offer intriguing skills from which to build. All will likely stay in the lower minors for a few seasons. Paris, in particular, is young for the class—he didn't turn 18 until November—but he is starting to grow into his lean frame and should be able to stick at SS. The Angels focused on college arms in rounds 5 through 12. If a few of these pitchers pan out, potentially in the bullpen, this could be one of the more underrated draft hauls.

Sleeper: RHP Greg Veliz (15) was transitioned to the bullpen in his last year in college and thrived in that role. He works off of a low-to-mid 90s fastball and solid-average slider. He showed flashes in 13 appearances with Low-A Burlington in his debut.

Grade: C

MINNESOTA TWINS

The need for athletic infielders was satisfied with shortstops being taken with four of the Twins top eight selections, headlined by SS Keoni Cavaco (1) with the 13th overall pick. Two other college shortstops are also highly-regarded: Spencer Steer (3) from Oregon and Will Holland (5) from Auburn. There was also have a heavy dose of college performers - Cavaco was the only high school prospect signed by Minnesota. RHP Matt Canterino (2) was the highest-drafted pitcher by the Twins and he was highly impressive in five starts in Low-A: 1.35 ERA, 3.2 Ctl and 11.3 Dom. OF Matt Wallner (S-1) is a prototypical RF with plus power potential and an extremely strong arm.

Sleeper: 2B Eduoard Julien (18) was inked to a signing bonus just under $500k out of Auburn and has a chance to be a power-hitting infielder, though he underwent Tommy John surgery in August.

Grade: B

NEW YORK YANKEES

Some thought the Yankees reached a bit when they selected prep SS Anthony Volpe (1) with the 30th overall pick. Signed to a $2.7M bonus from a New Jersey high school, he struggled in his pro debut, but many scouts love his makeup, defensive abilities, and instincts. After that, the Yankees focused on college prospects and didn't select another high school player until the 20th round. They added three left-handed pitchers to the system in their first six picks. Highlighted by LHP TJ Sikkema (S-1), the Yankees also opted for LHP Jake Agnos (4) and LHP Ken Waldichuk (5). They have high hopes for college 2B Josh Smith (2) who has high OBP skills with above-average raw power.

Sleeper: RHP Mitch Spence (10) was a starter in college, but the Yankees appear to prefer him in the bullpen. His pro career got off to a great start with a 3.54 ERA, 4 saves, 1.3 Ctl, and 9.3 Dom in 16 games. He touches the mid-90s and gets a ton of grounders.

Grade: C-

OAKLAND ATHLETICS

Few organizations can match the eclectic mix of prospects the Athletics selected. With a strong mix of high schoolers and college players to pitchers and position players, Oakland spread out their bonus pool effectively and efficiently. SS Logan Davidson (1) and RHP Tyler Baum (2) were the top two selections and both have impressive pedigrees and upsides. Davidson is a true shortstop who can hit and Baum has excellent pure stuff. Two college catchers, Kyle McCann (4) and Drew Millas (7), have opposite skill sets from one another. McCann is better with the bat while Millas is a standout defensively. OF Marcus Smith (3) may be a project, but he is among the fastest draftees and is a terrific CF.

Sleeper: 1B/3B Dustin Harris (11) was a junior college selection who exceeded expectations with his hitting acumen. He batted .330/.407/.425 with 2 HR and 9 SB between rookie ball and short-season.

Grade: B

SEATTLE MARINERS

There is a pitching need in the organization and the Mariners added a number of excellent arms by selecting pitchers with their first five selections and nine of their first 11. The first nine picks all signed for six-figure bonuses, headlined by RHP George Kirby (1) who inked a $3.2M bonus. He had the best strikeout to walk ratio in NCAA and carried that into pro ball where he didn't walk a batter in 23 innings. He uses four offerings with his change-up possibly being the best. LHP Brandon Williamson (2) was considered a stretch with the 59th overall pick, but he offers projection and a deep repertoire. RHP Isaiah Campbell (S-2) may be the best overall hurler of the lot and has the potential of a mid-rotation starter.

Sleeper: C Carter Bins (11) was known mostly for his above-average defense going into the draft, yet he stood out for his improved stroke and power. There are some flaws, but he was better than anticipated in his pro debut.

Grade: B-

TAMPA BAY RAYS

Only a few organizations can match the haul selected by the Rays. With three of the first 40 overall picks and 5 of the first 99, the Rays filled in a lot of gaps in the organization. They opted for pitching with eight of their first 11 picks, including three college left-handers in the first five rounds. They eventually signed four prospects to a seven-figure bonus. The gem may be SS Greg Jones (1), a switch-hitting infielder who may be the fastest player in the draft. He hit .330/.407/.454 in his debut. LHP John Doxakis (2) was a standout as a pro as well, posting a 1.93 ERA in 32.2 innings. He is more about deception than pure heat and he throws consistent strikes. Keep an eye on RHP J.J. Goss (S-1) who has pure arm strength and a terrific slider.

Sleeper: 1B Jake Guenther (7) stands 6'4" 230 pounds and has a mature approach from the left side of the plate. Scouts question his power, but he makes easy, hard contact and runs well for his size.

Grade: A-

TEXAS RANGERS

The Rangers selected two college third basemen in the first and supplemental first rounds. 3B Josh Jung (1) immediately becomes one of their top prospects while 3B Davis Wendzel (S-1) also offers upside. After those two picks, the Rangers selected two college right-handed pitchers, including RHP Ryan Garcia (2) and Justin Slaten (3). Garcia isn't blessed with great size, but he has a deep pitch mix and should advance quickly. SS Cody Freeman (4), a high school selection, is a very polished, instinctual prospect who makes easy contact with a simple stroke. From rounds six through 18, the Rangers drafted nothing but pitchers, 11 from college and seven from high school. Despite the top two selections as position prospects, this was a very pitching-heavy draft.

Sleeper: RHP Gavin Collyer (12) is an undersized pitcher from the high school ranks, but he has the arm strength and speed to fire fastballs into the low 90s. He may take a few years to add strength to his frame, but has excellent upside.

Grade: B+

TORONTO BLUE JAYS

Nearly the opposite of the Rangers draft, the Blue Jays chose power arms with their first two selections before focusing on position players with their next nine picks. RHP Alek Manoah (1) and RHP Kendall Williams (2) give the Blue Jays two high-upside pitchers with different trajectories. Manoah, from West Virginia, has a very large frame and arm to match. Williams, from IMG Academy in Florida, has more projection. College hitters were selected in rounds 4 through 9 with OF Will Robertson (4) and SS Tanner Morris (5) the best of the lot. One draftee with intriguing upside is OF Dasan Brown (3), a Canadian high schooler who brings exciting tools, though not performance yet, to the table.

Sleeper: C Philip Clarke (9) swings a solid stick and has improved his glovework behind the plate. If he can continue to show improvement defensively, he has a chance to be a sound all-around backstop.

Grade: A-

NATIONAL LEAGUE

ARIZONA DIAMONDBACKS

The Diamondbacks had the largest draft budget in the 2019 draft and owned seven of the first 75 picks. They landed high school CF Corbin Carroll (#16), then took prep hurlers Blake Walston (#26) and Brennan Malone (#33) before ending round one with Ball State RHP Drey Jameson (#34). The club also added Oregon RHP Ryne Nelson (2), Michigan LHP and College World Series standout Tommy Henry (2), before adding Arkansas CF Dominic Fletcher (2). While none of the picks are likely to be superstars, they all project to be major league regulars and Carroll has game-changing speed. Overall, the Diamondbacks utilized their $16M draft budget effectively and transformed a bottom-third farm system into one of the deepest in the NL.

Sleeper: RHP Nick Snyder (11) dominated in the Big 12 as a draft-eligible sophomore, and owns a plus 94-98 mph fastball. He missed plenty of bats in his pro debut, going 2-0 with a 0.53 ERA and 9 BB/30 K in 17 IP.

Grade: A+

ATLANTA BRAVES

The Braves had $11.5M to spend and nabbed Baylor C Shea Langeliers at #8 and added Texas A&M SS Braden Shewmake with pick #21. The club inked Lengeliers to an under-slot deal and used the extra money to sign prep hurlers RHP Tyler Owens (13) and Joey Estes (16). The Braves went college heavy in rounds 2-10, highlighted by Oregon State SS Beau Phillip (2), Texas A&M RHP Kasey Kalich (4), and Seton Hall RHP Rickey DeVito (8). Langeliers was the best defensive backstop in the draft with a cannon for an arm and superb (1.8) pop times. Shewmake is a natural hitter and had a career line of .3232/.381/.487 in three years at A&M.

Sleeper: RHP Tyler Owens (13) is an undersized high school RHP. He comes at hitters with a solid three-pitch mix, highlighted by a 92-94 mph fastball and could develop into a back-end starter.

Grade: B+

CINCINNATI REDS

The Reds added the top arm in the class, TCU LHP Nick Lodolo, at #7. The club then went over slot to land two exciting high school position players, 3B Rece Hinds (2) and 2B Tyler Callihan (3). Lodolo impressed in his pro debut, posting a 2.45 ERA with 0 BB/30 K in 18.1 innings of work. He has three plus offerings, highlighted by a low-to-mid 90s sinker. He has the size and projectability to develop into a #2 starter. JuCo SS Ivan Johnson (4) doesn't wow with his physical tools, but is a switch-hitting infielder with a bit of pop, solid speed, a good glove, and had a respectable debut (.255/.327/.415 with 6 HR/11 SB). If Hinds and Callihan reach their potential as everyday regulars, this will be an impressive draft. If not, Lodolo will have to carry this class by himself, which he is perfectly capable of doing.

Sleeper: SS Yan Contreras (12) was one of the better Puerto Rican position players available, but fell to the Reds where he signed an above-slot deal. Contreras has above-average raw power with a strong arm, but might not be able to stick at SS.

Grade: A

CHICAGO CUBS

The Cubs had just $5.8M to spend on the draft and not surprisingly secured a relatively uninspiring haul. They had to wait to the end of round one to land Fresno State RHP Ryan Jensen (#27). The club then added UCLA 2B Chase Strumpf (2) and Louisville RHP Michael McAvene (3). Strumpf had a solid career at UCLA (.297/.409/.507) with good contact skills, but lacks the power needed to be an impact player at the next level. Jensen has a plus to double-plus fastball that tops out at 98 mph, but struggles with command and posted a 4.2 Ctl in college. The Cubs did go over slot to land high school catcher Ethan Hearn (6), who shows signs of being a plus defender with good power, but was overmatched in his pro debut (.163/.286/.275 in 80 AB).

Sleeper: OF Zac Taylor (25) led Illinois to an NCAA tournament appearance, hitting a career-best .321/.405/.612 with 10 HR. He's a double-plus runner with surprising pop for his size and played at four different levels in his pro debut.

Grade: C-

COLORADO ROCKIES

The Rockies continued their focus of stocking their system with college players. They added UCLA 1B Michael Toglia (1), Georgia 3B Aaron Schunk (2), and Michigan RHP Karl Kaufmann with their CBB pick (2). The 6'5" Toglia had the best raw power in the 2019 draft class with some evaluators projecting 30+ HR down the road. Schunk was a two-way standout at Georgia, providing plus defense while closing games with a 95 mph heater. Kaufman has three above-average offerings and some of the best secondary stuff the system. Connecticut RHP Jacob Wallace (3) and Shepherd University OF Brenton Doyle were other notable selections.

Sleeper: C Colin Simpson (29) primarily a catcher for Oklahoma State, but also saw action in LF, both in college and in his pro debut. He has above-average power with 18 HR and was named the MVP of the Pioneer League, but there is also a lot of swing-and-miss to his game.

Grade: B

LOS ANGELES DODGERS

Not surprisingly, the Dodgers went college heavy in 2019, taking just one prep player in their first twenty picks. They added Tulane 3B Kody Hoese at #25 and North Carolina 2B Michael Busch at #31. Busch struggled as a pro, but has a solid track record and drew more walks than strikeouts in his three years at UNC. Hoese is a fringe Top-100 prospect and slashed .299/.380/.483 in his debut. The Dodgers then added prep RHP Jimmy Lewis (2), Butler righty Ryan Pepiot (3), and UC Irvine slugger Brandon Lewis (4). While there are no superstars in this mix, Hoese and Busch project as everyday players and Jimmy Lewis has a projectable arm that is worth watching.

Sleeper: OF Joe Varnesh (15) was a two-sport star in high school and had a breakout season as a junior for St. Mary's, hitting .327/.437/.640 with 16 doubles and 15 home runs. He continued his hot hitting in the Pioneer League, slashing .329/.460/.468 and showed a discerning eye at the plate.

Grade: B+

MIAMI MARLINS

The Marlins landed four pre-draft Top 100 prospects, highlighted by Vanderbilt OF J.J. Bleday at #4. Bleday was considered the third-best hitting prospect in the draft after compiling a career line of .327/.448/.555 with more walks than strikeouts. They also added Missouri OF Cameron Misner, high school SS Nasim Nunez (2), Wright State OF Peyton Burdick (3), and NC State 1B Evan Edwards (4), before taking their first pitcher high school RHP Evan Fitterer (5). Burdick didn't get a lot of pre-draft hype, but was impressive in his debut hitting .308/.407/.542 with 20 double and 11 home runs between Rookie Ball and Low-A. Overall, this was an impressive haul and Bleday has the size, power, selectivity, and track record to be a middle-of-the-order hitter for years to come.

Sleeper: RHP Chris Mokma (12) is a 6'4" prep right-hander with an above-average 91-93 mph fastball. He posted a solid debut in the AZL, going 0-1 with a 2.19 ERA and 12 K in 12.1 IP.

Grade: A

MILWAUKEE BREWERS

The Brewers reached an under-slot deal with Mississippi State senior LHP Ethan Small (#28) before adding JuCo LHP Antoine Kelly (2), Washington C Nick Kahle (4), and Mississippi OF Thomas Dillard (5). Small was better than anticipated in his debut, posting a 0.86 ERA with 4 BB/36 K in 21 IP and has a nice three-pitch mix. Kelly has a projectable frame and already tops out at 98 mph and he topped the JuCo circuit with a ridiculous 19.1 Dom and then struck out 45 in 31.2 IP in his pro debut. Dillard has some experience behind the plate with above-average raw power, but his below-average speed limits him to LF.

Sleeper: OF Andre Nnebe (28) agreed to a $190,000 bonus. The 6'6", 230-pound outfielder from West Coast Conference powerhouse Santa Clara University has plus raw power, but also a lot of contact issues. He impressed in his pro debut, hitting .302/.392/.496 with 4 HR in 129 AB in the AZL.

Grade: C-

NEW YORK METS

The Mets have never been shy about taking high school players early in the draft and doubled-down on that approach in 2019, landing prep slugger 3B Brett Batty with the 12th overall pick and then adding high school right-handers Josh Wolf (2) and Matthew Allan (3). All three players were considered Top 50 pre-draft prospects. They also added 2019 College World Series standout Jake Magnum (4) for just $20,000. The switch-hitting OF is a plus athlete with an advanced understanding of the strike zone, but has bottom-of-the-scale power and hit just 5 home runs in his four years at Mississippi State. Overall, the decision to focus on long-term upside with Batty, Allan, and Wolf is a bold one. We won't know for several years if this approach was a success or not, but give the Mets kudos for thinking outside the box.

Sleeper: RHP Jace Beck (22) has a projectable 6'9", 220-pound frame and already owns an above-average 90-93 mph fastball. He dominated as a high school senior, going 13-0 with a 0.99 ERA and 134 K in 90 IP. He also fared well in a limited pro debut, putting up a 3.38 ERA with 1 BB/10 K in 8 IP.

Grade: A

PHILADELPHIA PHILLIES

The Phillies took UNLV SS Bryson Stott with the 14th pick in the draft and then had to wait until round three before adding high school SS Jamari Baylor (3). The Phillies look to have found a gem with Stanford LHP Erik Miller (4). The 6'5" lefty can run the ball up at 96-97 mph with a plus slider and average change-up. He struggles with command and could move to relief down the road, but dominated in his debut, going 1-0 with a 1.50 ERA and 15 BB/52 K in 36 IP. The club then went over-slot to land JuCo RHP Gunner Mayer (5) and Tennessee RHP Andrew Schultz (6). Stott is the only sure thing in this draft class and had a solid pro debut, hitting .295/.391/.494.

Sleeper: OF Hunter Markwardt (13) is a LHH speedster out of Oklahoma Christian University. He swiped 21 bases as a junior and then went 6-for-7 in SB in his pro debut while hitting .306/.324/.355 in short-season ball.

Grade: C-

PITTSBURGH PIRATES

The Pirates went the high school route with both of their first-round picks, adding RHP Quinn Priester (#18) and OF Sam Siani (#37). Priester has a fastball that sits in the low-90s but has been clocked as high as 96 mph in the past. Siani, the brother of Reds prospect Mike Siani, owns an advanced hit tool, but doesn't yet generate much power from his 6'0", 195-pound frame. Not surprisingly, the Pirates went with collegiate picks in rounds 2-10, adding Indiana OF Matt Gorski (2), Houston INF Jared Triolo (2), Arizona OF Matt Frazier (3), and Florida State RHP J.C. Flowers (4). Gorski has the potential to be a 20/20 OF, but needs to make more consistent contact to reach that potential.

Sleeper: High school OF Jasiah Dixon (23) has plus-plus speed and opened eyes in his pro debut, hitting .329/.417/.425 with 8 SB in the GCL. His approach at the plate needs to be refined, but he's a plus defender and could be a steal this late in the draft.

Grade: C+

SAN DIEGO PADRES

The Padres had the 6th pick in the draft and were thrilled to find high school SS C.J. Abrams still available. Abrams was a three-sport star in high school and has double-plus speed (3.9 to 1B). He currently projects to have below-average power, but profiles as an old school top-of-the-order hitter. The Padres also landed prep OF Joshua Mears (2), George Mason C Logan Driscoll (2), before going well over slot ($3 million) for high school OF Hudson Head (3). The club then added a number of college seniors at below slot deals in rounds 4-10. Mears has plus raw power and hit 7 HR in 43 games in his debut, but also struck out 59 times in 166 AB. Head was one of the better all-around athletes in the draft class and hit .615 as a high school senior. Even if no one else from this group contributes at the next level, Abrams has the tools to be an impact player.

Sleeper: RHP Blake Baker (23) is a hard-throwing reliever from Miami Dade Community College. Baker struggles to control his mid-90s heater, but has enough velocity to miss bats and posted a 2.35 ERA with 13 BB/34 K in 23 IP.

Grade: A

SAN FRANCISCO GIANTS

With the 10th pick in the 2019 draft, the Giants added Arizona State OF Hunter Bishop. The left-handed hitting Bishop slashed .342/.479/.748 with 22 HR in his junior year and has an intriguing mix of power and speed. The Giants also added Louisville 1B Logan Wyatt (2), a patient hitter who continued that trend in his pro debut, posting a .388 OBP. The club signed both Bishop and Wyatt to below-slot deals and used the savings to land prep 1B Garrett Frechette (5), Dilan Rosario (6), and RHP Trevor McDonald (11). Long-term, Bishop has a chance to be a middle-of-the-order hitter and Wyatt an offensive-minded OBP machine.

Sleeper: RHP Trevor McDonald (11) has a low-90s fastball that touches 95 mph and a potentially plus curveball. He has the size and stuff to be a back-end starter.

Grade: A-

ST. LOUIS CARDINALS

The Cardinals played this one straight down the middle. They had to wait until pick #19, where they landed Kentucky LHP Zack Thompson, then added high school CF Trejyn Fletcher (2) and then went heavy on college pitching with the rest of their slotted picks (7 of their first 10 picks were collegiate pitchers). Thompson is a strong-bodied lefty who projects as a mid-rotation starter and was a steal at #19, while Fletcher is a plus athlete who, if he can hit, has 20/20 potential. Georgia RHP Tony Locey (3) has a mid-90s fastball that touched 98 mph in his pro debut and UC Irvine RHP Andre Pallante (4) is a strike-thrower with a solid four-pitch mix. Thompson has the potential to be a Top 100 prospect down the road and Fletcher has exciting tools, but posted an alarming 57% ct% and will need to rework his swing.

Sleeper: OF Patrick Romeri (12) is an athletic, projectable OF from the IMG Academy in Florida. He's a plus runner and defender and uses a toe-tap and quick stroke to shoot lines drives to all fields.

Grade: C+

WASHINGTON NATIONALS

The Nationals landed a decent crop of prospects in 2019 despite the absence of a 2nd round pick as compensation for signing Patrick Corbin. First-rounder Jackson Rutledge (#17) was the highest-ranked JuCo player since Bryce Harper and owns a nasty four-pitch mix, highlighted by a plus 94-97 mph fastball that has been clocked a high as 102 mph. He looked right at home in his debut, going 2-0 with a 3.13 ERA and 15 BB/39 K in 37.1 IP at three different levels. The Nationals also scooped up Florida State stalwart 3B Drew Mendoza, who was unexpectedly still on the board in round three. The club stayed the college route through rounds 4-10 and didn't add a high school senior until round 23. Arkansas closer LHP Matt Cronin looks like a steal at pick #123. His fastball/power curve mix enabled him to dominate in his debut, posting a 0.82 ERA with 11 BB/41 K in 22 IP.

Sleeper: OF Jake Randa (13) is the son of former major leaguer Joe Randa. The LHH Randa hit .412 with 13 home runs as a freshman and followed that up hitting .368 with 5 HR and 20 BB/19 K. There isn't a ton of upside, but Randa has good pop and a discerning eye at the plate.

Grade: A-

College Players to Watch in 2020

by Chris Lee

Here's our list of 2020 draft-eligible college players who project as top MLB fantasy prospects heading into the 2020 season, which begins the weekend of Feb. 14-16 and ends with the College World Series (June 12-24) in Omaha, Neb. The MLB Draft will also be in Omaha for the first time, and run June 10-12.

All stats are from the 2019 college season unless noted.

1. Austin Martin, IF/OF — *Vanderbilt, R/R, 6-0, 170*
Martin can do everything and is a legit 1/1 candidate with an outstanding approach (87% ct%, 14 bb%, 1.20 Eye) that translates into elite production (.392/.486/.604) thanks to an uncanny ability to hit the ball hard with regularity. Martin stole 41 bases his first two collegiate seasons and added the long ball (10 HR) to his arsenal late last year. He was outstanding at third base in 2019, may play center this year and could play there, or perhaps at shortstop, in the bigs.

2. Emerson Hancock, RHP — *Georgia, R/R, 6-4, 213*
A mid-season lat problem was about the only damper on Hancock's phenomenal sophomore year, during which he flashed a 9.7 Dom and a 5.4 Cmd. Hancock's a polished, four-pitch guy who can get into the high-90s with his fastball—it's his best pitch, and hitters have a tough time seeing it until it's too late—might be the first arm taken in 2020.

3. Spencer Torkelson, 1B — *Arizona St., R/R, 6-1, 220*
Torkelson's mashed 48 homers in two college seasons, and slashed .351/.446/.707 in 2019. He gets Andrew Vaughn comps, but the Eye (0.90) and patience (14% bb%), while good, aren't at Vaughn's level. There's plenty of power and likely and some batting average, too.

4. Garrett Mitchell, OF — *UCLA, L/R, 6-3, 204*
Mitchell's shown more of promise than production, but the latter's starting to catch up, when his raw power and speed tools began to show last year (6 HR, 18 SB, 12 triples) to go with a huge jump in Eye (0.30 to 0.70) and ct% (75% to 84%). Mitchell's a Type 1 diabetic and that's a concern, but he's a potential across-the-board fantasy star.

5. Nick Gonzales, 2B — *New Mexico St., R/R, 5-10, 190*
The former walk-on produced (.432/.532/.773, 16 HR) in a ridiculously-favorable hitting environment, but blew up as a prospect with a .351/.451/.630 showing in the Cape Cod league last summer, with 7 HR and 6 SB. Gonzales, a mature player with a compact swing who showed tremendous growth in Eye (0.60 to 1.50), profiles as a second baseman who can hit for average and some power.

6. Asa Lacy, LHP — *Texas A&M, L/L, 6-4, 214*
The highly-competitive lefty who nearly untouchable (13.7 Dom, .162 oppBA) last season. His mid-90s fastball headlines a four-pitch mix that includes a slider that's particularly tough on lefties. Command is the knock on Lacy—his motion is more over the top, and at times, it looks as if he struggles to find a consistent release point—but there's big upside.

7. Reid Detmers, LHP — *L/L, Louisville, 6-2, 210*
Detmers posted a phenomenal 13.3 Dom, 5.1 Cmd and a .177 average against as a sophomore. His fastball sits in the low-90s, but can be tough to hit thanks to terrific arm-side run that can be particularly effective against right-handers—and he complements it with a loopy breaking ball that he loves to use against lefties, plus a change-up. He's a smart competitor who matured a sophomore and can adjust when it's not his best day.

8. Casey Martin, SS — *Arkansas, R/R, 5-11, 175*
The most high-risk, high-reward player on the list, Martin has home-run power, (28 HR in two seasons) and big-steal upside (he swiped 10 bags in 2019 and he has top-of-the-scale speed). Martin needs a lot of needs refining at the plate (72% ct%, 0.40 Eye) and seems to get sped up in the field, but some blame that on an adjustment that came from playing at a low level of high school baseball. There's a 20/20 guy in here who'll play on the left side of the dirt if it works out.

9. J.T. Ginn, RHP — *Mississippi St., R/R, 6-2, 192*
Ginn, who the Dodgers took 30th overall in 2019, is a draft-eligible sophomore. He missed a lot of the 2019 postseason with shoulder discomfort. Before that, he earned Southeastern Conference Freshman of the Year honors thanks to a 10.9 Dom and a 5.5 Cmd. His best grades come on a curve and a fastball he can run into the high-90s.

10. Tanner Burns, RHP — *Auburn, R/R, 6-0, 205*
Burns' best pitches are a fastball and a curve that he commands well—as good a pitcher as there is in college baseball when he's healthy. But health's the problem: Burns had a sore shoulder that hampered him from late-April on, and wasn't the same when he returned. He posted an 11.7 Dom and was competitive enough to want the ball during Auburn's postseason run, when he had far less than his best self.

11. Heston Kjerstad, OF — *Arkansas, L/R, 6-3, 200*
Kjerstad, who's mashed 31 HR in two seasons, is one of the best power-hitting prospects in the draft. That's where is value's going to lie—a ct% of 76% and Eye of 0.30, and below-average speed limit the rest—but that's enough to put him on the radar.

12. Garrett Crochet, LHP — *Tennessee, L/L, 6-6, 218*
Crochet has pitched mostly out of the bullpen, but a high-spin-rate fastball that started touching 100 this fall has excited scouts, and he adds a slider and a change.

More to watch:
C.J. Van Eyk, RHP, Florida St.
Aaron Sabato, 1B, North Carolina
Cole Henry, RHP, LSU
Justin Foscue, 2B, Mississippi St.

2020's TOP FANTASY PROSPECTS

1	Wander Franco	SS	TAM		51	Nick Madrigal	2B	CHW
2	Jo Adell	OF	LAA		52	Riley Greene	OF	DET
3	Luis Robert	OF	CHW		53	Ryan Mountcastle	1B	BAL
4	Gavin Lux	SS	LA		54	Ke'Bryan Hayes	3B	PIT
5	MacKenzie Gore	LHP	SD		55	Jordan Groshans	SS	TOR
6	Royce Lewis	SS	MIN		56	Ronny Mauricio	SS	NYM
7	Jarred Kelenic	OF	SEA		57	Daniel Lynch	LHP	KC
8	Adley Rutschman	C	BAL		58	Xavier Edwards	SS	TAM
9	Forrest Whitley	RHP	HOU		59	Matthew Liberatore	LHP	STL
10	Julio Rodriguez	OF	SEA		60	D.L. Hall	LHP	BAL
11	Jesus Luzardo	LHP	OAK		61	Alek Thomas	OF	ARI
12	Andrew Vaughn	1B	CHW		62	Brennen Davis	OF	CHC
13	Casey Mize	RHP	DET		63	Hunter Greene	RHP	CIN
14	Carter Kieboom	SS	WAS		64	Deivi Garcia	RHP	NYY
15	Dylan Carlson	OF	STL		65	Logan Gilbert	RHP	SEA
16	Nate Pearson	RHP	TOR		66	Nico Hoerner	SS	CHC
17	Dustin May	RHP	LA		67	Kyle Wright	RHP	ATL
18	Alex Kirilloff	OF	MIN		68	George Valera	OF	CLE
19	Bobby Witt, Jr.	SS	KC		69	Sean Murphy	C	OAK
20	Marco Luciano	SS	SF		70	Corbin Carroll	OF	ARI
21	Joey Bart	C	SF		71	Keibert Ruiz	C	LA
22	Michael Kopech	RHP	CHW		72	Josiah Gray	RHP	LA
23	Cristian Pache	OF	ATL		73	Josh Jung	3B	TEX
24	Matt Manning	RHP	DET		74	Evan White	1B	SEA
25	C.J. Abrams	SS	SD		75	Tyler Freeman	SS	CLE
26	Sixto Sanchez	RHP	MIA		76	Luis Garcia	SS	WAS
27	Drew Waters	OF	ATL		77	Shane Baz	RHP	TAM
28	Alec Bohm	3B	PHI		78	Daulton Varsho	C	ARI
29	Brendan McKay	LHP/DH	TAM		79	Triston Casas	1B	BOS
30	Kristian Robinson	OF	ARI		80	Nick Lodolo	LHP	CIN
31	Vidal Brujan	2B	TAM		81	Hans Crouse	RHP	TEX
32	A.J. Puk	LHP	OAK		82	Tarik Skubal	LHP	DET
33	Brendan Rodgers	SS	COL		83	Brandon Marsh	OF	LAA
34	Luis Patino	RHP	SD		84	Jeter Downs	SS	LA
35	Spencer Howard	RHP	PHI		85	Greg Jones	SS	TAM
36	J.J. Bleday	OF	MIA		86	Luis Campusano	C	SD
37	Nolan Gorman	3B	STL		87	Clarke Schmidt	RHP	NYY
38	Heliot Ramos	OF	SF		88	Noelvi Marte	SS	SEA
39	Jazz Chisholm	SS	MIA		89	Jordan Balazovic	RHP	MIN
40	Mitch Keller	RHP	PIT		90	Ethan Hankins	RHP	CLE
41	Nolan Jones	3B	CLE		91	Sherten Apostel	3B	TEX
42	Taylor Trammell	OF	SD		92	Robert Puason	SS	OAK
43	Jasson Dominguez	OF	NYY		93	Brent Honeywell	RHP	TAM
44	Grayson Rodriguez	RHP	BAL		94	Brady Singer	RHP	KC
45	Brusdar Graterol	RHP	MIN		95	Leody Taveras	OF	TEX
46	Ian Anderson	RHP	ATL		96	Francisco Alvarez	C	NYM
47	Oneil Cruz	SS	PIT		97	Geraldo Perdomo	SS	ARI
48	Jesus Sanchez	OF	MIA		98	Adrian Morejon	LHP	SD
49	Hunter Bishop	OF	SF		99	Monte Harrison	OF	MIA
50	Trevor Larnach	OF	MIN		100	Brailyn Marquez	LHP	CHC

Sleepers Outside the HQ100

by Alec Dopp

Every year, the final practice in creating the *Minor League Baseball Analyst* is the production of the HQ100, wherein each member of the BaseballHQ prospect team ranks what they perceive to be the Top 100 prospects in dynasty formats for the coming year.

The goal of this practice isn't to pat ourselves on the back for agreeing with one another. Instead, the goal is to see how different eyes can evaluate the same players. Projection is often an inexact science, but through this process, we can divulge how we as a team value the best minor league talent. Fantasy owners, in turn, reap the benefits.

That doesn't mean future talent is limited solely to the HQ100, though. Below are a handful of names that did not crack the 2020 HQ100, but could be on this list a year from now.

AMERICAN LEAGUE

One of the best pure athletes at any level of the minors, **Jordyn Adams (OF, LAA)** just missed the cut for the HQ100 after slashing .257/.351/.369 with 8 HR and 16 SB in 109 G in 2019, the majority of which were spent in the Low-A Midwest League (MWL). Along with his elite speed, Adams brings to the table solid plate discipline skills and some twitchy bat speed that should allow him to grow into 15-20 HR at his peak as he matures physically. He is still working on his bat-to-ball skills and overall feel for hitting, but he should be a .250+ BA type whose timeline to the majors is pushed more than normal due to his plus defensive ability in centerfield.

Younger brother to Josh, **Bo Naylor (C, CLE)** made his full-season debut in the MWL last summer after signing for above slot value as a first-rounder back in 2018. Even for a 19-year-old at that level, he slashed .243/.313/.421 with a 40% x/h% in 107 games along with a solid 37% caught stealing rate behind the plate. Naylor's youth combined with a strong arm and framing acumen should allow him to stick at catcher, and his plus contact skills and strong plate discipline should allow him to be a BA/OBP contributor. He's more athletic than his body would let on, and he could have sneaky SB value along with burgeoning HR pop.

Alek Manoah (RHP, TOR) posted a scintillating junior year with West Virginia and wound up going 11th overall in the 2019 amateur draft, after which he pitched effectively in short-season ball with a 2.65 ERA, 1.06 WHIP and 14.3 Dom/2.6 Ctl split in 17 IP. The 21-year-old right-hander is physically imposing at 6-6, 260 pounds and got leaner during his final collegiate season. His plus-plus fastball lives in the mid-90s with good arm-side movement and a late-breaking slider gives him a second plus pitch, though his change-up will require work. He lives around the zone and could have big Dom potential as a #3 SP at his peak.

Yet to make his stateside debut, **Erick Peña (OF, KC)** was touted among his fellow international cohorts as a toolsy outfielder with considerable projection required, and he ended up with a $3.8 million signing bonus in July 2019. There's potential for multi-category impact in his profile, which is headlined by plus raw power and a smooth, level swing that allows him to impact the baseball consistently with good bat speed. Peña is currently an above-average runner with an outside chance to stay in centerfield, but the expectation is for him to bulk up a bit and lose a step. He should still be a double-digit SB contributor as an everyday right-fielder.

Boston's farm system has been deeper in prior years, but **Gilberto Jimenez (OF, BOS)** could be a name who shoots up their 2020 Organization Report with a strong intro to full-season ball in 2020. A 2017 July 2 signee from the Dominican Republic, Jimenez led the NYPL with a .359 BA and also stole 14 bases across 59 G as a mere 19-year-old. He is a switch-hitter with natural feel for hitting and a predominantly slap approach from either side, which allows for double-plus contact but also limits his raw power. He is a solid defender with elite speed and should stay in centerfield, which gives him a leadoff-type profile with BA/SB ability.

Misael Urbina (OF, MIN) was one of the more coveted bats in the 2017 July 2 international signing period and eventually inked a $2.75 million bonus with Minnesota. He made his pro debut last summer in the Dominican Republic, hitting .279 with 19 SB and a 92% ct% across 183 AB. That stat line is remarkably descriptive of his actual scouting report, as the 17-year-old is a plus runner capable of SB impact and quality range for centerfield. His bat-to-ball skills are advanced for his age and he has a solid foundational knowledge of the strike zone. He's still learning to get his power into games, but he has solid everyday upside at his peak.

NATIONAL LEAGUE

The jump from High-A to Double-A is generally viewed as the toughest for pitchers, but **Edward Cabrera (RHP, MIA)** made it look nearly seamless during his breakout 2019 campaign, going 9-4 with a 2.23 ERA, 0.99 WHIP and 10.8 Dom across nearly 100 IP combined between both levels. The 21-year-old righty made significant gains with his command and further augmented feel for his power curve in 2019, and he shows an ability to touch 98 mph with sink to his plus heater. His change-up demonstrates more flash than consistency at this point, but it projects to be at least average and his upside is a solid mid-rotation starter with Dom skills.

The general stigma attached to Colorado pitching prospects is legitimate, but **Ryan Rolison (LHP, COL)** is one arm that could shoot up the HQ100 a year from now based on his skills and development. The 21-year-old lefty pitched most of 2019 in the hitter-friendly CAL and posted solid peripherals (9.1 Dom, 2.9 Ctl, 44% grounders), which was masked by an ugly 4.87 ERA in 116 IP. Rolison has a chance for three above-average pitches at maturity, including a swing and miss curveball, a solid fading change-up and fastball around 91-94 mph that added some movement last year. At his peak, he could be #3/4 SP with innings-eating ability.

A breakout performer for Baylor during the 2019 College World Series, **Shea Langeliers (C, ATL)** signed for below-slot value as the 9th overall pick in last summer's draft and had a shaky offensive debut as a pro, slashing .255/.310/.343 with a 27% x/h% in 54 games in the SAL. The reason to potentially buy low Langeliers' profile is that his cannon arm and defensive skills will allow him to stick at catcher, which enhances his fantasy value. Moreover, he has plus raw pop via a pull-heavy approach and posted a solid 82% ct% in college and could hit for a .270-.280 BA at full maturity. Next season will be a good litmus test as he heads to the High-A Florida State League.

Andres Gimenez (SS, NYM) was No. 56 on this list a year ago, though trials during his first Double-A assignment — he hit .250/.309/.387 with a marked drop in ct% — have bruised his stock heading into 2020. The 21-year-old SS rebounded nicely in his AFL campaign, however, looking more like the hitter that was formerly projected as a July 2 signee. Gimenez projects to have solid SB value with his plus speed, and he can pick it at short, allowing him to stay up the middle long-term. His HR projection is in the mid-teens and an aggressive approach may cap his OBP, but he has natural bat-to-ball skills and should hit for a sound BA.

One of the top prep arms in the 2019 amateur draft, **Brennan Malone (RHP, ARI)** signed as the 33rd overall pick for at-slot value and made his pro debut in the Arizona League (rookie) last summer, striking out seven in as many innings before ending his abbreviated campaign in the short-season Northwest League. Malone is tall and physically advanced for his age and can touch 99 mph with his fastball and sit 94-96 fairly comfortably, and he shows aptitude for spinning a plus slider. His curve and change-up are back burners to the slider among his secondaries, but they project to be solid offerings. Malone could peak with elite velocity and four pitches that are above-average as a #2/3 SP.

Bryson Stott (SS, PHI) was Philadelphia's top overall pick in the 2019 draft after a stellar career at UNLV, slashing .274/.370/.446 with 5 HR and 5 SB in 44 G in the NYPL to finish out his debut. Stott has a fluid, low-effort swing from the left side that is conducive to an all-fields approach and he walked more often than he struck out over three years as a college starter. Though there lacks a standout tool in the profile, Stott is a good enough athlete where 20+ SB could be in his future as a glove who could have positional flexibility across the infield, along with average HR output and high-volume doubles power at his peak.

POSITIONS: Up to four positions are listed for each batter and represent those for which he appeared (in order) the most games at in 2019. Positions are shown with their numeric designation (2=CA, 3=1B, 7=LF, 0=DH, etc.)

BATS: Shows which side of the plate he bats from—right (R), left (L) or switch-hitter (S).

AGE: Player's age, as of April 1, 2020.

DRAFTED: The year, round, and school that the player performed at as an amateur if drafted, or where the player was signed from, if a free agent.

EXP MLB DEBUT: The year a player is expected to debut in the major leagues.

H/W: The player's height and weight.

FUT: The role that the batter is expected to have for the majority of his major league career, not necessarily his greatest upside.

SKILLS: Each skill a player possesses is graded and designated with a "+", indicating the quality of the skills, taking into context the batter's age and level played. An average skill will receive three "+" marks.

- **PWR:** Measures the player's ability to drive the ball and hit for power.
- **BAVG:** Measures the player's ability to hit for batting average and judge the strike zone.
- **SPD:** Measures the player's raw speed and base-running ability. When we've measured run times (point of bat-to-ball contact to foot hitting first base), we've included these next to the SPD box.
- **DEF:** Measures the player's overall defense, which includes arm strength, arm accuracy, range, agility, hands, and defensive instincts.

PLAYER STAT LINES: Player statistics for the last five teams that he played for (if applicable), including college and the major leagues.

TEAM DESIGNATIONS: Each team that the player performed for during a given year is included.

LEVEL DESIGNATIONS: The level for each team a player performed is included. "AAA" means Triple-A, "AA" means Double-A, "A+" means high Class-A, "A-" means low Class-A, and "Rk" means rookie level.

SABERMETRIC CATEGORIES: Descriptions of all the sabermetric categories appear in the glossary.

CAPSULE COMMENTARIES: For each player, a brief analysis of their skills/statistics, and their future potential is provided.

ELIGIBILITY: Eligibility for inclusion is the less than 130 major league at-bats.

POTENTIAL RATINGS: The Potential Ratings are a two-part system in which a player is assigned a number rating based on his upside potential (1-10) and a letter rating based on the probability of reaching that potential (A-E).

Potential

10:	Hall of Famer	5:	MLB reserve
9:	Elite player	4:	Top minor leaguer
8:	Solid regular	3:	Average minor leaguer
7:	Average regular	2:	Minor league reserve
6:	Platoon player	1:	Minor league roster filler

Probability Rating

A: 90% probability of reaching potential
B: 70% probability of reaching potential
C: 50% probability of reaching potential
D: 30% probability of reaching potential
E: 10% probability of reaching potential

SKILLS: Scouts usually grade a player's skills on the 20-80 scale, and while most of the grades are subjective, there are grades that can be given to represent a certain hitting statistic or running speed. These are indicated on this chart:

Scout Grade	HR	BA	Speed (L)	Speed (R)
80	39+	.320+	3.9	4.0
70	32-38	.300-.319	4.0	4.1
60	25-31	.286-.299	4.1	4.2
50 (avg)	17-24	.270-.285	4.2	4.3
40	11-16	.250-.269	4.3	4.4
30	6-10	.220-.249	4.4	4.5
20	0-5	.219-	4.5	4.6

CATCHER POP TIMES: Catchers are timed (in seconds) from the moment the pitch reaches the catcher's mitt until the time that the middle infielder receives the baseball at second base. This number assists both teams in assessing whether a base-runner should steal second base or not.

1.85	+
1.95	MLB average
2.05	–

Abrams,CJ | 6 | San Diego

EXP MLB DEBUT: 2023 | H/W: 6-2 185 | FUT: Starting SS | 9D

Bats L Age 19
2019 (1) HS (GA)

- Pwr +++
- BAvg ++++
- Spd +++++
- Def +++

Year	Lev	Team	AB	R	H	HR	RBI	Avg	OB	Slg	OPS	bb%	ct%	Eye	SB	CS	x/h%	Iso	RC/G
2019	Rk	AZL Padres	142	40	57	3	22	401	441	662	1103	7	90	0.71	14	6	40	261	8.86
2019	A	Fort Wayne	8	1	2	0	0	250	333	375	708	11	100		1	0	50	125	5.15

Wiry-strong athlete with an elite run tool and up-the-middle defensive utility. Hands explode to the ball and displays plus contact skills, with an ability to backspin the ball to gaps. Will be able to add strength to lower half and with added loft could produce average power. Solid range with a plus arm, he should be able to stick to SS.

Abreu,Pablo | 8 | Milwaukee

EXP MLB DEBUT: 2023 | H/W: 6-0 170 | FUT: Starting OF | 7D

Bats R Age 20
2016 FA (DR)

- Pwr ++
- BAvg ++
- Spd +++
- Def +++

Year	Lev	Team	AB	R	H	HR	RBI	Avg	OB	Slg	OPS	bb%	ct%	Eye	SB	CS	x/h%	Iso	RC/G
2017	Rk	AZL Brewers	19	1	6	0	2	316	381	474	855	10	74	0.40	1	0	50	158	6.59
2018	Rk	Helena	208	33	52	7	33	250	339	418	757	12	71	0.46	9	1	40	168	5.12
2019	Rk	AZL BrewersG	53	7	12	1	10	226	305	396	701	10	60	0.29	0	0	50	170	4.82
2019	A	Wisconsin	102	13	19	0	11	186	252	245	497	8	66	0.26	3	0	26	59	1.38

High-profile July 2 signee from 2016 who has raw tools but struggles with swing-and-miss and approach. Strong, developed body for age. Plus bat speed lends itself to good raw power, but lack of barrel control may limit his HR output. Has athletic actions for moderate SB impact and range for CF now, but could profile well in RF with strong arm.

Acosta,Maximo | 6 | Texas

EXP MLB DEBUT: 2023 | H/W: 6-1 170 | FUT: Starting SS | 9E

Bats R Age 17
2019 FA (VZ)

- Pwr +++
- BAvg ++++
- Spd ++++
- Def +++

Year	Lev	Team	AB	R	H	HR	RBI	Avg	OB	Slg	OPS	bb%	ct%	Eye	SB	CS	x/h%	Iso	RC/G
2019		Did not play in U.S.																	

A significant international signing in 2019, he is an already-physical SS with a short, powerful swing and collection of plus tools. Strength for future power, whole-field awareness and pitch recognition skills for future plus hit, speed and agility on the bases and in the field. A bevy of intangibles help round out an advanced package.

Adams,Jordyn | 8 | Los Angeles (A)

EXP MLB DEBUT: 2022 | H/W: 6-2 180 | FUT: Starting CF | 9D

Bats R Age 20
2018 (1) HS (NC)

- Pwr +++
- BAvg +++
- Spd +++++
- Def ++++

Year	Lev	Team	AB	R	H	HR	RBI	Avg	OB	Slg	OPS	bb%	ct%	Eye	SB	CS	x/h%	Iso	RC/G
2018	Rk	Orem	35	5	11	0	8	314	385	486	870	10	80	0.57	0	1	45	171	6.68
2018	Rk	AZL Angels	70	8	17	0	5	243	338	329	666	13	67	0.43	5	2	24	86	4.10
2019	Rk	AZL Angels	13	4	7	0	4	538	571	615	1187	7	77	0.33	4	0	14	77	10.43
2019	A	Burlington	372	52	93	7	31	250	339	358	696	12	75	0.53	12	5	26	108	4.27
2019	A+	Inland Empire	35	7	8	1	1	229	325	400	725	13	60	0.36	0	1	38	171	5.16

Uber-athletic OF prospect who was among the youngest hitters to appear in CAL in 2019. Was highly touted HS football star and now utilizes his 80-grade speed to play a premium CF and potentially make elite SB impact. Working on barrel control but has plus bat speed and a solid approach, which should help him reach his upside of average raw power.

Adams,Riley | 2 | Toronto

EXP MLB DEBUT: 2021 | H/W: 6-4 225 | FUT: Starting C | 7E

Bats R Age 23
2017 (3) San Diego

- Pwr ++
- BAvg ++
- Spd +
- Def +++

Year	Lev	Team	AB	R	H	HR	RBI	Avg	OB	Slg	OPS	bb%	ct%	Eye	SB	CS	x/h%	Iso	RC/G
2017	NCAA	San Diego	202	45	63	13	47	312	409	564	973	14	72	0.58	2	0	40	252	8.06
2017	A-	Vancouver	203	26	62	3	35	305	362	438	800	8	75	0.36	1	1	32	133	5.54
2018	A+	Dunedin	349	49	86	4	43	246	341	361	702	13	73	0.54	3	0	36	115	4.47
2019	A+	Dunedin	65	12	18	3	12	277	405	462	867	18	72	0.78	1	0	33	185	6.78
2019	AA	New Hampshire	287	46	74	11	39	258	332	439	771	10	63	0.30	3	1	38	181	5.54

Under the radar backstop who set easy career high in HR in breakout campaign. Takes advantage of good athleticism behind plate where he controls running game with catch and throw skills and average arm. Blocks and receives well and could continue to improve as footwork progresses. Willing to draw walks, though contact skills aren't polished.

Adell,Jo | 89 | Los Angeles (A)

EXP MLB DEBUT: 2020 | H/W: 6-3 215 | FUT: Starting OF | 9B

Bats R Age 20
2017 (1) HS (KY)

- Pwr ++++
- BAvg +++
- Spd ++++
- Def +++

Year	Lev	Team	AB	R	H	HR	RBI	Avg	OB	Slg	OPS	bb%	ct%	Eye	SB	CS	x/h%	Iso	RC/G
2018	A+	Inland Empire	238	46	69	12	42	290	332	546	878	6	74	0.24	9	2	49	256	6.40
2018	AA	Mobile	63	14	15	2	6	238	304	429	733	9	65	0.27	2	0	53	190	4.91
2019	A+	Inland Empire	25	4	7	2	5	280	308	560	868	4	60	0.10	0	0	43	280	6.92
2019	AA	Mobile	159	28	49	8	23	308	382	553	935	11	74	0.46	6	0	47	245	7.37
2019	AAA	Salt Lake	121	22	32	0	8	264	321	355	676	8	64	0.23	1	0	34	91	4.17

Freak athlete who has potential for plus tools across the board and dynamic fantasy impact. Strong, chiseled frame produces elite all-fields raw power; has a chance to get even more into games as he fortifies his ct% skills. Quick to full speed and is plus runner. Drafted as CF, he likely slides to RF with range and arm to be above-average glove.

Ademan,Aramis | 6 | Chicago (N)

EXP MLB DEBUT: 2021 | H/W: 5-11 160 | FUT: Starting SS | 7C

Bats L Age 21
2015 FA (DR)

- Pwr ++
- BAvg +++
- Spd +++
- Def +++

Year	Lev	Team	AB	R	H	HR	RBI	Avg	OB	Slg	OPS	bb%	ct%	Eye	SB	CS	x/h%	Iso	RC/G
2017	A-	Eugene	161	23	46	4	27	286	343	466	809	8	81	0.47	10	6	37	180	5.54
2017	A	South Bend	127	13	31	3	15	244	267	378	645	3	81	0.17	4	2	32	134	3.20
2018	A+	Myrtle Beach	396	49	82	3	38	207	276	273	549	9	76	0.40	9	5	21	66	2.23
2019	A+	Myrtle Beach	362	40	80	5	39	221	312	334	646	12	75	0.52	16	9	29	113	3.65

Glove-first SS prospect who repeated Hi-A assignment and improved marginally. Lacks plus tool but has well-rounded game. Smooth, level LH stroke conducive to gap power and liners to all fields. Bat speed presently average and will need to add strength to slender frame. Athletic enough for SB value with enough PT volume, but has average speed.

Adolfo,Micker | 9 | Chicago (A)

EXP MLB DEBUT: 2020 | H/W: 6-4 255 | FUT: Starting OF | 7D

Bats R Age 23
2013 FA (DR)

- Pwr ++++
- BAvg +++
- Spd ++
- Def +

Year	Lev	Team	AB	R	H	HR	RBI	Avg	OB	Slg	OPS	bb%	ct%	Eye	SB	CS	x/h%	Iso	RC/G
2016	A	Kannapolis	247	30	54	5	21	219	261	340	601	5	64	0.16	0	1	35	121	2.79
2017	A	Kannapolis	424	60	112	16	68	264	314	453	767	7	65	0.21	2	0	41	189	5.30
2018	A+	Winston-Salem	291	48	82	11	50	282	357	464	821	10	68	0.37	2	1	37	182	6.04
2019	Rk	AZL White Sox	50	8	13	2	3	260	351	480	831	12	58	0.33	0	0	54	220	7.10
2019	AA	Birmingham	78	5	16	0	9	205	326	295	621	15	54	0.39	0	3	44	90	3.93

Powerful, big-bodied slugger continues to struggle with injury. This time, it was a 2nd elbow surgery. When healthy, imposing figure in batting box. Big double-plus power plays to all fields. Long, lumbering uppercut swing limits hit tool. Pull-oriented approach limits bat to .250 or less average. Defensively challenged, likely DH bat.

Alcantara,Kevin | 8 | New York (A)

EXP MLB DEBUT: 2024 | H/W: 6-6 188 | FUT: Starting OF | 8E

Bats R Age 17
2018 FA (DR)

- Pwr +++
- BAvg ++
- Spd ++++
- Def +++

Year	Lev	Team	AB	R	H	HR	RBI	Avg	OB	Slg	OPS	bb%	ct%	Eye	SB	CS	x/h%	Iso	RC/G
2019	Rk	GCL Yankees	123	19	32	1	13	260	278	358	636	2	78	0.11	3	3	25	98	3.09

Quick-twitch, super-athletic OF made stateside debut in '19. Toolshed is abundant but extremely raw. Quick, loose hands create plus bat speed. Very lean frame but with above-average current strength. Could be a raw power producer with hit tool refinement and added muscle. Plus runner who may eventually outgrow tool. Solid defender in CF.

Alcantara,Sergio | 46 | Detroit

EXP MLB DEBUT: 2020 | H/W: 5-9 170 | FUT: Starting SS | 7C

Bats B Age 23
2012 FA (DR)

- Pwr +
- BAvg ++
- Spd ++
- Def ++++

Year	Lev	Team	AB	R	H	HR	RBI	Avg	OB	Slg	OPS	bb%	ct%	Eye	SB	CS	x/h%	Iso	RC/G
2016	A+	Visalia	15	2	4	0	0	267	389	333	722	17	87	1.50	0	1	25	67	5.14
2017	A+	Visalia	340	44	95	3	28	279	345	362	707	9	83	0.60	11	10	21	82	4.36
2017	A+	Lakeland	126	18	29	0	7	230	307	278	585	10	82	0.61	4	3	17	48	2.93
2018	AA	Erie	441	53	120	1	37	272	335	333	669	9	79	0.45	8	5	18	61	3.84
2019	AA	Erie	324	46	80	2	27	247	344	296	640	13	78	0.68	7	6	15	49	3.64

Compact, plus-plus defender with one of the strongest arms in the organization. Fluid actions at shortstop with advanced footwork and accuracy to first that continues to improve. Has maintained contact rate in Double-A, but tools failed to shine in 2019 as they have in the past. Added muscle in 2019, able to steal bases, but lacks discipline.

Alemais,Stephen | 46 | Pittsburgh

EXP MLB DEBUT: 2020 | H/W: 5-11 190 | FUT: Reserve IF | 6C

Bats R Age 24
2016 (3) Tulane

- Pwr +
- BAvg +++
- Spd +++
- Def ++++

Year	Lev	Team	AB	R	H	HR	RBI	Avg	OB	Slg	OPS	bb%	ct%	Eye	SB	CS	x/h%	Iso	RC/G
2017	Rk	GCL Pirates	27	6	7	0	2	259	355	370	725	13	81	0.80	0	0	43	111	4.92
2017	A	West Virginia	121	14	27	3	12	223	254	380	634	4	74	0.16	5	3	41	157	3.12
2017	A+	Bradenton	101	10	32	1	20	317	400	406	806	12	86	1.00	5	2	22	89	5.78
2018	AA	Altoona	402	56	112	1	34	279	350	346	696	10	83	0.64	16	9	19	67	4.30
2019	AA	Altoona	45	4	12	0	2	267	283	267	549	2	80	0.11	2	0	0	0	1.91

Athletic INF who ended year in April after shoulder surgery. Known for glove as he ranges well to both sides. Possesses strong arm that is suitable for any INF spot. Quick, textbook footwork to make routine and tough plays. Hitting lags behind, however. Little to no power in profile and lacks punch in bat for xbh. Draws walks and tough to fan.

Alexander,Blaze — 46 — Arizona

EXP MLB DEBUT: 2022 | H/W: 6-0 160 | FUT: Starting SS | 7C

Bats R Age 20
2018 (11) HS (FL)
- Pwr +++
- BAvg ++
- Spd ++
- Def ++++

Year	Lev	Team	AB	R	H	HR	RBI	Avg	OB	Slg	OPS	bb%	ct%	Eye	SB	CS	x/h%	Iso	RC/G
2018	Rk	Missoula	116	27	35	3	17	302	367	509	876	9	73	0.39	3	0	43	207	6.72
2018	Rk	AZL DBacks	94	25	34	2	25	362	469	574	1043	17	78	0.90	7	3	41	213	9.26
2019	A	Kane County	343	56	90	7	47	262	343	382	725	11	74	0.47	14	4	26	120	4.62

Glove-first MIF prospect with elite arm strength and plus defensive ability. Offensive game predicated on average speed and ability to work counts. Could be BA liability with pervasive swing-and-miss issues and pull-heavy approach. Possesses average raw power now and will have a chance to add mass, with potentially more to come.

Alexander,CJ — 35 — Atlanta

EXP MLB DEBUT: 2021 | H/W: 6-5 215 | FUT: Reserve 3B | 6C

Bats L Age 23
2018 (20) State JC of FL
- Pwr +++
- BAvg ++
- Spd +++
- Def +++

Year	Lev	Team	AB	R	H	HR	RBI	Avg	OB	Slg	OPS	bb%	ct%	Eye	SB	CS	x/h%	Iso	RC/G
2018	Rk	GCL Braves	34	6	14	1	8	412	500	618	1118	15	88	1.50	0	0	21	206	9.60
2018	Rk	Danville	82	10	29	0	12	354	442	488	930	14	74	0.62	1	1	24	134	7.79
2018	A+	Florida	80	5	26	1	7	325	386	450	836	9	79	0.47	3	1	27	125	6.00
2019	A+	Florida	60	4	8	0	1	133	297	150	447	19	70	0.78	3	1	13	17	0.91
2019	AA	Mississippi	68	6	7	2	7	103	197	206	403	11	63	0.32	0	0	43	103	-0.33

Tall, athletic 3B struggled in first full season with injury and performance after lighting world on fire in '18 debut. Missed time due to elbow and thumb strains. Swing appeared much slower than previous swing, struggling to get barrel out in front, depressing hit tool. There's power in frame and could come to swing. Plays a solid 3B.

Alfonzo,Eliezer — 2 — Detroit

EXP MLB DEBUT: 2023 | H/W: 5-10 155 | FUT: Reserve C | 7D

Bats B Age 20
2016 FA (VZ)
- Pwr ++
- BAvg +++
- Spd +
- Def ++

Year	Lev	Team	AB	R	H	HR	RBI	Avg	OB	Slg	OPS	bb%	ct%	Eye	SB	CS	x/h%	Iso	RC/G
2018	Rk	DSL Tigers 2	110	22	43	0	21	391	485	500	985	15	93	2.50	3	1	26	109	8.20
2018	Rk	GCL Tigers W	69	7	15	1	12	217	308	275	583	12	87	1.00	3	1	13	58	3.07
2019	A-	Connecticut	179	16	57	1	24	318	348	374	722	4	91	0.47	2	2	14	56	4.32

Venezuelan CA with projectable, solid frame behind the plate with average arm and cat-like defensive reflexes. Advanced ability to lead pitchers with solid framing and game-calling. Maturing switch-hitter able to barrel the ball from both sides of the plate. Swing path is progressing.

Alford,Anthony — 89 — Toronto

EXP MLB DEBUT: 2017 | H/W: 6-1 215 | FUT: Starting CF | 8E

Bats R Age 25
2012 (3) HS (MS)
- Pwr ++
- BAvg ++
- Spd ++++
- Def +++

Year	Lev	Team	AB	R	H	HR	RBI	Avg	OB	Slg	OPS	bb%	ct%	Eye	SB	CS	x/h%	Iso	RC/G
2018	AAA	Buffalo	375	52	90	5	34	240	296	344	640	7	70	0.27	17	7	31	104	3.38
2018	MLB	Toronto	19	3	2	0	1	105	190	105	296	10	53	0.22	1	0	0	0	-2.37
2019	Rk	GCL Blue Jays	13	3	5	1	1	385	467	923	1390	13	92	2.00	0	0	80	538	12.43
2019	AAA	Buffalo	282	46	73	7	37	259	332	411	744	10	67	0.33	22	8	36	152	5.04
2019	MLB	Toronto	28	3	5	1	1	179	207	286	493	3	61	0.09	2	0	20	107	0.92

Regressing OF who can't stay healthy. Formerly an elite prospect, continues to show glimpses of potential with athleticism and speed. Swings fast bat and exhibits plus raw power at times. Swing and miss profile mutes BA potential and doesn't get on base enough to use speed. Good OF who can play all spots with ample range, but fringy arm strength.

Allen,Austin — 2 — Oakland

EXP MLB DEBUT: 2019 | H/W: 6-2 220 | FUT: Starting 1B | 7A

Bats L Age 26
2015 (4) Florida Tech
- Pwr ++++
- BAvg +++
- Spd +
- Def ++

Year	Lev	Team	AB	R	H	HR	RBI	Avg	OB	Slg	OPS	bb%	ct%	Eye	SB	CS	x/h%	Iso	RC/G
2017	A+	Lake Elsinore	463	71	131	22	81	283	345	497	842	9	76	0.40	0	1	41	214	5.92
2018	AA	San Antonio	451	59	131	22	56	290	344	506	850	8	78	0.38	0	3	40	215	5.90
2019	AAA	El Paso	270	52	89	21	67	330	380	663	1043	8	79	0.39	0	0	54	333	8.24
2019	MLB	San Diego	65	4	14	0	3	215	282	277	559	8	68	0.29	0	0	29	62	2.31

Bat-first CA prospect who posted elite x/h% and career-best BA, albeit in hitter-friendly PCL. Could be future HR/RBI source with plus raw power that plays well to CF/RF. Approach leans toward aggressive and overall bat to ball skills are only average. Fringe arm allowed for only a 11% CS rate in debut. May move to 1B, which hurts his value.

Allen,Nick — 6 — Oakland

EXP MLB DEBUT: 2021 | H/W: 5-9 166 | FUT: Starting MIF | 7C

Bats R Age 21
2017 (3) HS (CA)
- Pwr +
- BAvg +++
- Spd +++
- Def ++++

Year	Lev	Team	AB	R	H	HR	RBI	Avg	OB	Slg	OPS	bb%	ct%	Eye	SB	CS	x/h%	Iso	RC/G
2017	Rk	AZL Athletics	138	26	35	1	14	254	318	326	644	9	80	0.46	7	3	17	72	3.51
2018	A	Beloit	460	51	110	0	34	239	291	302	594	7	82	0.40	24	8	21	63	2.89
2019	A+	Stockton	288	45	84	3	25	292	354	434	788	9	82	0.54	13	5	36	142	5.42

Precocious, slender SS has the arm and range to be cornerstone defender. A solid hitter in the CAL despite his young age, flashing high-volume contact ability via a lightning-quick stroke and all-fields approach. Clear lack of physicality and power likely caps his HR at single digits, but works counts well and has athleticism to steal some bags.

Alvarez,Francisco — 2 — New York (N)

EXP MLB DEBUT: 2023 | H/W: 5-11 220 | FUT: Starting C | 9D

Bats R Age 18
2018 FA (VZ)
- Pwr +++
- BAvg ++++
- Spd ++
- Def ++++

Year	Lev	Team	AB	R	H	HR	RBI	Avg	OB	Slg	OPS	bb%	ct%	Eye	SB	CS	x/h%	Iso	RC/G
2019	Rk	GCL Mets	26	8	12	2	10	462	533	846	1379	13	85	1.00	0	1	50	385	12.56
2019	Rk	Kingsport	131	24	37	5	16	282	365	443	808	11	75	0.52	1	1	30	160	5.65

Top CA in lower minors exploded on scene with advanced assignment as 17-year-old. Physically mature and strong with stocky build, he utilizes a quick, compact swing. Has solid control of the barrel showing ability to drive ball to the opposite field. There's above-average-to-plus power in frame. Defensively advanced; controls SB game.

Amaya,Jacob — 46 — Los Angeles (N)

EXP MLB DEBUT: 2021 | H/W: 6-0 180 | FUT: Utility player | 6C

Bats R Age 21
2017 (11) HS (CA)
- Pwr +
- BAvg +++
- Spd +++
- Def +++

Year	Lev	Team	AB	R	H	HR	RBI	Avg	OB	Slg	OPS	bb%	ct%	Eye	SB	CS	x/h%	Iso	RC/G
2017	Rk	AZL Dodgers	118	17	30	2	14	254	358	356	714	14	79	0.76	4	2	23	102	4.62
2018	Rk	Ogden	127	41	44	3	24	346	461	535	996	18	77	0.93	11	4	34	189	8.64
2018	A	Great Lakes	98	13	26	1	5	265	390	306	696	17	82	1.11	3	3	8	41	4.59
2019	A	Great Lakes	386	68	101	6	58	262	380	394	774	16	78	0.89	4	4	35	132	5.58
2019	A+	RanchoCuca	80	14	20	1	13	250	310	375	685	8	81	0.47	1	3	30	125	4.06

Undersized infielder has a solid understanding of the strike zone and patient approach. Upright stance with hands low and uses a quick trigger and a short stroke to make consistent contact, but without much power. Moves well with good instincts, range, and enough arm strength to stay up the middle. Hard worker profiles as a utility type.

Amaya,Miguel — 2 — Chicago (N)

EXP MLB DEBUT: 2022 | H/W: 6-1 185 | FUT: Starting C | 8C

Bats R Age 21
2015 FA (PN)
- Pwr +++
- BAvg +++
- Spd +
- Def +++

Year	Lev	Team	AB	R	H	HR	RBI	Avg	OB	Slg	OPS	bb%	ct%	Eye	SB	CS	x/h%	Iso	RC/G
2017	A-	Eugene	228	21	52	3	26	228	264	338	601	5	79	0.22	1	0	35	110	2.77
2018	A	South Bend	414	54	106	12	52	256	336	403	740	11	78	0.55	1	0	33	147	4.75
2019	A+	Myrtle Beach	341	50	80	11	57	235	339	402	741	14	80	0.78	2	0	44	167	4.93

Defensively advanced CA with plus arm strength who continues to grow into his bat. Has thrown out more than 33% of baserunners as a pro; blocks and receives well. Hands and lower half work well together in smooth RH swing with some feel to hit. Good strike-zone eye; works counts well. Chance to add more strength. Speed is below-average.

Americaan,Edmond — 89 — Chicago (N)

EXP MLB DEBUT: 2022 | H/W: 6-1 170 | FUT: Starting OF | 8E

Bats L Age 23
2018 (35) Chipola JC
- Pwr +++
- BAvg ++
- Spd +++
- Def +++

Year	Lev	Team	AB	R	H	HR	RBI	Avg	OB	Slg	OPS	bb%	ct%	Eye	SB	CS	x/h%	Iso	RC/G
2018	Rk	AZL Cubs	112	22	33	0	9	295	368	375	743	10	73	0.43	11	6	21	80	4.99
2019	A-	Eugene	255	38	72	4	32	282	332	435	767	7	75	0.29	16	7	36	153	5.09
2019	A	South Bend	25	0	4	0	0	160	250	200	450	11	64	0.33	0	0	25	40	0.65

Long, athletic OF prospect who was a bit old for the level, but showed speed and gap pop in short-season ball. Already possesses above-average bat speed and should grow into at least average HR with added strength to lower half. Has fringy bat to ball skills, but works counts and may be valued higher in OBP formats. Plus runner and athlete.

Antuna,Yasel — 6 — Washington

EXP MLB DEBUT: 2023 | H/W: 6-0 170 | FUT: Starting SS | 8E

Bats B Age 20
2016 FA (DR)
- Pwr ++
- BAvg +++
- 4.25 Spd ++
- Def ++

Year	Lev	Team	AB	R	H	HR	RBI	Avg	OB	Slg	OPS	bb%	ct%	Eye	SB	CS	x/h%	Iso	RC/G
2017	Rk	GCL Nationals	173	25	52	1	17	301	383	399	781	12	83	0.79	5	5	23	98	5.48
2018	A	Hagerstown	323	44	71	6	27	220	290	331	621	9	76	0.41	8	7	31	111	3.15
2019	Rk	GCL Nationals	6	1	1	0	0	167	375	167	542	25	83	2.00	0	0	0	0	3.11

Missed almost all of 2019 recovering from Tommy John surgery and a leg injury. Smooth-swinging switch-hitter, and gets to some power even from his thin build. Made plays at SS with a strong arm and footwork. Staying healthy and proving his injuries are behind him are current goals.

Apostel,Sherten — 5 — Texas

EXP MLB DEBUT: 2021 | H/W: 6-4 200 | FUT: Starting 3B | 9D

Bats R Age 21
2015 FA (CC)
Pwr ++++
BAvg ++
4.51 Spd +
Def ++

Year	Lev	Team	AB	R	H	HR	RBI	Avg	OB	Slg	OPS	bb%	ct%	Eye	SB	CS	x/h%	Iso	RC/G
2018	Rk	Bristol	139	28	36	7	26	259	398	460	858	19	70	0.76	3	1	39	201	6.76
2018	A-	Spokane	37	7	13	1	10	351	478	459	938	20	78	1.13	0	1	15	108	7.81
2019	A	Hickory	283	38	73	15	43	258	325	470	795	9	75	0.39	2	1	40	212	5.29
2019	A+	Down East	135	18	32	4	16	237	348	378	726	15	64	0.47	0	0	31	141	4.95

Broad-shouldered and barrel-chested, he caught fire after a cool start in his first full season, and finished in High-A. All-fields power is the show here; he squares balls up with regularity. Pitch recognition is still shaky at times, but it improved through the season. Has a third-baseman's arm and enough glove to stick.

Arauz,Jonathan — 456 — Boston

EXP MLB DEBUT: 2021 | H/W: 6-0 150 | FUT: Starting MIF | 7D

Bats B Age 21
2014 FA (PN)
Pwr ++
BAvg ++
Spd +++
Def +++

Year	Lev	Team	AB	R	H	HR	RBI	Avg	OB	Slg	OPS	bb%	ct%	Eye	SB	CS	x/h%	Iso	RC/G
2017	A	Quad Cities	127	23	28	0	4	220	327	276	602	14	86	1.11	0	1	18	55	3.49
2018	A	Quad Cities	204	31	61	4	29	299	389	471	859	13	81	0.79	7	6	34	172	6.50
2018	A+	Buies Creek	233	25	39	4	18	167	221	288	508	6	85	0.44	1	2	44	120	1.91
2019	A+	Fayetteville	317	41	80	8	42	252	317	388	705	9	78	0.43	5	4	34	136	4.21
2019	AA	Corpus Christi	108	12	26	3	13	241	305	389	694	8	82	0.53	1	1	31	148	4.11

Athletic, lithe INF who set new high in HR in improving season. Mostly known for steady glovework with sufficient SS range and average arm. Fundamentally sound with footwork and positioning. Still filling out frame and could become average hitter in time. Understands strike zone and has level stroke. Could become more than utility infielder.

Arias,Gabriel — 6 — San Diego

EXP MLB DEBUT: 2022 | H/W: 6-1 201 | FUT: Starting SS | 8D

Bats R Age 20
2016 FA (VZ)
Pwr +++
BAvg ++
Spd +++
Def ++++

Year	Lev	Team	AB	R	H	HR	RBI	Avg	OB	Slg	OPS	bb%	ct%	Eye	SB	CS	x/h%	Iso	RC/G
2017	Rk	AZL Padres 2	153	18	42	0	13	275	319	353	672	6	67	0.20	4	6	21	78	3.94
2017	A	Fort Wayne	62	8	15	0	4	242	266	258	524	3	74	0.13	1	0	7	16	1.56
2018	A	Fort Wayne	455	54	109	6	55	240	302	352	654	8	67	0.28	3	3	33	112	3.68
2019	A+	Lake Elsinore	477	62	144	17	75	302	337	470	806	5	73	0.20	8	4	29	168	5.36

Defensively advanced SS had full breakout with the bat in hitter-friendly CAL. Added roughly 10 points to his fly-ball rate and even flashed some pop to the opposite field, and power is intriguing. Can be overly aggressive early in counts and despite smooth cut and bat speed, bat to ball skills will need work. Good athlete with physical projection.

Armenteros,Lazaro — 7 — Oakland

EXP MLB DEBUT: 2022 | H/W: 6-0 182 | FUT: Starting OF | 8D

Bats R Age 20
2016 FA (CU)
Pwr +++
BAvg ++
Spd ++++
Def ++

Year	Lev	Team	AB	R	H	HR	RBI	Avg	OB	Slg	OPS	bb%	ct%	Eye	SB	CS	x/h%	Iso	RC/G
2017	Rk	AZL Athletics	156	24	45	4	22	288	355	474	829	9	69	0.33	10	1	38	186	6.21
2018	A	Beloit	292	43	81	8	39	277	357	401	757	11	61	0.31	8	6	22	123	5.54
2019	A+	Stockton	459	65	102	17	61	222	329	403	732	14	51	0.32	22	6	43	181	6.10

Twitchy, chiseled athlete with some bat speed but also pervasive ct% issues. Sexiest tool in the profile is plus speed, and he should be a solid SB source, as he likes to run. Has plus raw pop and will flash ability to opposite field, but can get pull-happy. Willing to take a walk and will have more OBP value. Big upside if ct% woes are addressed.

Arozarena,Randy — 89 — Tampa Bay

EXP MLB DEBUT: 2019 | H/W: 5-11 170 | FUT: Starting OF | 7B

Bats R Age 25
2016 FA (CU)
Pwr +++
BAvg +++
Spd +++
Def +++

Year	Lev	Team	AB	R	H	HR	RBI	Avg	OB	Slg	OPS	bb%	ct%	Eye	SB	CS	x/h%	Iso	RC/G
2018	AA	Springfield	91	22	36	7	21	396	433	681	1114	6	73	0.24	9	3	33	286	9.44
2018	AAA	Memphis	267	42	62	5	28	232	305	348	653	9	78	0.47	17	5	34	116	3.62
2019	AA	Springfield	97	14	30	3	15	309	391	515	906	12	76	0.57	8	5	40	206	7.09
2019	AAA	Memphis	246	51	88	12	38	358	415	593	1008	9	80	0.50	9	7	36	236	7.94
2019	MLB	St. Louis	20	4	6	1	2	300	364	500	864	9	80	0.50	2	1	33	200	6.10

Underrated player can do a bit of everything and had breakout season. Aggressive approach is mitigated by quick hands and ability to barrel the ball. Gap-to-gap approach, size, and poor pitch recognition limit power profile. Above-average speed, arm, and range give him the tools to play all three OF slots. Traded from STL to TAM in January.

Avelino,Abiatal — 456 — San Francisco

EXP MLB DEBUT: 2018 | H/W: 5-11 195 | FUT: Utility player | 6A

Bats R Age 25
2011 FA (DR)
Pwr ++
BAvg +++
Spd +++
Def +++

Year	Lev	Team	AB	R	H	HR	RBI	Avg	OB	Slg	OPS	bb%	ct%	Eye	SB	CS	x/h%	Iso	RC/G
2018	AAA	Scranton/WB	274	33	69	5	38	252	288	372	660	5	78	0.23	10	2	25	120	3.48
2018	AAA	Sacramento	13	2	2	0	1	154	154	154	308	0	77	0.00	2	0	0	0	-1.26
2018	MLB	SF Giants	11	1	3	0	0	273	273	273	545	0	73	0.00	0	0	0	0	1.63
2019	AAA	Sacramento	473	70	134	12	62	283	317	444	761	5	82	0.27	17	5	33	161	4.71
2019	MLB	SF Giants	7	0	2	0	1	286	375	286	661	13	57	0.33	0	0	0	0	4.23

Versatile INF with offensive ability but somewhat muted by impatient approach. Has shown some pop in revised swing and makes decent contact. Can steal bases on basis of speed/instincts combo. Reaching seats more often as he is pulling more. Has smooth actions in field with soft, quick hands. Owns very strong arm that works well at any spot.

Azocar,Jose — 89 — Detroit

EXP MLB DEBUT: 2020 | H/W: 6-0 185 | FUT: Reserve OF | 7C

Bats R Age 23
2012 FA (VZ)
Pwr +
BAvg ++
Spd +++
Def +++

Year	Lev	Team	AB	R	H	HR	RBI	Avg	OB	Slg	OPS	bb%	ct%	Eye	SB	CS	x/h%	Iso	RC/G
2016	A	West Michigan	501	56	141	0	51	281	316	335	651	5	76	0.21	14	5	13	54	3.39
2017	A+	Lakeland	431	38	95	3	37	220	245	292	537	3	72	0.11	12	6	20	72	1.77
2018	A	West Michigan	104	19	33	1	16	317	349	490	839	5	80	0.24	6	2	30	173	5.85
2018	A+	Lakeland	300	34	87	1	34	290	311	367	677	3	79	0.14	5	2	21	77	3.63
2019	AA	Erie	504	65	144	10	58	286	314	399	713	4	74	0.16	10	3	24	113	4.10

Extremely high-energy outfielder who doesn't seem to have a gear for slowing down. Quick-twitch profile brings pros and cons on both sides of the ball, including success on the base paths, but more swing-and-miss than is acceptable. Speed-first defender with a cannon of an arm.

Baddoo,Akil — 8 — Minnesota

EXP MLB DEBUT: 2022 | H/W: 6-1 210 | FUT: Starting OF | 7D

Bats L Age 21
2016 (2) HS (GA)
Pwr +++
BAvg +++
Spd ++++
Def +++

Year	Lev	Team	AB	R	H	HR	RBI	Avg	OB	Slg	OPS	bb%	ct%	Eye	SB	CS	x/h%	Iso	RC/G
2016	Rk	GCL Twins	107	15	19	2	15	178	296	271	567	14	66	0.50	8	1	21	93	2.45
2017	Rk	GCL Twins	75	18	20	1	10	267	345	440	785	11	83	0.69	4	0	40	173	5.52
2017	Rk	Elizabethton	126	39	45	3	19	357	471	579	1050	18	85	1.42	5	4	44	222	9.14
2018	A	Cedar Rapids	437	83	106	11	40	243	352	419	771	14	72	0.60	24	5	42	176	5.50
2019	A+	Fort Myers	117	15	25	4	9	214	287	393	680	9	67	0.31	6	2	40	179	4.02

Toolsy, athletic OF missed most of '19 after left elbow surgery. When healthy, there's plus bat speed in profile. However, unorthodox swing mechanics cause poor swing path. A patient hitter, works favorable counts, can't cash in. Average power potential. Plus speed is carry tool with SB instincts. Solid CF defender.

Bae,Ji-Hwan — 46 — Pittsburgh

EXP MLB DEBUT: 2022 | H/W: 6-1 170 | FUT: Starting MIF | 7C

Bats L Age 20
2017 FA (KR)
Pwr +
BAvg +++
Spd ++++
Def +++

Year	Lev	Team	AB	R	H	HR	RBI	Avg	OB	Slg	OPS	bb%	ct%	Eye	SB	CS	x/h%	Iso	RC/G
2018	Rk	GCL Pirates	129	24	35	0	13	271	347	349	696	10	88	0.94	10	4	23	78	4.48
2019	A	Greensboro	328	69	106	0	38	323	402	430	831	12	77	0.56	31	11	28	107	6.22

Speedy INF who led SAL and org in BA. Successful first full year in minors by showcasing plus speed and dynamic glovework. Split time between 2B and SS with good fundamentals. Has enough arm for SS and range for either spot. Hasn't yet hit HR as pro and rarely drives ball. Simple swing with plus hand-eye; and profiles as leadoff hitter.

Baker,Luken — 3 — St. Louis

EXP MLB DEBUT: 2021 | H/W: 6-4 265 | FUT: Reserve 1B | 7D

Bats R Age 23
2018 (2) TCU
Pwr ++++
BAvg +++
Spd +
Def ++

Year	Lev	Team	AB	R	H	HR	RBI	Avg	OB	Slg	OPS	bb%	ct%	Eye	SB	CS	x/h%	Iso	RC/G
2018	Rk	GCL Cardinals	24	10	12	1	7	500	556	708	1264	11	83	0.75	0	0	25	208	11.11
2018	A	Peoria	139	16	40	3	15	288	361	417	779	10	78	0.52	0	0	30	129	5.27
2019	A+	Palm Beach	439	47	107	10	53	244	324	390	713	11	74	0.46	1	1	40	146	4.47

Big bodied thumper has good raw power, but struggled in full-season debut and hit just 10 HR. A discerning eye at the plate, and all-fields power give him a chance to make an impact with the bat, but bottom of the scale speed and below-average defense limit him to 1B. Has the size and tools to develop into an solid offensive player.

Ball,Bryce — 3 — Atlanta

EXP MLB DEBUT: 2022 | H/W: 6-6 235 | FUT: Starting 1B | 7E

Bats L Age 21
2019 (24) Dallas Baptist
Pwr ++++
BAvg ++
Spd +
Def +

Year	Lev	Team	AB	R	H	HR	RBI	Avg	OB	Slg	OPS	bb%	ct%	Eye	SB	CS	x/h%	Iso	RC/G
2019	NCAA	Dallas Baptist	228	54	74	18	54	325	448	614	1062	18	77	0.96	3	2	41	289	9.17
2019	Rk	Danville	145	37	47	13	38	324	413	676	1089	13	79	0.73	0	0	53	352	9.09
2019	A	Rome	86	14	29	4	14	337	367	547	913	4	77	0.20	0	0	34	209	6.57

Big-bodied, power-oriented 1B had impressive draft year debut, feasting on FBs and laying off breaking pitches. Power is real and massive. Plus-plus potential in frame and swing. Struggles getting bat going and will likely be susceptible to velocity and spin as he moves up. Sprays ball well for power bat. Poor speed and poor defender at 1B.

Banfield,Will — 2 — Miami
EXP MLB DEBUT: 2023 | H/W: 6-0 200 | FUT: Starting C | 7E

Bats R Age 20
2018 (2) HS (GA)
Pwr ++++
BAvg ++
Spd +
Def ++++

Year	Lev	Team	AB	R	H	HR	RBI	Avg	OB	Slg	OPS	bb%	ct%	Eye	SB	CS	x/h%	Iso	RC/G
2018	Rk	GCL Marlins	82	7	21	0	14	256	315	378	693	8	66	0.25	0	1	43	122	4.45
2018	A	Greensboro	48	5	10	3	4	208	269	396	665	8	69	0.27	0	0	30	188	3.40
2019	A	Clinton	397	44	79	9	55	199	246	310	556	6	70	0.21	0	0	30	111	2.05

Defensive-oriented CA with some raw power potential struggled with aggressive full-season assignment. Very elongated swing. Struggled in '18 with ct% against older talent. Didn't fare better in Single-A. Lots of power in frame and sells out to it in swing. Plus defender with a plus throwing arm. Not a runner.

Banks,Nick — 79 — Washington
EXP MLB DEBUT: 2020 | H/W: 6-0 215 | FUT: Reserve OF | 7C

Bats L Age 25
2016 (4) Texas A&M
Pwr ++
BAvg ++
Spd +++
Def +++

Year	Lev	Team	AB	R	H	HR	RBI	Avg	OB	Slg	OPS	bb%	ct%	Eye	SB	CS	x/h%	Iso	RC/G
2017	A	Hagerstown	440	52	111	7	58	252	301	373	674	7	80	0.34	14	7	32	120	3.78
2018	A	Hagerstown	200	25	52	6	27	260	305	395	700	6	78	0.29	10	4	29	135	3.97
2018	A+	Potomac	232	27	61	4	30	263	305	379	684	6	78	0.27	1	0	28	116	3.83
2019	A+	Potomac	280	41	76	9	35	271	318	443	761	6	81	0.35	2	2	39	171	4.78
2019	AA	Harrisburg	156	19	45	1	21	288	351	410	761	9	74	0.37	6	0	33	122	5.15

Corner outfielder finally showed some offensive potential in second tour of High-A; then held his own upon promotion. Simple swing from the left side, he started turning on pitches and finding success with a pull approach. Makes good contact, and flat swing plane bodes toward more line drives than long HR. Good defender and some current speed.

Bannon,Rylan — 45 — Baltimore
EXP MLB DEBUT: 2020 | H/W: 5-7 180 | FUT: Utility player | 7C

Bats R Age 23
2017 (8) Xavier
Pwr ++
BAvg +++
Spd +++
Def ++

Year	Lev	Team	AB	R	H	HR	RBI	Avg	OB	Slg	OPS	bb%	ct%	Eye	SB	CS	x/h%	Iso	RC/G
2017	Rk	Ogden	149	39	50	10	30	336	411	591	1001	11	81	0.66	5	0	36	255	7.88
2018	A+	RanchoCuca	338	58	100	20	61	296	401	559	960	15	70	0.57	4	4	43	263	8.12
2018	AA	Bowie	98	16	20	2	11	204	350	327	677	18	76	0.92	0	0	40	122	4.28
2019	AA	Bowie	388	45	99	8	42	255	336	394	730	11	81	0.65	8	4	34	139	4.71
2019	AAA	Norfolk	82	18	26	3	17	317	341	549	890	4	83	0.21	0	1	50	232	6.19

Undersized, UT type inched closer to MLB debut. Above-average hit tool with solid plate skills carries versatile profile. Below-average power but a solid base; think 10-18 HR at maturity. Defensively challenged on IF but athletically sound. Fills in well at several positions. Average speed.

Barber,Colin — 8 — Houston
EXP MLB DEBUT: 2024 | H/W: 6-0 185 | FUT: Starting OF | 8E

Bats L Age 19
2019 (4) HS (CA)
Pwr +++
BAvg ++
Spd +++
Def +++

Year	Lev	Team	AB	R	H	HR	RBI	Avg	OB	Slg	OPS	bb%	ct%	Eye	SB	CS	x/h%	Iso	RC/G
2019	Rk	GCL Astros	99	19	26	2	6	263	381	394	775	16	71	0.66	2	1	31	131	5.63

Speedy leadoff OF with upside, but a long way away from reaching ceiling. Owns disciplined eye at plate and knows which pitches to drive. Focuses on contact and using entire field in simple approach. Runs very well and should develop power as he learns to read pitches better. Can play CF, but likely to end up in corner with solid average arm.

Barrera,Luis — 8 — Oakland
EXP MLB DEBUT: 2020 | H/W: 6-0 205 | FUT: Starting CF | 7C

Bats L Age 24
2012 FA (DR)
Pwr +
BAvg +++
Spd ++++
Def ++++

Year	Lev	Team	AB	R	H	HR	RBI	Avg	OB	Slg	OPS	bb%	ct%	Eye	SB	CS	x/h%	Iso	RC/G
2017	A	Beloit	278	41	77	3	22	277	316	406	723	5	78	0.26	13	7	30	129	4.39
2017	A+	Stockton	114	15	26	4	16	228	279	351	630	7	78	0.32	3	1	23	123	3.03
2018	A+	Stockton	313	51	89	3	46	284	351	415	766	9	80	0.51	10	4	31	131	5.16
2018	AA	Midland	131	24	43	0	18	328	371	450	822	6	86	0.50	13	3	28	122	5.70
2019	AA	Midland	224	35	72	4	24	321	356	513	869	5	79	0.25	9	7	33	192	6.24

Athletic, glove-first OF has a chance to be special glove but has lower offensive ceiling. Can flash plus speed in centerfield and on the bases and could have moderate SB value. Approach is line-drive oriented, with a high-probability barrel path conducive to high contact. Lacks leverage or physicality for HR, but will pepper the gaps.

Barrera,Tres — 2 — Washington
EXP MLB DEBUT: 2019 | H/W: 6-0 215 | FUT: Starting C | 7C

Bats R Age 25
2016 (6) Texas
Pwr +++
BAvg ++
Spd +
Def +++

Year	Lev	Team	AB	R	H	HR	RBI	Avg	OB	Slg	OPS	bb%	ct%	Eye	SB	CS	x/h%	Iso	RC/G
2016	A-	Auburn	164	19	40	3	17	244	307	366	673	8	87	0.68	0	0	33	122	3.98
2017	A	Hagerstown	237	28	66	8	27	278	342	464	806	9	76	0.40	1	0	41	186	5.57
2018	A+	Potomac	259	36	68	6	24	263	320	386	706	8	80	0.42	3	0	29	124	4.19
2019	AA	Harrisburg	357	42	89	8	46	249	318	381	699	9	81	0.52	1	2	35	132	4.20
2019	MLB	Washington	2	0	0	0	0	0	0	0	0	0	100		0	0		0	-2.66

Under-the-radar catching prospect that has methodically moved through the system before getting a cup of coffee in majors in 2019. Features a patient approach at plate with improving contact rate. Gap power from a solid RH swing, and good enough defender to project a big-league role.

Barrosa,Jorge — 89 — Arizona
EXP MLB DEBUT: 2023 | H/W: 5-9 165 | FUT: Reserve OF | 6B

Bats B Age 19
2017 FA (VZ)
Pwr +
BAvg +++
Spd +++
Def +++

Year	Lev	Team	AB	R	H	HR	RBI	Avg	OB	Slg	OPS	bb%	ct%	Eye	SB	CS	x/h%	Iso	RC/G
2018	Rk	DSL DBacks	204	57	61	3	21	299	376	412	787	11	83	0.74	37	6	23	113	5.44
2018	Rk	AZL DBacks	43	4	10	0	1	233	283	326	608	7	86	0.50	2	2	20	93	3.22
2018	Rk	Missoula	18	3	3	0	1	167	211	278	488	5	72	0.20	0	0	33	111	1.37
2019	A-	Hillsboro	223	25	56	1	26	251	316	336	652	9	86	0.66	8	4	27	85	3.78

Contact-oriented switch hitter who projects as fourth-OF type with defensive value. Looks to put the ball in play with limited hand load in swing and level barrel path to ball. Has plus defensive instincts required to stick in CF and has shown to be an adept base stealer in past. Clear lack of power in profile limits his overall upside.

Bart,Joey — 2 — San Francisco
EXP MLB DEBUT: 2020 | H/W: 6-3 235 | FUT: Starting C | 9C

Bats R Age 23
2018 (1) Georgia Tech
Pwr ++++
BAvg +++
Spd ++
Def ++++

Year	Lev	Team	AB	R	H	HR	RBI	Avg	OB	Slg	OPS	bb%	ct%	Eye	SB	CS	x/h%	Iso	RC/G
2018	NCAA	Georgia Tech	220	55	79	16	38	359	460	632	1092	16	75	0.73	3	0	35	273	9.59
2018	Rk	AZL Giants O	23	3	6	0	1	261	292	391	683	4	70	0.14	0	0	33	130	4.05
2018	A-	Salem-Keizer	181	35	54	13	39	298	342	613	955	6	78	0.30	2	1	54	315	7.14
2019	A+	San Jose	234	37	62	12	37	265	306	479	785	6	79	0.28	5	2	39	214	4.95
2019	AA	Richmond	79	9	25	4	11	316	372	544	916	8	73	0.33	0	2	36	228	6.98

All-around CA who can impact game with bat and glove. Missed time early due to fractured hand and broke thumb in AFL. Destroys LHP with mammoth power and can shorten swing to focus on contact to all fields. Has chance to hit for power, BA and OBP but will need to work counts more. Athletic behind plate and is adept receiver with plus arm strength.

Basabe,Luis — 78 — Chicago (A)
EXP MLB DEBUT: 2020 | H/W: 6-0 160 | FUT: Starting OF | 7D

Bats B Age 23
2012 FA (VZ)
Pwr +++
BAvg ++
Spd ++++
Def +++

Year	Lev	Team	AB	R	H	HR	RBI	Avg	OB	Slg	OPS	bb%	ct%	Eye	SB	CS	x/h%	Iso	RC/G
2017	A+	Winston-Salem	375	52	83	5	36	221	311	320	631	12	72	0.47	17	6	27	99	3.40
2018	A+	Winston-Salem	207	36	55	9	30	266	369	502	872	14	69	0.53	7	8	47	237	6.94
2018	AA	Birmingham	231	41	58	6	26	251	337	394	731	11	67	0.39	9	4	31	143	4.86
2019	A	Kannapolis	20	2	6	0	1	300	417	400	817	17	65	0.57	1	1	17	100	6.69
2019	AA	Birmingham	256	31	63	3	30	246	323	336	659	10	67	0.34	9	4	25	90	3.79

Quick-twitch, switch hitting OF struggled with health, contact and hard-hit rate in '19. Short, compact swing but struggles with consistent swing path and pitch recognition skills, which have been exposed in Double-A. Has altered swing trajectory to try and cash in on above-average power potential. Doesn't reach it in games, however. Plus runner.

Baty,Brett — 5 — New York (N)
EXP MLB DEBUT: 2022 | H/W: 6-3 210 | FUT: Starting 3B | 8C

Bats L Age 20
2019 (1) HS (TX)
Pwr ++++
BAvg +++
Spd ++
Def ++

Year	Lev	Team	AB	R	H	HR	RBI	Avg	OB	Slg	OPS	bb%	ct%	Eye	SB	CS	x/h%	Iso	RC/G
2019	Rk	GCL Mets	20	5	7	1	8	350	480	650	1130	20	70	0.83	0	0	57	300	11.02
2019	Rk	Kingsport	158	30	35	6	22	222	324	437	761	13	65	0.43	0	0	57	215	5.48
2019	A-	Brooklyn	10	2	2	0	3	200	500	300	800	38	70	2.00	0	0	50	100	6.83

LHH corner IF struggled in debut, mostly trying to do too much. Disciplined hitter with good plate skills. Controls barrel well and power plays to all fields. Could hit 30+ HR at projection. but long-term defensive questions. May fit best at 1B, though strong arm could work at 3B too.

Bautista,Mariel — 79 — Cincinnati
EXP MLB DEBUT: 2022 | H/W: 6-3 194 | FUT: Starting OF | 7D

Bats R Age 22
2014 FA (DR)
Pwr +++
BAvg +++
Spd ++++
Def +++

Year	Lev	Team	AB	R	H	HR	RBI	Avg	OB	Slg	OPS	bb%	ct%	Eye	SB	CS	x/h%	Iso	RC/G
2017	Rk	AZL Reds	147	29	47	0	20	320	342	395	737	3	84	0.21	16	1	21	75	4.40
2018	Rk	Billings	209	43	69	8	37	330	378	541	918	7	86	0.55	16	3	35	211	6.67
2019	Rk	AZL Reds	19	6	7	0	1	368	429	526	955	10	84	0.67	4	1	43	158	7.55
2019	A	Dayton	386	43	90	8	33	233	285	332	617	7	77	0.32	19	11	22	98	2.96

Toolsy, athletic OF struggled in Single-A debut with finding barrel. Quick wrists and loose hands aid dynamic swing speed. Struggles with bat path and extending early, depressing hard contact. Plus power in wiry frame and swing. Added mass last off-season, is a plus runner but doesn't have feel for SB ability yet.

Beard,James

8 | Chicago (A) | EXP MLB DEBUT: 2023 | H/W: 5-10 170 | FUT: Starting OF | 7E

Bats R Age 19
2019 (4) HS (MS)

- Pwr ++
- BAvg +++
- Spd +++++
- Def ++

Year	Lev	Team	AB	R	H	HR	RBI	Avg	OB	Slg	OPS	bb%	ct%	Eye	SB	CS	x/h%	Iso	RC/G
2019	Rk	AZL White Sox	127	19	27	2	12	213	259	307	566	6	57	0.15	9	3	26	94	2.49

Speedy OF struggled with hit tool in pro debut. '19 draft pick. Regarded as fastest prospect in draft. Elite run tool, Billy Hamilton-esque. Like Hamilton, hit tool extremely raw. Loose actions but inconsistent swing plane. Contact rate will need to improve. Likely below average power if hit tool develops. Raw defender.

Beck,Austin

8 | Oakland | EXP MLB DEBUT: 2021 | H/W: 6-1 200 | FUT: Starting OF | 8D

Bats R Age 21
2017 (1) HS (NC)

- Pwr +++
- BAvg ++
- Spd ++++
- Def +++

Year	Lev	Team	AB	R	H	HR	RBI	Avg	OB	Slg	OPS	bb%	ct%	Eye	SB	CS	x/h%	Iso	RC/G
2017	Rk	AZL Athletics	152	23	32	2	28	211	290	349	639	10	66	0.33	7	1	41	138	3.58
2018	A	Beloit	493	58	146	2	60	296	337	383	720	6	76	0.26	8	6	24	87	4.36
2019	A+	Stockton	338	40	85	8	49	251	301	411	712	7	63	0.19	2	2	40	160	4.68

Athletic, toosly OF with five-category value if things break right. Has Javy Baez-esque bat speed from right side that should translate to plus raw power. Iffy bat to ball skills that will need to be addressed to actualize HR potential. Plus speed; among best athletes in the system. Plus arm for any OF spot, though refining routes to remain in CF.

Beer,Seth

37 | Arizona | EXP MLB DEBUT: 2020 | H/W: 6-3 195 | FUT: Starting 1B | 7A

Bats L Age 23
2018 (1) Clemson

- Pwr ++++
- BAvg ++
- Spd +
- Def ++

Year	Lev	Team	AB	R	H	HR	RBI	Avg	OB	Slg	OPS	bb%	ct%	Eye	SB	CS	x/h%	Iso	RC/G
2018	A	Quad Cities	112	15	39	3	16	348	425	491	916	12	85	0.88	1	0	26	143	6.98
2018	A+	Buies Creek	107	15	28	5	19	262	288	439	728	4	79	0.18	0	1	32	178	4.09
2019	A+	Fayetteville	128	24	42	9	34	328	394	602	996	10	77	0.47	0	3	40	273	7.87
2019	AA	Jackson	88	8	18	1	17	205	271	318	589	8	72	0.32	0	1	44	114	2.74
2019	AA	Corpus Christi	234	40	70	16	52	299	364	543	907	9	75	0.41	0	0	36	244	6.69

Light-tower power prospect who swatted 26 HR and posted 95th percentile OBP among AA bats. Chance for elite HR output via plus bat speed and tremendous loft in swing; pop plays to all fields. Has made approach improvements with new org, though overall contact skills may only be fringe-average. Limited athletically to 1B or LF with his poor arm.

Bello,Micah

9 | Milwaukee | EXP MLB DEBUT: 2023 | H/W: 5-11 165 | FUT: Starting OF | 7C

Bats R Age 19
2018 (2) HS (HI)

- Pwr +
- BAvg +++
- Spd +++
- Def +++

Year	Lev	Team	AB	R	H	HR	RBI	Avg	OB	Slg	OPS	bb%	ct%	Eye	SB	CS	x/h%	Iso	RC/G
2018	Rk	AZL Brewers	154	25	37	1	15	240	320	325	644	10	73	0.44	10	1	22	84	3.58
2019	Rk	Rocky Mountain	177	30	41	6	20	232	303	418	721	9	73	0.38	5	4	44	186	4.48

Lean, athletic OF whose game is predicated on high-volume contact and a plus run tool. Smooth, level stroke through zone produces line-drive contact and ability to use all fields. Power projects to be mostly limited to the gaps, but has room to add strength. Displays reads and range necessary to stick at CF long-term.

Benson,Will

79 | Cleveland | EXP MLB DEBUT: 2022 | H/W: 6-5 225 | FUT: Starting OF | 7D

Bats L Age 21
2016 (1) HS (GA)

- Pwr ++++
- BAvg ++
- Spd +++
- Def +++

Year	Lev	Team	AB	R	H	HR	RBI	Avg	OB	Slg	OPS	bb%	ct%	Eye	SB	CS	x/h%	Iso	RC/G
2016	Rk	AZL Indians	158	31	33	6	27	209	306	424	730	12	62	0.37	10	2	58	215	5.09
2017	A-	MahoningVal	202	29	48	10	36	238	339	475	814	13	60	0.39	7	1	48	238	6.53
2018	A	Lake County	416	54	75	22	58	180	315	370	685	16	63	0.54	12	6	45	190	4.15
2019	A	Lake County	217	44	59	18	55	272	378	604	982	15	64	0.47	18	2	56	332	8.74
2019	A+	Lynchburg	217	29	41	4	23	189	290	304	594	13	66	0.42	9	2	37	115	2.87

Poweful, athletic corner OF prospect had jekyll and hyde season, split between A-Ball affiliates. Contact rate and BB% held steady throughout season. Hands struggle getting back to hit position, depressing reaction speed and quick stroke. Raw double-plus power in frame and swing. It plays in game but bat must react to pitches to reach barrel. SB threat.

Bishop,Braden

8 | Seattle | EXP MLB DEBUT: 2019 | H/W: 6-1 190 | FUT: Starting CF | 7D

Bats R Age 26
2015 (3) Washington

- Pwr ++
- BAvg +++
- Spd ++++
- Def ++++

Year	Lev	Team	AB	R	H	HR	RBI	Avg	OB	Slg	OPS	bb%	ct%	Eye	SB	CS	x/h%	Iso	RC/G
2017	AA	Arkansas	125	18	42	1	11	336	407	448	855	11	88	1.00	6	1	26	112	6.31
2018	AA	Arkansas	345	70	98	8	33	284	353	412	765	10	80	0.54	5	2	29	128	5.03
2019	A+	Modesto	25	7	6	0	3	240	296	360	656	7	64	0.22	0	0	33	120	3.95
2019	AAA	Tacoma	185	29	51	8	31	276	356	486	842	11	76	0.52	2	2	45	211	6.09
2019	MLB	Seattle	56	3	6	0	4	107	153	107	260	5	63	0.14	0	0	0	0	-2.55

Defensively-skilled CF prospect has limited offensive profile. Athletic build is near projection. Has flat, line drive oriented swing, conducive for heavy top spin contact but will occasional lower hands to get to trajectory. Frame doesn't suggest more than above-average power. Plus runner, doesn't use legs enough on bases.

Bishop,Hunter

8 | San Francisco | EXP MLB DEBUT: 2022 | H/W: 6-5 210 | FUT: Starting CF | 9D

Bats L Age 21
2019 (1) Arizona St

- Pwr ++++
- BAvg +++
- Spd ++++
- Def +++

Year	Lev	Team	AB	R	H	HR	RBI	Avg	OB	Slg	OPS	bb%	ct%	Eye	SB	CS	x/h%	Iso	RC/G
2019	Rk	AZL Giants O	20	4	5	1	3	250	483	550	1033	31	45	0.82	2	0	80	300	13.52
2019	A-	Salem-Keizer	85	21	19	4	9	224	421	400	821	25	67	1.04	6	2	32	176	6.48

Athletic OF with All-Star potential. Has all five tools at disposal with speed and power grading highest. Owns plus bat speed and making better contact as he ages. Can go to all fields, but double plus raw power is the highlight. Can be too patient at plate. Runs well and has 20 SB potential. Possesses plus range in CF with strong, accurate arm.

Blanco,Dairon

78 | Kansas City | EXP MLB DEBUT: 2020 | H/W: 6-0 170 | FUT: Reserve OF | 6C

Bats R Age 27
2018 FA (CU)

- Pwr ++
- BAvg +++
- Spd ++++
- Def +++

Year	Lev	Team	AB	R	H	HR	RBI	Avg	OB	Slg	OPS	bb%	ct%	Eye	SB	CS	x/h%	Iso	RC/G
2018	A+	Stockton	313	39	91	1	37	291	343	406	749	7	79	0.38	22	2	26	115	4.87
2019	AA	NW Arkansas	126	10	29	0	5	230	276	302	578	6	67	0.19	6	6	28	71	2.54
2019	AA	Midland	301	57	83	7	44	276	339	468	808	9	68	0.31	27	7	39	193	5.96

Older, speedy OF prospect with solid hit tool was acquired mid-season from OAK. All-fields approach. Gap-to-gap hitter with some plate discipline. Hit skills likely not to improve much. Average power in frame but doesn't get to it unless selling out to pull-side. Double-plus runner. Solid defender.

Blankenhorn,Travis

47 | Minnesota | EXP MLB DEBUT: 2020 | H/W: 6-2 228 | FUT: Starting 2B | 7B

Bats L Age 23
2015 (3) HS (PA)

- Pwr +++
- BAvg +++
- Spd +++
- Def +++

Year	Lev	Team	AB	R	H	HR	RBI	Avg	OB	Slg	OPS	bb%	ct%	Eye	SB	CS	x/h%	Iso	RC/G
2016	A	Cedar Rapids	91	11	26	1	12	286	343	418	761	8	69	0.29	2	1	31	132	5.22
2017	A	Cedar Rapids	438	68	110	13	69	251	324	441	764	10	73	0.39	13	2	42	189	5.15
2018	A+	Fort Myers	442	52	102	11	57	231	286	387	673	7	71	0.27	6	4	40	156	3.79
2019	A+	Fort Myers	52	6	14	1	3	269	377	404	781	15	77	0.75	0	0	36	135	5.58
2019	AA	Pensacola	388	50	108	18	51	278	310	474	785	4	76	0.19	11	0	35	196	4.93

Offensive-oriented 2B prospect with OF versatility had career season as power began showing up in game. Made swing adjustment, gaining trajectory without losing hit tool approach. Likely a fringe average hit tool. Power is in frame, may verify as above-average at maturity. Think 25 HR+. Solid runner, will sneak SB due to headiness over foot speed.

Bleday,JJ

9 | Miami | EXP MLB DEBUT: 2021 | H/W: 6-3 205 | FUT: Starting OF | 8B

Bats L Age 22
2019 (1) Vanderbilt

- Pwr ++++
- BAvg ++++
- Spd +++
- Def +++

Year	Lev	Team	AB	R	H	HR	RBI	Avg	OB	Slg	OPS	bb%	ct%	Eye	SB	CS	x/h%	Iso	RC/G
2019	NCAA	Vanderbilt	254	77	89	26	69	350	464	717	1181	18	79	1.02	1	1	45	366	10.46
2019	A+	Jupiter	140	13	36	3	19	257	311	379	690	7	79	0.38	0	0	31	121	3.96

LHH with refined hit tool added in-game plus power to land in the Top 5 of last year's draft. Athletic with a high baseball IQ, he controls the zone and the barrel with a quick, compact swing, generating loft. Hit/power tools both are plus. Average runner who can sneak SBs.

Bohm,Alec

35 | Philadelphia | EXP MLB DEBUT: 2020 | H/W: 6-5 225 | FUT: Starting 1B | 9C

Bats R Age 23
2018 (1) Wichita St

- Pwr ++++
- BAvg ++++
- 4.63 Spd +
- Def ++

Year	Lev	Team	AB	R	H	HR	RBI	Avg	OB	Slg	OPS	bb%	ct%	Eye	SB	CS	x/h%	Iso	RC/G
2018	Rk	GCL Phillies	27	7	11	0	5	407	429	519	947	4	85	0.25	2	0	18	111	6.89
2018	A-	Williamsport	107	9	24	0	12	224	291	290	580	9	82	0.53	1	0	25	65	2.84
2019	A	Lakewood	79	13	29	3	11	367	451	595	1045	13	82	0.86	3	0	41	228	8.72
2019	A+	Clearwater	158	25	52	4	27	329	394	506	901	10	87	0.81	1	2	33	177	6.71
2019	AA	Reading	238	38	64	14	42	269	346	500	846	11	84	0.74	2	2	41	231	5.92

Sped through three levels in first full season with outstanding hit/power tool combination. Tall, lanky, and powerful, showed impressive ability to use the opposite field when pitched away, and exhibited excellent strike-zone judgement. Fringy range and footwork, odd throwing motion will likely eventually push him to 1B; bat will still carry him.

Bolt,Skye
89 | Oakland | EXP MLB DEBUT: 2019 | H/W: 6-2 187 | FUT: Reserve OF | 6A

Bats B Age 26	Year	Lev	Team	AB	R	H	HR	RBI	Avg	OB	Slg	OPS	bb%	ct%	Eye	SB	CS	x/h%	Iso	RC/G
2015 (4) North Carolina	2017	A+	Stockton	432	76	105	15	66	243	326	435	761	11	69	0.40	9	8	44	192	5.22
Pwr +++	2018	A+	Stockton	169	28	45	9	32	266	380	521	901	16	72	0.66	9	3	47	254	7.20
BAvg ++	2018	AA	Midland	285	41	73	10	37	256	321	446	766	9	74	0.36	10	1	42	189	5.05
Spd ++++	2019	AAA	Las Vegas	305	57	82	11	61	269	348	459	807	11	69	0.39	7	5	40	190	5.85
Def +++	2019	MLB	Oakland	10	1	1	0	0	100	182	200	382	9	70	0.33	0	0	100	100	-0.09

Lean, athletic switch-hitter whose burgeoning offensive skills could net him a fourth OF role long-term. One of the system's more disciplined hitters, allowing him to get on base at a solid clip. Plus runner who can steal a base. More power as LH, but ct% skills are average from both sides. Likely the strong side of an OF platoon at his peak.

Bracho,Aaron
4 | Cleveland | EXP MLB DEBUT: 2023 | H/W: 5-11 175 | FUT: Starting 2B | 8C

Bats B Age 18	Year	Lev	Team	AB	R	H	HR	RBI	Avg	OB	Slg	OPS	bb%	ct%	Eye	SB	CS	x/h%	Iso	RC/G
2018 FA (VZ)																				
Pwr ++++																				
BAvg ++++																				
Spd +++	2019	Rk	AZL Indians 2	108	25	32	6	29	296	420	593	1012	18	81	1.10	4	1	56	296	8.57
Def +++	2019	A-	MahoningVal	27	5	6	2	4	222	344	481	825	16	70	0.63	0	0	50	259	5.97

Polished and poised MIF handled rookie ball assignment. Solid frame, will add strength too. Advanced approach and great zone discipline; recognizes spin. Short, compact uppercut swing geared towards creating loft and barreled contact. Raw plus power potential, has flashed in games; think 25+ HR at projection. Average runner, range limits him to 2B.

Bradley,Bobby
3 | Cleveland | EXP MLB DEBUT: 2019 | H/W: 6-1 225 | FUT: Starting 1B | 7C

Bats L Age 23	Year	Lev	Team	AB	R	H	HR	RBI	Avg	OB	Slg	OPS	bb%	ct%	Eye	SB	CS	x/h%	Iso	RC/G
2014 (3) HS (MS)	2017	AA	Akron	467	66	117	23	89	251	330	465	794	11	74	0.45	3	3	44	214	5.42
Pwr ++++	2018	AA	Akron	369	49	79	24	64	214	300	477	776	11	72	0.43	1	0	58	263	5.17
BAvg ++	2018	AAA	Columbus	114	11	29	3	19	254	320	430	750	9	62	0.26	0	0	41	175	5.37
Spd ++	2019	AAA	Columbus	402	65	106	33	74	264	339	567	906	10	62	0.30	0	0	53	303	7.56
Def +++	2019	MLB	Cleveland	45	4	8	1	4	178	245	356	600	8	56	0.20	0	0	75	178	3.35

Big-bodied slugging 1B-only prospect struggled in MLB debut. Dead FB hitter, pitchers quickly adjusted game plan by throwing steady diet of breaking pitches. Solid approach with plate discipline. Swing doesn't adjust well or lend itself to anything more than below-average hit tool. Double-plus power in frame, plays plus because of hit tool.

Breaux,Josh
2 | New York (A) | EXP MLB DEBUT: 2023 | H/W: 6-1 220 | FUT: Starting C | 7D

Bats R Age 22	Year	Lev	Team	AB	R	H	HR	RBI	Avg	OB	Slg	OPS	bb%	ct%	Eye	SB	CS	x/h%	Iso	RC/G
2018 (2) McLennan JC																				
Pwr +++																				
BAvg +++	2018	Rk	GCL Yankees	8	0	1	0	0	125	222	125	347	11	88	1.00	0	0	0	0	0.40
Spd +	2018	A-	Staten Island	100	6	28	0	13	280	301	370	671	3	80	0.15	0	0	32	90	3.62
Def ++	2019	A	Charleston (Sc)	199	28	54	13	49	271	322	518	840	7	70	0.25	0	0	43	246	5.90

Offensive-minded CA prospect made strides with hit tool in '19 shortening up swing and using more of the field. Super-aggressive approach. Will expand on anything close. Raw plus power plays to pull side. Will be close to above-average if hit tool continues development. Improved defensively. Base clogger.

Brewer,Jordan
89 | Houston | EXP MLB DEBUT: 2022 | H/W: 6-1 195 | FUT: Starting OF | 7C

Bats R Age 22	Year	Lev	Team	AB	R	H	HR	RBI	Avg	OB	Slg	OPS	bb%	ct%	Eye	SB	CS	x/h%	Iso	RC/G
2019 (3) Michigan																				
Pwr +++																				
BAvg ++																				
Spd ++++																				
Def +++	2019	A-	Tri City	54	5	7	1	3	130	161	185	346	4	89	0.33	2	0	14	56	0.04

Very athletic OF who struggled in debut, but has tools that could lead to 20 HR/20 SB seasons. Best tool is plus speed. Ranges well in CF, though routes need polish, Brings good approach to plate with strength and bat speed to profile for power. Expands strike zone at times and can struggle with breaking balls. Long swing can be exploited.

Brito,Marcos
6 | Oakland | EXP MLB DEBUT: 2022 | H/W: 6-0 165 | FUT: Starting MIF | 7D

Bats B Age 20	Year	Lev	Team	AB	R	H	HR	RBI	Avg	OB	Slg	OPS	bb%	ct%	Eye	SB	CS	x/h%	Iso	RC/G
2016 FA (DR)																				
Pwr +																				
BAvg +++	2017	Rk	AZL Athletics	171	30	40	1	17	234	318	298	616	11	75	0.50	4	1	18	64	3.21
Spd +++	2018	A-	Vermont	212	29	51	1	20	241	326	288	614	11	76	0.54	7	6	14	47	3.20
Def +++	2019	A	Beloit	204	21	37	2	13	181	261	250	511	10	67	0.33	3	4	27	69	1.55

Loose, projectable INF with some feel to hit and up-the-middle defensive ability. Approach is advanced for age and smooth, level swing lends itself to high volume grounders and contact. Utilizes all fields, but will need to turn on more pitches and bulk up to hit for more power. Played all '19 at SS, though arm may work better from 2B.

Brown,Dasan
8 | Toronto | EXP MLB DEBUT: 2024 | H/W: 6-0 185 | FUT: Starting CF | 8E

Bats R Age 18	Year	Lev	Team	AB	R	H	HR	RBI	Avg	OB	Slg	OPS	bb%	ct%	Eye	SB	CS	x/h%	Iso	RC/G
2019 (3) HS (ON)																				
Pwr +																				
BAvg ++																				
Spd +++++																				
Def +++	2019	Rk	GCL Blue Jays	45	8	10	0	5	222	352	356	707	17	62	0.53	6	2	40	133	5.11

Extraordinarily fast OF project who could pay immense dividends. Explosive speed allows for plus range in CF and could be elite defender down road. Raw hitter with lackluster power and inability to drive to all fields. Struggles with breaking balls and content to bury ball into ground. Has some strength and could develop OK hit tool with avg pop.

Brujan,Vidal
46 | Tampa Bay | EXP MLB DEBUT: 2020 | H/W: 5-9 155 | FUT: Starting 2B | 9D

Bats B Age 22	Year	Lev	Team	AB	R	H	HR	RBI	Avg	OB	Slg	OPS	bb%	ct%	Eye	SB	CS	x/h%	Iso	RC/G
2014 FA (DR)	2017	A-	Hudson Valley	260	51	74	3	20	285	367	415	783	12	86	0.94	16	8	31	131	5.51
Pwr ++	2018	A	Bowling Green	377	86	118	5	41	313	391	427	818	11	86	0.91	43	15	24	114	5.86
BAvg ++++	2018	A+	Charlotte	98	26	34	4	12	347	434	582	1015	13	85	1.00	12	4	38	235	8.28
Spd +++++	2019	A+	Charlotte	176	28	51	1	15	290	352	386	739	9	85	0.65	24	5	24	97	4.80
Def +++	2019	AA	Montgomery	207	28	55	3	25	266	330	391	722	9	83	0.57	24	8	29	126	4.55

Switch-hitting IF with exceptional foot speed and bat control inched closer to big leagues. LH swing short, compact with no wasted effort. Patient and will spray low liners and ground balls across diamond. RH swing lags behind. Slight build but strong with some pull-power potential. Double-plus run tool. Could steal 50 bases in MLB. Solid defender.

Burdick,Peyton
79 | Miami | EXP MLB DEBUT: 2022 | H/W: 6-0 210 | FUT: Starting OF | 7C

Bats R Age 23	Year	Lev	Team	AB	R	H	HR	RBI	Avg	OB	Slg	OPS	bb%	ct%	Eye	SB	CS	x/h%	Iso	RC/G
2019 (3) Wright St																				
Pwr +++																				
BAvg +++	2019	NCAA	Wright St	214	79	87	15	72	407	536	729	1265	22	84	1.71	24	3	41	322	11.86
Spd +++	2019	A-	Batavia	22	3	7	1	5	318	375	545	920	8	77	0.40	1	1	29	227	6.93
Def +++	2019	A	Clinton	238	57	73	10	59	307	389	542	931	12	72	0.48	6	6	45	235	7.56

Picked up where his college season left off in pro debut, mashing in Single-A. Easy setup at the plate, makes up for average bat speed by having no wasted movement. Hands may not be quick enough to handle velocity. Solidly built and generates power from base. 20-25 HR power if hit skills allow it. Average runner; fits best in LF.

Burger,Jake
5 | Chicago (A) | EXP MLB DEBUT: 2021 | H/W: 6-2 210 | FUT: Starting 1B | 7E

Bats R Age 23	Year	Lev	Team	AB	R	H	HR	RBI	Avg	OB	Slg	OPS	bb%	ct%	Eye	SB	CS	x/h%	Iso	RC/G
2017 (1) Missouri St	2017	NCAA	Missouri St	247	69	81	22	65	328	428	648	1075	15	85	1.13	3	1	43	320	8.80
Pwr ++++	2017	Rk	AZL White Sox	13	4	2	1	2	154	214	462	676	7	85	0.50	0	0	100	308	3.70
BAvg +++	2017	A	Kannapolis	181	21	49	4	27	271	320	409	728	7	85	0.46	0	1	31	138	4.47
Spd ++	2018		Did not play - injury																	
Def +++	2019		Did not play - injury																	

Physically strong power-first corner IF has missed 2 seasons due to leg injuries. Tore achilles in same leg twice in '18 and couldn't get on the field in '19 due to heel injury in same leg. Patient hitter with solid ct% skills. Power plays, mostly to pull-side in game. Solid hands but likely 1B long term due to range limitations.

Busch,Michael
4 | Los Angeles (N) | EXP MLB DEBUT: 2022 | H/W: 6-0 207 | FUT: Starting 2B | 7C

Bats L Age 22	Year	Lev	Team	AB	R	H	HR	RBI	Avg	OB	Slg	OPS	bb%	ct%	Eye	SB	CS	x/h%	Iso	RC/G
2019 (1) North Carolina																				
Pwr +++																				
BAvg +++																				
Spd ++	2019	Rk	AZL Dodgers	13	1	1	0	0	77	143	77	220	7	85	0.50	0	0	0	0	-1.47
Def ++	2019	A	Great Lakes	11	4	2	0	0	182	182	182	364	0	82	0.00	0	0	0	0	-0.33

Professional hitter had a breakout in 2018 Cape Cod League (.322/.450/.567), but a tough pro debut. Doesn't wow with athleticism and bat will be key to long-term development. Lack of speed, arm, and range limit him to 2B but has the bat to ball skills and enough raw power to make an impact at the plate.

Bush,Bryce
59 | **Chicago (A)** | EXP MLB DEBUT: 2023 | H/W: 6-0 200 | FUT: Starting OF | **7E**

Bats R Age 20	Year	Lev	Team	AB	R	H	HR	RBI	Avg	OB	Slg	OPS	bb%	ct%	Eye	SB	CS	x/h%	Iso	RC/G
2018 (33) HS (MI)																				
Pwr +++	2018	Rk	AZL White Sox	43	8	19	1	8	442	529	605	1134	16	91	2.00	1	2	26	163	9.79
BAvg +++	2018	Rk	Great Falls	96	16	24	2	10	250	321	385	706	9	78	0.48	3	0	33	135	4.31
Spd ++	2019	Rk	AZL White Sox	9	0	0	0	0	0	0	0	0	0	78	0.00	0	0		0	-4.97
Def +++	2019	A	Kannapolis	254	29	51	5	33	201	278	346	624	10	64	0.29	4	1	43	146	3.35

Bat-speed darling struggled with ct%, eye-sight and injuries during first season in Single-A. Quick, whippy bat with big power potential. Uses lower half well in uppercut-oriented swing. Swing plane is geared for loft but can get under ball and is prone to swing-and-miss. Likely moving off 3B completely soon. Arm fits in RF with enough athleticism.

Cabello,Antonio
7 | **New York (A)** | EXP MLB DEBUT: 2023 | H/W: 5-10 160 | FUT: Starting OF | **8E**

Bats R Age 19	Year	Lev	Team	AB	R	H	HR	RBI	Avg	OB	Slg	OPS	bb%	ct%	Eye	SB	CS	x/h%	Iso	RC/G
2018 FA (VZ)																				
Pwr +++																				
BAvg +++	2018	Rk	GCL Yankees W	137	21	44	5	20	321	411	555	966	13	75	0.62	5	5	41	234	8.01
Spd +++	2018	Rk	DSL Yankees	22	5	5	0	1	227	393	318	711	21	73	1.00	5	1	20	91	5.04
Def +++	2019	Rk	Pulaski	227	31	48	3	19	211	272	330	603	8	66	0.25	5	4	35	119	2.93

Five-tool prospect regressed in terrible 2019 season. Hasn't been quite right since '18 shoulder injury. Bat speed has been sapped, which propelled hit tool to a plus projection previously. Struggles with pitch selection too. Looked to be primed for CF but has lost a step already. Still, if some of his tools come back, projects as a solid MLB OF.

Callihan,Tyler
45 | **Cincinnati** | EXP MLB DEBUT: 2023 | H/W: 6-1 205 | FUT: Starting 3B | **8E**

Bats L Age 19	Year	Lev	Team	AB	R	H	HR	RBI	Avg	OB	Slg	OPS	bb%	ct%	Eye	SB	CS	x/h%	Iso	RC/G
2019 (3) HS (FL)																				
Pwr ++++																				
BAvg ++																				
Spd +++	2019	Rk	Billings	20	3	8	1	7	400	429	650	1079	5	80	0.25	2	0	25	250	8.54
Def ++	2019	Rk	Greeneville	204	27	51	5	26	250	282	422	703	4	77	0.20	9	3	39	172	4.03

IF prospect showcased raw plus power in pro debut. LH swing sells out to flyball trajectory. Struggles with over-aggresive approach and with spin, especially from LHP. Best position bet is at 3B, but has caught in HS but not ideal size or agility.

Cameron,Daz
89 | **Detroit** | EXP MLB DEBUT: 2020 | H/W: 6-2 195 | FUT: Starting OF | **8C**

Bats R Age 23	Year	Lev	Team	AB	R	H	HR	RBI	Avg	OB	Slg	OPS	bb%	ct%	Eye	SB	CS	x/h%	Iso	RC/G
2015 (1) HS (GA)	2017	A	Quad Cities	446	79	121	14	73	271	338	466	804	9	76	0.42	32	12	42	195	5.60
Pwr ++	2018	A+	Lakeland	216	35	56	3	20	259	336	370	706	10	68	0.36	10	4	27	111	4.50
BAvg +++	2018	AA	Erie	200	32	57	5	35	285	364	470	834	11	74	0.47	12	5	39	185	6.20
Spd +++	2018	AAA	Toledo	57	8	12	0	6	211	237	316	553	3	74	0.13	2	2	42	105	2.16
Def ++	2019	AAA	Toledo	448	68	96	13	43	214	310	377	687	12	66	0.41	17	8	43	163	4.25

Athletic outfielder able to maximize above-average speed and arm to hold down centerfield with little issue. Produced elevated rate of hard contact before challenging offensive season in 2019. Keen eye for pitch recognition and level of raw power that projects to increase later on.

Campusano,Luis
2 | **San Diego** | EXP MLB DEBUT: 2021 | H/W: 5-10 215 | FUT: Starting C | **8C**

Bats R Age 21	Year	Lev	Team	AB	R	H	HR	RBI	Avg	OB	Slg	OPS	bb%	ct%	Eye	SB	CS	x/h%	Iso	RC/G
2017 (2) HS (GA)																				
Pwr +++	2017	Rk	AZL Padres	121	7	34	4	24	281	360	413	774	11	80	0.63	0	2	24	132	5.13
BAvg +++	2017	Rk	AZL Padres 2	13	1	2	0	1	154	154	154	308	0	92	0.00	0	0	0	0	-0.30
Spd +	2018	A	Fort Wayne	260	26	75	3	40	288	337	365	702	7	83	0.44	0	1	19	77	4.14
Def +++	2019	A+	Lake Elsinore	422	63	137	15	81	325	399	509	908	11	86	0.91	0	0	34	185	6.81

Thick, strong CA who grew into his power and made palpable approach gains in Hi-A. Swings hard and has tremendous bat speed, but also shows natural feel to hit. Below-average runner; potential base-clogger. Has plus arm and transfer times have improved behind plate. Receiving and blocking will require more work, but has a chance to stick at CA.

Canario,Alexander
8 | **San Francisco** | EXP MLB DEBUT: 2022 | H/W: 6-1 165 | FUT: Starting OF | **8D**

Bats R Age 19	Year	Lev	Team	AB	R	H	HR	RBI	Avg	OB	Slg	OPS	bb%	ct%	Eye	SB	CS	x/h%	Iso	RC/G
2016 FA (DR)																				
Pwr ++++																				
BAvg +++	2018	Rk	AZL Giants	176	36	44	6	19	250	350	403	753	13	71	0.53	8	5	30	153	5.08
Spd +++	2019	Rk	AZL Giants O	43	13	17	7	14	395	422	1000	1422	4	79	0.22	1	0	65	605	12.46
Def +++	2019	A-	Salem-Keizer	193	38	58	9	40	301	360	539	899	9	63	0.25	3	1	47	238	7.54

Has yet to appear in full-season and continues to dominate lower ranks. Finished 2nd in NWL in HR and SLG with incredible bat speed. Has hit for BA, but lacks strike zone knowledge and frontline pitch recognition. Can sell out for power as well and lengthen swing. Could play CF or RF on basis of range and strong arm. Routes and reads need polish.

Cancel,Gabriel
4 | **Kansas City** | EXP MLB DEBUT: 2020 | H/W: 6-0 185 | FUT: Reserve IF | **6C**

Bats R Age 23	Year	Lev	Team	AB	R	H	HR	RBI	Avg	OB	Slg	OPS	bb%	ct%	Eye	SB	CS	x/h%	Iso	RC/G
2015 (7) HS (PR)																				
Pwr +++	2016	Rk	Burlington	172	28	50	5	26	291	348	494	842	8	81	0.47	1	2	48	203	5.95
BAvg ++	2017	A	Lexington	401	70	111	14	49	277	316	466	782	5	75	0.23	9	8	41	190	5.07
Spd +++	2018	A+	Wilmington	455	54	118	8	73	259	312	385	697	7	80	0.38	7	4	34	125	4.09
Def ++	2019	AA	NW Arkansas	464	70	114	18	69	246	297	427	724	7	69	0.24	15	2	42	181	4.45

Versatile, heady IF prospect sold out to swing trajectory, posting career HR total. Stocky, powerful frame. New swing, plus cutting off outer half of plate caused ct% to drop. Above-average power in frame and gets to enough bat speed for 20 HR potential. Fringe-average defender who plays multiple positions.

Canning,Gage
89 | **Washington** | EXP MLB DEBUT: 2022 | H/W: 5-10 175 | FUT: Reserve OF | **6C**

Bats L Age 22	Year	Lev	Team	AB	R	H	HR	RBI	Avg	OB	Slg	OPS	bb%	ct%	Eye	SB	CS	x/h%	Iso	RC/G
2018 (5) Arizona St	2018	NCAA	Arizona St	236	47	87	9	45	369	427	648	1075	9	77	0.44	8	7	43	280	9.16
Pwr ++	2018	A-	Auburn	54	13	17	2	7	315	373	593	965	8	67	0.28	0	2	47	278	8.42
BAvg ++	2018	A	Hagerstown	112	15	25	4	16	223	293	411	703	9	68	0.31	2	0	52	188	4.32
Spd +++	2019	A	Hagerstown	41	7	10	1	5	244	295	341	637	7	68	0.23	6	0	20	98	3.19
Def ++	2019	A+	Potomac	369	44	88	3	40	238	299	341	641	8	69	0.28	8	4	30	103	3.47

Thin frame with no projection left; hits from a wide stance and doesn't engage lower half in a noisy swing. Bat plane flat also, giving him very little future power. Consistent 30%+ K rates in last two seasons. Has a bit of speed, but well end up at COR OF due to poor arm; not enough bat to compensate.

Cannon,Cameron
46 | **Boston** | EXP MLB DEBUT: 2021 | H/W: 5-10 196 | FUT: Starting 2B | **7D**

Bats R Age 22	Year	Lev	Team	AB	R	H	HR	RBI	Avg	OB	Slg	OPS	bb%	ct%	Eye	SB	CS	x/h%	Iso	RC/G
2019 (2) Arizona																				
Pwr ++																				
BAvg +++	2019	NCAA	Arizona	232	71	92	8	56	397	476	651	1127	13	88	1.21	0	1	43	254	9.60
Spd +++	2019	Rk	GCL Red Sox	9	0	1	0	0	111	111	111	222	0	44	0.00	0	0	0	0	-3.68
Def ++	2019	A-	Lowell	161	17	33	3	21	205	260	335	596	7	77	0.32	1	0	45	130	2.78

Instinctual INF with solid fundamentals, but no overwhelming tools. Makes clean, easy contact with enough pull power to warrant long look. Not the most fleet of foot and not much of a threat on base. Likely 2B long-term due to average range and arm, though hands and footwork work well. Can make careless errors that need to be cleaned up.

Capel,Conner
78 | **St. Louis** | EXP MLB DEBUT: 2021 | H/W: 6-1 185 | FUT: Reserve OF | **6C**

Bats L Age 22	Year	Lev	Team	AB	R	H	HR	RBI	Avg	OB	Slg	OPS	bb%	ct%	Eye	SB	CS	x/h%	Iso	RC/G
2016 (5) HS (TX)	2017	A	Lake County	439	73	108	22	61	246	313	478	792	9	75	0.40	15	10	47	232	5.31
Pwr +++	2018	A+	Palm Beach	117	11	29	1	19	248	290	342	632	6	74	0.23	0	1	28	94	3.19
BAvg +++	2018	A+	Lynchburg	322	47	84	6	44	261	358	388	747	13	78	0.68	15	10	31	127	5.04
Spd +++	2019	AA	Springfield	341	39	79	9	40	232	280	352	632	6	75	0.27	9	4	28	120	3.10
Def +++	2019	AAA	Memphis	30	5	13	2	7	433	452	800	1252	3	80	0.17	1	0	54	367	10.61

Lean, athletic OF has average to above tools across the board, but none of them are plus. Quick bat, contact ability, and raw power should allow him to double digit HR in the majors, but 6% BB cuts into BA upside. Above-average speed and arm allow him to play all three OF positions, but without an uptick in power his likely upside is as a 4th OF.

Carlson,Dylan
8 | **St. Louis** | EXP MLB DEBUT: 2020 | H/W: 6-3 205 | FUT: Starting CF | **8B**

Bats B Age 21	Year	Lev	Team	AB	R	H	HR	RBI	Avg	OB	Slg	OPS	bb%	ct%	Eye	SB	CS	x/h%	Iso	RC/G
2016 (1) HS (CA)	2017	A	Peoria	383	63	92	7	42	240	331	347	678	12	70	0.45	6	6	28	107	4.06
Pwr ++++	2018	A	Peoria	47	5	11	2	9	234	368	426	794	18	79	1.00	2	0	45	191	5.73
BAvg +++	2018	A+	Palm Beach	376	63	93	9	53	247	339	386	724	12	79	0.67	6	3	33	138	4.67
Spd +++	2019	AA	Springfield	417	81	117	21	59	281	360	518	878	11	76	0.53	18	7	44	237	6.54
Def +++	2019	AAA	Memphis	72	14	26	5	9	361	410	681	1091	8	75	0.33	2	1	42	319	9.17

Breakout campaign was only a matter of time after being pushed aggressively early in career. Posted career highs en route to first 20/20 season. Plus bat speed and a powerful frame result in above-average raw power. BB rate and contact skills justify this level of production. Switch-hitter improved from the LH side and can play all three OF slots.

Carpio, Luis — 46 — New York (N)

EXP MLB DEBUT: 2021 | H/W: 5-11 190 | FUT: Reserve IF | 6C

Bats R Age 22
2013 FA (VZ)
Pwr ++
BAvg +++
Spd +++
Def +++

Year	Lev	Team	AB	R	H	HR	RBI	Avg	OB	Slg	OPS	bb%	ct%	Eye	SB	CS	x/h%	Iso	RC/G
2017	A	Columbia	474	53	110	3	36	232	309	302	611	10	80	0.56	17	5	22	70	3.19
2018	A+	St. Lucie	389	38	85	12	40	219	291	365	656	10	79	0.50	8	9	39	147	3.61
2018	AA	Binghamton	4	1	1	0	0	250	400	250	650	20	75	1.00	1	0	0	0	4.03
2019	A+	St. Lucie	94	13	31	1	12	330	394	426	820	10	84	0.67	2	3	19	96	5.76
2019	AA	Binghamton	243	28	64	3	22	263	339	362	702	10	80	0.57	2	6	28	99	4.33

Defense-oriented IF who has struggled to regain electricity in swing since '16 shoulder injury. Below-average swing speed, has tried to tap into loft in recent years, increasing swing trajectory to mixed results. Has added bulk to frame, hoping for over-the-fence power. Below average hit/power tool. Role evolving based on defensive versatility.

Carreras, Julio — 56 — Colorado

EXP MLB DEBUT: 2023 | H/W: 6-2 190 | FUT: Starting 3B | 8E

Bats R Age 20
2018 FA (DR)
Pwr +++
BAvg +++
Spd +++
Def ++++

Year	Lev	Team	AB	R	H	HR	RBI	Avg	OB	Slg	OPS	bb%	ct%	Eye	SB	CS	x/h%	Iso	RC/G
2019	Rk	Grand Junction	262	51	77	5	38	294	355	466	821	9	76	0.40	14	8	35	172	5.86

Wiry athlete with some quick-twitch attributes, but remains raw. Will have more real life value than fantasy value, as he is a plus defender at SS/3B with a strong arm. Currently a solid runner who should sustain speed even as he fills out his lean frame. Will need to work through kinks in swing, but shows bat speed and ability to make contact.

Carroll, Corbin — 8 — Arizona

EXP MLB DEBUT: 2023 | H/W: 5-10 165 | FUT: Starting CF | 8B

Bats L Age 19
2019 (1) HS (WA)
Pwr ++
BAvg ++++
Spd +++
Def +++

Year	Lev	Team	AB	R	H	HR	RBI	Avg	OB	Slg	OPS	bb%	ct%	Eye	SB	CS	x/h%	Iso	RC/G
2019	Rk	AZL DBacks	111	23	32	2	14	288	415	450	865	18	74	0.83	16	1	34	162	6.98
2019	A-	Hillsboro	43	13	14	0	6	326	396	581	977	10	72	0.42	2	0	50	256	8.60

High profile 2019 1st-rounder with elite run tool and natural feel to hit. Has compact, level stroke and sprays hard grounders and line-drives to all fields. Power limited to gaps, but will be able to add strength. Advanced approach for age and will have on-base value. Speed and base-running acumen point to SB upside. Projects as plus CF glove.

Cartaya, Diego — 2 — Los Angeles (N)

EXP MLB DEBUT: 2024 | H/W: 6-2 199 | FUT: Starting C | 8D

Bats R Age 18
2018 FA (VZ)
Pwr ++
BAvg +++
Spd +
Def ++++

Year	Lev	Team	AB	R	H	HR	RBI	Avg	OB	Slg	OPS	bb%	ct%	Eye	SB	CS	x/h%	Iso	RC/G
2019	Rk	AZL DodgersM	135	25	40	3	13	296	349	437	786	8	77	0.35	1	0	33	141	5.23

Venezuelan teen impressed in state-side debut. Shows good pitch recognition and plate discipline and should develop average power, though for now he has more of a line-drive, all-fields approach. Moves well behind the plate with good blocking and framing skills and a plus arm. Lots to like here, but work to do as well.

Casas, Triston — 3 — Boston

EXP MLB DEBUT: 2022 | H/W: 6-4 238 | FUT: Starting 1B | 8C

Bats L Age 20
2018 (1) HS (FL)
Pwr ++++
BAvg +++
Spd +
Def ++

Year	Lev	Team	AB	R	H	HR	RBI	Avg	OB	Slg	OPS	bb%	ct%	Eye	SB	CS	x/h%	Iso	RC/G
2018	Rk	GCL Red Sox	4	0	0	0	0	0	200	0	200	20	50	0.50	0	0		0	-4.89
2019	A	Greenville	422	64	107	19	78	254	344	472	815	12	73	0.50	3	2	46	218	5.87
2019	A+	Salem	7	2	3	1	3	429	429	1000	1429	0	71	0.00	0	0	67	571	13.35

Big, strong 1B finished 3rd in SAL in HR with mammoth, all-fields pop. Decent athlete for size and can make in-game adjustments to swing. Brings advanced eye to plate with chance to hit for moderate BA. Strikes out in bunches, but power makes up for it. Very little foot speed, though is passable defender with average arm.

Castro, Rodolfo — 46 — Pittsburgh

EXP MLB DEBUT: 2022 | H/W: 6-0 200 | FUT: Starting MIF | 7D

Bats B Age 20
2015 FA (DR)
Pwr +++
BAvg ++
Spd +++
Def ++

Year	Lev	Team	AB	R	H	HR	RBI	Avg	OB	Slg	OPS	bb%	ct%	Eye	SB	CS	x/h%	Iso	RC/G
2017	Rk	GCL Pirates	188	27	52	6	32	277	333	479	812	8	75	0.34	4	3	42	202	5.65
2018	A	West Virginia	385	47	89	12	50	231	280	395	675	6	74	0.26	6	3	39	164	3.71
2019	A	Greensboro	215	33	52	14	46	242	300	516	817	8	68	0.26	6	5	56	274	5.76
2019	A+	Bradenton	202	26	49	5	27	243	288	391	679	6	73	0.24	1	0	39	149	3.80

Powerful, versatile INF who set new high in HR between A- and A+. Switch hitter who offers more power from right as he zones in on LHP. Good bat control, but struggles with pitch recognition and swing-happy approach. May not provide impact with BA. Plays all INF spots but 1B, but not a standout. Body control and arm are average.

Castro, Willi — 6 — Detroit

EXP MLB DEBUT: 2019 | H/W: 6-1 205 | FUT: Starting SS | 8C

Bats B Age 22
2013 FA (PR)
Pwr ++
BAvg +++
Spd +++
Def +++

Year	Lev	Team	AB	R	H	HR	RBI	Avg	OB	Slg	OPS	bb%	ct%	Eye	SB	CS	x/h%	Iso	RC/G
2018	AA	Erie	476	67	125	9	52	263	312	397	709	7	77	0.31	17	5	34	134	4.21
2018	AA	Akron	371	55	91	5	39	245	298	350	649	7	77	0.33	13	4	30	105	3.46
2018	AAA	Toledo	21	0	6	0	0	286	286	286	571	0	76	0	1	0	0	0	1.99
2019	AAA	Toledo	465	75	140	11	62	301	353	467	819	7	76	0.34	17	4	34	166	5.70
2019	MLB	Detroit	100	10	23	1	8	230	274	340	614	6	66	0.18	0	1	35	110	3.05

Pure shortstop with feel to hold his post into the future. Quick hands and feet work well. Occasional miscues indicate continued need for polish. Switch-hitter with above-average speed who made his major league debut in August 2019. Ability to drive to the gaps with developing power.

Cavaco, Keoni — 6 — Minnesota

EXP MLB DEBUT: 2023 | H/W: 6-2 195 | FUT: Starting 3B | 8D

Bats R Age 18
2019 (1) HS (CA)
Pwr ++++
BAvg +++
Spd +++
Def +++

Year	Lev	Team	AB	R	H	HR	RBI	Avg	OB	Slg	OPS	bb%	ct%	Eye	SB	CS	x/h%	Iso	RC/G
2019	Rk	GCL Twins	87	9	15	1	6	172	209	253	462	4	60	0.11	1	1	33	80	0.68

1st round pick with tons of power potential struggled in pro debut. Combination of swing speed, uppercut trajectory and powerful lower half carries double-plus power tool. With swing speed comes looseness, which causes swing path to be inconsistent. Above-average defender with solid foot speed. Has plus arm at 3B.

Celestino, Gilberto — 89 — Minnesota

EXP MLB DEBUT: 2022 | H/W: 6-0 170 | FUT: Starting CF | 7C

Bats R Age 21
2015 FA (DR)
Pwr ++
BAvg +++
Spd ++++
Def ++++

Year	Lev	Team	AB	R	H	HR	RBI	Avg	OB	Slg	OPS	bb%	ct%	Eye	SB	CS	x/h%	Iso	RC/G
2018	Rk	Elizabethton	109	13	29	1	13	266	304	349	653	5	85	0.38	8	2	21	83	3.53
2018	A-	Tri City	127	18	41	4	21	323	372	480	853	7	80	0.40	14	0	29	157	5.94
2018	AA	Corpus Christi	8	0	0	0	0	0	0	0	0	0	38	0.00	0	0		0	-9.15
2019	A	Cedar Rapids	450	52	124	10	51	276	345	409	754	10	82	0.59	14	8	30	133	4.92
2019	A+	Fort Myers	30	6	9	0	3	300	344	433	777	6	87	0.50	0	0	44	133	5.20

Defensively skilled CF showed off bat-to-ball skills and patience. Has advanced feel for hitting with above-average hit tool. Average power should verify at maturity. 18-25 HR potential. Plus runner, doesn't show up on SB%. Plus defender, handles CF well.

Chang, Yu — 456 — Cleveland

EXP MLB DEBUT: 2019 | H/W: 6-1 180 | FUT: Utility player | 6B

Bats R Age 24
2013 FA (TW)
Pwr ++
BAvg +++
Spd +++
Def +++

Year	Lev	Team	AB	R	H	HR	RBI	Avg	OB	Slg	OPS	bb%	ct%	Eye	SB	CS	x/h%	Iso	RC/G
2016	A+	Lynchburg	417	78	108	13	70	259	331	463	794	10	74	0.41	11	3	47	204	5.55
2017	AA	Akron	440	72	97	24	66	220	303	461	764	11	70	0.39	11	4	55	241	5.11
2018	AAA	Columbus	457	56	117	13	62	256	321	411	733	9	68	0.31	4	3	37	155	4.73
2019	AAA	Columbus	253	45	64	9	39	253	323	427	749	9	74	0.39	4	1	39	174	4.83
2019	MLB	Cleveland	73	8	13	1	6	178	286	274	560	13	70	0.50	0	0	31	96	2.40

Versatile IF with some hit skills made MLB debut in '19. Didn't fare well in MLB due to speed of game, mostly at the plate. Contact-oriented hitter with good plate discipline. Has struggled maintaining power rate in upper minors. Has average power in medium frame. Solid defender. Doesn't excel or hurt at any IF position.

Chatham, C.J. — 46 — Boston

EXP MLB DEBUT: 2020 | H/W: 6-3 185 | FUT: Starting MIF | 7C

Bats R Age 25
2016 (2) Florida Atlantic
Pwr ++
BAvg +++
Spd +++
Def +++

Year	Lev	Team	AB	R	H	HR	RBI	Avg	OB	Slg	OPS	bb%	ct%	Eye	SB	CS	x/h%	Iso	RC/G
2017	A	Greenville	3	0	1	0	2	333	333	333	667	0	100		0	1	0	0	3.67
2018	A	Greenville	75	13	23	0	9	307	333	413	747	4	81	0.21	1	1	30	107	4.62
2018	A+	Salem	362	42	114	3	43	315	352	384	736	5	80	0.29	10	4	16	69	4.45
2019	AA	Portland	350	39	104	3	36	297	332	403	734	5	81	0.27	7	1	29	106	4.46
2019	AAA	Pawtucket	86	11	26	2	10	302	333	430	764	4	76	0.19	0	0	31	128	4.75

Lanky INF who led EL in BA and org in doubles. Spent most of season at SS, but also saw time at 2B due to org need. Possesses feel for barrel with simple, clean stroke and produces hard line drives to gaps. Power not part of game due to lack of strength in frame. Can be standout defender at times with quick feet and outstanding body control.

Chisholm,Jazz

6 | **Miami** | EXP MLB DEBUT: 2020 | H/W: 5-11 165 | FUT: Starting SS | **9D**

Bats L Age 22
2015 FA (BM)
Pwr ++++
BAvg +++
Spd +++
Def +++

Year	Lev	Team	AB	R	H	HR	RBI	Avg	OB	Slg	OPS	bb%	ct%	Eye	SB	CS	x/h%	Iso	RC/G
2017	A	Kane County	109	14	27	1	12	248	311	358	669	8	64	0.26	3	0	30	110	4.04
2018	A	Kane County	307	52	75	15	43	244	312	472	784	9	68	0.31	8	2	48	228	5.41
2018	A+	Visalia	149	27	49	10	27	329	367	597	964	6	65	0.17	9	2	37	268	8.06
2019	AA	Jacksonville	81	6	23	3	10	284	370	494	863	12	70	0.46	3	0	39	210	6.69
2019	AA	Jackson	314	51	64	18	44	204	296	427	723	12	61	0.33	13	4	45	223	4.80

Quick-twitch, athletic SS acquired in trade with ARI. Struggled mightily with contact and extreme flyball swing in 1st half. Recovered value going back to pre-2019 trajectory. Despite struggles, improved BB% and Eye. Plus power plays, mostly to pull field; 30+ HR at maturity. Double-digit SB threat and plays solid defensive SS.

Clemens,Kody

4 | **Detroit** | EXP MLB DEBUT: 2021 | H/W: 6-1 170 | FUT: Starting 2B | **7C**

Bats L Age 23
2018 (3) Texas
Pwr +++
BAvg ++
Spd ++
Def +++

Year	Lev	Team	AB	R	H	HR	RBI	Avg	OB	Slg	OPS	bb%	ct%	Eye	SB	CS	x/h%	Iso	RC/G
2018	NCAA	Texas	248	58	87	24	72	351	443	726	1169	14	80	0.82	5	0	48	375	10.12
2018	A	West Michigan	149	18	45	4	17	302	388	477	865	12	82	0.78	3	1	36	174	6.47
2018	A+	Lakeland	42	6	10	1	3	238	273	357	630	5	71	0.17	1	0	30	119	3.02
2019	A+	Lakeland	411	43	98	11	59	238	314	411	725	10	75	0.45	11	3	43	173	4.59
2019	AA	Erie	47	5	8	1	4	170	264	277	541	11	62	0.33	0	0	38	106	1.98

Gritty infielder with exceptional defensive instincts. Aggressive play helps to hide limited speed and range. Shows enough feel to be able to stick at second. Made improvements to swing path and ability to pull the ball. Power has struggled to stay consistent, but improved enough to earn promotion to Double-A in 2019.

Clement,Ernie

46 | **Cleveland** | EXP MLB DEBUT: 2020 | H/W: 6-0 170 | FUT: Reserve IF | **6C**

Bats R Age 24
2017 (4) Virginia
Pwr +
BAvg +++
Spd ++++
Def +++

Year	Lev	Team	AB	R	H	HR	RBI	Avg	OB	Slg	OPS	bb%	ct%	Eye	SB	CS	x/h%	Iso	RC/G
2018	A	Lake County	221	34	59	1	15	267	336	353	689	9	90	1.10	11	6	27	86	4.39
2018	A+	Lynchburg	133	29	46	1	13	346	412	421	833	10	95	2.14	5	3	17	75	6.07
2018	AA	Akron	65	9	16	0	5	246	279	354	633	4	89	0.43	2	1	38	108	3.49
2019	AA	Akron	394	46	103	1	24	261	307	322	629	6	92	0.79	16	10	18	61	3.54
2019	AAA	Columbus	11	3	6	0	4	545	615	636	1252	15	91	2.00	1	0	17	91	11.20

Contact-oriented singles hitter with excellent bat-to-ball skills has struggled with plate aggressiveness and lack of power to help carry profile. Quick hands and compact swing aid with ct%. Expands a lot and can't lay off out pitches. Has a flat swing plane with no power. Relies on legs for 10+ SB ability. Average defender, will move around IF.

Clementina,Hendrik

2 | **Cincinnati** | EXP MLB DEBUT: 2022 | H/W: 6-0 250 | FUT: Reserve C | **6C**

Bats R Age 22
2014 FA (CC)
Pwr +++
BAvg ++
Spd +
Def ++

Year	Lev	Team	AB	R	H	HR	RBI	Avg	OB	Slg	OPS	bb%	ct%	Eye	SB	CS	x/h%	Iso	RC/G
2016	Rk	AZL Dodgers	157	22	34	6	23	217	281	369	650	8	73	0.33	2	0	32	153	3.37
2017	Rk	Ogden	92	17	34	4	25	370	431	554	986	10	83	0.63	0	0	26	185	7.63
2017	Rk	Billings	96	13	23	2	10	240	291	365	656	7	74	0.28	0	0	35	125	3.50
2018	A	Dayton	340	38	91	18	59	268	327	497	824	8	71	0.30	1	0	45	229	5.80
2019	A+	Daytona	338	30	84	14	54	249	289	411	700	5	73	0.21	1	0	32	163	3.90

Power-first CA prospect struggled with finding barrels, depressing power numbers and average in '19. XXL physical profile. Will struggle to stay in CA shape. Raw plus-plus power in frame, plays average due to hit tool limitations. Long, slow swings. Has solid knowledge of zone and works pitchers. Defensively limited due to size.

Cluff,Jackson

6 | **Washington** | EXP MLB DEBUT: 2022 | H/W: 6-0 185 | FUT: Reserve IF | **7D**

Bats L Age 23
2019 (6) Brigham Young
Pwr +++
BAvg ++
Spd ++++
Def ++

Year	Lev	Team	AB	R	H	HR	RBI	Avg	OB	Slg	OPS	bb%	ct%	Eye	SB	CS	x/h%	Iso	RC/G
2019	NCAA	Brigham Young	199	57	65	4	56	327	432	518	950	16	80	0.95	12	0	42	191	7.85
2019	A	Hagerstown	240	33	55	5	19	229	305	367	671	10	74	0.41	11	5	33	138	3.87

Well-proportioned infielder with some feel to hit and surprising pop for his size. Was away from game for 2+ years on a church mission but had a great year at BYU. Average runner with great instincts leads to SB ability. Sound defensively with good range in middle infield spots.

Collins,Darryl

7 | **Kansas City** | EXP MLB DEBUT: 2024 | H/W: 6-2 185 | FUT: Starting OF | **7E**

Bats L Age 18
2019 FA (NT)
Pwr ++
BAvg +++
Spd +++
Def +++

Year	Lev	Team	AB	R	H	HR	RBI	Avg	OB	Slg	OPS	bb%	ct%	Eye	SB	CS	x/h%	Iso	RC/G
2019	Rk	AZL Royals	181	24	58	0	25	320	394	436	831	11	83	0.73	1	2	24	116	6.10

Raw, athletic OF prospect made pro debut in the Arizona League. Dutch born player has advanced bat-to-ball skills. Does a solid job shooting balls to gaps and letting his above-average speed do the rest. Scouts split on power tool, with half saying it will come and the other half saying not. Arm limits to LF, meaning tweener risk exists.

Collins,Zack

2 | **Chicago (A)** | EXP MLB DEBUT: 2019 | H/W: 6-3 220 | FUT: Starting C | **7D**

Bats L Age 25
2016 (1) Miami
Pwr +++
BAvg ++
Spd +
Def +

Year	Lev	Team	AB	R	H	HR	RBI	Avg	OB	Slg	OPS	bb%	ct%	Eye	SB	CS	x/h%	Iso	RC/G
2017	A+	Winston-Salem	341	63	76	17	48	223	365	443	807	18	65	0.64	0	2	50	220	6.17
2017	AA	Birmingham	34	7	8	2	5	235	422	471	893	24	68	1.00	0	0	50	235	7.50
2018	AA	Birmingham	418	58	98	15	68	234	383	404	788	19	62	0.64	5	0	41	170	6.12
2019	AAA	Charlotte	294	56	83	19	74	282	407	548	955	17	67	0.63	0	0	47	265	8.29
2019	MLB	Chi White Sox	86	10	16	3	12	186	300	349	649	14	55	0.36	0	0	44	163	4.08

Former 1st round pick made MLB debut despite struggling with contact and hard-hit rate. Had best year in Triple-A but was completely over-matched in MLB. Big hitch in setup, causing swing to slow considerably. Double-plus plate discipline with huge BB% potential. Can get to plus power if contact quality improves but doubtful. Likely DH.

Conine,Griffin

9 | **Toronto** | EXP MLB DEBUT: 2021 | H/W: 6-1 200 | FUT: Starting OF | **8D**

Bats L Age 22
2018 (2) Duke
Pwr ++++
BAvg ++
Spd ++
Def +++

Year	Lev	Team	AB	R	H	HR	RBI	Avg	OB	Slg	OPS	bb%	ct%	Eye	SB	CS	x/h%	Iso	RC/G
2018	NCAA	Duke	227	54	65	18	52	286	400	608	1008	16	67	0.58	0	1	54	322	8.92
2018	Rk	GCL Blue Jays	8	1	3	0	3	375	444	500	944	11	75	0.50	0	0	33	125	7.78
2018	A-	Vancouver	206	24	49	7	30	238	302	427	729	8	69	0.30	5	0	47	189	4.65
2019	A	Lansing	304	59	86	22	64	283	363	576	938	11	59	0.30	2	0	50	293	8.57

Big, strong OF who led MWL in HR and SLG despite serving suspension for violating drug policy. Posts very high K rate due to ultra aggressive approach. Can send any ball over fence due to loft and leverage in swing. Could post moderate BA as he knows K zone, but needs to improve against LHP. Not much value with glove, though has arm strength.

Contreras,William

2 | **Atlanta** | EXP MLB DEBUT: 2021 | H/W: 6-0 180 | FUT: Starting C | **8E**

Bats R Age 22
2015 FA (VZ)
Pwr ++++
BAvg +++
Spd ++
Def +++

Year	Lev	Team	AB	R	H	HR	RBI	Avg	OB	Slg	OPS	bb%	ct%	Eye	SB	CS	x/h%	Iso	RC/G
2017	Rk	Danville	169	29	49	4	25	290	378	432	810	12	82	0.80	1	0	31	142	5.78
2018	A	Rome	307	54	90	11	39	293	354	463	817	9	76	0.40	1	1	32	169	5.62
2018	A+	Florida	83	3	21	0	10	253	303	337	641	7	81	0.38	0	0	33	84	3.48
2019	A+	Florida	190	26	50	3	22	263	314	368	682	7	77	0.32	0	0	28	105	3.86
2019	AA	Mississippi	191	24	47	3	17	246	301	340	641	7	79	0.38	0	0	26	94	3.36

Athletic catcher who struggled with bat in High-A and Double-A. Generates solid bat speed with loose hands, sometimes effecting swing path. Will expand zone, especially against spin. Has a power in frame and swing, though he struggled reaching it, mostly due to not finding barrel enough against advanced pitching. Defense continues to improve.

Craig,Will

3 | **Pittsburgh** | EXP MLB DEBUT: 2020 | H/W: 6-3 212 | FUT: Starting 1B | **7C**

Bats R Age 25
2016 (1) Wake Forest
Pwr ++++
BAvg ++
Spd +
Def ++

Year	Lev	Team	AB	R	H	HR	RBI	Avg	OB	Slg	OPS	bb%	ct%	Eye	SB	CS	x/h%	Iso	RC/G
2016	NCAA	Wake Forest	182	53	69	16	66	379	507	731	1237	21	81	1.34	0	1	46	352	11.42
2016	A-	West Virginia	218	28	61	2	23	280	394	362	756	16	83	1.11	2	0	23	83	5.37
2017	A+	Bradenton	458	59	124	6	61	271	358	371	729	12	77	0.58	1	3	27	100	4.75
2018	AA	Altoona	480	73	119	20	102	248	308	448	756	8	73	0.33	6	3	45	200	4.85
2019	AAA	Indianapolis	494	69	123	23	78	249	310	435	746	8	70	0.30	2	3	37	186	4.70

Patient, strong hitter who is all about power. Set new career high in HR. Puts jolt into ball, though swing tends to get long and result in Ks. More of an all-or-nothing approach, but can work counts. Some hope for BA potential with tweaked bat plane, though may detract from power. Tried RF to hasten major league arrival, but best suited for 1B.

Cron,Kevin

3 | **Arizona** | EXP MLB DEBUT: 2019 | H/W: 6-5 250 | FUT: Starting 1B | **7A**

Bats R Age 27
2014 (14) TCU
Pwr ++++
BAvg ++
Spd +
Def +++

Year	Lev	Team	AB	R	H	HR	RBI	Avg	OB	Slg	OPS	bb%	ct%	Eye	SB	CS	x/h%	Iso	RC/G
2017	AA	Jackson	515	76	146	25	91	283	354	497	851	10	74	0.42	1	0	41	214	6.15
2018	AAA	Reno	392	57	121	22	97	309	367	554	920	8	74	0.36	1	0	42	245	6.97
2019	Rk	AZL DBacks	5	1	1	1	2	200	200	800	1000	0	60	0.00	0	0	100	600	8.37
2019	AAA	Reno	305	81	101	38	105	331	443	777	1220	17	75	0.79	1	2	58	446	11.12
2019	MLB	Arizona	71	12	15	6	16	211	253	521	774	5	61	0.14	0	1	67	310	5.42

Tall, hulking 1B prospect with massive raw power but also excessive contact woes. Creates leverage and torque in swing and produced elite barrel rate in rookie debut. Struggled mightily with pitch ID and was free-swinger despite previous gains in AAA. Possesses upside of 25-30 HR with solid-average OBP ability as everyday 1B.

Cronenworth,Jake

6 | San Diego | EXP MLB DEBUT: 2020 | H/W: 6-1 185 | FUT: Utility player | 7C

Bats L Age 26
2015 (7) Michigan
Pwr ++
BAvg +++
Spd +++
Def +++

Year	Lev	Team	AB	R	H	HR	RBI	Avg	OB	Slg	OPS	bb%	ct%	Eye	SB	CS	x/h%	Iso	RC/G
2017	AA	Montgomery	158	15	45	1	20	285	362	342	703	11	88	1.00	1	1	16	57	4.51
2018	AA	Montgomery	418	75	106	4	50	254	323	344	668	9	83	0.62	21	3	25	91	3.93
2018	AAA	Durham	25	4	6	0	2	240	269	360	629	4	80	0.20	1	0	50	120	3.24
2019	Rk	GCL Rays	12	2	2	0	0	167	231	250	481	8	83	0.50	0	0	50	83	1.68
2019	AAA	Durham	344	75	115	10	45	334	417	520	938	12	82	0.79	12	5	35	186	7.37

Versatile, athletic IF enjoyed best season as pro. Quick, compact LHH, cashed in on some below-average power potential. Solid defender at 3 positions. Athletic enough for OF duty. Above-average runner. A two-way player in college, TAM developed him as a MIF until 2019. Sat 92-95 MPH on mound with plus breaking-pitch in limited action.

Crook,Narciso

789 | Cincinnati | EXP MLB DEBUT: 2020 | H/W: 6-3 220 | FUT: Reserve OF | 6C

Bats R Age 24
2013 (23) Gloucester Cty CC
Pwr ++
BAvg +++
Spd +++
Def +++

Year	Lev	Team	AB	R	H	HR	RBI	Avg	OB	Slg	OPS	bb%	ct%	Eye	SB	CS	x/h%	Iso	RC/G
2018	A	Dayton	80	11	21	3	19	263	337	525	862	10	66	0.33	3	0	67	263	6.94
2018	A+	Daytona	48	5	10	1	3	208	255	354	609	6	77	0.27	1	1	40	146	2.91
2018	AA	Pensacola	161	18	46	2	22	286	358	379	736	10	75	0.44	4	4	20	93	4.76
2019	AA	Chattanooga	71	11	21	0	6	296	342	437	779	7	75	0.28	1	1	38	141	5.35
2019	AAA	Louisville	275	38	75	10	35	273	320	484	803	6	69	0.23	9	2	43	211	5.64

Over-achieving, athletic OF knocking on door to MLB debut. 4th or 5th OF profile. Does a little bit of everything to help. Solid, contact-oriented bat with gap-to-gap approach. HR power completely pull-oriented. Above-average runner who has some SB ability. Best defensively in RF.

Cruz,Oneil

6 | Pittsburgh | EXP MLB DEBUT: 2021 | H/W: 6-7 175 | FUT: Starting 3B | 9D

Bats L Age 21
2015 FA (DR)
Pwr ++++
BAvg +++
Spd ++++
Def +++

Year	Lev	Team	AB	R	H	HR	RBI	Avg	OB	Slg	OPS	bb%	ct%	Eye	SB	CS	x/h%	Iso	RC/G
2017	A	Great Lakes	342	51	82	8	36	240	297	342	639	8	68	0.25	8	7	22	102	3.29
2018	A	West Virginia	402	66	115	14	59	286	342	488	829	8	75	0.34	11	5	40	201	5.84
2019	Rk	GCL Pirates	10	0	6	0	1	600	636	700	1336	9	90	1.00	1	0	17	100	11.57
2019	A+	Bradenton	136	21	41	7	16	301	340	515	855	6	72	0.21	7	3	34	213	6.03
2019	AA	Altoona	119	14	32	1	17	269	351	412	763	11	71	0.43	3	1	38	143	5.39

Long, strong SS who missed time with fractured foot but showed superstar ability. Offers boatloads of raw pop and runs well enough to project to 20/20 player. Unusual height for SS and will likely move positions, but improving at SS with strong arm and could play 3B. Holes in swing and will strike out, but should hit for BA/power.

Cumberland,Brett

2 | Baltimore | EXP MLB DEBUT: 2021 | H/W: 5-11 205 | FUT: Reserve C | 6C

Bats B Age 24
2016 (2) California
Pwr +++
BAvg ++
Spd +
Def ++

Year	Lev	Team	AB	R	H	HR	RBI	Avg	OB	Slg	OPS	bb%	ct%	Eye	SB	CS	x/h%	Iso	RC/G
2018	AA	Mississippi	18	1	2	0	0	111	158	111	269	5	72	0.20	0	0	0	0	-1.84
2018	AA	Bowie	42	6	8	3	7	190	261	405	666	9	71	0.33	0	0	38	214	3.38
2019	A-	Aberdeen	14	0	4	0	1	286	333	286	619	7	71	0.25	0	0	0	0	2.95
2019	A+	Frederick	44	7	12	1	3	273	373	477	850	14	80	0.78	0	0	58	205	6.47
2019	AA	Bowie	125	21	31	4	20	248	365	408	773	16	73	0.68	0	0	39	160	5.45

Switch-hitting, offensive-oriented backstop showed improvement with glove skills. Has shortened up swing, improving the quality of contact off the bat. There's raw power in frame but consistently reaches and overextends for it. Doesn't get bat head out in front enough. Gives good target behind the plate and has improved footwork.

Dalbec,Bobby

35 | Boston | EXP MLB DEBUT: 2020 | H/W: 6-4 225 | FUT: Starting 3B | 8C

Bats R Age 24
2016 (4) Arizona
Pwr ++++
BAvg ++
Spd ++
Def ++++

Year	Lev	Team	AB	R	H	HR	RBI	Avg	OB	Slg	OPS	bb%	ct%	Eye	SB	CS	x/h%	Iso	RC/G
2017	A	Greenville	284	48	70	13	39	246	331	437	768	11	57	0.29	4	5	40	190	5.97
2018	A+	Salem	344	59	88	26	85	256	366	573	939	15	62	0.46	3	1	63	317	8.30
2018	AA	Portland	111	14	29	6	24	261	299	514	813	5	59	0.13	0	0	52	252	6.47
2019	AA	Portland	359	57	84	20	57	234	356	454	810	16	69	0.62	6	4	44	220	5.92
2019	AAA	Pawtucket	113	12	29	7	16	257	288	478	766	4	74	0.17	0	2	38	221	4.61

Powerful slugger who led org in HR; was 3rd in EL. Crushes fastballs to all fields and possesses disciplined eye to work counts and find quality pitches. Will swing and miss; contact issues likely to result in below average BA. Plus, strong arm ideal for 3B and can be elite defender in time. HR, BB, and defense is a solid combo for future success.

Davidson,Logan

6 | Oakland | EXP MLB DEBUT: 2021 | H/W: 6-3 185 | FUT: Starting SS | 7B

Bats B Age 22
2019 (1) Clemson
Pwr +++
BAvg ++
Spd +++
Def +++

Year	Lev	Team	AB	R	H	HR	RBI	Avg	OB	Slg	OPS	bb%	ct%	Eye	SB	CS	x/h%	Iso	RC/G
2019	A-	Vermont	205	42	49	4	12	239	339	332	671	13	73	0.56	5	0	22	93	3.94

Well-rounded, switch-hitting SS can do a bit of everything but lacks a plus tool. Taps into above-average power more as LH, where his wiry-strong frame produces plus bat speed. Shows good strike-zone awareness and willing to walk. Will swing over quality breakers, leading to potential ct% concerns. Moves well with a good arm and should stick at SS.

Davis,Brennen

78 | Chicago (N) | EXP MLB DEBUT: 2022 | H/W: 6-4 175 | FUT: Starting OF | 9E

Bats R Age 20
2018 (2) HS (AZ)
Pwr +++
BAvg +++
Spd ++++
Def +++

Year	Lev	Team	AB	R	H	HR	RBI	Avg	OB	Slg	OPS	bb%	ct%	Eye	SB	CS	x/h%	Iso	RC/G
2018	Rk	AZL Cubs 2	57	9	17	0	3	298	403	333	736	15	79	0.83	6	1	12	35	5.04
2019	A	South Bend	177	33	54	8	30	305	369	525	895	9	79	0.47	4	1	37	220	6.61

Uber-athletic OF prospect with physical gifts required for multi-category impact. Speed is plus tool and projects to have SB skills; can cover ground in CF. Arm is strong and could improve with more strength. Will need to improve contact, but shows plus raw power via smooth, leveraged stroke. Missed time in 2019 with finger injury.

Davis,Jaylin

79 | San Francisco | EXP MLB DEBUT: 2019 | H/W: 6-1 190 | FUT: Reserve OF | 7D

Bats R Age 25
2015 (24) Appalachian St
Pwr ++++
BAvg ++
Spd +++
Def +++

Year	Lev	Team	AB	R	H	HR	RBI	Avg	OB	Slg	OPS	bb%	ct%	Eye	SB	CS	x/h%	Iso	RC/G
2018	AA	Chattanooga	240	30	66	6	34	275	333	425	758	8	71	0.30	5	2	33	150	5.00
2019	AA	Pensacola	212	34	58	10	25	274	379	458	837	15	70	0.56	7	3	33	184	6.28
2019	AAA	Sacramento	102	21	34	10	27	333	414	686	1100	12	73	0.50	1	1	47	353	9.51
2019	AAA	Rochester	154	39	51	15	42	331	391	708	1098	9	70	0.33	2	0	53	377	9.58
2019	MLB	SF Giants	42	2	7	1	3	167	222	238	460	7	74	0.27	1	2	14	71	0.75

Trade deadline acquisition who finished 4th in minors in HR. Set easy career high in HR and SB. Has raw ingredients to be sound prospect, but has significant issues with making contact. Power and BA potential muted by very long swing and has trouble with spin. Added value with ability to play all OF spots, but better in corner due to raw instincts.

Dawson,Ronnie

8 | Houston | EXP MLB DEBUT: 2020 | H/W: 6-2 225 | FUT: Starting OF | 7D

Bats L Age 24
2016 (2) Ohio St
Pwr +++
BAvg ++
Spd +++
Def +++

Year	Lev	Team	AB	R	H	HR	RBI	Avg	OB	Slg	OPS	bb%	ct%	Eye	SB	CS	x/h%	Iso	RC/G
2017	A+	Buies Creek	52	7	17	0	5	327	375	423	798	7	83	0.44	1	3	24	96	5.43
2018	A+	Buies Creek	332	51	82	10	49	247	326	398	724	11	71	0.41	29	11	35	151	4.58
2018	AA	Corpus Christi	114	18	33	6	14	289	325	518	843	5	70	0.18	6	3	39	228	5.95
2019	AA	Corpus Christi	392	71	83	17	50	212	296	403	699	11	64	0.33	13	10	47	191	4.36
2019	AAA	Round Rock	34	1	5	0	3	147	216	176	393	8	68	0.27	1	0	20	29	-0.20

Powerful OF with high HR/high K potential. Led org in K while also setting high in HR. Struggled to hit for BA as he has ton of swing and miss in game and can get pull happy. Only hit .111 against LHP in AAA. Produces quality pop to the pull side due to bat speed and natural strength. Owns good speed and can be an above average defender in CF.

Daza,Yonathan

8 | Colorado | EXP MLB DEBUT: 2019 | H/W: 6-2 210 | FUT: Starting OF | 7C

Bats R Age 26
2010 FA (VZ)
Pwr +
BAvg ++++
Spd ++++
Def ++++

Year	Lev	Team	AB	R	H	HR	RBI	Avg	OB	Slg	OPS	bb%	ct%	Eye	SB	CS	x/h%	Iso	RC/G
2016	A+	Modesto	33	1	8	0	3	242	265	303	568	3	79	0.14	1	1	25	61	2.29
2017	A+	Lancaster	519	93	177	3	87	341	377	466	843	5	83	0.34	31	8	27	125	5.85
2018	AA	Hartford	219	27	67	4	29	306	327	461	789	3	89	0.29	4	5	36	155	5.01
2019	AAA	Albuquerque	387	67	141	11	48	364	403	548	951	6	87	0.48	12	9	32	183	7.00
2019	MLB	Colorado	97	7	20	0	3	206	260	237	497	7	78	0.33	1	0	10	31	1.53

Athletic, high-contact spray hitter with below-average power and attractive defensive value. Quick hands to the ball, level stroke produce line drives required for high-volume doubles. Makes plus contact and displays good plate coverage. Near-elite speed will translate to SB. Cannon arm and good defensive range will get him PT.

De Jesus,Alex

56 | Los Angeles (N) | EXP MLB DEBUT: 2023 | H/W: 6-2 170 | FUT: Starting 3B | 7D

Bats R Age 18
2019 FA (DR)
Pwr +++
BAvg +++
Spd ++
Def ++

Year	Lev	Team	AB	R	H	HR	RBI	Avg	OB	Slg	OPS	bb%	ct%	Eye	SB	CS	x/h%	Iso	RC/G
2019	Rk	AZL Dodgers	163	13	45	2	25	276	326	374	700	7	64	0.21	5	1	24	98	4.39

Impressive pro debut in the DSL and then in 44 games in the AZL. Worked hard to become stronger and more athletic. Short leg kick, good balance, and above-average power allow him to made hard contact, mostly to the pull-side. Approach can be overly aggressive (67% ct%) and will need to be addressed. Average range but enough arm to play SS or 3B.

de la Rosa, Jeremy — 79 — Washington

EXP MLB DEBUT: 2024 | H/W: 5-11 160 | FUT: Starting OF | 8D
Bats L | Age 18 | 2018 FA (DR)
Pwr +++ | BAvg +++ | Spd | Def ++

Year	Lev	Team	AB	R	H	HR	RBI	Avg	OB	Slg	OPS	bb%	ct%	Eye	SB	CS	x/h%	Iso	RC/G
2019	Rk	GCL Nationals	82	14	19	2	10	232	330	366	696	13	65	0.41	3	2	26	134	4.44

Athletically developed teenager from 2018 international class. Has a smooth lefthanded swing from a wide base that projects to both future power and BA. More present strength than most teenagers, though frame is not large by any means. Will settle in a corner OF spot; one to keep an eye on.

Dean, Justin — 8 — Atlanta

EXP MLB DEBUT: 2022 | H/W: 5-6 185 | FUT: Reserve OF | 6C
Bats R | Age 23 | 2018 (17) Lenoir-Rhyne
Pwr ++ | BAvg ++ | Spd ++++ | Def ++++

Year	Lev	Team	AB	R	H	HR	RBI	Avg	OB	Slg	OPS	bb%	ct%	Eye	SB	CS	x/h%	Iso	RC/G
2018	Rk	Danville	130	28	40	1	15	308	408	454	862	14	75	0.69	7	6	33	146	6.81
2018	A	Rome	113	20	29	0	8	257	323	363	685	9	76	0.41	9	3	24	106	4.16
2019	A	Rome	429	85	122	9	46	284	375	431	806	13	73	0.54	47	10	30	147	5.87

Athletic, speed-oriented OF prospect posted solid returns in 2nd pro season. Average bat speed with solid strike zone discipline, did solid job finding barrels and spraying field. Struggles with spin recognition and higher velocities. Below-average power potential. Speed carries profile. Plus run tool translate to 20-plus SB with playing time.

Deatherage, Brock — 8 — Detroit

EXP MLB DEBUT: 2021 | H/W: 6-1 175 | FUT: Starting OF | 7D
Bats L | Age 24 | 2018 (10) N Carolina St
Pwr ++ | BAvg ++ | Spd ++++ | Def ++

Year	Lev	Team	AB	R	H	HR	RBI	Avg	OB	Slg	OPS	bb%	ct%	Eye	SB	CS	x/h%	Iso	RC/G
2018	NCAA	NC St	228	47	70	14	41	307	383	548	931	11	67	0.37	18	8	34	241	7.66
2018	Rk	GCL Tigers W	9	6	5	4	7	556	600	1889	2489	10	89	1.00	0	0	80	1333	22.82
2018	A	West Michigan	176	25	55	2	18	313	363	443	806	7	72	0.28	15	3	25	131	5.73
2018	A+	Lakeland	45	12	15	1	6	333	412	467	878	12	71	0.46	4	0	20	133	6.88
2019	A+	Lakeland	451	62	103	7	41	228	266	357	623	5	70	0.17	45	11	32	129	3.06

Aggressive outfielder with near-elite speed and above-average overall defensive profile. Thrives off speed in the outfield and on the base paths. Contact rate suffered in return to Florida State League, holding him there for all of 2019. Swing path is good, but over-aggression leads to too much swing-and-miss and needs to be slowed down.

Decker, Nick — 9 — Boston

EXP MLB DEBUT: 2023 | H/W: 6-0 200 | FUT: Starting OF | 7D
Bats L | Age 20 | 2018 (2) HS (NJ)
Pwr +++ | BAvg +++ | Spd ++ | Def +++

Year	Lev	Team	AB	R	H	HR	RBI	Avg	OB	Slg	OPS	bb%	ct%	Eye	SB	CS	x/h%	Iso	RC/G
2018	Rk	GCL Red Sox	4	1	1	0	0	250	400	500	900	20	75	1.00	0	0	100	250	7.83
2019	A-	Lowell	170	23	42	6	25	247	330	471	800	11	65	0.36	4	5	50	224	6.04

Sleeper OF with good tools, but far from majors. Hasn't yet seen full season ball. Has power and bat to potentially be impact, middle-of-order producer. Can be beaten by good fastballs and can flail against breakers. Has bat speed and swing path to hit for BA some day. 20+ HR potential as well. Not enough for speed for CF, but enough arm for RF.

Deichmann, Greg — 9 — Oakland

EXP MLB DEBUT: 2020 | H/W: 6-2 190 | FUT: Starting OF | 7B
Bats L | Age 24 | 2017 (2) Louisiana St
Pwr ++++ | BAvg ++ | Spd +++ | Def ++

Year	Lev	Team	AB	R	H	HR	RBI	Avg	OB	Slg	OPS	bb%	ct%	Eye	SB	CS	x/h%	Iso	RC/G
2017	NCAA	LSU	266	54	82	19	73	308	420	579	999	16	77	0.82	7	3	41	271	8.24
2017	A-	Vermont	164	31	45	8	30	274	380	530	911	15	76	0.70	4	1	49	256	7.22
2018	Rk	AZL Athletics	38	9	11	1	7	289	372	526	898	12	79	0.63	0	0	45	237	7.00
2018	A+	Stockton	166	18	33	6	21	199	273	392	665	9	62	0.27	0	1	61	193	3.95
2019	AA	Midland	301	42	66	11	36	219	299	375	674	10	66	0.33	19	5	35	156	3.90

Smooth-swinging lefty dismantled AFL pitching after showing power and sneaky speed in AA. Stroke is quiet and compact and even started lifting the ball to all fields more consistency this past year. Elite raw power on contact. Contact skills are average, and has OPS of roughly .550 vs. LHP in full season ball. Fringe athlete and strong arm; RF profile.

Delgado, Raynel — 456 — Cleveland

EXP MLB DEBUT: 2023 | H/W: 6-2 185 | FUT: Reserve 3B | 6C
Bats B | Age 20 | 2018 (6) HS (FL)
Pwr +++ | BAvg ++ | Spd +++ | Def +++

Year	Lev	Team	AB	R	H	HR	RBI	Avg	OB	Slg	OPS	bb%	ct%	Eye	SB	CS	x/h%	Iso	RC/G
2018	Rk	AZL Indians 2	173	34	53	1	21	306	409	382	790	15	75	0.68	10	2	21	75	5.78
2019	A-	MahoningVal	200	19	48	2	17	240	312	345	657	10	70	0.35	5	4	31	105	3.74
2019	A	Lake County	64	7	16	0	6	250	273	313	585	3	80	0.15	1	0	25	63	2.53

Versatile, switch-hitting IF with a chance at starting role likely headed to bench spot. Plays 3 IF positions well and shows good reactions at 3B. Aggressive hitter who tries to use middle-of-the-field. Pull power plays and could be above-average at maturity, especially if he transfers the energy in his hitters load consistently. Average runner.

Deveaux, Trent — 78 — Los Angeles (A)

EXP MLB DEBUT: 2022 | H/W: 6-0 160 | FUT: Starting OF | 8E
Bats R | Age 19 | 2017 FA (BA)
Pwr ++ | BAvg ++ | Spd ++++ (4.34) | Def ++

Year	Lev	Team	AB	R	H	HR	RBI	Avg	OB	Slg	OPS	bb%	ct%	Eye	SB	CS	x/h%	Iso	RC/G
2018	Rk	AZL Angels	166	20	33	1	11	199	300	247	547	13	59	0.35	7	4	18	48	2.20
2019	Rk	Orem	29	4	5	1	2	172	226	310	536	6	48	0.13	1	0	40	138	2.42
2019	Rk	AZL Angels	215	38	53	6	23	247	322	437	759	10	65	0.32	14	6	47	191	5.43

Toolsy teenage OF started to find his swing during his second tour of AZL. Among the best pure athletes in the system and is plus-plus runner underway; will be SB threat. Likes the ball out front, where his above-avg raw power works best. Still learning his feel for hitting and ironing out his approach. Chance to stay in CF even as he fills out.

Devers, Jose — 6 — Miami

EXP MLB DEBUT: 2022 | H/W: 6-0 155 | FUT: Starting SS | 7D
Bats L | Age 20 | 2016 FA (DR)
Pwr + | BAvg +++ | Spd ++++ | Def ++++

Year	Lev	Team	AB	R	H	HR	RBI	Avg	OB	Slg	OPS	bb%	ct%	Eye	SB	CS	x/h%	Iso	RC/G
2018	A	Greensboro	337	46	92	0	24	273	304	332	636	4	85	0.31	13	6	17	59	3.32
2018	A+	Jupiter	8	1	2	0	2	250	333	250	583	11	100		0	0	0	0	3.73
2019	Rk	GCL Marlins	40	7	11	0	2	275	341	400	741	9	90	1.00	3	1	36	125	5.03
2019	A	Clinton	11	5	5	0	2	455	538	636	1175	15	82	1.00	0	0	40	182	10.81
2019	A+	Jupiter	126	13	41	0	8	325	366	365	731	6	84	0.40	5	0	10	40	4.46

Wiry, athletic SS struggled with injury bug once again but showed improvement with hit tool. Solid, compact swing with a flat trajectory, uses entire field to spray liners and ground balls. Has solid understanding of zone and lays off out pitches. No power projection in frame. Plus runner, although it hasn't popped in SB situations. Plus defender.

Diaz, Danny — 5 — Boston

EXP MLB DEBUT: 2023 | H/W: 6-1 170 | FUT: Starting 1B | 8E
Bats R | Age 19 | 2017 FA (VZ)
Pwr ++++ | BAvg ++ | Spd | Def +++

Year	Lev	Team	AB	R	H	HR	RBI	Avg	OB	Slg	OPS	bb%	ct%	Eye	SB	CS	x/h%	Iso	RC/G
2019	Rk	GCL Red Sox	105	15	22	1	12	210	245	343	588	5	71	0.17	0	0	55	133	2.64

Signed for huge bonus ($1.7M) in '17 and has enticing power to dream on. Swings with double plus bat speed and has the size and strength for impact potential. 3B now, but likely to move to 1B as he grows. Not a threat on base and could slow down more in time. Hit tool shows potential and needs to polish swing mechanics for BA growth.

Diaz, Jordan — 5 — Oakland

EXP MLB DEBUT: 2023 | H/W: 5-10 175 | FUT: Starting 1B | 8E
Bats R | Age 19 | 2016 FA (CB)
Pwr +++ | BAvg +++ | Spd | Def ++

Year	Lev	Team	AB	R	H	HR	RBI	Avg	OB	Slg	OPS	bb%	ct%	Eye	SB	CS	x/h%	Iso	RC/G
2017	Rk	AZL Athletics	27	2	5	0	2	185	185	185	370	0	85	0.00	1	0	0	0	-0.07
2018	Rk	AZL Athletics	159	23	44	1	25	277	354	390	744	11	86	0.86	0	2	32	113	5.02
2019	A-	Vermont	277	31	73	9	47	264	308	430	738	6	83	0.39	2	2	37	166	4.49

Young 3B who flashed power and ct% ability in NYPL tour. Has strong arm for third base, but lack of ideal lateral mobility could move him to 1B. Good news is his above-average raw power fits well there, and his smooth, level stroke should enable an avg BA. Below-averge legs; won't be an SB source. Power could blossom as he learns to work counts.

Diaz, Lewin — 3 — Miami

EXP MLB DEBUT: 2020 | H/W: 6-4 225 | FUT: Starting 1B | 8C
Bats L | Age 23 | 2013 FA (DR)
Pwr ++++ | BAvg ++ | Spd ++ | Def ++++

Year	Lev	Team	AB	R	H	HR	RBI	Avg	OB	Slg	OPS	bb%	ct%	Eye	SB	CS	x/h%	Iso	RC/G
2017	A	Cedar Rapids	466	47	136	12	68	292	328	444	772	5	83	0.31	2	1	34	152	4.86
2018	A+	Fort Myers	294	21	66	6	35	224	250	344	594	3	81	0.18	1	0	30	119	2.60
2019	A+	Fort Myers	214	34	62	13	36	290	333	533	866	6	81	0.35	0	0	40	243	5.91
2019	AA	Pensacola	126	12	38	6	26	302	343	587	931	6	82	0.35	0	0	61	286	6.87
2019	AA	Jacksonville	115	16	23	8	14	200	270	461	731	9	76	0.39	0	1	61	261	4.35

Slugging 1B slimmed down last off-season and saw skills skyrocket. Acquired mid-season from MIN. All-field power comes with limited ct% risk; a 30-HR bat at projection. Aggressive hitter who will expand the zone, but has a spray approach that should allow for average hit, too. Below-average runner but has good actions and plays a plus 1B.

Diaz,Yusniel — 9 — Baltimore

EXP MLB DEBUT: 2020 | H/W: 6-1 195 | FUT: Starting OF | 7C

Bats R Age 23
2015 FA (CU)

- Pwr +++
- BAvg +++
- Spd ++
- Def +++

Year	Lev	Team	AB	R	H	HR	RBI	Avg	OB	Slg	OPS	bb%	ct%	Eye	SB	CS	x/h%	Iso	RC/G
2018	AA	Tulsa	220	36	69	6	30	314	421	477	899	16	82	1.05	8	8	29	164	7.08
2018	AA	Bowie	134	23	32	5	15	239	329	403	732	12	79	0.64	4	5	34	164	4.66
2019	A-	Aberdeen	9	0	3	0	0	333	400	667	1067	10	89	1.00	0	0	100	333	9.06
2019	A+	Frederick	22	0	6	0	2	273	360	273	633	12	68	0.43	0	0	0	0	3.41
2019	AA	Bowie	286	45	75	11	53	262	336	472	809	10	77	0.48	0	3	45	210	5.64

Electric swing speed but he has yet to sustain prolonged success. Trying to find power stroke to avoid tweener label. Quick wrists and strong hands carry hit tool. HR pop still lags despite bat speed and power in frame. Below-average runner, likely future RF due to strong arm. Not a SB threat.

Dillard,Thomas — 3 — Milwaukee

EXP MLB DEBUT: 2021 | H/W: 6-0 230 | FUT: Starting OF | 7C

Bats B Age 22
2019 (5) Mississippi

- Pwr ++++
- BAvg ++
- Spd +++
- Def ++

Year	Lev	Team	AB	R	H	HR	RBI	Avg	OB	Slg	OPS	bb%	ct%	Eye	SB	CS	x/h%	Iso	RC/G
2019	Rk	AZL BrewersB	18	2	5	1	4	278	316	611	927	5	83	0.33	1	0	80	333	6.77
2019	A	Wisconsin	171	27	42	6	24	246	397	386	783	20	71	0.86	7	0	29	140	5.75

Muscular, stocky 1B/OF with massive raw pop as switch-hitter and some on-base ability. Owns plus bat speed and drives the ball to all fields. Speed is below-average but is adept base runner and could offer double-digit SB at next level. Limited to corner OF spot long-term. Should be valued higher in OBP formats than traditional.

Dominguez,Jasson — 789 — New York (A)

EXP MLB DEBUT: 2024 | H/W: 5-10 190 | FUT: Starting OF | 9E

Bats R Age 16
2019 FA (DR)

- Pwr ++++
- BAvg ++++
- Spd ++++
- Def ++++

Year	Lev	Team	AB	R	H	HR	RBI	Avg	OB	Slg	OPS	bb%	ct%	Eye	SB	CS	x/h%	Iso	RC/G
2019		Did not play in U.S.																	

Uber-talented, athletic OF signed with NYY as international free agent from DR. Has an all-world toolshed. Built like an NFL RB with double-plus raw tools across the board, scouts have dropped Bo Jackson, Yasiel Puig and even Mickey Mantle comps on his profile. Supposedly, well-polished too. Has yet to debut in pro ball.

Downs,Jeter — 6 — Los Angeles (N)

EXP MLB DEBUT: 2021 | H/W: 5-11 180 | FUT: Starting 2B | 8D

Bats R Age 21
2017 (1) HS (FL)

- Pwr +++
- BAvg +++
- Spd +++
- Def +++

Year	Lev	Team	AB	R	H	HR	RBI	Avg	OB	Slg	OPS	bb%	ct%	Eye	SB	CS	x/h%	Iso	RC/G
2017	Rk	Billings	172	31	46	6	29	267	367	424	791	14	81	0.84	8	5	26	157	5.53
2018	A	Dayton	455	63	117	13	47	257	333	402	736	10	77	0.50	37	10	32	145	4.67
2019	A+	RanchoCuca	412	78	111	19	75	269	354	507	861	12	76	0.56	23	8	50	238	6.39
2019	AA	Tulsa	48	14	16	5	11	333	407	688	1095	11	79	0.60	1	0	44	354	8.91

Athletic infielder came over in the Puig/Kemp deal and posted career-highs in doubles and HR and his first 20/20 season. Patient, all-fields approach and a quick bat results in surprising power. Average speed plays up due to advanced base-running skills. Solid defender with good instincts and soft hands, but arm might be a bit light to stick at SS.

Dubon,Mauricio — 46 — San Francisco

EXP MLB DEBUT: 2019 | H/W: 6-0 160 | FUT: Starting MIF | 7B

Bats R Age 25
2013 (26) HS (CA)

- Pwr +++
- BAvg ++++
- Spd +++
- Def +++

Year	Lev	Team	AB	R	H	HR	RBI	Avg	OB	Slg	OPS	bb%	ct%	Eye	SB	CS	x/h%	Iso	RC/G
2018	AAA	Col Springs	108	18	37	4	18	343	355	574	929	2	82	0.11	6	3	41	231	6.53
2019	AAA	San Antonio	404	59	120	16	47	297	327	475	802	4	85	0.31	9	6	33	178	5.08
2019	AAA	Sacramento	99	23	32	4	9	323	385	485	870	9	91	1.11	1	2	25	162	6.19
2019	MLB	SF Giants	104	12	29	4	9	279	312	442	754	5	82	0.26	3	1	31	163	4.52
2019	MLB	Milwaukee	2	0	0	0	0	0	0	0	0	0	50	0.00	0	0		0	-7.85

Aggressive INF who had best pro season. Exhibits quick, compact stroke to make easy, hard contact and uses entire field. More leverage in swing resulted in easy career high in HR and has the whippy bat to add more pop. Runs well underway, though not a burner, and SB output dropped. Very solid defender at 2B and SS with quick hands and feet.

Duran,Ezequiel — 4 — New York (A)

EXP MLB DEBUT: 2023 | H/W: 5-11 185 | FUT: Starting 2B | 8D

Bats R Age 20
2017 FA(DR)

- Pwr +++
- BAvg +++
- Spd +++
- Def ++++

Year	Lev	Team	AB	R	H	HR	RBI	Avg	OB	Slg	OPS	bb%	ct%	Eye	SB	CS	x/h%	Iso	RC/G
2018	Rk	Pulaski	219	34	44	4	20	201	232	311	543	4	70	0.14	7	0	32	110	1.84
2019	A-	Staten Island	246	49	63	13	37	256	325	496	821	9	69	0.32	11	4	46	240	5.92

Strong-bodied MIF led New York Penn Lg in HR. Gap hitter who found power selling out to pull-side on inside FB. Raw hit tool, struggles with pitch selection and bat path. Plus-defender at 2B but will be limited due to arm strength. Above-average runner.

Duran,Jarren — 8 — Boston

EXP MLB DEBUT: 2020 | H/W: 6-2 200 | FUT: Starting CF | 7B

Bats L Age 23
2018 (7) Long Beach St

- Pwr ++
- BAvg ++++
- Spd ++++
- Def +++

Year	Lev	Team	AB	R	H	HR	RBI	Avg	OB	Slg	OPS	bb%	ct%	Eye	SB	CS	x/h%	Iso	RC/G
2018	NCAA	Long Beach St	222	42	67	2	22	302	362	392	754	9	86	0.66	17	2	19	90	4.94
2018	A-	Lowell	155	28	54	2	20	348	392	548	940	7	83	0.42	12	4	31	200	7.14
2018	A	Greenville	128	24	47	1	15	367	391	477	868	4	83	0.23	12	6	23	109	5.96
2019	A+	Salem	199	49	77	4	19	387	450	543	993	10	78	0.52	18	5	26	156	8.09
2019	AA	Portland	320	41	80	1	19	250	300	325	625	7	74	0.27	28	8	21	75	3.17

Emerging OF who started year on fire before cooling upon AA promotion. Led org in SB and triples; 2nd in BA. Best tool is plus speed and can be above average CF despite fringy arm. Knows strike zone and get on base. Lack of punch not a concern, as he hits hard line drives with level swing path. Could become top of order hitter with high OBP.

Duran,Rodolfo — 2 — Philadelphia

EXP MLB DEBUT: 2022 | H/W: 5-9 181 | FUT: Reserve C | 7D

Bats R Age 22
2014 FA (DR)

- Pwr ++++
- BAvg ++
- Spd +
- Def +++

Year	Lev	Team	AB	R	H	HR	RBI	Avg	OB	Slg	OPS	bb%	ct%	Eye	SB	CS	x/h%	Iso	RC/G
2016	Rk	GCL Phillies	73	14	23	3	14	315	351	493	844	5	81	0.29	1	1	26	178	5.64
2016	A-	Williamsport	9	1	2	0	0	222	222	222	444	0	89	0.00	0	0	0	0	0.93
2017	A-	Williamsport	159	14	40	0	6	252	287	346	633	5	77	0.22	0	1	30	94	3.26
2018	A	Lakewood	311	44	81	18	46	260	305	495	800	6	76	0.27	1	1	44	235	5.19
2019	A+	Clearwater	233	25	56	6	23	240	272	369	641	4	77	0.19	0	0	30	129	3.14

Plus thump out of a classic catcher's frame, but poor plate discipline casts doubt on whether it can continue at higher levels. Aggressive approach but struggles with offspeed offerings. Average defender behind the dish, but a strong arm and excellent throwing mechanics led to gunning down 41% of attempted base stealers.

Edwards,Xavier — 46 — Tampa Bay

EXP MLB DEBUT: 2021 | H/W: 5-10 175 | FUT: Starting MIF | 8B

Bats B Age 20
2018 (1) HS (FL)

- Pwr +
- BAvg ++++
- Spd +++++
- Def +++

Year	Lev	Team	AB	R	H	HR	RBI	Avg	OB	Slg	OPS	bb%	ct%	Eye	SB	CS	x/h%	Iso	RC/G
2018	Rk	AZL Padres	73	19	28	0	11	384	477	466	942	15	86	1.30	12	1	18	82	7.68
2018	A-	Tri-City	86	21	27	0	5	314	433	360	793	17	83	1.20	10	0	15	47	5.95
2019	A	Fort Wayne	307	44	103	1	30	336	395	414	808	9	89	0.86	20	9	17	78	5.64
2019	A+	Lake Elsinore	196	32	59	0	13	301	348	367	715	7	90	0.74	14	2	15	66	4.48

Short, compact MIF prospect who pairs elite contact skills with blinding speed. Stroke is short and hands are lightning quick to the ball; shows ability to pepper the gaps both as RHB/LHB. High ground-ball profile; likely capped at single-digit HR even at his peak. Has spent time at 2B/SS in A-Ball. Average arm and build profile at 2B long-term.

Eierman,Jeremy — 46 — Oakland

EXP MLB DEBUT: 2021 | H/W: 6-0 205 | FUT: Starting MIF | 7C

Bats R Age 23
2018 (2) Missouri St

- Pwr +++
- BAvg ++
- Spd +++
- Def +++

Year	Lev	Team	AB	R	H	HR	RBI	Avg	OB	Slg	OPS	bb%	ct%	Eye	SB	CS	x/h%	Iso	RC/G
2018	NCAA	Missouri St	223	48	64	10	49	287	364	516	880	11	79	0.57	21	3	45	229	6.52
2018	A-	Vermont	247	36	58	8	26	235	273	381	654	5	72	0.19	10	4	31	146	3.33
2019	A+	Stockton	501	57	104	13	64	208	265	357	622	7	65	0.22	11	3	40	150	3.17

Former power-speed college bat struggled with Hi-A, posting a near 33% K-rate and BA near the Mendoza line. Most attractive tool is his plus raw power and a swing that is conducive to tons of fly balls. Some speed to offer, but lack of OBP ability caps his potential impact. Org believes in SS glove, but looks like UTIL guy until further notice.

Encarnacion,JC — 5 — Baltimore

EXP MLB DEBUT: 2023 | H/W: 6-3 195 | FUT: Reserve IF | 6D

Bats R Age 22
2016 FA (DR)

- Pwr +++
- BAvg ++
- Spd +++
- Def +

Year	Lev	Team	AB	R	H	HR	RBI	Avg	OB	Slg	OPS	bb%	ct%	Eye	SB	CS	x/h%	Iso	RC/G
2017	Rk	GCL Braves	103	16	36	2	16	350	374	563	937	4	79	0.18	4	2	39	214	7.02
2017	Rk	Danville	93	14	27	1	6	290	313	355	667	3	77	0.14	3	5	15	65	3.42
2018	A	Rome	361	45	104	10	57	288	313	463	775	3	72	0.13	5	5	37	175	5.00
2018	A	Delmarva	462	55	126	12	64	273	297	439	736	3	71	0.12	5	5	37	167	4.51
2019	A	Delmarva	450	53	108	9	50	240	285	356	640	6	68	0.19	12	3	29	116	3.30

Lanky, corner IF prospect didn't follow up encouraging '18 campaign. Uber-aggressive approach with little pitch recognition skills. Loose hands but struggles with consistent swing plane. Plus power in frame, struggles reaching it due to hit tool. Above-average runner despite awkward gait and has another gear. Stone hands defensively.

Encarnacion,Jerar | 79 | Miami | EXP MLB DEBUT: 2022 | H/W: 6-4 219 | FUT: Starting OF | 8E

Bats R Age 22 — 2015 FA (DR)

Pwr ++++ · BAvg ++ · Spd ++ · Def +++

Year	Lev	Team	AB	R	H	HR	RBI	Avg	OB	Slg	OPS	bb%	ct%	Eye	SB	CS	x/h%	Iso	RC/G
2017	Rk	GCL Marlins	154	25	41	5	26	266	311	448	759	6	67	0.20	3	3	37	182	5.09
2018	A-	Batavia	183	30	52	4	24	284	299	448	748	2	69	0.07	1	1	38	164	4.73
2018	A	Greensboro	54	3	4	0	2	74	153	74	227	8	57	0.22	0	0	0	0	-3.38
2019	A	Clinton	255	34	76	10	43	298	356	478	835	8	73	0.33	3	1	34	180	5.92
2019	A+	Jupiter	253	27	64	6	28	253	300	372	672	6	72	0.24	3	2	27	119	3.66

Tall, toolsy OF started showing skill in full-season ball. Physically strong, calling card is light-tower power. Hit tool is raw. Quick-twitch, loose hands, inconsistent swing path and length; will likely be low-average slugger. Raw plus-plus power, should play if hit tool improves. Solid range for corner OF and cannon arm for RF.

Erceg,Lucas | 5 | Milwaukee | EXP MLB DEBUT: 2020 | H/W: 6-3 210 | FUT: Starting 3B | 7C

Bats L Age 24 — 2016 (2) Menlo College

Pwr +++ · BAvg ++ · Spd +++ · Def +++

Year	Lev	Team	AB	R	H	HR	RBI	Avg	OB	Slg	OPS	bb%	ct%	Eye	SB	CS	x/h%	Iso	RC/G
2016	A	Wisconsin	167	17	47	7	29	281	330	497	827	7	77	0.32	1	3	40	216	5.65
2017	A+	Carolina	496	66	127	15	81	256	305	417	722	7	81	0.37	2	3	39	161	4.33
2017	AAA	Col Springs	10	2	4	0	2	400	455	600	1055	9	90	1.00	0	0	50	200	8.61
2018	AA	Biloxi	463	52	115	13	51	248	304	382	686	7	82	0.45	3	1	30	134	3.92
2019	AAA	San Antonio	357	55	78	15	52	218	304	398	702	11	71	0.43	2	2	42	179	4.22

Former small-school, 2nd-round pick who struggled offensively in PCL despite the juiced baseball. Profile is carried by plus raw power from left side that will show almost exclusively to his pull-side. BA bottomed-out to career low in 2019 by way of over-aggressiveness and fringy ct%. Has plus arm and good range for 3B, but he will need to hit.

Ernesto,Larry | 8 | Milwaukee | EXP MLB DEBUT: 2023 | H/W: 6-2 175 | FUT: Starting OF | 7D

Bats B Age 19 — 2017 FA (DR)

Pwr +++ · BAvg ++ · Spd +++ · Def +++

Year	Lev	Team	AB	R	H	HR	RBI	Avg	OB	Slg	OPS	bb%	ct%	Eye	SB	CS	x/h%	Iso	RC/G
2018	Rk	AZL Brewers	20	4	7	0	2	350	381	450	831	5	70	0.17	0	1	29	100	6.05
2018	Rk	DSL Brewers	203	38	48	5	20	236	286	394	680	6	67	0.21	9	4	42	158	3.99
2019	Rk	AZL BrewersG	122	15	21	2	9	172	217	246	463	5	52	0.12	5	1	24	74	0.84

Skinny, high-waisted OF with potential for moderate impact in all categories down the road. Switch hitter with above-avg raw power but mostly shows as LHH. Approach and pitch ID skills will require significant work, and will need time to add mass to projectable frame. Has a chance for SB value with long, fluid strides and some burst.

Estevez,Omar | 46 | Los Angeles (N) | EXP MLB DEBUT: 2021 | H/W: 5-10 185 | FUT: Utility player | 7D

Bats R Age 22 — 2015 FA (CU)

Pwr ++ · BAvg +++ · Spd ++ · Def +++

Year	Lev	Team	AB	R	H	HR	RBI	Avg	OB	Slg	OPS	bb%	ct%	Eye	SB	CS	x/h%	Iso	RC/G
2017	A+	RanchoCuca	457	56	117	4	47	256	306	348	654	7	79	0.34	2	2	26	92	3.55
2018	A+	RanchoCuca	515	87	143	15	84	278	336	456	792	8	73	0.33	3	1	42	179	5.42
2019	Rk	AZL DodgersM	20	7	6	0	3	300	364	400	764	9	60	0.25	0	0	33	100	5.92
2019	AA	Tulsa	299	34	87	6	36	291	358	431	789	9	77	0.44	0	2	34	140	5.40

Cuban infielder has solid bat-to-ball skills with a short, compact stroke and should continue to hit for average. Surprising pop for size, but line-drive, all-fields approach limits power upside. Average defender who continues to split time at 2B and SS and his future is in a utility role. None of his tools profile as plus.

Fabian,Sandro | 9 | San Francisco | EXP MLB DEBUT: 2022 | H/W: 6-1 180 | FUT: Starting OF | 8E

Bats R Age 22 — 2014 FA (DR)

Pwr ++ · BAvg +++ · Spd ++ · Def +++

Year	Lev	Team	AB	R	H	HR	RBI	Avg	OB	Slg	OPS	bb%	ct%	Eye	SB	CS	x/h%	Iso	RC/G
2016	Rk	AZL Giants	159	30	54	2	35	340	367	522	889	4	82	0.25	3	1	37	182	6.37
2017	A	Augusta	480	51	133	11	61	277	292	408	700	2	82	0.11	5	4	31	131	3.80
2018	A+	San Jose	406	47	81	10	35	200	248	325	573	6	74	0.24	1	2	37	126	2.33
2019	Rk	AZL Giants	32	4	7	2	8	219	324	500	824	14	59	0.38	0	0	71	281	6.71
2019	A+	San Jose	167	20	48	5	33	287	343	413	756	8	80	0.42	3	1	21	126	4.73

Smart, aggressive OF who repeated A+ and saw success upon return in July. Improved ability to put bat to ball, but often results in weak contact. Has strength and bat speed to offer power potential and may need to pull ball to realize. Needs to work counts, but reads spin. Plays a solid RF and covers lots of ground to go along with very strong arm.

Fairchild,Stuart | 8 | Cincinnati | EXP MLB DEBUT: 2021 | H/W: 6-0 190 | FUT: Starting OF | 7C

Bats R Age 24 — 2017 (2) Wake Forest

Pwr +++ · BAvg +++ · Spd +++ · Def +++

Year	Lev	Team	AB	R	H	HR	RBI	Avg	OB	Slg	OPS	bb%	ct%	Eye	SB	CS	x/h%	Iso	RC/G
2017	Rk	Billings	204	36	62	3	23	304	363	412	775	9	83	0.54	12	4	19	108	5.13
2018	A	Dayton	235	40	65	7	37	277	361	460	820	12	72	0.48	17	4	37	183	6.02
2018	A+	Daytona	220	25	55	2	20	250	304	350	654	7	71	0.27	6	2	31	100	3.58
2019	A+	Daytona	248	32	64	8	37	258	326	440	766	9	76	0.42	3	5	42	181	5.05
2019	AA	Chattanooga	153	25	42	4	17	275	355	444	799	11	85	0.83	3	2	40	170	5.59

All-around solid OF prospect doesn't flash a true carrying tool, but a hard worker. Grinds AB and utilizes solid approach to go deep into counts and find barrels in short, compact swing. Above-average power potential; flashes it occasionally but struggles to maintain. Average runner; better as COR OF but power will need to come.

Feliciano,Mario | 2 | Milwaukee | EXP MLB DEBUT: 2020 | H/W: 6-1 195 | FUT: Starting C | 8C

Bats R Age 21 — 2016 (2) HS (PR)

Pwr ++++ · BAvg +++ · Spd ++ · Def +++

Year	Lev	Team	AB	R	H	HR	RBI	Avg	OB	Slg	OPS	bb%	ct%	Eye	SB	CS	x/h%	Iso	RC/G
2017	A	Wisconsin	402	47	101	4	36	251	310	331	640	8	82	0.47	10	2	22	80	3.46
2018	Rk	AZL Brewers	14	0	4	0	2	286	375	357	732	13	79	0.67	0	1	25	71	4.90
2018	A+	Carolina	146	20	30	3	12	205	270	329	599	8	60	0.22	2	0	37	123	3.00
2019	A+	Carolina	440	62	120	19	81	273	318	477	795	6	68	0.21	2	1	40	205	5.47
2019	AA	Biloxi	12	2	2	0	0	167	167	333	500	0	67	0.00	0	0	50	167	1.47

Young, offense-minded backstop who made AA debut at just 20 years old last summer. Became more aggressive and looked to drive pitches in 2019, resulting in career-high HR but also less ct%. Will show plus bat speed with good barrel control, but expands the zone often. Good athlete behind plate. Will require more reps to stick at CA.

Fernandez,Eduarqui | 8 | Milwaukee | EXP MLB DEBUT: 2024 | H/W: 6-2 176 | FUT: Starting OF | 8E

Bats R Age 18 — 2019 FA (DR)

Pwr +++ · BAvg ++ · Spd +++ · Def +++

Year	Lev	Team	AB	R	H	HR	RBI	Avg	OB	Slg	OPS	bb%	ct%	Eye	SB	CS	x/h%	Iso	RC/G
2019		Did not play in U.S.																	

Advanced-hitting CF prospect who nearly led DSL in both HR and SB. Potential for average or better tools across the board, headlined by plus speed and good raw power. Aggressive, pull oriented hitter. Shows bat to ball skills and some HR upside as he adds strength. A move to a corner OF spot may ideally suit his defensive ability.

Fitzgerald,Tyler | 6 | San Francisco | EXP MLB DEBUT: 2022 | H/W: 6-3 205 | FUT: Starting MIF | 7D

Bats R Age 22 — 2019 (4) Louisville

Pwr ++ · BAvg +++ · Spd +++ · Def +++

Year	Lev	Team	AB	R	H	HR	RBI	Avg	OB	Slg	OPS	bb%	ct%	Eye	SB	CS	x/h%	Iso	RC/G
2019	Rk	AZL Giants	11	2	3	1	5	273	333	636	970	8	100		0	0	67	364	7.20
2019	A-	Salem-Keizer	102	20	29	0	16	284	376	431	807	13	76	0.63	2	1	45	147	6.04
2019	A	Augusta	72	11	19	0	9	264	338	306	643	10	76	0.47	4	0	16	42	3.55

Tall, consistent INF who made it to A- in pro debut. Has body and strength to offer power potential, though seems content with hard line drives. Has ability to differentiate between balls and strikes and draw walks. Owns average speed and will steal occasional base. May not stick at SS due to fringy range, but makes routine plays with instincts.

Fletcher,Dominic | 89 | Arizona | EXP MLB DEBUT: 2022 | H/W: 5-9 185 | FUT: Starting OF | 7D

Bats L Age 22 — 2019 (2) Arkansas

Pwr +++ · BAvg +++ · Spd ++ · Def +++

Year	Lev	Team	AB	R	H	HR	RBI	Avg	OB	Slg	OPS	bb%	ct%	Eye	SB	CS	x/h%	Iso	RC/G
2019	A	Kane County	214	33	68	5	28	318	381	463	844	9	77	0.44	1	1	29	145	6.09

Arkansas product taken in 2nd round of 2019 draft with a good CF glove and average blend of skills. Taps into his average raw power in games well and drives balls well to his pull-side. Swing can elongate at times and overall barrel control will require improvement. Could stick in CF despite lack of elite speed, but won't be SB source.

Fletcher,Trejyn | 8 | St. Louis | EXP MLB DEBUT: 2024 | H/W: 6-2 200 | FUT: Starting CF | 8E

Bats R Age 18 — 2019 (2) HS (ME)

Pwr +++ · BAvg ++ · Spd ++++ · Def ++++

Year	Lev	Team	AB	R	H	HR	RBI	Avg	OB	Slg	OPS	bb%	ct%	Eye	SB	CS	x/h%	Iso	RC/G
2019	Rk	Johnson City	123	9	28	2	18	228	269	325	594	5	52	0.12	7	1	25	98	3.36
2019	Rk	GCL Cardinals	37	6	11	2	8	297	366	541	906	10	54	0.24	0	0	45	243	8.82

Premium athlete has exciting raw tools and was a two-way standout in HS. Above-average bat speed and plus raw power to the pull-side. Ball jumps off his bat with loud contact, but extreme contact issues are huge red flag. Plus arm (up to 95 mph in HS) and speed should allow him to stick in CF. Over slot bonus lured him away from Vanderbilt.

Flores,Antoni

46 | **Boston** | EXP MLB DEBUT: 2023 | H/W: 6-1 190 | FUT: Starting SS | **9E**

Bats R Age 19
2017 FA (VZ)
Pwr +++
BAvg +++
Spd +++
Def +++

Year	Lev	Team	AB	R	H	HR	RBI	Avg	OB	Slg	OPS	bb%	ct%	Eye	SB	CS	x/h%	Iso	RC/G
2019	A-	Lowell	181	14	35	0	12	193	291	227	518	12	67	0.42	1	3	14	33	1.76

Athletic, high-upside INF who struggled all year - hit under .200 each month. Spent most of season at SS with some 2B exposure. Owns exciting tools for age with potential for significant rise in status. Will continue to grow and can put charge in ball with fast bat. Loft in swing and natural strength should lead to power and has keen eye at plate.

Florial,Estevan

8 | **New York (A)** | EXP MLB DEBUT: 2021 | H/W: 6-1 185 | FUT: Starting OF | **8D**

Bats L Age 22
2015 FA (HT)
Pwr +++
BAvg ++
Spd ++++
Def +++

Year	Lev	Team	AB	R	H	HR	RBI	Avg	OB	Slg	OPS	bb%	ct%	Eye	SB	CS	x/h%	Iso	RC/G
2017	A+	Tampa	76	13	23	2	14	303	376	461	837	11	68	0.38	6	1	26	158	6.36
2018	Rk	GCL YankeesW	31	10	17	3	8	548	600	1000	1600	11	84	0.80	5	0	41	452	15.02
2018	Rk	GCL Yankees	17	5	11	2	5	647	684	1294	1978	11	88	1.00	3	0	55	647	18.94
2018	A+	Tampa	294	45	75	3	27	255	352	361	713	13	70	0.51	11	10	29	105	4.67
2019	A+	Tampa	274	38	65	8	38	237	299	383	682	8	64	0.24	9	5	32	146	4.07

Tantalizing OF prospect continues to battle injury bug. Athleticism and double-plus bat speed remain. However, refinement is extremely raw, especially at plate. Struggles with spin and over-aggressiveness. Raw plus power should start playing again in games. Still has plus run tool.

Fox,Lucius

6 | **Tampa Bay** | EXP MLB DEBUT: 2020 | H/W: 6-1 180 | FUT: Starting SS | **7C**

Bats B Age 22
2015 FA (BM)
Pwr +
BAvg +++
Spd +++++
Def +++

Year	Lev	Team	AB	R	H	HR	RBI	Avg	OB	Slg	OPS	bb%	ct%	Eye	SB	CS	x/h%	Iso	RC/G
2017	A+	Charlotte	115	19	27	1	12	235	307	287	594	9	71	0.36	3	3	15	52	2.75
2018	A+	Charlotte	351	54	99	2	30	282	359	353	712	11	77	0.53	23	7	20	71	4.49
2018	AA	Montgomery	104	14	23	1	9	221	277	298	575	7	81	0.40	6	2	22	77	2.59
2019	AA	Montgomery	365	60	84	3	33	230	328	342	670	13	76	0.60	37	11	32	112	4.07
2019	AAA	Durham	42	6	6	0	1	143	250	190	440	13	64	0.40	2	0	17	48	0.55

Speed-first, hit-over-power switch-hitter struggled mightily against advanced pitching. Solid plate skills helped keep offensive skills afloat but struggled to get bat head out in front. There is minimal power in frame/swing. Does steal bags; plus-plus run tool and solid defensive skill push his profile.

Fraley,Jake

789 | **Seattle** | EXP MLB DEBUT: 2019 | H/W: 6-0 195 | FUT: Starting OF | **8C**

Bats L Age 24
2016 (2) Louisiana St
Pwr +++
BAvg +++
Spd ++++
Def +++

Year	Lev	Team	AB	R	H	HR	RBI	Avg	OB	Slg	OPS	bb%	ct%	Eye	SB	CS	x/h%	Iso	RC/G
2017	A+	Charlotte	94	6	16	1	12	170	228	255	483	7	74	0.29	1	3	31	85	1.25
2018	A+	Charlotte	225	39	78	4	41	347	414	547	961	10	80	0.59	11	8	38	200	7.69
2019	AA	Arkansas	230	40	72	11	47	313	375	539	915	9	76	0.42	16	5	39	226	6.92
2019	AAA	Tacoma	152	28	42	8	33	276	325	553	878	7	78	0.32	6	2	55	276	6.31
2019	MLB	Seattle	40	3	6	0	1	150	150	200	350	0	65	0.00	0	0	33	50	-1.04

Contact-oriented OF mostly put leg injury history in rearview mirror, eventually making MLB debut. Solid approach and smooth swing. Has added uppercut trajectory to swing, which has helped push pull-oriented above-average power. A plus runner, stole 22 SB. Average defender.

Franco,Wander

6 | **Tampa Bay** | EXP MLB DEBUT: 2020 | H/W: 5-10 190 | FUT: Starting 3B | **10C**

Bats B Age 19
2017 FA (DR)
Pwr ++++
BAvg +++++
Spd +++
Def +++

Year	Lev	Team	AB	R	H	HR	RBI	Avg	OB	Slg	OPS	bb%	ct%	Eye	SB	CS	x/h%	Iso	RC/G
2018	Rk	Princeton	242	46	85	11	57	351	416	587	1003	10	92	1.42	4	3	33	236	7.78
2019	A	Bowling Green	233	42	74	6	29	318	395	506	902	11	91	1.50	14	9	36	189	6.87
2019	A+	Charlotte	192	40	65	3	24	339	417	464	881	12	92	1.73	4	5	25	125	6.68

Stocky, switch-hitting phenom with rare double-plus hit tool beat up on lower level full-season competition in '19. Exceptional and excellent describe every aspect of hitting skill. Shows plus power in BP to all fields; in-game HR should begin to show up as trajectory is added to swing. Likely 2B or 3B long term.

Frechette,Garrett

3 | **San Francisco** | EXP MLB DEBUT: 2023 | H/W: 6-3 200 | FUT: Starting 1B | **7E**

Bats L Age 19
2019 (5) HS (CA)
Pwr ++
BAvg +++
Spd ++
Def +++

Year	Lev	Team	AB	R	H	HR	RBI	Avg	OB	Slg	OPS	bb%	ct%	Eye	SB	CS	x/h%	Iso	RC/G
2019	Rk	AZL Giants	145	23	42	0	20	290	340	366	705	7	76	0.31	1	0	21	76	4.26

Large-framed 1B who is more of a BA hitter than power. Owns pretty lefty stroke and works deep counts. Racks up a lot of Ks as he can be too passive at plate. Swing mechanics need to be reworked for him to generate pop. Moves well for large frame and is decent defender. Very intriguing profile, but will take time to develop skills across board.

Freeman,Cole

48 | **Washington** | EXP MLB DEBUT: 2021 | H/W: 5-9 175 | FUT: Reserve 2B | **7E**

Bats R Age 25
2017 (4) Louisiana St
Pwr ++
BAvg +++
4.17 Spd ++++
Def +++

Year	Lev	Team	AB	R	H	HR	RBI	Avg	OB	Slg	OPS	bb%	ct%	Eye	SB	CS	x/h%	Iso	RC/G
2018	A	Hagerstown	447	78	119	3	43	266	336	371	707	10	87	0.80	26	8	32	105	4.52
2019	A+	Potomac	453	82	141	3	49	311	383	404	787	10	87	0.88	31	6	23	93	5.49

Slightly-built, his game is built on a solid hit tool, athleticism to handle both 2B and CF, and footspeed. Very little current or future HR power, but gap-to-gap pop comes from quick hands that can catch up to plus velocity. Works counts/gets on base, and can fly. Will be uphill battle, but could see a MLB UT future.

Freeman,Tyler

6 | **Cleveland** | EXP MLB DEBUT: 2021 | H/W: 6-0 170 | FUT: Starting MIF | **8B**

Bats R Age 20
2017 (2) HS (CA)
Pwr ++
BAvg ++++
Spd +++
Def +++

Year	Lev	Team	AB	R	H	HR	RBI	Avg	OB	Slg	OPS	bb%	ct%	Eye	SB	CS	x/h%	Iso	RC/G
2017	Rk	AZL Indians	128	19	38	2	14	297	333	414	747	5	91	0.58	5	1	29	117	4.69
2018	A-	MahoningVal	270	49	95	2	38	352	371	511	882	3	92	0.36	14	3	37	159	6.10
2019	A	Lake County	236	51	69	3	24	292	343	424	766	7	88	0.64	11	4	32	131	5.04
2019	A+	Lynchburg	257	38	82	0	20	319	340	397	737	3	90	0.32	8	1	22	78	4.47

Athletic, contact-oriented SS making low minors look easy. Double-plus hit potential with better plate discipline, lightning quick compact swing finds the barrel, even outside of zone. Gap power for now but room to grow in frame and hitting skill should allow for more power. Average runner with base running IQ. Fringe range at SS.

Friedl,TJ

9 | **Cincinnati** | EXP MLB DEBUT: 2020 | H/W: 5-10 180 | FUT: Reserve OF | **6C**

Bats L Age 24
2016 FA (U of Nevada)
Pwr +
BAvg +++
Spd ++++
Def +++

Year	Lev	Team	AB	R	H	HR	RBI	Avg	OB	Slg	OPS	bb%	ct%	Eye	SB	CS	x/h%	Iso	RC/G
2017	A	Dayton	250	47	71	5	25	284	358	472	830	10	82	0.63	14	8	44	188	6.01
2017	A+	Daytona	179	15	46	2	13	257	296	346	643	5	78	0.26	2	1	22	89	3.29
2018	A+	Daytona	228	40	67	3	35	294	395	412	807	14	81	0.86	11	4	25	118	5.91
2018	AA	Pensacola	261	47	72	2	16	276	346	360	706	10	79	0.50	19	5	21	84	4.36
2019	AA	Chattanooga	226	38	53	5	28	235	322	385	707	11	78	0.58	13	4	38	150	4.43

Speedy OF struggled through injuries in 2nd go at Double-A. Missed the last two months of '19 after ankle surgery. Contact-oriented bat with good strike zone discipline. Works the entire field with a groundball/line drive heavy approach. Will power up swing on middle-in FB early in count. Below-average power in frame. Plus runner with OBP skills.

Fuentes,Josh

35 | **Colorado** | EXP MLB DEBUT: 2019 | H/W: 6-2 209 | FUT: Starting 3B | **6B**

Bats R Age 26
2014 FA (Miss. Baptist)
Pwr +++
BAvg ++
Spd ++
Def ++

Year	Lev	Team	AB	R	H	HR	RBI	Avg	OB	Slg	OPS	bb%	ct%	Eye	SB	CS	x/h%	Iso	RC/G
2016	A+	Modesto	291	44	81	9	44	278	316	450	766	5	81	0.30	1	1	35	172	4.79
2017	AA	Hartford	414	48	127	15	72	307	345	517	862	5	78	0.26	8	5	39	210	6.05
2018	AAA	Albuquerque	551	93	180	14	95	327	351	517	869	4	81	0.20	3	5	36	191	6.00
2019	AAA	Albuquerque	402	66	102	17	64	254	297	448	745	6	71	0.21	1	1	41	194	4.65
2019	MLB	Colorado	55	8	12	3	7	218	232	400	632	2	64	0.05	1	0	33	182	2.94

Aggressive, power-oriented corner INF who made debut last year. Uses big leg kick as timing mechanism to tap into plus raw pop to pull-side. Expands the zone often and overall quality of at-bats is questionable; could be OBP liability. Contact skills are fringe-average and struggles vs. quality breakers. Has good arm and enough range for 3B.

Garcia,Adolis

789 | **Texas** | EXP MLB DEBUT: 2018 | H/W: 6-1 180 | FUT: Starting CF | **8E**

Bats R Age 27
2017 FA (CU)
Pwr ++++
BAvg +
Spd ++++
Def ++++

Year	Lev	Team	AB	R	H	HR	RBI	Avg	OB	Slg	OPS	bb%	ct%	Eye	SB	CS	x/h%	Iso	RC/G
2017	AA	Springfield	309	43	88	12	55	285	340	476	816	8	75	0.34	12	8	40	191	5.61
2017	AAA	Memphis	136	21	41	3	10	301	336	478	814	5	77	0.23	3	1	39	176	5.50
2018	AAA	Memphis	406	62	104	22	71	256	281	500	781	3	76	0.14	10	3	49	244	4.86
2018	MLB	St. Louis	17	3	2	0	1	118	118	176	294	0	59	0.00	0	0	50	59	-2.00
2019	AAA	Memphis	491	96	124	32	96	253	285	517	802	4	68	0.14	14	10	48	265	5.43

Continues to elicit mixed reviews. Those who believe, point to plus speed, power, and athleticism. Launched 32 HR with 14 SB with an .818 OPS. Skeptics point to his highly aggressive, pull-heavy approach and doubt he can make enough contact in the majors. His plus speed, defense, and arm should at least get him a chance to prove his critics wrong.

Garcia,Aramis | 23 | San Francisco | EXP MLB DEBUT: 2018 | H/W: 6-2 220 | FUT: Reserve C | 6B

Bats R Age 27 — 2014 (2) Florida Intl
Pwr +++ · BAvg ++ · Spd + · Def +++

Year	Lev	Team	AB	R	H	HR	RBI	Avg	OB	Slg	OPS	bb%	ct%	Eye	SB	CS	x/h%	Iso	RC/G
2018	AA	Richmond	301	36	70	11	33	233	280	395	676	6	75	0.26	0	1	37	163	3.66
2018	AAA	Sacramento	38	5	9	0	4	237	275	263	538	5	68	0.17	0	0	11	26	1.81
2018	MLB	SF Giants	63	8	18	4	9	286	308	492	800	3	51	0.06	0	0	28	206	7.04
2019	AAA	Sacramento	332	52	90	16	55	271	339	488	827	9	66	0.30	0	2	42	217	6.19
2019	MLB	SF Giants	42	5	6	2	5	143	217	310	527	9	50	0.19	0	0	50	167	1.93

Large backstop who has been prospect for years. Obvious deficiencies in game - long swing, hit tool, receiving - but has tools to give him chance to stick. Admirable pop with loft in swing. May strike out in bunches, but can give ball a ride. Exhibits plus arm strength with good catch and throw skills. Projects as backup catcher who can hit.

Garcia,David | 2 | Texas | EXP MLB DEBUT: 2024 | H/W: 5-11 170 | FUT: Starting C | 7C

Bats B Age 20 — 2016 FA (VZ)
Pwr ++ · BAvg +++ · Spd + · Def +++

Year	Lev	Team	AB	R	H	HR	RBI	Avg	OB	Slg	OPS	bb%	ct%	Eye	SB	CS	x/h%	Iso	RC/G
2018	Rk	AZL Rangers	119	10	32	1	20	269	320	361	682	7	78	0.35	0	1	28	92	3.91
2019	A-	Spokane	184	33	51	5	29	277	351	435	786	10	77	0.50	1	1	37	158	5.36

Defensive-minded backstop who made some steps forward with the bat in short-season league. Switch-hitter with lots of moving parts in setup and swing; decent bat control and plate approach, but still projects to below-average power. Skilled blocker/receiver with a strong arm. Bat will need to develop further to become MLB-level starter.

Garcia,Eduardo | 6 | Milwaukee | EXP MLB DEBUT: 2024 | H/W: 6-2 160 | FUT: Starting SS | 8E

Bats R Age 17 — 2018 FA (VZ)
Pwr ++ · BAvg +++ · Spd ++ · Def ++++

Year	Lev	Team	AB	R	H	HR	RBI	Avg	OB	Slg	OPS	bb%	ct%	Eye	SB	CS	x/h%	Iso	RC/G
2019		Did not play in U.S.																	

Uber-young Venezuelan SS who made his pro debut in the DSL last summer. Requires extensive physical projection to his skinny frame, but tools show potential. Profile is presently defense-first with arm strength and range for SS. Lean and athletic enough to steal bases and shows some feel to hit. Power projects to be fringe-average.

Garcia,Jose | 6 | Cincinnati | EXP MLB DEBUT: 2021 | H/W: 6-2 175 | FUT: Starting SS | 8D

Bats R Age 22 — 2017 FA (CU)
Pwr ++ · BAvg +++ · Spd +++ · Def ++++

Year	Lev	Team	AB	R	H	HR	RBI	Avg	OB	Slg	OPS	bb%	ct%	Eye	SB	CS	x/h%	Iso	RC/G
2018	A	Dayton	482	61	118	6	53	245	273	344	618	4	77	0.17	13	9	27	100	2.90
2019	A+	Daytona	404	58	113	8	55	280	322	436	757	6	79	0.30	15	2	41	156	4.80

Wiry, athletic SS prospect has the defensive chops and hit tool to make it as MLB SS. He may not add much more weight to his frame but generates power by utilizing lower-half leverage. Solid swing allows for plenty of barrel contact. Gap-to-gap approach complements skill set well. Above-average runner with potential plus ability defensively.

Garcia,Luis V. | 46 | Washington | EXP MLB DEBUT: 2021 | H/W: 6-2 190 | FUT: Starting 2B | 8C

Bats L Age 19 — 2016 FA (DR)
Pwr +++ · BAvg ++++ · Spd +++ · Def ++++

Year	Lev	Team	AB	R	H	HR	RBI	Avg	OB	Slg	OPS	bb%	ct%	Eye	SB	CS	x/h%	Iso	RC/G
2017	Rk	GCL Nationals	199	25	60	1	22	302	332	387	719	4	84	0.28	11	2	20	85	4.24
2018	A	Hagerstown	296	48	88	3	31	297	340	402	742	6	83	0.39	8	5	24	105	4.61
2018	A+	Potomac	204	34	61	4	23	299	338	412	750	6	84	0.36	4	1	21	113	4.61
2019	AA	Harrisburg	525	66	135	4	30	257	280	337	618	3	84	0.20	11	5	22	80	2.96

"Held his own" is a huge compliment for a 19-year-old at Double-A. Has a smooth and balanced swing, with more punch than 2019's SLG implies, and makes very good contact. Power still the question. Body type likely eventually eats into his range at SS, though enough good hands, arm, instincts for 2B. Not likely to be SB threat in the majors.

Garcia,Luis J. | 46 | Philadelphia | EXP MLB DEBUT: 2023 | H/W: 5-11 170 | FUT: Starting SS | 8E

Bats B Age 19 — 2018 FA (DR)
Pwr ++ · BAvg +++ · 4.30 Spd +++ · Def ++++

Year	Lev	Team	AB	R	H	HR	RBI	Avg	OB	Slg	OPS	bb%	ct%	Eye	SB	CS	x/h%	Iso	RC/G
2018	Rk	GCL PhilliesW	168	33	62	1	32	369	421	488	909	8	88	0.71	12	8	24	119	6.76
2019	A	Lakewood	467	36	87	4	36	186	256	255	511	9	72	0.33	9	8	24	69	1.61

After sky-high rookie league debut, 2019 was a flat-out disaster. Consistently overmatched; was late on fastballs, off-time on breaking balls, and too passive on hittable pitches. Will never be power hitter, but needs to add strength and focus on the middle of the field. Good instincts with glove and has an up-the-middle future. Still very young.

Garcia,Reivaj | 4 | Chicago (N) | EXP MLB DEBUT: 2022 | H/W: 5-11 175 | FUT: Starting 2B | 7E

Bats B Age 18 — 2017 FA (MX)
Pwr + · BAvg +++ · Spd +++ · Def +++

Year	Lev	Team	AB	R	H	HR	RBI	Avg	OB	Slg	OPS	bb%	ct%	Eye	SB	CS	x/h%	Iso	RC/G
2018	Rk	AZL Cubs 2	172	28	52	0	13	302	358	355	713	8	79	0.42	7	3	17	52	4.37
2019	Rk	AZL Cubs 2	85	7	21	0	10	247	264	306	570	2	88	0.20	3	0	24	59	2.53
2019	A-	Eugene	37	3	6	0	2	162	205	162	367	5	73	0.20	1	0	0	0	-0.49

High-contact MIF prospect who struggled upon his aggressive assignment to A-ball in 2019. Has short, ultra-compact swing as LH/RH with intention of sneaking grounders through the infield. Should be BA asset. Slender build with chance to add strength, but likely capped at 8-10 HR. Solid range and average arm profile him best at 2B long-term.

Garcia,Robel | 457 | Chicago (N) | EXP MLB DEBUT: 2019 | H/W: 6-0 168 | FUT: Utility player | 7B

Bats B Age 27 — 2010 FA (DR)
Pwr +++ · BAvg ++ · Spd ++ · Def ++

Year	Lev	Team	AB	R	H	HR	RBI	Avg	OB	Slg	OPS	bb%	ct%	Eye	SB	CS	x/h%	Iso	RC/G
2019	AA	Tennessee	78	12	23	6	26	295	389	590	979	13	72	0.55	1	1	48	295	8.05
2019	AAA	Iowa	260	51	73	21	52	281	355	585	940	10	62	0.31	3	3	48	304	8.08
2019	MLB	Chi Cubs	72	8	15	5	11	208	278	500	778	9	51	0.20	0	0	60	292	6.74

Older prospect who made his debut in 2019 and showed power upside but also a free-swinging approach. Has above-average raw pop and natural leverage in bat path, but swing can elongate and often swings over the top of quality breaking balls. Projects to be utility defender with average arm and fringe athleticism. Likely won't be an SB source.

Genoves,Ricardo | 2 | San Francisco | EXP MLB DEBUT: 2022 | H/W: 6-2 190 | FUT: Starting C | 7D

Bats R Age 20 — 2015 FA (VZ)
Pwr +++ · BAvg ++ · Spd + · Def +++

Year	Lev	Team	AB	R	H	HR	RBI	Avg	OB	Slg	OPS	bb%	ct%	Eye	SB	CS	x/h%	Iso	RC/G
2017	Rk	AZL Giants	135	20	34	2	19	252	313	356	668	8	79	0.43	0	1	26	104	3.78
2018	A-	Salem-Keizer	177	22	43	1	13	243	298	311	609	7	78	0.36	0	0	23	68	2.99
2019	A-	Salem-Keizer	131	19	33	7	31	252	310	481	791	8	82	0.46	1	0	45	229	5.14
2019	A	Augusta	65	9	19	2	14	292	352	446	798	8	74	0.35	0	0	32	154	5.45

Defensive-oriented CA with advanced glove for age. Receives well and is considered solid framer. Owns cannon that is fairly accurate and keeps baserunners in check. If offensive game develops, he could be a good one. Has bat speed for average power, but exhibits crude swing and chases breaking balls. Focuses more on contact than driving ball.

Gigliotti,Michael | 8 | Kansas City | EXP MLB DEBUT: 2022 | H/W: 6-2 173 | FUT: Starting CF | 7D

Bats L Age 23 — 2017 (4) Lipscomb
Pwr + · BAvg +++ · Spd ++++ · Def ++++

Year	Lev	Team	AB	R	H	HR	RBI	Avg	OB	Slg	OPS	bb%	ct%	Eye	SB	CS	x/h%	Iso	RC/G
2017	A	Lexington	86	14	26	1	8	302	362	419	780	9	77	0.40	7	5	27	116	5.27
2018	A	Lexington	17	3	4	1	2	235	435	471	905	26	71	1.20	1	0	50	235	7.64
2019	Rk	AZL Royals	14	3	6	0	2	429	529	500	1029	18	79	1.00	2	0	17	71	9.12
2019	A	Lexington	236	42	73	1	23	309	380	411	791	10	79	0.55	29	7	29	102	5.54
2019	A+	Wilmington	87	8	16	0	5	184	253	230	483	8	74	0.35	5	3	19	46	1.30

Light-hitting, On-base machine struggled once again with health in solid full-season effort. Plus bat-to-ball and spray approach push hit tool. Flat swing plan ideal for ground ball and line drive contact. No power growth expected given approach, frame and trajectory. Near double-plus runner. Stole 36 bases in 46 attempts.

Gil,Mateo | 6 | St. Louis | EXP MLB DEBUT: 2022 | H/W: 6-1 180 | FUT: Utility player | 6C

Bats R Age 19 — 2018 (3) HS (TX)
Pwr + · BAvg +++ · Spd ++ · Def +++

Year	Lev	Team	AB	R	H	HR	RBI	Avg	OB	Slg	OPS	bb%	ct%	Eye	SB	CS	x/h%	Iso	RC/G
2018	Rk	GCL Cardinals	171	27	43	1	20	251	330	316	646	10	70	0.39	2	2	19	64	3.58
2019	Rk	Johnson City	204	42	55	7	30	270	326	431	757	8	73	0.30	1	3	31	162	4.86
2019	A+	Palm Beach	6	0	0	0	0	0	0	0	0	0	67	0.00	0	0		0	-6.12

Smart, hard-working player has solid all-around skills, but none stand out. Quick hands and a knack for barreling the ball, but below-average power likely relegates him to a UT role. Quick first step and a strong arm should all him to stick at short where he is a tick above-average on defense.

Gimenez, Andres — 6 — New York (N)

EXP MLB DEBUT: 2020 | H/W: 6-0 161 | FUT: Starting MIF | 7A

Bats L Age 21 2015 FA (VZ)
Pwr ++ | BAvg +++ | Spd ++++ | Def ++++

Year	Lev	Team	AB	R	H	HR	RBI	Avg	OB	Slg	OPS	bb%	ct%	Eye	SB	CS	x/h%	Iso	RC/G
2017	A	Columbia	347	49	92	4	31	265	320	349	669	7	82	0.46	14	8	18	84	3.78
2018	A+	St. Lucie	308	43	87	6	30	282	330	432	762	7	77	0.31	28	11	34	149	4.92
2018	AA	Binghamton	137	19	38	0	16	277	322	358	680	6	84	0.41	10	3	26	80	3.95
2019	AA	Binghamton	432	54	108	9	37	250	289	387	676	5	76	0.24	28	16	33	137	3.71

Defensively sound, he saw his ct% and bb% drop against Double-A pitching. Was out of sorts mechanically with swing, trying to reach for more pop. Swing was improved in AFL and he was able to tap into some pull power while maintaining a line drive/gap approach. Likely 12-18 HR at maturity. Plus runner and defender.

Gomez, Antonio — 2 — New York (A)

EXP MLB DEBUT: 2024 | H/W: 6-2 210 | FUT: Starting C | 8E

Bats R Age 18 2018 FA (VZ)
Pwr +++ | BAvg +++ | Spd ++ | Def ++++

Year	Lev	Team	AB	R	H	HR	RBI	Avg	OB	Slg	OPS	bb%	ct%	Eye	SB	CS	x/h%	Iso	RC/G
2019	Rk	GCL Yankees	47	9	12	1	7	255	300	404	704	6	85	0.43	0	0	42	149	4.18

Spectacular defensive catcher also has solid hitting toolshed. Contact-oriented approach with an inside-out approach. There's power in frame even though swing generates mostly topspin contact presently. Double-plus arm and receiving skills. Defense could push profile if hit tools lag.

Gomez, Moises — 79 — Tampa Bay

EXP MLB DEBUT: 2021 | H/W: 5-11 200 | FUT: Starting OF | 7C

Bats R Age 21 2015 FA (VZ)
Pwr ++++ | BAvg ++ | Spd ++ | Def ++

Year	Lev	Team	AB	R	H	HR	RBI	Avg	OB	Slg	OPS	bb%	ct%	Eye	SB	CS	x/h%	Iso	RC/G
2016	Rk	GCL Rays	168	20	37	1	10	220	272	327	600	7	78	0.32	4	3	35	107	2.91
2017	Rk	Princeton	211	37	58	5	28	275	317	398	715	6	75	0.25	10	1	28	123	4.19
2018	A	Bowling Green	471	67	132	19	82	280	329	503	832	7	71	0.25	4	3	45	223	5.97
2019	A+	Charlotte	428	55	94	16	66	220	298	402	700	10	62	0.29	3	3	47	182	4.52

Strong-bodied, pull-oriented power hitter didn't live up to '18 helium in '19. Calmed aggressive approach some, not a lot. Sells out to loft with long, uppercut swing. Contact rate fell, mostly from steadier diet of off-speed pitches. Big HR potential in swing if he can muster more hitting skills. Below-average runner and arm. LF only defensively.

Gonzalez, Luis — 789 — Chicago (A)

EXP MLB DEBUT: 2020 | H/W: 6-1 195 | FUT: Starting CF | 7C

Bats L Age 24 2017 (3) New Mexico
Pwr +++ | BAvg +++ | Spd +++ | Def ++++

Year	Lev	Team	AB	R	H	HR	RBI	Avg	OB	Slg	OPS	bb%	ct%	Eye	SB	CS	x/h%	Iso	RC/G
2017	Rk	Great Falls	17	3	2	0	3	118	286	176	462	19	82	1.33	0	0	50	59	1.85
2017	A	Kannapolis	233	26	57	2	12	245	351	361	711	14	79	0.76	2	3	33	116	4.70
2018	A	Kannapolis	230	35	69	8	26	300	359	491	850	8	75	0.37	7	2	38	191	6.12
2018	A+	Winston-Salem	252	50	79	6	45	313	380	504	884	10	82	0.59	3	5	42	190	6.59
2019	AA	Birmingham	473	63	117	9	59	247	301	359	675	9	81	0.53	17	9	26	112	3.90

Athletic, LHH CF prospect struggled in Double-A. Has solid approach at plate with good sense of zone. Bat speed backed up and he struggled getting hands around on velocity early in the season. Will spray the field with hits but power is all pull-oriented. Hangs in well against LHP. Plus defender, mostly due to route running and arm. SB threat.

Gonzalez, Oscar — 79 — Cleveland

EXP MLB DEBUT: 2021 | H/W: 6-2 180 | FUT: Reserve OF | 6C

Bats R Age 22 2014 FA (DR)
Pwr ++ | BAvg ++ | Spd +++ | Def +++

Year	Lev	Team	AB	R	H	HR	RBI	Avg	OB	Slg	OPS	bb%	ct%	Eye	SB	CS	x/h%	Iso	RC/G
2016	A-	MahoningVal	3	0	0	0	0	250	250	250	500	25	67	1.00	0	0	0	0	-2.42
2017	A-	MahoningVal	237	20	67	3	34	283	298	388	686	2	74	0.08	0	0	28	105	3.69
2018	A	Lake County	462	52	135	13	52	292	310	435	745	3	77	0.11	5	6	29	143	4.37
2019	A+	Lynchburg	385	46	123	8	61	319	340	455	795	3	83	0.18	7	5	27	135	4.99
2019	AA	Akron	96	7	18	1	9	188	212	271	483	3	82	0.18	0	0	33	83	1.33

Bat-to-ball OF prospect enjoyed career year in High-A but crashed in Double-A small sample. Ultra-aggressive hitter who struggles finding barrel consistently. Increased his ct% by adjusting better to spin. Strong frame. Swing plane only allows for average power. Average speed. Will settle in COF, likely RF.

Gordon, Nick — 46 — Minnesota

EXP MLB DEBUT: 2020 | H/W: 6-0 170 | FUT: Reserve IF | 6B

Bats L Age 24 2014 (1) HS (FL)
Pwr | BAvg +++ | Spd +++ | Def +++

Year	Lev	Team	AB	R	H	HR	RBI	Avg	OB	Slg	OPS	bb%	ct%	Eye	SB	CS	x/h%	Iso	RC/G
2016	A+	Fort Myers	461	56	134	3	52	291	324	386	710	5	81	0.26	19	13	24	95	4.16
2017	AA	Chattanooga	519	80	140	9	66	270	337	408	746	9	74	0.40	13	7	33	139	4.89
2018	AA	Chattanooga	162	22	54	5	20	333	376	525	900	6	83	0.41	7	2	33	191	6.48
2018	AAA	Rochester	382	40	81	2	29	212	257	283	540	6	79	0.28	13	3	23	71	2.05
2019	AAA	Rochester	292	49	87	4	40	298	339	459	798	6	78	0.28	14	4	41	161	5.39

Former 1st round pick hasn't lived up to draft pedigree but had solid '19 season in Triple-A. Hit-over-power, his bat trajectory is geared towards line-drive top-spin heavy contact. Mostly a short stroke but will elongate path, especially reaching for pull power. Below-average power potential. 10-15 HR if regular playing time.

Gorman, Nolan — 5 — St. Louis

EXP MLB DEBUT: 2022 | H/W: 6-1 210 | FUT: Starting 3B | 9D

Bats L Age 19 2018 (1) HS (AZ)
Pwr +++++ | BAvg +++ | Spd + | Def +++

Year	Lev	Team	AB	R	H	HR	RBI	Avg	OB	Slg	OPS	bb%	ct%	Eye	SB	CS	x/h%	Iso	RC/G
2018	Rk	Johnson City	143	41	50	11	28	350	443	664	1107	14	74	0.65	1	3	44	315	9.78
2018	A	Peoria	94	8	19	6	16	202	279	426	704	10	59	0.26	0	2	47	223	4.53
2019	A	Peoria	241	41	58	10	41	241	330	448	778	12	67	0.41	2	0	47	207	5.51
2019	A+	Palm Beach	215	24	55	5	21	256	298	428	726	6	66	0.18	0	1	44	172	4.71

Top prospect from 2018 took a step back. Has some of best bat speed and power in the minors, but aggressive approach results in swing-and-miss and will need to make more contact to reach potential. Thick frame results in average speed and stiff actions at 3B, but does have strong arm and should be able to stick on the dirt.

Gorski, Matt — 78 — Pittsburgh

EXP MLB DEBUT: 2022 | H/W: 6-4 198 | FUT: Starting OF | 8E

Bats R Age 22 2019 (2) Indiana
Pwr +++ | BAvg ++ | Spd ++++ | Def ++

Year	Lev	Team	AB	R	H	HR	RBI	Avg	OB	Slg	OPS	bb%	ct%	Eye	SB	CS	x/h%	Iso	RC/G
2019	A-	West Virginia	179	32	40	3	22	223	298	346	644	10	73	0.40	11	3	35	123	3.51

Projectable, fast OF with exciting tools and ideal frame for big league OF. Needs pro AB to polish approach and long swing. Stroke gets out of whack when attempting to hit for additional pop. Offers good strength and can give ball a ride. Should evolve into solid CF with above average arm. Not a lottery ticket per se, but a high risk/reward scenario.

Gray, Joe — 8 — Milwaukee

EXP MLB DEBUT: 2023 | H/W: 6-1 195 | FUT: Starting OF | 8E

Bats R Age 20 2018 (2) HS (MS)
Pwr +++ | BAvg ++ | Spd +++ | Def +++

Year	Lev	Team	AB	R	H	HR	RBI	Avg	OB	Slg	OPS	bb%	ct%	Eye	SB	CS	x/h%	Iso	RC/G
2018	Rk	AZL Brewers	77	14	14	2	9	182	337	325	662	19	68	0.72	6	0	50	143	4.00
2019	Rk	Rocky Mountain	110	19	18	3	9	164	252	300	552	11	67	0.36	3	2	44	136	2.13

Raw, pure athlete with physical tools but lacks polish at present. Possesses plus bat speed and explosive hands through zone and will light up exit velocity leaderboards. Swing can elongate often and still working on barrel control; pitch recognition and approach remain in question. Above-average runner with cannon arm for ideal RF profile.

Greene, Riley — 8 — Detroit

EXP MLB DEBUT: 2023 | H/W: 6-3 200 | FUT: Starting CF | 8C

Bats L Age 19 2019 (1) HS (FL)
Pwr +++ | BAvg +++ | Spd +++ | Def +++

Year	Lev	Team	AB	R	H	HR	RBI	Avg	OB	Slg	OPS	bb%	ct%	Eye	SB	CS	x/h%	Iso	RC/G
2019	Rk	GCL TigersW	37	9	13	2	8	351	429	595	1023	12	68	0.42	0	0	38	243	9.10
2019	A-	Connecticut	88	12	26	1	7	295	374	386	760	11	72	0.44	1	0	19	91	5.20
2019	A	West Michigan	96	13	21	2	13	219	265	344	608	6	73	0.23	4	0	29	125	2.83

Outfielder with advanced understanding for defensive responsibilities with a gritty style of play. Wiry frame has room to add more muscle, but still manages to produce a deceptive degree of raw power. Vaulted through three affiliates in summer debut and handled the challenge. Average speed with sub-par arm, complemented by advanced instincts.

Green, Ryder — 78 — New York (A)

EXP MLB DEBUT: 2023 | H/W: 6-0 200 | FUT: Starting OF | 8E

Bats R Age 19 2018 (3) HS (TN)
Pwr ++++ | BAvg ++ | Spd +++ | Def +++

Year	Lev	Team	AB	R	H	HR	RBI	Avg	OB	Slg	OPS	bb%	ct%	Eye	SB	CS	x/h%	Iso	RC/G
2018	Rk	GCL Yankees	79	11	16	3	10	203	300	392	692	12	56	0.31	3	2	44	190	4.82
2019	Rk	Pulaski	225	45	59	8	28	262	336	444	780	10	70	0.37	10	3	41	182	5.39

Strong, powerful OF prospect had better 2nd season in rookie ball. Raw plus-plus power in swing and frame. Uses leverage well to power ball out of the park. Cut down swing length some, which helped getting to barrels. Will need to cut more to get to velocity. Solid runner who showed some SB aptitude.

Grenier,Cadyn — 46 — Baltimore
EXP MLB DEBUT: 2022 | H/W: 5-11 188 | FUT: Starting SS | 7E

Bats R Age 23 — 2018 (1) Oregon St

Pwr ++ | BAvg ++ | Spd +++ | Def ++++

Year	Lev	Team	AB	R	H	HR	RBI	Avg	OB	Slg	OPS	bb%	ct%	Eye	SB	CS	x/h%	Iso	RC/G
2018	NCAA	Oregon St	273	70	87	6	47	319	394	462	856	11	79	0.60	9	1	29	143	6.30
2018	A	Delmarva	162	23	35	1	13	216	291	333	624	9	67	0.32	3	2	43	117	3.36
2019	A	Delmarva	308	49	78	7	39	253	354	399	753	13	65	0.45	5	1	36	146	5.38
2019	A+	Frederick	77	11	16	1	4	208	307	325	631	13	60	0.35	2	1	38	117	3.68

Future starting caliber SS with no true offensive carry skill outside of plate discipline. Swing is long. Either contact is poor or doesn't make enough contact. Struggles laying off pitcher pitches. Swing trajectory geared towards generating loft. 10-15 HR at maturity. Defensive standout, carries profile.

Grissom,Vaughn — 6 — Atlanta
EXP MLB DEBUT: 2023 | H/W: 6-3 180 | FUT: Starting 3B | 7E

Bats R Age 19 — 2019 (11) HS (FL)

Pwr ++ | BAvg ++ | Spd +++ | Def +++

Year	Lev	Team	AB	R	H	HR	RBI	Avg	OB	Slg	OPS	bb%	ct%	Eye	SB	CS	x/h%	Iso	RC/G
2019	Rk	GCL Braves	160	22	46	3	23	288	352	400	752	9	83	0.59	3	0	24	113	4.87

Contact-oriented SS who likely fits at 3B if hit and power tool develop. Fringe-average-to-average toolshed across the board. Has a knack for barreled contact. Has a flat swing trajectory and loose hands, contributing to inconsistent swing path. Power is in frame but swing likely limits to 12-18 HR at projection. Average runner and defender.

Groshans,Jaxx — 2 — Boston
EXP MLB DEBUT: 2022 | H/W: 6-0 209 | FUT: Starting C | 7E

Bats R Age 21 — 2019 (5) Kansas

Pwr +++ | BAvg ++ | Spd ++ | Def ++

Year	Lev	Team	AB	R	H	HR	RBI	Avg	OB	Slg	OPS	bb%	ct%	Eye	SB	CS	x/h%	Iso	RC/G
2019	NCAA	Kansas	197	49	67	12	46	340	480	604	1084	21	80	1.33	0	3	40	264	9.66
2019	A-	Lowell	148	15	32	4	23	216	322	345	666	13	77	0.68	1	1	31	128	3.91

Athletic backstop who has improved in each nuance of game. Has acceptable agility and mobility behind plate along with solid arm, but needs to upgrade receiving. Swings good bat with some pop, but mostly to pull side. Despite plate patience, doesn't read breaking balls well and BA in question.

Groshans,Jordan — 6 — Toronto
EXP MLB DEBUT: 2022 | H/W: 6-3 205 | FUT: Starting SS | 9D

Bats R Age 20 — 2018 (1) HS (TX)

Pwr +++ | BAvg ++++ | Spd +++ | Def +++

Year	Lev	Team	AB	R	H	HR	RBI	Avg	OB	Slg	OPS	bb%	ct%	Eye	SB	CS	x/h%	Iso	RC/G
2018	Rk	GCL Blue Jays	142	17	47	4	39	331	387	500	887	8	80	0.45	0	0	34	169	6.51
2018	Rk	Bluefield	44	4	8	1	4	182	217	273	490	4	82	0.25	0	0	25	91	1.37
2019	A	Lansing	83	12	28	2	13	337	427	482	909	14	75	0.62	1	1	29	145	7.25

Athletic SS who ended season in May due to foot injury. Can shine with both bat and glove. Should become top hitter who puts ball in play with ease while showcasing natural power to all fields. No obvious weakness in overall game. Runs fairly well and is sound defender with strong arm. Has look and production of future All-Star.

Grullon,Deivy — 2 — Philadelphia
EXP MLB DEBUT: 2019 | H/W: 6-1 180 | FUT: Reserve C | 7D

Bats R Age 24 — 2012 FA (DR)

Pwr +++ | BAvg ++ | Spd + | Def ++++

Year	Lev	Team	AB	R	H	HR	RBI	Avg	OB	Slg	OPS	bb%	ct%	Eye	SB	CS	x/h%	Iso	RC/G
2017	A+	Clearwater	271	31	69	8	24	255	286	395	681	4	77	0.20	0	1	32	140	3.64
2017	AA	Reading	83	10	19	4	13	229	273	410	682	6	77	0.26	0	0	37	181	3.63
2018	AA	Reading	326	36	89	21	59	273	311	515	826	5	75	0.22	0	0	40	242	5.45
2019	AAA	Lehigh Valley	407	55	115	21	77	283	354	496	850	10	67	0.34	1	0	39	214	6.42
2019	MLB	Philadelphia	9	0	1	0	1	111	111	222	333	0	78	0.00	0	0	100	111	-0.63

A second 20+ HR season in the high minors warrants a mention, as he was previously known for his standout defense but suspect bat. Perhaps the AAA ball was involved for 2019, but he also doubled his walk rate and has a simple, strong swing. That along with his solid glove should result in some major league time, even as a backup.

Guzman,Alvin — 8 — Arizona
EXP MLB DEBUT: 2024 | H/W: 6-1 166 | FUT: Starting CF | 8E

Bats R Age 18 — 2018 FA (DR)

Pwr +++ | BAvg ++ | Spd ++++ | Def ++++

Year	Lev	Team	AB	R	H	HR	RBI	Avg	OB	Slg	OPS	bb%	ct%	Eye	SB	CS	x/h%	Iso	RC/G
2019		Did not play in U.S.																	

Lean, tooled-up OF who has chance to be special CF defender with rocket arm and intriguing offensive skill-set. Flashes plus bat speed via loose wrists and extends well through the ball. Learning to tone back aggressive approach at plate. Has plus speed and will be SB source. Power restricted to gaps for now, but has projectable body for strength.

Guzman,Jeison — 6 — Kansas City
EXP MLB DEBUT: 2023 | H/W: 6-2 180 | FUT: Starting 2B | 7E

Bats B Age 21 — 2015 FA (DR)

Pwr ++ | BAvg +++ | Spd ++++ | Def +++

Year	Lev	Team	AB	R	H	HR	RBI	Avg	OB	Slg	OPS	bb%	ct%	Eye	SB	CS	x/h%	Iso	RC/G
2016	Rk	AZL Royals	188	35	49	1	19	261	325	378	703	9	77	0.41	5	3	31	117	4.35
2017	Rk	Burlington	193	21	40	0	15	207	285	249	534	10	77	0.47	3	3	15	41	2.12
2018	Rk	Burlington	106	17	30	2	8	283	356	368	724	10	85	0.75	14	1	13	85	4.58
2018	A	Lexington	209	27	50	2	21	239	300	349	649	8	72	0.31	12	4	32	110	3.55
2019	A	Lexington	450	51	114	7	48	253	293	373	666	5	78	0.26	15	13	31	120	3.60

Athletic, contact-oriented hitter back-tracked slightly last season. Above-average bat-to-ball skills allow average bat speed to reach mostly everything. Struggled with spin, causing BB% to drop. Room to grow in frame. Could find fringe-average power at projection. Plus-runner who doesn't have quality burst, depressing SB%. Likely a 2B long term.

Guzman,Jonathan — 46 — Philadelphia
EXP MLB DEBUT: 2023 | H/W: 6-0 156 | FUT: Starting MIF | 7C

Bats R Age 20 — 2015 FA (DR)

Pwr + | BAvg +++ | Spd +++ | Def ++++

Year	Lev	Team	AB	R	H	HR	RBI	Avg	OB	Slg	OPS	bb%	ct%	Eye	SB	CS	x/h%	Iso	RC/G
2017	Rk	GCL Phillies	153	17	38	1	13	248	299	320	619	7	84	0.46	5	1	18	72	3.21
2017	A-	Williamsport	19	2	5	1	2	263	391	421	812	17	84	1.33	0	1	20	158	5.87
2017	A+	Clearwater	3	0	0	0	0	0	0	0	0	0	0	0.00	0	0		0	
2018	A-	Williamsport	243	28	51	2	14	210	241	272	513	4	75	0.16	3	4	20	62	1.49
2019	A	Lakewood	475	55	119	3	40	251	298	316	614	6	80	0.33	31	11	19	65	3.00

Small-framed player who split time at both MIF positions. Excellent range and actions around the bag, makes both routine and difficult plays. Very good bat-to-ball ability; can catch up to velocity and rarely swings through pitches. Flat bat plane more conducive to gap-to-gap power, there is some hitting utility here and has SB ability.

Haase,Eric — 2 — Cleveland
EXP MLB DEBUT: 2018 | H/W: 5-10 210 | FUT: Reserve C | 6D

Bats R Age 27 — 2011 (7) HS (MI)

Pwr +++ | BAvg + | Spd + | Def +++

Year	Lev	Team	AB	R	H	HR	RBI	Avg	OB	Slg	OPS	bb%	ct%	Eye	SB	CS	x/h%	Iso	RC/G
2017	AAA	Columbus	6	1	2	1	2	333	429	833	1262	14	67	0.50	0	0	50	500	12.13
2018	AAA	Columbus	433	54	102	20	71	236	287	443	730	7	67	0.22	3	1	46	208	4.59
2018	MLB	Cleveland	16	0	2	0	1	125	125	125	250	0	63	0.00	0	0	0	0	-2.76
2019	AAA	Columbus	350	67	79	28	60	226	309	517	826	11	59	0.30	1	1	54	291	6.49
2019	MLB	Cleveland	16	1	1	1	3	63	118	250	368	6	50	0.13	0	0	100	188	-1.28

Power-oriented backup CA prospect has not fared well in small MLB sample. FB hitter. Struggles getting bat started, which throws off the timing of reacting to off-speed pitches. High-barrel rate when he connects with ball. However, 59% ct% in Triple-A isn't ideal. Plus-power but the strikeouts won't allow it to verify. Improved defensively.

Haggerty,Sam — 45 — New York (N)
EXP MLB DEBUT: 2019 | H/W: 5-11 175 | FUT: Utility player | 6B

Bats B Age 25 — 2015 (24) New Mexico

Pwr + | BAvg +++ | Spd ++++ | Def +++

Year	Lev	Team	AB	R	H	HR	RBI	Avg	OB	Slg	OPS	bb%	ct%	Eye	SB	CS	x/h%	Iso	RC/G
2018	AAA	Columbus	17	3	3	0	2	176	263	176	440	11	65	0.33	2	0	0	0	0.41
2019	A-	Brooklyn	21	5	7	0	4	333	440	476	916	16	62	0.50	0	0	43	143	8.60
2019	AA	Binghamton	247	39	64	2	13	259	362	356	719	14	68	0.51	19	4	23	97	4.84
2019	AAA	Syracuse	42	9	13	1	9	310	370	524	893	9	76	0.40	4	0	46	214	6.83
2019	MLB	NY Mets	4	2	0	0	0	0	0	0	0	0	25	0.00	0	0		0	-10.45

Over-achieving utility IF made most of opportunity, making MLB debut in process. Solid gap-to-gap approach utilizing short, compact swing. Works deep counts and gets on base. There's not much power projection in short, athletic frame. Probably never reaches double digit HR, even in regular role. Plus runner who SB efficiently. Versatile defender.

Hall,Adam — 46 — Baltimore
EXP MLB DEBUT: 2022 | H/W: 6-0 170 | FUT: Starting MIF | 7C

Bats R Age 20 — 2017 (2) HS (ON)

Pwr ++ | BAvg +++ | Spd ++++ | Def +++

Year	Lev	Team	AB	R	H	HR	RBI	Avg	OB	Slg	OPS	bb%	ct%	Eye	SB	CS	x/h%	Iso	RC/G
2017	Rk	GCL Orioles	9	4	6	0	2	667	667	1000	1667	0	78	0.00	1	0	33	333	16.18
2018	A-	Aberdeen	222	35	65	1	24	293	343	374	717	7	74	0.29	22	5	20	81	4.41
2019	A	Delmarva	463	78	138	5	45	298	360	395	755	9	75	0.38	33	9	22	97	4.97

Solid, athletic prospect handled full-season debut without hiccup. Average-to-above-average tools across the board, minus power potential. Patient hitter who works counts and will spray balls to gaps. HR power taps out at 10-15 HR at projection. Solid defender at 2B and SS. A 55-grade runner has been aggressive on bases; could steal 10-15 in bigs.

Hannah,Jameson — 89 — Cincinnati

EXP MLB DEBUT: 2022 | H/W: 5-9 185 | FUT: Starting OF | 7C

Bats L Age 22 — 2018 (2) Dallas Baptist

Pwr + | BAvg +++ | Spd +++ | Def +++

Year	Lev	Team	AB	R	H	HR	RBI	Avg	OB	Slg	OPS	bb%	ct%	Eye	SB	CS	x/h%	Iso	RC/G
2018	NCAA	Dallas Baptist	236	62	85	6	45	360	443	555	998	13	85	1.00	8	1	36	195	8.12
2018	A-	Vermont	86	14	24	1	10	279	347	384	731	9	72	0.38	6	0	25	105	4.72
2019	A+	Stockton	375	48	106	2	31	283	334	381	715	7	77	0.33	6	7	28	99	4.39
2019	A+	Daytona	67	6	15	0	6	224	316	299	614	12	76	0.56	2	1	27	75	3.31

Short-statured, athletic OF brings a solid approach and good zone recognition to hit tool. Wiry frame. Will struggle to add strength, limiting power potential. Flat, ground ball/line drive swing plane also not conducive to better power. Above-average defender in CF with above-average run tool. Arm is poor-to-below-average; tweener profile.

Harris,Michael — 89 — Atlanta

EXP MLB DEBUT: 2023 | H/W: 6-0 195 | FUT: Reserve OF | 7E

Bats B Age 19 — 2019 (3) HS (GA)

Pwr +++ | BAvg ++ | Spd ++++ | Def +++

Year	Lev	Team	AB	R	H	HR	RBI	Avg	OB	Slg	OPS	bb%	ct%	Eye	SB	CS	x/h%	Iso	RC/G
2019	Rk	GCL Braves	109	15	38	2	16	349	398	514	912	8	82	0.45	5	2	29	165	6.80
2019	A	Rome	82	11	15	0	11	183	264	232	495	10	73	0.41	3	0	20	49	1.52

Athletic, toolsy OF is sushi-raw despite solid pro debut. Slim, athletic frame, should grow into power. Lightning quick hands and some bat-to-ball skills. Swing plane is completely haywire and will need total reconstruction. Average power in frame, completely to pull-side. Plus runner but will likely settle into a COF profile if hits.

Harris,Trey — 79 — Atlanta

EXP MLB DEBUT: 2021 | H/W: 5-8 215 | FUT: Reserve OF | 7C

Bats R Age 24 — 2018 (32) Missouri

Pwr ++ | BAvg +++ | Spd +++ | Def +++

Year	Lev	Team	AB	R	H	HR	RBI	Avg	OB	Slg	OPS	bb%	ct%	Eye	SB	CS	x/h%	Iso	RC/G
2018	Rk	GCL Braves	105	24	33	1	18	314	429	467	895	17	88	1.62	4	3	36	152	7.23
2018	A	Rome	84	10	24	0	11	286	341	393	734	8	85	0.54	3	0	38	107	4.73
2019	A	Rome	202	38	74	8	44	366	423	594	1017	9	84	0.63	4	4	35	228	8.02
2019	A+	Florida	122	20	37	4	17	303	366	443	808	9	79	0.46	3	0	24	139	5.47
2019	AA	Mississippi	146	15	41	2	12	281	300	411	711	3	77	0.12	1	2	29	130	4.06

Late-round pick from 2018 surprised many with this breakout. Slashed .323/.389/.498 between 3 levels; continued to hit in AFL. Student of analytics, he understands relationship of trajectory & loft with his swing, enabling for barreled contact. Gets most power out of stocky frame. Average runner, fits best in RF. Tweener bat projects as 4th OF.

Harrison,Monte — 89 — Miami

EXP MLB DEBUT: 2020 | H/W: 6-3 220 | FUT: Starting CF | 8D

Bats R Age 24 — 2014 (2) HS (MO)

Pwr ++++ | BAvg ++ | Spd ++++ | Def ++++

Year	Lev	Team	AB	R	H	HR	RBI	Avg	OB	Slg	OPS	bb%	ct%	Eye	SB	CS	x/h%	Iso	RC/G
2017	A	Wisconsin	223	32	59	11	32	265	349	475	825	12	69	0.41	11	3	41	211	6.06
2017	A+	Carolina	230	41	64	10	35	278	320	487	807	6	70	0.20	16	1	42	209	5.54
2018	AA	Jacksonville	521	85	125	19	48	240	299	399	698	8	59	0.20	28	9	34	159	4.58
2019	A+	Jupiter	7	2	1	0	0	143	143	143	286	0	86	0.00	3	0	0	0	-0.98
2019	AAA	New Orleans	215	41	59	9	24	274	350	451	801	10	66	0.34	20	2	31	177	5.81

Quick-twitch, athletic OF recovered from ugly 2018 to post solid returns in injury-riddled season, which ended after wrist surgery. Quieted big leg kick and also ironed out some swing plane issues and cut K% in process. Raw plus power plays big from CF to pull side. Plus runner with SB aptitude. Was 20 for 22 in SB attempts; smooth in CF.

Hayes,Ke'Bryan — 5 — Pittsburgh

EXP MLB DEBUT: 2020 | H/W: 6-1 210 | FUT: Starting 3B | 8B

Bats R Age 23 — 2015 (1) HS (TX)

Pwr +++ | BAvg ++++ | Spd +++ | Def +++++

Year	Lev	Team	AB	R	H	HR	RBI	Avg	OB	Slg	OPS	bb%	ct%	Eye	SB	CS	x/h%	Iso	RC/G
2016	A	West Virginia	247	27	65	6	37	263	308	393	701	6	79	0.31	6	5	29	130	4.02
2017	A+	Bradenton	421	66	117	2	43	278	342	363	705	9	82	0.54	27	5	21	86	4.36
2018	AA	Altoona	437	64	128	7	47	293	374	444	818	12	81	0.68	12	5	35	151	5.91
2019	A-	West Virginia	9	1	1	0	2	111	273	222	495	18	78	1.00	1	0	100	111	2.06
2019	AAA	Indianapolis	427	64	113	10	53	265	332	415	746	9	79	0.48	12	1	37	150	4.81

Intriguing INF who has advanced one level per year and on verge of majors. Offers all five tools, including speed, but stands out for elite defense. Could win future awards; owns cannon arm and has instincts and footwork. Hit tool ahead of power and brings solid approach to plate. Set new high in HR while hitting lot of doubles. SB threat as well.

Hays,Austin — 89 — Baltimore

EXP MLB DEBUT: 2017 | H/W: 6-1 195 | FUT: Starting OF | 8C

Bats R Age 24 — 2016 (3) Jacksonville

Pwr ++++ | BAvg ++ | Spd +++ | Def +++

Year	Lev	Team	AB	R	H	HR	RBI	Avg	OB	Slg	OPS	bb%	ct%	Eye	SB	CS	x/h%	Iso	RC/G
2019	A-	Aberdeen	18	5	5	2	4	278	316	722	1038	5	100		0	1	80	444	7.61
2019	A+	Frederick	37	3	6	2	6	162	184	324	509	3	70	0.09	0	0	33	162	1.07
2019	AA	Bowie	56	9	15	3	11	268	328	518	846	8	80	0.45	3	1	53	250	5.88
2019	AAA	Norfolk	240	43	61	10	27	254	287	454	741	4	75	0.18	6	4	44	200	4.45
2019	MLB	Baltimore	68	12	21	4	13	309	373	574	947	9	81	0.54	2	0	48	265	7.16

Aggressive hitter with plus bat speed regained prospect luster with solid 2019 season. Stopped selling completely out to power and also showed improved patience. Still, struggles laying off pitcher's pitches, resulting in lower average. Plus raw power in frame and swing. Could hit 30+ HR. Solid runner who is average defensively.

Head,Hudson — 8 — San Diego

EXP MLB DEBUT: 2023 | H/W: 6-1 180 | FUT: Starting OF | 7D

Bats L Age 18 — 2019 (3) HS (TX)

Pwr ++ | BAvg +++ | Spd +++ | Def ++

Year	Lev	Team	AB	R	H	HR	RBI	Avg	OB	Slg	OPS	bb%	ct%	Eye	SB	CS	x/h%	Iso	RC/G
2019	Rk	AZL Padres	120	19	34	1	12	283	363	417	780	11	76	0.52	3	3	32	133	5.49

Young OF prospect who inked record-breaking signing bonus in 2019's third round. Held his own in AZL debut, showing advanced plate discipline and flaunting good bat speed. Lean, wiry athlete with plus speed that should materialize in SB value. Tons of room for muscle, which should allow for presently gap-pop to turn into at least average power.

Hearn,Ethan — 2 — Chicago (N)

EXP MLB DEBUT: 2023 | H/W: 6-0 200 | FUT: Starting C | 7E

Bats L Age 19 — 2019 (6) HS (AL)

Pwr ++ | BAvg ++ | Spd ++ | Def ++++

Year	Lev	Team	AB	R	H	HR	RBI	Avg	OB	Slg	OPS	bb%	ct%	Eye	SB	CS	x/h%	Iso	RC/G
2019	Rk	AZL Cubs	80	10	13	2	14	163	280	275	555	14	55	0.36	1	1	38	113	2.33

Teen CA prospect taken in the sixth round has solid defensive foundation and offensive profile built on some power. Pop times are above-avg and arm accuracy should help him control the running game. Bat speed is average, but produces natural loft and projects to have moderate HR value. Can struggle with contact and speed is not a part of his game.

Heim,Jonah — 2 — Oakland

EXP MLB DEBUT: 2020 | H/W: 6-4 220 | FUT: Reserve C | 6A

Bats B Age 24 — 2013 (4) HS (NY)

Pwr ++ | BAvg +++ | Spd ++ | Def ++++

Year	Lev	Team	AB	R	H	HR	RBI	Avg	OB	Slg	OPS	bb%	ct%	Eye	SB	CS	x/h%	Iso	RC/G
2017	A+	Charlotte	55	3	12	0	8	218	259	273	531	5	69	0.18	1	0	25	55	1.79
2018	A+	Stockton	312	41	91	7	49	292	352	433	785	9	81	0.48	3	1	32	141	5.23
2018	AA	Midland	137	16	25	1	11	182	238	234	472	7	84	0.45	0	0	20	51	1.43
2019	AA	Midland	181	20	51	5	34	282	366	431	797	12	85	0.89	0	1	33	149	5.56
2019	AAA	Las Vegas	106	22	38	4	19	358	419	557	975	9	83	0.61	0	0	34	198	7.54

Quality defensive CA gunned down 52% of baserunners and also hit .300 in the upper minors. Glove is advanced and shows ability to handle a big-league rotation. Bat speed is average, though simple, level stroke leads to line drives and gap power. Likely maxes out at 10-12 HR with a solid-average BA sans speed as a backup-catcher type profile.

Henderson,Gunnar — 6 — Baltimore

EXP MLB DEBUT: 2024 | H/W: 6-3 195 | FUT: Starting 3B | 8D

Bats L Age 18 — 2019 (2) HS (AL)

Pwr +++ | BAvg +++ | Spd +++ | Def +++

Year	Lev	Team	AB	R	H	HR	RBI	Avg	OB	Slg	OPS	bb%	ct%	Eye	SB	CS	x/h%	Iso	RC/G
2019	Rk	GCL Orioles	108	21	28	1	11	259	328	370	698	9	74	0.39	2	2	29	111	4.27

Solid athletic, young SS prospect made professional debut in short-season ball. Above-average offensive skills. Compact swing with a flat swing plane. Does good job finding barrels. There is raw plus power in frame; swing will have to adjust to create loft. Solid defensive actions. However, arm and body better suited for 3B. Average runner.

Henry,Payton — 2 — Milwaukee

EXP MLB DEBUT: 2021 | H/W: 6-1 215 | FUT: Starting C | 7C

Bats R Age 22 — 2016 (6) HS (UT)

Pwr ++++ | BAvg ++ | Spd + | Def +++

Year	Lev	Team	AB	R	H	HR	RBI	Avg	OB	Slg	OPS	bb%	ct%	Eye	SB	CS	x/h%	Iso	RC/G
2016	Rk	AZL Brewers	82	15	21	0	17	256	307	341	648	7	77	0.32	0	1	33	85	3.54
2017	Rk	Helena	207	38	50	7	33	242	338	435	772	13	67	0.43	1	0	50	193	5.55
2018	A	Wisconsin	337	44	79	10	41	234	312	380	692	10	63	0.31	1	3	34	145	4.32
2019	A+	Carolina	430	49	104	14	75	242	285	395	680	6	67	0.18	1	1	36	153	3.85

Strong, durable backstop who made significant defensive strides at CA in 2019. Calling card is his plus raw power that plays to all fields, and fly-ball rate has increased each of the last three years. Barrel control and pitch recognition skills are questionable, but willing to take a walk. After slimming down, he projects to stay behind the plate.

Hermosillo,Michael — 8 — Los Angeles (A)

EXP MLB DEBUT: 2018 | H/W: 6-0 205 | FUT: Starting OF | 7D

Bats R Age 25	Year	Lev	Team	AB	R	H	HR	RBI	Avg	OB	Slg	OPS	bb%	ct%	Eye	SB	CS	x/h%	Iso	RC/G
2013 (28) HS (IL)	2018	AAA	Salt Lake	273	43	73	12	46	267	340	480	820	10	68	0.34	10	5	41	212	6.01
Pwr +++	2018	MLB	LA Angels	57	7	12	1	1	211	250	333	583	5	70	0.18	0	1	42	123	2.48
BAvg ++	2019	A+	Inland Empire	9	0	2	0	0	222	300	333	633	10	89	1.00	0	0	50	111	3.84
Spd ++++	2019	AAA	Salt Lake	259	51	63	15	43	243	312	471	783	9	66	0.30	6	4	41	228	5.42
Def +++	2019	MLB	Los Angeles	36	7	5	0	3	139	244	222	466	12	47	0.26	2	0	40	83	1.26

Athletic OF made his debut in 2018 but has yet to nail down a starting job in the bigs. Best tool is his plus speed; should have moderate SB value given his propensity for solid walk rates. Projects to have average power but struggles to tap into it consistently with fringy ct% skills. Solid defender who looks like a quality fourth-OF type.

Hernandez,Adrian — 8 — New York (N)

EXP MLB DEBUT: 2024 | H/W: 5-9 210 | FUT: Starting OF | 7E

Bats R Age 19	Year	Lev	Team	AB	R	H	HR	RBI	Avg	OB	Slg	OPS	bb%	ct%	Eye	SB	CS	x/h%	Iso	RC/G
2017 FA (DR)																				
Pwr +++																				
BAvg +++																				
Spd ++++																				
Def +++	2019	Rk	GCL Mets	14	3	4	1	1	286	333	643	976	7	71	0.25	2	1	75	357	7.89

Strong, toolsy top 2017 International signing missed most of '19 with severe knee injury. Projects for above-average-to-plus power at projection. Hit tool is fringe average with length concerns. Plus runner in past. Recovery from knee injury may take away from speed. Solid defensive OF.

Hernandez,Heriberto — 9 — Texas

EXP MLB DEBUT: 2023 | H/W: 6-1 180 | FUT: Starting OF | 8E

Bats R Age 20	Year	Lev	Team	AB	R	H	HR	RBI	Avg	OB	Slg	OPS	bb%	ct%	Eye	SB	CS	x/h%	Iso	RC/G
2018 FA (DR)																				
Pwr ++++																				
BAvg ++																				
Spd +++	2019	Rk	AZL Rangers	192	42	66	11	48	344	425	646	1070	12	70	0.47	3	3	48	302	9.64
Def ++	2019	A-	Spokane	8	4	3	0	1	375	500	375	875	20	63	0.67	3	0	0	0	7.80

Bat-first prospect led the AZL in total bases and was second in HR. Has good power but strikes out a lot; not hugely built but strong with plus bat speed. Doesn't have a clear defensive home; played C/1B/OF, and will likely settle in OF.

Hernandez,Ronaldo — 2 — Tampa Bay

EXP MLB DEBUT: 2021 | H/W: 6-1 185 | FUT: Starting C | 8D

Bats R Age 22	Year	Lev	Team	AB	R	H	HR	RBI	Avg	OB	Slg	OPS	bb%	ct%	Eye	SB	CS	x/h%	Iso	RC/G
2014 FA (CB)																				
Pwr ++++																				
BAvg +++	2017	Rk	Princeton	223	42	74	5	40	332	377	507	883	7	83	0.41	2	2	38	175	6.36
Spd +	2018	A	Bowling Green	405	68	115	21	79	284	335	494	829	7	83	0.45	10	4	37	210	5.53
Def ++	2019	A+	Charlotte	393	43	104	9	60	265	295	397	692	4	83	0.26	7	0	30	132	3.85

Physically mature CA with offense-minded profile. Struggled with plate skills in '19, chasing out-of-zone breaking pitches. Plus bat/ball skills prevented swings and misses but couldn't carry hard contact rate. Plus power plays in any league; 30-HR potential at maturity. Defensively challenged despite controlling running game due to strong arm.

Herrera,Ivan — 2 — St. Louis

EXP MLB DEBUT: 2022 | H/W: 6-0 180 | FUT: Starting C | 8D

Bats R Age 19	Year	Lev	Team	AB	R	H	HR	RBI	Avg	OB	Slg	OPS	bb%	ct%	Eye	SB	CS	x/h%	Iso	RC/G
2016 FA (PN)																				
Pwr +++	2018	Rk	GCL Cardinals	112	23	39	1	25	348	407	500	907	9	82	0.55	1	1	28	152	6.88
BAvg ++++	2018	AA	Springfield	4	0	0	0	0	0	0	0	0	0	50	0.00	0	0		0	-7.85
Spd +	2019	A	Peoria	248	41	71	8	42	286	375	423	798	12	77	0.63	1	1	25	137	5.55
Def ++	2019	A+	Palm Beach	58	7	16	1	5	276	333	328	661	8	72	0.31	0	0	6	52	3.52

Offensive-minded backstop had an excellent full-season debut. Quick bat and an advanced understanding of the strike zone allow him to barrel balls consistently with average to above power. Blocking and receiving are a work in progress and arm is only average. Will need to work hard in order to stay behind the plate, but the tools are there.

Hicklen,Brewer — 789 — Kansas City

EXP MLB DEBUT: 2021 | H/W: 6-2 208 | FUT: Starting OF | 7D

Bats R Age 24	Year	Lev	Team	AB	R	H	HR	RBI	Avg	OB	Slg	OPS	bb%	ct%	Eye	SB	CS	x/h%	Iso	RC/G
2017 (7) Alabama-Birmingh	2017	Rk	Idaho Falls	87	19	26	1	10	299	365	471	836	9	75	0.41	3	1	42	172	6.21
Pwr +++	2017	Rk	AZL Royals	69	19	24	3	13	348	423	609	1032	12	65	0.38	13	3	38	261	9.61
BAvg +++	2018	A	Lexington	306	59	94	17	65	307	358	552	910	7	68	0.24	29	6	40	245	7.16
Spd +++	2018	A+	Wilmington	71	11	15	1	3	211	253	310	563	5	63	0.15	6	0	33	99	2.26
Def +++	2019	A+	Wilmington	419	70	110	14	51	263	348	427	775	12	67	0.39	39	14	31	165	5.51

Former 2-sport athlete (NCAA Division 1 WR)took steps forward during 2019 season by mproving plate skills and discipline. Is more cerebral hitter than stats indicate. Raw plus power in frame, likely doesn't reach it due to swing plane limitations. Has plus run tool but doesn't accelerate well out of box, on OF jumps or SB attempts.

Hilliard,Sam — 89 — Colorado

EXP MLB DEBUT: 2019 | H/W: 6-5 238 | FUT: Starting OF | 8D

Bats L Age 26	Year	Lev	Team	AB	R	H	HR	RBI	Avg	OB	Slg	OPS	bb%	ct%	Eye	SB	CS	x/h%	Iso	RC/G
2015 (15) Wichita St	2016	A	Asheville	461	71	123	17	83	267	346	449	795	11	67	0.37	30	12	37	182	5.73
Pwr ++++	2017	A+	Lancaster	536	95	161	21	92	300	360	487	847	9	71	0.32	37	17	32	187	6.18
BAvg ++	2018	AA	Hartford	435	58	114	9	40	262	326	389	714	9	65	0.27	23	14	30	126	4.60
Spd ++++	2019	AAA	Albuquerque	500	109	131	35	101	262	334	558	892	10	67	0.33	22	5	54	296	7.00
Def +++	2019	MLB	Colorado	77	13	21	7	13	273	349	649	998	10	70	0.39	2	0	62	377	8.30

Tooled-up OF whose closest physical comp is an NFL tight end. Plus raw power is the carrying tool in profile, owning plus bat speed from a smooth LH stroke that plays to all fields. Good athlete for his size and runs well. Discerning eye at plate; works counts. Strong arm and range for either CF or RF. Contact skills could remain fringe-average.

Hilson,P.J. — 8 — San Francisco

EXP MLB DEBUT: 2023 | H/W: 5-11 175 | FUT: Starting CF | 8E

Bats R Age 19	Year	Lev	Team	AB	R	H	HR	RBI	Avg	OB	Slg	OPS	bb%	ct%	Eye	SB	CS	x/h%	Iso	RC/G
2018 (6) HS (AR)																				
Pwr +																				
BAvg ++																				
Spd ++++	2018	Rk	AZL Giants O	161	25	30	4	19	186	251	335	587	8	58	0.21	5	2	43	149	2.85
Def ++++	2019	Rk	AZL Giants O	127	23	28	2	15	220	288	346	634	9	58	0.23	13	2	36	126	3.73

Quick, athletic OF with as much speed as any. Can be standout defender who can track down any flyball. Accentuates defense with strong, accurate arm and sound instincts. Lot of upside here, but has lot of development time with bat ahead of him. Strikes out a lot and doesn't read spin. Looked better at end of season, but needs to drive ball more.

Hinds,Rece — 56 — Cincinnati

EXP MLB DEBUT: 2024 | H/W: 6-4 215 | FUT: Starting 3B | 8E

Bats R Age 19	Year	Lev	Team	AB	R	H	HR	RBI	Avg	OB	Slg	OPS	bb%	ct%	Eye	SB	CS	x/h%	Iso	RC/G
2019 (2) HS (FL)																				
Pwr ++++																				
BAvg ++																				
Spd +++																				
Def ++	2019	Rk	Greeneville	8	1	0	0	1	0	200	0	200	20	63	0.67	0	0		0	-3.59

Physical IF struggled with a quad injury in professional debut. Exceptional power potential carries profile; it plays to all fields and should show up in games. Hit tool is the question: Struggled with spin and aggressiveness in high school; bat-to-ball skills must improve. Average runner, will likely grow out of speed. 3B or RF in future.

Hiraldo,Miguel — 46 — Toronto

EXP MLB DEBUT: 2023 | H/W: 5-11 170 | FUT: Starting 2B | 8D

Bats R Age 19	Year	Lev	Team	AB	R	H	HR	RBI	Avg	OB	Slg	OPS	bb%	ct%	Eye	SB	CS	x/h%	Iso	RC/G
2017 FA (DR)																				
Pwr +++	2018	Rk	DSL Blue Jays	214	41	67	2	33	313	380	453	833	10	86	0.77	15	6	34	140	6.01
BAvg +++	2018	Rk	GCL Blue Jays	39	3	9	0	3	231	250	333	583	3	69	0.08	3	0	44	103	2.53
Spd ++	2019	Rk	Bluefield	237	43	71	7	37	300	339	481	820	6	85	0.39	11	3	39	181	5.47
Def ++	2019	A	Lansing	4	0	1	0	0	250	250	750	1000	0	100		0	0	100	500	7.78

Natural-hitting INF who split time between 2B and SS. Shows quickness and fluidity, though may be best suited for 2B as he matures. Needs to clean up careless glovework. Possesses sufficient bat speed that plays at any level. Swings bat aggressively, though has tendency to pull ball too often. Drives ball and should grow into above average power.

Hoerner,Nico — 46 — Chicago (N)

EXP MLB DEBUT: 2019 | H/W: 5-11 200 | FUT: Starting SS | 8C

Bats R Age 22	Year	Lev	Team	AB	R	H	HR	RBI	Avg	OB	Slg	OPS	bb%	ct%	Eye	SB	CS	x/h%	Iso	RC/G
2018 (1) Stanford	2018	A-	Eugene	22	6	7	1	2	318	444	545	990	19	86	1.67	4	1	29	227	8.26
Pwr ++	2018	A	South Bend	15	1	6	1	3	400	471	667	1137	12	93	2.00	0	0	33	267	9.24
BAvg +++	2019	Rk	AZL Cubs 2	20	2	8	0	0	400	429	450	879	5	95	1.00	0	0	13	50	6.12
Spd +++	2019	AA	Tennessee	268	37	76	3	22	284	336	399	735	7	88	0.68	8	4	29	116	4.70
Def +++	2019	MLB	Chi Cubs	78	13	22	3	17	282	309	436	745	4	86	0.27	0	0	23	154	4.36

First-rounder from 2018 who skipped AAA en route to big league debut. Makes plus contact from quick hands and short RH stroke. Does not produce a ton of raw power from shorter, slender frame, but learning to impact the ball consistently for high-volume doubles. Likes to swing. Plus runner with some burst; could move off SS to 2B sans plus arm.

Hoese,Kody — 5 — Los Angeles (N)

EXP MLB DEBUT: 2021 | H/W: 6-4 200 | FUT: Starting 3B | 8C

Bats R Age 22 — 2019 (1) Tulane

Pwr ++++ | BAvg +++ | Spd + | Def ++

Year	Lev	Team	AB	R	H	HR	RBI	Avg	OB	Slg	OPS	bb%	ct%	Eye	SB	CS	x/h%	Iso	RC/G
2019	NCAA	Tulane	235	72	92	23	61	391	478	779	1257	14	86	1.15	4	1	48	387	10.92
2019	Rk	AZL DodgersM	56	14	20	3	13	357	455	643	1097	15	80	0.91	1	0	45	286	9.52
2019	A	Great Lakes	91	15	24	2	16	264	323	385	708	8	85	0.57	0	0	25	121	4.29

Strong-bodied 3B had some of the best raw power in the 2019 class. Loads hands low with a short stride that results in a quick, balanced, powerful stroke. Below average speed and fringe defense limit him to 3B, but has the arm and power to stick at the position. Smart player with advanced power and should move through the system relatively quickly.

Holland,Will — 6 — Minnesota

EXP MLB DEBUT: 2023 | H/W: 5-10 181 | FUT: Starting SS | 7E

Bats R Age 21 — 2019 (5) Auburn

Pwr +++ | BAvg ++ | Spd ++++ | Def ++++

Year	Lev	Team	AB	R	H	HR	RBI	Avg	OB	Slg	OPS	bb%	ct%	Eye	SB	CS	x/h%	Iso	RC/G
2019	Rk	Elizabethton	125	22	24	7	16	192	273	376	649	10	65	0.32	8	1	38	184	3.38

Athletic, defensively sound SS struggled mightily in '19 before and after 5th round selection in draft. Plus bat speed but inconsistent swing plane and over-aggressiveness severely depress hit tool. Uppercut swing trajectory, gets to above-average power in BP. Could hit 20-25 HR if hit tool verifies. Plus runner with SB ability.

Howell,Korry — 48 — Milwaukee

EXP MLB DEBUT: 2022 | H/W: 6-3 180 | FUT: Utility player | 7E

Bats R Age 21 — 2018 (12) Kirkwood CC

Pwr + | BAvg ++ | Spd ++++ | Def ++

Year	Lev	Team	AB	R	H	HR	RBI	Avg	OB	Slg	OPS	bb%	ct%	Eye	SB	CS	x/h%	Iso	RC/G
2018	Rk	AZL Brewers	103	15	32	0	6	311	393	350	743	12	77	0.58	12	4	13	39	4.96
2019	A	Wisconsin	293	35	69	2	22	235	321	317	639	11	68	0.39	19	8	25	82	3.55

Skinny, explosive, up-the-middle glove best known for an elite run tool but noticeable lack of power. Uses low-effort, line-drive approach for above-average contact skills. Has improved plate skills and SB value will be closely tied to OBP. May be capped at 6-8 HR annually. Projects to be BA/SB contributor at multiple defensive positions.

Howlett,Brandon — 5 — Boston

EXP MLB DEBUT: 2023 | H/W: 6-1 205 | FUT: Starting 3B | 7D

Bats R Age 20 — 2018 (21) HS (FL)

Pwr +++ | BAvg +++ | Spd + | Def ++

Year	Lev	Team	AB	R	H	HR	RBI	Avg	OB	Slg	OPS	bb%	ct%	Eye	SB	CS	x/h%	Iso	RC/G
2018	Rk	GCL Red Sox	137	24	42	5	25	307	403	526	928	14	72	0.58	0	1	48	219	7.63
2018	A-	Lowell	15	5	2	1	2	133	381	400	781	29	80	2.00	1	0	100	267	5.82
2019	A	Greenville	390	48	90	8	35	231	327	356	684	13	63	0.39	1	5	36	126	4.33

Strong 3B who took step back in first year in full-season ball. Finished 2nd in org in Ks and had trouble with breaking balls. Can shorten swing at times, but leads to weak contact. Willing to work counts to get on base and can go to opposite field as needed. Has bat speed and strength that project well. Lacks quickness, though possesses strong arm.

Huff,Sam — 2 — Texas

EXP MLB DEBUT: 2021 | H/W: 6-4 230 | FUT: Starting C | 8C

Bats R Age 22 — 2016 (7) HS (AZ)

Pwr ++++ | BAvg ++ | Spd + | Def +++

Year	Lev	Team	AB	R	H	HR	RBI	Avg	OB	Slg	OPS	bb%	ct%	Eye	SB	CS	x/h%	Iso	RC/G
2016	Rk	AZL Rangers	97	19	32	1	17	330	425	485	909	14	70	0.55	0	0	38	155	7.67
2017	Rk	AZL Rangers	197	34	49	9	31	249	330	452	782	11	66	0.36	3	2	41	203	5.53
2018	A	Hickory	415	53	100	18	55	241	281	439	719	5	66	0.16	9	1	43	198	4.42
2019	A	Hickory	108	22	36	15	29	333	368	796	1165	5	66	0.16	4	1	56	463	10.60
2019	A+	Down East	367	49	96	13	43	262	312	425	737	7	68	0.23	2	5	33	163	4.67

Bat-first backstop broke out in a huge way (28 HR over two A-ball stops) and on the big stage (game-tying HR in the Futures Game). Easy plus power with high exit velocities from his long levers and big frame. Doesn't draw enough walks, and there are strikeouts aplenty, so upper-minors pitching will be a test. But big upside for a CA.

Hulsizer,Niko — 79 — Tampa Bay

EXP MLB DEBUT: 2022 | H/W: 6-2 225 | FUT: Starting OF | 7C

Bats R Age 23 — 2018 (18) Morehead St

Pwr ++++ | BAvg ++ | Spd +++ | Def +++

Year	Lev	Team	AB	R	H	HR	RBI	Avg	OB	Slg	OPS	bb%	ct%	Eye	SB	CS	x/h%	Iso	RC/G
2018	Rk	Ogden	160	47	45	9	32	281	395	531	926	16	68	0.58	12	2	49	250	7.80
2019	Rk	GCL Rays	9	0	1	0	1	111	273	111	384	18	56	0.50	0	1	0	0	-0.78
2019	A	Great Lakes	209	46	56	15	49	268	378	574	952	15	64	0.49	4	1	59	306	8.36
2019	A+	RanchoCuca	85	15	22	5	18	259	330	506	836	10	61	0.27	3	2	50	247	6.63
2019	A+	Charlotte	34	4	8	1	4	235	316	382	698	11	68	0.36	0	1	38	147	4.29

Beefy, power-hitting OF destroyed Single-A pitching. Double-plus power plays. However, swing-and-miss struggles temper power impact. Using lower half to gain solid leverage in upper-cut oriented swing. Has solid plate skills despite ct% issues. An average runner, arm and athleticism fits LF.

Hunt,Blake — 2 — San Diego

EXP MLB DEBUT: 2022 | H/W: 6-3 215 | FUT: Starting C | 7D

Bats R Age 21 — 2017 (2) HS (CA)

Pwr ++ | BAvg +++ | Spd + | Def +++

Year	Lev	Team	AB	R	H	HR	RBI	Avg	OB	Slg	OPS	bb%	ct%	Eye	SB	CS	x/h%	Iso	RC/G
2017	Rk	AZL Padres 2	144	28	34	3	23	236	290	403	693	7	62	0.20	1	0	47	167	4.49
2017	Rk	AZL Padres	28	7	6	1	4	214	290	393	683	10	54	0.23	0	0	50	179	4.84
2018	A-	Tri-City	207	34	56	3	25	271	355	377	732	12	73	0.48	2	1	29	106	4.79
2019	A	Fort Wayne	333	40	85	5	39	255	326	381	707	10	80	0.52	4	1	34	126	4.38

Defense-first CA prospect whose plus arm helped him gun-down 33% of would-be base stealers in MWL. Has big, athletic frame and made strides with receiving and framing in 2019. Offensive tools aren't loud, making average contact and drawing walks at a league-avg rate. Grew into his power some in full-season ball and projects for double-digit HR.

India,Jonathan — 5 — Cincinnati

EXP MLB DEBUT: 2020 | H/W: 6-0 200 | FUT: Starting 3B | 7A

Bats R Age 23 — 2018 (1) Florida

Pwr +++ | BAvg +++ | Spd +++ | Def +++

Year	Lev	Team	AB	R	H	HR	RBI	Avg	OB	Slg	OPS	bb%	ct%	Eye	SB	CS	x/h%	Iso	RC/G
2018	Rk	Greeneville	46	11	12	3	12	261	443	543	986	25	74	1.25	1	0	50	283	8.66
2018	Rk	Billings	8	1	2	0	0	250	250	250	500	0	50	0.00	0	1	0	0	1.64
2018	A	Dayton	96	17	22	3	11	229	321	396	717	12	71	0.46	5	0	45	167	4.56
2019	A+	Daytona	317	50	81	8	30	256	333	410	743	10	74	0.44	7	5	35	155	4.87
2019	AA	Chattanooga	111	24	30	3	14	270	391	378	769	17	77	0.85	4	0	20	108	5.40

Polished, athletic prospect made it to Double-A in first full minor league season. Hit tool, plate discipline and approach carry profile. Struggles against higher velocity (ct% troubles) but adjusts well to spin. Average power plays inconsistently; also has average speed. Plus arm and solid reactions make for above-average 3B.

Isabel,Ibandel — 379 — Cincinnati

EXP MLB DEBUT: 2021 | H/W: 6-4 225 | FUT: Reserve 1B | 6C

Bats R Age 24 — 2013 FA (DR)

Pwr +++++ | BAvg + | Spd ++ | Def +

Year	Lev	Team	AB	R	H	HR	RBI	Avg	OB	Slg	OPS	bb%	ct%	Eye	SB	CS	x/h%	Iso	RC/G
2017	A+	RanchoCuca	444	62	115	28	87	259	320	489	809	8	61	0.23	0	2	39	230	6.06
2018	A+	RanchoCuca	21	1	5	1	3	238	304	476	781	9	57	0.22	0	0	60	238	6.20
2018	A+	Daytona	376	62	97	35	75	258	323	566	889	9	60	0.24	1	1	47	309	7.37
2019	AA	Chattanooga	334	52	81	26	69	243	297	518	815	7	54	0.17	0	0	48	275	6.85

Big, lumbering power 1B continues to struggle with ct% with promotion to upper levels. Exceptional power potential in XXL frame. Finds it easily in games. Swing trajectory geared towards creating loft. Swing is like a big, jumbo fan blade on low. Lots of force, takes awhile. Struggles defensively at 1B, LF & RF.

Isbel,Kyle — 89 — Kansas City

EXP MLB DEBUT: 2021 | H/W: 5-11 183 | FUT: Starting CF | 7D

Bats L Age 23 — 2018 (3) UNLV

Pwr ++ | BAvg +++ | Spd +++ | Def +++

Year	Lev	Team	AB	R	H	HR	RBI	Avg	OB	Slg	OPS	bb%	ct%	Eye	SB	CS	x/h%	Iso	RC/G
2018	NCAA	UNLV	238	59	85	14	56	357	438	643	1080	13	82	0.79	6	3	42	286	9.02
2018	Rk	Idaho Falls	105	27	40	4	18	381	454	610	1063	12	84	0.82	12	3	38	229	8.79
2018	A	Lexington	159	30	46	3	14	289	339	434	773	7	73	0.28	12	3	35	145	5.16
2019	Rk	AZL Royals	25	9	9	2	7	360	407	680	1087	7	80	0.40	3	1	44	320	8.70
2019	A+	Wilmington	194	26	42	5	23	216	273	361	634	7	77	0.34	8	3	36	144	3.24

Athletic, strong OF prospect can't reach physical strength due to barrel issues. Line-drive swing trajectory, geared towards top-spin contact. Average bat speed, doesn't cover zone, depressing hit and power tools. Above-average runner and defender. 10+ SB potential.

Jackson,Alex — 2 — Atlanta

EXP MLB DEBUT: 2019 | H/W: 6-2 215 | FUT: Starting C | 7D

Bats R Age 24 — 2014 (1) HS (CA)

Pwr ++++ | BAvg + | Spd ++ | Def ++

Year	Lev	Team	AB	R	H	HR	RBI	Avg	OB	Slg	OPS	bb%	ct%	Eye	SB	CS	x/h%	Iso	RC/G
2017	AA	Mississippi	110	12	28	5	20	255	317	427	744	8	71	0.31	0	0	32	173	4.66
2018	AA	Mississippi	225	27	45	5	24	200	265	329	594	8	65	0.26	0	0	40	129	2.75
2018	AAA	Gwinnett	108	15	22	3	17	204	283	426	709	10	61	0.29	0	0	73	222	4.91
2019	AAA	Gwinnett	306	52	70	28	65	229	276	533	809	6	61	0.17	1	0	53	304	5.82
2019	MLB	Atlanta	13	0	0	0	0	0	71	0	71	7	62	0.20	0	0		0	-5.59

Powerful CA prospect made brief MLB debut. Continues to sell out hit tool for power. Long, lumbering swing can be beat with velocity and is pull-oriented. Trajectory generates tremendous loft, contributing to tape-measured HR. Power plays mostly from CF to pull side. Defensively improved but still below-average defender.

Jackson,Jeremiah

46 | Los Angeles (A) | EXP MLB DEBUT: 2022 | H/W: 6-0 165 | FUT: Starting MIF | 8C

Bats R Age 20
2018 (2) HS (AL)
Pwr +++
BAvg +++
Spd +++
Def ++

Year	Lev	Team	AB	R	H	HR	RBI	Avg	OB	Slg	OPS	bb%	ct%	Eye	SB	CS	x/h%	Iso	RC/G
2018	Rk	AZL Angels	82	13	26	5	14	317	371	598	968	8	70	0.28	6	1	42	280	7.93
2018	Rk	Orem	91	13	18	2	9	198	263	396	658	8	63	0.24	4	1	61	198	3.98
2019	Rk	Orem	256	47	68	23	60	266	329	605	934	9	63	0.25	5	1	57	340	7.88

Young MIF prospect who led Pioneer League in HR and x/h% and will make full-season debut in 2020. Chance for average or better tools, headlined by potentially plus raw power from a lean, skinny frame. Approach and bat to ball skills remain raw but has loose, level cut and uses all fields. Decent runner and athlete who may move to 3B as he fills out.

Javier,Wander

6 | Minnesota | EXP MLB DEBUT: 2023 | H/W: 6-1 165 | FUT: Starting MIF | 8E

Bats R Age 21
2015 FA (DR)
Pwr ++
BAvg +++
Spd ++++
Def +++

Year	Lev	Team	AB	R	H	HR	RBI	Avg	OB	Slg	OPS	bb%	ct%	Eye	SB	CS	x/h%	Iso	RC/G
2017	Rk	Elizabethton	157	34	47	4	22	299	375	471	846	11	69	0.39	4	3	38	172	6.52
2018	Rk	Did not play - injury																	
2019	A	Cedar Rapids	300	43	53	11	37	177	263	323	586	10	61	0.30	2	0	40	147	2.61

Quick-twitch, athletic SS had disastrous Single-A season after missing all of '18 with a torn left shoulder. Swing speed remains but reactions were rough. Struggled maintaining swing plane and recognizing spin. Below-average power in frame. Defensively, likely fits best at 2B despite arm due to poor reactions. Plus runner.

Jeffers,Ryan

2 | Minnesota | EXP MLB DEBUT: 2021 | H/W: 6-4 230 | FUT: Starting C | 7C

Bats R Age 22
2018 (2) UNC-Wilmington
Pwr +++
BAvg +++
Spd +
Def ++

Year	Lev	Team	AB	R	H	HR	RBI	Avg	OB	Slg	OPS	bb%	ct%	Eye	SB	CS	x/h%	Iso	RC/G
2018	NCAA	UNC Wilmington	219	53	69	16	59	315	444	635	1079	19	80	1.16	2	1	55	320	9.40
2018	Rk	Elizabethton	102	29	43	3	16	422	516	578	1095	16	84	1.25	0	1	23	157	9.48
2018	A	Cedar Rapids	139	19	40	4	17	288	353	446	799	9	78	0.47	0	0	35	158	5.44
2019	A+	Fort Myers	281	35	72	10	40	256	324	402	726	9	77	0.44	0	0	29	146	4.42
2019	AA	Pensacola	87	13	25	4	9	287	354	483	837	9	78	0.47	0	0	36	195	5.84

Offensive-oriented backstop posted solid returns in A+/AA. Solid hitting approach to go along with good bat-to-ball skills. Struggles getting bat speed up to handle velocity. Power in swing and frame; likely gets to average power at maturity. Defensively, really clunky behind plate but presents solid target for pitchers.

Jenista,Greyson

79 | Atlanta | EXP MLB DEBUT: 2021 | H/W: 6-3 210 | FUT: Reserve OF | 7D

Bats L Age 23
2018 (2) Wichita St
Pwr +++
BAvg ++
Spd +++
Def ++

Year	Lev	Team	AB	R	H	HR	RBI	Avg	OB	Slg	OPS	bb%	ct%	Eye	SB	CS	x/h%	Iso	RC/G
2018	Rk	Danville	40	10	10	3	7	250	348	500	848	13	78	0.67	0	1	40	250	6.00
2018	A	Rome	117	20	39	1	23	333	386	453	839	8	85	0.59	4	1	23	120	5.92
2018	A+	Florida	66	3	10	0	4	152	233	227	460	10	77	0.47	0	0	40	76	1.24
2019	A+	Florida	202	24	45	4	29	223	314	361	676	12	65	0.39	1	4	42	139	4.15
2019	AA	Mississippi	222	18	54	5	26	243	325	338	663	11	66	0.36	2	4	19	95	3.78

Tall, powerful athletic OF struggled translating power into swing. Hit tool took step backwards. Patient approach with solid plate skills disappeared as trajectory in swing increased. Unable to get bat head out in front, struggled with hard contact rate and losing spray approach. Power in frame is for real. Above-average runner despite size.

Jimenez,Gilberto

8 | Boston | EXP MLB DEBUT: 2023 | H/W: 5-11 160 | FUT: Starting CF | 8D

Bats B Age 19
2017 FA (DR)
Pwr +
BAvg ++++
Spd ++++
Def +++

Year	Lev	Team	AB	R	H	HR	RBI	Avg	OB	Slg	OPS	bb%	ct%	Eye	SB	CS	x/h%	Iso	RC/G
2019	A-	Lowell	234	35	84	3	19	359	393	470	863	5	84	0.34	14	6	20	111	5.96

Breakout, athletic OF who led NYPL in BA while hitting at least .341 each month. Has barrel awareness and strike zone knowledge for easy contact with slap approach. Very little power projection, but ability to hit from both sides enhances offense. Could be leadoff guy with easy plus speed. Plays solid CF and needs time to polish routes and jumps.

Jimenez,Leonardo

46 | Toronto | EXP MLB DEBUT: 2023 | H/W: 5-11 160 | FUT: Starting MIF | 7D

Bats R Age 18
2017 FA (PN)
Pwr +
BAvg +++
Spd +++
Def +++

Year	Lev	Team	AB	R	H	HR	RBI	Avg	OB	Slg	OPS	bb%	ct%	Eye	SB	CS	x/h%	Iso	RC/G
2018	Rk	GCL Blue Jays	132	13	33	0	19	250	331	341	672	11	87	0.94	0	0	30	91	4.24
2019	Rk	Bluefield	215	34	64	0	22	298	360	377	737	9	80	0.50	2	1	23	79	4.77
2019	A	Lansing	6	0	1	0	0	167	167	167	333	0	67	0.00	0	0	0	0	-1.38

Savvy INF who does everything well but hit for power. Plays game with strong fundamentals and natural feel for hitting. Uses all fields with line drive approach and rarely chases pitches. Should hit for nice BA, though could stand to add strength to enhance well below avg pop. Hasn't yet hit HR and doesn't steal many bases despite avg speed.

Johnson,Daniel

89 | Cleveland | EXP MLB DEBUT: 2020 | H/W: 5-10 200 | FUT: Starting OF | 7C

Bats L Age 24
2016 (5) New Mexico St
Pwr +++
BAvg +++
Spd ++++
Def +++

Year	Lev	Team	AB	R	H	HR	RBI	Avg	OB	Slg	OPS	bb%	ct%	Eye	SB	CS	x/h%	Iso	RC/G
2017	A+	Potomac	170	22	50	5	20	294	344	459	803	7	82	0.43	10	2	36	165	5.35
2018	Rk	GCL Nationals	20	3	6	1	4	300	364	450	814	9	90	1.00	1	0	17	150	5.45
2018	AA	Harrisburg	356	48	95	6	31	267	311	410	721	6	75	0.26	21	4	34	143	4.41
2019	AA	Akron	146	25	37	10	33	253	327	534	861	10	73	0.41	6	3	51	281	6.25
2019	AAA	Columbus	337	51	103	9	44	306	369	496	865	9	77	0.43	6	7	40	190	6.40

Toolsy athlete continues to refine swing and tighten up game. A late-bloomer, he has improved plate discipline to go with solid ct%. Compact swing but cuts off outer half and has average pull power. Struggles with spin, specifically against LHP and may likely be more of a platoon bat. Double-plus runner without SB aptitude. Think 10+ SB.

Johnson,Ivan

46 | Cincinnati | EXP MLB DEBUT: 2023 | H/W: 6-0 190 | FUT: Starting MIF | 7C

Bats B Age 21
2019 (4) Chipola JC
Pwr +++
BAvg +++
Spd +++
Def +++

Year	Lev	Team	AB	R	H	HR	RBI	Avg	OB	Slg	OPS	bb%	ct%	Eye	SB	CS	x/h%	Iso	RC/G
2019	NCAA	Chipola College	189	54	72	9	49	381	475	587	1063	15	80	0.92	14	6	28	206	9.03
2019	Rk	Greeneville	188	27	48	6	22	255	320	415	735	9	76	0.39	11	4	35	160	4.60

Athletic, slugging MIF prospect showed power in pro debut after 4th rd selection. Switch-hitter. Added power to frame last off-season. Now, raw plus power potential carries profile. Plus bat speed but struggles with consistent path and spin recognition. Average runner. Likely a 2B long term.

Johnson,Osiris

6 | Miami | EXP MLB DEBUT: 2023 | H/W: 6-0 181 | FUT: Starting SS | 7D

Bats R Age 19
2018 (2) HS (CA)
Pwr +++
BAvg ++
Spd ++++
Def +++

Year	Lev	Team	AB	R	H	HR	RBI	Avg	OB	Slg	OPS	bb%	ct%	Eye	SB	CS	x/h%	Iso	RC/G
2018	Rk	GCL Marlins	103	12	31	1	13	301	327	447	774	4	82	0.21	7	2	35	146	4.93
2018	A	Greensboro	85	4	16	2	6	188	198	294	492	1	60	0.03	0	2	31	106	1.03
2019		Did not play - injury																	

Quick-twitch toolsy SS missed all of '19 after having surgery to repair a right tibial stress fracture. Aggressive approach with swing and miss issues. Plus bat speed makes up for swing path conerns in lower minors but will need to refine to reach MLB ceiling. Plus raw power in swing and frame and was plus runner prior to injury.

Jones,Greg

6 | Tampa Bay | EXP MLB DEBUT: 2022 | H/W: 6-2 175 | FUT: Starting SS | 9D

Bats B Age 22
2019 (1) UNC-Wilmington
Pwr ++
BAvg ++++
Spd +++++
Def ++++

Year	Lev	Team	AB	R	H	HR	RBI	Avg	OB	Slg	OPS	bb%	ct%	Eye	SB	CS	x/h%	Iso	RC/G
2019	NCAA	UNC Wilmington	223	70	76	5	36	341	471	543	1014	20	80	1.25	42	10	34	202	8.93
2019	A-	Hudson Valley	191	39	64	1	24	335	404	461	864	10	71	0.39	19	8	28	126	6.79

Double-plus athlete made strides with hit tool during debut. Switch-hitter with solid plate skills, has excellent feel for barrel and ability to spray ball around. He has learned to be more aggressive as pro. Below-average raw power may play up due to hit tool. Stole bases in 40% of pro games. Plus range at SS, but could end up in CF.

Jones,Jahmai

4 | Los Angeles (A) | EXP MLB DEBUT: 2021 | H/W: 5-11 205 | FUT: Starting 2B | 7A

Bats R Age 22
2015 (2) HS (GA)
Pwr ++
BAvg +++
Spd ++++
Def ++

Year	Lev	Team	AB	R	H	HR	RBI	Avg	OB	Slg	OPS	bb%	ct%	Eye	SB	CS	x/h%	Iso	RC/G
2017	A	Burlington	346	54	94	9	30	272	333	425	758	8	82	0.51	18	7	33	153	4.90
2017	A+	Inland Empire	172	32	52	5	17	302	351	488	840	7	75	0.30	9	6	37	186	5.97
2018	A+	Inland Empire	298	47	70	8	35	235	331	383	714	13	79	0.68	13	3	33	148	4.54
2018	AA	Mobile	184	33	45	2	20	245	332	375	707	12	72	0.47	11	1	36	130	4.53
2019	AA	Mobile	482	66	113	5	50	234	306	324	630	9	77	0.46	9	11	27	89	3.35

Athletic, squatty 2B had down year statistically in AA but possesses well-rounded game needed for moderate impact. A former HS football star who displays plus speed on the bases. Shows proclivity to walk; knows the strike zone. Has level barrel path geared toward hard line drives and mostly gap power. Fringe arm and range profile well at 2B.

Jones,Nolan — 5 — Cleveland

EXP MLB DEBUT: 2020 | H/W: 6-2 185 | FUT: Starting 3B | 9C

Bats L Age 21 — 2016 (2) HS (PA)

Pwr ++++ | BAvg +++ | Spd +++ | Def +++

Year	Lev	Team	AB	R	H	HR	RBI	Avg	OB	Slg	OPS	bb%	ct%	Eye	SB	CS	x/h%	Iso	RC/G
2017	A-	MahoningVal	218	41	69	4	33	317	429	482	911	16	72	0.72	1	0	36	165	7.61
2018	A	Lake County	323	46	90	16	49	279	396	464	861	16	70	0.65	2	1	31	186	6.68
2018	A+	Lynchburg	104	23	31	3	17	298	438	471	910	20	67	0.76	0	0	39	173	7.92
2019	A+	Lynchburg	252	48	72	7	41	286	432	425	857	21	66	0.76	5	3	28	139	7.13
2019	AA	Akron	178	33	45	8	22	253	364	466	830	15	65	0.49	2	0	44	213	6.52

Slugging 3B continued march to MLB. Big, athletic build. Has natural strength oozing throughout game. Power plays and will likely correlate to 30+ HR production. Hit tool has regressed as he's continued to grab for more power. BB% and Eye are strong. Put lot of work in on defense. Average defender with double-plus arm.

Jones,Taylor — 37 — Houston

EXP MLB DEBUT: 2020 | H/W: 6-7 225 | FUT: Reserve IF | 6B

Bats R Age 26 — 2016 (19) Gonzaga

Pwr +++ | BAvg +++ | Spd + | Def +++

Year	Lev	Team	AB	R	H	HR	RBI	Avg	OB	Slg	OPS	bb%	ct%	Eye	SB	CS	x/h%	Iso	RC/G
2017	A	Quad Cities	174	23	38	5	28	218	288	351	639	9	71	0.34	0	0	34	132	3.30
2017	A+	Buies Creek	191	17	43	2	17	225	324	293	617	13	73	0.55	0	0	19	68	3.24
2018	AA	Corpus Christi	309	45	97	13	63	314	401	528	929	13	75	0.58	2	0	40	214	7.40
2018	AAA	Fresno	143	16	30	5	17	210	289	378	667	10	68	0.35	0	0	43	168	3.79
2019	AAA	Round Rock	447	86	130	22	84	291	384	501	886	13	75	0.61	0	1	38	210	6.76

Versatile, under-radar prospect who gets on base, hits for power and destroys LHP. Mostly plays 1B and has seen action at 3B and LF. Has disciplined eye that gets him on base via walk. Swing has gotten quicker and shorter while adding more strength to his slender frame. Won't steal bases and likely not a starter in majors over long-term.

Jung,Josh — 5 — Texas

EXP MLB DEBUT: 2021 | H/W: 6-2 215 | FUT: Starting 3B | 9D

Bats R Age 22 — 2019 (1) Texas Tech

Pwr ++++ | BAvg +++ | Spd ++ | Def +++

Year	Lev	Team	AB	R	H	HR	RBI	Avg	OB	Slg	OPS	bb%	ct%	Eye	SB	CS	x/h%	Iso	RC/G
2019	Rk	AZL Rangers	17	5	10	1	5	588	632	941	1573	11	82	0.67	0	0	30	353	14.96
2019	A	Hickory	157	18	45	1	23	287	353	389	741	9	82	0.55	4	1	31	102	4.83

Hit the ground running after drafted #8 overall and will likely be a quick mover given his experience and drive to improve. Physically developed, was still learning to turn on pitches and utilize the strength in his frame to his for power at the pro level. Good pitch recognition, patience at the plate, and good enough to stick at the hot corner.

Kelenic,Jarred — 89 — Seattle

EXP MLB DEBUT: 2020 | H/W: 6-0 196 | FUT: Starting CF | 9C

Bats L Age 20 — 2018 (1) HS (WI)

Pwr +++ | BAvg ++++ | Spd +++ | Def +++

Year	Lev	Team	AB	R	H	HR	RBI	Avg	OB	Slg	OPS	bb%	ct%	Eye	SB	CS	x/h%	Iso	RC/G
2018	Rk	Kingsport	174	33	44	5	33	253	337	431	768	11	78	0.56	11	1	39	178	5.20
2018	Rk	GCL Mets	46	9	19	1	9	413	460	609	1069	8	76	0.36	4	0	26	196	9.06
2019	A	West Virginia	191	33	59	11	29	309	389	586	975	12	76	0.56	7	4	47	277	7.84
2019	A+	Modesto	169	36	49	6	22	290	355	485	840	9	71	0.35	10	3	41	195	6.19
2019	AA	Arkansas	83	11	21	6	17	253	319	542	861	9	80	0.47	3	0	52	289	6.01

Potential superstar OF accelerated through 3 levels with polished approach and plus hitting tools. A hand placement adjustment pushed hit tool to next level. Compact line drive swing. Still learning to incorporate lift into swing but will turn on inside FB to pull field. Above-average power potential. Also, an above-average runner with SB ability.

Kendall,Jeren — 8 — Los Angeles (N)

EXP MLB DEBUT: 2022 | H/W: 5-11 190 | FUT: Starting CF | 8E

Bats L Age 24 — 2017 (1) Vanderbilt

Pwr +++ | BAvg + | Spd ++++ | Def +++++

Year	Lev	Team	AB	R	H	HR	RBI	Avg	OB	Slg	OPS	bb%	ct%	Eye	SB	CS	x/h%	Iso	RC/G
2017	NCAA	Vanderbilt	261	59	80	15	53	307	365	556	920	8	72	0.32	20	4	38	249	7.11
2017	Rk	Ogden	22	5	10	1	7	455	455	727	1182	0	86	0.00	4	0	30	273	9.11
2017	A	Great Lakes	140	21	31	2	18	221	288	400	688	8	70	0.31	5	8	45	179	4.24
2018	A+	RanchoCuca	438	68	94	12	42	215	298	356	654	11	64	0.33	37	14	37	142	3.74
2019	A+	RanchoCuca	352	51	77	19	63	219	318	469	786	13	58	0.35	24	7	52	250	6.19

Athletic 1st rounder has failed to hit as a pro. Plus bat speed and above-average power allowed him to stroke a career-best 19 HR, but extreme contact issues and an aggressive approach make it unlikely he will hit enough. Plus range and arm give him the tools to be a gold glove CF.

Kennedy,Buddy — 5 — Arizona

EXP MLB DEBUT: 2022 | H/W: 6-1 190 | FUT: Starting 3B | 7D

Bats R Age 21 — 2017 (5) HS (NJ)

Pwr +++ | BAvg +++ | Spd ++ | Def ++

Year	Lev	Team	AB	R	H	HR	RBI	Avg	OB	Slg	OPS	bb%	ct%	Eye	SB	CS	x/h%	Iso	RC/G
2017	Rk	AZL DBacks	178	29	48	0	20	270	340	410	750	10	74	0.40	7	2	35	140	5.16
2018	Rk	Missoula	226	46	74	4	32	327	397	465	861	10	85	0.76	2	0	30	137	6.30
2019	A	Kane County	385	50	101	7	49	262	343	384	727	11	79	0.58	4	4	29	122	4.66

Strong, stocky 3B who hit well in his introduction to full-season MWL. Has unorthodox load in hands, but swing is short and compact and yields hard line-drive contact. Power limited to his pull-side and may be capped at 10-12 HR annually. Has plus arm required for his current position, though range is fringy and could get reps at CA.

Kessinger,Grae — 456 — Houston

EXP MLB DEBUT: 2022 | H/W: 6-2 200 | FUT: Starting 2B | 7D

Bats R Age 22 — 2019 (2) Mississippi

Pwr ++ | BAvg +++ | Spd ++ | Def +++

Year	Lev	Team	AB	R	H	HR	RBI	Avg	OB	Slg	OPS	bb%	ct%	Eye	SB	CS	x/h%	Iso	RC/G
2019	NCAA	Mississippi	270	67	89	7	50	330	418	474	892	13	87	1.17	16	3	28	144	6.80
2019	A-	Tri City	41	5	11	0	3	268	318	366	684	7	90	0.75	1	1	36	98	4.21
2019	A	Quad Cities	170	25	38	2	17	224	327	294	621	13	81	0.81	8	2	21	71	3.46

Tall INF who makes consistent contact with short, compact stroke. Hasn't produced much power, but some potential for long balls. Could add more leverage to stroke to realize pop potential. Hits line drives to gaps and could be doubles machine without adjustments. Plays all INF spots, though lacks natural SS actions to stick there long-term.

Kieboom,Carter — 46 — Washington

EXP MLB DEBUT: 2019 | H/W: 6-2 190 | FUT: Starting 2B | 8A

Bats R Age 22 — 2016 (1) HS (GA)

Pwr +++ | BAvg +++ | Spd ++ | Def +++

Year	Lev	Team	AB	R	H	HR	RBI	Avg	OB	Slg	OPS	bb%	ct%	Eye	SB	CS	x/h%	Iso	RC/G
2017	A	Hagerstown	179	36	53	8	26	296	391	497	889	14	78	0.70	2	2	38	201	6.77
2018	A+	Potomac	245	48	73	11	46	298	388	494	882	13	80	0.72	6	1	36	196	6.60
2018	AA	Harrisburg	248	36	65	5	23	262	322	395	717	8	76	0.37	3	1	34	133	4.39
2019	AAA	Fresno	412	79	125	16	79	303	402	493	895	14	76	0.68	5	2	34	189	6.98
2019	MLB	Washington	39	4	5	2	2	128	209	282	491	9	59	0.25	0	0	40	154	0.90

Long/lean infielder rose quickly through the minors—a bit too quickly given his rough 39-AB MLB debut. But flourished at AAA, showing good pitch recognition, a patient approach and developing power. Has improved defensively but many scouts think his long-term future is as an everyday second baseman with pop.

Kirilloff,Alex — 39 — Minnesota

EXP MLB DEBUT: 2020 | H/W: 6-2 195 | FUT: Starting OF | 9D

Bats L Age 22 — 2016 (1) HS (PA)

Pwr ++++ | BAvg ++++ | Spd +++ | Def +++

Year	Lev	Team	AB	R	H	HR	RBI	Avg	OB	Slg	OPS	bb%	ct%	Eye	SB	CS	x/h%	Iso	RC/G
2016	Rk	Elizabethton	216	33	66	7	33	306	339	454	793	5	85	0.34	0	1	26	148	5.02
2017		Did not play - injury																	
2018	A	Cedar Rapids	252	36	84	13	56	333	391	607	998	9	81	0.51	1	1	45	274	7.82
2018	A+	Fort Myers	260	39	94	7	45	362	394	550	944	5	85	0.36	3	2	35	188	6.90
2019	AA	Pensacola	375	47	106	9	43	283	334	413	747	7	80	0.38	7	6	27	131	4.67

Forgettable season for top prospect as wrist injury majorly affected natural hitting stroke. Showed solid plate skills with ct% ability and power pre-injury. Afterwards, swing was a wreck as he tried to compensate. Power is still present and showed up in BP and August run. 25-plus HR power at projection. May shift to 1B defensively.

Kirk,Alejandro — 2 — Toronto

EXP MLB DEBUT: 2021 | H/W: 5-9 220 | FUT: Reserve C | 6B

Bats R Age 21 — 2016 FA (MX)

Pwr ++ | BAvg +++ | Spd + | Def ++

Year	Lev	Team	AB	R	H	HR	RBI	Avg	OB	Slg	OPS	bb%	ct%	Eye	SB	CS	x/h%	Iso	RC/G
2017	Rk	GCL Blue Jays	2	0	0	0	0	0	0	0	0	0	100		0	0		0	-2.66
2018	Rk	Bluefield	206	31	73	10	57	354	444	558	1002	14	90	1.57	2	0	29	204	7.99
2019	A	Lansing	77	15	23	3	8	299	432	519	951	19	90	2.25	1	0	43	221	7.87
2019	A+	Dunedin	233	26	67	4	36	288	387	446	834	14	87	1.23	2	0	43	159	6.27

Short, stocky CA who has elevated prospect status due to offensive production. Has walked more than fanned for each of last two seasons and is doubles machine. Brings keen approach to plate and quick, clean stroke has led to solid BA. Not much of HR threat, but should reach double figures. Glove needs upgrade as he is below average athlete.

Knizner,Andrew — 2 — St. Louis

EXP MLB DEBUT: 2019 | H/W: 6-1 200 | FUT: Starting C | 7B

Bats R Age 25 — 2016 (7) NC State

Pwr +++ | BAvg ++ | Spd + | Def +++

Year	Lev	Team	AB	R	H	HR	RBI	Avg	OB	Slg	OPS	bb%	ct%	Eye	SB	CS	x/h%	Iso	RC/G
2017	AA	Springfield	182	27	59	4	22	324	372	462	834	7	85	0.52	0	1	29	137	5.72
2018	AA	Springfield	281	39	88	7	41	313	365	434	799	8	86	0.58	0	1	23	121	5.30
2018	AAA	Memphis	54	3	17	0	4	315	362	407	769	7	85	0.50	0	0	29	93	5.08
2019	AAA	Memphis	246	41	68	12	34	276	341	463	804	9	85	0.65	2	0	32	187	5.34
2019	MLB	St. Louis	53	7	12	2	7	226	281	377	658	7	74	0.29	2	0	33	151	3.42

Patient hitter continues to put up solid numbers, but looked overmatched in MLB debut. Bat to ball skills are among the best in the system and he should continue to hit for average with 15-20 HR power at his peak. Continues to improve behind the plate but footwork and blocking remain inconsistent and arm strength is just a tick above average.

Knowles, D'Shawn — 8 — Los Angeles (A)
EXP MLB DEBUT: 2023 | H/W: 6-0 165 | FUT: Starting CF | 8E

Bats B | Age 19 | 2017 FA (BM)
Pwr ++ | BAvg ++ | Spd ++++ | Def +++

Year	Lev	Team	AB	R	H	HR	RBI	Avg	OB	Slg	OPS	bb%	ct%	Eye	SB	CS	x/h%	Iso	RC/G
2019	Rk	Orem	253	38	61	6	28	241	312	387	699	9	70	0.34	5	4	34	146	4.27

Rangy, speed-focused prospect who profiles as everyday CF and switch-hitting, top of the order type bat. Best tool is his elite running ability, which is complemented by solid approach and ability to get on base. Bat-to-ball skills from both sides are fringy and does not possess a ton of raw power, but has lean frame with projection for strength.

Kramer, Kevin — 47 — Pittsburgh
EXP MLB DEBUT: 2018 | H/W: 6-0 200 | FUT: Utility player | 6B

Bats L | Age 26 | 2015 (2) UCLA
Pwr ++ | BAvg +++ | Spd ++ | Def +++

Year	Lev	Team	AB	R	H	HR	RBI	Avg	OB	Slg	OPS	bb%	ct%	Eye	SB	CS	x/h%	Iso	RC/G
2017	AA	Altoona	202	31	60	6	27	297	352	500	852	8	75	0.34	7	2	43	203	6.18
2018	AAA	Indianapolis	476	73	148	15	59	311	362	492	853	7	73	0.30	13	5	36	181	6.19
2018	MLB	Pittsburgh	37	5	5	0	5	135	179	135	315	5	46	0.10	0	0	0	0	-1.93
2019	AAA	Indianapolis	393	49	102	10	54	260	333	417	750	10	70	0.37	4	5	40	158	5.00
2019	MLB	Pittsburgh	42	5	7	0	5	167	271	190	461	13	60	0.35	0	1	14	24	0.76

Versatile prospect who has spent parts of last two seasons with PIT. Plays multiple positions, though a master of none. Added more power by revising swing path. Drives ball to gaps and has strength to reach seats. Strikes out as swing tends to lengthen and struggles with good breaking balls. Not enough range for SS, but plays a solid 2B and LF.

Labour, Franklin — 9 — San Francisco
EXP MLB DEBUT: 2022 | H/W: 6-1 190 | FUT: Starting OF | 7D

Bats R | Age 21 | 2015 FA (DR)
Pwr +++ | BAvg ++ | Spd +++ | Def +++

Year	Lev	Team	AB	R	H	HR	RBI	Avg	OB	Slg	OPS	bb%	ct%	Eye	SB	CS	x/h%	Iso	RC/G
2018	Rk	AZL Giants	130	23	35	1	20	269	358	431	789	12	69	0.45	7	1	49	162	5.90
2019	A-	Salem-Keizer	166	37	51	14	34	307	375	639	1014	10	74	0.42	2	1	49	331	8.20
2019	A	Augusta	107	16	23	1	11	215	270	299	569	7	63	0.20	0	0	30	84	2.42

Offensive-oriented OF who dominated NWL by leading in HR and SLG (by 100 pts) before late promotion to full-season A. Promising hitter with plus raw power to all fields and ability to make easy contact from compact stroke. Some swing and miss in profile, but can work counts. Owns average RF arm, but just an average outfielder with below average speed.

Langeliers, Shea — 2 — Atlanta
EXP MLB DEBUT: 2021 | H/W: 6-0 190 | FUT: Starting C | 7B

Bats R | Age 22 | 2019 (1) Baylor
Pwr ++++ | BAvg ++ | Spd ++ | Def ++++

Year	Lev	Team	AB	R	H	HR	RBI	Avg	OB	Slg	OPS	bb%	ct%	Eye	SB	CS	x/h%	Iso	RC/G
2019	NCAA	Baylor	187	36	62	13	53	332	393	604	997	9	85	0.68	4	2	39	273	7.58
2019	A	Rome	216	27	55	2	34	255	309	343	652	7	75	0.31	0	0	27	88	3.51

Strong CA made debut after Top-10 draft selection in June. Power-oriented swing with average bat speed, but sells out on his pull side. Best when he keeps swing short and compact, and relies on gap-to-gap skills. Home runs play in BP, and will come in games. Defensively skilled, manages pitching staff and controls running game well.

Lantigua, Danny — 9 — Cincinnati
EXP MLB DEBUT: 2023 | H/W: 6-1 165 | FUT: Starting OF | 7E

Bats B | Age 21 | 2016 FA (DR)
Pwr +++ | BAvg ++ | Spd +++ | Def +++

Year	Lev	Team	AB	R	H	HR	RBI	Avg	OB	Slg	OPS	bb%	ct%	Eye	SB	CS	x/h%	Iso	RC/G
2018	Rk	AZL Reds	197	26	44	8	37	223	271	467	738	6	62	0.17	5	4	59	244	5.13
2019	Rk	Greeneville	195	19	36	3	18	185	213	313	526	3	50	0.07	1	2	39	128	2.33

Overaggressive, athletic switch-hitter struggled first time away from CIN complex. Raw plus power carries profile. Swing is long and struggles with spin. Aggressiveness causes expansion of zone. Solid CF, but mostly played RF in '19. Will likely stay in RF since speed is fringe-average. Will never be a big SB threat.

Larnach, Trevor — 79 — Minnesota
EXP MLB DEBUT: 2020 | H/W: 6-4 223 | FUT: Starting OF | 8B

Bats L | Age 23 | 2018 (1) Oregon St
Pwr +++ | BAvg +++ | Spd ++ | Def +++

Year	Lev	Team	AB	R	H	HR	RBI	Avg	OB	Slg	OPS	bb%	ct%	Eye	SB	CS	x/h%	Iso	RC/G
2018	NCAA	Oregon St	256	72	89	19	77	348	454	652	1107	16	74	0.76	4	2	44	305	9.89
2018	Rk	Elizabethton	61	10	19	2	16	311	408	492	900	14	82	0.91	2	0	37	180	6.97
2018	A	Cedar Rapids	91	17	27	3	10	297	373	505	878	11	81	0.65	1	0	44	209	6.54
2019	A+	Fort Myers	320	33	101	6	44	316	383	459	842	10	77	0.47	4	1	33	144	6.14
2019	AA	Pensacola	156	26	46	7	22	295	382	455	837	12	68	0.44	0	0	24	160	6.26

Polished, former 1st round pick made it to Double-A in first full season. Plus approach with spray ability. Quick, compact swing will get to above-average hit tool at projection. Plus-power in frame but swing geared towards above-average potential, given spray approach of hit tool. Think 20-25 HR, maybe more with juiced ball.

Lavigne, Grant — 3 — Colorado
EXP MLB DEBUT: 2022 | H/W: 6-4 220 | FUT: Starting 1B | 8D

Bats L | Age 20 | 2018 (1) HS (NH)
Pwr +++ | BAvg +++ | Spd + | Def +++

Year	Lev	Team	AB	R	H	HR	RBI	Avg	OB	Slg	OPS	bb%	ct%	Eye	SB	CS	x/h%	Iso	RC/G
2018	Rk	Grand Junction	206	45	72	6	38	350	466	519	986	18	81	1.13	12	7	29	170	8.34
2019	A	Asheville	440	52	104	7	64	236	339	327	666	13	71	0.53	8	9	25	91	3.92

Bat-first 1B prospect with plus raw power and advanced strike zone awareness. Has struggled lifting ball consistently as a pro but long levers, strong base and bat speed project him to tap into it with more reps. Contact skills regressed in full-season ball but overall bat to ball skills remain solid. Limited athleticism; relegated to 1B long-term.

Lee, Khalil — 789 — Kansas City
EXP MLB DEBUT: 2020 | H/W: 5-10 170 | FUT: Starting OF | 8D

Bats L | Age 21 | 2016 (3) HS (VA)
Pwr +++ | BAvg +++ | Spd +++ | Def +++

Year	Lev	Team	AB	R	H	HR	RBI	Avg	OB	Slg	OPS	bb%	ct%	Eye	SB	CS	x/h%	Iso	RC/G
2016	Rk	AZL Royals	182	43	49	6	29	269	381	484	865	15	69	0.58	8	4	43	214	6.99
2017	A	Lexington	451	71	107	17	61	237	333	430	763	13	62	0.38	20	18	44	193	5.60
2018	A+	Wilmington	244	42	66	4	41	270	390	406	796	16	69	0.64	14	3	32	135	6.04
2018	AA	NW Arkansas	102	15	25	2	10	245	319	353	672	10	73	0.39	2	2	28	108	3.83
2019	AA	NW Arkansas	470	74	124	8	51	264	353	372	726	12	67	0.42	53	12	26	109	4.83

Continues to hold own with aggressive assignments despite continuing concerns with hit tool. Patient, but struggles getting hands in hitting position. Improved bat path but still has ct% issues. Athletic, strong frame. Doesn't get to average power in frame due to lack of leverage in lower half. Surprised with SB, but hasn't gotten faster.

Lee, Korey — 2 — Houston
EXP MLB DEBUT: 2022 | H/W: 6-2 205 | FUT: Starting C | 7C

Bats R | Age 21 | 2019 (1) California
Pwr +++ | BAvg ++ | Spd ++ | Def +++

Year	Lev	Team	AB	R	H	HR	RBI	Avg	OB	Slg	OPS	bb%	ct%	Eye	SB	CS	x/h%	Iso	RC/G
2019	NCAA	California	198	34	67	15	57	338	415	626	1041	12	79	0.62	1	0	40	288	8.44
2019	A-	Tri City	224	31	60	3	28	268	349	371	720	11	78	0.57	8	5	22	103	4.59

Surprising 1st round pick, but fits HOU profile with patience and power potential. Could move quickly thanks to mature approach and ability to recognize spin. Though improving as backstop, still work to be done with blocking and receiving. Owns cannon for an arm. Not blessed with natural hitting skills, but could hit 20+ HR with moderately high OBP.

Lewis, Brandon — 35 — Los Angeles (N)
EXP MLB DEBUT: 2022 | H/W: 6-3 215 | FUT: Starting 1B | 7E

Bats R | Age 21 | 2019 (4) UC Irvine
Pwr ++++ | BAvg ++ | Spd + | Def +++

Year	Lev	Team	AB	R	H	HR	RBI	Avg	OB	Slg	OPS	bb%	ct%	Eye	SB	CS	x/h%	Iso	RC/G
2019	Rk	AZL Dodgers	41	5	9	0	2	220	304	244	548	11	80	0.63	0	0	11	24	2.45
2019	Rk	Ogden	130	32	48	12	39	369	414	723	1137	7	73	0.29	0	2	46	354	9.75
2019	A	Great Lakes	48	9	8	1	5	167	231	271	502	8	69	0.27	0	0	38	104	1.33

Plus bat speed and massive raw power are his calling card and he slugged 28 HR between college and pro ball. Can be beat with high heat and aggressive approach results in plenty of swing-and-miss. Other tools grade out below average and he's unlikely to stick at 3B. RHB/1B only is a tough profile and will need to continue to mash to have value.

Lewis, Kyle — 789 — Seattle
EXP MLB DEBUT: 2019 | H/W: 6-4 210 | FUT: Starting OF | 8D

Bats R | Age 24 | 2016 (1) Mercer
Pwr +++ | BAvg ++ | Spd +++ | Def +++

Year	Lev	Team	AB	R	H	HR	RBI	Avg	OB	Slg	OPS	bb%	ct%	Eye	SB	CS	x/h%	Iso	RC/G
2017	A+	Modesto	149	20	38	6	24	255	323	403	726	9	74	0.39	2	1	26	148	4.39
2018	A+	Modesto	196	21	51	5	32	260	300	429	728	5	72	0.20	0	0	45	168	4.48
2018	AA	Arkansas	132	18	29	4	20	220	309	371	680	11	76	0.53	1	0	41	152	3.99
2019	AA	Arkansas	457	61	120	11	62	263	343	398	741	11	67	0.37	3	2	32	136	5.01
2019	MLB	Seattle	71	10	19	6	13	268	297	592	889	4	59	0.10	0	0	58	324	7.44

Athletic, slugging OF lost formerly plus run tool after serious knee injury a few seasons ago. High hard-contact rate makes up for ct% issues. Has bat speed but hitch in swing makes it hard not to be anything more than guess hitter. Has solid zone judgement and is mostly a pull-oriented power hitter. Big power potential, think 35+ HR seasons.

Lewis,Royce

68 | Minnesota | EXP MLB DEBUT: 2020 | H/W: 6-2 200 | FUT: Starting SS | 9B

Bats R Age 20 — 2017 (1) HS (CA) — Pwr +++ — BAvg +++ — Spd ++++ — Def ++++

Year	Lev	Team	AB	R	H	HR	RBI	Avg	OB	Sig	OPS	bb%	ct%	Eye	SB	CS	x/h%	Iso	RC/G
2017	A	Cedar Rapids	71	16	21	1	10	296	351	394	745	8	77	0.38	3	1	19	99	4.71
2018	A	Cedar Rapids	295	50	93	9	53	315	367	485	852	8	83	0.49	22	4	34	169	5.94
2018	A+	Fort Myers	188	33	48	5	21	255	324	399	723	9	81	0.54	6	4	29	144	4.48
2019	A+	Fort Myers	383	55	91	10	35	238	288	376	664	7	77	0.30	16	8	33	138	3.57
2019	AA	Pensacola	134	18	31	2	14	231	290	358	648	8	75	0.33	6	2	39	127	3.50

Quick-twitch, super-athletic former 1st overall pick struggled for 1st time in pro career. Missed most of spring training due to injury and took 2 months to get right. Lots of moving parts in swing and spin recognition caused struggles against RHP. Power plays to the gap and pull-side. Above-average power at maturity. Plus runner and it plays.

Leyba,Domingo

46 | Arizona | EXP MLB DEBUT: 2019 | H/W: 5-11 160 | FUT: Utility player | 6A

Bats B Age 24 — 2012 FA (DR) — Pwr + — BAvg +++ — Spd +++ — Def +++

Year	Lev	Team	AB	R	H	HR	RBI	Avg	OB	Sig	OPS	bb%	ct%	Eye	SB	CS	x/h%	Iso	RC/G
2017	A-	Hillsboro	28	4	8	1	6	286	375	429	804	13	93	2.00	0	0	25	143	5.75
2017	AA	Jackson	58	11	16	2	9	276	333	448	782	8	90	0.83	0	0	38	172	5.18
2018	AA	Jackson	320	43	86	5	30	269	341	381	722	10	86	0.76	5	2	28	113	4.62
2019	AAA	Reno	457	85	137	19	77	300	346	519	864	7	83	0.41	0	2	43	219	6.02
2019	MLB	Arizona	25	6	7	0	5	280	379	440	819	14	64	0.44	0	0	43	160	6.80

Switch-hitting MIF prospect whose power showed up in PCL en route to big-league debut. Good feel for the barrel and shows mostly line-drive power to fill up the gaps at present. Will expand the zone and be over-aggressive, which could cap his walk rate and hence overall OBP value. Has the overall look of a platoon INF with solid BA value.

Lipcius,Andre

45 | Detroit | EXP MLB DEBUT: 2022 | H/W: 6-1 190 | FUT: Starting MIF | 7D

Bats R Age 21 — 2019 (3) Tennessee — Pwr +++ — BAvg ++ — Spd ++ — Def +++

Year	Lev	Team	AB	R	H	HR	RBI	Avg	OB	Sig	OPS	bb%	ct%	Eye	SB	CS	x/h%	Iso	RC/G
2019	NCAA	Tennessee	237	51	73	17	58	308	388	586	975	12	86	0.94	10	1	44	278	7.45
2019	A	West Michigan	253	32	69	2	29	273	343	360	703	10	77	0.47	3	2	26	87	4.31

Athletic, lean infielder out of the University of Tennessee. Although he produces dependable defense in the field, his overall profile fall short of his offensive contribution. Lacks speed, but above-average arm and instincts balance that out a bit. Access to deceptive power, but frame doesn't support much beyond that.

Longhi,Nick

379 | Boston | EXP MLB DEBUT: 2020 | H/W: 6-2 205 | FUT: Utility player | 6C

Bats R Age 24 — 2013 (30) HS (FL) — Pwr ++ — BAvg +++ — Spd ++ — Def +++

Year	Lev	Team	AB	R	H	HR	RBI	Avg	OB	Sig	OPS	bb%	ct%	Eye	SB	CS	x/h%	Iso	RC/G
2017	AA	Portland	237	26	62	6	33	262	300	401	701	5	83	0.33	0	1	34	139	4.01
2017	AA	Pensacola	19	2	6	1	7	316	409	526	935	14	74	0.60	0	0	33	211	7.47
2018	AA	Pensacola	176	20	44	2	28	250	302	335	637	7	78	0.34	0	0	25	85	3.30
2018	AAA	Louisville	90	8	21	0	8	233	250	289	539	2	70	0.07	1	0	24	56	1.78
2019	AAA	Louisville	389	51	110	12	51	283	334	463	797	7	74	0.29	0	1	39	180	5.41

Utility player had best season of career in Triple-A. Contact-oriented corner player. Doesn't have power to carry profile. Does well working counts and spraying the ball across the diamond. Flat swing plane limits power potential. Can play COF and 1B. Fits best between 1B & 3B but no tool carries profile.

Lopez,Otto

46 | Toronto | EXP MLB DEBUT: 2022 | H/W: 5-10 160 | FUT: Utility player | 6B

Bats R Age 21 — 2016 FA (DR) — Pwr ++ — BAvg +++ — Spd +++ — Def +++

Year	Lev	Team	AB	R	H	HR	RBI	Avg	OB	Sig	OPS	bb%	ct%	Eye	SB	CS	x/h%	Iso	RC/G
2017	Rk	GCL Blue Jays	178	30	49	1	15	275	345	360	705	10	87	0.83	7	3	20	84	4.48
2018	Rk	Bluefield	33	8	12	0	6	364	364	636	1000	0	85	0.00	1	0	58	273	7.56
2018	A-	Vancouver	175	31	52	3	22	297	388	434	822	13	88	1.24	13	6	27	137	6.05
2019	A	Lansing	447	61	145	5	50	324	372	425	797	7	86	0.54	20	15	21	101	5.33

Steady INF who led MWL and org in BA in consistent campaign. Stood out for his easy bat to ball skills and fundamental glovework at both 2B and SS. Seems to fit more of a utility profile as he lacks HR punch and may lack range for SS. Despite 20 SB, was caught 15 times. Flies under the radar, but plays game aggressively and is fun to watch.

Lora,Bayron

9 | Texas | EXP MLB DEBUT: 2024 | H/W: 6-3 190 | FUT: Starting OF | 9E

Bats R Age 17 — 2019 FA (DR) — Pwr ++++ — BAvg +++ — Spd ++ — Def ++

Year	Lev	Team	AB	R	H	HR	RBI	Avg	OB	Sig	OPS	bb%	ct%	Eye	SB	CS	x/h%	Iso	RC/G
2019		Did not play in U.S.																	

In a big-league slugger's body, he has the massive power associated with his broad-shouldered frame. With a simple setup and swing and plus bat speed, he hits the ball far even when he doesn't square it up. Long-levered, he still has some holes in his swing he'll need too close up. But massive HR potential.

Lowe,Josh

8 | Tampa Bay | EXP MLB DEBUT: 2020 | H/W: 6-4 205 | FUT: Starting OF | 8C

Bats L Age 22 — 2016 (1) HS (GA) — Pwr ++++ — BAvg +++ — Spd ++++ — Def ++++

Year	Lev	Team	AB	R	H	HR	RBI	Avg	OB	Sig	OPS	bb%	ct%	Eye	SB	CS	x/h%	Iso	RC/G
2016	Rk	Princeton	80	11	19	3	11	238	371	400	771	18	60	0.53	1	1	26	163	5.91
2016	Rk	GCL Rays	93	14	24	2	15	258	389	409	798	18	71	0.74	1	1	38	151	6.04
2017	A	Bowling Green	456	60	122	8	55	268	329	386	715	8	68	0.29	22	8	30	118	4.51
2018	A+	Charlotte	399	62	95	6	47	238	318	361	679	11	71	0.40	18	6	36	123	4.07
2019	AA	Montgomery	448	70	113	18	62	252	339	442	781	12	71	0.45	30	9	40	190	5.42

Athletic OF struggled early but emerged late as plate skills and power blossomed. May never be high average guy but has simple swing that finds barrels despite ct% risk. Power plays to the gaps and to the pull side; has 30+ HR potential. Has bulked up and may have lost step but still a plus runner. Enough defensive skill for CF.

Luciano,Marco

6 | San Francisco | EXP MLB DEBUT: 2022 | H/W: 6-2 178 | FUT: Starting SS | 9C

Bats R Age 18 — 2018 FA (DR) — Pwr ++++ — BAvg ++++ — Spd +++ — Def +++

Year	Lev	Team	AB	R	H	HR	RBI	Avg	OB	Sig	OPS	bb%	ct%	Eye	SB	CS	x/h%	Iso	RC/G
2019	Rk	AZL Giants O	146	46	47	10	38	322	428	616	1044	16	73	0.69	8	6	45	295	9.08
2019	A-	Salem-Keizer	33	6	7	0	4	212	316	333	649	13	82	0.83	1	0	57	121	4.01

High-ceiling INF who has all tools to be All-Star. Athletic, fast, strong, projection; has it all. With lightning stroke, can reach seats to all fields and has speed to steal bases. Should hit for BA and power and could move thru minors quickly. Has glove to be SS, but could move to 3B as he grows. Double plus arm strength with quick feet.

Lugo,Matthew

6 | Boston | EXP MLB DEBUT: 2024 | H/W: 6-1 185 | FUT: Starting SS | 8E

Bats R Age 18 — 2019 (2) HS (PR) — Pwr ++ — BAvg +++ — Spd +++ — Def +++

Year	Lev	Team	AB	R	H	HR	RBI	Avg	OB	Sig	OPS	bb%	ct%	Eye	SB	CS	x/h%	Iso	RC/G
2019	Rk	GCL Red Sox	136	19	35	1	12	257	331	331	662	10	74	0.42	3	0	20	74	3.77
2019	A-	Lowell	8	0	2	0	1	250	250	250	500	0	75	0.00	0	0	0	0	1.07

Projectable SS with tantalizing upside, but very raw at present. Slender frame could add significant strength down the road while bat speed and hitting instincts could lead to high BA. Runs well underway and owns quick feet to enhance SS actions. May move around diamond for exposure and has athleticism, hands and arm for any position.

Lutz,Tristen

89 | Milwaukee | EXP MLB DEBUT: 2022 | H/W: 6-2 210 | FUT: Starting OF | 7B

Bats R Age 21 — 2017 (1) HS (TX) — Pwr ++++ — BAvg ++ — Spd ++ — Def +++

Year	Lev	Team	AB	R	H	HR	RBI	Avg	OB	Sig	OPS	bb%	ct%	Eye	SB	CS	x/h%	Iso	RC/G
2017	Rk	AZL Brewers	68	12	19	3	11	279	319	559	878	6	69	0.19	1	0	53	279	6.75
2017	Rk	Helena	93	23	31	6	16	333	410	559	969	11	77	0.57	2	4	26	226	7.55
2018	A	Wisconsin	444	63	109	13	63	245	316	421	737	9	69	0.33	9	3	45	176	4.85
2019	A+	Carolina	420	62	107	13	54	255	328	419	747	10	67	0.34	3	2	37	164	5.02

Strong, physically mature 21-year-old OF prospect with intriguing power upside. Swing packs a punch with strong forearms and lower half; limited physical projection remaining. Aggressive approach and fringy ct% could limit his ability to hit for a high average, but willing to take a walk. Plus arm, restricted athleticism project him to RF.

Lux,Gavin

46 | Los Angeles (N) | EXP MLB DEBUT: 2019 | H/W: 6-2 190 | FUT: Starting SS | 8A

Bats L Age 22 — 2016 (1) HS (WI) — Pwr +++ — BAvg ++++ — Spd +++ — Def ++++

Year	Lev	Team	AB	R	H	HR	RBI	Avg	OB	Sig	OPS	bb%	ct%	Eye	SB	CS	x/h%	Iso	RC/G
2018	A+	RanchoCuca	358	64	116	11	48	324	397	520	916	11	81	0.63	11	7	35	196	7.01
2018	AA	Tulsa	105	21	34	4	9	324	403	495	899	12	81	0.70	2	2	26	171	6.75
2019	AA	Tulsa	259	45	81	13	37	313	380	521	901	10	77	0.47	7	3	30	208	6.70
2019	AAA	Oklahoma City	199	54	78	13	39	392	478	719	1197	14	79	0.79	3	3	45	327	10.77
2019	MLB	Los Angeles	75	12	18	2	9	240	305	400	705	9	68	0.29	2	0	39	160	4.36

Breakout season for former 1st rounder. Started strong and then obliterated pitching once moved up to AAA. Smooth lefty stroke and advanced understanding of strike zone resulted in career-highs in BA/OB/SLG. Speed has taken a back seat to power and BA, but remains a plus runner. Has the chops to stick at short.

Maciel,Gabriel — 89 — Minnesota

EXP MLB DEBUT: 2022 | H/W: 5-10 170 | FUT: Starting CF | 7E

Bats B | Age 21 | 2016 FA (BR)

Pwr + | BAvg +++ | Spd ++++ | Def ++++

Year	Lev	Team	AB	R	H	HR	RBI	Avg	OB	Slg	OPS	bb%	ct%	Eye	SB	CS	x/h%	Iso	RC/G
2017	Rk	Missoula	217	40	70	3	25	323	390	438	828	10	84	0.71	9	8	26	115	5.88
2018	A	Kane County	279	44	80	1	16	287	356	333	689	10	82	0.60	14	5	14	47	4.16
2018	A	Cedar Rapids	397	60	111	3	23	280	338	348	686	8	82	0.49	16	10	17	68	4.02
2019	A	Cedar Rapids	162	28	50	0	17	309	395	377	771	12	81	0.74	8	2	14	68	5.40
2019	A+	Fort Myers	199	29	52	3	17	261	332	357	689	10	85	0.70	14	7	21	95	4.17

Super-athletic CF is rawer than High-A performance suggests. Brazilian prospect was quite a find by ARI international scouting department. Plus bat-to-ball skills and plus run tool dominate profile. Struggles offensively finding the barrel, resulting in lots of light contact. There isn't much power projection in swing or frame. 20+ SB potential.

Madrigal,Nick — 6 — Chicago (A)

EXP MLB DEBUT: 2020 | H/W: 5-7 165 | FUT: Starting 2B | 8B

Bats R | Age 23 | 2018 (1) Oregon St

Pwr + | BAvg ++++ | Spd ++++ | Def +++++

Year	Lev	Team	AB	R	H	HR	RBI	Avg	OB	Slg	OPS	bb%	ct%	Eye	SB	CS	x/h%	Iso	RC/G
2018	A	Kannapolis	44	9	15	0	6	341	356	409	765	2	100		2	2	20	68	4.92
2018	A+	Winston-Salem	98	14	30	0	9	306	340	347	687	5	95	1.00	6	3	13	41	4.14
2019	A+	Winston-Salem	191	20	52	2	27	272	332	377	709	8	97	2.83	17	4	27	105	4.71
2019	AA	Birmingham	164	30	56	1	16	341	393	451	844	8	97	2.80	14	6	25	110	6.11
2019	AAA	Charlotte	118	26	39	1	12	331	397	424	821	10	96	2.60	4	3	21	93	5.96

Athletic contact darling excelled at three levels, including late Triple-A stint. Mostly inside-out swing, peppers RCF with line drives. Has great plate discipline and solid spray skills; no power in swing. Doesn't pull enough to even cash in on 10-15 HRs. Plus runner with SB efficiency. Double-plus defender at 2B.

Maitan,Kevin — 45 — Los Angeles (A)

EXP MLB DEBUT: 2022 | H/W: 6-2 190 | FUT: Starting 3B | 8E

Bats B | Age 20 | 2016 FA (VZ)

Pwr +++ | BAvg ++ | Spd ++ | Def +++

Year	Lev	Team	AB	R	H	HR	RBI	Avg	OB	Slg	OPS	bb%	ct%	Eye	SB	CS	x/h%	Iso	RC/G
2017	Rk	Danville	127	10	28	2	15	220	272	323	595	7	69	0.23	1	0	29	102	2.68
2017	Rk	GCL Braves	35	5	11	0	3	314	351	400	751	5	71	0.20	1	0	27	86	4.89
2018	Rk	Orem	262	42	65	8	26	248	299	397	696	7	75	0.29	1	2	34	149	3.98
2019	A	Burlington	486	56	104	12	46	214	272	323	595	7	66	0.24	7	4	25	109	2.66

Post-hype prospect struggled in his first tour of full-season ball. Has moved off SS to 3B, where his still plus raw power and strong arm profile best. Has added strength to previously lean frame but also has also added weight in his midsection, limiting the athleticism in his swing and leading to ct% issues. Still young, but it's time to produce.

Mann,Devin — 45 — Los Angeles (N)

EXP MLB DEBUT: 2022 | H/W: 6-3 180 | FUT: Starting 2B | 7D

Bats R | Age 23 | 2018 (5) Louisville

Pwr +++ | BAvg ++ | Spd ++ | Def +++

Year	Lev	Team	AB	R	H	HR	RBI	Avg	OB	Slg	OPS	bb%	ct%	Eye	SB	CS	x/h%	Iso	RC/G
2018	Rk	AZL Dodgers	5	0	1	0	0	200	333	200	533	17	40	0.33	0	1	0	0	3.07
2018	A	Great Lakes	224	26	54	2	30	241	341	335	676	13	78	0.68	7	4	30	94	4.15
2019	Rk	AZL DodgersM	1	0	0	0	0	0	500	0	500	50	100		0	0		0	4.75
2019	Rk	AZL DodgersL	13	2	7	0	1	538	571	692	1264	7	92	1.00	0	1	29	154	10.57
2019	A+	RanchoCuca	367	63	102	19	63	278	357	496	853	11	75	0.48	5	4	39	218	6.19

Pop-up prospect had a breakout season. Solid bat-to-ball skills in college and a line-drive swing made him a 5th round pick, but a more aggressive approach and better use of lower half raises power profile. Hunts for pitches he can drive, but now has more swing-and-miss. Moves well for his size and with solid fundamentals at 2B.

Marcano,Tucupita — 456 — San Diego

EXP MLB DEBUT: 2021 | H/W: 6-0 170 | FUT: Starting MIF | 8D

Bats L | Age 20 | 2016 FA (VZ)

Pwr + | BAvg ++++ | Spd +++ | Def +++

Year	Lev	Team	AB	R	H	HR	RBI	Avg	OB	Slg	OPS	bb%	ct%	Eye	SB	CS	x/h%	Iso	RC/G
2018	Rk	AZL Padres 2	124	33	49	0	17	395	500	444	944	17	92	2.60	10	7	10	48	7.83
2018	A-	Tri-City	70	12	22	1	9	314	351	429	780	5	91	0.67	5	0	18	114	5.08
2019	A	Fort Wayne	460	55	124	2	45	270	321	337	658	7	90	0.78	15	16	19	67	3.86

Skinny, wiry SS posted lowest K-rate in MWL. Combines elite contact ability with patient, discerning eye. Works deep into counts and can put bat on ball in any quadrant of strike zone. Has slender build and spray-hitter mentality that isn't conducive to much raw power. Good athlete with some speed to provide moderate SB impact.

Marchan,Rafael — 2 — Philadelphia

EXP MLB DEBUT: 2022 | H/W: 5-9 170 | FUT: Starting C | 8C

Bats B | Age 21 | 2015 FA (VZ)

Pwr ++ | BAvg ++++ | 4.53 Spd ++ | Def ++++

Year	Lev	Team	AB	R	H	HR	RBI	Avg	OB	Slg	OPS	bb%	ct%	Eye	SB	CS	x/h%	Iso	RC/G
2017	Rk	GCL Phillies	84	10	20	0	10	238	273	298	570	5	90	0.50	1	0	25	60	2.77
2018	A-	Williamsport	196	28	59	0	12	301	338	362	700	5	91	0.61	9	6	17	61	4.23
2019	A	Lakewood	236	21	64	0	20	271	338	339	677	9	87	0.77	1	3	25	68	4.16
2019	A+	Clearwater	78	6	18	0	3	231	286	282	568	7	90	0.75	1	2	22	51	2.86

Rode an advanced hit tool through full-season debut and finished year in High-A. Can manipulate the barrel, catch up to velocity, stay on offspeed, and go with pitches with ease. Has a catcher's frame, but has shown little current power (zero pro HR). Rocket arm; but blocking/receiving still need work. Athleticism points to future improvement.

Marsh,Brandon — 89 — Los Angeles (A)

EXP MLB DEBUT: 2020 | H/W: 6-4 215 | FUT: Starting CF | 8B

Bats L | Age 22 | 2016 (2) HS (GA)

Pwr +++ | BAvg +++ | Spd +++ | Def +++

Year	Lev	Team	AB	R	H	HR	RBI	Avg	OB	Slg	OPS	bb%	ct%	Eye	SB	CS	x/h%	Iso	RC/G
2017	Rk	Orem	177	47	62	4	44	350	382	548	930	5	80	0.26	10	2	35	198	6.88
2018	A	Burlington	132	26	39	3	24	295	392	470	862	14	70	0.53	4	0	41	174	6.87
2018	A+	Inland Empire	371	59	95	7	46	256	348	385	733	12	68	0.44	10	4	29	129	4.94
2019	Rk	AZL Angels	21	1	1	0	2	48	48	48	95	0	62	0.00	1	0	0	0	-5.15
2019	AA	Mobile	360	48	108	7	43	300	381	428	809	12	74	0.51	18	5	28	128	5.80

Athletic, toolsy OF was two-sport HS athlete before signing for slot value as 2nd rounder in 2016. Swing is geared toward high ct% and an up-the-middle approach; shows BA upside. Owns quality walk rates and is discerning at plate. Learning to tap into power, but lack of leverage likely caps him at fringe HR. Has range and arm for CF profile.

Marte,Jelfry — 6 — Tampa Bay

EXP MLB DEBUT: 2024 | H/W: 5-10 130 | FUT: Starting SS | 7E

Bats B | Age 19 | 2017 FA (DR)

Pwr + | BAvg ++ | Spd ++++ | Def +++

Year	Lev	Team	AB	R	H	HR	RBI	Avg	OB	Slg	OPS	bb%	ct%	Eye	SB	CS	x/h%	Iso	RC/G
2018	Rk	GCL Rays	153	16	43	0	14	281	308	314	622	4	83	0.23	7	4	9	33	3.01
2019	Rk	Princeton	176	24	33	0	9	188	255	222	477	8	69	0.30	2	5	15	34	1.08
2019	Rk	GCL Rays	19	2	6	0	7	316	381	632	1013	10	63	0.29	0	0	50	316	10.11

Switch-hitting, quick-twitch SS struggled in stateside debut with speed of game and hit tool. Documented vision issues caused '17 deal with MIN to be voided. Quick hands and loose swing create plus bat speed. Struggles creating consistent swing path. Below-average power in wiry frame. Plus runner and above-average at SS.

Marte,Noelvi — 6 — Seattle

EXP MLB DEBUT: 2024 | H/W: 6-1 181 | FUT: Starting 3B | 9E

Bats R | Age 18 | 2018 FA (DR)

Pwr ++++ | BAvg +++ | Spd ++++ | Def +++

Year	Lev	Team	AB	R	H	HR	RBI	Avg	OB	Slg	OPS	bb%	ct%	Eye	SB	CS	x/h%	Iso	RC/G
2019		Did not play in U.S.																	

Athletic, toolsy power hitting SS made Dominican Summer League debut. Power drives hit tool. Has a solid, uppercut swing, primed for generating loft. Does well incorporating leverage in swing. Plus runner. Expected to fill out frame and eventually lose speed and move to 3B. Is on similar trajectory path as Julio Rodriguez was after signing.

Martin,Jason — 78 — Pittsburgh

EXP MLB DEBUT: 2019 | H/W: 5-9 185 | FUT: Reserve OF | 6B

Bats L | Age 24 | 2013 (8) HS (CA)

Pwr +++ | BAvg ++ | Spd +++ | Def ++

Year	Lev	Team	AB	R	H	HR	RBI	Avg	OB	Slg	OPS	bb%	ct%	Eye	SB	CS	x/h%	Iso	RC/G
2017	AA	Corpus Christi	300	38	82	11	37	273	317	483	800	6	73	0.23	7	6	46	210	5.43
2018	AA	Altoona	255	49	83	9	34	325	392	522	914	10	76	0.46	7	8	33	196	7.03
2018	AAA	Indianapolis	213	20	45	4	21	211	270	319	589	7	76	0.33	5	4	27	108	2.64
2019	AAA	Indianapolis	370	47	96	8	50	259	313	419	732	7	79	0.37	9	6	40	159	4.56
2019	MLB	Pittsburgh	36	5	9	0	2	250	325	306	631	10	72	0.40	2	0	22	56	3.38

Short, strong OF who ended season in September after dislocating shoulder. Packs power into fast bat and uses hands well in clean swing. Tends to get pull-conscious at times and can flail at breakers. Possesses average speed on base and in OF. More of a tweener - not enough range for CF, but gets good jumps. Good value with utility profile.

Martin,Mason — 3 — Pittsburgh

EXP MLB DEBUT: 2022 | H/W: 6-0 201 | FUT: Starting 1B | 7D

Bats L | Age 20 | 2017 (17) HS (WA)

Pwr ++++ | BAvg ++ | Spd + | Def +

Year	Lev	Team	AB	R	H	HR	RBI	Avg	OB	Slg	OPS	bb%	ct%	Eye	SB	CS	x/h%	Iso	RC/G
2017	Rk	GCL Pirates	127	37	39	11	22	307	447	630	1076	20	68	0.78	2	2	49	323	10.03
2018	Rk	Bristol	223	42	52	10	40	233	355	422	776	16	61	0.48	2	2	40	188	5.85
2018	A	West Virginia	150	16	30	4	18	200	286	333	619	11	59	0.29	1	1	40	133	3.35
2019	A	Greensboro	301	58	79	23	83	262	360	575	935	13	66	0.45	8	2	57	312	7.85
2019	A+	Bradenton	176	32	42	12	46	239	323	528	852	11	63	0.34	0	1	62	290	6.75

Strong 1B who led SAL in HR in first full season experience. Finished 4th in minors in HR while also showing discerning eye at plate. Draws lot of walks, though expect a ton of whiffs. Bat only prospect at present as he is very slow and exhibits poor glovework. Doesn't receive much pub, but could surprise if he rounds out his overall game.

Martinez,Juan Pablo

78	Texas	EXP MLB DEBUT: 2021	H/W: 5-9 174	FUT: Starting CF	7C

Bats L Age 24
2018 FA (CU)

- Pwr +++
- BAvg ++
- Spd ++++
- Def +++

Year	Lev	Team	AB	R	H	HR	RBI	Avg	OB	Slg	OPS	bb%	ct%	Eye	SB	CS	x/h%	Iso	RC/G
2018	Rk	DSL Rangers	22	10	9	1	3	409	581	682	1262	29	68	1.29	2	3	33	273	13.77
2018	A-	Spokane	234	49	59	8	21	252	347	436	783	13	71	0.49	11	6	37	184	5.54
2019	A	Hickory	40	7	10	1	5	250	302	400	702	7	70	0.25	4	1	30	150	4.21
2019	A+	Down East	407	59	101	14	58	248	314	423	737	9	65	0.27	28	12	39	174	4.92

Thin and small-framed, can catch up to velocity with quick hands but offspeed gives him fits. More HR (and Ks) than expected with this profile; leads to questions on how/if he'll adjust to upper-level pitching. Speed for SBs, but OBP problematic. 4th OF downside.

Martinez,Orelvis

56	Toronto	EXP MLB DEBUT: 2023	H/W: 6-1 188	FUT: Starting 3B	9E

Bats R Age 18
2018 FA (DR)

- Pwr ++++
- BAvg +++
- Spd ++
- Def +++

Year	Lev	Team	AB	R	H	HR	RBI	Avg	OB	Slg	OPS	bb%	ct%	Eye	SB	CS	x/h%	Iso	RC/G
2019	Rk	GCL Blue Jays	142	20	39	7	32	275	340	549	889	9	80	0.48	2	0	51	275	6.56

Outstanding pro debut for 2018 bonus baby ($3.5M). Finished 2nd in HR and SLG in GCL and has significant projection. Exhibits quality athleticism, though isn't a great runner. Very high ceiling predicated on explosive bat speed. Should hit for BA as well. Projects as 3B with strong arm and soft hands. High risk due to youth, but also high reward.

Martinez,Pedro

46	Chicago (N)	EXP MLB DEBUT: 2023	H/W: 5-11 165	FUT: Utility player	7D

Bats B Age 19
2018 FA (VZ)

- Pwr ++
- BAvg ++++
- Spd +++
- Def +++

Year	Lev	Team	AB	R	H	HR	RBI	Avg	OB	Slg	OPS	bb%	ct%	Eye	SB	CS	x/h%	Iso	RC/G
2019	Rk	AZL Cubs	108	12	38	2	17	352	417	519	935	10	75	0.44	8	5	29	167	7.47
2019	A-	Eugene	98	15	26	0	7	265	345	347	692	11	63	0.33	11	5	19	82	4.57

Switch-hitting, slender MIF proficient in bat control and speed. Distributes low line drives and ground balls to all fields. Power projects as below-average but has projectable frame and can add strength. Uses big leg kick for timing and could be starting point to tap into more power. Has enough arm and range to stick on left side of the infield.

Mateo,Jorge

6	Oakland	EXP MLB DEBUT: 2020	H/W: 6-0 192	FUT: Starting SS	7A

Bats R Age 24
2012 FA (DR)

- Pwr ++
- BAvg +++
- Spd +++++
- Def +++

Year	Lev	Team	AB	R	H	HR	RBI	Avg	OB	Slg	OPS	bb%	ct%	Eye	SB	CS	x/h%	Iso	RC/G
2017	A+	Tampa	275	39	66	4	11	240	282	400	682	5	71	0.20	28	3	42	160	3.97
2017	AA	Trenton	120	26	36	4	26	300	378	525	903	11	73	0.47	11	7	44	225	7.13
2017	AA	Midland	137	25	40	4	20	292	336	518	854	6	76	0.27	13	3	40	226	6.16
2018	AAA	Nashville	470	50	108	3	45	230	275	353	628	6	70	0.21	25	10	33	123	3.25
2019	AAA	Las Vegas	532	95	154	19	78	289	326	504	830	5	73	0.20	24	11	40	214	5.81

Loose, wiry SS was dynamic force in hitter-friendly PCL and is almost ready to contribute. Owns perhaps the best speed in the minors and projects to be top-tier SB source. Has aggressive approach and ct% skills are fringe-average; quality breakers give him fits. Power surge related to the ball and park environment and may only have fringe HR value.

Matias,Seuly

9	Kansas City	EXP MLB DEBUT: 2022	H/W: 6-3 198	FUT: Starting OF	7E

Bats R Age 21
2015 FA (DR)

- Pwr ++++
- BAvg +
- Spd +++
- Def +++

Year	Lev	Team	AB	R	H	HR	RBI	Avg	OB	Slg	OPS	bb%	ct%	Eye	SB	CS	x/h%	Iso	RC/G
2016	Rk	AZL Royals	172	32	43	8	29	250	335	477	812	11	58	0.30	2	4	49	227	6.73
2017	Rk	Burlington	222	27	54	7	36	243	294	423	718	7	68	0.22	2	1	43	180	4.48
2018	A	Lexington	338	62	78	31	63	231	282	550	832	7	61	0.18	6	0	58	320	6.26
2019	A+	Wilmington	189	23	28	4	22	148	248	307	555	12	48	0.26	2	4	64	159	2.95

Physically-strong, athletic RF didn't come close to hitting his body weight last season. Broke hand in June, ended miserable season. Only hit 4 HR in 57 games. Light-tower power pushes profile. However, holes in swing keep power potential in check. Struggled getting bat head out in front to make hard contact. Defensively, arm is suited for RF.

Matijevic,J.J.

37	Houston	EXP MLB DEBUT: 2020	H/W: 6-0 206	FUT: Reserve OF	6B

Bats L Age 24
2017 (2) Arizona

- Pwr +++
- BAvg ++
- Spd ++
- Def +

Year	Lev	Team	AB	R	H	HR	RBI	Avg	OB	Slg	OPS	bb%	ct%	Eye	SB	CS	x/h%	Iso	RC/G
2017	A	Quad Cities	24	2	3	1	4	125	160	250	410	4	63	0.11	0	1	33	125	-0.39
2018	A	Quad Cities	48	8	17	3	5	354	446	708	1155	14	79	0.80	3	0	59	354	10.28
2018	A+	Buies Creek	335	58	89	19	57	266	337	513	850	10	69	0.35	10	13	47	248	6.32
2019	A+	Fayetteville	18	3	6	2	2	333	400	722	1122	10	78	0.50	0	0	50	389	9.26
2019	AA	Corpus Christi	281	41	69	9	35	246	312	423	735	9	65	0.28	8	0	45	178	4.90

Strong hitter who is all about power. Missed time due to 50-game suspension for drug of abuse. Struggles with BA as pitch recognition falls short and can be beaten with good fastballs. Can sell out for power and fan in bunches. When contact made, drives ball a long way. Limited defensively with sub-par athleticism.

Maton,Nick

46	Philadelphia	EXP MLB DEBUT: 2021	H/W: 6-1 165	FUT: Starting MIF	7C

Bats L Age 23
2017 (7) Lincoln Land JC

- Pwr +++
- BAvg ++
- Spd ++
- Def +++

Year	Lev	Team	AB	R	H	HR	RBI	Avg	OB	Slg	OPS	bb%	ct%	Eye	SB	CS	x/h%	Iso	RC/G
2017	NCAA	LincolnLandJC	169	60	69	8	46	408	507	722	1229	17	84	1.26	33	2	42	314	11.21
2017	A-	Williamsport	210	34	53	2	13	252	346	333	679	13	78	0.64	10	5	23	81	4.13
2018	A	Lakewood	406	52	104	8	51	256	327	404	731	10	75	0.42	5	3	38	148	4.69
2019	A+	Clearwater	337	35	93	5	45	276	354	380	734	11	79	0.58	11	8	24	104	4.75
2019	AA	Reading	62	6	13	2	6	210	310	355	665	13	77	0.64	1	1	38	145	3.83

No standout tools, but broad base and they are improving with time. Has good AB, enough sting out of wiry frame to approach double-digit HR. Enough bat speed for BA; solid Eye for OBA; and speed and baseball IQ net him SB. Has improved agility and range on defense, making him an adequate defender up the middle with a plus arm and instincts.

Matos,Luis

8	San Francisco	EXP MLB DEBUT: 2024	H/W: 5-11 160	FUT: Starting CF	8E

Bats R Age 18
2018 FA (VZ)

- Pwr +++
- BAvg +++
- Spd +++
- Def +++

Year	Lev	Team	AB	R	H	HR	RBI	Avg	OB	Slg	OPS	bb%	ct%	Eye	SB	CS	x/h%	Iso	RC/G
2019	Rk	DOSL Giants	235	60	85	7	47	362	409	570	980	7	87	0.63	20	2	39	209	7.46
2019	Rk	AZL Giants	16	5	7	0	1	438	471	500	971	6	94	1.00	1	1	14	63	7.18

Quick, athletic OF who impressed in all facets of game in pro debut. Exhibits contact-oriented approach with electric bat speed and strike zone knowledge. Should grow into more power as he adds strength to lithe frame. Runs very well and plays solid defense in CF. Arm strength sufficient for any outfield spot.

Mauricio,Ronny

6	New York (N)	EXP MLB DEBUT: 2022	H/W: 6-3 166	FUT: Starting 3B	9C

Bats B Age 19
2017 FA (DR)

- Pwr ++++
- BAvg +++
- Spd ++
- Def +++

Year	Lev	Team	AB	R	H	HR	RBI	Avg	OB	Slg	OPS	bb%	ct%	Eye	SB	CS	x/h%	Iso	RC/G
2018	Rk	GCL Mets	197	26	55	3	31	279	314	421	735	5	84	0.32	1	6	35	142	4.49
2018	Rk	Kingsport	30	6	7	0	4	233	303	333	636	9	70	0.33	1	0	43	100	3.53
2019	A	Columbia	470	62	126	4	37	268	302	357	660	5	79	0.23	6	10	23	89	3.50

Tall, long switch-hitting teenager held own in full-season debut. Big power potential with long levers and a good frame to add to. Solid athlete with quick twitch skills, especially from LH side of plate. Swing from RH side a bit crude. From LH side, does well with power transfer, waiting on trajectory to increase and tap into power. Likely 3B long-term.

Mazeika,Patrick

2	New York (N)	EXP MLB DEBUT: 2020	H/W: 6-3 208	FUT: Reserve C	6C

Bats L Age 26
2015 (8) Stetson

- Pwr +++
- BAvg ++
- Spd +
- Def ++

Year	Lev	Team	AB	R	H	HR	RBI	Avg	OB	Slg	OPS	bb%	ct%	Eye	SB	CS	x/h%	Iso	RC/G
2016	A	Columbia	239	34	73	3	35	305	401	402	802	14	84	0.97	2	0	23	96	5.80
2017	A+	St. Lucie	352	45	101	7	50	287	373	406	779	12	85	0.91	2	2	28	119	5.39
2017	AA	Binghamton	21	3	7	0	5	333	391	571	963	9	71	0.33	0	0	71	238	8.32
2018	AA	Binghamton	295	32	68	9	39	231	320	363	683	12	88	1.11	0	0	31	132	4.25
2019	AA	Binghamton	413	50	101	16	69	245	307	426	733	8	78	0.42	1	0	42	182	4.50

Tall, big-bodied CA saw power production climb, tapping to more pull-dominated power. Below-average bat speed but with solid plate skills. Can shoot the gaps if the bat head can get around quick enough. There's average power in frame and swing and has good sense of zone. Bulky catcher. Not quiet but presents quality target. Fringe MLB player.

McCann,Kyle

23	Oakland	EXP MLB DEBUT: 2022	H/W: 6-2 217	FUT: Reserve 1B	7D

Bats L Age 22
2019 (4) Georgia Tech

- Pwr ++++
- BAvg ++
- Spd +
- Def ++

Year	Lev	Team	AB	R	H	HR	RBI	Avg	OB	Slg	OPS	bb%	ct%	Eye	SB	CS	x/h%	Iso	RC/G
2019	Rk	AZL A's G	20	10	8	2	7	400	520	1000	1520	20	70	0.83	0	0	75	600	16.71
2019	A-	Vermont	198	23	38	7	25	192	283	343	626	11	59	0.31	0	0	39	152	3.38

Strong CA hit for massive power in ACC en route to over-slot bonus. Plus raw power is legit, working best to CF/RF with a natural ability to lift the ball. Swing can get stiff and will be shifted heavily with high pull-rate, leading to questions about BA value. More of an OBP target with 25-30 HR ability, though may move to 1B.

McCarthy, Jake — 8 — Arizona
EXP MLB DEBUT: 2021 | H/W: 6-2 195 | FUT: Reserve OF | 7E
Bats L | Age 22 | 2018 (1) Virginia
Pwr ++ | BAvg +++ | Spd ++++ | Def +++

Year	Lev	Team	AB	R	H	HR	RBI	Avg	OB	Slg	OPS	bb%	ct%	Eye	SB	CS	x/h%	Iso	RC/G
2018	NCAA	Virginia	82	17	27	0	12	329	402	415	817	11	89	1.11	9	0	26	85	5.92
2018	Rk	AZL DBacks	11	1	3	0	4	273	333	455	788	8	91	1.00	1	0	33	182	5.60
2018	A-	Hillsboro	208	33	60	3	18	288	357	442	799	10	81	0.55	20	8	38	154	5.57
2019	A+	Visalia	195	29	54	2	30	277	335	405	740	8	73	0.33	18	2	33	128	4.81

Speed-centric CF prospect with some feel to hit, but comes with checkered injury past. Flat barrel path leads to high-volume grounders and low line drives the other way. Power is below average but body is still projectable enough for added strength. If the bat progresses a bit, will be everyday CF with speed value. If not, is fourth-OF type.

McCarthy, Joe — 79 — San Francisco
EXP MLB DEBUT: 2020 | H/W: 6-3 220 | FUT: Reserve OF | 6B
Bats L | Age 26 | 2015 (5) Virginia
Pwr ++ | BAvg ++ | Spd ++ | Def ++

Year	Lev	Team	AB	R	H	HR	RBI	Avg	OB	Slg	OPS	bb%	ct%	Eye	SB	CS	x/h%	Iso	RC/G
2018	A+	Charlotte	10	0	0	0	0	0	231	0	231	23	60	0.75	1	0	0	0	-3.39
2018	AAA	Durham	160	31	43	8	25	269	368	513	880	14	73	0.58	3	1	51	244	6.80
2019	A+	Charlotte	8	0	1	0	0	125	125	125	250	0	50	0.00	0	0	0	0	-3.11
2019	AAA	Sacramento	79	10	13	1	4	165	241	241	482	9	62	0.27	0	0	31	76	1.04
2019	AAA	Durham	148	24	29	6	23	196	328	385	713	16	64	0.54	1	0	48	189	4.74

Injury-riddled OF can't stay on field, but has some value in plate approach. Draws walks and is high OBP buy. Knows strike zone, but struggles to hit with consistent pop. Despite natural strength, has never hit 10 HR. Has OK instincts, but back injuries have muted any speed and has limited range in corner. Could become average hitter at best.

McConnell, Brady — 6 — Kansas City
EXP MLB DEBUT: 2023 | H/W: 6-3 195 | FUT: Starting MIF | 8E
Bats R | Age 21 | 2019 (2) Florida
Pwr ++++ | BAvg ++ | Spd ++++ | Def +++

Year	Lev	Team	AB	R	H	HR	RBI	Avg	OB	Slg	OPS	bb%	ct%	Eye	SB	CS	x/h%	Iso	RC/G
2019	NCAA	Florida	229	51	76	15	48	332	378	576	954	7	75	0.30	6	2	34	245	7.21
2019	Rk	Idaho Falls	152	25	32	4	22	211	277	382	659	8	57	0.21	5	3	53	171	4.23
2019	Rk	AZL Royals	8	3	2	1	1	250	333	750	1083	11	75	0.50	0	0	100	500	9.04

Made pro debut flashing plus power and speed with hit tool question marks. Has above-average bat speed but struggles with spin recognition and getting hands started. Swing path uneven and cuts bat off plate, and geared towards maximizing power to pull-side. 25+ HR if hit tool allows it. Plus speed but not a premium SB threat.

McCoy, Mason — 46 — Baltimore
EXP MLB DEBUT: 2020 | H/W: 6-0 175 | FUT: Reserve IF | 6C
Bats L | Age 25 | 2017 (6) Iowa
Pwr + | BAvg ++ | Spd +++ | Def +++

Year	Lev	Team	AB	R	H	HR	RBI	Avg	OB	Slg	OPS	bb%	ct%	Eye	SB	CS	x/h%	Iso	RC/G
2017	A-	Aberdeen	186	34	56	1	29	301	387	409	795	12	85	0.93	4	3	27	108	5.71
2018	A	Delmarva	482	66	128	4	47	266	328	369	698	9	80	0.47	13	2	25	104	4.23
2019	A+	Frederick	116	21	44	2	17	379	419	509	928	6	86	0.50	3	0	25	129	6.77
2019	AA	Bowie	429	60	114	2	31	266	323	343	665	8	80	0.43	10	3	19	77	3.77

UT IF with scrappy profile continues march to big leagues. Works counts deep and maximizes limited hit tools by coaxing pitchers into mistakes. Power is limited and so is bat speed. Defensively sound but isn't special at any position. Is a threat to steal bases despite average run tool.

McCray, Grant — 8 — San Francisco
EXP MLB DEBUT: 2024 | H/W: 6-2 170 | FUT: Starting OF | 8E
Bats L | Age 19 | 2019 (3) HS (FL)
Pwr ++ | BAvg +++ | Spd ++++ | Def +++

Year	Lev	Team	AB	R	H	HR	RBI	Avg	OB	Slg	OPS	bb%	ct%	Eye	SB	CS	x/h%	Iso	RC/G
2019	Rk	AZL Giants	185	43	50	1	11	270	372	335	707	14	71	0.56	17	13	16	65	4.61

Raw, lanky OF offers tools, but will need lot of time to reach ceiling. Has blazing speed with graceful actions. Tracks balls and takes efficient routes. Swing can get choppy and long and lacks strength to drive ball. Will need to add strength to frame to realize average power potential. Despite speed, gets caught stealing far too often.

McGuire, Reese — 2 — Toronto
EXP MLB DEBUT: 2018 | H/W: 6-0 215 | FUT: Starting C | 7C
Bats L | Age 25 | 2013 (1) HS (WA)
Pwr ++ | BAvg +++ | Spd + | Def ++++

Year	Lev	Team	AB	R	H	HR	RBI	Avg	OB	Slg	OPS	bb%	ct%	Eye	SB	CS	x/h%	Iso	RC/G
2017	AA	New Hampshire	115	19	32	6	20	278	366	496	862	12	83	0.84	2	1	38	217	6.25
2018	AAA	Buffalo	322	31	75	7	37	233	304	339	643	9	76	0.43	3	2	24	106	3.41
2018	MLB	Toronto	31	5	9	2	4	290	333	581	914	6	71	0.22	1	0	56	290	6.56
2019	AAA	Buffalo	243	30	60	5	29	247	317	366	683	9	82	0.57	4	0	30	119	4.03
2019	MLB	Toronto	97	14	29	5	11	299	346	526	872	7	81	0.39	0	0	41	227	6.07

Fundamentally-sound receiver who was better in majors than minors. Has all requisite attributes to be above average backstop with strong arm and quick release. Blocks and receives with aplomb. Doesn't have much oomph in short stroke, but makes contact and can lace line drives to gaps. If power develops, could become primary catcher in system.

McKay, Brendan — 3 — Tampa Bay
EXP MLB DEBUT: 2019 | H/W: 6-2 212 | FUT: Starting 1B | 7C
Bats L | Age 24 | 2017 (1) Louisville
Pwr +++ | BAvg ++ | Spd + | Def +++

Year	Lev	Team	AB	R	H	HR	RBI	Avg	OB	Slg	OPS	bb%	ct%	Eye	SB	CS	x/h%	Iso	RC/G
2018	A	Bowling Green	63	12	16	1	16	254	484	333	817	31	79	2.15	0	0	19	79	6.82
2018	A+	Charlotte	119	19	25	5	21	210	304	403	707	12	68	0.42	0	0	48	193	4.40
2019	A	Montgomery	78	8	13	0	8	167	235	192	428	8	65	0.26	0	1	15	26	0.25
2019	AAA	Durham	67	11	16	5	11	239	338	493	830	13	64	0.42	1	0	44	254	6.23
2019	MLB	Tampa	10	2	2	1	1	200	273	500	773	9	80	0.50	0	0	50	300	4.68

Two-way prospect became exclusively a DH as a hitter in '20. Work on mound outpaces offensive upside. Battled with length in swing, causing hit tool to slump. Plus-power potential remains in frame and BP. However, hit tool won't allow him to reach for it in games. Two-way novelty running out.

McKenna, Ryan — 789 — Baltimore
EXP MLB DEBUT: 2020 | H/W: 5-11 185 | FUT: Starting CF | 8D
Bats R | Age 23 | 2015 (4) HS (NH)
Pwr ++ | BAvg +++ | Spd ++++ | Def +++

Year	Lev	Team	AB	R	H	HR	RBI	Avg	OB	Slg	OPS	bb%	ct%	Eye	SB	CS	x/h%	Iso	RC/G
2016	A-	Aberdeen	220	29	53	1	26	241	310	309	619	9	73	0.37	17	6	23	68	3.16
2017	A	Delmarva	468	62	120	7	42	256	319	380	699	9	73	0.34	20	2	35	124	4.23
2018	A+	Frederick	257	60	97	8	37	377	456	556	1012	13	82	0.82	5	6	29	179	8.26
2018	AA	Bowie	213	35	51	3	16	239	331	338	669	12	74	0.52	4	1	25	99	3.93
2019	AA	Bowie	488	78	113	9	54	232	314	365	679	11	75	0.49	25	11	36	133	4.04

Undersized, athletic CF struggled in Double-A after taking big step forward in 2018. Compact swing remains in virtually same delivery, spray approach. Struggled getting bat out in front of the plate, depressing barrels. Below-average power in frame and flat swing plane; 10-14 HR at projection. Double-plus runner but low SB%. Will stick in CF.

Meadows, Parker — 89 — Detroit
EXP MLB DEBUT: 2022 | H/W: 6-5 205 | FUT: Starting OF | 8E
Bats L | Age 20 | 2018 (2) HS (GA)
Pwr +++ | BAvg ++ | Spd ++++ | Def +++

Year	Lev	Team	AB	R	H	HR	RBI	Avg	OB	Slg	OPS	bb%	ct%	Eye	SB	CS	x/h%	Iso	RC/G
2018	Rk	GCL Tigers W	74	16	21	4	8	284	354	500	854	10	66	0.32	3	1	33	216	6.51
2018	A-	Connecticut	19	4	6	0	2	316	381	368	749	10	68	0.33	0	0	17	53	5.11
2019	A	West Michigan	443	52	98	4	40	221	296	312	607	10	74	0.42	14	8	24	90	2.97

Younger brother to Austin Meadows with two extra inches to his build and surprising plus speed from his tall frame. Carries plus raw power. Swing is a bit long, but should shorten up as he gets more exposure at the plate. Above-average arm plays well with speed and impressive defensive feel.

Mears, Joshua — 9 — San Diego
EXP MLB DEBUT: 2023 | H/W: 6-3 230 | FUT: Starting OF | 8E
Bats R | Age 19 | 2019 (2) HS (WA)
Pwr ++++ | BAvg ++ | Spd +++ | Def +++

Year	Lev	Team	AB	R	H	HR	RBI	Avg	OB	Slg	OPS	bb%	ct%	Eye	SB	CS	x/h%	Iso	RC/G
2019	Rk	AZL Padres	166	30	42	7	24	253	344	440	784	12	64	0.39	9	1	33	187	5.71

Strong, physically advanced teenage OF with monster bat speed and HR upside. Chance to grow into double-plus raw power with ability to clear fences the opposite way. A better athlete than the body will let on and could have moderate SB value. Will need to be more consistent with bat to ball skills as he transitions to full-season MWL competition.

Medina, Luis — 8 — Milwaukee
EXP MLB DEBUT: 2024 | H/W: 6-2 168 | FUT: Starting OF | 8E
Bats L | Age 17 | 2019 FA (VZ)
Pwr +++ | BAvg +++ | Spd ++ | Def ++

Year	Lev	Team	AB	R	H	HR	RBI	Avg	OB	Slg	OPS	bb%	ct%	Eye	SB	CS	x/h%	Iso	RC/G
2019		Did not play in U.S.																	

High profile Venezuelan OF who signed for $1.3 million at July 2 signing period and has yet to make pro debut. Features potential plus raw power from smooth, easy LH swing through zone. Shows ability to use all fields consistently with solid ct% skills. Physical projection remaining on lean frame. Arm and average range could profile at any OF spot.

Melendez, MJ — 2 — Kansas City

EXP MLB DEBUT: 2023 | H/W: 6-1 185 | FUT: Starting C | 7E

Bats L · Age 21 · 2017 (2) HS (FL)

Pwr	++++
BAvg	+
Spd	++
Def	+++

Year	Lev	Team	AB	R	H	HR	RBI	Avg	OB	Slg	OPS	bb%	ct%	Eye	SB	CS	x/h%	Iso	RC/G
2017	Rk	AZL Royals	168	25	44	4	30	262	361	417	777	13	64	0.43	4	2	34	155	5.81
2018	A	Lexington	419	52	105	19	73	251	320	492	812	9	66	0.30	4	6	51	241	6.04
2019	A+	Wilmington	363	34	59	9	54	163	253	311	564	11	55	0.27	7	5	58	149	2.64

Powerful CA saw his already shaky ct% plummet as swing backed up from '19. Doesn't get his hands in good position to attack baseball. Swing is all upper body and he struggles extending his hands early away from his body. Has feel for zone. Plus power is real and verifies in BP. Doesn't get to barrel enough in game. Plus arm controls running game.

Mena, Ismael — 8 — San Diego

EXP MLB DEBUT: 2024 | H/W: 6-3 185 | FUT: Starting CF | 7C

Bats L · Age 17 · 2019 FA (DR)

Pwr	++
BAvg	++
Spd	++++
Def	++++

Year	Lev	Team	AB	R	H	HR	RBI	Avg	OB	Slg	OPS	bb%	ct%	Eye	SB	CS	x/h%	Iso	RC/G
2019		Did not play in U.S.																	

Athletic, wiry OF prospect shows plus range and arm for defensive impact in CF. Offensively, has a chance to be quality SB threat with elite speed and burst. Has a good idea of the strike zone and shows gap-to-gap power right now, could yield average HR output as he bulks up a bit. Remains raw and requires a lot of projection, but has upside.

Mendick, Danny — 4567 — Chicago (A)

EXP MLB DEBUT: 2019 | H/W: 5-10 189 | FUT: Reserve IF | 6C

Bats R · Age 26 · 2015 (22) Mass/Lowell

Pwr	++
BAvg	+++
Spd	++
Def	+++

Year	Lev	Team	AB	R	H	HR	RBI	Avg	OB	Slg	OPS	bb%	ct%	Eye	SB	CS	x/h%	Iso	RC/G
2017	A+	Winston-Salem	263	45	76	7	30	289	364	468	832	11	85	0.78	11	4	38	179	5.95
2017	AA	Birmingham	147	14	29	3	21	197	280	293	573	10	80	0.63	1	2	28	95	2.69
2018	AA	Birmingham	453	62	112	14	59	247	331	395	727	11	80	0.63	20	10	35	148	4.60
2019	AAA	Charlotte	477	75	133	17	64	279	366	444	811	12	80	0.69	19	8	33	166	5.70
2019	MLB	Chi White Sox	39	6	12	2	4	308	325	462	787	3	72	0.09	0	0	17	154	4.81

Utility IF defied long odds to make MLB debut. Signed for $2500 as a senior-sign in '15. Has been steady climber. Contact-oriented hitter who tapped into some Triple-A power, like everyone else. Solid hitter who doesn't offer much in starting role. Can defend a few positions while not hurting lineup in short spurts. He is a below-average runner.

Mendoza, Drew — 3 — Washington

EXP MLB DEBUT: 2022 | H/W: 6-5 230 | FUT: Starting 1B | 7D

Bats L · Age 22 · 2019 (3) Florida St

Pwr	+++
BAvg	+++
4.62 Spd	+
Def	++

Year	Lev	Team	AB	R	H	HR	RBI	Avg	OB	Slg	OPS	bb%	ct%	Eye	SB	CS	x/h%	Iso	RC/G
2019	A	Hagerstown	201	23	53	4	25	264	370	383	753	14	72	0.60	3	0	30	119	5.21

Tall and lean cornerman who was drafted as third baseman put played mostly at first as a pro. Developed his power throughout college and has present strength, but questions on how he'll handle advanced pitching given his swing and miss. Good patience and a frame for impact, but still has to prove it in pro ball.

Mesa Jr., Victor — 8 — Miami

EXP MLB DEBUT: 2024 | H/W: 5-11 175 | FUT: Starting OF | 7D

Bats L · Age 18 · 2019 FA (CU)

Pwr	+++
BAvg	+++
Spd	+++
Def	+++

Year	Lev	Team	AB	R	H	HR	RBI	Avg	OB	Slg	OPS	bb%	ct%	Eye	SB	CS	x/h%	Iso	RC/G
2019	Rk	GCL Marlins	176	39	50	1	24	284	370	398	768	12	72	0.49	7	4	28	114	5.43

Brother of Victor Victor Mesa, with solid bat-to-ball skills, thought doesn't have same athletic profile as brother. Still, solid athletic frame. Has bat wrap in load, which will cause issue against upper-division pitchers. Excellent sense of zone and advanced feel for spin. Average runner, likely to lose speed. COF if power plays.

Mesa, Victor Victor — 8 — Miami

EXP MLB DEBUT: 2021 | H/W: 5-10 165 | FUT: Reserve OF | 6C

Bats R · Age 23 · 2018 FA (CU)

Pwr	+
BAvg	+++
Spd	++++
Def	++++

Year	Lev	Team	AB	R	H	HR	RBI	Avg	OB	Slg	OPS	bb%	ct%	Eye	SB	CS	x/h%	Iso	RC/G
2019	A+	Jupiter	357	37	90	0	26	252	290	283	573	5	87	0.40	15	2	9	31	2.63
2019	AA	Jacksonville	107	8	19	0	3	178	200	196	396	3	85	0.19	3	0	11	19	0.40

Short-statured, athletic CF had trouble living up to $5.25M signing bonus. Struggled mightily with hit tool in High-A. Has quick hands and plus bat-to-ball skills. Aggressive approach, lack of barrel control and limited strength cause hit tool to flutter. Zero power in frame. Doesn't use base for leverage. Superior defender and plus runner.

Mieses, Luis — 9 — Chicago (A)

EXP MLB DEBUT: 2023 | H/W: 6-3 180 | FUT: Starting OF | 7E

Bats L · Age 19 · 2016 FA (DR)

Pwr	+++
BAvg	+++
Spd	+++
Def	+++

Year	Lev	Team	AB	R	H	HR	RBI	Avg	OB	Slg	OPS	bb%	ct%	Eye	SB	CS	x/h%	Iso	RC/G
2018	Rk	AZL White Sox	195	19	44	2	26	226	241	328	569	2	82	0.11	3	0	32	103	2.32
2019	Rk	Great Falls	220	24	53	4	28	241	264	359	623	3	79	0.15	0	1	34	118	2.93

Ultra-aggressive LHH has struggled in short-season ball so far. Grip-it-and-rip-it approach with strong bat-to-ball skills. Has hard contact ability when swinging at pitches in zone. Unfortunately, expands a lot. There's above-average power potential in swing and path. Hasn't tapped into it at all. Average runner with arm for RF.

Miller, Brian — 78 — Miami

EXP MLB DEBUT: 2020 | H/W: 6-1 186 | FUT: Reserve OF | 6B

Bats L · Age 24 · 2017 (1) North Carolina

Pwr	+
BAvg	+++
Spd	++++
Def	+++

Year	Lev	Team	AB	R	H	HR	RBI	Avg	OB	Slg	OPS	bb%	ct%	Eye	SB	CS	x/h%	Iso	RC/G
2017	NCAA	North Carolina	271	61	93	7	49	343	424	502	926	12	87	1.09	24	6	28	159	7.15
2017	A	Greensboro	233	42	75	1	28	322	383	416	799	9	85	0.66	21	6	25	94	5.53
2018	A+	Jupiter	256	28	83	0	29	324	359	398	758	5	89	0.52	19	6	19	74	4.84
2018	AA	Jacksonville	262	29	70	0	14	267	314	313	627	6	85	0.46	21	7	14	46	3.32
2019	AA	Jacksonville	449	52	119	2	39	265	321	354	675	8	82	0.46	22	9	26	89	3.93

Slap-hitting, athletic OF continues progression to eventual MLB bench role. Versatile athlete, capable of fielding several defensive roles, including 1B. Not much power in frame or swing. Makes solid ground ball and low line drive contact. Plus runner who is an asset on the bases; 20-SB role player potential.

Miller, Jalen — 4 — San Francisco

EXP MLB DEBUT: 2021 | H/W: 6-0 190 | FUT: Starting 2B | 7D

Bats R · Age 23 · 2015 (3) HS (GA)

Pwr	++
BAvg	++
Spd	++++
Def	+++

Year	Lev	Team	AB	R	H	HR	RBI	Avg	OB	Slg	OPS	bb%	ct%	Eye	SB	CS	x/h%	Iso	RC/G
2015	Rk	AZL Giants	174	28	38	0	13	218	288	259	547	9	76	0.40	11	2	16	40	2.22
2016	A	Augusta	457	65	102	5	44	223	265	322	587	5	77	0.24	11	5	29	98	2.59
2017	A+	San Jose	431	61	98	6	44	227	279	346	625	7	77	0.31	6	4	36	118	3.16
2018	A+	San Jose	511	73	141	14	62	276	312	434	747	5	76	0.22	11	4	36	159	4.58
2019	AA	Richmond	491	55	106	11	48	216	287	332	619	9	78	0.46	27	13	30	116	3.14

Ultra athletic INF who reached AA after two full years in A+. Set high in SB, though is far too inefficient as baserunner. Always been low BA guy as he offers little plate discipline and chases pitches. Making harder contact and can reach seats with average bat speed. Solid-average defender who has ample range and fringy arm.

Miller, Owen — 46 — San Diego

EXP MLB DEBUT: 2020 | H/W: 6-0 190 | FUT: Utility player | 7B

Bats R · Age 23 · 2018 (3) Illinois St

Pwr	++
BAvg	+++
Spd	+++
Def	+++

Year	Lev	Team	AB	R	H	HR	RBI	Avg	OB	Slg	OPS	bb%	ct%	Eye	SB	CS	x/h%	Iso	RC/G
2018	NCAA	Illinois St	229	45	88	6	35	384	429	537	966	7	90	0.78	8	2	25	153	7.20
2018	A-	Tri-City	191	22	64	2	20	335	383	440	823	7	87	0.63	4	4	20	105	5.66
2018	A	Fort Wayne	107	18	36	2	13	336	360	495	856	4	84	0.24	0	0	36	159	5.80
2019	AA	Amarillo	507	76	147	13	68	290	349	430	779	8	83	0.53	5	5	29	140	5.12

Fundamentally sound, high-volume contact hitter with potential for average tools across the board. Provides defensive versatility via instinctual reads, solid range and just enough arm for any INF spot. HR power limited to pull-side and projects as high-volume doubles type. Athletic to steal a handful of bases, but not an active runner.

Miranda, Jose — 45 — Minnesota

EXP MLB DEBUT: 2021 | H/W: 6-2 210 | FUT: Reserve IF | 6C

Bats R · Age 21 · 2016 (2) HS (PR)

Pwr	+++
BAvg	+++
Spd	++
Def	+++

Year	Lev	Team	AB	R	H	HR	RBI	Avg	OB	Slg	OPS	bb%	ct%	Eye	SB	CS	x/h%	Iso	RC/G
2017	Rk	Elizabethton	223	43	63	11	43	283	331	484	815	7	89	0.67	2	3	33	202	5.38
2018	A	Cedar Rapids	401	52	111	13	72	277	321	434	755	6	87	0.51	0	1	32	157	4.71
2018	A+	Fort Myers	102	9	22	3	10	216	252	353	605	5	89	0.45	0	2	36	137	3.00
2019	A+	Fort Myers	440	48	109	8	55	248	287	364	650	5	88	0.44	0	1	31	116	3.54
2019	AA	Pensacola	5	1	3	0	0	600	600	800	1400	0	100		0	0	33	200	11.01

Contact-oriented, versatile IF struggled with hard-contact rate in High-A. Excellent bat-to-ball skills with solid swing plane but is over-aggressive, expanding out of the zone. Below-average power to pull field. 8-12 HR at maturity. Below average runner. Lacks carry tool for even MIF profile.

Misner,Kameron | 8 | Miami

EXP MLB DEBUT: 2022 | H/W: 6-4 219 | FUT: Starting OF | 9D

Bats L Age 22	Year	Lev	Team	AB	R	H	HR	RBI	Avg	OB	Slg	OPS	bb%	ct%	Eye	SB	CS	x/h%	Iso	RC/G
2019 (1) Missouri																				
Pwr ++++																				
BAvg +++	2019	NCAA	Missouri	206	54	59	10	32	286	435	481	915	21	72	0.93	20	1	34	194	7.62
Spd +++	2019	Rk	GCL Marlins	29	2	7	0	4	241	421	310	731	24	76	1.29	3	0	29	69	5.42
Def +++	2019	A	Clinton	134	25	37	2	20	276	374	373	747	14	74	0.60	8	0	24	97	5.07

Tall, powerful OF struggled in draft year as strikeouts caused reason for alarm. Resolved ct% issues in Single-A sample during debut. Big power potential with some timing issues. However, swing trajectory, swing plane and feel for strikezone play both hit and power tool up. Above-average runner who defends well. Likely ends up in RF because of arm.

Mitchell,Cal | 9 | Pittsburgh

EXP MLB DEBUT: 2022 | H/W: 6-0 209 | FUT: Starting OF | 7C

Bats L Age 21	Year	Lev	Team	AB	R	H	HR	RBI	Avg	OB	Slg	OPS	bb%	ct%	Eye	SB	CS	x/h%	Iso	RC/G
2017 (2) HS (CA)																				
Pwr +++																				
BAvg +++	2017	Rk	GCL Pirates	159	17	39	2	20	245	344	352	696	13	78	0.69	2	3	33	107	4.41
Spd ++	2018	A	West Virginia	443	55	124	10	65	280	341	427	768	8	75	0.38	4	5	34	147	5.08
Def ++	2019	A+	Bradenton	451	54	113	15	64	251	300	406	706	7	69	0.23	1	1	34	155	4.21

Emerging OF who has bright future despite jump in Ks. Advancing as expected and has chance to develop into sound player. Power increased while maintaining proficient hitting approach. Hit tool has chance to develop into asset thanks to feel for strike zone and making hard contact. Not blessed with great defense, but has shown RF range with OK arm.

Moniak,Mickey | 89 | Philadelphia

EXP MLB DEBUT: 2021 | H/W: 6-2 185 | FUT: Starting CF | 7B

Bats L Age 21	Year	Lev	Team	AB	R	H	HR	RBI	Avg	OB	Slg	OPS	bb%	ct%	Eye	SB	CS	x/h%	Iso	RC/G
2016 (1) HS (CA)																				
Pwr ++	2016	Rk	GCL Phillies	176	27	50	1	28	284	326	409	735	6	80	0.31	10	4	32	125	4.60
BAvg +++	2017	A	Lakewood	466	53	110	5	44	236	279	341	621	6	77	0.26	11	7	30	105	3.06
Spd ++	2018	A+	Clearwater	433	50	117	5	55	270	305	383	689	5	77	0.22	6	5	31	113	3.89
Def +++	2019	AA	Reading	465	63	117	11	67	252	301	439	740	7	76	0.30	15	3	44	187	4.68

Continued to take small steps forward as hard-hit balls increased due to stronger frame. More balanced against breaking stuff and beginning to know when to turn on inside heaters. Still struggles vLHP, and continued swing/miss quells the plus-hit-tool draft day pronouncements. But should stick in CF and will see majors soon.

Montero,Elehuris | 5 | St. Louis

EXP MLB DEBUT: 2021 | H/W: 6-3 215 | FUT: Starting 3B | 8D

Bats R Age 21	Year	Lev	Team	AB	R	H	HR	RBI	Avg	OB	Slg	OPS	bb%	ct%	Eye	SB	CS	x/h%	Iso	RC/G
2014 FA (DR)	2017	Rk	GCL Cardinals	173	30	48	5	36	277	359	468	827	11	81	0.67	0	2	46	191	5.95
Pwr ++++	2018	A	Peoria	382	68	123	15	69	322	376	529	905	8	79	0.41	2	0	37	207	6.68
BAvg +++	2018	A+	Palm Beach	98	13	28	1	13	286	320	408	729	5	78	0.23	1	0	36	122	4.42
Spd ++	2019	Rk	GCL Cardinals	13	1	4	0	0	308	357	308	665	7	85	0.50	0	0	0	0	3.70
Def ++	2019	AA	Springfield	224	23	42	7	18	188	235	317	552	6	67	0.19	0	1	36	129	1.94

Impact bat despite a disastrous 2019. Slowed by wrist and hamstring injuries and never got going. Owns a quick bat and excellent bat-to-ball skills with above-average raw power. Needs to be more selective for hit tool to develop, but has the frame and strength to mash 25+ HR. Fringe defender needs to improve footwork and range to stick at 3B.

Morel,Christopher | 5 | Chicago (N)

EXP MLB DEBUT: 2022 | H/W: 6-0 140 | FUT: Starting 3B | 7C

Bats R Age 20	Year	Lev	Team	AB	R	H	HR	RBI	Avg	OB	Slg	OPS	bb%	ct%	Eye	SB	CS	x/h%	Iso	RC/G
2015 FA (DR)																				
Pwr ++																				
BAvg +++	2018	Rk	AZL Cubs	113	20	29	2	12	257	323	363	685	9	75	0.39	1	4	28	106	3.99
Spd +++	2018	A-	Eugene	91	7	15	1	8	165	165	220	385	0	68	0.00	0	1	20	55	-0.58
Def +++	2019	A	South Bend	257	36	73	6	31	284	313	467	780	4	77	0.18	9	6	38	183	5.04

Young 3B who has decent foundation of tools and physical projection remaining. Wiry frame with lots of room for strength in lower half. Has above-average bat speed and hands work well, but can get overly pull-happy and will need to learn to use RF. Power projects as average. Will need to iron out approach. Projects as average 3B glove defensively.

Moreno,Gabriel | 2 | Toronto

EXP MLB DEBUT: 2022 | H/W: 5-11 160 | FUT: Starting C | 8D

Bats R Age 20	Year	Lev	Team	AB	R	H	HR	RBI	Avg	OB	Slg	OPS	bb%	ct%	Eye	SB	CS	x/h%	Iso	RC/G
2016 FA (VZ)																				
Pwr +++																				
BAvg +++	2018	Rk	Bluefield	61	10	17	2	14	279	313	459	772	5	79	0.23	1	0	41	180	4.84
Spd ++	2018	Rk	GCL Blue Jays	92	14	38	2	22	413	438	652	1090	4	92	0.57	1	1	42	239	8.42
Def ++	2019	A	Lansing	307	47	86	12	52	280	328	485	814	7	88	0.58	7	1	40	205	5.44

Offense-first C who had solid debut at full-season affiliate despite fading down the stretch. Shows excellent bat with hand-eye coordination and level, balanced stroke. Hits for good power and should evolve into more as he fills out. Very aggressive approach, but makes incredibly easy, hard contact. Owns average arm, but receiving needs work.

Morris,Tanner | 46 | Toronto

EXP MLB DEBUT: 2022 | H/W: 6-2 190 | FUT: Starting 2B | 7D

Bats L Age 21	Year	Lev	Team	AB	R	H	HR	RBI	Avg	OB	Slg	OPS	bb%	ct%	Eye	SB	CS	x/h%	Iso	RC/G
2019 (5) Virginia																				
Pwr ++																				
BAvg +++																				
Spd ++	2019	NCAA	Virginia	223	56	77	5	38	345	447	507	954	16	83	1.08	3	1	34	161	7.78
Def +++	2019	A-	Tri-City	240	37	59	2	28	246	374	346	720	17	77	0.88	4	2	32	100	4.92

Instinctual INF who has potential to be offensive-oriented 2B. Has discerning eye at plate and works deep counts. Can be too passive at times. Focuses on hitting hard line drives, though could add more HR if he pulls ball more. Hits loads of doubles, though doesn't run well. Lacks range for SS, but has enough arm that plays at 2B or possibly 3B.

Mountcastle,Ryan | 37 | Baltimore

EXP MLB DEBUT: 2020 | H/W: 6-3 195 | FUT: Starting 1B | 8B

Bats R Age 23	Year	Lev	Team	AB	R	H	HR	RBI	Avg	OB	Slg	OPS	bb%	ct%	Eye	SB	CS	x/h%	Iso	RC/G
2015 (1) HS (FL)	2016	A	Delmarva	455	53	128	10	51	281	319	426	745	5	79	0.26	5	4	33	145	4.57
Pwr ++++	2017	A+	Frederick	360	63	113	15	47	314	340	542	881	4	83	0.23	8	2	45	228	6.05
BAvg +++	2017	AA	Bowie	153	18	34	3	15	222	237	366	603	2	77	0.09	0	0	47	144	2.65
Spd +++	2018	AA	Bowie	394	63	117	13	59	297	340	464	805	6	80	0.33	2	0	31	168	5.30
Def ++	2019	AAA	Norfolk	520	81	162	25	83	312	342	527	869	4	75	0.18	2	1	38	215	6.07

Offensive-minded, defensively-challenged IF tapped into power in '19. Quick wrists and strong hands propel plus swing speed. Improved hard hit contact rate and swing path working with technology. Changed trajectory of swing to reach power. 30+ HR potential at maturity. Defensively, he'll pass in 1B or LF if the bat plays, which it should.

Murphy,Sean | 2 | Oakland

EXP MLB DEBUT: 2019 | H/W: 6-3 232 | FUT: Starting C | 8A

Bats R Age 25	Year	Lev	Team	AB	R	H	HR	RBI	Avg	OB	Slg	OPS	bb%	ct%	Eye	SB	CS	x/h%	Iso	RC/G
2016 (3) Wright St	2018	AAA	Nashville	8	2	2	0	0	250	455	250	705	27	75	1.50	0	0	0	0	5.11
Pwr +++	2019	Rk	AZL A's Gr	2	1	1	0	0	500	800	500	1300	60	50	3.00	0	0	0	0	20.02
BAvg +++	2019	Rk	AZL A's Gd	28	8	6	1	1	214	313	393	705	13	86	1.00	0	0	50	179	4.51
Spd ++	2019	AAA	Las Vegas	120	25	37	10	30	308	385	625	1010	11	74	0.48	0	1	46	317	8.20
Def ++++	2019	MLB	Oakland	53	14	13	4	8	245	322	566	888	10	70	0.38	0	0	69	321	6.79

Defensively advanced CA made his debut in 2019 and continues to grow into his bat. Has elite arm strength, transfer to stymie the running game and solid athletic actions to smother balls in the dirt. Has compact, simple stroke conducive to contact and high volume gap power; potential HR value as he learns to lift. Good approach; will be OBP asset.

Muzziotti,Simon | 8 | Philadelphia

EXP MLB DEBUT: 2021 | H/W: 6-1 175 | FUT: Starting CF | 8C

Bats L Age 21	Year	Lev	Team	AB	R	H	HR	RBI	Avg	OB	Slg	OPS	bb%	ct%	Eye	SB	CS	x/h%	Iso	RC/G
2016 FA (VZ)	2017	Rk	GCL Phillies	134	20	36	0	14	269	305	388	693	5	94	0.88	8	3	28	119	4.32
Pwr +	2017	A+	Clearwater	7	2	2	0	0	286	286	286	571	0	71	0.00	1	0	0	0	1.97
BAvg +++	2018	Rk	GCL Phillies	22	2	2	0	2	91	167	91	258	8	95	2.00	1	0	0	0	-0.09
Spd ++++	2018	A	Lakewood	278	33	73	1	20	263	298	331	629	5	86	0.35	18	4	21	68	3.26
Def +++	2019	A+	Clearwater	425	52	122	3	28	287	337	372	709	7	86	0.53	21	12	22	85	4.32

Throwback CF with little power, but knows his game is slashing/bunting/running. Excellent footspeed should yield 20+ SB in the majors, and runs down balls in the gaps. Patience is improving and makes good contact, with hands that work and a balanced overall swing.

Naylor,Bo | 2 | Cleveland

EXP MLB DEBUT: 2022 | H/W: 6-0 195 | FUT: Starting C | 8C

Bats L Age 20	Year	Lev	Team	AB	R	H	HR	RBI	Avg	OB	Slg	OPS	bb%	ct%	Eye	SB	CS	x/h%	Iso	RC/G
2018 (1) HS (ON)																				
Pwr +++																				
BAvg +++																				
Spd +++	2018	Rk	AZL Indians 2	117	17	32	2	17	274	384	402	786	15	76	0.75	5	1	25	128	5.68
Def +++	2019	A	Lake County	399	60	97	11	65	243	317	421	738	10	74	0.41	7	5	40	178	4.77

Athletic, former IF continues growing as full-time catcher. Hit-over-power profile at plate. Struggled getting barrel to ball in full-season debut against advanced competition. Has advanced feel for the zone and doesn't chase. There's average power in projection and swing path is consistently produces loft. Improved drastically at C.

Neuse, Sheldon — 45 — Oakland
EXP MLB DEBUT: 2019 | H/W: 6-0 218 | FUT: Starting 3B | 7A
Bats R | Age 25 | 2016 (2) Oklahoma
Pwr +++ | BAvg +++ | Spd ++ | Def +++

Year	Lev	Team	AB	R	H	HR	RBI	Avg	OB	Slg	OPS	bb%	ct%	Eye	SB	CS	x/h%	Iso	RC/G
2017	A+	Stockton	83	21	32	7	22	386	446	675	1120	10	70	0.36	2	0	31	289	9.93
2017	AA	Midland	67	9	25	0	6	373	425	433	857	8	66	0.29	0	0	16	60	6.61
2018	AAA	Nashville	499	48	131	5	55	263	307	357	664	6	66	0.19	4	1	26	94	3.78
2019	AAA	Las Vegas	498	99	158	27	102	317	386	550	936	10	73	0.42	3	3	38	233	7.33
2019	MLB	Oakland	56	3	14	0	7	250	300	304	604	7	66	0.21	0	0	21	54	2.91

Stocky, strong-armed 3B who made significant offensive strides in PCL en route to MLB debut. Set career high HR by way of added contact and more patient approach, though swing is more geared toward high-volume liners to all fields. Fringe runner and overall athlete. Has enough range and first-step quickness for 3B but has spent time at 2B.

Neustrom, Robert — 79 — Baltimore
EXP MLB DEBUT: 2022 | H/W: 6-2 208 | FUT: Reserve OF | 6C
Bats L | Age 23 | 2018 (5) Iowa
Pwr +++ | BAvg ++ | Spd +++ | Def ++

Year	Lev	Team	AB	R	H	HR	RBI	Avg	OB	Slg	OPS	bb%	ct%	Eye	SB	CS	x/h%	Iso	RC/G
2018	NCAA	Iowa	212	43	66	11	36	311	384	538	922	11	84	0.74	4	0	39	226	6.88
2018	A-	Aberdeen	228	29	62	4	29	272	311	404	715	5	80	0.29	1	3	34	132	4.22
2019	A-	Aberdeen	16	0	1	0	1	63	63	63	125	0	69	0.00	0	0	0	0	-4.18
2019	A	Delmarva	179	27	51	5	36	285	363	453	816	11	79	0.59	5	0	37	168	5.77
2019	A+	Frederick	122	10	29	2	10	238	285	344	629	6	75	0.27	0	1	31	107	3.13

Powerful, corner OF prospect who struggling to bring HR power to game. Rare high ct% power hitter, although strikeouts rose in High-A sample. Raw plus HR power completely to pull side. Solid runner but defensively likely LF only profile.

Nevin, Tyler — 3 — Colorado
EXP MLB DEBUT: 2020 | H/W: 6-4 200 | FUT: Starting 1B | 7C
Bats R | Age 22 | 2015 (1) HS (CA)
Pwr +++ | BAvg +++ | Spd + | Def ++

Year	Lev	Team	AB	R	H	HR	RBI	Avg	OB	Slg	OPS	bb%	ct%	Eye	SB	CS	x/h%	Iso	RC/G
2016	A-	Boise	1	1	1	0	0	1000			3000	0	100		0	0	100	1000	27.71
2017	A-	Boise	30	4	7	1	6	233	233	433	667	0	70	0.00	0	1	57	200	3.44
2017	A	Asheville	298	45	91	4	47	305	363	456	819	8	81	0.48	10	5	31	151	5.65
2018	A+	Lancaster	378	59	124	13	62	328	383	503	886	8	80	0.44	4	3	31	175	6.44
2019	AA	Hartford	466	60	117	13	61	251	343	399	742	12	81	0.72	6	2	35	148	4.88

Corner INF prospect with some feel for the barrel and an advanced approach. Quick hands to the ball allows him to cover all quadrants of the zone and pepper the outfield gaps. Lacks ideal loft in swing for impact HR and is only a fringe runner. Defensively, he profiles best at 1B long-term as he lacks mobility and arm strength for the hot corner.

Newton, Shervyen — 456 — New York (N)
EXP MLB DEBUT: 2023 | H/W: 6-4 180 | FUT: Starting 3B | 7D
Bats B | Age 20 | 2015 FA (NT)
Pwr ++++ | BAvg ++ | Spd +++ | Def +++

Year	Lev	Team	AB	R	H	HR	RBI	Avg	OB	Slg	OPS	bb%	ct%	Eye	SB	CS	x/h%	Iso	RC/G
2018	Rk	Kingsport	207	50	58	5	41	280	411	449	860	18	59	0.55	4	0	40	169	7.70
2019	A	Columbia	382	35	80	9	32	209	279	330	609	9	64	0.27	1	4	33	120	2.99

Tall, toolsy switch-hitting infielder had trouble with Single-A. Missed early part of season due to shoulder injury and never recovered. Strong-bodied swing with plus raw power potential in his frame. Struggles with swing path, spin and swing length despite quality bat speed. Will need to refine swing soon.

Noel, Jhonkensy — 35 — Cleveland
EXP MLB DEBUT: 2024 | H/W: 6-1 180 | FUT: Starting 1B | 7E
Bats R | Age 18 | 2017 FA (DR)
Pwr ++++ | BAvg ++ | Spd ++ | Def +++

Year	Lev	Team	AB	R	H	HR	RBI	Avg	OB	Slg	OPS	bb%	ct%	Eye	SB	CS	x/h%	Iso	RC/G
2019	Rk	AZL Indians 2	178	32	51	6	42	287	352	455	807	9	78	0.46	5	1	35	169	5.52

Power-driven 1B-only prospect showed exceptional power potential. Big, long body. Looks like a man child because of face, frame and always having fun. Long levers leave some to worry about his future hit tool. Uppercut oriented swing not always on the same plane. Swing generates solid loft. With refinement and frame, could be huge HR source.

Northcut, Nick — 5 — Boston
EXP MLB DEBUT: 2023 | H/W: 6-1 200 | FUT: Starting 3B | 7E
Bats R | Age 20 | 2018 (11) HS (OH)
Pwr ++ | BAvg ++ | Spd ++ | Def +++

Year	Lev	Team	AB	R	H	HR	RBI	Avg	OB	Slg	OPS	bb%	ct%	Eye	SB	CS	x/h%	Iso	RC/G
2018	Rk	GCL Red Sox	142	13	33	1	20	232	306	317	623	10	68	0.33	0	0	30	85	3.25
2018	A-	Lowell	24	3	4	1	5	167	200	333	533	4	58	0.10	0	0	50	167	1.74
2019	A-	Lowell	194	20	41	1	22	211	285	299	584	9	69	0.33	1	1	32	88	2.71

Aggressive 3B who has yet to experience full season ball. Has struggled to hit for BA due to long swing and impatient plate approach. Raw tools are impressive, highlighted by natural strength. Owns loft in stroke that projects to future above average power. Very slow runner and lacks fluidity at 3B. Owns soft hands, strong arm and makes routine plays.

Nova, Freudis — 456 — Houston
EXP MLB DEBUT: 2022 | H/W: 6-1 180 | FUT: Starting SS | 8D
Bats R | Age 20 | 2016 FA (DR)
Pwr +++ | BAvg +++ | Spd ++++ | Def +++

Year	Lev	Team	AB	R	H	HR	RBI	Avg	OB	Slg	OPS	bb%	ct%	Eye	SB	CS	x/h%	Iso	RC/G
2018	Rk	GCL Astros	146	21	45	6	28	308	336	466	801	4	86	0.29	9	5	22	158	5.00
2019	A	Quad Cities	282	35	73	3	29	259	296	369	665	5	76	0.22	10	7	33	110	3.60

High-upside, aggressive INF with above average tools and present skills. Rotated between multiple INF spots and likely to stick at SS long-term due to double-plus arm strength and quickness. Despite impatient, swing-early approach, has bat speed and above average power potential. Leveraged, lofty stroke will lead to Ks, but payoff could be huge.

Nunez, Malcom — 5 — St. Louis
EXP MLB DEBUT: 2022 | H/W: 5-11 205 | FUT: Starting 3B | 8E
Bats R | Age 19 | 2018 FA (CU)
Pwr ++++ | BAvg +++ | Spd + | Def ++

Year	Lev	Team	AB	R	H	HR	RBI	Avg	OB	Slg	OPS	bb%	ct%	Eye	SB	CS	x/h%	Iso	RC/G
2019	Rk	Johnson City	130	14	33	2	13	254	322	385	706	9	75	0.41	3	2	39	131	4.34
2019	A	Peoria	71	5	13	0	5	183	237	197	434	7	79	0.33	0	0	8	14	0.73

Teenager has above-average power and hit tools, but struggled in full-season ball. Quick bat and muscular frame allows him to punish balls over the plate. Can be beat up and in but has a decent understanding of the strike zone and makes consistent contact. Below average speed and defense will make it hard to stick at 3B, but does have a strong arm.

Nunez, Nasim — 6 — Miami
EXP MLB DEBUT: 2023 | H/W: 5-9 160 | FUT: Starting SS | 7E
Bats B | Age 19 | 2019 (2) HS (GA)
Pwr ++ | BAvg +++ | Spd ++++ | Def ++++

Year	Lev	Team	AB	R	H	HR	RBI	Avg	OB	Slg	OPS	bb%	ct%	Eye	SB	CS	x/h%	Iso	RC/G
2019	Rk	GCL Marlins	175	37	37	0	12	211	340	251	591	16	75	0.79	28	2	16	40	3.12
2019	A-	Batavia	10	1	0	0	0	0	91	0	91	9	50	0.20	0	0	0	0	-6.50

Defensive-plus SS prospect taken in 2nd rd of '19 draft. Solid bat to ball skills with good spray skills, which should help push hit tool to fringe-average at projection. Lean, athletic frame not expected to add much strength, severely depressing any power potential. Plus-plus runner with 20-plus SB potential.

Ockimey, Josh — 3 — Boston
EXP MLB DEBUT: 2020 | H/W: 6-1 215 | FUT: Reserve 1B | 6C
Bats L | Age 24 | 2014 (5) HS (PA)
Pwr ++++ | BAvg ++ | Spd + | Def +

Year	Lev	Team	AB	R	H	HR	RBI	Avg	OB	Slg	OPS	bb%	ct%	Eye	SB	CS	x/h%	Iso	RC/G
2017	A+	Salem	349	56	96	11	63	275	390	438	829	16	68	0.60	1	4	34	163	6.41
2017	AA	Portland	103	12	28	3	11	272	375	427	802	14	68	0.52	0	0	36	155	5.98
2018	AA	Portland	311	43	79	15	56	254	373	473	846	16	64	0.53	0	1	46	219	6.82
2018	AAA	Pawtucket	93	10	20	5	15	215	298	398	696	11	60	0.30	1	0	35	183	4.33
2019	AAA	Pawtucket	377	64	77	25	57	204	346	459	805	18	63	0.59	0	2	57	255	6.10

Power-only 1B who set career-high in HR while leading IL in BB. Only hit .100 against LHP, though could be platoon option. Possesses mammoth power to all fields and crushes mistakes. Lack of contact minimizes potential - at least 129 K each of last 4 seasons. Lacks consistent bat path and swing mechanics. Not much upside, but solid HR/OBP profile.

O'Hoppe, Logan — 2 — Philadelphia
EXP MLB DEBUT: 2024 | H/W: 6-2 185 | FUT: Reserve C | 7D
Bats R | Age 20 | 2018 HS (NY)
Pwr ++++ | BAvg ++ | Spd ++ | Def +++

Year	Lev	Team	AB	R	H	HR	RBI	Avg	OB	Slg	OPS	bb%	ct%	Eye	SB	CS	x/h%	Iso	RC/G
2018	Rk	GCL PhilliesW	109	19	40	2	21	367	420	532	952	8	74	0.36	2	1	33	165	7.63
2019	A-	Williamsport	162	20	35	5	26	216	270	407	678	7	70	0.24	3	0	54	191	3.89

Pure power-over-hit catching prospect from cold-weather state. Natural strength from a tall frame, but hitting skills have a long way to go as the strikeouts mount. Solid fundamentals behind the plate; only an average arm with strong footwork and a student of the game. The hope is bat-to-ball skills improve enough to make in-game use of the power.

Oliva,Jared — 8 — Pittsburgh

EXP MLB DEBUT: 2020 | H/W: 6-3 203 | FUT: Starting CF | **7B**

Bats R Age 24
2017 (7) Arizona

- Pwr ++
- BAvg +++
- Spd ++++
- Def +++

Year	Lev	Team	AB	R	H	HR	RBI	Avg	OB	Slg	OPS	bb%	ct%	Eye	SB	CS	x/h%	Iso	RC/G
2017	NCAA	Arizona	243	56	78	4	54	321	387	498	885	10	83	0.62	10	3	41	177	6.63
2017	A-	West Virginia	222	30	59	0	17	266	318	374	692	7	74	0.30	15	4	29	108	4.17
2018	A+	Bradenton	396	75	109	9	47	275	342	424	766	9	77	0.44	33	8	34	149	5.08
2019	AA	Altoona	447	70	124	6	42	277	339	398	738	9	77	0.40	36	10	29	121	4.72

AFL standout finished 2nd in EL in SB with new career high. Best tool is speed and helps him on base and in CF. Solid defensive CF with ample range and strong, accurate arm. May strike out too much for someone with fringy power, but has wiry strength that could develop. Controls bat well and draws walks with solid batting eye.

Olivares,Edward — 89 — San Diego

EXP MLB DEBUT: 2020 | H/W: 6-2 186 | FUT: Starting OF | **8C**

Bats R Age 24
2014 FA (VZ)

- Pwr +++
- BAvg ++
- Spd +++
- Def +++

Year	Lev	Team	AB	R	H	HR	RBI	Avg	OB	Slg	OPS	bb%	ct%	Eye	SB	CS	x/h%	Iso	RC/G
2016	Rk	Bluefield	55	8	15	1	6	273	333	418	752	8	78	0.42	1	2	33	145	4.87
2017	A	Lansing	426	82	118	17	65	277	313	500	813	5	81	0.27	18	7	44	223	5.35
2017	A+	Dunedin	68	11	15	0	7	221	303	265	567	11	75	0.47	2	2	13	44	2.56
2018	A+	Lake Elsinore	531	79	147	12	62	277	314	429	744	5	81	0.28	21	8	32	153	4.55
2019	AA	Amarillo	488	85	138	18	77	283	341	453	794	8	80	0.44	35	10	33	170	5.24

Toolsy OF prospect who flashed power and speed in first tour of the upper minors. Chance to be impact SB source with plus speed from his athletic, wiry frame. Covers real estate and has strong arm for any OF spot. Approach is aggressive and overall contact skills vs. off-speed is fringy. Owns good bat speed and power plays well to LF/CF.

Ornelas,Jonathan — 46 — Texas

EXP MLB DEBUT: 2022 | H/W: 6-1 178 | FUT: Starting MIF | **8D**

Bats R Age 19
2018 (3) HS (AZ)

- Pwr +++
- BAvg +++
- Spd +++
- Def +++

Year	Lev	Team	AB	R	H	HR	RBI	Avg	OB	Slg	OPS	bb%	ct%	Eye	SB	CS	x/h%	Iso	RC/G
2018	Rk	AZL Rangers	172	34	52	3	28	302	391	459	850	13	76	0.61	15	5	33	157	6.45
2019	A	Hickory	413	61	106	6	38	257	325	373	698	9	75	0.41	13	4	31	116	4.22

Explosive athlete with aggressive actions at the plate. Bat speed from strong hands/wrists; ability to turn on hard stuff but susceptible to pitches away. In-game power likely to come; slightly above average speed; athleticism to stick in middle infield.

Ornelas,Tirso — 9 — San Diego

EXP MLB DEBUT: 2022 | H/W: 6-3 200 | FUT: Starting OF | **8E**

Bats L Age 20
2016 FA (MX)

- Pwr +++
- BAvg +++
- Spd ++
- Def +++

Year	Lev	Team	AB	R	H	HR	RBI	Avg	OB	Slg	OPS	bb%	ct%	Eye	SB	CS	x/h%	Iso	RC/G
2017	Rk	AZL Padres 2	196	46	54	3	26	276	398	408	806	17	69	0.66	0	0	31	133	6.24
2018	A	Fort Wayne	309	45	78	8	40	252	338	392	730	11	78	0.59	5	1	31	139	4.68
2019	Rk	AZL Padres	88	6	18	0	11	205	278	227	506	9	75	0.41	4	0	11	23	1.64
2019	A+	Lake Elsinore	332	41	73	1	30	220	311	292	603	12	73	0.48	3	1	23	72	3.08

Young, toolsy OF whose production waned in the CAL, presumably due to nagging 2018 wrist injury. At his best, shows plus feel to hit with smooth LH stroke conducive to above-avg pull-side power. Patient hitter; has a plan with every AB. Chance to add more lean muscle to his tall frame. Fringe athlete and runner who likely profiles at LF long-term.

Ortiz,Jhailyn — 9 — Philadelphia

EXP MLB DEBUT: 2022 | H/W: 6-3 215 | FUT: Starting 1B | **8E**

Bats R Age 21
2015 FA (DR)

- Pwr ++++
- BAvg ++
- Spd ++
- Def ++

Year	Lev	Team	AB	R	H	HR	RBI	Avg	OB	Slg	OPS	bb%	ct%	Eye	SB	CS	x/h%	Iso	RC/G
2016	Rk	GCL Phillies	173	29	40	8	27	231	300	434	734	9	69	0.32	8	2	45	202	4.63
2017	A-	Williamsport	159	27	48	8	30	302	373	560	933	10	70	0.38	5	1	50	258	7.54
2018	A	Lakewood	405	51	91	13	47	225	286	375	662	8	63	0.24	2	2	36	151	3.76
2019	A+	Clearwater	430	57	86	19	65	200	262	381	643	8	65	0.24	2	3	43	181	3.34

Extreme power potential keeps hope alive, but factors against are piling up: second straight sub-.400 SLG season; persistent timing and pitch-recognition issues; bushels of Ks. Has crazy strength and all-fields power, but has been unable to actualize it in game situations. Still young, and more athletic than it would seem, but clock is ticking.

Pache,Cristian — 789 — Atlanta

EXP MLB DEBUT: 2020 | H/W: 6-2 185 | FUT: Starting CF | **8A**

Bats R Age 21
2015 FA (DR)

- Pwr +++
- BAvg ++++
- Spd +++
- Def ++++

Year	Lev	Team	AB	R	H	HR	RBI	Avg	OB	Slg	OPS	bb%	ct%	Eye	SB	CS	x/h%	Iso	RC/G
2017	A	Rome	469	60	132	0	42	281	337	343	680	8	78	0.38	32	14	16	62	3.94
2018	A+	Florida	369	46	105	8	40	285	313	431	743	4	81	0.22	7	6	31	146	4.47
2018	AA	Mississippi	104	10	27	1	7	260	294	337	630	5	73	0.18	0	2	19	77	3.07
2019	AA	Mississippi	392	50	109	11	53	278	336	474	810	8	73	0.33	8	11	43	196	5.71
2019	AAA	Gwinnett	95	13	26	1	8	274	337	411	747	9	81	0.50	0	0	38	137	4.89

Athletic, defensively-skilled OF made tremendous strides with hit and power production. Calmed approach, increasing BB% and Eye while not losing ct% or hard hit rate. Adjusted swing to reach more power, mostly pull-oriented. Could reach 20-25 HR at with high BA. Speed diminished, above-average at present; plus defender in CF.

Packard,Bryant — 7 — Detroit

EXP MLB DEBUT: 2022 | H/W: 6-3 200 | FUT: Starting OF | **7C**

Bats L Age 22
2019 (5) East Carolina

- Pwr +++
- BAvg ++
- Spd ++
- Def ++

Year	Lev	Team	AB	R	H	HR	RBI	Avg	OB	Slg	OPS	bb%	ct%	Eye	SB	CS	x/h%	Iso	RC/G
2019	A-	Connecticut	37	5	13	0	2	351	442	405	847	14	76	0.67	1	0	15	54	6.51
2019	A	West Michigan	81	14	25	3	12	309	404	494	898	14	70	0.54	1	0	36	185	7.23
2019	A+	Lakeland	17	2	2	0	2	118	211	118	328	11	71	0.40	0	0	0	0	-0.99

Bat-first collegiate profile selected in the fifth-round of the 2019 MLB draft out of East Carolina. Projects as an average defender, although raw offensive power is poised to outshine defensive contributions as his pitch recognition improves. Speed and arm-strength grade out as below-average, but play well off defensive instincts.

Padlo,Kevin — 35 — Tampa Bay

EXP MLB DEBUT: 2020 | H/W: 6-2 205 | FUT: Starting 3B | **7C**

Bats R Age 23
2014 (5) HS (CA)

- Pwr +++
- BAvg ++
- Spd +++
- Def +++

Year	Lev	Team	AB	R	H	HR	RBI	Avg	OB	Slg	OPS	bb%	ct%	Eye	SB	CS	x/h%	Iso	RC/G
2017	Rk	GCL Rays	17	3	2	0	1	118	250	235	485	15	94	3.00	1	0	50	118	2.75
2017	A+	Charlotte	220	28	49	6	34	223	329	391	720	14	73	0.58	4	5	45	168	4.70
2018	A+	Charlotte	385	54	86	8	54	223	308	353	661	11	69	0.39	5	0	40	130	3.79
2019	AA	Montgomery	220	39	55	12	35	250	382	505	887	18	68	0.67	11	4	58	255	7.25
2019	AAA	Durham	131	25	38	9	27	290	388	595	984	14	65	0.46	1	0	55	305	8.78

Patient, power-oriented hitter had breakout season in upper minors after struggling in '17 & '18. Slow setup leads to swing-and-miss and average concerns. Added aggressiveness in FB counts aided power and hit tool surge. Rarely swings at pitches out of the zone until 2-strikes. Average runner and average defender.

Palacios,Richard — 4 — Cleveland

EXP MLB DEBUT: 2022 | H/W: 5-11 180 | FUT: Utility player | **7D**

Bats L Age 22
2018 (3) Towson

- Pwr ++
- BAvg +++
- Spd ++++
- Def +++

Year	Lev	Team	AB	R	H	HR	RBI	Avg	OB	Slg	OPS	bb%	ct%	Eye	SB	CS	x/h%	Iso	RC/G
2018	NCAA	Towson	196	56	59	8	31	301	448	515	963	21	92	3.25	25	1	44	214	8.14
2018	Rk	AZL Indians	16	4	7	2	6	438	591	875	1466	27	88	3.00	2	0	43	438	14.18
2018	A-	MahoningVal	73	12	30	2	17	411	488	589	1077	13	84	0.92	2	1	27	178	9.09
2018	A	Lake County	80	10	24	2	7	300	317	425	742	2	84	0.15	3	0	21	125	4.29
2019		Did not play - injury																	

Contact-oriented 2B missed all of '19 after spring shoulder surgery. Short-statured player with limited room to build onto frame. Excellent bat-to-ball profile. Showed zone discipline and will spray the ball the other way on occasion. Average raw power at best. Likely plays in 10-18 HR range at maturity. Plus runner with SB aptitude.

Palmer,Jaylen — 56 — New York (N)

EXP MLB DEBUT: 2023 | H/W: 6-3 195 | FUT: Starting 3B | **7E**

Bats R Age 19
2018 (22) HS (NY)

- Pwr ++++
- BAvg ++
- Spd +++
- Def +++

Year	Lev	Team	AB	R	H	HR	RBI	Avg	OB	Slg	OPS	bb%	ct%	Eye	SB	CS	x/h%	Iso	RC/G
2018	Rk	GCL Mets	87	13	27	1	11	310	368	414	782	8	69	0.30	5	2	22	103	5.49
2019	Rk	Kingsport	242	41	63	7	28	260	344	413	758	11	55	0.29	1	3	33	153	6.06

Long, powerful IF prospect has showcased big power despite significant swing-and-miss concerns. Long and lumbering swing is an understatement; will need to shorten it tremendously to continue to hit enough. Uses lower half well to get leverage in swing. Likely 3B long term.

Paredes,Isaac — 56 — Detroit

EXP MLB DEBUT: 2020 | H/W: 5-11 225 | FUT: Starting MIF | **8C**

Bats R Age 21
2015 FA (MX)

- Pwr +++
- BAvg +++
- Spd ++
- Def +++

Year	Lev	Team	AB	R	H	HR	RBI	Avg	OB	Slg	OPS	bb%	ct%	Eye	SB	CS	x/h%	Iso	RC/G
2017	A	West Michigan	115	16	25	4	21	217	297	348	645	10	89	1.00	0	0	28	130	3.70
2017	A	South Bend	337	49	89	7	49	264	322	401	723	8	84	0.54	2	1	36	136	4.48
2018	A+	Lakeland	301	50	78	12	48	259	330	455	785	10	82	0.59	1	0	42	196	5.25
2018	AA	Erie	131	20	42	3	22	321	407	458	865	13	83	0.86	1	0	29	137	6.46
2019	AA	Erie	478	63	135	13	66	282	359	416	775	11	87	0.93	5	3	27	134	5.25

Athletic shortstop with ability to defend beyond his years. Has maxed on his physical development with a rock-solid, compact frame and broad shoulders. Accurate arm with good footwork despite size. Works the entire field with advanced ability to barrel the ball. Impressive plate discipline.

Paris, Kyren — 6 — Los Angeles (A)

EXP MLB DEBUT: 2023 | H/W: 6-0 165 | FUT: Starting SS | **8D**

Bats R Age 18
2019 (2) HS (CA)

			Pwr	++
BAvg	+++
Spd	+++
Def	+++

Year	Lev	Team	AB	R	H	HR	RBI	Avg	OB	Slg	OPS	bb%	ct%	Eye	SB	CS	x/h%	Iso	RC/G
2019	Rk	AZL Angels	10	4	3	0	2	300	462	400	862	23	60	0.75	0	0	33	100	7.99

Young, slender SS who displays quality defensive skills to stick and solid-average offensive upside. Approach is contact-oriented and geared toward line drives. Bat speed is average. Likely capped at gap power and will need to add mass and more leverage in swing to tap into power more consistently. Shows good understanding of the strike zone.

Patino, Wilderd — 8 — Arizona

EXP MLB DEBUT: 2023 | H/W: 6-1 175 | FUT: Starting OF | **8E**

Bats R Age 18
2017 FA (VZ)

			Pwr	++
BAvg	+++
Spd	++++
Def	+++

Year	Lev	Team	AB	R	H	HR	RBI	Avg	OB	Slg	OPS	bb%	ct%	Eye	SB	CS	x/h%	Iso	RC/G
2019	Rk	Missoula	35	6	8	0	4	229	270	371	642	5	60	0.14	1	1	38	143	3.93
2019	Rk	AZL DBacks	106	18	37	1	21	349	410	472	882	9	70	0.34	13	3	22	123	6.99

Athletic, chiseled OF with across-the-board tools required for a breakout in full-season ball. Presently a plus runner with burst to cover ground in CF and do damage on bases. Displays good pitch ID skills. Compact, level stroke yields gap power at present. Bat-to-ball skills are fringy right now, but should hit for a solid average with more reps.

Peguero, Liover — 6 — Arizona

EXP MLB DEBUT: 2023 | H/W: 6-2 190 | FUT: Starting SS | **8D**

Bats R Age 19
2017 FA (DR)

			Pwr	++
BAvg	++++
Spd	+++
Def	+++

Year	Lev	Team	AB	R	H	HR	RBI	Avg	OB	Slg	OPS	bb%	ct%	Eye	SB	CS	x/h%	Iso	RC/G
2018	Rk	AZL DBacks	66	8	13	0	5	197	254	197	450	7	74	0.29	3	2	0	0	0.74
2018	Rk	DSL DBacks	81	14	25	1	16	309	356	457	813	7	85	0.50	4	1	28	148	5.57
2019	Rk	Missoula	143	34	52	5	27	364	413	559	972	8	76	0.35	8	1	29	196	7.65
2019	A-	Hillsboro	84	13	22	0	11	262	326	357	683	9	80	0.47	3	1	27	95	4.12

Glove-first SS prospect who is plus athlete and runner with some feel to hit. Works middle of field with smooth RH swing. Shows aptitude for reading spin and demonstrates plate discipline. Has good contact skills, which should help power develop a bit as he grows into his lean frame. Lacks elite tool but overall skill-set is well-rounded for value.

Pena, Erick — 89 — Kansas City

EXP MLB DEBUT: 2025 | H/W: 6-3 180 | FUT: Starting OF | **9E**

Bats L Age 17
2019 FA (DR)

			Pwr	++++
BAvg	++++
Spd	+++
Def	+++

Year	Lev	Team	AB	R	H	HR	RBI	Avg	OB	Slg	OPS	bb%	ct%	Eye	SB	CS	x/h%	Iso	RC/G
2019		Did not play in U.S.																	

Quick-twitch, toolsy OF signed as 16-year-old in July 2019. Athletic build with good body for development. Quick, loose swing carries profile. Raw plus power based on swing profile and projected body development. Scalds baseballs, finding barrel more than not. Above-average runner, scouts believe moves off CF as bulk is added. Likely RF.

Pena, Jeremy — 6 — Houston

EXP MLB DEBUT: 2021 | H/W: 6-0 179 | FUT: Utility player | **6A**

Bats R Age 22
2018 (3) Maine

			Pwr	+
BAvg	+++
Spd	+++
Def	++++

Year	Lev	Team	AB	R	H	HR	RBI	Avg	OB	Slg	OPS	bb%	ct%	Eye	SB	CS	x/h%	Iso	RC/G
2018	NCAA	Maine	211	50	65	5	28	308	387	469	856	11	80	0.64	10	0	29	161	6.32
2018	A-	Tri City	136	22	34	1	10	250	338	309	646	12	86	0.95	3	0	18	59	3.85
2019	A	Quad Cities	242	44	71	5	41	293	383	421	804	13	76	0.61	17	6	24	128	5.75
2019	A+	Fayetteville	167	28	53	2	13	317	363	467	830	7	80	0.36	3	4	34	150	5.80

Defensive-oriented INF who is mostly a bottom-of-the-order singles hitter. Nevertheless, carries value due to nimble defensive abilities. Offers quick, soft hands and plus arm from any INF spot. Works counts to get on base, but makes weak contact. Not much present pop nor potential. Runs bases well and could become valued utility infielder down road.

Pena, Viandel — 46 — Washington

EXP MLB DEBUT: 2024 | H/W: 5-8 148 | FUT: Starting 2B | **8E**

Bats B Age 19
2017 FA (DR)

			Pwr	+
BAvg	+++
Spd	++++
Def	++++

Year	Lev	Team	AB	R	H	HR	RBI	Avg	OB	Slg	OPS	bb%	ct%	Eye	SB	CS	x/h%	Iso	RC/G
2019	Rk	GCL Nationals	131	27	47	0	15	359	447	481	928	14	76	0.68	6	3	28	122	7.67

Tiny build, but led GCL in BA and showed a knack for getting on base due to good strike zone judgement. Struggles with quality offspeed, typical for rookie-ball teenager. Line drives come from a flat swing; little power projection. Average runner.

Peraza, Oswald — 6 — New York (A)

EXP MLB DEBUT: 2022 | H/W: 6-0 176 | FUT: Starting SS | **8C**

Bats R Age 19
2016 FA (VZ)

			Pwr	+++
BAvg	+++
Spd	++++
Def	++++

Year	Lev	Team	AB	R	H	HR	RBI	Avg	OB	Slg	OPS	bb%	ct%	Eye	SB	CS	x/h%	Iso	RC/G
2017	Rk	GCL Yankees	184	34	49	0	24	266	325	332	657	8	80	0.44	12	2	22	65	3.70
2018	Rk	Pulaski	140	25	35	1	11	250	318	321	640	9	71	0.34	8	1	17	71	3.43
2019	A-	Staten Island	79	7	19	2	7	241	286	354	640	6	89	0.56	5	2	21	114	3.44
2019	A	Charleston (Sc)	183	31	50	2	13	273	332	333	665	8	85	0.57	18	5	14	60	3.78

Athletic, polished prospect aggressively promoted to full-season ball late. Short, compact swing with solid plate skills, discipline and gap-to-gap power. Has strength in wiry, lean frame to find average power at maturity. Sound defensively, could move quick with deep range and strong arm at SS. 30-plus SB ability.

Perdomo, Geraldo — 6 — Arizona

EXP MLB DEBUT: 2022 | H/W: 6-3 184 | FUT: Starting SS | **9E**

Bats R Age 20
2016 FA (DR)

			Pwr	++
BAvg	++++
Spd	+++
Def	+++

Year	Lev	Team	AB	R	H	HR	RBI	Avg	OB	Slg	OPS	bb%	ct%	Eye	SB	CS	x/h%	Iso	RC/G
2018	Rk	Missoula	22	3	10	0	2	455	586	545	1132	24	82	1.75	1	1	10	91	10.84
2018	Rk	AZL DBacks	86	20	27	1	8	314	410	442	852	14	80	0.82	14	1	26	128	6.49
2018	A-	Hillsboro	103	20	31	3	14	301	405	456	861	15	78	0.78	9	4	26	155	6.57
2019	A	Kane County	314	48	84	2	36	268	378	357	735	15	82	1.00	20	8	25	89	5.09
2019	A+	Visalia	93	15	28	1	11	301	393	387	780	13	88	1.27	6	5	21	86	5.55

Loose, wiry athlete with feel to hit from both sides and advanced knowledge of strike zone. Plus bat-to-ball skills and works entire field consistently. Plus speed gives him a second intriguing tool, while his range and good arm strength project the glove to stay at SS long-term. Working on tapping into his power and has projectable frame.

Pereira, Everson — 8 — New York (A)

EXP MLB DEBUT: 2023 | H/W: 6-0 191 | FUT: Starting OF | **8E**

Bats R Age 18
2017 FA (VZ)

			Pwr	+++
BAvg	+++
Spd	+++
Def	+++

Year	Lev	Team	AB	R	H	HR	RBI	Avg	OB	Slg	OPS	bb%	ct%	Eye	SB	CS	x/h%	Iso	RC/G
2018	Rk	Pulaski	167	21	44	3	26	263	324	389	713	8	64	0.25	3	2	30	126	4.66
2019	A-	Staten Island	70	9	12	1	3	171	216	257	473	5	63	0.15	3	0	33	86	0.84

Athletic OF with power projection had a forgettable '19 after emerging as 17-year-old in Appy league in 2018. Struggled through performance and injury. Underlying tools remain including bat-to-ball skills and compact swing. Swing path and discipline will need to improve to reach hit projections. An above-average runner, could stick in CF.

Perez, Delvin — 6 — St. Louis

EXP MLB DEBUT: 2022 | H/W: 6-3 175 | FUT: Reserve SS | **6C**

Bats R Age 21
2016 (1) HS (PR)

			Pwr	+
BAvg	++
Spd	+++
Def	+++

Year	Lev	Team	AB	R	H	HR	RBI	Avg	OB	Slg	OPS	bb%	ct%	Eye	SB	CS	x/h%	Iso	RC/G
2016	Rk	GCL Cardinals	163	19	48	0	19	294	343	393	735	7	83	0.43	12	1	25	98	4.67
2017	Rk	Johnson City	76	7	14	0	4	184	295	224	519	14	82	0.86	3	4	14	39	2.28
2017	Rk	GCL Cardinals	42	7	10	0	5	238	319	357	676	11	76	0.50	2	1	30	119	4.15
2018	A-	State College	239	22	51	1	21	213	296	272	568	10	77	0.52	8	6	18	59	2.60
2019	A	Peoria	458	64	123	1	30	269	309	325	635	6	74	0.23	22	9	17	57	3.21

23rd overall pick from 2016 has been a rare Cardinals miss. Had his best season as a pro, slashing .273/.332/.329 but lack of power remains a red flag - just 1 career HR in 982 AB. Athletic player has a quick bat and above-average speed, but aggressive approach was exploited by pitchers in the MWL. Needs to show more in 2020 to remain a prospect.

Perez, Wenceel — 6 — Detroit

EXP MLB DEBUT: 2022 | H/W: 5-11 195 | FUT: Starting SS | **7B**

Bats B Age 20
2016 FA (DR)

			Pwr	+
BAvg	+++
Spd	+++
Def	++

Year	Lev	Team	AB	R	H	HR	RBI	Avg	OB	Slg	OPS	bb%	ct%	Eye	SB	CS	x/h%	Iso	RC/G
2018	Rk	GCL TigersW	81	20	31	1	14	383	462	543	1006	13	83	0.86	2	1	29	160	8.22
2018	A-	Connecticut	82	8	20	1	8	244	287	305	592	6	85	0.42	7	3	15	61	2.80
2018	A	West Michigan	68	8	21	0	9	309	329	441	770	3	88	0.25	4	1	29	132	4.89
2019	A	West Michigan	459	59	107	6	30	233	302	314	615	9	81	0.52	21	13	23	81	3.21

High-energy infielder with advanced understanding for play on both sides of the ball. Footwork and arm accuracy have both improved, although overall profile is still quite raw. Rushes himself at times, but works off athleticism to overshadow immaturity. Able to barrel the ball with an exceptional eye and ability to draw walks.

Peters, DJ — 89 — Los Angeles (N)

Bats R Age 24 2016 (4) Western NV CC
EXP MLB DEBUT: 2020 H/W: 6-6 225 FUT: Starting CF 8E

Pwr ++++
BAvg ++
Spd +++
Def +++

Year	Lev	Team	AB	R	H	HR	RBI	Avg	OB	Slg	OPS	bb%	ct%	Eye	SB	CS	x/h%	Iso	RC/G
2016	Rk	Ogden	262	63	92	13	48	351	428	615	1042	12	75	0.53	5	3	43	263	8.88
2017	A+	RanchoCuca	504	91	139	27	82	276	357	514	871	11	63	0.34	3	3	44	238	7.18
2018	AA	Tulsa	491	79	116	29	60	236	300	473	773	8	61	0.23	1	2	47	236	5.57
2019	AA	Tulsa	249	31	60	11	42	241	318	422	739	10	63	0.30	1	0	37	181	5.01
2019	AAA	OklahomaCity	208	40	54	12	39	260	361	490	851	14	64	0.44	1	1	43	231	6.76

Huge, athletic OF has above-average to plus power and bat speed, but ultra aggressive approach limits in-game results. Career 69 ct% makes it unlikely he will ever hit for average and could limit him to a 4th OF role. Runs well for his size with a plus arm and continues to stick in CF, giving him added value. Does draw his fair share of walks.

Peterson, Dustin — 379 — Detroit

Bats R Age 25 2013 (2) HS (AZ)
EXP MLB DEBUT: 2018 H/W: 6-2 210 FUT: Reserve OF 6A

Pwr ++
BAvg ++
Spd +
Def +++

Year	Lev	Team	AB	R	H	HR	RBI	Avg	OB	Slg	OPS	bb%	ct%	Eye	SB	CS	x/h%	Iso	RC/G
2018	AAA	Gwinnett	406	46	109	11	55	268	319	406	725	7	76	0.31	3	0	31	138	4.37
2018	MLB	Detroit	2	0	0	0	0	0	0	0	0	0	50	0.00	0	0	0	0	-7.85
2018	MLB	Atlanta	2	0	0	0	0	0	0	0	0	0	50	0.00	0	0	0	0	-7.85
2019	AAA	Toledo	301	31	86	11	49	286	317	439	756	4	74	0.18	1	1	28	153	4.60
2019	MLB	Detroit	44	3	10	0	6	227	261	318	579	4	68	0.14	1	0	40	91	2.53

Solid framed former third baseman turned outfielder. Athleticism complements what would otherwise be viewed as an average tool set. Easy raw power with dependable defensive resume. Major League experience both in 2018 and 2019 between Braves and Tigers.

Philip, Beau — 6 — Atlanta

Bats R Age 21 2019 (2) Oregon St
EXP MLB DEBUT: 2023 H/W: 6-0 190 FUT: Starting SS 7E

Pwr +++
BAvg ++
Spd +++
Def +++

Year	Lev	Team	AB	R	H	HR	RBI	Avg	OB	Slg	OPS	bb%	ct%	Eye	SB	CS	x/h%	Iso	RC/G
2019	NCAA	Oregon St	177	32	55	5	31	311	371	486	857	9	80	0.47	6	3	36	175	6.16
2019	Rk	Danville	207	27	40	4	20	193	283	280	563	11	75	0.51	5	5	25	87	2.42

Struggled in pro debut. Shows solid plate skills despite poor pitch recognition. Can get beat expanding the zone with 2 strikes with considerable swing-and-miss potential if spin issues continue. There is power in frame and swing, potentially average HR power at projection. Over-aggressive base runner with above-average run tool.

Pie, Alejandro — 6 — Tampa Bay

Bats R Age 18 2018 FA (DR)
EXP MLB DEBUT: 2024 H/W: 6-4 175 FUT: Starting SS 8E

Pwr +++
BAvg +++
Spd +++
Def ++++

Year	Lev	Team	AB	R	H	HR	RBI	Avg	OB	Slg	OPS	bb%	ct%	Eye	SB	CS	x/h%	Iso	RC/G
2019		Did not play in U.S.																	

Toolsy, athletic quick-twitch SS made pro debut in Dominican Summer League. Features above-average-or-better tools across the board. Quick wrists creates above-average bat speed. Swing is uneven and inconsistent. There is raw plus-power potential in frame. Double-plus runner could be SB threat. Plus defender with strong arm.

Pie, Juan — 79 — Pittsburgh

Bats R Age 19 2017 FA (DR)
EXP MLB DEBUT: 2024 H/W: 6-2 170 FUT: Starting OF 8E

Pwr ++
BAvg ++
Spd +++
Def +++

Year	Lev	Team	AB	R	H	HR	RBI	Avg	OB	Slg	OPS	bb%	ct%	Eye	SB	CS	x/h%	Iso	RC/G
2019	Rk	GCL Pirates	121	14	28	2	16	231	306	347	653	10	78	0.48	6	5	25	116	3.65
2019	A-	West Virginia	14	3	5	0	5	357	438	571	1009	13	64	0.40	1	1	60	214	9.82

Toolsy OF with upside. Spent first year in US and impressed with projectable frame and defensive instincts. Has chance to grow into plus power if his slight build fills out. Bat speed more than sufficient to get to any fastball. Runs well now, though could slow down in future. Could fit the classic RF profile due to strong arm and pop potential.

Planez, Alexfri — 89 — Cleveland

Bats R Age 18 2017 FA (VZ)
EXP MLB DEBUT: 2024 H/W: 6-2 180 FUT: Starting OF 8E

Pwr ++++
BAvg ++
Spd +++
Def +++

Year	Lev	Team	AB	R	H	HR	RBI	Avg	OB	Slg	OPS	bb%	ct%	Eye	SB	CS	x/h%	Iso	RC/G
2019	Rk	AZL Indians	24	3	8	1	3	333	360	542	902	4	71	0.14	0	0	38	208	6.74

Long, powerful OF made stateside debut but missed most of season with broken wrist. Big power in frame and swing. Double-plus power at projection if the hit tool materializes. Long limbs equals a bevy of moving parts. Swing path is very uneven. Aggressive approach with some spin recognition issues. Moves well for size with likely COF outcome.

Pomares, Jairo — 9 — San Francisco

Bats L Age 19 2018 FA (CU)
EXP MLB DEBUT: 2023 H/W: 6-1 185 FUT: Starting OF 7D

Pwr ++
BAvg ++
Spd +++
Def ++

Year	Lev	Team	AB	R	H	HR	RBI	Avg	OB	Slg	OPS	bb%	ct%	Eye	SB	CS	x/h%	Iso	RC/G
2019	Rk	AZL Giants	155	17	57	3	33	368	406	542	948	6	83	0.38	5	3	30	174	7.09
2019	A-	Salem-Keizer	58	7	12	0	4	207	220	259	479	2	71	0.06	0	0	25	52	0.94

Raw OF who finished 2nd in AZL in BA in first pro experience. Focuses on line drives with level swing, but has quick stroke and natural strength to project well. Uses all fields in swing-happy approach and brings slightly above average speed. Average arm, though takes crude routes to balls. Probable LF long-term, but bat/speed could play.

Potts, Hudson — 45 — San Diego

Bats R Age 21 2016 (1) HS (TX)
EXP MLB DEBUT: 2021 H/W: 6-3 205 FUT: Starting 3B 8D

Pwr +++
BAvg ++
Spd ++
Def +++

Year	Lev	Team	AB	R	H	HR	RBI	Avg	OB	Slg	OPS	bb%	ct%	Eye	SB	CS	x/h%	Iso	RC/G
2017	A	Fort Wayne	491	67	124	20	69	253	286	438	724	4	71	0.16	0	1	38	185	4.27
2018	A+	Lake Elsinore	406	66	114	17	58	281	341	498	838	8	72	0.33	3	1	46	217	6.04
2018	AA	San Antonio	78	5	12	2	5	154	250	231	481	11	58	0.30	1	0	17	77	0.87
2019	Rk	AZL Padres	12	3	8	1	6	667	667	1000	1667	0	75	0.00	0	0	25	333	15.83
2019	AA	Amarillo	409	56	93	16	59	227	283	406	689	7	69	0.25	3	1	43	178	3.97

Big-bodied 3B prospect who has good raw power but also lacks plate skills and ideal contact. Continues to post quality x/h% despite being young for each level. Loves to get the bat head out front, allowing power to flourish, but struggles covering the outer half. Aggressive, often free swinging mentality. Glove works at 3B, but could move to LF/RF.

Pratto, Nick — 3 — Kansas City

Bats L Age 21 2017 (1) HS (CA)
EXP MLB DEBUT: 2022 H/W: 6-1 195 FUT: Starting 1B 7D

Pwr +++
BAvg ++
Spd +++
Def +++

Year	Lev	Team	AB	R	H	HR	RBI	Avg	OB	Slg	OPS	bb%	ct%	Eye	SB	CS	x/h%	Iso	RC/G
2017	Rk	AZL Royals	198	25	49	4	34	247	329	414	743	11	71	0.41	10	4	45	167	5.01
2018	A	Lexington	485	79	136	14	62	280	342	443	785	8	69	0.30	22	5	36	163	5.46
2019	A+	Wilmington	419	48	80	9	46	191	276	310	586	10	61	0.30	17	7	39	119	2.75

LHH 1B with solid plate skills and discipline struggled with spin recognition and long, lumbering swing. Contact cratered, causing all other hit skills to crater with it, except BB% and Eye. Needs to rework swing to allow approach to work. Above-average power in frame and trajectory of swing. Can't get to it because of barrel issues. SB threat for a first baseman.

Preciado, Reginald — 6 — San Diego

Bats B Age 16 2019 FA (PN)
EXP MLB DEBUT: 2025 H/W: 6-4 185 FUT: Starting 3B 7D

Pwr +++
BAvg +++
Spd +++
Def +++

Year	Lev	Team	AB	R	H	HR	RBI	Avg	OB	Slg	OPS	bb%	ct%	Eye	SB	CS	x/h%	Iso	RC/G
2019		Did not play in U.S.																	

Long, lean SS who is long-term project but shows across-the-board ability. At 16, remains physically raw and will need ample time to grow into his frame. Is switch-hitter with fluid, level stroke from both sides and employs low-line drive approach to all fields. Chance for at least average power. Good athlete who may move to 3B as he gains weight.

Puason, Robert — 6 — Oakland

Bats B Age 17 2019 FA (DR)
EXP MLB DEBUT: 2024 H/W: 6-3 165 FUT: Starting SS 9E

Pwr +++
BAvg +++
Spd ++++
Def +++

Year	Lev	Team	AB	R	H	HR	RBI	Avg	OB	Slg	OPS	bb%	ct%	Eye	SB	CS	x/h%	Iso	RC/G
2019		Did not play in U.S.																	

Touted international SS signed for a hefty $5 million out of the D.R. Lean, projectable and athletic frame with room for added strength. Smooth, aqueous swing as RH/LH with special feel for hitting. Has actions, instincts for shortstop and a strong arm for the left side. Already a potential impact bat, his plus speed could net some SB value.

Quinn,Heath | 79 | San Francisco | EXP MLB DEBUT: 2020 | H/W: 6-3 220 | FUT: Reserve OF | 6B

Bats R Age 24
2016 (3) Samford
Pwr +++
BAvg +++
Spd ++
Def +++

Year	Lev	Team	AB	R	H	HR	RBI	Avg	OB	Slg	OPS	bb%	ct%	Eye	SB	CS	x/h%	Iso	RC/G
2017	A+	San Jose	272	24	62	10	29	228	281	371	652	7	68	0.23	0	0	31	143	3.38
2018	A+	San Jose	357	53	107	14	51	300	373	485	858	11	73	0.43	4	1	36	185	6.38
2019	Rk	AZL Giants O	25	5	7	2	7	280	357	640	997	11	80	0.60	0	0	71	360	7.86
2019	A+	San Jose	190	17	55	5	30	289	363	463	826	10	69	0.37	1	1	38	174	6.20
2019	AA	Richmond	97	6	20	2	9	206	306	330	636	13	64	0.40	0	0	35	124	3.54

Athletic OF can't stay on field due to litany of ailments. Demoted to A+ in June and turned season around. Offers above average raw power, but can be beaten with good fastballs. Knows the strike zone and draws enough walks. Has slowed down a bit and not much of a threat to steal. Solid LF with average arm and honed instincts.

Quintana,Nick | 5 | Detroit | EXP MLB DEBUT: 2022 | H/W: 5-10 187 | FUT: Starting 3B | 7D

Bats R Age 22
2019 (2) Arizona
Pwr ++
BAvg +++
Spd +++
Def +++

Year	Lev	Team	AB	R	H	HR	RBI	Avg	OB	Slg	OPS	bb%	ct%	Eye	SB	CS	x/h%	Iso	RC/G
2019	NCAA	Arizona	222	65	76	15	77	342	453	626	1079	17	76	0.83	3	0	43	284	9.49
2019	A-	Connecticut	86	12	22	1	4	256	347	372	719	12	64	0.39	1	0	36	116	4.94
2019	A	West Michigan	146	14	23	1	13	158	226	226	452	8	65	0.25	3	1	30	68	0.64

Athletic infielder selected as the Tigers second-round pick in 2019 out of the University of Arizona. Struggled to produce as advertised over short-season and Class A assignments. Quintana is a pure athlete who showed enough feel for the infield in college to avoid any panic in his debut miscues. Above-average arm and clean hands.

Quintero,Ronnier | 2 | Chicago (N) | EXP MLB DEBUT: 2025 | H/W: 6-0 175 | FUT: Starting C | 8E

Bats L Age 17
2019 FA (VZ)
Pwr +++
BAvg ++
Spd +
Def ++

Year	Lev	Team	AB	R	H	HR	RBI	Avg	OB	Slg	OPS	bb%	ct%	Eye	SB	CS	x/h%	Iso	RC/G
2019		Did not play in U.S.																	

Young CA who at 17 inked a club-record bonus in 2019's July 2 signing period. Developed body and is strong throughout; limited physical projection. Bat speed is above average and shows ability to impact the baseball with good raw power. Some feel to hit, but swing has slight hitch that will need to be ironed out. Good arm, but needs reps at CA.

Quiroz,Esteban | 4 | San Diego | EXP MLB DEBUT: 2020 | H/W: 5-7 175 | FUT: Utility player | 6A

Bats L Age 28
2017 FA (MX)
Pwr ++
BAvg +++
Spd ++
Def ++

Year	Lev	Team	AB	R	H	HR	RBI	Avg	OB	Slg	OPS	bb%	ct%	Eye	SB	CS	x/h%	Iso	RC/G
2018	Rk	GCL Red Sox	19	3	4	0	7	211	400	316	716	24	84	2.00	0	0	25	105	5.42
2018	AA	Portland	87	19	26	7	24	299	390	598	988	13	78	0.68	1	1	46	299	7.83
2019	AAA	El Paso	306	64	83	19	66	271	377	539	916	15	73	0.63	3	1	53	268	7.27

Older prospect with quality BA ability who posted above-average walk rate and fly ball rate in PCL. Does not turn heads with physical ability, but is strong and compact and should be a versatile INF glove when called upon. Avg power works best to RF but will flash oppo pop. Hits LH/RF equally well, but profiles as solid utility bat.

Raleigh,Cal | 2 | Seattle | EXP MLB DEBUT: 2021 | H/W: 6-3 215 | FUT: Starting C | 7C

Bats B Age 23
2018 (3) Florida St
Pwr +++
BAvg ++
Spd ++
Def +++

Year	Lev	Team	AB	R	H	HR	RBI	Avg	OB	Slg	OPS	bb%	ct%	Eye	SB	CS	x/h%	Iso	RC/G
2018	NCAA	Florida St	230	44	75	13	54	326	448	583	1031	18	81	1.19	2	1	43	257	8.76
2018	A-	Everett	146	25	42	8	29	288	366	534	900	11	80	0.62	1	1	45	247	6.70
2019	A+	Modesto	310	48	81	22	66	261	332	535	868	10	78	0.48	4	0	51	274	6.16
2019	AA	Arkansas	145	16	33	7	16	228	296	414	709	9	68	0.30	0	0	39	186	4.27

Power-driven CA prospect struggled with hit tool in late-season taste of Double-A. Switch-hitter with good understanding of zone. Struggled getting bat around against velocity, contributing to AA ct% woes. Above-average power played big in Cal League and should play in bigs. Improved defensively and looks to have enough to catch in big leagues.

Raley,Luke | 379 | Minnesota | EXP MLB DEBUT: 2020 | H/W: 6-4 235 | FUT: Reserve OF | 6C

Bats L Age 25
2016 (7) Lake Erie
Pwr +++
BAvg +++
Spd ++
Def ++

Year	Lev	Team	AB	R	H	HR	RBI	Avg	OB	Slg	OPS	bb%	ct%	Eye	SB	CS	x/h%	Iso	RC/G
2017	A+	Lancaster																	
2018	AA	Tulsa	386	65	106	17	53	275	317	477	794	6	73	0.23	3	0	37	202	5.24
2018	AA	Chattanooga	98	15	27	3	16	276	355	449	804	11	67	0.38	1	0	30	173	5.92
2019	Rk	GCL Twins	19	1	7	1	2	368	368	526	895	0	89	0.00	0	0	14	158	5.63
2019	AAA	Rochester	126	28	38	7	21	302	338	516	854	5	67	0.17	4	0	34	214	6.27

Over-achieving, 1B/OF prospect missed most of season due to ankle injury. Bulking prospect who is maxed out physically. Struggles creating loft off bat due to line-drive, top-spin-heavy swing trajectory. Patient hitter with good plate skills. Doesn't have carry tool to stick at corners or DH. Below average runner will sneak a SB here and there.

Ramirez,Alexander | 8 | Los Angeles (A) | EXP MLB DEBUT: 2024 | H/W: 6-2 180 | FUT: Starting OF | 8E

Bats R Age 17
2018 FA (DR)
Pwr +++
BAvg ++
Spd +++
Def +++

Year	Lev	Team	AB	R	H	HR	RBI	Avg	OB	Slg	OPS	bb%	ct%	Eye	SB	CS	x/h%	Iso	RC/G
2019		Did not play in U.S.																	

Uber-young July 2 signee from 2018 has yet to make stateside debut, but has intriguing tools. Long, lean levers produce natural lift in swing; could have plus power at peak as he bulks up. Bat control is raw and will need time to develop ct% skills, but shows pitch ID ability. Good athlete who can play CF now, but has ideal RF build and skill-set.

Ramos,Heliot | 8 | San Francisco | EXP MLB DEBUT: 2020 | H/W: 6-0 188 | FUT: Starting OF | 8B

Bats R Age 20
2017 (1) HS (PR)
Pwr ++++
BAvg +++
Spd +++
Def +++

Year	Lev	Team	AB	R	H	HR	RBI	Avg	OB	Slg	OPS	bb%	ct%	Eye	SB	CS	x/h%	Iso	RC/G
2017	Rk	AZL Giants	138	33	48	6	27	348	392	645	1037	7	65	0.21	10	2	48	297	9.53
2018	A	Augusta	485	61	119	11	52	245	296	396	692	7	72	0.26	8	7	36	151	4.04
2019	A+	San Jose	294	51	90	13	40	306	374	500	874	10	71	0.38	6	7	34	194	6.60
2019	AA	Richmond	95	13	23	3	15	242	314	421	735	10	65	0.30	2	3	43	179	4.94

Exciting power/speed prospect who does everything well on diamond. Has controlled swing to make acceptable contact while also adding power to repertoire. Solid situational hitter and goes opposite way at will. Offers plus bat speed and natural strength. Runs well, though not a big SB artist. Probable RF down line, but good CF with very strong arm.

Ramos,Roberto | 3 | Colorado | EXP MLB DEBUT: 2020 | H/W: 6-3 220 | FUT: Starting 1B | 6A

Bats L Age 25
2014 (16) CollegeCanyons JC
Pwr ++++
BAvg ++
Spd +
Def +++

Year	Lev	Team	AB	R	H	HR	RBI	Avg	OB	Slg	OPS	bb%	ct%	Eye	SB	CS	x/h%	Iso	RC/G
2016	A+	Modesto	78	7	18	2	9	231	318	397	716	11	67	0.38	0	0	50	167	4.69
2017	A+	Lancaster	478	72	142	13	68	297	353	444	796	8	74	0.33	3	2	30	146	5.40
2018	A+	Lancaster	214	44	65	17	43	304	394	640	1034	13	70	0.49	3	1	54	336	9.03
2018	AA	Hartford	199	26	46	15	34	231	320	503	823	12	62	0.35	2	1	52	271	6.22
2019	AAA	Albuquerque	431	77	133	30	105	309	394	580	974	12	67	0.43	0	1	43	271	8.29

Pure-slugging 1B who has massive raw power and questionable contact ability. Has collected 62 HR in past two seasons by way of steep uppercut bat path and ability to clear fences to opposite field. Willing to take a walk and work counts; will have more value in OBP leagues. Has favoritism for RHP, which could cut into his PT.

Randolph,Corneilus | 79 | Philadelphia | EXP MLB DEBUT: 2020 | H/W: 5-11 205 | FUT: Reserve OF | 6B

Bats L Age 22
2015 (1) HS (GA)
Pwr ++
BAvg ++
Spd ++
Def ++

Year	Lev	Team	AB	R	H	HR	RBI	Avg	OB	Slg	OPS	bb%	ct%	Eye	SB	CS	x/h%	Iso	RC/G
2016	Rk	GCL Phillies	12	1	1	0	0	83	214	83	298	14	75	0.67	0	0	0	0	-1.03
2016	A	Lakewood	241	33	66	2	27	274	345	357	701	10	76	0.46	5	4	23	83	4.29
2017	A+	Clearwater	440	47	110	13	55	250	333	402	736	11	72	0.44	7	3	33	152	4.77
2018	AA	Reading	410	52	99	5	40	241	321	322	643	10	78	0.52	3	3	23	80	3.53
2019	AA	Reading	348	42	86	10	44	247	319	399	719	10	71	0.36	9	5	34	152	4.50

Repeating Double-A, achieved a marginally better slash line, though HR and SB ticked up. Once in a while can break out an on-time swing and send an extra-base hit into the gap or over the wall, but mostly it's weak contact when it's contact at all. Defensively, he's a LF only, with questionable routes/decisions. A 5th OF if he makes it at all.

Ray,Corey | 8 | Milwaukee | EXP MLB DEBUT: 2020 | H/W: 6-0 195 | FUT: Starting OF | 8C

Bats L Age 25
2016 (1) Louisville
Pwr +++
BAvg ++
Spd ++++
Def +++

Year	Lev	Team	AB	R	H	HR	RBI	Avg	OB	Slg	OPS	bb%	ct%	Eye	SB	CS	x/h%	Iso	RC/G
2017	A+	Carolina	449	56	107	7	48	238	312	367	679	10	65	0.31	24	10	37	129	4.17
2018	AA	Biloxi	532	86	128	27	75	241	318	479	797	10	67	0.34	37	7	52	239	5.72
2019	Rk	AZL BrewersG	15	5	8	1	4	533	563	933	1496	6	80	0.33	0	0	50	400	13.90
2019	AA	Biloxi	40	5	10	0	0	250	348	325	673	13	65	0.43	3	2	30	75	4.25
2019	AAA	San Antonio	207	23	39	7	21	188	260	329	588	9	57	0.22	3	1	38	140	2.80

Former top-five overall pick missed significant time on IL with finger injury and struggled in AAA play. Still possesses plus-plus speed for dynamic impact on bases and plus raw power gives him two intriguing tools. Contact woes persisted in PCL (57% ct% in 200 AB) and BA downside signals high risk. Upside remains, but with big question marks.

Read,Raudy — 2 — Washington

EXP MLB DEBUT: 2017 | H/W: 6-0 170 | FUT: Reserve C | 6A

Bats R | Age 26 | 2011 FA (DR)

Pwr +++ | BAvg +++ | Spd + | Def ++

Year	Lev	Team	AB	R	H	HR	RBI	Avg	OB	Slg	OPS	bb%	ct%	Eye	SB	CS	x/h%	Iso	RC/G
2017	MLB	Washington	11	1	3	0	0	273	273	273	545	0	73	0.00	0	0	0	0	1.63
2018	AA	Harrisburg	147	14	42	3	24	286	335	435	771	7	80	0.37	0	0	33	150	5.01
2018	AAA	Syracuse	50	2	13	0	2	260	275	300	575	2	84	0.13	0	0	15	40	2.39
2019	AAA	Fresno	306	52	84	20	60	275	313	546	858	5	81	0.29	1	1	48	271	5.78
2019	MLB	Washington	11	0	1	0	0	91	91	91	182	0	55	0.00	0	0	0	0	-4.21

Good power and contact skills from a catcher cements his place here, but questionable defense will likely continue keep him from an everyday MLB job. Has a short compact swing with strength to drive the ball out; aggression in the box will be tested at highest level. Bench bat with occasional HR.

Reed,Buddy — 78 — Oakland

EXP MLB DEBUT: 2020 | H/W: 6-4 210 | FUT: Reserve OF | 6A

Bats B | Age 24 | 2016 (2) Florida

Pwr ++ | BAvg ++ | Spd ++++ | Def ++++

Year	Lev	Team	AB	R	H	HR	RBI	Avg	OB	Slg	OPS	bb%	ct%	Eye	SB	CS	x/h%	Iso	RC/G
2016	A-	Tri-City	205	31	52	0	13	254	326	337	663	10	74	0.42	15	5	25	83	3.86
2017	A	Fort Wayne	316	48	74	6	35	234	286	396	682	7	69	0.24	12	8	42	161	4.02
2018	A+	Lake Elsinore	315	54	102	12	47	324	372	549	921	7	73	0.29	33	7	39	225	7.11
2018	AA	San Antonio	179	21	32	1	15	179	230	235	465	6	65	0.19	18	3	25	56	0.77
2019	AA	Amarillo	381	49	87	14	50	228	305	388	693	10	67	0.33	23	8	36	160	4.16

Raw, pure athlete with elite speed and future value as dynamic OF glove. Will show good raw power to all fields in BP, but poor feel for hitting and persistent contact woes limit his ability to tap into it consistently. Can work counts and willing to take a walk; projects to have more value in OBP formats. A fourth OF type if ct% doesn't improve.

Rios,Edwin — 35 — Los Angeles (N)

EXP MLB DEBUT: 2019 | H/W: 6-3 220 | FUT: Reserve 1B | 8E

Bats L | Age 25 | 2015 (6) Florida Intl

Pwr ++++ | BAvg ++ | Spd + | Def ++

Year	Lev	Team	AB	R	H	HR	RBI	Avg	OB	Slg	OPS	bb%	ct%	Eye	SB	CS	x/h%	Iso	RC/G
2017	AA	Tulsa	306	47	97	15	62	317	353	533	886	5	77	0.25	1	1	37	216	6.24
2017	AAA	Oklahoma City	169	23	50	9	29	296	364	533	896	10	75	0.43	0	1	44	237	6.71
2018	AAA	Oklahoma City	309	45	94	10	55	304	352	482	835	7	64	0.21	0	1	37	178	6.40
2019	AAA	Oklahoma City	393	72	106	31	91	270	333	575	908	9	61	0.24	2	2	53	305	7.67
2019	MLB	Los Angeles	47	10	13	4	8	277	393	617	1010	16	55	0.43	0	0	54	340	10.41

Strong-bodied LH masher has some of the best raw power in the system, but aggressive all-out approach results in few BB and plenty of swing-and-miss. Despite the strikeouts, he has a surprisingly robust .295/.348/.539 career slash line. Bottom-of-the-scale run tool limits him to 1B/DH where he needs to continue to mash.

Rivas,Leonardo — 6 — Los Angeles (A)

EXP MLB DEBUT: 2021 | H/W: 5-10 150 | FUT: Utility player | 6B

Bats B | Age 22 | 2014 FA (VZ)

Pwr + | BAvg +++ | Spd ++++ | Def +++

Year	Lev	Team	AB	R	H	HR	RBI	Avg	OB	Slg	OPS	bb%	ct%	Eye	SB	CS	x/h%	Iso	RC/G
2017	A	Burlington	90	24	24	0	7	267	400	322	722	18	76	0.91	8	1	21	56	5.03
2018	Rk	AZL Angels	8	2	2	1	3	250	250	750	1000	0	75	0.00	0	0	100	500	7.40
2018	A	Burlington	454	62	106	4	34	233	353	326	679	16	70	0.61	16	10	25	93	4.28
2019	Rk	AZL Angels	16	6	1	0	0	63	375	63	438	33	75	2.00	1	0	0	0	1.26
2019	A+	Inland Empire	297	44	70	6	26	236	324	377	702	12	70	0.43	4	2	36	141	4.42

Slender INF with solid run tool and has the look of a solid utility bat down the road. Employs disciplined, though almost too passive approach as switch hitter that leads to high bb% but also questionable ct%. Not a big power threat, as he lacks leverage and bat speed to impact the ball. Will have positional flexibility, which increases his value.

Robert,Luis — 8 — Chicago (A)

EXP MLB DEBUT: 2020 | H/W: 6-3 185 | FUT: Starting CF | 9C

Bats R | Age 22 | 2017 FA (CU)

Pwr ++++ | BAvg +++ | Spd ++++ | Def ++++

Year	Lev	Team	AB	R	H	HR	RBI	Avg	OB	Slg	OPS	bb%	ct%	Eye	SB	CS	x/h%	Iso	RC/G
2018	A	Kannapolis	45	5	13	0	4	289	347	400	747	8	73	0.33	4	2	31	111	4.98
2018	A+	Winston-Salem	123	21	30	0	11	244	290	309	599	6	70	0.22	8	2	23	65	2.80
2019	A+	Winston-Salem	75	21	34	8	24	453	481	920	1401	5	73	0.20	8	2	47	467	13.20
2019	AA	Birmingham	226	43	71	8	29	314	351	518	869	5	76	0.24	21	6	38	204	6.19
2019	AAA	Charlotte	202	44	60	16	39	297	333	634	967	5	73	0.20	7	3	52	337	7.47

Strong, athletic CF is knocking on door of MLB call up. True five-tool talent. Has above-average-or-better tools across the board. Whippy, electric bat speed. Does solid job maintaining bat plane despite looseness of hands. Doesn't react well to spin. Double-plus power plays to all fields. Combine HR power with plus speed, potential 30/30 player.

Robertson,Will — 9 — Toronto

EXP MLB DEBUT: 2022 | H/W: 6-2 215 | FUT: Starting OF | 7C

Bats L | Age 22 | 2019 (4) Creighton

Pwr +++ | BAvg +++ | Spd ++ | Def ++

Year	Lev	Team	AB	R	H	HR	RBI	Avg	OB	Slg	OPS	bb%	ct%	Eye	SB	CS	x/h%	Iso	RC/G
2019	NCAA	Creighton	222	53	69	15	67	311	381	599	980	10	82	0.64	1	1	49	288	7.53
2019	A-	Vancouver	228	33	61	6	33	268	355	404	759	12	79	0.63	1	2	30	136	5.07

Aggressive OF with brute strength and natural raw power to all fields. Quick stroke produces decent contact, though Ks will always be part of profile as he can sell out for power. Has chance to hit for HR and BA, though not likely to steal many bases due to lack of foot speed. Likely limited to LF long-term with sub-par range and average arm.

Robinson,Kristian — 89 — Arizona

EXP MLB DEBUT: 2022 | H/W: 6-3 190 | FUT: Starting OF | 9D

Bats R | Age 19 | 2017 FA (BM)

Pwr ++++ | BAvg ++ | Spd ++++ | Def +++

Year	Lev	Team	AB	R	H	HR	RBI	Avg	OB	Slg	OPS	bb%	ct%	Eye	SB	CS	x/h%	Iso	RC/G
2018	Rk	Missoula	60	13	18	3	10	300	408	467	875	15	65	0.52	5	3	22	167	7.10
2018	Rk	AZL DBacks	162	35	44	4	31	272	337	414	751	9	72	0.35	7	5	34	142	4.92
2019	A-	Hillsboro	163	29	52	9	35	319	403	558	962	12	71	0.49	14	3	38	239	7.93
2019	A	Kane County	92	14	20	5	16	217	280	435	715	8	67	0.27	3	2	45	217	4.32

Tall, explosive OF with quick-twitch attributes for dynamic impact, but comes with risk. Has elite raw power that plays to all fields and bat speed required to make contact. Still sorting out swing and miss and approach issues. Plus runner who may lose a step as he fills out, but speed is an asset. Has arm and range to profile at any OF spot.

Robson,Jacob — 789 — Detroit

EXP MLB DEBUT: 2020 | H/W: 5-10 180 | FUT: Reserve OF | 7C

Bats L | Age 25 | 2016 (8) Mississippi St

Pwr ++ | BAvg ++ | Spd +++ | Def ++

Year	Lev	Team	AB	R	H	HR	RBI	Avg	OB	Slg	OPS	bb%	ct%	Eye	SB	CS	x/h%	Iso	RC/G
2017	A	West Michigan	228	38	75	1	27	329	409	395	804	12	74	0.53	5	9	16	66	5.82
2017	A+	Lakeland	224	27	62	2	18	277	344	388	733	9	74	0.39	16	9	27	112	4.75
2018	AA	Erie	262	46	75	7	32	286	379	450	829	13	70	0.50	11	4	35	164	6.28
2018	AAA	Toledo	220	36	67	4	15	305	370	427	798	9	72	0.37	7	6	27	123	5.62
2019	AAA	Toledo	409	61	109	9	52	267	351	399	749	11	68	0.40	25	10	30	132	5.13

Compact outfielder with ability to make tools look bigger than they are through gritty approach. Undersized frame isn't built to produce much power, but tight plate discipline and an ability to maximize use the whole field have continued to position him as an asset. Above-average speed with sub-par arm, complemented by sound defensive instincts.

Rocchio,Brayan — 6 — Cleveland

EXP MLB DEBUT: 2023 | H/W: 5-10 150 | FUT: Starting SS | 8D

Bats B | Age 19 | 2017 FA (VZ)

Pwr ++ | BAvg ++++ | Spd ++++ | Def +++

Year	Lev	Team	AB	R	H	HR	RBI	Avg	OB	Slg	OPS	bb%	ct%	Eye	SB	CS	x/h%	Iso	RC/G
2018		Did not play																	
2019	A-	MahoningVal	268	33	67	5	27	250	302	373	675	7	85	0.50	14	8	30	123	3.88

Short-statured, contact-oriented MIF brings headiness to table. Athletic, wiry frame; will not add much bulk. Switch-hitter with solid plate skills despite a little too much aggressiveness. Sprays the entire field and relies on his plus run tool to get XBH and SB. Does well to incorporate lower half and has below-average power projection.

Rodgers,Brendan — 4 — Colorado

EXP MLB DEBUT: 2019 | H/W: 6-0 180 | FUT: Starting MIF | 8A

Bats R | Age 23 | 2015 (1) HS (FL)

Pwr +++ | BAvg +++ | Spd +++ | Def +++

Year	Lev	Team	AB	R	H	HR	RBI	Avg	OB	Slg	OPS	bb%	ct%	Eye	SB	CS	x/h%	Iso	RC/G
2017	AA	Hartford	150	20	39	6	17	260	297	413	711	5	76	0.22	0	2	28	153	3.99
2018	AA	Hartford	357	49	98	17	62	275	331	493	824	8	79	0.39	12	3	43	218	5.60
2018	AAA	Albuquerque	69	5	16	0	5	232	243	290	533	1	77	0.06	0	0	25	58	1.73
2019	AAA	Albuquerque	143	34	50	9	21	350	408	622	1030	9	81	0.52	0	0	40	273	8.12
2019	MLB	Colorado	76	8	17	0	7	224	263	250	513	5	64	0.15	0	0	12	26	1.44

Former top-five draft pick struggled in debut and required season-ending shoulder surgery mid year. Blends solid skill-set including above-average power via plus bat speed and hard line-drive contact to all fields. Free-swinger who will need to get into better counts for power to flourish. Not a plus runner, but good instincts and arm for 2B/SS.

Rodriguez,Alfredo — 6 — Cincinnati

EXP MLB DEBUT: 2020 | H/W: 6-0 190 | FUT: Reserve IF | 6B

Bats R | Age 25 | 2016 FA (CU)

Pwr + | BAvg +++ | Spd ++++ | Def ++++

Year	Lev	Team	AB	R	H	HR	RBI	Avg	OB	Slg	OPS	bb%	ct%	Eye	SB	CS	x/h%	Iso	RC/G
2018	Rk	AZL Reds	20	3	5	0	3	250	286	400	686	5	85	0.33	0	0	60	150	4.08
2018	A+	Daytona	111	12	23	2	12	207	261	324	585	7	80	0.36	4	0	35	117	2.68
2018	AA	Pensacola	26	4	5	0	0	192	250	192	442	7	73	0.29	0	0	0	0	0.60
2019	AA	Chattanooga	409	50	117	1	25	286	323	347	670	5	85	0.35	13	9	18	61	3.72
2019	AAA	Louisville	77	5	13	0	9	169	238	221	459	8	83	0.54	3	0	31	52	1.39

Speedy, defensive specialist struggled with lapses of poor judgement despite some hit gains in '19. Contact-oriented bar with above-average bat-to-ball skills. Flat swing trajectory doesn't allow for much loft. Uses field well in singles/doubles attack. Plus runner and defender. Will take off plays and will get burned in all facets of game.

Rodriguez, Carlos — 8 — Milwaukee
EXP MLB DEBUT: 2023 | H/W: 5-10 150 | FUT: Starting CF | 8E
Bats L · Age 19 · 2017 FA (VZ)
Pwr + | BAvg +++ | Spd +++ | Def +++

Year	Lev	Team	AB	R	H	HR	RBI	Avg	OB	Slg	OPS	bb%	ct%	Eye	SB	CS	x/h%	Iso	RC/G
2018	Rk	DSL Brewers	217	38	70	2	32	323	344	419	763	3	91	0.37	12	8	23	97	4.74
2018	Rk	AZL Brewers	20	4	7	0	1	350	409	350	759	9	95	2.00	2	1	0	0	5.16
2019	Rk	AZL BrewersG	22	5	7	0	1	318	318	364	682	0	91	0.00	1	1	14	45	3.61
2019	Rk	Rocky Mountain	151	20	50	3	12	331	348	424	772	3	87	0.20	4	6	14	93	4.63

Shorter, slender OF whose profile is currently driven by his glove and speed but could develop into offensive threat. Plus runner and overall athlete with good range and instincts to thrive in CF long-term. Sprays low line drives to all fields and shows good plate coverage. Power is well below-average at present but room for muscle in lean frame.

Rodriguez, Gabriel — 6 — Cleveland
EXP MLB DEBUT: 2023 | H/W: 6-2 174 | FUT: Starting SS | 8E
Bats R · Age 18 · 2018 FA (VZ)
Pwr ++++ | BAvg +++ | Spd +++ | Def +++

Year	Lev	Team	AB	R	H	HR	RBI	Avg	OB	Slg	OPS	bb%	ct%	Eye	SB	CS	x/h%	Iso	RC/G
2019	Rk	AZL Indians	65	7	14	0	10	215	261	262	522	6	66	0.18	1	1	21	46	1.66

Long-levers, power-driven SS prospect made stateside debut. Solid approach, will spray ball to all fields and take walks. Maybe too aggressive within zone. Power projection over right now. Double-plus raw power in frame. Fringe-average runner. Not flashy at SS but good reads on balls; could move to 3B if range becomes issue.

Rodriguez, Johnathan — 9 — Cleveland
EXP MLB DEBUT: 2023 | H/W: 6-3 180 | FUT: Starting OF | 7E
Bats R · Age 20 · 2017 (3) HS (PR)
Pwr +++ | BAvg +++ | Spd +++ | Def ++

Year	Lev	Team	AB	R	H	HR	RBI	Avg	OB	Slg	OPS	bb%	ct%	Eye	SB	CS	x/h%	Iso	RC/G
2017	Rk	AZL Indians	96	13	24	0	11	250	385	333	718	18	76	0.91	0	1	25	83	5.05
2018	Rk	AZL Indians	187	36	55	1	22	294	368	406	775	11	76	0.50	8	3	27	112	5.38
2019	A-	MahoningVal	231	36	57	6	27	247	310	424	734	8	71	0.31	4	2	44	177	4.73

Strong, switch-hitting OF with raw baseball skills had so-so season in short-season A. Powerful frame. Plus-power projection shows up in BP and some in games. Has solid approach and will work pitchers but doesn't have bat speed to more than a fringe-average hitter. Smooth swing plane with natural uppercut. Should generate more loft with experience.

Rodriguez, Julio — 89 — Seattle
EXP MLB DEBUT: 2021 | H/W: 6-4 225 | FUT: Starting OF | 9C
Bats R · Age 19 · 2017 FA (DR)
Pwr ++++ | BAvg +++ | Spd +++ | Def +++

Year	Lev	Team	AB	R	H	HR	RBI	Avg	OB	Slg	OPS	bb%	ct%	Eye	SB	CS	x/h%	Iso	RC/G
2018	Rk	DSL Mariners	219	50	69	5	36	315	398	525	923	12	82	0.75	10	0	39	210	7.26
2019	A	West Virginia	263	50	77	10	50	293	343	490	833	7	75	0.30	1	3	40	198	5.82
2019	A+	Modesto	65	13	30	2	19	462	500	738	1238	7	85	0.50	0	0	37	277	10.60

Dynamic OF prospect made waves in full-season and stateside debut. Power driven profile. Does a good job finding barrel and driving balls to gaps. Mostly flat swing trajectory during season. Has started implementing lift in swing to go with bulk added last off-season. Could be Double-plus HR hitter. Runs well for size but fits best in RF.

Rodriguez, Julio E. — 2 — St. Louis
EXP MLB DEBUT: 2021 | H/W: 6-0 197 | FUT: Starting C | 7D
Bats R · Age 22 · 2016 FA (DR)
Pwr ++ | BAvg ++ | Spd + | Def ++++

Year	Lev	Team	AB	R	H	HR	RBI	Avg	OB	Slg	OPS	bb%	ct%	Eye	SB	CS	x/h%	Iso	RC/G
2017	Rk	Johnson City	182	28	51	5	36	280	342	451	792	9	83	0.55	0	0	39	170	5.33
2017	A+	Palm Beach	3	0	0	0	0	0	0	0	0	0	100		0	0	0	0	-2.66
2018	A	Peoria	291	26	75	8	47	258	289	405	695	4	79	0.22	0	0	33	148	3.85
2019	A+	Palm Beach	268	28	74	7	31	276	317	407	724	4	80	0.30	0	0	28	131	4.26
2019	AA	Springfield	45	2	10	1	7	222	255	311	566	4	67	0.13	0	0	20	89	2.10

Dominican backstop has been slow to develop, but put up solid numbers in the pitcher-friendly FSL earning a mid-season All-Star nod. Above-average defender with good blocking and receiving skills, a quick release and a strong, accurate arm. Aggressive approach at the plate leads to contact issues, but does show moderate pull-side power.

Rodriguez, Luis — 8 — Los Angeles (N)
EXP MLB DEBUT: 2024 | H/W: 6-2 175 | FUT: Starting CF | 8D
Bats R · Age 17 · 2019 FA (VZ)
Pwr +++ | BAvg +++ | Spd +++ | Def +++

Year	Lev	Team	AB	R	H	HR	RBI	Avg	OB	Slg	OPS	bb%	ct%	Eye	SB	CS	x/h%	Iso	RC/G
2019		Did not play in U.S.																	

Athletic Venezuelan OF was inked to a $2.7 million bonus in 2019 and has yet to make his pro debut. Widely regarded as one of the top international free agents available with above-average tools across the board. Advanced bat-to-ball skills should develop average power as he matures and moves up with the ability to play all three OF slots.

Roederer, Cole — 8 — Chicago (N)
EXP MLB DEBUT: 2022 | H/W: 6-0 175 | FUT: Starting OF | 8E
Bats L · Age 20 · 2018 (2) HS (CA)
Pwr +++ | BAvg +++ | Spd +++ | Def ++

Year	Lev	Team	AB	R	H	HR	RBI	Avg	OB	Slg	OPS	bb%	ct%	Eye	SB	CS	x/h%	Iso	RC/G
2018	Rk	AZL Cubs 2	142	30	39	5	24	275	356	465	821	11	74	0.49	13	4	33	190	5.92
2019	A	South Bend	384	45	86	9	60	224	317	365	681	12	71	0.46	16	5	37	141	4.09

Former 2nd-rounder who posted subpar OPS in MWL debut, but has some feel to hit and can run a bit. Has added mass to lean frame, but still has strength projection and could have above average power. Swing works best when he gets the bat head out front. Bat path can be inconsistent; still ironing out his approach. Currently CF, but could move off to LF.

Rogers, Jake — 2 — Detroit
EXP MLB DEBUT: 2019 | H/W: 6-1 205 | FUT: Starting C | 7C
Bats R · Age 24 · 2016 (3) Tulane
Pwr +++ | BAvg +++ | Spd + | Def +++

Year	Lev	Team	AB	R	H	HR	RBI	Avg	OB	Slg	OPS	bb%	ct%	Eye	SB	CS	x/h%	Iso	RC/G
2017	A+	Buies Creek	313	43	83	12	55	265	356	457	813	12	77	0.61	13	8	40	192	5.77
2018	AA	Erie	352	57	77	11	56	219	300	412	712	10	68	0.37	7	1	43	193	4.36
2019	AA	Erie	86	17	26	5	21	302	429	535	963	18	70	0.73	0	0	35	233	8.27
2019	AAA	Toledo	166	29	37	9	31	223	299	458	757	10	68	0.34	0	0	54	235	5.02
2019	MLB	Detroit	112	11	14	4	8	125	216	259	475	10	54	0.25	0	0	50	134	0.81

Highly advanced defensive-minded backstop. Filled defensive need for Detroit's farm with accurate arm and advanced receiving and framing skills. Flashed power at the plate, but hit tool still lags behind. Can use all fields with good swing path, but lacks feel for contact.

Rojas, Johan — 8 — Philadelphia
EXP MLB DEBUT: 2023 | H/W: 6-1 165 | FUT: Starting CF | 8E
Bats R · Age 19 · 2018 FA (DR)
Pwr ++++ | BAvg +++ | Spd ++++ (4.30) | Def +++

Year	Lev	Team	AB	R	H	HR	RBI	Avg	OB	Slg	OPS	bb%	ct%	Eye	SB	CS	x/h%	Iso	RC/G
2019	A-	Williamsport	164	17	40	2	11	244	266	384	650	3	82	0.17	11	4	33	140	3.39
2019	Rk	GCL PhilliesW	74	13	23	0	4	311	386	527	913	11	84	0.75	3	2	48	216	7.24

Pop-up player with raw tools who turned some heads in two short-season stops. Good present strength with a frame to take on more. Plus raw power and bat speed, hit tool currently capped by typical teenage pitch recognition struggles. Has speed for SB and covers ground in CF, along with a strong, accurate arm. A worthy follow.

Rooker, Brent — 37 — Minnesota
EXP MLB DEBUT: 2020 | H/W: 6-3 215 | FUT: Starting OF | 8D
Bats R · Age 25 · 2017 (1) Mississippi St
Pwr ++++ | BAvg +++ | Spd ++ | Def ++

Year	Lev	Team	AB	R	H	HR	RBI	Avg	OB	Slg	OPS	bb%	ct%	Eye	SB	CS	x/h%	Iso	RC/G
2017	Rk	Elizabethton	85	19	24	7	17	282	365	588	953	11	75	0.52	2	2	50	306	7.39
2017	A+	Fort Myers	143	23	40	11	35	280	352	552	905	10	67	0.34	0	0	43	273	7.08
2018	AA	Chattanooga	503	72	128	22	79	254	329	465	794	10	70	0.37	6	1	45	211	5.56
2019	Rk	GCL Twins	6	2	2	0	0	333	429	333	762	14	100		0	0	0	0	5.78
2019	AAA	Rochester	228	41	64	14	47	281	376	535	912	13	58	0.37	2	0	47	254	6.99

Big-bodied power hitter without defensive position missed time last season due to leg injury. XBH machine when things going well. Has GB tendencies when things aren't going good. Lumbering swing finds barrel when making contact but has swing-and-miss in profile. 30-HR potential but weak defensively at 2 positions; most passable in LF.

Rortvedt, Ben — 2 — Minnesota
EXP MLB DEBUT: 2021 | H/W: 5-10 205 | FUT: Reserve C | 6C
Bats L · Age 22 · 2016 (2) HS (WI)
Pwr ++ | BAvg ++ | Spd ++ | Def ++++

Year	Lev	Team	AB	R	H	HR	RBI	Avg	OB	Slg	OPS	bb%	ct%	Eye	SB	CS	x/h%	Iso	RC/G
2017	A	Cedar Rapids	308	33	69	4	30	224	276	315	591	7	81	0.37	1	0	29	91	2.75
2018	A	Cedar Rapids	145	14	40	1	16	276	323	386	709	6	76	0.29	1	0	30	110	4.28
2018	A+	Fort Myers	172	20	43	4	27	250	332	372	704	11	83	0.72	0	0	28	122	4.37
2019	A+	Fort Myers	80	13	19	2	10	238	337	438	774	13	80	0.75	0	0	58	200	5.44
2019	AA	Pensacola	197	14	47	5	19	239	318	355	674	10	74	0.45	0	0	28	117	3.85

Defensive-oriented backstop with plus catch/throws skills struggled offensively in '19. Contact-oriented swing with solid bat-to-ball skills. Struggled with hard hit rate for first time in career. Below-average power projection. 10-15 HR at projection with playing time. Catcher speed.

Rosario,Dilan | 6 | San Francisco

EXP MLB DEBUT: 2024 | H/W: 6-0 175 | FUT: Starting SS | 7E

Bats R Age 18
2019 (6) HS (PR)
Pwr ++
BAvg ++
Spd +++
Def +++

Year	Lev	Team	AB	R	H	HR	RBI	Avg	OB	Slg	OPS	bb%	ct%	Eye	SB	CS	x/h%	Iso	RC/G
2019	Rk	AZL Giants	187	22	40	5	30	214	258	364	621	6	61	0.15	9	3	40	150	3.21

Young, instinctual INF who has advanced skills. Expands strike zone and subject to high amount of Ks, but has quick stroke and goes gap to gap in present approach. Could add more power to mix with more leverage. Mostly pull pop now. Good defensive SS with sure, steady hands and body control. Good skills, but needs time to put them all together.

Rosario,Eguy | 56 | San Diego

EXP MLB DEBUT: 2021 | H/W: 5-9 150 | FUT: Utility player | 7D

Bats R Age 20
2015 FA (DR)
Pwr ++
BAvg +++
Spd +++
Def ++

Year	Lev	Team	AB	R	H	HR	RBI	Avg	OB	Slg	OPS	bb%	ct%	Eye	SB	CS	x/h%	Iso	RC/G
2017	Rk	AZL Padres 2	206	36	58	1	33	282	357	422	779	10	79	0.56	16	7	34	141	5.45
2017	A	Fort Wayne	180	15	37	0	13	206	285	278	563	10	72	0.39	17	5	30	72	2.47
2018	A+	Lake Elsinore	457	60	109	9	45	239	297	363	660	8	74	0.32	9	8	35	125	3.61
2018	AA	San Antonio	11	2	2	0	2	182	308	182	490	15	55	0.40	1	0	0	0	1.23
2019	A+	Lake Elsinore	464	60	129	7	72	278	331	412	743	7	78	0.36	21	9	31	134	4.72

Shorter, stocky INF prospect who shows ability in all areas but lacks plus tool. Hunts pitches early in counts and employs aggressive approach; OBP may suffer in the long-term. Likes the ball out front and fringy power limited to LF, but could rack up doubles. Bat-to-ball skills are solid and projects for a .275-.280 BA at his peak with some SB.

Rosario,Jeisson | 8 | San Diego

EXP MLB DEBUT: 2022 | H/W: 6-1 191 | FUT: Starting CF | 8C

Bats L Age 20
2016 FA (DR)
Pwr ++
BAvg ++++
Spd ++++
Def ++++

Year	Lev	Team	AB	R	H	HR	RBI	Avg	OB	Slg	OPS	bb%	ct%	Eye	SB	CS	x/h%	Iso	RC/G
2017	Rk	AZL Padres	187	31	56	1	24	299	405	369	774	15	81	0.92	8	6	20	70	5.53
2018	A	Fort Wayne	436	79	118	3	34	271	367	353	720	13	75	0.61	18	12	21	83	4.72
2019	A+	Lake Elsinore	430	67	104	3	35	242	369	314	683	17	73	0.76	11	4	20	72	4.37

Premium athlete with "plus CF defender" written all over him and also led A-ball hitters with 17% walk rate. Excruciatingly patient hitter who works deep into counts consistently. Smooth, level swing geared toward line drives the opposite way and has ct% foundation to tweak swing for future average power. Plus runner who projects to have SB value.

Ruiz,Esteury | 4 | San Diego

EXP MLB DEBUT: 2021 | H/W: 6-0 169 | FUT: Starting 2B | 8D

Bats R Age 21
2015 FA (DR)
Pwr +++
BAvg ++
Spd ++++
Def ++

Year	Lev	Team	AB	R	H	HR	RBI	Avg	OB	Slg	OPS	bb%	ct%	Eye	SB	CS	x/h%	Iso	RC/G
2017	Rk	AZL Royals	86	22	36	3	23	419	444	779	1224	4	77	0.20	9	0	53	360	10.94
2017	Rk	AZL Padres	120	23	36	1	16	300	349	475	824	7	72	0.26	17	6	42	175	6.07
2018	A	Fort Wayne	439	63	111	12	53	253	312	403	716	8	68	0.27	49	11	33	150	4.47
2019	A+	Lake Elsinore	339	45	81	6	36	239	293	357	650	7	70	0.26	34	11	32	118	3.48

Wiry utility prospect who plays with all-out style and possesses an intriguing combination of tools. Has whippy, plus bat speed and shows good raw power to pull-side. Inconsistent barrel path and effort in swing can lead to contact issues; also willing to expand the zone. Likes to run and is aggressive on bases. Still searching for a defensive home.

Ruiz,Keibert | 2 | Los Angeles (N)

EXP MLB DEBUT: 2020 | H/W: 6-0 200 | FUT: Starting C | 8C

Bats B Age 21
2014 FA (VZ)
Pwr ++
BAvg ++++
Spd ++
Def ++++

Year	Lev	Team	AB	R	H	HR	RBI	Avg	OB	Slg	OPS	bb%	ct%	Eye	SB	CS	x/h%	Iso	RC/G
2017	A	Great Lakes	227	34	72	2	24	317	367	423	790	7	87	0.60	0	0	26	106	5.30
2017	A+	RanchoCuca	149	24	47	6	27	315	346	497	843	4	85	0.30	0	0	30	181	5.56
2018	AA	Tulsa	377	44	101	12	47	268	315	401	716	6	91	0.79	0	1	26	133	4.35
2019	AA	Tulsa	276	33	70	4	25	254	322	330	652	9	92	1.33	0	0	19	76	3.94
2019	AAA	Oklahoma City	38	6	12	2	9	316	350	474	824	5	97	2.00	0	0	17	158	5.40

Started slow before a broken finger ended his season in August and the emergence of Will Smith clouds his future. Disciplined, contact-oriented approach at the plate and average power should keep him on track for a 2020 MLB debut. Moves well behind the plate with good framing skills, signal calling, and a quick release, but just an average arm.

Rutherford,Blake | 789 | Chicago (A)

EXP MLB DEBUT: 2021 | H/W: 6-2 210 | FUT: Reserve OF | 6C

Bats L Age 22
2016 (1) HS (CA)
Pwr ++
BAvg +++
Spd +++
Def +++

Year	Lev	Team	AB	R	H	HR	RBI	Avg	OB	Slg	OPS	bb%	ct%	Eye	SB	CS	x/h%	Iso	RC/G
2016	Rk	Pulaski	89	13	34	2	9	382	439	618	1057	9	73	0.38	0	2	38	236	9.27
2017	A	Kannapolis	122	11	26	0	5	213	289	254	543	10	83	0.62	1	0	19	41	2.43
2017	A	Charleston (Sc)	274	41	77	2	30	281	341	391	732	8	80	0.45	9	4	31	109	4.66
2018	A+	Winston-Salem	447	67	131	7	78	293	343	436	779	7	80	0.38	15	8	31	143	5.15
2019	AA	Birmingham	438	50	116	7	49	265	322	365	687	8	73	0.31	9	2	23	100	3.98

Hit-tool-first OF prospect hasn't exactly hit much despite 1st round pedigree. Line drive oriented swing plane with lots of top spin contact, depressing average power potential. Got out of sorts trying for more loft, struggled mightily. Average runner. Arm is light and likely best in LF. No carry tool exists.

Rutschman,Adley | 2 | Baltimore

EXP MLB DEBUT: 2021 | H/W: 6-2 216 | FUT: Starting C | 9C

Bats B Age 22
2019 (1) Oregon St
Pwr ++++
BAvg ++++
Spd +++
Def ++++

Year	Lev	Team	AB	R	H	HR	RBI	Avg	OB	Slg	OPS	bb%	ct%	Eye	SB	CS	x/h%	Iso	RC/G
2019	NCAA	Oregon St	185	57	76	17	58	411	582	751	1334	29	79	2.00	0	2	37	341	13.34
2019	Rk	GCL Orioles	14	3	2	1	3	143	250	357	607	13	86	1.00	1	0	50	214	3.09
2019	A-	Aberdeen	77	11	25	1	15	325	416	481	896	13	79	0.75	0	0	36	156	7.07
2019	A	Delmarva	39	5	6	2	8	154	267	333	600	13	77	0.67	0	0	50	179	2.87

Switch-hitting catching phenom made pro debut after being taken 1st overall. Offensive juggernaut. Easy, uppercut swing creates loft and hard barrel contact. Double-plus plate skills and strong plate discipline. Adept at spraying the field. Plus power should play; think 30+ HR at maturity. Sound defensively with good throwing mechanics.

Salinas,Raimfer | 8 | New York (A)

EXP MLB DEBUT: 2024 | H/W: 6-0 175 | FUT: Starting CF | 8D

Bats R Age 19
2017 FA (VZ)
Pwr +++
BAvg +++
Spd ++++
Def ++++

Year	Lev	Team	AB	R	H	HR	RBI	Avg	OB	Slg	OPS	bb%	ct%	Eye	SB	CS	x/h%	Iso	RC/G
2018	Rk	DSL Yankees	21	4	2	0	2	95	269	143	412	19	76	1.00	4	2	50	48	0.80
2018	Rk	GCL YankeesW	16	0	2	0	0	125	222	125	347	11	69	0.40	0	1	0	0	-0.81
2019	Rk	GCL YankeesW	159	25	43	3	15	270	301	415	716	4	72	0.16	11	5	35	145	4.28

Quick-twitch CF prospect flashed all-around skills in US debut. Quick wrists, strong hands propel plus bat speed and solid swing path. Expands the zone and struggles with spin. Raw above-average power in lean frame. Currently, gap-to-gap power. Plus runner and defender who should stick in CF long-term.

Sanchez,Ali | 2 | New York (N)

EXP MLB DEBUT: 2020 | H/W: 6-0 196 | FUT: Reserve C | 6C

Bats R Age 23
2013 FA (VZ)
Pwr +
BAvg +++
Spd ++
Def ++++

Year	Lev	Team	AB	R	H	HR	RBI	Avg	OB	Slg	OPS	bb%	ct%	Eye	SB	CS	x/h%	Iso	RC/G
2017	A	Columbia	182	20	42	1	15	231	282	264	546	7	86	0.50	2	3	10	33	2.34
2018	A	Columbia	193	26	50	4	22	259	296	389	684	5	88	0.43	1	1	32	130	3.91
2018	A+	St. Lucie	135	11	37	2	16	274	300	385	685	4	89	0.33	1	1	30	111	3.86
2019	AA	Binghamton	270	28	75	1	30	278	334	337	672	8	81	0.44	1	0	19	59	3.83
2019	AAA	Syracuse	56	5	10	0	3	179	246	250	496	8	80	0.45	0	1	40	71	1.75

Defensive-oriented CA with contact skills is on cusp of MLB consideration. Light hitter but solid bat-to-ball skills. More of a punch and judy hitter who inside-outs a lot of pitches for bloop hits the opposite field. Power is minimal and exclusively to the pull side. Plus receiver with a double-plus arm. Controls running game extremely well.

Sanchez,Jesus | 9 | Miami

EXP MLB DEBUT: 2020 | H/W: 6-3 230 | FUT: Starting OF | 8B

Bats L Age 22
2014 FA (DR)
Pwr ++++
BAvg +++
Spd +++
Def +++

Year	Lev	Team	AB	R	H	HR	RBI	Avg	OB	Slg	OPS	bb%	ct%	Eye	SB	CS	x/h%	Iso	RC/G
2018	A+	Charlotte	359	56	108	10	64	301	329	462	791	4	80	0.21	6	3	33	162	5.03
2018	AA	Montgomery	98	14	21	1	11	214	294	327	620	10	79	0.52	1	1	43	112	3.31
2019	AA	Montgomery	287	32	79	8	49	275	331	404	735	8	77	0.37	5	4	25	129	4.51
2019	AAA	New Orleans	65	11	16	4	9	246	338	446	784	12	77	0.60	0	0	31	200	5.17
2019	AAA	Durham	63	6	13	1	5	206	275	317	593	9	68	0.30	0	0	31	111	2.75

Strong-bodied, athletic OF acquired in mid-season trade with TAM. High-ball hitter with solid hand/eye skills. Has calmed chase rate and doesn't miss FB. Trying to tap into power, he has struggled achieving loft but eventually, the power will play plus. Average runner with no SB feel. Arm projects to RF but bat will need power for relevance.

Sanchez,Lolo | 78 | Pittsburgh

EXP MLB DEBUT: 2022 | H/W: 5-11 168 | FUT: Starting OF | 7C

Bats R Age 20
2015 FA (DR)
Pwr ++
BAvg +++
Spd ++++
Def ++++

Year	Lev	Team	AB	R	H	HR	RBI	Avg	OB	Slg	OPS	bb%	ct%	Eye	SB	CS	x/h%	Iso	RC/G
2017	Rk	GCL Pirates	204	42	58	4	20	284	351	417	768	9	91	1.11	14	7	29	132	5.20
2018	A	West Virginia	378	57	92	4	34	243	317	328	645	10	81	0.57	30	13	25	85	3.61
2019	A	Greensboro	226	43	68	4	26	301	350	451	801	7	88	0.61	20	10	29	150	5.41
2019	A+	Bradenton	163	21	32	1	9	196	276	270	546	10	81	0.58	13	5	22	74	2.42

Speed merchant who stood out in low-A before struggles in A+. Outstanding defender with plus speed and above average arm. Steals bases with good instincts. Hitting approach may be sound, but lacks strength to put jolt into ball. Can handle fastballs, but breaking balls give him fits. Tough to whiff and could be best served by keeping ball on ground.

Sanchez,Yolbert

6	Chicago (A)	EXP MLB DEBUT: 2021	H/W: 5-11 176	FUT: Starting SS	7D

Bats R Age 23
2019 FA (CU)

- Pwr ++
- BAvg +++
- Spd +++
- Def ++++

Year	Lev	Team	AB	R	H	HR	RBI	Avg	OB	Slg	OPS	bb%	ct%	Eye	SB	CS	x/h%	Iso	RC/G
2019		Did not play in U.S.																	

Defensively skilled Cuban defector signed with CHW last spring. Made debut in Dominican League despite advanced age due to visa issues. Glove carries profile. However, has plus bat-to-ball skills, a solid approach and a feel for the zone. Hard hit rate has always been concern. Power is below-average at best. Has above-average run tool.

Sanquintin,Junior

56	Cleveland	EXP MLB DEBUT: 2024	H/W: 6-0 182	FUT: Starting 3B	8E

Bats B Age 18
2018 FA (DR)

- Pwr ++++
- BAvg +++
- Spd ++
- Def ++++

Year	Lev	Team	AB	R	H	HR	RBI	Avg	OB	Slg	OPS	bb%	ct%	Eye	SB	CS	x/h%	Iso	RC/G
2019		Did not play in U.S.																	

Switch-hitting power prospect struggled in Dominican League. Hit tool less refined than other top prospects. Scouts believe it will come. Power plays in BP at both sides of the place. Should be able to bring to games in coming years. Potential plus defender at 3B with good reactions and strong arm. Below-average runner, likely to get worse.

Santana,Cristian

35	Los Angeles (N)	EXP MLB DEBUT: 2020	H/W: 6-2 175	FUT: Reserve 3B	7E

Bats R Age 23
2014 FA (DR)

- Pwr ++++
- BAvg ++
- Spd +
- Def ++

Year	Lev	Team	AB	R	H	HR	RBI	Avg	OB	Slg	OPS	bb%	ct%	Eye	SB	CS	x/h%	Iso	RC/G
2016	Rk	AZL Dodgers	172	26	44	8	24	256	277	453	730	3	73	0.11	0	1	36	198	4.20
2017	Rk	Ogden	41	18	22	5	16	537	596	1000	1596	13	85	1.00	0	0	36	463	14.74
2017	A	Great Lakes	174	18	56	5	25	322	341	460	801	3	76	0.12	0	1	25	138	5.08
2018	A+	RanchoCuca	548	75	150	24	109	274	299	447	746	4	74	0.14	2	2	31	173	4.40
2019	AA	Tulsa	399	45	120	10	57	301	318	436	754	2	78	0.11	0	0	28	135	4.47

Solid follow-up to breakout in 2018. Strong frame, quick bat, and good contact skills give him above-average power, but overly aggressive approach prevents him from realizing potential. Needs to be more selective and too often makes weak contact. Below average runner, but hands and plus arm should allow him to stick at 3B.

Santana,Luis

45	Houston	EXP MLB DEBUT: 2022	H/W: 5-8 175	FUT: Starting 2B	7E

Bats R Age 20
2016 FA (DR)

- Pwr ++
- BAvg +++
- Spd ++
- Def +++

Year	Lev	Team	AB	R	H	HR	RBI	Avg	OB	Slg	OPS	bb%	ct%	Eye	SB	CS	x/h%	Iso	RC/G
2018	Rk	Kingsport	204	34	71	4	35	348	424	471	895	12	89	1.17	8	3	24	123	6.75
2019	A-	Tri City	165	19	44	2	15	267	324	352	676	8	85	0.58	4	2	23	85	3.93
2019	AA	Corpus Christi	57	5	13	0	2	228	302	263	565	10	84	0.67	0	0	15	35	2.73

Offensive-oriented INF who uses all fields in simple, contact approach. Tough to strike out due to plate patience and ability to recognize pitches. Includes some power potential as he swings hard and lines balls to gaps. Reliable, steady defender with limited arm, but ranges well. Fun player to watch with graceful actions and aggressive nature.

Schnell,Nick

8	Tampa Bay	EXP MLB DEBUT: 2022	H/W: 6-3 180	FUT: Starting OF	8E

Bats L Age 20
2018 (1) HS (IN)

- Pwr +++
- BAvg +++
- Spd +++
- Def +++

Year	Lev	Team	AB	R	H	HR	RBI	Avg	OB	Slg	OPS	bb%	ct%	Eye	SB	CS	x/h%	Iso	RC/G
2018	Rk	GCL Rays	67	8	16	1	4	239	370	373	744	17	66	0.61	2	6	38	134	5.40
2019	Rk	GCL Rays	21	4	4	0	1	190	190	381	571	0	57	0.00	0	0	50	190	3.01
2019	Rk	Princeton	147	28	42	5	27	286	364	503	867	11	65	0.35	5	2	45	218	7.06
2019	A	Bowling Green	55	7	13	0	3	236	263	327	590	4	56	0.08	0	1	31	91	3.13

Struggled with a knee injury early, showed promise late. Average-to-above-average toolshed across the board. Loose wrists generates plus swing speed. Swing is uneven and prone to swing-and-miss; solid knowledge of zone. Above-average power in frame may play up with refined swing. Leg injuries have sapped plus speed.

Schunk,Aaron

5	Colorado	EXP MLB DEBUT: 2022	H/W: 6-2 205	FUT: Starting 3B	7C

Bats R Age 22
2019 (2) Georgia

- Pwr +++
- BAvg +++
- Spd ++
- Def +++

Year	Lev	Team	AB	R	H	HR	RBI	Avg	OB	Slg	OPS	bb%	ct%	Eye	SB	CS	x/h%	Iso	RC/G
2019	NCAA	Georgia	230	49	78	15	58	339	377	604	981	6	87	0.48	3	1	37	265	7.14
2019	A-	Boise	173	31	53	6	23	306	358	503	861	7	86	0.56	4	1	38	197	6.05

Two-way collegiate prospect taken in 2nd round and spent all of pro debut at 3B. Provides defensive value at hot corner with plus arm; range should improve with full-time reps. Owns above-average raw power that should play consistently with solid contact skills. Still has some physical projection remaining to add strength. Below-average speed.

Scott,Connor

8	Miami	EXP MLB DEBUT: 2022	H/W: 6-4 180	FUT: Starting CF	8D

Bats L Age 20
2018 (1) HS (FL)

- Pwr +++
- BAvg ++
- Spd ++++
- Def ++++

Year	Lev	Team	AB	R	H	HR	RBI	Avg	OB	Slg	OPS	bb%	ct%	Eye	SB	CS	x/h%	Iso	RC/G
2018	Rk	GCL Marlins	103	15	23	0	8	223	316	311	627	12	72	0.48	8	5	22	87	3.47
2018	A	Greensboro	76	4	16	1	5	211	302	276	579	12	64	0.37	1	3	19	66	2.58
2019	A	Clinton	378	56	95	4	36	251	308	368	676	8	76	0.34	21	9	34	116	3.89
2019	A+	Jupiter	98	12	23	1	5	235	312	327	638	10	73	0.42	2	1	26	92	3.46

Lean, athletic 2018 1st rounder has struggled with quality contact since debut. Tall frame with a projectable body. Swing mechanics are average but the swing speed is below average, which tightens his margin of error. Above-average power potential in frame, but will need to find barrels to reach it. Plus runner with plus potential in CF. SB threat.

Seigler,Anthony

2	New York (A)	EXP MLB DEBUT: 2023	H/W: 6-0 200	FUT: Starting C	8D

Bats B Age 20
2018 (1) HS (GA)

- Pwr +++
- BAvg +++
- Spd +++
- Def ++++

Year	Lev	Team	AB	R	H	HR	RBI	Avg	OB	Slg	OPS	bb%	ct%	Eye	SB	CS	x/h%	Iso	RC/G
2018	Rk	Pulaski	43	4	9	0	5	209	333	233	566	16	88	1.60	0	0	11	23	3.25
2018	Rk	GCL YankeesW	36	7	12	1	4	333	429	472	901	14	81	0.86	0	0	25	139	6.99
2019	A	Charleston (Sc)	97	10	17	0	6	175	316	206	522	17	71	0.71	1	0	18	31	2.05

Athletic, switch-hitting catcher struggled in full-season debut. Swing is short and compact. Patient to a fault, could be more aggressive earlier in counts. Good plate skills. Barrel rate will need to improve to reach average power. A solid defender, should be able to defend run game with plus pop times.

Severino,Yunior

4	Minnesota	EXP MLB DEBUT: 2023	H/W: 6-1 189	FUT: Starting MIF	7E

Bats B Age 20
2016 FA (DR)

- Pwr +++
- BAvg +++
- Spd ++
- Def +++

Year	Lev	Team	AB	R	H	HR	RBI	Avg	OB	Slg	OPS	bb%	ct%	Eye	SB	CS	x/h%	Iso	RC/G
2017	Rk	GCL Braves	189	27	54	3	27	286	341	444	786	8	68	0.26	0	1	41	159	5.64
2018	Rk	Elizabethton	198	32	52	8	28	263	321	424	745	8	74	0.33	0	1	31	162	4.62
2019	Rk	GCL Twins	22	2	5	1	2	227	227	500	727	0	73	0.00	0	0	60	273	4.24
2019	A	Cedar Rapids	78	7	19	0	8	244	306	333	639	8	65	0.26	0	0	37	90	3.60

Switch-hitting MIF struggled and missed time with broken thumb in full-season debut. LH swing ahead of RH swing. Hit tool from either side of plate struggles with swing plane. Surprising power in frame. Potential average power at maturity. 2B or 3B likely long term due to lacking range for SS. Below-average runner.

Shaw,Chris

37	San Francisco	EXP MLB DEBUT: 2018	H/W: 6-3 226	FUT: Starting 1B	7C

Bats L Age 26
2015 (1) Boston College

- Pwr ++++
- BAvg ++
- Spd +
- Def ++

Year	Lev	Team	AB	R	H	HR	RBI	Avg	OB	Slg	OPS	bb%	ct%	Eye	SB	CS	x/h%	Iso	RC/G
2018	AAA	Sacramento	394	55	102	24	65	259	296	505	801	5	63	0.15	0	0	46	246	5.73
2018	MLB	SF Giants	54	2	10	1	7	185	279	278	556	11	57	0.30	1	0	30	93	2.33
2019	AA	Richmond	160	25	46	7	24	288	363	500	863	11	79	0.58	2	2	39	213	6.28
2019	AAA	Sacramento	282	52	84	21	70	298	344	592	937	7	72	0.26	0	0	48	294	7.12
2019	MLB	SF Giants	18	0	1	0	0	56	150	56	206	10	56	0.25	0	0	0	0	-3.89

Hulking hitter who continues to bash, but not in majors. Led org in HR and RBI while setting career bests. Spent most of last 3 years in AAA. Too much swing and miss in aggressive approach, but crushes balls when contact made. Offers desirable power to all fields and plus arm strength, but fringy defender with little foot speed.

Sheets,Gavin

3	Chicago (A)	EXP MLB DEBUT: 2020	H/W: 6-4 230	FUT: Starting 1B	7D

Bats L Age 23
2017 (2) Wake Forest

- Pwr +++
- BAvg +++
- Spd +
- Def +++

Year	Lev	Team	AB	R	H	HR	RBI	Avg	OB	Slg	OPS	bb%	ct%	Eye	SB	CS	x/h%	Iso	RC/G
2017	NCAA	Wake Forest	240	57	76	21	84	317	427	629	1056	16	85	1.24	1	0	42	313	8.65
2017	Rk	AZL White Sox	12	3	6	1	3	500	600	917	1517	20	100		0	0	50	417	13.90
2017	A	Kannapolis	192	16	51	3	25	266	335	365	699	9	82	0.59	0	0	25	99	4.25
2018	A+	Winston-Salem	437	58	128	6	61	293	368	407	775	11	81	0.64	1	0	28	114	5.29
2019	AA	Birmingham	464	56	124	16	83	267	344	414	757	10	79	0.55	3	1	28	147	4.91

Contact-oriented 1B/DH only prospect showed flashes of MLB talent in Double-A. Swing started incorporating lower half more in '19. Still, doesn't get enough strength and bat speed from lower half, depressing hard hit rate. Has solid plate discipline. Power in frame is big in BP but not so much in game. Mostly pull-dominant in game. Slow runner.

Shewmake,Braden

6 | **Atlanta** | EXP MLB DEBUT: 2021 | H/W: 6-4 190 | FUT: Starting MIF | **7B**

Bats L Age 22
2019 (1) Texas A&M
Pwr ++
BAvg +++
Spd +++
Def +++

Year	Lev	Team	AB	R	H	HR	RBI	Avg	OB	Slg	OPS	bb%	ct%	Eye	SB	CS	x/h%	Iso	RC/G
2019	NCAA	Texas A&M	249	45	78	6	47	313	376	474	850	9	89	0.93	9	3	31	161	6.08
2019	A	Rome	201	37	64	3	39	318	383	473	856	9	86	0.72	11	3	36	154	6.23
2019	AA	Mississippi	46	7	10	0	1	217	280	217	497	8	76	0.36	2	0	0	0	1.47

Tall, lanky first-round pick brought high ct% and fundamental play to full-season in debut. Solid approach with spray skills. Flat swing trajectory, generates top heavy line drives. Controls barrel well and has solid gap-to-gap tendencies. Below-average physical strength. HR totals could play up with hit tool. Double-digit SB ability.

Short,Zack

6 | **Chicago (N)** | EXP MLB DEBUT: 2020 | H/W: 5-10 180 | FUT: Utility player | **7A**

Bats R Age 24
2016 (17) Sacred Heart
Pwr +++
BAvg ++
Spd +++
Def +++

Year	Lev	Team	AB	R	H	HR	RBI	Avg	OB	Slg	OPS	bb%	ct%	Eye	SB	CS	x/h%	Iso	RC/G
2017	A+	Myrtle Beach	232	34	61	6	21	263	371	414	785	15	78	0.80	3	5	33	151	5.58
2018	AA	Tennessee	436	68	99	17	59	227	349	417	767	16	69	0.60	8	3	47	190	5.43
2019	Rk	AZL Cubs	16	5	6	0	3	375	583	500	1083	33	75	2.00	0	0	33	125	11.07
2019	AA	Tennessee	64	7	16	0	5	250	342	359	702	12	72	0.50	0	1	31	109	4.58
2019	AAA	Iowa	133	22	28	6	17	211	318	414	732	14	62	0.42	2	1	54	203	5.02

Athletic, utility MIF doesn't stand out for his raw tools, but gets the most out of his ability. Employs uber-patient approach and owns stellar 15% bb% in upper minors. Can get pull happy, but generates tons of fly balls and has surprising bat speed for his size. Above-average runner whose high OBP could lead to sneaky SB value.

Siani,Mike

8 | **Cincinnati** | EXP MLB DEBUT: 2022 | H/W: 6-1 188 | FUT: Starting CF | **8D**

Bats L Age 20
2018 (4) HS (PA)
Pwr +++
BAvg +++
Spd ++++
Def ++++

Year	Lev	Team	AB	R	H	HR	RBI	Avg	OB	Slg	OPS	bb%	ct%	Eye	SB	CS	x/h%	Iso	RC/G
2018	Rk	Greeneville	184	24	53	2	13	288	345	386	731	8	81	0.46	6	4	21	98	4.58
2019	A	Dayton	466	75	118	6	39	253	320	339	659	9	77	0.42	45	15	19	86	3.66

Athletic, LHH prospect struggled with swing length in full-season debut. Medium frame though should grow into it. Known more for defensive skill and run tool than offensive prowess. Despite long swing, does good job making contact, but struggles to find the barrel. Average power potential; hit tool needs refinement. 75% SB success rate.

Siani,Sammy

78 | **Pittsburgh** | EXP MLB DEBUT: 2023 | H/W: 6-0 195 | FUT: Starting OF | **8D**

Bats L Age 19
2019 (1) HS (PA)
Pwr ++
BAvg +++
Spd +++
Def +++

Year	Lev	Team	AB	R	H	HR	RBI	Avg	OB	Slg	OPS	bb%	ct%	Eye	SB	CS	x/h%	Iso	RC/G
2019	Rk	GCL Pirates	133	21	32	0	9	241	365	308	673	16	69	0.63	5	0	19	68	4.28

Smallish OF with solid overall tools and chance to patrol CF in big leagues. Has simple, compact stroke to make acceptable contact, though can lengthen swing at times. Could develop at least average power as he learns to read pitches better and tweak swing mechanics. Has the plate patience to draw walks and hits hard line drives to gaps.

Simmons,Kendall

45 | **Philadelphia** | EXP MLB DEBUT: 2023 | H/W: 6-2 180 | FUT: Starting 2B | **8D**

Bats R Age 19
2018 (6) HS (GA)
Pwr ++++
BAvg ++
Spd +++
Def +++

Year	Lev	Team	AB	R	H	HR	RBI	Avg	OB	Slg	OPS	bb%	ct%	Eye	SB	CS	x/h%	Iso	RC/G
2018	Rk	GCL Phillies	95	21	22	3	11	232	298	400	698	9	68	0.30	2	4	45	168	4.22
2019	A-	Williamsport	171	31	40	12	34	234	314	520	835	10	68	0.37	5	6	55	287	6.09

An athletic and twitchy infielder with a strong lower half and a leveraged RH swing. It resulted in easy power; finished tied for 2d in HR in NYPL. Questions remain on his hit tool; was plenty patient but also struck out a lot. Though he likely doesn't have enough range for SS, his glove is solid and could heading towards a multi-position future.

Siri,Jose

8 | **Cincinnati** | EXP MLB DEBUT: 2020 | H/W: 6-2 175 | FUT: Starting OF | **7C**

Bats R Age 24
2012 FA (DR)
Pwr +++
BAvg ++
Spd ++++
Def ++++

Year	Lev	Team	AB	R	H	HR	RBI	Avg	OB	Slg	OPS	bb%	ct%	Eye	SB	CS	x/h%	Iso	RC/G
2017	A	Dayton	498	92	146	24	76	293	337	530	867	6	74	0.25	46	12	40	237	6.24
2018	A+	Daytona	119	15	31	1	9	261	285	395	680	3	73	0.13	9	1	39	134	3.80
2018	AA	Pensacola	253	42	58	12	34	229	296	474	770	9	64	0.26	14	5	50	245	5.48
2019	AA	Chattanooga	366	46	92	11	50	251	313	388	701	8	66	0.26	21	6	29	137	4.29
2019	AAA	Louisville	102	10	19	0	3	186	252	245	497	8	62	0.23	5	2	26	59	1.38

Five-tool prospect can't seem to put them all to work at same time. Athletic, muscular frame; calmed aggressiveness as season wore on. Struggled with consistent bat path and extending early, causing contact to occur late in pitch progression. Plus raw power doesn't verify because of unpredictability of swing. Double-plus runner, but with no feel for SB.

Smith,Canaan

7 | **New York (A)** | EXP MLB DEBUT: 2022 | H/W: 6-0 215 | FUT: Starting OF | **7C**

Bats L Age 20
2017 (4) HS (TX)
Pwr +++
BAvg +++
Spd +++
Def ++

Year	Lev	Team	AB	R	H	HR	RBI	Avg	OB	Slg	OPS	bb%	ct%	Eye	SB	CS	x/h%	Iso	RC/G
2017	Rk	GCL Yankees	187	29	54	5	28	289	429	422	852	20	76	1.05	5	3	28	134	6.71
2018	A-	Staten Island	152	13	29	3	16	191	281	316	596	11	66	0.37	0	0	41	125	2.87
2019	A	Charleston (Sc)	449	67	138	11	74	307	405	465	871	14	76	0.69	16	4	33	158	6.75

Professional hitter who doesn't look refined but stats and sound off his bat say differently. Short, compact swing finds barrel despite uneven swing path and flailing away from pitches. Patient hitter who doesn't offer at many pitches out of zone. Average power projection if he can get under the ball more. Average runner.

Smith,Josh

6 | **New York (A)** | EXP MLB DEBUT: 2022 | H/W: 5-10 172 | FUT: Starting 2B | **7C**

Bats L Age 22
2019 (2) Louisiana St
Pwr ++
BAvg +++
Spd +++
Def +++

Year	Lev	Team	AB	R	H	HR	RBI	Avg	OB	Slg	OPS	bb%	ct%	Eye	SB	CS	x/h%	Iso	RC/G
2019	A-	Staten Island	111	17	36	3	15	324	449	477	926	18	85	1.47	6	3	28	153	7.56

Patient, gap hitting SS made pro debut after successful SEC season. Short, compact swing with a consistent swing path, great bat-to-ball skills, and gap power. However, hit tool may push power tool upward. Solid defensive actions at SS but lacking arm. Likely a 2B or UT. An average runner.

Smith,Kevin

6 | **Toronto** | EXP MLB DEBUT: 2020 | H/W: 5-11 188 | FUT: Starting SS | **8E**

Bats R Age 23
2017 (4) Maryland
Pwr +++
BAvg ++
Spd +++
Def +++

Year	Lev	Team	AB	R	H	HR	RBI	Avg	OB	Slg	OPS	bb%	ct%	Eye	SB	CS	x/h%	Iso	RC/G
2017	NCAA	Maryland	194	38	52	13	48	268	317	552	869	7	75	0.29	4	0	50	284	6.14
2017	Rk	Bluefield	262	43	71	8	43	271	313	466	779	6	73	0.23	9	0	48	195	5.15
2018	A	Lansing	183	36	65	7	44	355	410	639	1049	9	82	0.52	12	1	52	284	8.55
2018	A+	Dunedin	340	57	93	18	49	274	320	468	787	6	74	0.26	17	5	30	194	5.04
2019	AA	New Hampshire	430	49	90	19	61	209	259	402	662	6	65	0.19	11	6	48	193	3.62

Versatile INF who took major step back after exciting 2018. K rate drastically rose while walk rate fell dramatically. As expected, power output and BA dropped. Exhibits fast bat with plus raw power and can drive ball to all fields. Sound defender with strong arm and quickness at SS. Poor AFL campaign didn't ease concerns about 2018 being fluke.

Solak,Nick

457 | **Texas** | EXP MLB DEBUT: 2019 | H/W: 5-11 190 | FUT: Starting OF | **7B**

Bats R Age 25
2016 (2) Louisville
Pwr +++
BAvg +++
Spd ++
Def +++

Year	Lev	Team	AB	R	H	HR	RBI	Avg	OB	Slg	OPS	bb%	ct%	Eye	SB	CS	x/h%	Iso	RC/G
2017	AA	Trenton	119	16	34	2	9	286	341	429	770	8	80	0.42	1	1	35	143	5.07
2018	AA	Montgomery	478	91	135	19	76	282	372	450	822	12	77	0.61	21	6	29	167	5.85
2019	AAA	Nashville	118	23	41	10	27	347	379	653	1032	5	79	0.24	2	0	39	305	7.82
2019	AAA	Durham	301	56	80	17	47	266	350	485	835	11	73	0.49	3	2	39	219	5.97
2019	MLB	Texas	116	19	34	5	17	293	374	491	865	11	75	0.52	2	0	35	198	6.43

Multi-positioner who has grown into power the past several seasons, tanking 32 between AAA/majors in 2019. Always been a hitter; a compact swing and decent ct% rates, and though SB declined, he's a safe HR and BA bet. Where to play him will be the question, he's below average at 2B; OF is likely his most frequent destination.

Sosa,Edmundo

6 | **St. Louis** | EXP MLB DEBUT: 2018 | H/W: 5-11 170 | FUT: Utility player | **6B**

Bats R Age 24
2012 FA (PN)
Pwr ++
BAvg +++
Spd +++
Def +++

Year	Lev	Team	AB	R	H	HR	RBI	Avg	OB	Slg	OPS	bb%	ct%	Eye	SB	CS	x/h%	Iso	RC/G
2018	AA	Springfield	261	34	72	7	32	276	300	429	729	3	80	0.17	1	2	35	153	4.23
2018	AAA	Memphis	191	31	50	5	27	262	309	408	717	6	78	0.31	5	2	36	147	4.26
2018	MLB	St. Louis	2	1	0	0	0	0	333	0	333	33	50	1.00	0	0		0	-2.91
2019	AAA	Memphis	453	70	132	17	62	291	317	466	783	4	79	0.18	2	3	30	174	4.85
2019	MLB	St. Louis	8	2	2	0	0	250	333	250	583	11	75	0.50	1	0	0	0	2.72

Defensive-minded player slugged a career-high 17 HR in second full season at AAA. Slick defender has range, soft hands, and enough arm strength for SS, 2B, and 3B. Quick hands and a contact oriented approach allows him to put the ball into play, but lack of selectivity means few base on balls.

Sosa,Lenyn — 6 — Chicago (A)

EXP MLB DEBUT: 2022 | H/W: 6-0 180 | FUT: Reserve IF | **6C**

Bats R Age 20 — 2016 FA (VZ)

Rating		Year	Lev	Team	AB	R	H	HR	RBI	Avg	OB	Slg	OPS	bb%	ct%	Eye	SB	CS	x/h%	Iso	RC/G
Pwr	+++																				
BAvg	+++	2017	Rk	AZL White Sox	159	19	43	2	23	270	329	358	688	8	85	0.58	3	4	19	88	4.09
Spd	++	2018	Rk	Great Falls	276	44	81	4	35	293	311	406	717	2	87	0.19	2	2	25	112	4.10
Def	++	2019	A	Kannapolis	501	72	126	7	51	251	290	371	661	5	80	0.26	6	6	35	120	3.56

Solid, contact-oriented hitter played as a 19-year-old season at full-season Single-A. Ultra-aggressive hitter coming in, calmed down some of those tendencies. Gap-to-gap doubles power. Wears out LHP especially. Average raw power in frame and swing. Below average runner. Passable defender at maturity.

Soto,Livan — 46 — Los Angeles (A)

EXP MLB DEBUT: 2022 | H/W: 6-0 160 | FUT: Utility player | **7D**

Bats L Age 19 — 2016 FA (VZ)

Rating		Year	Lev	Team	AB	R	H	HR	RBI	Avg	OB	Slg	OPS	bb%	ct%	Eye	SB	CS	x/h%	Iso	RC/G
Pwr	+	2017	Rk	GCL Braves	173	24	39	0	14	225	330	254	584	14	85	1.04	7	3	13	29	3.20
BAvg	+++	2018	Rk	Orem	172	31	50	0	11	291	378	349	726	12	86	1.00	9	3	20	58	4.89
Spd	+++	2019	Rk	AZL Angels	28	4	6	0	1	214	241	286	527	3	86	0.25	0	2	33	71	2.06
Def	+++	2019	A	Burlington	245	24	54	1	20	220	310	253	564	12	84	0.80	6	2	11	33	2.76

Instinctual SS with some feel to hit and good athletic attributes. Loose, level stroke allows for all-fields approach and demonstrates exceptional plate discipline to get into favorable counts. Very slight of frame and HR will be capped at single digits. Above-average runner. Can pick it at short but has internal clock and feel to play anywhere in INF.

Steer,Spencer — 5 — Minnesota

EXP MLB DEBUT: 2022 | H/W: 5-11 185 | FUT: Utility player | **7D**

Bats R Age 22 — 2019 (3) Oregon

Rating		Year	Lev	Team	AB	R	H	HR	RBI	Avg	OB	Slg	OPS	bb%	ct%	Eye	SB	CS	x/h%	Iso	RC/G
Pwr	++																				
BAvg	+++	2019	NCAA	Oregon	215	40	75	6	57	349	429	502	931	12	85	0.91	6	2	27	153	7.20
Spd	+++	2019	Rk	Elizabethton	77	14	25	2	13	325	435	506	941	16	94	3.00	0	1	36	182	7.67
Def	+++	2019	A	Cedar Rapids	173	26	45	2	20	260	333	387	721	10	84	0.68	5	1	36	127	4.64

Advanced college bat handled lower minor pitching in pro debut. Short, compact swing with strong bat-to-ball skills. Has solid zone discipline and sprays the ball well. Below-average power potential. Likely 10-15 HR at projection. Above-average runner with SB ability. Athleticism to play 3 IF positions & possibly OF.

Stephen,Josh — 7 — Philadelphia

EXP MLB DEBUT: 2022 | H/W: 6-0 185 | FUT: Reserve OF | **7D**

Bats L Age 22 — 2016 (11) HS (CA)

Rating		Year	Lev	Team	AB	R	H	HR	RBI	Avg	OB	Slg	OPS	bb%	ct%	Eye	SB	CS	x/h%	Iso	RC/G
Pwr	+++	2016	Rk	GCL Phillies	162	21	41	2	26	253	328	370	698	10	76	0.46	6	6	29	117	4.28
BAvg	++	2017	A-	Williamsport	239	23	59	2	28	247	283	364	647	5	79	0.24	4	3	32	117	3.41
Spd	++	2018	A	Lakewood	314	28	76	4	35	242	285	347	632	6	77	0.27	4	1	30	105	3.20
Def	+	2019	AA	Reading	362	48	98	12	47	271	342	483	825	10	70	0.35	7	6	48	213	6.13

Bat-first OF underwent surprising emergence after skipping High-A. Newfound power in hitter-friendly Reading will come under scrutiny, but his simple LH stroke and ability to use opposite field was always a fine starting point. Defense in LF is rough so he'll have to hit to gain playing time.

Stephenson,Tyler — 2 — Cincinnati

EXP MLB DEBUT: 2020 | H/W: 6-4 225 | FUT: Starting C | **8D**

Bats R Age 23 — 2015 (1) HS (GA)

Rating		Year	Lev	Team	AB	R	H	HR	RBI	Avg	OB	Slg	OPS	bb%	ct%	Eye	SB	CS	x/h%	Iso	RC/G
		2016	Rk	AZL Reds	20	4	5	1	2	250	318	450	768	9	65	0.29	0	0	40	200	5.27
Pwr	+++	2016	A	Dayton	139	17	30	3	16	216	278	324	602	8	68	0.27	0	0	27	108	2.79
BAvg	+++	2017	A	Dayton	295	39	82	6	50	278	372	414	785	13	80	0.76	2	1	34	136	5.52
Spd	+	2018	A+	Daytona	388	60	97	11	59	250	328	392	720	10	75	0.46	1	0	33	142	4.48
Def	++	2019	AA	Chattanooga	312	47	89	6	44	285	361	410	771	11	81	0.62	0	0	29	125	5.20

Big-bodied, contact-oriented CA had best offensive season at Double-A. Maxed out physically, his lack of mobility limits defensive skill. Patient hitter with solid up-the-middle approach. There's significant power in frame but swing trajectory doesn't always allow for it to play. Could end up a 15-20 HR guy at peak.

Stevenson,Cal — 78 — Houston

EXP MLB DEBUT: 2021 | H/W: 5-10 175 | FUT: Reserve OF | **6B**

Bats L Age 23 — 2018 (10) Arizona

Rating		Year	Lev	Team	AB	R	H	HR	RBI	Avg	OB	Slg	OPS	bb%	ct%	Eye	SB	CS	x/h%	Iso	RC/G
		2018	NCAA	Arizona	174	47	51	1	26	293	411	397	808	17	91	2.19	8	5	20	103	6.24
Pwr	+	2018	Rk	GCL Blue Jays	19	12	9	0	2	474	667	579	1246	37	84	3.67	1	0	22	105	13.23
BAvg	++++	2018	Rk	Bluefield	195	61	70	2	29	359	496	518	1014	21	89	2.52	20	1	30	159	8.96
Spd	+++	2019	A+	Fayetteville	81	18	20	0	9	247	390	346	736	19	84	1.46	2	3	35	99	5.41
Def	+++	2019	A+	Dunedin	336	59	100	5	50	298	389	393	781	13	85	0.96	11	6	18	95	5.48

Steady, breakout prospect who finished 2nd in FSL in BA and OBP. More BB than K in consistent year by controlling strike zone and recognizing pitches. Makes easy contact with compact stroke, though offers well below average power. XBH mostly due to speed and instincts. Can be sound defender who gets good jumps and takes efficient routes to ball.

Stott,Bryson — 6 — Philadelphia

EXP MLB DEBUT: 2021 | H/W: 6-3 200 | FUT: Starting 2B | **8C**

Bats L Age 22 — 2019 (1) UNLV

Rating		Year	Lev	Team	AB	R	H	HR	RBI	Avg	OB	Slg	OPS	bb%	ct%	Eye	SB	CS	x/h%	Iso	RC/G
Pwr	+++																				
BAvg	+++																				
4.30 Spd	++	2019	Rk	GCL Phillies	9	3	6	1	3	667	727	1333	2061	18	100		0	0	50	667	19.43
Def	+++	2019	A-	Williamsport	157	27	43	5	24	274	363	446	809	12	75	0.56	5	3	35	172	5.78

Physically developed collegian with a strong core and moderate hit/power ability. Gritty type who plays game aggressively with corresponding positives/negatives. Overswings at times, but has good pitch recognition and plate coverage, and willing to use the whole field. Only an average runner, his body type points more towards a future at 2B/3B.

Stowers,Josh — 89 — New York (A)

EXP MLB DEBUT: 2023 | H/W: 6-0 200 | FUT: Starting OF | **7D**

Bats R Age 23 — 2018 (2) Louisville

Rating		Year	Lev	Team	AB	R	H	HR	RBI	Avg	OB	Slg	OPS	bb%	ct%	Eye	SB	CS	x/h%	Iso	RC/G
Pwr	+++																				
BAvg	++	2018	NCAA	Louisville	220	72	74	9	60	336	463	559	1022	19	83	1.41	36	0	36	223	8.78
Spd	+++	2018	A-	Everett	200	32	52	5	28	260	376	410	786	16	72	0.65	20	4	38	150	5.72
Def	+++	2019	A	Charleston (Sc)	385	61	105	7	40	273	376	400	776	14	68	0.52	35	16	31	127	5.67

Athletic OF brings solid but unspectacular tool shed to table. Has solid patience at plate and a quick bat. Struggles with pitch selection and getting beat by velocity in. There's average power in frame if he can get out in front of the ball. Aggressive with above-average run tool on bases. Stole 35 bases in 51 attempts.

Stowers,Kyle — 79 — Baltimore

EXP MLB DEBUT: 2022 | H/W: 6-3 200 | FUT: Starting OF | **7D**

Bats L Age 22 — 2019 (2) Stanford

Rating		Year	Lev	Team	AB	R	H	HR	RBI	Avg	OB	Slg	OPS	bb%	ct%	Eye	SB	CS	x/h%	Iso	RC/G
Pwr	+++																				
BAvg	++																				
Spd	++																				
Def	+++	2019	A-	Aberdeen	204	19	44	6	23	216	286	377	663	9	74	0.38	5	1	45	162	3.68

Power-hitting OF prospect struggled in pro debut. Generates solid bat speed but swing has length to it. Aggressive approach leads to low ct%. Raw plus power plays to all fields. Hit tool may limit game impact. Corner OF prospect may be limited to LF or even 1B due to poor throwing arm.

Strumpf,Chase — 4 — Chicago (N)

EXP MLB DEBUT: 2022 | H/W: 6-1 191 | FUT: Utility player | **7C**

Bats R Age 22 — 2019 (2) UCLA

Rating		Year	Lev	Team	AB	R	H	HR	RBI	Avg	OB	Slg	OPS	bb%	ct%	Eye	SB	CS	x/h%	Iso	RC/G
Pwr	++																				
BAvg	+++	2019	Rk	AZL Cubs 2	22	5	4	0	1	182	379	318	697	24	68	1.00	0	0	75	136	4.95
Spd	+++	2019	A-	Eugene	89	17	26	2	14	292	394	449	844	14	69	0.54	2	0	38	157	6.66
Def	+++	2019	A	South Bend	24	3	3	1	2	125	160	292	452	4	71	0.14	0	0	67	167	0.49

Well-rounded but not elite 2B who was productive three-year starter at UCLA. Makes above-average contact from a compact, simple stroke that projects for high-volume doubles and line drives. Fringe power, limited to pull-side. Keen eye at plate enables him to reach base at a high clip. Average athleticism and arm; could be 2B or UTIL-bound.

Stubbs,Garrett — 2 — Houston

EXP MLB DEBUT: 2019 | H/W: 5-10 175 | FUT: Starting C | **7D**

Bats L Age 26 — 2015 (8) USC

Rating		Year	Lev	Team	AB	R	H	HR	RBI	Avg	OB	Slg	OPS	bb%	ct%	Eye	SB	CS	x/h%	Iso	RC/G
		2017	AA	Corpus Christi	263	36	62	4	25	236	319	331	649	11	83	0.73	8	0	27	95	3.74
Pwr	++	2017	AAA	Fresno	77	11	17	0	12	221	318	286	604	13	81	0.73	3	0	29	65	3.29
BAvg	+++	2018	AAA	Fresno	297	60	92	4	38	310	383	455	837	11	82	0.66	6	0	32	145	6.09
Spd	+++	2019	AAA	Round Rock	204	33	49	7	23	240	320	397	717	11	81	0.63	12	2	37	157	4.44
Def	+++	2019	MLB	Houston	35	8	7	0	2	200	282	286	568	10	80	0.57	1	0	43	86	2.75

Short, versatile CA who bucks typical profile. Offers athleticism and speed for position while showcasing gun for an arm. High CS% behind plate and is consistent, textbook receiver. Can play 2B and OF as needed due to smarts and arm. Very limited power in tool box, but is decent hitter for BA. Knows strike zone and doesn't swing at bad pitches.

Swaggerty,Travis — 8 — Pittsburgh

EXP MLB DEBUT: 2021 | H/W: 5-11 180 | FUT: Starting CF | 8C

Bats L Age 22
2018 (1) South Alabama

- Pwr +++
- BAvg +++
- Spd ++++
- Def ++++

Year	Lev	Team	AB	R	H	HR	RBI	Avg	OB	Slg	OPS	bb%	ct%	Eye	SB	CS	x/h%	Iso	RC/G
2018	NCAA	South Alabama	213	57	63	13	38	296	438	526	964	20	82	1.42	9	5	37	230	7.94
2018	A-	West Virginia	139	22	40	4	15	288	357	453	810	10	71	0.38	9	3	35	165	5.80
2018	A	West Virginia	62	6	8	1	5	129	217	226	443	10	71	0.39	0	0	38	97	0.66
2019	A+	Bradenton	457	79	121	9	40	265	346	381	727	11	75	0.49	23	8	26	116	4.65

All-around OF with no obvious weakness in game. Tends to fly under radar as he doesn't own any overwhelming tool. Uses short stroke to make contact and has bat speed and patience to drive good pitches. Power starting to develop and has chance to post high BA and OBP while flashing average pop. Runs bases very well and covers a lot of ground in CF.

Taveras,Leody — 89 — Texas

EXP MLB DEBUT: 2021 | H/W: 6-1 171 | FUT: Starting CF | 9D

Bats B Age 21
2015 FA (DR)

- Pwr +++
- BAvg +++
- 4.26 Spd ++++
- Def ++++

Year	Lev	Team	AB	R	H	HR	RBI	Avg	OB	Slg	OPS	bb%	ct%	Eye	SB	CS	x/h%	Iso	RC/G
2016	A-	Spokane	123	14	28	0	9	228	275	293	567	6	79	0.31	3	1	25	65	2.47
2017	A	Hickory	522	73	130	8	50	249	311	360	671	8	82	0.51	20	6	27	111	3.87
2018	A+	Down East	521	65	128	5	48	246	313	332	645	9	82	0.53	19	11	22	86	3.58
2019	A+	Down East	255	44	75	2	25	294	371	376	747	11	76	0.50	21	5	17	82	4.96
2019	AA	Frisco	264	32	70	3	31	265	324	375	699	8	77	0.38	11	8	27	110	4.19

Bat finally showed some life in 1H in repeat of High-A, but still a surprising lack of in-game power given a bevy of pro reps. Top-shelf athleticism, bat speed and hard contact potentially can pair with excellent defense and plate patience/OBP. Showed off his wheels in 2019, too. It's still 5-tool impact potential for young-for-his-level player.

Taylor,Samad — 4 — Toronto

EXP MLB DEBUT: 2021 | H/W: 5-10 160 | FUT: Starting 2B | 7D

Bats R Age 21
2016 (10) HS (CA)

- Pwr ++
- BAvg ++
- Spd ++++
- Def +++

Year	Lev	Team	AB	R	H	HR	RBI	Avg	OB	Slg	OPS	bb%	ct%	Eye	SB	CS	x/h%	Iso	RC/G
2017	Rk	Bluefield	16	1	4	0	3	250	368	250	618	16	63	0.50	1	0	0	0	3.38
2017	A-	Vancouver	68	7	20	2	8	294	342	426	769	7	74	0.28	2	2	25	132	4.94
2017	A-	MahoningVal	120	18	36	4	19	300	328	467	795	4	80	0.21	4	2	31	167	5.03
2018	A	Lansing	460	67	105	9	53	228	313	387	700	11	78	0.58	44	16	46	159	4.37
2019	A+	Dunedin	319	48	69	7	38	216	321	364	684	13	66	0.46	26	10	43	147	4.28

Short, wiry 2B with unique punch-speed combo for frame. Brings patient approach to plate and gets on base consistently. Should hit for moderate BA as he can use all fields with quick bat. BA has been limited due to poor pitch recognition and inability to hit breaking balls. Acceptable defensive tools that play at 2B. Speed is easy plus.

Taylor,Tyrone — 89 — Milwaukee

EXP MLB DEBUT: 2019 | H/W: 6-0 185 | FUT: Starting OF | 7B

Bats R Age 26
2012 (2) HS (CA)

- Pwr +++
- BAvg +++
- Spd +++
- Def +++

Year	Lev	Team	AB	R	H	HR	RBI	Avg	OB	Slg	OPS	bb%	ct%	Eye	SB	CS	x/h%	Iso	RC/G
2017	AA	Biloxi	85	15	21	1	6	247	312	376	688	9	79	0.44	2	1	38	129	4.12
2018	AAA	Col Springs	446	73	124	20	80	278	319	504	824	6	83	0.36	13	4	42	226	5.47
2019	Rk	AZL BrewersG	12	1	5	0	0	417	462	500	962	8	83	0.50	0	0	20	83	7.38
2019	AAA	San Antonio	334	44	90	14	59	269	326	461	787	8	75	0.33	5	0	39	192	5.20
2019	MLB	Milwaukee	10	1	4	0	1	400	455	600	1055	9	90	1.00	0	0	50	200	8.61

Well-rounded OF prospect who lacks plus tool but could contribute in several categories. Makes plus contact via quick, level stroke and sprays balls to all fields. Added leg kick and loft to swing in upper minors and could have 25 HR upside. Good athlete who runs well with 10+ SB value. Potentially sneaky bat who could have nice value in 2020.

Tejeda,Anderson — 6 — Texas

EXP MLB DEBUT: 2021 | H/W: 5-11 160 | FUT: Starting SS | 8D

Bats B Age 21
2014 FA (DR)

- Pwr ++++
- BAvg ++
- Spd +++
- Def +++

Year	Lev	Team	AB	R	H	HR	RBI	Avg	OB	Slg	OPS	bb%	ct%	Eye	SB	CS	x/h%	Iso	RC/G
2016	Rk	AZL Rangers	133	22	39	1	21	293	333	496	830	6	73	0.22	1	0	49	203	6.09
2016	A-	Spokane	94	15	26	8	19	277	313	553	866	5	65	0.15	1	0	35	277	6.39
2017	A	Hickory	401	68	99	8	53	247	309	411	720	8	67	0.27	10	7	41	165	4.70
2018	A+	Down East	467	76	121	19	74	259	329	439	768	9	70	0.35	11	4	34	180	5.16
2019	A+	Down East	158	22	37	4	24	234	309	386	695	10	63	0.29	9	4	41	152	4.42

Was on his way to a breakout HR/SB season before shoulder injury shut him down for the year in May. Contact not a strong suit, walk rate has improved and able to get to his power. Shortstop actions on defense with quick hands, great arm, and plus athleticism. Shoulder adds risk to profile.

Tena,Jose — 6 — Cleveland

EXP MLB DEBUT: 2023 | H/W: 5-9 159 | FUT: Starting MIF | 7E

Bats L Age 19
2017 FA (DR)

- Pwr +++
- BAvg +++
- Spd +++
- Def +++

Year	Lev	Team	AB	R	H	HR	RBI	Avg	OB	Slg	OPS	bb%	ct%	Eye	SB	CS	x/h%	Iso	RC/G
2019	Rk	AZL Indians 2	191	30	62	1	18	325	345	440	785	3	77	0.14	6	2	23	115	5.06

Ultra-aggressive, barrel-contact machine performed in Arizona League. Above-average bat-to-ball skills with a heavy opposite field approach. Peppers line drives to the LCF gap. Short, stockier frame, likely finds power as body matures. Swing trajectory currently geared towards heavy top spin contact. Solid range at SS. Arm may move over to 2B.

Terry,Curtis — 3 — Texas

EXP MLB DEBUT: 2021 | H/W: 6-3 264 | FUT: Starting 1B | 8D

Bats R Age 23
2015 (13) HS (GA)

- Pwr ++++
- BAvg +++
- 4.62 Spd +
- Def ++

Year	Lev	Team	AB	R	H	HR	RBI	Avg	OB	Slg	OPS	bb%	ct%	Eye	SB	CS	x/h%	Iso	RC/G
2016	A-	Spokane	31	4	6	1	3	194	194	323	516	0	52	0.00	0	0	33	129	1.81
2017	A-	Spokane	229	26	59	12	30	258	280	467	747	3	74	0.12	3	0	41	210	4.38
2018	A-	Spokane	246	51	83	15	60	337	414	606	1019	12	74	0.50	1	1	41	268	8.50
2019	A	Hickory	232	39	61	15	47	263	305	560	865	6	71	0.21	0	1	64	297	6.27
2019	A+	Down East	239	35	77	10	33	322	382	515	896	9	79	0.46	0	1	31	192	6.57

After four years in short-season ball, hulking 1Bman blew through two levels of full-season A-ball. Big power from strong legs, but improvements in contact at High-A are possibly the most intriguing for his future. Will take a walk too, but size limits him to 1B only. Competitive and a hard worker, but will be uphill battle.

Thomas,Alek — 8 — Arizona

EXP MLB DEBUT: 2022 | H/W: 5-11 175 | FUT: Starting OF | 8C

Bats L Age 19
2018 (2) HS (IL)

- Pwr +++
- BAvg +++
- Spd ++++
- Def +++

Year	Lev	Team	AB	R	H	HR	RBI	Avg	OB	Slg	OPS	bb%	ct%	Eye	SB	CS	x/h%	Iso	RC/G
2018	Rk	AZL DBacks	123	24	40	0	10	325	390	431	821	10	85	0.72	8	2	20	106	5.88
2018	Rk	Missoula	123	26	42	2	17	341	396	496	891	8	85	0.58	4	3	33	154	6.55
2019	A	Kane County	353	63	110	8	48	312	386	479	865	11	80	0.60	11	6	33	167	6.44
2019	A+	Visalia	94	13	24	2	7	255	320	340	661	9	65	0.27	4	5	17	85	3.70

Shorter, slender OF who led MWL in SLG and OPS at just 19 years old. Well-rounded but not elite skill-set includes plus speed, solid-average contact ability via a compact, level stroke. Utilizes all-fields approach. Raw power is below-average and body is not super projectable. Plays a solid CF but may have to move to the corners with fringy arm.

Thompson,Bubba — 78 — Texas

EXP MLB DEBUT: 2022 | H/W: 6-1 180 | FUT: Starting CF | 8D

Bats R Age 21
2017 (1) HS (AL)

- Pwr +++
- BAvg ++
- Spd ++++
- Def +++

Year	Lev	Team	AB	R	H	HR	RBI	Avg	OB	Slg	OPS	bb%	ct%	Eye	SB	CS	x/h%	Iso	RC/G
2017	Rk	AZL Rangers	113	23	29	3	12	257	294	434	728	5	75	0.21	5	5	41	177	4.40
2018	A	Hickory	332	52	96	8	42	289	335	446	781	6	69	0.22	32	7	32	157	5.37
2019	A+	Down East	202	24	36	5	21	178	256	312	567	9	64	0.29	12	3	42	134	2.36

Youth, injuries (hamate and foot) can partially be blamed for 2019, and he looked better in the AFL while making up missed AB. But strikeout rose to concerning levels as pitch recognition problems persisted. Premium athlete with impact power/speed potential, but needs to stay on field and get on base.

Thompson-Williams,Dom — 789 — Seattle

EXP MLB DEBUT: 2020 | H/W: 6-0 190 | FUT: Reserve OF | 6C

Bats L Age 24
2016 (5) South Carolina

- Pwr +++
- BAvg ++
- Spd +++
- Def +++

Year	Lev	Team	AB	R	H	HR	RBI	Avg	OB	Slg	OPS	bb%	ct%	Eye	SB	CS	x/h%	Iso	RC/G
2017	A-	Staten Island	141	17	39	3	22	277	358	390	749	11	79	0.60	7	6	26	113	4.91
2017	A	Charleston (Sc)	80	6	15	0	6	188	270	213	482	10	81	0.60	2	2	13	25	1.62
2018	A	Charleston (Sc)	37	7	14	5	9	378	410	811	1221	5	81	0.29	3	2	43	432	9.80
2018	A+	Tampa	331	56	96	17	65	290	351	517	867	9	71	0.33	17	7	39	227	6.42
2019	AA	Arkansas	432	46	101	12	41	234	291	391	682	7	65	0.23	15	2	40	157	4.08

Muscular, power-centric prospect struggled with ct% and hardcontact. Raw plus power pushes profile. However, long, uneven swing doesn't allow for high BA. Struggles with spin recognition as well. Stocky frame. Likely grows out of average speed. Corner-only profile.

Toglia,Michael — 3 — Colorado

EXP MLB DEBUT: 2022 | H/W: 6-5 226 | FUT: Starting 1B | 8E

Bats B Age 21
2019 (1) UCLA

- Pwr ++++
- BAvg ++
- Spd ++
- Def +++

Year	Lev	Team	AB	R	H	HR	RBI	Avg	OB	Slg	OPS	bb%	ct%	Eye	SB	CS	x/h%	Iso	RC/G
2019	A-	Boise	145	25	36	9	26	248	370	483	853	16	69	0.62	1	1	44	234	6.54

Tall, long-levered 1B with big-time raw power and a chance to move quickly. Strong, chiseled lower half allows him to generate bat speed and loft into swing from both sides; looks a bit more polished as LHH. Contact skills remain somewhat raw, but shows plate discipline needed for OBP value. Moves well for his size and could man corner OF or 1B.

Toribio,Luis

5 | San Francisco | EXP MLB DEBUT: 2023 | H/W: 6-1 165 | FUT: Starting 3B | 8D

Bats L Age 19
2017 FA (DR)
Pwr +++
BAvg ++++
Spd ++
Def ++

Year	Lev	Team	AB	R	H	HR	RBI	Avg	OB	Slg	OPS	bb%	ct%	Eye	SB	CS	x/h%	Iso	RC/G
2019	Rk	AZL Giants O	185	45	55	3	33	297	435	459	894	20	71	0.83	4	5	38	162	7.61
2019	A-	Salem-Keizer	11	2	3	0	0	273	385	364	748	15	55	0.40	0	0	33	91	6.29

Strong-swinging 3B who is all about bat production. Demonstrates proficiency with pitch recognition and advanced feel for zone. Could develop into middle of order guy with plus power. Needs to add muscle to frame, but can be above average hitter. Not much in the way of speed or defense as he makes careless errors. May profile best at 2B.

Toro,Abraham

345 | Houston | EXP MLB DEBUT: 2019 | H/W: 6-1 190 | FUT: Starting 3B | 8C

Bats B Age 23
2016 (5) Seminole St JC
Pwr +++
BAvg ++++
Spd +
Def ++

Year	Lev	Team	AB	R	H	HR	RBI	Avg	OB	Slg	OPS	bb%	ct%	Eye	SB	CS	x/h%	Iso	RC/G
2018	A+	Buies Creek	296	54	76	14	56	257	355	473	828	13	79	0.73	5	1	46	216	5.95
2018	AA	Corpus Christi	178	16	41	2	22	230	297	371	668	9	74	0.37	3	3	46	140	3.89
2019	AA	Corpus Christi	376	65	115	16	70	306	384	513	898	11	80	0.62	4	1	37	207	6.76
2019	AAA	Round Rock	66	17	28	1	10	424	500	606	1106	13	92	2.00	0	1	36	182	9.33
2019	MLB	Houston	78	13	17	2	9	218	299	385	683	10	76	0.47	1	1	41	167	4.06

Breakout prospect who led TL in OBP and set new high in HR and leading org in BA. Becoming weapon from both sides of plate. Offers above average pop and willing to work deep counts. Makes acceptable contact and drives ball to all fields. Question is defensive home. Not a good defender with limited range and quickness.

Torres,Jhon

79 | St. Louis | EXP MLB DEBUT: 2022 | H/W: 6-4 199 | FUT: Starting OF | 8D

Bats R Age 20
2016 FA (CB)
Pwr ++++
BAvg ++
Spd ++
Def +++

Year	Lev	Team	AB	R	H	HR	RBI	Avg	OB	Slg	OPS	bb%	ct%	Eye	SB	CS	x/h%	Iso	RC/G
2018	Rk	GCL Cardinals	63	11	25	4	14	397	465	683	1147	11	79	0.62	1	1	40	286	9.85
2018	Rk	AZL Indians 2	99	16	27	4	16	273	345	424	770	10	76	0.46	3	0	26	152	5.01
2019	Rk	Johnson City	112	24	32	6	17	286	389	527	916	15	68	0.53	0	2	47	241	7.59
2019	A	Peoria	66	4	11	0	8	167	247	212	459	10	56	0.24	0	1	27	45	0.77

Came over as part of the Mercado trade. Was over-matched in MWL assignment, posting a 39% K rate, but regrouped when sent to Rookie ball. Plus bat speed and impressive all-fields power are his carrying tools. Shows some feel for barreling the ball, but needs to make more contact. Average speed and a plus arm give him a RF profile.

Trammell,Taylor

78 | San Diego | EXP MLB DEBUT: 2020 | H/W: 6-2 215 | FUT: Starting OF | 8B

Bats L Age 22
2016 (1) HS (GA)
Pwr +++
BAvg +++
Spd ++++
Def ++++

Year	Lev	Team	AB	R	H	HR	RBI	Avg	OB	Slg	OPS	bb%	ct%	Eye	SB	CS	x/h%	Iso	RC/G
2016	Rk	Billings	228	39	69	2	34	303	367	421	788	9	75	0.40	24	7	25	118	5.47
2017	A	Dayton	491	80	138	13	77	281	372	450	822	13	75	0.58	41	12	34	169	6.03
2018	A+	Daytona	397	71	110	8	41	277	369	406	775	13	74	0.55	25	10	28	128	5.41
2019	AA	Chattanooga	318	47	75	6	33	236	347	336	683	15	73	0.63	17	4	23	101	4.19
2019	AA	Amarillo	118	14	27	4	10	229	305	381	687	10	69	0.36	3	4	33	153	4.02

Athletic, tooled-up OF who fits top-of-the-order prototype. Best skill is plus-plus speed, which pairs nicely with his ability to work counts and draw walks. Swing is short, compact and geared toward spraying liners to the gaps. Lacks ideal leverage in swing for power, but should be 10-15 HR type. May move off CF to LF with lack of arm strength.

Triolo,Jared

56 | Pittsburgh | EXP MLB DEBUT: 2022 | H/W: 6-3 212 | FUT: Starting 3B | 7C

Bats R Age 22
2019 (2) Houston
Pwr ++
BAvg ++
Spd +++
Def +++

Year	Lev	Team	AB	R	H	HR	RBI	Avg	OB	Slg	OPS	bb%	ct%	Eye	SB	CS	x/h%	Iso	RC/G
2019	NCAA	Houston	217	46	72	7	44	332	415	512	927	13	86	1.03	13	2	35	180	7.15
2019	A-	West Virginia	234	30	56	2	34	239	318	389	707	10	79	0.55	3	1	46	150	4.52

Tall, patient INF who can play both SS and 3B. Walked more than he fanned in college, though power hasn't yet translated to game action. Has the frame and natural strength to realize power, but may not have the bat speed or leverage to do so. Has nice swing and knows the strike zone. Possesses average range at 3B with solid arm strength.

Turang,Brice

46 | Milwaukee | EXP MLB DEBUT: 2022 | H/W: 6-0 173 | FUT: Starting SS | 8C

Bats L Age 20
2018 (1) HS (CA)
Pwr ++
BAvg ++++
Spd +++
Def ++++

Year	Lev	Team	AB	R	H	HR	RBI	Avg	OB	Slg	OPS	bb%	ct%	Eye	SB	CS	x/h%	Iso	RC/G
2018	Rk	Helena	112	26	30	1	11	268	388	348	736	16	75	0.79	6	1	20	80	5.08
2018	Rk	AZL Brewers	47	11	15	0	7	319	429	362	790	16	87	1.50	8	1	13	43	5.89
2019	A	Wisconsin	303	57	87	2	31	287	386	376	763	14	82	0.91	21	4	22	89	5.36
2019	A+	Carolina	170	25	34	1	6	200	333	276	610	17	72	0.72	9	1	26	76	3.33

Defensively advanced, strike-zone savvy MIF prospect with former first-round status. Has slender, athletic frame with projection for added strength toward average power. Batted ball profile leans toward line drives to all fields. Works counts well, identifies spin out of hand and knows how to get on base. Above-average athlete with plus speed.

Urbina,Misael

8 | Minnesota | EXP MLB DEBUT: 2024 | H/W: 6-0 175 | FUT: Starting CF | 8D

Bats R Age 17
2018 FA (VZ)
Pwr ++
BAvg +++
Spd ++++
Def ++++

Year	Lev	Team	AB	R	H	HR	RBI	Avg	OB	Slg	OPS	bb%	ct%	Eye	SB	CS	x/h%	Iso	RC/G
2019		Did not play in U.S.																	

Contact-oriented, defensively skilled CF had solid summer in Dominican League. Plus bat-to-ball skills with good bat speed. Spray approach, doesn't get for barrel as much due to uneven swing plane. Average power in frame. Will need rework of swing mechanics to reach it in game. Speedy runner who excels in CF with clean routes. Fringe throwing arm.

Valdez,Freddy

9 | New York (N) | EXP MLB DEBUT: 2024 | H/W: 6-3 212 | FUT: Starting OF | 8E

Bats R Age 18
2018 FA (DR)
Pwr ++++
BAvg ++
Spd ++
Def +++

Year	Lev	Team	AB	R	H	HR	RBI	Avg	OB	Slg	OPS	bb%	ct%	Eye	SB	CS	x/h%	Iso	RC/G
2019	Rk	GCL Mets	10	4	4	1	3	400	538	800	1338	23	70	1.00	0	1	50	400	13.91

Big power bat made late season US debut after successful Dominican Summer League season. Improved approach, quelling aggressiveness but is still a very pull-dominant hitter. Power is big and plays in any stadium. Has been popping more game power of late. Current CF; run tool likely pushes profile to a corner.

Valera,George

8 | Cleveland | EXP MLB DEBUT: 2023 | H/W: 5-10 160 | FUT: Starting OF | 9D

Bats L Age 19
2017 FA (DR)
Pwr ++++
BAvg +++
Spd +++
Def +++

Year	Lev	Team	AB	R	H	HR	RBI	Avg	OB	Slg	OPS	bb%	ct%	Eye	SB	CS	x/h%	Iso	RC/G
2018	Rk	AZL Indians 2	18	4	6	1	6	333	429	556	984	14	83	1.00	1	1	33	222	7.85
2019	A-	MahoningVal	157	22	37	8	29	236	355	446	801	16	67	0.56	6	2	43	210	5.90
2019	A	Lake County	23	1	2	0	3	87	160	174	334	8	61	0.22	0	2	50	87	-1.20

Short-statured, big power bat struggled with contact despite advanced hit skills. Loose hands contribute to inconsistent swing path, but swing is smooth, majestic & compact when he tightens up his hands and explodes on the ball. But spin recognition contributes to low ct%, though raw plus power plays. Average runner, a RF long term.

Vargas,Alexander

6 | New York (A) | EXP MLB DEBUT: 2024 | H/W: 5-11 148 | FUT: Starting SS | 7D

Bats B Age 18
2018 FA (CU)
Pwr +
BAvg +++
Spd ++++
Def ++++

Year	Lev	Team	AB	R	H	HR	RBI	Avg	OB	Slg	OPS	bb%	ct%	Eye	SB	CS	x/h%	Iso	RC/G
2019	Rk	GCL Yankees	155	23	34	1	16	219	284	335	620	8	86	0.64	13	0	32	116	3.43

Athletic SS known more for stellar glove than offensive tools. Bottom-of-the-order type bat due to limited strength in lean frame and concerns power will never come. Solid, contact-oriented hitter who must spray ball to carry hitting value. Plus runner who was 14 for 14 in SB attempts. Gold-Glove-good at SS.

Vargas,Miguel

5 | Los Angeles (N) | EXP MLB DEBUT: 2022 | H/W: 6-3 205 | FUT: Starting 1B | 7D

Bats R Age 20
2017 FA (CU)
Pwr +++
BAvg +++
Spd ++
Def ++

Year	Lev	Team	AB	R	H	HR	RBI	Avg	OB	Slg	OPS	bb%	ct%	Eye	SB	CS	x/h%	Iso	RC/G
2018	Rk	Ogden	94	25	37	2	22	394	441	596	1037	8	86	0.62	6	1	38	202	8.22
2018	Rk	AZL Dodgers	31	6	13	0	2	419	500	581	1081	14	90	1.67	1	0	31	161	9.24
2018	A	Great Lakes	75	4	16	0	6	213	306	253	559	12	73	0.50	0	0	13	40	2.46
2019	A	Great Lakes	280	53	91	5	45	325	400	464	864	11	85	0.81	9	1	30	139	6.39
2019	A+	RanchoCuca	211	23	60	2	32	284	346	408	754	9	81	0.50	4	3	35	123	4.96

Cuban-born player held his own in A-ball, splitting time between 3B and 1B. Improved conditioning resulted in more power though of the gap, opposite-field variety. Discerning eye at the plate and willing to use the whole field. Arm, range, and defense make 1B his likely destination, which means power must continue to develop.

Varsho,Daulton — 2 — Arizona

EXP MLB DEBUT: 2020 | H/W: 5-10 190 | FUT: Starting C | 8B

Bats L Age 23 | 2017 (2) Wisc-Milwaukee | Pwr +++ | BAvg +++ | Spd +++ | Def +++

Year	Lev	Team	AB	R	H	HR	RBI	Avg	OB	Slg	OPS	bb%	ct%	Eye	SB	CS	x/h%	Iso	RC/G
2017	NCAA	UW Milwaukee	199	47	72	11	39	362	482	643	1125	19	80	1.18	10	0	39	281	10.09
2017	A-	Hillsboro	193	36	60	7	39	311	367	534	900	8	84	0.57	7	2	43	223	6.59
2018	Rk	AZL DBacks	12	4	6	1	1	500	500	1083	1583	0	92	0.00	0	0	67	583	13.38
2018	A+	Visalia	304	44	87	11	44	286	350	451	801	9	77	0.42	19	3	29	164	5.42
2019	AA	Jackson	396	85	119	18	58	301	368	520	888	10	84	0.67	21	5	39	220	6.46

Sleeper CA prospect who projects to have value in all 5x5 categories. Shows above-average raw power to pull side via strong lower half and natural loft. Works counts well, displays plus contact skills and has discerning eye at the plate. Owns surprising athleticism and will have speed value. May never be a plus backstop, but should stick there.

Vaughn,Andrew — 3 — Chicago (A)

EXP MLB DEBUT: 2021 | H/W: 6-0 214 | FUT: Starting 1B | 9C

Bats R Age 22 | 2019 (1) California | Pwr ++++ | BAvg ++++ | Spd ++ | Def +++

Year	Lev	Team	AB	R	H	HR	RBI	Avg	OB	Slg	OPS	bb%	ct%	Eye	SB	CS	x/h%	Iso	RC/G
2019	NCAA	California	176	49	67	15	50	381	536	716	1252	25	81	1.79	2	0	43	335	11.91
2019	Rk	AZL White Sox	15	3	9	1	4	600	600	933	1533	0	80	0.00	0	0	33	333	13.61
2019	A	Kannapolis	83	14	21	2	11	253	361	410	770	14	78	0.78	0	0	43	157	5.40
2019	A+	Winston-Salem	107	16	27	3	21	252	350	411	761	13	84	0.94	0	1	41	159	5.21

Top 3 pick in 2019 has plus hit and power package at 1B. High floor with power ceiling left. Very easy bat speed in compact power swing. Has control of barrel and will use gaps well. Easily adjusts swing path to cover zone. 30-plus HR potential. Should verify at maturity. Solid at 1B but undersized; likely 1B-only profile.

Vavra,Terrin — 46 — Colorado

EXP MLB DEBUT: 2021 | H/W: 6-1 185 | FUT: Starting 2B | 7B

Bats L Age 22 | 2018 (3) Minnesota | Pwr ++ | BAvg ++++ | Spd ++ | Def +++

Year	Lev	Team	AB	R	H	HR	RBI	Avg	OB	Slg	OPS	bb%	ct%	Eye	SB	CS	x/h%	Iso	RC/G
2018	NCAA	Minnesota	223	55	86	10	59	386	458	614	1073	12	90	1.36	8	1	31	229	8.70
2018	A-	Boise	169	22	51	4	26	302	395	467	862	13	76	0.65	9	1	31	166	6.60
2019	A	Asheville	374	79	119	10	52	318	415	489	904	14	83	1.00	18	9	36	171	7.06

Lean, slender 2B/SS who led SAL in OBP and Eye in 2019. Excels at pitch ID, while patience often allows him to get into favorable counts. Approach is geared toward all fields and peppering gaps with line drives. Has loose, level swing with which produces plus contact. Good athlete with room for some muscle, he's likely a 2B down the road.

Velazquez,Nelson — 9 — Chicago (N)

EXP MLB DEBUT: 2023 | H/W: 6-0 190 | FUT: Starting OF | 8E

Bats R Age 21 | 2017 (5) HS (PR) | Pwr ++++ | BAvg ++ | Spd ++ | Def +++

Year	Lev	Team	AB	R	H	HR	RBI	Avg	OB	Slg	OPS	bb%	ct%	Eye	SB	CS	x/h%	Iso	RC/G
2017	Rk	AZL Cubs	110	26	26	8	17	236	328	536	864	12	65	0.38	5	2	58	300	6.83
2018	A-	Eugene	264	35	66	11	33	250	310	458	768	8	69	0.28	12	4	47	208	5.15
2018	A	South Bend	112	6	21	0	7	188	235	196	432	6	62	0.16	3	0	5	9	0.17
2019	Rk	AZL Cubs 2	19	4	6	2	5	316	381	684	1065	10	74	0.40	0	0	50	368	8.76
2019	A	South Bend	262	33	75	4	34	286	339	424	763	7	71	0.27	5	3	32	137	5.13

Toolsy OF with plus raw power and fringe athleticism that profile for an OF corner. Strong and physically developed for his age. Plus arm strength. Chiseled lower half and forearms lend themselves to some bat speed, but swing requires some effort and lacks natural feel to hit. Able to steal a base now, but projects to have fringe speed at maturity.

Verdugo,Luis — 6 — Chicago (N)

EXP MLB DEBUT: 2023 | H/W: 6-0 172 | FUT: Starting SS | 7D

Bats R Age 19 | 2017 FA (MX) | Pwr ++ | BAvg +++ | Spd +++ | Def ++++

Year	Lev	Team	AB	R	H	HR	RBI	Avg	OB	Slg	OPS	bb%	ct%	Eye	SB	CS	x/h%	Iso	RC/G
2018	Rk	AZL Cubs 2	176	28	34	4	20	193	264	295	560	9	74	0.38	5	3	26	102	2.25
2019	Rk	AZL Cubs 2	197	40	60	5	38	305	366	447	812	9	80	0.49	8	2	27	142	5.57

Young SS who made strides on both sides of the ball in second go-around in the AZL. Chance to be an impact defender with a plus arm, range and footwork for either SS or 3B. Lean athlete with room to fill out lower half. Still working on timing of swing, and bat speed is average. Chance to add moderate SB value, but lacks premium offensive tool.

Vientos,Mark — 5 — New York (N)

EXP MLB DEBUT: 2022 | H/W: 6-4 185 | FUT: Starting 3B | 8C

Bats R Age 20 | 2017 (2) HS (FL) | Pwr ++++ | BAvg +++ | Spd ++ | Def ++

Year	Lev	Team	AB	R	H	HR	RBI	Avg	OB	Slg	OPS	bb%	ct%	Eye	SB	CS	x/h%	Iso	RC/G
2017	Rk	Kingsport	17	1	5	0	2	294	333	412	745	6	76	0.25	0	0	40	118	4.77
2017	Rk	GCL Mets	174	22	45	4	24	259	314	397	710	7	76	0.33	0	2	36	138	4.25
2018	Rk	Kingsport	223	32	64	11	52	287	388	489	877	14	81	0.86	1	0	36	202	6.58
2019	A	Columbia	416	48	106	12	62	255	292	411	703	5	74	0.20	1	4	38	156	4.04

Tall, powerful COR IF overcame early struggles to post solid returns. Good bat speed with a pull-oriented approach. Reads zone well and improved his spin recognition. Will cut off plate, trying to tap into raw plus-plus power. The power plays and could end up in the 30-40 HR range if the hit tool is refined. Defensive questions; may require a move to 1B.

Vilade,Ryan — 56 — Colorado

EXP MLB DEBUT: 2021 | H/W: 6-2 194 | FUT: Starting 3B | 7A

Bats R Age 21 | 2017 (2) HS (OK) | Pwr ++ | BAvg +++ | Spd +++ | Def +++

Year	Lev	Team	AB	R	H	HR	RBI	Avg	OB	Slg	OPS	bb%	ct%	Eye	SB	CS	x/h%	Iso	RC/G
2017	Rk	Grand Junction	117	23	36	5	21	308	438	496	933	19	74	0.87	5	5	28	188	7.78
2018	A	Asheville	457	77	125	5	44	274	344	368	711	10	79	0.51	17	13	23	94	4.42
2019	A+	Lancaster	509	92	154	12	71	303	372	466	837	10	81	0.59	24	7	32	163	5.99

Versatile INF glove with strong arm and average mix of offensive skills. Owns good raw power and started tapping into fly-ball angles in 2019; projects as high-volume doubles bat. Patient hitter with solid overall bat to ball ability. SB value could be sneaky, as he is not a plus runner but picks his spots well and gets on base at a high clip.

Volpe,Anthony — 6 — New York (A)

EXP MLB DEBUT: 2023 | H/W: 5-11 180 | FUT: Starting SS | 8D

Bats R Age 18 | 2019 (1) HS (NJ) | Pwr +++ | BAvg +++ | Spd +++ | Def ++++

Year	Lev	Team	AB	R	H	HR	RBI	Avg	OB	Slg	OPS	bb%	ct%	Eye	SB	CS	x/h%	Iso	RC/G
2019	Rk	Pulaski	121	19	26	2	11	215	340	355	696	16	69	0.61	6	1	42	140	4.54

Athletic, smart SS with solid plate skills and high ct% aided by short stroke with line drive swing trajectory. Fringe-average power, could play up due to approach. Smart, heady runner who is more quick than fast. Plus defender and polished for age/level.

Wade Jr,LaMonte — 789 — Minnesota

EXP MLB DEBUT: 2019 | H/W: 6-1 180 | FUT: Reserve OF | 6B

Bats L Age 26 | 2015 (9) Maryland | Pwr ++ | BAvg ++ | Spd +++ | Def +++

Year	Lev	Team	AB	R	H	HR	RBI	Avg	OB	Slg	OPS	bb%	ct%	Eye	SB	CS	x/h%	Iso	RC/G
2018	AAA	Rochester	253	24	58	4	21	229	330	336	666	13	79	0.70	5	1	28	107	3.98
2019	A	Cedar Rapids	15	1	2	0	0	133	278	133	411	17	67	0.60	0	0	0	0	0.14
2019	AA	Pensacola	21	3	5	0	3	238	333	381	714	13	86	1.00	0	0	60	143	4.88
2019	AAA	Rochester	264	47	65	5	24	246	378	356	734	18	82	1.17	7	2	28	110	5.11
2019	MLB	Minnesota	56	10	11	2	5	196	328	375	703	16	84	1.22	0	1	45	179	4.65

Tweener OF prospect made MLB debut after subpar Triple-A season. Can play all 3 OF positions well; glove carries profile. Has solid bat-to-ball skills and a line drive swing trajectory. Struggles getting bat speed up on higher velocity. Average raw power; plays below-average in game. Above-average runner but unlikely to steal bases.

Walker,Steele — 8 — Texas

EXP MLB DEBUT: 2021 | H/W: 5-11 190 | FUT: Starting OF | 7C

Bats L Age 23 | 2018 (2) Oklahoma | Pwr +++ | BAvg +++ | Spd +++ | Def +++

Year	Lev	Team	AB	R	H	HR	RBI	Avg	OB	Slg	OPS	bb%	ct%	Eye	SB	CS	x/h%	Iso	RC/G
2018	Rk	Great Falls	34	4	7	2	4	206	229	412	640	3	79	0.14	1	1	43	206	2.94
2018	Rk	AZL White Sox	11	0	5	0	0	455	500	455	955	8	91	1.00	0	0	0	0	7.12
2018	A	Kannapolis	113	13	21	3	17	186	240	310	549	7	74	0.28	5	1	38	124	2.03
2019	A	Kannapolis	74	6	27	0	11	365	427	581	1008	10	80	0.53	4	2	48	216	8.45
2019	A+	Winston-Salem	383	59	103	10	51	269	341	426	767	10	84	0.67	9	5	37	157	5.10

Solid, all-around athlete made it up to High-A in 1st full pro season. LHH has average swing speed. Contact-oriented hitter with solid bat-to-ball skills. Does a good job of incorporating lower half, which may play up power potential. There is average HR potential in frame and swing. Doesn't find barrel enough to take advantage. Average runner.

Wallner,Matt — 9 — Minnesota

EXP MLB DEBUT: 2022 | H/W: 6-5 220 | FUT: Starting OF | 7D

Bats L Age 22 | 2019 (1) So Mississippi | Pwr ++++ | BAvg ++ | Spd ++ | Def ++++

Year	Lev	Team	AB	R	H	HR	RBI	Avg	OB	Slg	OPS	bb%	ct%	Eye	SB	CS	x/h%	Iso	RC/G
2019	Rk	Elizabethton	208	35	56	6	28	269	330	452	782	8	68	0.29	1	1	45	183	5.50
2019	A	Cedar Rapids	44	7	9	2	6	205	286	455	740	10	68	0.36	0	0	67	250	4.91

Powerful LHH former 2-way player who was drafted as a power first bat. Big-bodied, close to physical projection. Extreme uppercut swing trajectory sells out to loft. Average bat speed but long swing path; contact risk. Defensively suited for RF due to arm that touched 97 on mound. Below-average runner.

Walls,Taylor | 6 | Tampa Bay

EXP MLB DEBUT: 2020 | H/W: 5-10 180 | FUT: Utility player | 7B

Bats B Age 23 | 2017 (3) Florida St | Pwr ++ | BAvg +++ | Spd +++ | Def +++

Year	Lev	Team	AB	R	H	HR	RBI	Avg	OB	Slg	OPS	bb%	ct%	Eye	SB	CS	x/h%	Iso	RC/G
2017	NCAA	Florida St	260	82	71	8	47	273	422	423	845	20	83	1.49	10	2	28	150	6.63
2017	A-	Hudson Valley	164	22	35	1	21	213	332	287	618	15	68	0.55	5	4	29	73	3.36
2018	A	Bowling Green	467	87	142	6	57	304	390	428	819	12	83	0.83	31	12	28	124	5.95
2019	A+	Charlotte	156	22	42	4	26	269	349	417	765	11	82	0.68	13	6	31	147	5.12
2019	AA	Montgomery	211	42	57	6	20	270	350	479	829	11	76	0.51	15	9	47	209	6.06

Switch-hitting, UT IF continued to showcase all-around average tools in 2019. Contact-oriented hitter with a solid approach and good plate skills. LHH swing caught up with RHH swing and may even edge it out. Has average raw power in swing and frame from RH side. Above-average runner with SB instincts. Athletic enough to play OF, too.

Walsh,Jared | 3 | Los Angeles (A)

EXP MLB DEBUT: 2019 | H/W: 6-0 210 | FUT: Starting 1B | 7A

Bats L Age 26 | 2015 (39) Georgia | Pwr ++++ | BAvg +++ | Spd ++ | Def +++

Year	Lev	Team	AB	R	H	HR	RBI	Avg	OB	Slg	OPS	bb%	ct%	Eye	SB	CS	x/h%	Iso	RC/G
2018	A+	Inland Empire	149	28	41	13	36	275	376	604	980	14	66	0.48	0	1	54	329	8.41
2018	AA	Mobile	149	26	43	8	26	289	376	537	913	12	68	0.44	1	0	49	248	7.48
2018	AAA	Salt Lake	178	32	48	8	37	270	330	478	807	8	69	0.29	0	0	44	208	5.72
2019	AAA	Salt Lake	382	90	124	36	86	325	415	686	1101	13	70	0.51	0	0	53	361	9.87
2019	MLB	Los Angeles	79	6	16	1	5	203	259	329	588	7	56	0.17	0	0	44	127	3.10

Big-time power 1B was among PCL leaders in all offensive categories. Pummels pitches low and inside and displays ability to clear fences the opposite way with high volume fly balls. Has a good feel for the strike zone and should be valued a tick higher in OBP formats. Moves well for his stocky, strong frame and should be solid 1B glove.

Walton,Donnie | 46 | Seattle

EXP MLB DEBUT: 2019 | H/W: 5-10 184 | FUT: Reserve IF | 6B

Bats L Age 25 | 2016 (5) Oklahoma St | Pwr ++ | BAvg +++ | Spd +++ | Def +++

Year	Lev	Team	AB	R	H	HR	RBI	Avg	OB	Slg	OPS	bb%	ct%	Eye	SB	CS	x/h%	Iso	RC/G
2017	A+	Modesto	242	37	65	2	24	269	342	368	710	10	80	0.55	6	6	29	99	4.45
2018	A+	Modesto	217	35	67	3	19	309	393	433	826	12	83	0.81	8	3	27	124	6.02
2018	AA	Arkansas	208	22	49	1	22	236	306	327	633	9	84	0.62	3	1	33	91	3.55
2019	AA	Arkansas	480	72	144	11	50	300	381	427	808	12	85	0.88	10	13	25	127	5.70
2019	MLB	Seattle	16	2	3	0	2	188	316	188	503	16	69	0.60	0	1	0	0	1.61

Over-achieving, contact-oriented bat made it to big leagues after good Double-A season. Employs spray approach with compact, line drive swing with flat trajectory. Will power up on middle-in FB but power exclusively to the pull side. Solid runner with sneaky SB ability. Fits best at 2B but likely reserve IF.

Ward,Je'Von | 79 | Milwaukee

EXP MLB DEBUT: 2022 | H/W: 6-5 190 | FUT: Starting OF | 8E

Bats L Age 20 | 2017 (12) HS (CA) | Pwr +++ | BAvg ++ | Spd +++ | Def +++

Year	Lev	Team	AB	R	H	HR	RBI	Avg	OB	Slg	OPS	bb%	ct%	Eye	SB	CS	x/h%	Iso	RC/G
2017	Rk	AZL Brewers	123	15	34	0	15	276	326	325	651	7	68	0.23	2	7	18	49	3.55
2018	Rk	Helena	238	40	73	2	21	307	389	403	792	12	76	0.56	13	5	23	97	5.63
2019	A	Wisconsin	373	35	84	2	46	225	312	322	634	11	71	0.44	7	6	30	97	3.50

Tall, high-waisted athlete with quick-twitch attributes but requires significant projection. Beautiful LH swing with potential for plus raw power when he extends properly through ball, but ct% skills remain a question mark. Plus runner with burst for future SB value. Easy to dream on HR/SB upside as everyday OF, but may still be 2-3 years away.

Waters,Drew | 789 | Atlanta

EXP MLB DEBUT: 2020 | H/W: 6-2 183 | FUT: Starting OF | 8C

Bats B Age 21 | 2017 (2) HS (GA) | Pwr +++ | BAvg +++ | Spd ++++ | Def +++

Year	Lev	Team	AB	R	H	HR	RBI	Avg	OB	Slg	OPS	bb%	ct%	Eye	SB	CS	x/h%	Iso	RC/G
2017	Rk	Danville	149	20	38	2	14	255	327	383	710	10	60	0.27	4	2	37	128	4.92
2018	A	Rome	337	58	102	9	36	303	344	513	857	6	79	0.29	20	5	46	211	6.09
2018	A+	Florida	123	14	33	0	3	268	313	374	687	6	73	0.24	3	0	30	106	4.06
2019	AA	Mississippi	420	63	134	5	41	319	362	481	843	6	71	0.23	13	6	37	162	6.24
2019	AAA	Gwinnett	107	17	29	2	11	271	339	374	713	9	60	0.26	3	0	24	103	4.87

Ultra-aggressive, athletic switch-hitting CF continues to produce with hit tool. Unorthodox swing from both sides. LH swing projects better than RH swing. Easy bat speed with line-drive skills; power will come. Has strength but not the trajectory currently. A plus runner, he has 15-SB potential. Is above-average defensively throughout the OF.

Watson,Zach | 8 | Baltimore

EXP MLB DEBUT: 2022 | H/W: 6-0 160 | FUT: Starting CF | 7D

Bats R Age 22 | 2019 (3) Louisiana St | Pwr ++ | BAvg ++ | Spd ++++ | Def ++++

Year	Lev	Team	AB	R	H	HR	RBI	Avg	OB	Slg	OPS	bb%	ct%	Eye	SB	CS	x/h%	Iso	RC/G
2019	A-	Aberdeen	55	17	13	2	9	236	288	418	706	7	71	0.25	5	1	46	182	4.18
2019	A	Delmarva	60	9	13	3	8	217	288	450	738	9	78	0.46	0	0	62	233	4.59

Defensive minded, athletic CF was somewhat limited due to hit tool concerns. Doesn't really get swing going. Susceptible to and cheats on velocity. Double-plus runner and exceptional defender. Glove and run tool carries profile. Could become more aggressive on bases. Speed and form point towards SB totals above 20.

Welker,Colton | 35 | Colorado

EXP MLB DEBUT: 2021 | H/W: 6-1 195 | FUT: Starting 3B | 7B

Bats R Age 22 | 2016 (4) HS (FL) | Pwr +++ | BAvg +++ | Spd ++ | Def +++

Year	Lev	Team	AB	R	H	HR	RBI	Avg	OB	Slg	OPS	bb%	ct%	Eye	SB	CS	x/h%	Iso	RC/G
2016	Rk	Grand Junction	210	38	69	5	36	329	368	490	858	6	87	0.46	6	4	32	162	5.93
2017	A	Asheville	254	32	89	6	33	350	393	500	893	7	83	0.43	5	7	28	150	6.40
2018	A+	Lancaster	454	74	151	13	82	333	389	489	878	8	77	0.41	5	1	30	156	6.43
2019	AA	Hartford	353	37	89	10	53	252	314	408	722	8	81	0.47	2	1	38	156	4.43

Strong corner INF with some feel to hit and limited physical projection. Has good bat speed and started tapping into fly-ball contact more in 2019 for plus raw power ability. Shows ability to cover all quadrants of zone via plus barrel control. Thick frame not conducive to SB value. Has arm strength for 3B but has received reps at 1B in AFL.

Wendzel,Davis | 5 | Texas

EXP MLB DEBUT: 2022 | H/W: 6-0 205 | FUT: Starting 3B | 8E

Bats R Age 22 | 2019 (1) Baylor | Pwr +++ | BAvg ++++ | Spd ++ | Def +++

Year	Lev	Team	AB	R	H	HR	RBI	Avg	OB	Slg	OPS	bb%	ct%	Eye	SB	CS	x/h%	Iso	RC/G
2019	Rk	AZL Rangers	9	4	4	1	2	444	545	889	1434	18	67	0.67	0	0	50	444	15.55
2019	A-	Spokane	10	4	2	0	0	200	385	200	585	23	70	1.00	2	1	0	0	3.07

Supplemental first-rounder with hit-over-power profile who missed most of 2019 post-draft with a thumb injury. Athletic and balanced skill set, has played SS and could also end up in an OF corner. Bat speed, coordination, instincts all plusses in his profile. Position and how much pop he ends up with are still question marks.

White,Eli | 68 | Texas

EXP MLB DEBUT: 2020 | H/W: 6-2 175 | FUT: Utility player | 7C

Bats R Age 25 | 2016 (11) Clemson | Pwr +++ | BAvg ++ | Spd +++ | Def +++

Year	Lev	Team	AB	R	H	HR	RBI	Avg	OB	Slg	OPS	bb%	ct%	Eye	SB	CS	x/h%	Iso	RC/G
2016	Rk	AZL Athletics	3	0	0	0	0	0	0	0	0	0	100		0	0		0	-2.66
2016	A-	Vermont	233	31	65	2	25	279	351	361	712	10	72	0.40	12	3	22	82	4.47
2017	A+	Stockton	448	71	121	4	36	270	331	395	726	8	73	0.34	12	5	35	125	4.66
2018	AA	Midland	504	81	154	9	55	306	382	450	832	11	77	0.53	18	9	31	145	6.07
2019	AAA	Nashville	438	63	111	14	43	253	320	418	738	9	68	0.31	14	5	35	164	4.79

Well-rounded, up-the-middle player who can handle both SS and CF, but who lacks any plus tools. Simple line-drive stroke, but got HR totals into double-digits in 2019 (insert 'Triple-A baseball' reference). SB history much more consistent; so could have fantasy value if he got MLB AB. But those AB might be hard to come by.

White,Evan | 3 | Seattle

EXP MLB DEBUT: 2020 | H/W: 6-3 205 | FUT: Starting 1B | 8C

Bats R Age 23 | 2017 (1) Kentucky | Pwr +++ | BAvg +++ | Spd +++ | Def ++++

Year	Lev	Team	AB	R	H	HR	RBI	Avg	OB	Slg	OPS	bb%	ct%	Eye	SB	CS	x/h%	Iso	RC/G
2017	NCAA	Kentucky	212	48	79	10	41	373	439	637	1076	11	85	0.81	5	2	44	264	8.77
2017	A-	Everett	47	6	13	3	12	277	358	532	890	11	87	1.00	1	1	38	255	6.49
2018	A+	Modesto	476	72	144	11	66	303	371	458	829	10	78	0.50	4	3	31	155	5.92
2018	AAA	Tacoma	18	0	4	0	0	222	222	333	556	0	72	0.00	0	0	50	111	2.05
2019	AA	Arkansas	365	61	107	18	55	293	345	488	833	7	75	0.32	2	0	31	195	5.71

Advanced hitter who signed contract extension this off-season, likely guaranteeing Opening Day roster spot. Advanced approach with terrific strike zone discipline. Sprays line drives with short, compact swing. Hand adjustment helped reach power in '19. Likely above-average power at maturity. Above-average runner. Exceptional defender at 1B.

Williams,Justin | 79 | St. Louis

EXP MLB DEBUT: 2018 | H/W: 6-2 215 | FUT: Starting OF | 7D

Bats L Age 24 | 2013 (2) HS (LA) | Pwr +++ | BAvg ++ | Spd ++ | Def +++

Year	Lev	Team	AB	R	H	HR	RBI	Avg	OB	Slg	OPS	bb%	ct%	Eye	SB	CS	x/h%	Iso	RC/G
2018	AAA	Memphis	69	8	15	3	11	217	270	391	662	7	75	0.29	0	1	40	174	3.45
2018	AAA	Durham	356	41	92	8	46	258	307	376	683	7	77	0.31	4	3	28	118	3.82
2018	MLB	Tampa Bay	1	0	0	0	0	0	0	0	0	0	100		0	0		0	-2.66
2019	AA	Springfield	57	7	11	1	3	193	246	263	509	7	70	0.24	1	0	18	70	1.38
2019	AAA	Memphis	102	20	36	7	26	353	441	608	1049	14	71	0.53	0	0	33	255	9.16

Hand injury limited him to 159 AB between AA/AAA. Didn't miss a beat when he returned and now owns a career line of .297/.342/.436. Professional hitter with natural power, but unorthodox mechanics and GB tendency leave many skeptical it will translate. Average runner with a strong arm fits as an everyday RF, but only if the power emerges.

Wilson,Izzy — 89 — Tampa Bay — EXP MLB DEBUT: 2022 — H/W: 6-3 185 — FUT: Reserve OF — 6C

Bats L Age 22	Year	Lev	Team	AB	R	H	HR	RBI	Avg	OB	Slg	OPS	bb%	ct%	Eye	SB	CS	x/h%	Iso	RC/G
2014 FA (NT)	2018	A	Rome	223	38	51	6	25	229	315	372	687	11	65	0.36	11	4	35	143	4.22
Pwr +++	2018	A+	Florida	135	16	29	2	10	215	289	311	600	9	68	0.33	5	1	28	96	2.85
BAvg +	2019	A	Bowling Green	85	11	20	3	13	235	323	376	699	11	67	0.39	7	2	25	141	4.28
Spd ++++	2019	A+	Florida	124	20	22	2	6	177	282	298	580	13	56	0.33	7	1	41	121	2.89
Def +++	2019	A+	Charlotte	63	7	17	1	8	270	378	429	807	15	70	0.58	3	2	41	159	6.16

Quick-twitch, athletic OF showed improvement after ATL release. Average-or-better tools across the ball. Extremely raw with ct% issues. Shortened swing in TAM look, resulted in smoother swing path and increased barrel rate. Hard to project hit tool further. Plus runner. 77% SB rate with feel for timing pitchers. Can play all OF positions.

Wilson,Marcus — 89 — Boston — EXP MLB DEBUT: 2020 — H/W: 6-2 175 — FUT: Starting OF — 7D

Bats R Age 23	Year	Lev	Team	AB	R	H	HR	RBI	Avg	OB	Slg	OPS	bb%	ct%	Eye	SB	CS	x/h%	Iso	RC/G
2014 (2) HS (CA)	2017	A	Kane County	383	56	113	9	54	295	384	446	830	13	77	0.61	15	7	31	151	6.10
Pwr +++	2018	A+	Visalia	447	60	105	10	48	235	303	369	673	9	68	0.31	16	6	36	134	3.89
BAvg ++	2019	A+	Salem	146	26	50	8	29	342	415	603	1017	11	68	0.38	4	3	42	260	8.97
Spd +++	2019	AA	Portland	206	35	46	8	22	223	316	408	724	12	60	0.34	6	0	48	184	5.02
Def +++	2019	AA	Jackson	34	4	8	2	7	235	333	529	863	13	62	0.38	3	1	63	294	7.20

Very athletic OF who was demoted from AA to A+ early before turning season around. Set career high in HR while showcasing speed and raw pop. Swing gets choppy at times, though puts charge in ball upon contact. Should stay in CF due to range, but fringy instincts could lead to OF corner. Strong makeup and ability to get on base are admirable.

Wilson,Will — 6 — San Francisco — EXP MLB DEBUT: 2022 — H/W: 6-0 184 — FUT: Starting MIF — 7C

Bats R Age 21	Year	Lev	Team	AB	R	H	HR	RBI	Avg	OB	Slg	OPS	bb%	ct%	Eye	SB	CS	x/h%	Iso	RC/G
2019 (1) NC State																				
Pwr +++																				
BAvg +++																				
Spd ++	2019	NCAA	NC St	128	30	45	9	38	352	424	664	1088	11	78	0.57	1	0	49	313	9.13
Def +++	2019	Rk	Orem	189	23	52	5	18	275	325	439	764	7	75	0.30	0	0	35	164	4.95

High-IQ, high makeup SS was standout three-year starter in ACC before being taken 15th overall. Tools are solid-average. Has compact, simple stroke but uses moderate leg kick to tap into average raw power and spray line drives to the gaps. Understands the strike zone. Fringe runner. Instinctual glove who could play either 2B/SS long-term.

Wiseman,Rhett — 9 — Washington — EXP MLB DEBUT: 2021 — H/W: 6-0 200 — FUT: Reserve OF — 6C

Bats L Age 25	Year	Lev	Team	AB	R	H	HR	RBI	Avg	OB	Slg	OPS	bb%	ct%	Eye	SB	CS	x/h%	Iso	RC/G
2015 (3) Vanderbilt	2016	A	Hagerstown	478	71	122	13	75	255	315	410	725	8	78	0.40	19	10	35	155	4.46
Pwr +++	2017	A+	Potomac	432	55	99	13	55	229	285	391	677	7	78	0.35	2	4	39	162	3.78
BAvg +	2018	A+	Potomac	407	65	103	21	63	253	353	484	837	13	70	0.52	8	2	47	231	6.27
Spd ++	2019	A-	Auburn	13	4	4	3	3	308	357	1000	1357	7	77	0.33	1	0	75	692	11.57
Def ++	2019	AA	Harrisburg	335	40	72	15	57	215	291	412	703	10	63	0.29	6	5	47	197	4.42

Crushed 9 HR in April, and launch-angle stories followed. But it was a one-month affair, and the price was heavy the rest of the season, which it could be argued it was the worst of his career. Will need to tame 2019's monstrous strikeout rate if he is to make it. At this point RF arm might be his best tool.

Witt Jr.,Bobby — 6 — Kansas City — EXP MLB DEBUT: 2023 — H/W: 6-1 190 — FUT: Starting SS — 9C

Bats R Age 19	Year	Lev	Team	AB	R	H	HR	RBI	Avg	OB	Slg	OPS	bb%	ct%	Eye	SB	CS	x/h%	Iso	RC/G
2019 (1) HS (TX)																				
Pwr ++++																				
BAvg +++																				
Spd ++++																				
Def ++++	2019	Rk	AZL Royals	164	30	43	1	27	262	316	354	670	7	79	0.37	9	1	19	91	3.80

Quick-twitch, athletic second-generation player was 2nd overall pick in 2019. 5-tool potential if tools actualize. Loose, quick swing. Struggles with swing path and spin recognition but uses legs and has feel for zone. Double-plus raw power but will take time to get there as swing smooths out. Double-plus speed; could be 30/30 threat.

Wong,Connor — 245 — Los Angeles (N) — EXP MLB DEBUT: 2021 — H/W: 6-1 181 — FUT: Reserve C — 6C

Bats R Age 23	Year	Lev	Team	AB	R	H	HR	RBI	Avg	OB	Slg	OPS	bb%	ct%	Eye	SB	CS	x/h%	Iso	RC/G
2017 (3) Houston	2017	Rk	AZL Dodgers	1	0	0	0	0	0	0	0	0	0	0	0.00	0	0		0	
Pwr +++	2017	A	Great Lakes	97	19	27	5	18	278	327	495	822	7	73	0.27	1	1	41	216	5.61
BAvg ++	2018	A+	RanchoCuca	383	64	103	19	60	269	335	480	815	9	64	0.28	6	2	40	211	6.09
Spd +++	2019	A+	RanchoCuca	274	39	67	15	51	245	298	507	806	7	66	0.23	9	2	54	263	5.80
Def +++	2019	AA	Tulsa	149	17	52	9	31	349	394	604	998	7	66	0.22	2	1	37	255	8.53

Athletic backstop moved from SS to C in college and had a breakout season in 2019, hitting .281 with 24 Doubles and 24 HR. Good power from the RH side and above-average speed allowed him to split time at 2B. Strong arm with solid receiving skills should allow him to stick behind the dish, but will need to make more contact as he moves up.

Woodrow,Danny — 7 — Detroit — EXP MLB DEBUT: 2020 — H/W: 5-10 170 — FUT: Reserve OF — 6B

Bats L Age 25	Year	Lev	Team	AB	R	H	HR	RBI	Avg	OB	Slg	OPS	bb%	ct%	Eye	SB	CS	x/h%	Iso	RC/G
2016 (12) Creighton	2016	A-	Connecticut	145	21	40	0	13	276	331	324	655	8	78	0.38	8	2	15	48	3.61
Pwr +	2017	A	West Michigan	469	73	127	0	47	271	342	324	666	10	80	0.55	31	11	17	53	3.90
BAvg +++	2018	A+	Lakeland	21	5	8	0	1	381	409	429	838	5	76	0.20	4	1	13	48	5.74
Spd ++++	2018	AA	Erie	342	48	107	3	37	313	370	395	765	8	79	0.44	19	13	18	82	5.00
Def +++	2019	AAA	Toledo	376	58	103	1	32	274	345	340	686	10	76	0.46	23	5	17	66	4.12

Compact, lean outfielder who thrives off speed on both sides of the ball. Advanced defensive feel plays off near-elite speed with ability to cover his entire post. Sound pitch recognition, but thin frame won't produce for genuine power. Needs to play towards line drive contact to earn the most offensive value.

Wyatt,Logan — 3 — San Francisco — EXP MLB DEBUT: 2021 — H/W: 6-4 230 — FUT: Starting 1B — 7C

Bats L Age 22	Year	Lev	Team	AB	R	H	HR	RBI	Avg	OB	Slg	OPS	bb%	ct%	Eye	SB	CS	x/h%	Iso	RC/G
2019 (2) Louisville																				
Pwr +++																				
BAvg +++																				
Spd +	2019	Rk	AZL Giants	24	7	9	0	9	375	464	417	881	14	75	0.67	0	1	11	42	6.98
Def +++	2019	A-	Salem-Keizer	67	10	19	2	12	284	377	403	780	13	87	1.11	0	1	21	119	5.40

Natural-hitting 1B who is more about contact than power. Patient approach has led to high OBP and likes to use entire field with hard line drives. Can be too passive, though finds good pitches to drive. Good defender with soft hands and average arm. Slow foot speed limits SB opps. Strength is there, but would need to tweak swing mechanics.

Young,Andy — 456 — Arizona — EXP MLB DEBUT: 2020 — H/W: 6-0 195 — FUT: Utility player — 7B

Bats R Age 25	Year	Lev	Team	AB	R	H	HR	RBI	Avg	OB	Slg	OPS	bb%	ct%	Eye	SB	CS	x/h%	Iso	RC/G
2016 (37) Indiana St	2017	AA	Springfield	3	2	2	0	1	667	750	667	1417	25	67	1.00	0	0	0	0	16.56
Pwr +++	2018	A+	Palm Beach	297	43	82	12	34	276	345	444	789	9	80	0.53	4	0	29	168	5.23
BAvg ++	2018	AA	Springfield	135	18	43	9	24	319	352	556	908	5	81	0.27	0	2	30	237	6.27
Spd ++	2019	AA	Jackson	223	36	58	8	28	260	315	453	768	7	76	0.34	1	1	43	193	4.98
Def ++	2019	AAA	Reno	239	53	67	21	53	280	346	611	957	9	72	0.35	2	2	51	331	7.50

Stocky, chiseled 2B prospect with OBP skills and good raw power. Effortful swing is geared toward big-time fly ball contact to all fields but also limits his contact skills to fringe-average; struggles with quality located breaking balls. Has bounced around the diamond, but lack of arm strength and limited athleticism project him to 2B long-term.

Young,Chavez — 89 — Toronto — EXP MLB DEBUT: 2022 — H/W: 6-0 195 — FUT: Starting OF — 7D

Bats B Age 22	Year	Lev	Team	AB	R	H	HR	RBI	Avg	OB	Slg	OPS	bb%	ct%	Eye	SB	CS	x/h%	Iso	RC/G
2016 (39) HS (GA)	2016	Rk	GCL Blue Jays	73	9	20	0	6	274	329	438	767	8	64	0.23	6	1	50	164	5.75
Pwr ++	2017	Rk	Bluefield	252	52	71	4	25	282	317	440	757	5	77	0.22	4	5	35	159	4.82
BAvg +++	2017	A-	Vancouver	13	3	4	0	5	308	308	538	846	0	62	0.00	0	0	50	231	7.11
Spd ++++	2018	A	Lansing	470	88	134	8	57	285	364	445	808	11	79	0.58	44	13	37	160	5.78
Def +++	2019	A+	Dunedin	401	53	99	6	43	247	307	354	661	8	75	0.34	24	11	27	107	3.66

Rangy OF who saw production fall with rise to A+. Still showcased plus speed, though baserunning instincts lag behind. Has offensive potential with mature approach and enough strength to reach seats. More power forthcoming has he learns to swing more consistently with loft. Profiles well in RF due to plus range and strong arm. Sleeper prospect.

Zagunis,Mark — 79 — Chicago (N) — EXP MLB DEBUT: 2017 — H/W: 6-0 215 — FUT: Reserve OF — 6A

Bats R Age 27	Year	Lev	Team	AB	R	H	HR	RBI	Avg	OB	Slg	OPS	bb%	ct%	Eye	SB	CS	x/h%	Iso	RC/G
2014 (3) Virginia Tech	2017	MLB	Chi Cubs	14	0	0	0	1	0	222	0	222	22	57	0.67	2	0		0	-3.82
Pwr ++	2018	AAA	Iowa	371	63	101	7	40	272	388	375	762	16	73	0.69	11	1	24	102	5.37
BAvg +++	2018	MLB	Chi Cubs	5	0	2	0	1	400	500	600	1100	17	80	1.00	0	0	50	200	10.07
Spd +++	2019	AAA	Iowa	255	35	75	6	43	294	355	475	829	9	63	0.26	6	3	44	180	6.60
Def ++	2019	MLB	Chi Cubs	36	2	9	0	5	250	325	333	658	10	56	0.25	0	0	33	83	4.46

Former 3rd round pick who had a solid year in AAA, but has struggled to stay on the 25-man roster and profiles as utility glove or bat. Possesses some of the best pitch ID and plate discipline skills in the system and should rack up walks. Makes good contact via short, compact stroke. Power is fringy, but his solid speed could result in SB value.

PITCHERS

Pitchers are classified as Starters (SP) or Relievers (RP).

THROWS: Handedness — right (RH) or left (LH).

AGE: Pitcher's age, as of April 1, 2020.

DRAFTED: The year, round, and school that the pitcher performed at as an amateur if drafted, or the year and country where the player was signed from, if a free agent.

EXP MLB DEBUT: The year a player is expected to debut in the major leagues.

H/W: The player's height and weight.

FUT: The role that the pitcher is expected to have for the majority of his major league career, not necessarily his greatest upside.

PITCHES: Each pitch that a pitcher throws is graded and designated with a "+", indicating the quality of the pitch, taking into context the pitcher's age and level pitched. Pitches are graded for their velocity, movement, and command. An average pitch will receive three "+" marks. If known, a pitcher's velocity for each pitch is indicated.

FB	fastball
CB	curveball
SP	split-fingered fastball
SL	slider
CU	change-up
CT	cut-fastball
KC	knuckle-curve
KB	knuckle-ball
SC	screwball
SU	slurve

PLAYER STAT LINES: Pitchers receive statistics for the last five teams that they played for (if applicable), including college and the major leagues.

TEAM DESIGNATIONS: Each team that the pitcher performed for during a given year is included.

LEVEL DESIGNATIONS: The level for each team a player performed is included. "AAA" means Triple-A, "AA" means Double-A, "A+" means high Class-A, "A-" means low Class-A and "Rk" means rookie level.

SABERMETRIC CATEGORIES: Descriptions of all the sabermetric categories appear in the glossary.

CAPSULE COMMENTARIES: For each pitcher, a brief analysis of their skills/statistics, and their future potential is provided.

ELIGIBILITY: Eligibility for inclusion is less than 50 innings pitched in the majors.

POTENTIAL RATINGS: The Potential Ratings are a two-part system in which a player is assigned a number rating based on his upside potential (1-10) and a letter rating based on the probability of reaching that potential (A-E).

Potential

10:	Hall of Famer	5:	MLB reserve
9:	Elite player	4:	Top minor leaguer
8:	Solid regular	3:	Average minor leaguer
7:	Average regular	2:	Minor league reserve
6:	Platoon player	1:	Minor league roster filler

Probability Rating

- A: 90% probability of reaching potential
- B: 70% probability of reaching potential
- C: 50% probability of reaching potential
- D: 30% probability of reaching potential
- E: 10% probability of reaching potential

FASTBALL: Scouts grade a fastball in terms of both velocity and movement. Movement of a pitch is purely subjective, but one can always watch the hitter to see how he reacts to a pitch or if he swings and misses. Pitchers throw four types of fastballs with varying movement. A two-seam fastball is often referred to as a sinker. A four-seam fastball appears to maintain its plane at high velocities. A cutter can move in different directions and is caused by the pitcher both cutting-off his extension out front and by varying the grip. A split-fingered fastball (forkball) is thrown with the fingers spread apart against the seams and demonstrates violent downward movement. Velocity is often graded on the 20-80 scale and is indicated by the chart below.

Scout Grade	Velocity (mph)
80	96+
70	94-95
60	92-93
50 (avg)	89-91
40	87-88
30	85-86
20	82-84

PITCHER RELEASE TIMES: The speed (in seconds) that a pitcher releases a pitch from the stretch is extremely important in terms of halting the running game and establishing good pitching mechanics. Pitchers are timed from the movement of the front leg until the baseball reaches the catcher's mitt. The phrases "slow to the plate" or "quick to the plate" may appear in the capsule commentary box.

1.0-1.2	+
1.3-1.4	MLB average
1.5+	–

Abbott,Cory

SP | **Chicago (N)** | EXP MLB DEBUT: 2020 | H/W: 6-2 220 | FUT: #5 SP/swingman | **7B**

Thrws R Age 24
2017 (2) Loyola Marymount

Velo	Pitch	Grade
91-93	FB	+++
86-88	CT	+++
80-82	CB	+++
84-85	CU	++

Year	Lev	Team	W	L	Sv	IP	K	ERA	WHIP	BF/G	OBA	H%	S%	xERA	Ctl	Dom	Cmd	hr/9	BPV
2017	NCAA	LoyolaMarymt	11	2	0	98	130	1.74	0.91	24.4	181	28	81	1.31	2.6	11.9	4.6	0.3	163
2017	A-	Eugene	0	0	0	14	18	3.86	1.21	11.3	262	38	69	3.43	1.9	11.6	6.0	0.6	174
2018	A	South Bend	4	1	0	47	57	2.48	1.02	20.1	209	28	81	2.56	2.5	10.9	4.4	1.0	147
2018	A+	Myrtle Beach	4	5	0	67	74	2.54	1.26	21.1	237	33	80	3.03	3.5	9.9	2.8	0.4	102
2019	AA	Tennessee	8	8	0	146	166	3.02	1.12	22.2	214	28	77	2.86	3.2	10.2	3.2	0.9	116

Strong, durable RH who led the Southern League in Dom and IP. Produced above-average SwK in 2020 via solid-average, four-pitch blend. Spots low-90s FB well and effective CT makes him hard to barrel up. CB and CU project as fringe-to-average offerings. Spent time as RP in college, but stuff should play well as a low-risk, back-end SP.

Abreu,Albert

SP | **New York (A)** | EXP MLB DEBUT: 2020 | H/W: 6-2 175 | FUT: #4 starter | **8D**

Thrws R Age 24
2013 FA (DR)

Velo	Pitch	Grade
96-98	FB	++++
82-86	CB	+++
86-89	CU	+++

Year	Lev	Team	W	L	Sv	IP	K	ERA	WHIP	BF/G	OBA	H%	S%	xERA	Ctl	Dom	Cmd	hr/9	BPV
2018	Rk	GCL YankeesW	0	3	0	5	5	23.40	3.20	10.0	498	61	19	12.64	3.6	9.0	2.5	0.0	83
2018	Rk	GCL Yankees	0	1	0	2	2	18.00	2.00	9.6	415	52	0	7.49	0.0	9.0		0.0	180
2018	A+	Tampa	4	3	0	62	65	4.20	1.33	19.9	235	29	73	4.03	4.2	9.4	2.2	1.3	74
2018	AA	Trenton	0	0	0	5	4	0.00	0.20	15.1	0	0	100		1.8	7.2	4.0	0.0	99
2019	AA	Trenton	5	8	0	96	91	4.30	1.62	18.6	275	34	75	4.87	5.0	8.5	1.7	0.8	37

Big bodied, hard-throwing RHP continues to go the wrong way in development. A short-strider, arm injuries have shortened the past two seasons. Durability concerns may push to RP role. Sits mid-to-high 90s with FB, though it flattens out as he adds velocity. 12-to-6 CB has inconsistent depth despite solid break. CU is late-fading offering.

Abreu,Bryan

SP | **Houston** | EXP MLB DEBUT: 2019 | H/W: 6-1 204 | FUT: #3 starter | **8C**

Thrws R Age 22
2013 FA (DR)

Velo	Pitch	Grade
92-96	FB	++++
83-85	CB	++++
85-87	SL	+++
83-85	CU	++

Year	Lev	Team	W	L	Sv	IP	K	ERA	WHIP	BF/G	OBA	H%	S%	xERA	Ctl	Dom	Cmd	hr/9	BPV
2018	A-	Tri City	2	0	0	16		1.13	1.06	15.5	196	28	100	2.67	3.4	12.4	3.7	1.1	150
2018	A	Quad Cities	4	1	3	38	68	1.65	1.02	14.6	170	34	86	1.63	4.0	16.1	4.0	0.5	199
2019	A+	Fayetteville	1	0	0	14	25	3.80	1.06	18.3	184	32	69	2.61	3.8	15.8	4.2	1.3	201
2019	AA	Corpus Christi	6	2	2	76	101	5.08	1.42	16.1	218	32	64	3.44	5.7	11.9	2.1	0.7	80
2019	MLB	Houston	0	0	0	8	13	1.10	0.85	4.3	147	28	86	0.53	3.3	14.3	4.3	0.0	186

Reached majors despite no IP above A- prior to 19. Moving quickly on basis of two plus offerings in FB and elite CB. Mixes in SL that also flashes plus, but doesn't consistently throw for strikes. Pitched out of pen with HOU and could be role if CU doesn't improve. Has been tough to hit, but walk rate a bit high. Owns very high ceiling.

Adon,Joan

SP | **Washington** | EXP MLB DEBUT: 2023 | H/W: 6-2 185 | FUT: #4 starter | **7D**

Thrws R Age 21
2016 FA (DR)

Velo	Pitch	Grade
91-94	FB	+++
83-85	SL	++
80-82	CU	++

Year	Lev	Team	W	L	Sv	IP	K	ERA	WHIP	BF/G	OBA	H%	S%	xERA	Ctl	Dom	Cmd	hr/9	BPV
2018	A-	Auburn	1	1	0	11	11	7.36	2.00	7.6	295	35	65	6.86	7.4	9.0	1.2	1.6	-19
2018	Rk	GCL Nationals	2	0	2	19	29	2.34	1.72	6.7	270	44	85	4.19	6.1	13.6	2.2	0.0	98
2019	A	Hagerstown	11	3	0	105	90	3.86	1.30	19.7	239	29	71	3.44	3.8	7.7	2.0	0.7	55

Strong, athletic frame with good mound presence from 3/4s slot. Some crossfire in delivery allows 91-94 FB to play up, some life but not yet a true swing-and-miss offering. SL/CU both show brief flashes of average potential. Mechanics inconsistent and lead to walks. With improvements, still time for back-of-rotation starter.

Adon,Melvin

RP | **San Francisco** | EXP MLB DEBUT: 2020 | H/W: 6-3 235 | FUT: Closer | **7C**

Thrws R Age 25
2015 FA (DR)

Velo	Pitch	Grade
95-100	FB	++++
87-89	SL	+++
87-88	CU	+

Year	Lev	Team	W	L	Sv	IP	K	ERA	WHIP	BF/G	OBA	H%	S%	xERA	Ctl	Dom	Cmd	hr/9	BPV
2017	A	Augusta	3	11	0	99	89	4.36	1.46	18.5	282	36	69	4.21	3.2	8.1	2.5	0.5	78
2018	Rk	AZL Giants O	0	1	0	4	8	8.57	2.86	11.9	432	70	67	9.95	6.4	17.1	2.7	0.0	153
2018	A+	San Jose	2	5	0	77	71	4.90	1.50	20.9	274	34	67	4.41	4.0	8.3	2.1	0.7	60
2019	AA	Richmond	2	6	14	45	59	2.60	1.42	5.3	230	35	82	3.31	5.2	11.8	2.3	0.4	90
2019	AAA	Sacramento	0	1	0	10	18	14.26	2.38	4.4	360	59	35	8.10	7.1	16.0	2.3	0.9	114

Large-framed RP who served as closer in AA before getting shelled in AAA. Moved to pen in 2019 and impressed with high K rate. Pitches off plus FB that often reaches triple digits. Features electric movement and can be tough to elevate. Difficulty has been throwing strikes. Lacks consistency with plate control. Uses wipeout SL when ahead in count.

Akin,Keegan

SP | **Baltimore** | EXP MLB DEBUT: 2020 | H/W: 6-0 225 | FUT: #4 starter | **7C**

Thrws L Age 25
2016 (2) Western Michigan

Velo	Pitch	Grade
89-92	FB	+++
83-84	SL	+++
80-84	CU	+++

Year	Lev	Team	W	L	Sv	IP	K	ERA	WHIP	BF/G	OBA	H%	S%	xERA	Ctl	Dom	Cmd	hr/9	BPV
2016	NCAA	WestMichigan	7	4	0	109	133	1.82	0.94	24.1	190	29	79	1.31	2.5	11.0	4.4	0.1	149
2016	A-	Aberdeen	0	1	0	26	29	1.04	0.85	10.6	170	25	86	0.79	2.4	10.0	4.1	0.0	133
2017	A+	Frederick	7	8	0	100	111	4.14	1.35	19.9	240	31	72	3.91	4.1	10.0	2.4	1.1	86
2018	AA	Bowie	14	7	0	137	142	3.28	1.25	22.4	228	29	78	3.49	3.8	9.3	2.4	1.0	83
2019	AAA	Norfolk	6	7	0	112	131	4.74	1.52	19.4	256	35	69	4.28	4.9	10.5	2.1	0.8	75

High 3/4s pitchability LHP was solid in Triple-A in 2019. Very repeatable delivery, commands three-pitch arsenal extremely well. Low 90s FB with minimal run must be commanded to corners and edges of zone. Best secondary is his CU, which projects as borderline plus with deception off FB and late fading action to the arm-side. SL is fringe-average.

Alcala,Jorge

RP | **Minnesota** | EXP MLB DEBUT: 2019 | H/W: 6-3 205 | FUT: Setup reliever | **7C**

Thrws R Age 24
2014 FA (DR)

Velo	Pitch	Grade
92-96	FB	++++
84-87	SL	++++
79-81	CB	++
	CU	++

Year	Lev	Team	W	L	Sv	IP	K	ERA	WHIP	BF/G	OBA	H%	S%	xERA	Ctl	Dom	Cmd	hr/9	BPV
2018	AA	Corpus Christi	2	3	1	40	37	3.58	1.32	18.5	241	31	71	3.06	3.8	8.3	2.2	0.2	64
2018	AA	Chattanooga	0	4	0	20	22	5.85	1.85	18.7	290	36	73	6.54	6.3	9.9	1.6	1.8	26
2019	AA	Pensacola	5	7	0	102	105	5.90	1.48	16.9	283	36	60	4.82	3.3	9.2	2.8	1.1	96
2019	AAA	Rochester	1	0	0	7	11	0.00	0.83	5.3	165	30	100	0.67	2.5	13.8	5.5	0.0	198
2019	MLB	Minnesota	0	0	0	1	1	0.00	1.67	2.7	228	30	100	3.57	7.5	7.5	1.0	0.0	-50

Lean RHP made full-time transition from SP to RP role mid-season, making MLB debut in September. 3/4s, max-effort delivery. Solid athlete. Mostly 2-pitch mix as RP. Relies on FB with solid late arm-side action. Flattens when up in zone. SL is late 2-plane breaker and is a plus pitch. CB has solid characteristics but struggles with slot.

Alexy,A.J.

SP | **Texas** | EXP MLB DEBUT: 2021 | H/W: 6-4 195 | FUT: #4 starter | **8D**

Thrws R Age 21
2016 (11) HS (PA)

Velo	Pitch	Grade
91-94	FB	+++
70-73	CB	++++
82-85	CU	++

Year	Lev	Team	W	L	Sv	IP	K	ERA	WHIP	BF/G	OBA	H%	S%	xERA	Ctl	Dom	Cmd	hr/9	BPV
2016	Rk	AZL Dodgers	1	0	0	13	12	4.77	1.52	8.2	314	37	72	5.67	2.0	8.2	4.0	1.4	110
2017	A	Hickory	1	1	0	20	27	3.12	1.39	17.0	186	25	84	3.57	6.7	12.0	1.8	1.3	54
2017	A	Great Lakes	2	6	0	73	86	3.69	1.13	15.2	182	26	66	2.00	4.5	10.6	2.3	0.4	86
2018	A	Hickory	6	8	0	108	138	3.58	1.31	20.3	226	34	72	2.98	4.3	11.5	2.7	0.4	108
2019	A+	Down East	0	3	0	19	23	5.18	1.41	16.2	206	30	62	3.07	6.1	10.8	1.8	0.5	48

Broad-shouldered and built for innings, he started slow in High-A and was shut down for the season with a lat strain in early May. Prior, showed a low-90s FB with some life, but best offering was 11-to-5 hammer curve with depth, a plus present pitch. Was working on mid-80s CU that he'll need to neutralize LHH. Will need to tighten control.

Allan,Matt

SP | **New York (N)** | EXP MLB DEBUT: 2023 | H/W: 6-3 225 | FUT: #2 starter | **9D**

Thrws R Age 18
2019 (3) HS (FL)

Velo	Pitch	Grade
92-96	FB	++++
77-81	CB	++++
84-87	CU	+++

Year	Lev	Team	W	L	Sv	IP	K	ERA	WHIP	BF/G	OBA	H%	S%	xERA	Ctl	Dom	Cmd	hr/9	BPV
2019	Rk	GCL Mets	1	0	0	8	11	1.11	1.11	6.4	180	30	89	1.55	4.4	12.2	2.8	0.0	118
2019	A-	Brooklyn	0	0	0	2	3	9.00	3.00	11.6	470	65	67	11.29	4.5	13.5	3.0	0.0	140

Athletic, hard-throwing 2019 draftee made pro debut. Repeats his high 3/4s delivery well. Sat 92-96 in pro debut with advanced command and late biting action on FB. CB flashes double-plus with 11-to-5 break and will be his primary out pitch. CU fades but lacks consistency. Athleticism should play up development.

Allen,Logan

SP | **Cleveland** | EXP MLB DEBUT: 2019 | H/W: 6-3 200 | FUT: #4 starter | **7C**

Thrws L Age 22
2015 (8) HS (FL)

Velo	Pitch	Grade
90-94	FB	+++
83-85	SL	+++
75-78	CB	++
81-84	CU	++++

Year	Lev	Team	W	L	Sv	IP	K	ERA	WHIP	BF/G	OBA	H%	S%	xERA	Ctl	Dom	Cmd	hr/9	BPV
2018	AAA	El Paso	4	0	0	27	26	1.65	1.25	22.1	215	25	97	3.59	4.3	8.6	2.0	1.3	57
2019	AAA	Columbus	1	1	0	22	18	7.74	1.95	21.1	332	36	65	8.08	4.9	7.3	1.5	2.4	18
2019	MLB	San Diego	2	3	0	25	14	6.81	1.83	14.6	318	34	64	6.64	4.7	5.0	1.1	1.4	-17
2019	MLB	Cleveland	0	0	0	2	3	0.00	1.43	8.9	336	51	100	4.49	0.0	12.9		0.0	249

Pitchability LHP made MLB debut but FB fell flat. Acquired in mid-season trade with SD. Easy, 3/4s crossfire delivery. Low 90s FB lost run for most of season and downward plane was enough to get hitters out. Best secondary is late-fading CU with solid separation off FB. SL projected as above-average pitch.

Alzolay,Adbert

SP | **Chicago (N)** | EXP MLB DEBUT: 2019 | H/W: 6-0 179 | FUT: Setup reliever | **7B**

Thrws R Age 25
2012 FA (VZ)

Velo	Pitch	Grade
92-94	FB	+++
78-80	CB	++++
83-85	CU	++

Year	Lev	Team	W	L	Sv	IP	K	ERA	WHIP	BF/G	OBA	H%	S%	xERA	Ctl	Dom	Cmd	hr/9	BPV
2017	AA	Tennessee	0	3	0	32	30	3.07	1.21	18.5	229	31	72	2.42	3.4	8.4	2.5	0.0	78
2018	AAA	Iowa	2	4	0	39	27	4.82	1.43	20.8	280	32	67	4.54	3.0	6.2	2.1	0.9	49
2019	A+	Myrtle Beach	0	1	0	4	3	11.25	2.25	20.3	383	42	50	9.59	4.5	6.8	1.5	2.3	18
2019	AAA	Iowa	2	4	0	65	91	4.42	1.29	17.8	224	32	70	3.82	4.3	12.6	2.9	1.4	129
2019	MLB	Chi Cubs	1	1	0	12	13	7.44	1.82	14.0	276	30	67	7.36	6.7	9.7	1.4	3.0	11

Oft injury-prone RH who missed time with biceps tweak after making his debut. Operates at 92-94 mph (t97) with FB; good 2-seam action when he gets on top. Plus CB flashes elite spin rate and has ability to command down in zone. CU is inconsistent and will need work. Plus FB/CB combo could ultimately work better from the bullpen.

Anderson,Ian | SP | Atlanta | EXP MLB DEBUT: 2020 | H/W: 6-3 170 | FUT: #3 starter | 8C

Thrws R Age 21	Year	Lev	Team	W	L	Sv	IP	K	ERA	WHIP	BF/G	OBA	H%	S%	xERA	Ctl	Dom	Cmd	hr/9	BPV
2016 (1) HS (NY)	2017	A	Rome	4	5	0	83	101	3.14	1.35	17.3	228	34	74	2.73	4.7	11.0	2.3	0.0	89
91-94 FB ++++	2018	A+	Florida	2	6	0	100	118	2.52	1.13	19.8	206	30	77	2.08	3.6	10.6	3.0	0.2	112
73-77 CB +++	2018	AA	Mississippi	2	1	0	19	24	2.36	1.20	19.2	206	32	78	2.10	4.2	11.3	2.7	0.0	107
84-86 CU ++++	2019	AA	Mississippi	7	5	0	111	147	2.68	1.16	21.0	208	31	79	2.61	3.8	11.9	3.1	0.6	130
	2019	AAA	Gwinnett	1	2	0	24	25	6.69	1.69	21.8	252	29	64	5.68	6.7	9.3	1.4	1.9	5

Former 1st-round pick inched closer to MLB debut. Over-the-top, online delivery with deception created by arm angle and solid extension. Sneaky-quick FB sits low 90s but plays louder. 12-to-6 CB carries a lighter spin rate but plays up due to arm slot and is average-to-above-average at maturity. CU is a late-fading, true out pitch.

Andrews,Clayton | RP | Milwaukee | EXP MLB DEBUT: 2021 | H/W: 5-6 160 | FUT: Middle reliever | 6B

Thrws L Age 23	Year	Lev	Team	W	L	Sv	IP	K	ERA	WHIP	BF/G	OBA	H%	S%	xERA	Ctl	Dom	Cmd	hr/9	BPV
2018 (17) Long Beach St	2018	NCAA	Long Beach St	7	7	0	99	118	2.00	0.96	25.0	218	31	80	1.96	1.5	10.7	6.9	0.4	169
87-89 FB +	2018	Rk	Helena	0	0	0	6	12	6.00	1.83	5.6	347	65	64	5.65	3.0	18.0	6.0	0.0	261
78-80 CB ++++	2018	A	Wisconsin	6	1	0	27	42	1.33	0.70	6.8	155	24	94	1.18	1.7	14.0	8.4	1.0	225
CU +++	2019	A+	Carolina	2	2	11	28	44	3.86	1.21	5.1	233	39	69	3.03	3.2	14.1	4.4	0.6	186
	2019	AA	Biloxi	3	0	0	31	33	2.60	1.09	7.2	178	23	81	2.33	4.3	9.5	2.2	0.9	73

Shorter, stocky two-way prospect who projects better on the mound than at the plate. Lacks ideal FB velocity in upper-80s but shows aptitude for spin on plus CB and deceptive, fading CU. Racked up Ks against AFL competition and could eventually morph into a swingman or long relief type with sneaky Dom.

Antone,Tejay | SP | Cincinnati | EXP MLB DEBUT: 2020 | H/W: 6-4 205 | FUT: #5 SP/swingman | 6C

Thrws R Age 26	Year	Lev	Team	W	L	Sv	IP	K	ERA	WHIP	BF/G	OBA	H%	S%	xERA	Ctl	Dom	Cmd	hr/9	BPV
2014 (5) Weatherford JC	2016	AAA	Louisville	0	1	0	5		1.80	1.20	20.1	175	25	83	1.76	5.4	9.0	1.7	0.0	34
89-93 FB +++	2017		Did not play -injured																	
84-86 SL +++	2018	A+	Daytona	6	3	0	96	82	4.03	1.29	23.2	260	32	69	3.56	2.7	7.7	2.8	0.6	83
78-81 CB ++	2019	AA	Chattanooga	7	4	0	74	63	3.40	1.15	22.6	231	29	70	2.75	2.7	7.6	2.9	0.5	83
84-85 CU +++	2019	AAA	Louisville	4	8	0	71	70	4.68	1.74	23.2	317	40	74	5.83	3.9	8.8	2.3	0.9	71

Older, 3/4s extreme crossfire RHP has emerged late in development due to increased velocity and high spin rates. Four-pitch pitcher. Does a good job mixing and matching, playing up arsenal. FB has heavy bore and sink in lower half of zone. SL is above-average offering with a longer angle break. CB and CU both workable. Could excel in RP role.

Aquino,Stiward | SP | Los Angeles (A) | EXP MLB DEBUT: 2023 | H/W: 6-6 170 | FUT: Middle reliever | 8E

Thrws R Age 20	Year	Lev	Team	W	L	Sv	IP	K	ERA	WHIP	BF/G	OBA	H%	S%	xERA	Ctl	Dom	Cmd	hr/9	BPV
2016 FA (DR)																				
91-94 FB +++																				
74-78 CB +++	2017	Rk	AZL Angels	1	0	0	5	2	1.73	1.73	11.8	254	28	89	4.11	6.9	3.5	0.5	0.0	-107
82-84 CU +++	2019	Rk	Orem	0	1	0	15	23	5.92	1.64	17.0	307	45	68	6.23	3.6	13.6	3.8	1.8	167
	2019	Rk	AZL Angels	0	4	0	21	26	7.71	1.76	12.0	313	44	53	5.38	4.3	11.1	2.6	0.4	103

Tall, projectable RH returned to short-season ball with mixed bag after missing 2018 from Tommy John surgery. Chance for three above-avg pitches. FB tops out at 96 mph but plays down due to lack of extension to plate. CB has solid 11-to-5 break; CU advanced for age. Stuff is hittable in zone and lack of athleticism may limit his ability to develop avg command.

Armenteros,Rogelio | SP | Houston | EXP MLB DEBUT: 2019 | H/W: 6-1 215 | FUT: #5 SP/swingman | 7D

Thrws R Age 25	Year	Lev	Team	W	L	Sv	IP	K	ERA	WHIP	BF/G	OBA	H%	S%	xERA	Ctl	Dom	Cmd	hr/9	BPV
2014 FA (CU)	2017	AA	Corpus Christi	2	3	1	65	74	1.94	1.04	18.0	211	30	83	2.15	2.6	10.2	3.9	0.4	131
88-92 FB +++	2017	AAA	Fresno	8	1	0	58	72	2.17	1.05	22.5	204	29	84	2.41	2.9	11.2	3.8	0.8	139
73-78 CB ++	2018	AAA	Fresno	8	1	1	118	134	3.74	1.31	22.1	242	31	76	3.88	3.7	10.2	2.8	1.1	103
84-86 SL ++	2019	AAA	Round Rock	6	7	0	84	85	4.82	1.44	18.9	275	33	71	5.01	3.3	9.1	2.7	1.5	92
80-82 CU ++++	2019	MLB	Houston	1	1	1	18	18	4.00	1.22	14.6	251	33	67	3.20	2.5	9.0	3.6	0.5	113

Durable arm succeeds with command and precise pitch location. CU is his go-to pitch and can sequence pitches backwards to keep hitters off balance. Can rear back for more velocity, but FB best in low 90s. Has missed lot of bats in career, though may be more moderate in majors. Both SL and CB are fringe average at best. Could be bullpen candidate.

Ashby,Aaron | SP | Milwaukee | EXP MLB DEBUT: 2021 | H/W: 6-2 181 | FUT: #3 starter | 7B

Thrws L Age 21	Year	Lev	Team	W	L	Sv	IP	K	ERA	WHIP	BF/G	OBA	H%	S%	xERA	Ctl	Dom	Cmd	hr/9	BPV
2018 (4) Crowder JC	2018	NCAA	Crowder JC	11	2	1	74	156	2.30	1.19	19.8	177	45	80	1.87	5.2	18.9	3.6	0.2	218
91-94 FB +++	2018	Rk	Helena	1	2	1	20	19	6.27	1.29	13.8	241	28	52	4.04	3.6	8.5	2.4	1.3	74
79-83 SL +++	2018	A	Wisconsin	1	1	0	37	47	2.18	1.32	21.9	277	40	83	3.53	2.2	11.4	5.2	0.2	164
71-75 CB ++++	2019	A	Wisconsin	3	4	0	61	80	3.54	1.23	22.5	215	32	72	2.81	4.1	11.8	2.9	0.6	119
CU +++	2019	A+	Carolina	2	6	0	65	55	3.46	1.32	20.7	228	29	72	2.82	4.4	7.6	1.7	0.1	35

JUCO southpaw taken in 2nd round of 2018 who carved up MWL hitters in 2019 en route to A+ bump. High three-quarters slot produces plus hammer CB for whiffs and will at times scrape 95 mph with plus FB. Change-up flashes above-average but will require more reps. Will need to find the strike zone more to realize his potential of a #3 SP.

Ashcraft,Braxton | SP | Pittsburgh | EXP MLB DEBUT: 2023 | H/W: 6-5 195 | FUT: #3 starter | 8D

Thrws R Age 20	Year	Lev	Team	W	L	Sv	IP	K	ERA	WHIP	BF/G	OBA	H%	S%	xERA	Ctl	Dom	Cmd	hr/9	BPV
2018 (2) HS (TX)																				
90-94 FB ++++																				
81-85 SL +++																				
81-83 CU ++	2018	Rk	GCL Pirates	0	1	0	17	12	4.71	1.22	13.9	248	28	63	3.70	2.6	6.3	2.4	1.0	60
	2019	A-	West Virginia	1	9	0	53	39	5.77	1.34	20.0	247	29	55	3.63	3.7	6.6	1.8	0.7	36

Athletic, tall SP who uses height to advantage by throwing on extreme plane to plate. Has potential for bigger FB as he adds strength. FB is top offering at present with good heat, angle and sink. SL has added power in past few seasons and spotted well low in zone. Repeats delivery well for age and should continue to develop at least average CU.

Avila,Pedro | SP | San Diego | EXP MLB DEBUT: 2019 | H/W: 5-11 190 | FUT: #5 SP/swingman | 7C

Thrws R Age 23	Year	Lev	Team	W	L	Sv	IP	K	ERA	WHIP	BF/G	OBA	H%	S%	xERA	Ctl	Dom	Cmd	hr/9	BPV
2014 FA (VZ)	2018	A+	Lake Elsinore	7	9	1	130	142	4.29	1.46	23.2	270	36	70	4.10	3.7	9.8	2.6	0.6	94
91-93 FB +++	2019	Rk	AZL Padres 2	0	0	0	2	3	9.00	1.50	8.6	262	27	50	7.76	4.5	13.5	3.0	4.5	140
74-77 CB +++	2019	Rk	AZL Padres	0	1	0	10	15	0.90	0.70	11.7	151	27	86	0.19	1.8	13.5	7.5	0.0	212
82-84 CU +++	2019	AA	Amarillo	0	2	0	12	13	8.25	1.67	17.9	293	32	56	7.25	4.5	9.8	2.2	3.0	72
	2019	MLB	San Diego	0	0	0	5	5	1.76	1.18	20.4	218	30	83	2.19	3.5	8.8	2.5	0.0	82

Breakout prospect from 2017 made spot-start debut in April, but missed significant time on IL with injuries. Shorter, stocky build; runs FB up to 96 mph in short stints but mostly operates in low 90s. Leans heavily on FB for secondaries, and both CB and CU project as above-average pitches. Has fly-ball profile, solid SwK floor but fringe command.

Aybar,Yoan | RP | Boston | EXP MLB DEBUT: 2022 | H/W: 6-3 165 | FUT: Setup reliever | 7D

Thrws L Age 22	Year	Lev	Team	W	L	Sv	IP	K	ERA	WHIP	BF/G	OBA	H%	S%	xERA	Ctl	Dom	Cmd	hr/9	BPV
2013 FA (DR)																				
94-98 FB ++++	2018	A-	Lowell	1	0	0	2	0	4.50	2.00	4.8	262	26	75	4.93	9.0	0.0	0.0	0.0	-225
83-87 SL +++	2018	Rk	GCL Red Sox	1	1	0	26	27	4.14	1.34	7.2	238	33	66	2.86	4.1	9.3	2.3	0.0	74
CU +	2019	A+	Salem	0	0	0	5	3	1.80	0.60	4.3	124	15	67		1.8	5.4	3.0	0.0	67
	2019	A	Greenville	1	3	0	51	67	4.92	1.45	5.5	191	30	63	2.68	7.0	11.8	1.7	0.2	40

Strong-armed RP who spent first full season as P after converting from INF in 2018. Got off to slow start but ended strong after cutting BB rate and upping K. Tough on RHH and LHH with quick FB and implementation of SL. As expected, owns inconsistent mechanics and arm slot with crude delivery. If FB command improves, watch out.

Baez,Michel | SP | San Diego | EXP MLB DEBUT: 2019 | H/W: 6-8 220 | FUT: #2 SP/closer | 8B

Thrws R Age 24	Year	Lev	Team	W	L	Sv	IP	K	ERA	WHIP	BF/G	OBA	H%	S%	xERA	Ctl	Dom	Cmd	hr/9	BPV
2016 FA (CU)	2017	A	Fort Wayne	6	2	0	58	82	2.47	0.84	21.3	200	29	80	2.26	1.2	12.7	10.3	1.2	213
93-96 FB ++++	2018	A+	Lake Elsinore	4	7	0	86	92	2.92	1.23	20.5	231	31	77	2.97	3.4	9.6	2.8	0.5	98
83-85 SL +++	2018	AA	San Antonio	0	3	0	18	21	7.46	1.88	21.3	301	37	63	6.96	6.0	10.4	1.8	2.0	45
76-80 CB +++	2019	AA	Amarillo	3	2	1	27	38	2.00	1.22	7.3	224	36	84	2.66	3.7	12.7	3.5	0.3	147
84-87 CU ++++	2019	MLB	San Diego	1	1	0	29	28	3.08	1.34	5.1	233	29	81	3.65	4.3	8.6	2.0	0.9	57

Tall, hard-throwing RHP who showed promise in MLB debut out of the 'pen. Maxes out at 98 mph on plus FB and produces whiffs at high rate on elite CU. CB/SL feel lags behind changeup, but both project to be useable pitches. Height and long levers make it difficult to repeat delivery at times. Groomed as SP, his future could be in the ninth inning.

Bahr,Jason | SP | Texas | EXP MLB DEBUT: 2021 | H/W: 6-5 190 | FUT: #5 SP/swingman | 7B

Thrws R Age 25	Year	Lev	Team	W	L	Sv	IP	K	ERA	WHIP	BF/G	OBA	H%	S%	xERA	Ctl	Dom	Cmd	hr/9	BPV
2017 (5) Central Florida	2018	A	Augusta	6	4	0	68	88	2.77	1.07	20.4	213	31	76	2.46	2.8	11.6	4.2	0.7	152
90-94 FB +++	2018	A+	San Jose	2	0	0	16	15	1.69	0.88	19.7	210	23	100	2.93	1.1	8.4	7.5	1.7	140
77-80 CB ++	2018	A+	Down East	2	4	0	35	32	5.88	1.53	19.2	297	36	62	5.14	3.1	8.2	2.7	1.0	82
82-84 CU ++	2019	A+	Down East	6	1	0	58	58	1.71	1.09	20.6	184	25	85	1.86	4.0	9.0	2.2	0.3	71
	2019	AA	Frisco	4	3	0	64	68	3.23	1.06	20.7	192	27	68	1.86	3.5	9.6	2.7	0.3	95

Flew through High-A and Double-A, limiting opponents to a .189 batting average against. Arsenal is only average; high-spin FB plays up a bit from its low-90s velocity; CB and CU are only flash average. High-waisted with simple mechanics, needs to limit the free passes as works his way through high minors. Lack of plus pitch keeps ceiling low.

Bailey,Brandon
SP | Baltimore | EXP MLB DEBUT: 2020 | H/W: 5-10 175 | FUT: #5 SP/swingman | 6B

Thrws R Age 25 — 2016 (6) Gonzaga
- 89-93 FB +++
- 85-87 SL ++
- 75-77 CB +++
- 81-84 CU +++

Year	Lev	Team	W	L	Sv	IP	K	ERA	WHIP	BF/G	OBA	H%	S%	xERA	Ctl	Dom	Cmd	hr/9	BPV
2017	A	Beloit	1	1	0	57	73	2.68	1.07	14.8	199	29	77	2.27	3.3	11.5	3.5	0.6	136
2017	A+	Stockton	2	1	1	34	47	4.24	1.12	14.9	226	33	65	3.10	2.6	12.4	4.7	1.1	170
2018	A+	Buies Creek	5	8	0	97	113	2.50	1.15	19.3	201	28	80	2.44	4.0	10.5	2.6	0.6	99
2018	AA	Corpus Christi	1	0	1	24	23	4.09	1.24	19.6	235	26	76	4.32	3.3	8.6	2.6	1.9	82
2019	AA	Corpus Christi	4	5	0	92	103	3.32	1.23	17.0	217	28	78	3.39	4.0	10.1	2.5	1.2	91

Small-framed SP who is all about pitchability rather than natural stuff. Posts low oppBA thanks to deception and ability to sequence pitches. Hitters can't get comfortable as he spots CB into zone and can change look and feel of SL/CT. Pitches exhibit lots of life, though can be tough to control. Will issue walks and needs better FB command.

Balazovic,Jordan
SP | Minnesota | EXP MLB DEBUT: 2021 | H/W: 6-5 215 | FUT: #3 starter | 8C

Thrws R Age 21 — 2016 (5) HS (ON)
- 93-96 FB ++++
- 82-84 SL ++++
- 87-90 CU ++

Year	Lev	Team	W	L	Sv	IP	K	ERA	WHIP	BF/G	OBA	H%	S%	xERA	Ctl	Dom	Cmd	hr/9	BPV
2017	Rk	GCL Twins	1	3	0	40	29	4.94	1.67	18.0	294	33	73	5.54	4.5	6.5	1.5	1.1	14
2018	A	Cedar Rapids	7	3	0	61	78	3.97	1.18	20.4	238	34	67	3.11	2.6	11.5	4.3	0.7	153
2019	A	Cedar Rapids	2	1	0	20	33	2.23	0.94	19.0	208	37	78	1.84	1.8	14.7	8.3	0.4	235
2019	A+	Fort Myers	6	4	0	73	96	2.84	1.00	18.6	202	31	71	1.87	2.6	11.8	4.6	0.4	161

Potential mid-rotation SP moving quickly through MIN farm system. Tall, projectable frame. Has long arm action but repeats 3/4s delivery relatively well. Four-seamer has ride and plays up due to extension in delivery. SL flashes plus 2-plane, tight break. CU is stiff and lacks movement.

Banda,Anthony
SP | Tampa Bay | EXP MLB DEBUT: 2017 | H/W: 6-2 225 | FUT: Middle reliever | 6B

Thrws L Age 26 — 2012 (10) San JacintoCol
- 91-96 FB ++++
- 80-85 CB ++
- 84-87 CU +++

Year	Lev	Team	W	L	Sv	IP	K	ERA	WHIP	BF/G	OBA	H%	S%	xERA	Ctl	Dom	Cmd	hr/9	BPV
2018	MLB	Tampa Bay	1	0	0	14		3.80	1.06	18.3	231	27	64	2.67	1.9	6.3	3.3	0.6	81
2019	Rk	GCL Rays	0	1	0	2	4	8.57	4.29	7.5	503	76	78	15.44	12.9	17.1	1.3	0.0	-21
2019	A+	Charlotte	0	0	0	2	2	0.00	0.45	3.6	139	19	100		0.0	8.2		0.0	165
2019	AAA	Durham	2	3	0	28	27	6.09	1.39	13.1	261	29	63	5.39	3.5	8.6	2.5	2.2	79
2019	MLB	Tampa Bay	0	0	0	4	2	6.75	1.50	5.8	347	39	50	4.95	0.0	4.5		0.0	99

Hard-throwing LHP returned late in 2019 after Tommy John surgery. Results weren't there in return with velocity drop from pre-TJS levels. With velocity down, stuff was down. Struggled with command of all pitches. 4-seam FB has late running action and is a plus-pitch thrown at top velocity. Best secondary is CU and struggles maintaining CB depth.

Baum,Tyler
SP | Oakland | EXP MLB DEBUT: 2022 | H/W: 6-2 195 | FUT: #4 starter | 7C

Thrws R Age 22 — 2019 (2) North Carolina
- 89-92 FB +++
- 77-80 CB +++
- 80-82 CU +++

Year	Lev	Team	W	L	Sv	IP	K	ERA	WHIP	BF/G	OBA	H%	S%	xERA	Ctl	Dom	Cmd	hr/9	BPV
2019	A-	Vermont	0	3	0	30	34	4.77	1.19	11.0	254	33	63	3.80	2.1	10.1	4.9	1.2	144

Medium-framed RH was org's second round pick in 2019 and has a chance to reach his #4 SP potential. Struck out more than a batter per inning in his debut. Runs FB up to 95 mph, cruising in low-90s with solid control. Can spin CB well, but feel for CU still developing. Athletic, repeatable delivery. Command projects to be above-average.

Baumann,Michael
SP | Baltimore | EXP MLB DEBUT: 2021 | H/W: 6-4 225 | FUT: #4 starter | 7C

Thrws R Age 24 — 2017 (3) Jacksonville
- 91-95 FB ++++
- 87-89 CT +++
- 74-77 CB +++
- 84-86 CU +++

Year	Lev	Team	W	L	Sv	IP	K	ERA	WHIP	BF/G	OBA	H%	S%	xERA	Ctl	Dom	Cmd	hr/9	BPV
2017	A-	Aberdeen	4	2	0	41	41	1.31	1.07	16.0	177	23	90	1.86	4.2	9.0	2.2	0.4	67
2018	A	Delmarva	5	0	0	38	47	1.42	0.95	20.5	177	28	83	1.11	3.1	11.1	3.6	0.0	135
2018	A+	Frederick	8	5	0	92	59	3.90	1.32	22.5	240	27	73	3.69	3.9	5.8	1.5	0.9	16
2019	A+	Frederick	1	4	0	54	77	3.83	1.19	19.7	208	34	66	2.37	4.0	12.8	3.2	0.3	141
2019	AA	Bowie	6	2	1	70	65	2.31	0.94	20.3	186	25	75	1.47	2.7	8.4	3.1	0.3	96

Physically-mature RHP posted solid returns split between High-A and Double-A. Utilizes over-the-top arm slot, his FB has natural downward plane and late movement. SL morphed into CT, which is tight and stays away from barrels. 12-to-6 CB has a solid depth profile and does well to change eye levels. CU is progressing, remaining tunneled with FB.

Baz,Shane
SP | Tampa Bay | EXP MLB DEBUT: 2021 | H/W: 6-2 190 | FUT: #3 starter | 8D

Thrws R Age 20 — 2017 (1) HS (TX)
- 93-98 FB ++++
- 88-91 CT +++
- 83-87 SL ++++
- 86-89 CU ++

Year	Lev	Team	W	L	Sv	IP	K	ERA	WHIP	BF/G	OBA	H%	S%	xERA	Ctl	Dom	Cmd	hr/9	BPV
2017	Rk	GCL Pirates	0	3	0	23	19	3.88	1.72	10.5	284	34	79	5.21	5.4	7.4	1.4	0.8	4
2018	Rk	Princeton	4	5	0	52	59	4.49	1.63	19.3	276	38	72	4.58	5.0	10.2	2.0	0.5	66
2018	Rk	Bristol	4	3	0	45	54	3.99	1.51	19.5	261	37	73	3.95	4.6	10.8	2.3	0.4	88
2019	A	Bowling Green	3	2	0	81	87	3.00	1.23	19.3	216	29	77	2.82	4.1	9.7	2.4	0.6	81

Projectable former 1st round pick took step forward in development. Has shifted repertoire, which works better with 3/4 arm slot. Strong base with plus arm speed. Struggles staying balanced in online delivery. Four-seam FB varies velocity but has awesome late break. Scrapped CB for SL with 2-plane break. CT and CU are works-in-progress.

Bazardo,Eduard
RP | Boston | EXP MLB DEBUT: 2020 | H/W: 6-0 155 | FUT: Middle reliever | 6B

Thrws R Age 24 — 2014 FA (VZ)
- 91-96 FB +++
- 78-79 CB +++
- 80-82 SL ++
- CU +

Year	Lev	Team	W	L	Sv	IP	K	ERA	WHIP	BF/G	OBA	H%	S%	xERA	Ctl	Dom	Cmd	hr/9	BPV
2018	A-	Lowell	5	3	0	49	56	2.38	0.85	20.1	206	27	81	2.25	1.1	10.2	9.3	1.1	173
2018	A	Greenville	1	2	0	28	28	3.21	1.07	21.8	262	34	71	3.10	0.6	9.0	14.0	0.6	163
2019	A+	Salem	1	1	4	41	53	1.76	0.93	9.0	201	31	81	1.53	2.0	11.6	5.9	0.2	174
2019	AA	Portland	4	1	0	32	35	2.80	1.25	6.2	230	31	79	3.03	3.6	9.8	2.7	0.6	96

Small-framed RP who has advanced quickly the last two years. Moved to pen full-time in 2019 and has taken to role. Thrives with solid-average FB and CB combo and isn't afraid to challenge hitters. Consistency in shape of CB has improved while exhibiting better FB location. Lacks effectiveness in erratic CU, but can succeed without.

Beasley,Jeremy
SP | Los Angeles (A) | EXP MLB DEBUT: 2020 | H/W: 6-3 215 | FUT: #5 SP/swingman | 7C

Thrws R Age 24 — 2017 (30) Clemson
- 90-92 FB ++
- 79-82 SL +++
- 80-83 SP ++++

Year	Lev	Team	W	L	Sv	IP	K	ERA	WHIP	BF/G	OBA	H%	S%	xERA	Ctl	Dom	Cmd	hr/9	BPV
2018	A	Burlington	0	2	0	23	19	2.35	1.00	14.6	198	26	74	1.52	2.7	7.4	2.7	0.0	78
2018	A+	Inland Empire	3	2	1	44	48	3.06	1.34	20.4	278	37	80	4.16	2.2	9.8	4.4	0.8	134
2018	AA	Mobile	3	3	0	44	37	2.45	1.04	17.0	205	25	79	2.29	2.9	7.6	2.6	0.6	77
2019	AA	Mobile	6	7	0	108	102	4.08	1.40	19.9	265	32	74	4.40	3.5	8.5	2.4	1.1	76
2019	AAA	Salt Lake	1	0	0	13	13	8.18	1.89	20.7	338	43	54	6.38	4.1	8.9	2.2	0.7	67

Developed, med-framed SP who has a high floor as back-end SP with good ratios. Thrives off feel for plus split-CU that falls off the table when on. FB is fringe-avg, lacking ideal velo nor movement to miss bats, and SL has average attributes. Aptitude for missing bats and keeping the ball on the ground makes him a potential deep-league streamer.

Beck,Tristan
SP | San Francisco | EXP MLB DEBUT: 2021 | H/W: 6-4 165 | FUT: #4 starter | 7C

Thrws R Age 23 — 2018 (4) Stanford
- 90-94 FB +++
- 75-79 CB +++
- 80-85 CU ++++

Year	Lev	Team	W	L	Sv	IP	K	ERA	WHIP	BF/G	OBA	H%	S%	xERA	Ctl	Dom	Cmd	hr/9	BPV
2018	NCAA	Stanford	8	4	0	90	73	2.99	1.22	24.3	237	29	77	3.12	3.1	7.3	2.4	0.6	66
2018	Rk	GCL Braves	0	0	0	4	7	0.00	1.43	5.9	252	45	100	3.21	4.3	15.0	3.5	0.0	172
2019	Rk	GCL Braves	0	0	0	9	14	4.00	1.44	19.2	262	44	69	3.39	4.0	14.0	3.5	0.0	162
2019	A+	San Jose	3	2	0	35	37	2.30	1.31	24.2	250	34	82	3.16	3.3	9.5	2.8	0.3	99
2019	A+	Florida	2	2	0	36	39	5.72	1.63	20.1	306	41	63	5.01	3.5	9.7	2.8	0.5	99

Trade deadline acquisition with solid command of average pitch mix. More command and control than power, though had sterling K rate. Locates relatively flat FB to both sides, though can be hittable due to lack of movement. Mixes in solid-average CB and CU with good separation. Rarely allows HR. Not frontline stuff, but has the savvy to advance.

Bello,Brayan
SP | Boston | EXP MLB DEBUT: 2022 | H/W: 6-1 170 | FUT: #3 starter | 8E

Thrws R Age 20 — 2017 FA (DR)
- 92-95 FB +++
- 82-85 SL +++
- 84-86 CU +++

Year	Lev	Team	W	L	Sv	IP	K	ERA	WHIP	BF/G	OBA	H%	S%	xERA	Ctl	Dom	Cmd	hr/9	BPV
2019	A	Greenville	5	10	0	117	119	5.45	1.48	20.1	290	37	62	4.57	2.9	9.1	3.1	0.7	104

Projectable, yet inconsistent SP who ended season hot. Throws strikes with all pitches and likes to use SL as swing-and-miss offering. FB has potential add a few more ticks as he gains strength and loose, quick arm offers hint of deception. CU has become at least avg with potential for more. Keeps ball low in zone and gets high amount of grounders.

Bettinger,Alec
SP | Milwaukee | EXP MLB DEBUT: 2020 | H/W: 6-2 210 | FUT: #5 SP/swingman | 7B

Thrws R Age 24 — 2017 (10) Virginia
- 90-93 FB ++
- 80-82 CB +++
- 85-88 CT +++

Year	Lev	Team	W	L	Sv	IP	K	ERA	WHIP	BF/G	OBA	H%	S%	xERA	Ctl	Dom	Cmd	hr/9	BPV
2017	NCAA	Virginia	8	0	1	63	71	2.43	1.10	11.7	176	24	81	2.16	4.4	10.1	2.3	0.7	81
2017	Rk	Helena	3	3	0	50	39	5.02	1.49	14.4	269	33	64	3.84	4.1	7.0	1.7	0.2	33
2018	A	Wisconsin	5	4	0	62	50	3.76	1.22	21.0	252	30	71	3.57	2.5	7.2	2.9	0.9	82
2018	A+	Carolina	1	6	0	54	56	6.97	1.61	18.4	314	38	58	6.17	2.8	9.3	3.3	1.7	109
2019	AA	Biloxi	5	7	0	146	157	3.45	1.07	21.8	227	30	70	2.78	2.2	9.7	4.5	0.8	134

Potential sleeper RH prospect whose ratios continue to improve against higher competition. Owns solid but not spectacular three-pitch mix with low-90s FB, above-avg CB and blends in CT for limited hard contact. Otherwise average SwK/GB% profile point to his limited upside, but projects to have quality ratios as back-end SP with a stable floor.

Bickford,Phil — RP — Milwaukee

EXP MLB DEBUT: 2020 | H/W: 6-4 200 | FUT: Setup reliever | 7C

Thrws R Age 24	Year	Lev	Team	W	L	Sv	IP	K	ERA	WHIP	BF/G	OBA	H%	S%	xERA	Ctl	Dom	Cmd	hr/9	BPV
2015 (1) CC of So. Nevada	2016	A+	San Jose	2	2	0	33	36	2.73	1.00	21.0	184	24	77	2.11	3.3	9.8	3.0	0.8	106
92-95 FB +++	2016	A+	Brevard County	2	1	0	27	30	3.67	1.52	19.5	255	35	75	3.83	5.0	10.0	2.0	0.3	63
78-81 SL +++	2017	Rk	AZL Brewers	1	0	0	17	16	2.12	1.41	12.0	226	30	83	2.89	5.3	8.5	1.6	0.0	28
84-86 CU ++	2018	A+	Carolina	0	0	0	34	41	4.74	1.61	7.2	277	38	71	4.79	4.7	10.8	2.3	0.8	84
	2019	A+	Carolina	3	0	1	32	53	2.52	1.06	6.2	202	36	78	2.16	3.1	14.8	4.8	0.6	202

Former lauded RH prospect finished 2019 on 26 IP scoreless streak from A+ bullpen. FB hums in around 92-95 mph with late life and SL has once again emerged as a swing-and-miss weapon. Not the high-profile SP prototype he once was, but could emerge as a productive bullpen piece with Dom value in 2020.

Bielak,Brandon — SP — Houston

EXP MLB DEBUT: 2020 | H/W: 6-1 210 | FUT: #4 starter | 7B

Thrws R Age 24	Year	Lev	Team	W	L	Sv	IP	K	ERA	WHIP	BF/G	OBA	H%	S%	xERA	Ctl	Dom	Cmd	hr/9	BPV
2017 (11) Notre Dame	2017	A-	Tri City	1	1	1	29	37	0.93	0.76	13.0	180	29	86	0.66	1.2	11.4	9.3	0.0	191
91-94 FB +++	2018	A+	Buies Creek	5	3	2	55	74	2.12	1.11	15.5	220	34	81	2.32	2.8	12.1	4.4	0.3	160
80-83 CB +++	2018	AA	Corpus Christi	2	5	0	61	57	2.36	1.21	22.4	232	29	83	3.01	3.2	8.4	2.6	0.6	82
84-85 SL +++	2019	AA	Corpus Christi	3	0	0	36	33	3.75	1.19	18.1	222	28	70	3.00	3.5	8.3	2.4	0.8	72
83-86 CU +++	2019	AAA	Round Rock	8	4	0	85	86	4.44	1.23	23.0	223	28	66	3.39	3.8	9.1	2.4	1.1	79

Durable SP who split 2019 between AA and AAA and put himself on map. May not own true knockout pitch, but has four quality offerings. Pitches to all quadrants of zone and knows how to mess with hitters timing. Throws from high slot which gives hint of deception. FB gets good late movement and mixes in SL and CB with differing velocities and shapes.

Bolanos,Ronald — SP — San Diego

EXP MLB DEBUT: 2019 | H/W: 6-3 220 | FUT: #4 starter | 8D

Thrws R Age 23	Year	Lev	Team	W	L	Sv	IP	K	ERA	WHIP	BF/G	OBA	H%	S%	xERA	Ctl	Dom	Cmd	hr/9	BPV
2016 FA (CU)	2017	A	Fort Wayne	5	2	0	69		4.43	1.43	18.4	250	30	68	3.64	4.4	6.6	1.5	0.4	18
92-95 FB ++++	2018	A+	Lake Elsinore	6	9	0	125	118	5.11	1.50	21.6	281	35	67	4.75	3.6	8.5	2.4	0.9	74
82-84 SL +++	2019	A+	Lake Elsinore	5	2	0	53	54	2.88	1.13	21.0	198	26	77	2.46	3.9	9.1	2.3	0.7	77
76-80 CB ++	2019	AA	Amarillo	8	5	0	76	88	4.25	1.33	21.1	248	34	69	3.72	3.5	10.4	2.9	0.8	109
82-84 CU ++	2019	MLB	San Diego	0	2	0	19	19	6.09	1.51	16.6	239	28	62	4.62	5.6	8.9	1.6	1.4	26

Strong, durable RHP who was aggressively promoted from Hi-A to MLB in 2019. Topped out at 99 mph in his debut but more comfortably sits 92-95 mph with armside movement on FB. CB/SL both project as average and CU remains a work in progress. Crossfire in delivery creates deception to plate, but command can suffer at times because of it.

Bolton,Cody — SP — Pittsburgh

EXP MLB DEBUT: 2021 | H/W: 6-3 185 | FUT: #4 starter | 7C

Thrws R Age 21	Year	Lev	Team	W	L	Sv	IP	K	ERA	WHIP	BF/G	OBA	H%	S%	xERA	Ctl	Dom	Cmd	hr/9	BPV
2017 (6) HS (CA)																				
90-95 FB ++++	2017	Rk	GCL Pirates	0	2	0	25	22	3.21	1.23	11.3	245	31	73	3.01	2.9	7.9	2.8	0.4	82
85-89 SL +++	2018	A	West Virginia	3	3	0	44	45	3.67	1.13	19.4	257	32	73	3.74	1.4	9.2	6.4	1.2	145
82-84 CU +++	2019	AA	Altoona	2	3	0	40	33	5.85	1.33	18.4	247	28	57	4.22	3.6	7.4	2.1	1.4	54
	2019	A+	Bradenton	6	3	0	61	69	1.62	0.87	18.8	184	27	81	1.14	2.1	10.1	4.9	0.1	145

Tall, lean SP who broke out in A+ only to struggle in AA. Owns solid-average three pitch mix, but K rate not likely sustainable. More focus on hitting spots than power or missing bats. Sinking FB spotted to any quadrant and features armside run. Hard SL can be effective against RHH while he has some feel for changing speeds.

Bowden,Ben — RP — Colorado

EXP MLB DEBUT: 2020 | H/W: 6-4 235 | FUT: Closer | 8C

Thrws L Age 25	Year	Lev	Team	W	L	Sv	IP	K	ERA	WHIP	BF/G	OBA	H%	S%	xERA	Ctl	Dom	Cmd	hr/9	BPV
2016 (2) Vanderbilt	2017	Rk	Did not pitch - injury																	
93-95 FB ++++	2018	A	Asheville	3	0	0	15	25	3.58	1.46	4.3	285	46	80	4.86	3.0	14.9	5.0	1.2	206
80-83 SL ++	2018	A+	Lancaster	4	2	0	36	53	4.23	1.38	4.5	255	37	75	4.55	3.7	13.2	3.5	1.5	154
CU ++++	2019	AA	Hartford	0	0	20	25	42	1.07	0.60	3.3	101	19	86		2.5	15.0	6.0	0.4	221
	2019	AAA	Albuquerque	1	3	1	26	37	5.88	1.77	5.4	283	41	69	5.82	5.9	12.8	2.2	1.4	90

Strong, physical RP with late-inning potential. Posted elite SwK in upper minors in 2019 by way of plus fading CU with ideal separation off FB, which tops out at 97 mph with sinking action. Lacks feel for SL at present, but may not need it in short stints. Hard to square up, though command is fringy and batted ball profile is fly-ball oriented.

Bowlan,Jonathan — SP — Kansas City

EXP MLB DEBUT: 2021 | H/W: 6-6 262 | FUT: #4 starter | 7C

Thrws R Age 23	Year	Lev	Team	W	L	Sv	IP	K	ERA	WHIP	BF/G	OBA	H%	S%	xERA	Ctl	Dom	Cmd	hr/9	BPV
2018 (2) Memphis																				
91-93 FB +++	2018	NCAA	Memphis	2	9	0	85	104	3.71	1.31	25.1	280	40	71	3.71	1.9	11.0	5.8	0.4	165
82-86 SL +++	2018	Rk	Idaho Falls	1	4	0	35	23	6.94	1.71	17.6	341	37	61	6.81	2.3	5.9	2.6	1.5	62
84-86 CU +++	2019	A	Lexington	6	2	1	69	74	3.38	0.94	20.0	220	30	64	2.10	1.3	9.6	7.4	0.5	156
	2019	A+	Wilmington	5	3	0	76	76	2.96	1.04	22.6	235	31	73	2.61	1.5	9.0	5.8	0.6	138

Big-bodied, tall innings-eater SP relies on pitchability over stuff. Tall-and-fall 3/4 RHP uses height well in delivery. FB relies on natural downward plane and plays up low with solid arm-side run. SL is an average offering; struggles with shape but still effective. CU has similar profile to FB, could use more velocity separation.

Bradish,Kyle — SP — Baltimore

EXP MLB DEBUT: 2021 | H/W: 6-4 190 | FUT: Middle reliever | 7C

Thrws R Age 23	Year	Lev	Team	W	L	Sv	IP	K	ERA	WHIP	BF/G	OBA	H%	S%	xERA	Ctl	Dom	Cmd	hr/9	BPV
2018 (4) New Mexico St																				
92-94 FB +++																				
80-83 CB +++																				
86-88 CU ++																				
	2019	A+	Inland Empire	6	7	0	101	120	4.28	1.42	17.8	240	33	71	3.81	4.7	10.7	2.3	0.8	83

Funky, high-effort RH who made debut as SP but has an overall package that projects for relief. Can touch 96 mph from overhand slot with FB that grades as solid-avg, but lack of balance in delivery limits his command of it. Repeatable arm slot is deceptive when throwing vertical CB. CU is raw and may not be necessary out of the bullpen.

Bradley,Taj — SP — Tampa Bay

EXP MLB DEBUT: 2023 | H/W: 6-2 190 | FUT: #4 starter | 8E

Thrws R Age 19	Year	Lev	Team	W	L	Sv	IP	K	ERA	WHIP	BF/G	OBA	H%	S%	xERA	Ctl	Dom	Cmd	hr/9	BPV
2018 (5) HS (GA)																				
91-94 FB ++++																				
74-78 CB +++																				
86-87 CU ++	2018	Rk	GCL Rays	1	4	0	23	24	5.09	1.65	10.3	286	38	68	4.67	4.7	9.4	2.0	0.4	60
	2019	Rk	Princeton	2	5	0	51	57	3.18	1.20	17.1	226	30	75	2.99	3.4	10.1	3.0	0.7	109

Projectable, physically-mature RHP made strides in in pro debut. One of the youngest players in 2018 draft class and the in the Appy League. Muscular build, probably throws 100 some day with a very athletic 3/4s delivery. Delivery is online and creates solid extension. 2-seam FB can miss bats and CB has makings of borderline plus potential.

Braymer,Ben — SP — Washington

EXP MLB DEBUT: 2020 | H/W: 6-2 215 | FUT: Middle reliever | 6A

Thrws L Age 25	Year	Lev	Team	W	L	Sv	IP	K	ERA	WHIP	BF/G	OBA	H%	S%	xERA	Ctl	Dom	Cmd	hr/9	BPV
2016 (18) Auburn	2017	A	Hagerstown	3	2	0	37	37	5.32	1.45	22.7	305	39	63	4.76	1.9	9.0	4.6	0.7	127
92-94 FB ++	2018	A	Hagerstown	3	0	0	25	25	1.79	0.91	13.4	202	26	86	2.01	1.8	8.9	5.0	0.7	131
79-81 CB +++	2018	A+	Potomac	6	3	2	89	93	2.43	1.15	16.8	225	30	80	2.58	2.9	9.4	3.2	0.4	108
83-85 CU ++	2019	AA	Harrisburg	4	4	0	79	69	2.51	0.97	23.1	201	24	79	2.24	2.4	7.9	3.3	0.8	95
	2019	AAA	Fresno	0	6	0	60	47	7.20	1.93	21.9	324	34	69	8.15	5.3	7.1	1.3	2.7	3

Tale of two halves - excelled at AA-Harrisburg, but was pummeled at AAA-Fresno, where he gave up 18 HR over 13 GS and gave up baserunners galore. CB is best pitch with 12-to-6 shape and bite, but FB still below average and CU is not effective. Destined for bullpen role though unlikely to have much impact.

Brown,Hunter — SP — Houston

EXP MLB DEBUT: 2022 | H/W: 6-2 203 | FUT: #3 starter | 8E

Thrws R Age 21	Year	Lev	Team	W	L	Sv	IP	K	ERA	WHIP	BF/G	OBA	H%	S%	xERA	Ctl	Dom	Cmd	hr/9	BPV
2019 (5) Wayne St																				
91-96 FB +++																				
83-87 SL ++																				
84-87 CU ++																				
	2019	A-	Tri City	2	2	0	23	33	4.66	1.34	8.0	166	29	61	1.96	7.0	12.8	1.8	0.0	60

Small college RHP with durable frame and potential to add to above average FB. Throws downhill and adds sink with quality two-seamer. SL has potential to grow into plus pitch, but far too inconsistent at present. Has trouble repeating mechanics, but could improve with reps and pro coaching. Has good feel for changing speeds with FB, but not CU.

Brown,Zack — SP — Milwaukee

EXP MLB DEBUT: 2020 | H/W: 6-1 180 | FUT: #4 starter | 7B

Thrws R Age 25	Year	Lev	Team	W	L	Sv	IP	K	ERA	WHIP	BF/G	OBA	H%	S%	xERA	Ctl	Dom	Cmd	hr/9	BPV
2016 (5) Kentucky	2017	A	Wisconsin	4	5	0	85	84	3.39	1.32	19.5	246	31	76	3.59	3.6	8.9	2.5	0.7	81
92-95 FB +++	2017	A+	Carolina	3	0	0	25	23	2.16	1.04	24.1	254	33	80	2.66	0.7	8.3	11.5	0.4	148
76-78 CB ++++	2018	Rk	AZL Brewers	0	0	0	2	3	0.00	2.00	9.6	347	53	100	6.12	4.5	13.5	3.0	0.0	140
84-86 CU +++	2018	AA	Biloxi	9	1	0	125	116	2.44	1.05	22.0	212	27	79	2.34	2.6	8.3	3.2	0.6	98
	2019	AAA	San Antonio	3	7	0	116	98	5.81	1.74	21.2	296	35	68	5.85	5.0	7.6	1.5	1.2	21

High-effort, ground-ball inducing RH whose baseline production succumbed to the PCL gopher ball. Comes after hitters with at times explosive low/mid-90s FB with arm-side life. Plus CB is his best pitch, with considerable late bite, and CU will flash plus. Up-tempo delivery and arm action could work out of bullpen, but has ingredients for #4/5 SP.

Brubaker,J.T.

SP | **Pittsburgh** | EXP MLB DEBUT: 2020 | H/W: 6-3 185 | FUT: #4 starter | **7D**

Thrws R Age 26
2015 (6) Akron

92-96	FB	++++
87-88	SL	+++
77-80	CB	++
81-82	CU	++

Year	Lev	Team	W	L	Sv	IP	K	ERA	WHIP	BF/G	OBA	H%	S%	xERA	Ctl	Dom	Cmd	hr/9	BPV
2017	AA	Altoona	7	6	0	129	109	4.46	1.51	21.5	292	36	70	4.63	3.1	7.6	2.4	0.6	70
2018	AA	Altoona	2	2	0	35	35	1.80	1.06	22.6	227	31	83	2.25	2.1	9.0	4.4	0.3	124
2018	AAA	Indianapolis	8	4	0	119	96	3.10	1.32	22.4	265	32	77	3.68	2.7	7.3	2.7	0.5	75
2019	A-	West Virginia	0	0	0	6	4	1.45	1.45	13.2	222	27	89	2.97	5.8	5.8	1.0	0.0	-34
2019	AAA	Indianapolis	2	1	0	21	20	2.57	1.10	20.6	243	30	81	3.11	1.7	8.6	5.0	0.9	126

Saw limited action due to elbow/forearm issues but will be ready for spring training. Has good extension to add effectiveness to FB. More of a pitch-to-contact guy than K pitcher. SL features hard break, though CB is a bit loose and may be scrapped. Firm CU needs to be upgraded to find spot in big league rotation.

Bubic,Kris

SP | **Kansas City** | EXP MLB DEBUT: 2021 | H/W: 6-3 220 | FUT: #4 starter | **7B**

Thrws L Age 22
2018 (1) Stanford

90-93	FB	+++
77-80	CB	+++
79-83	CU	++++

Year	Lev	Team	W	L	Sv	IP	K	ERA	WHIP	BF/G	OBA	H%	S%	xERA	Ctl	Dom	Cmd	hr/9	BPV
2018	NCAA	Stanford	8	1	0	86	101	2.62	1.07	22.3	198	28	77	2.16	3.3	10.6	3.2	0.5	118
2018	Rk	Idaho Falls	2	3	0	38	53	4.03	1.50	16.4	262	40	73	3.98	4.5	12.6	2.8	0.5	122
2019	A	Lexington	4	1	0	47	75	2.10	0.89	19.5	169	29	79	1.39	2.9	14.3	5.0	0.6	198
2019	A+	Wilmington	7	4	0	101	110	2.31	1.02	22.8	210	29	77	1.94	2.4	9.8	4.1	0.3	129

Funky, pitchability LHP dominated A-Ball level. Deceptive delivery with hesitation and arms/legs, achieves great extension. FB sits on the fringes of MLB average with solid arm-side movement. CU is double-plus offering with plus drop-off-the-table downward movement and excellent velocity separation. CB has average profile, changing eye levels.

Bukauskas,JB

SP | **Arizona** | EXP MLB DEBUT: 2020 | H/W: 6-0 196 | FUT: Closer | **9E**

Thrws R Age 23
2017 (1) North Carolina

93-97	FB	++++
84-87	SL	++++
89-91	CU	+++

Year	Lev	Team	W	L	Sv	IP	K	ERA	WHIP	BF/G	OBA	H%	S%	xERA	Ctl	Dom	Cmd	hr/9	BPV
2018	A	Quad Cities	1	2	0	15		4.20	1.47	16.1	262	41	68	3.46	4.2	12.6	3.0	0.0	131
2018	A+	Buies Creek	3	0	0	28	31	1.61	0.93	21.0	141	20	84	1.01	4.2	10.0	2.4	0.3	85
2018	AA	Corpus Christi	0	0	0	6	8	0.00	0.50	19.9	56	10	100		3.0	12.0	4.0	0.0	153
2019	AA	Jackson	0	1	0	7	11	7.71	2.14	17.4	336	53	60	6.28	6.4	14.1	2.2	0.0	99
2019	AA	Corpus Christi	2	4	1	85	98	5.28	1.58	18.8	252	34	67	4.44	5.7	10.4	1.8	0.8	50

Hard-throwing, short-armed RHP who ended 2019 on IL with elbow discomfort. Leans on power FB-SL combo to miss bats at a healthy clip, can touch 98 mph and breaker is legit plus offering. Blends in CT and CU and both are solid-average offerings. Has trouble finding zone at times. High-effort delivery and FB-SL combo point to RP future.

Burdi,Zack

RP | **Chicago (A)** | EXP MLB DEBUT: 2020 | H/W: 6-3 205 | FUT: Setup reliever | **7E**

Thrws R Age 25
2016 (1) Louisville

92-96	FB	++++
86-89	CB	++++
	CU	++

Year	Lev	Team	W	L	Sv	IP	K	ERA	WHIP	BF/G	OBA	H%	S%	xERA	Ctl	Dom	Cmd	hr/9	BPV
2016	AAA	Charlotte	1	0	1	16	22	2.25	1.25	7.2	166	28	80	1.75	6.2	12.4	2.0	0.0	74
2017	AAA	Charlotte	0	4	7	33	51	4.08	1.42	4.8	243	40	71	3.59	4.6	13.9	3.0	0.5	143
2018	Rk	AZL White Sox	0	1	0	6	7	2.95	1.48	3.7	225	33	78	3.02	5.9	10.3	1.8	0.0	45
2019	A	Kannapolis	1	1	0	3	6	9.00	1.67	4.5	321	62	40	4.79	3.0	18.0	6.0	0.0	261
2019	AA	Birmingham	0	3	3	19	24	6.56	1.93	5.4	307	39	72	7.50	6.1	11.3	1.8	2.3	56

Hard-throwing RHP has struggled with health in pro career, most recently dealing with knee issues. Velocity and effectiveness have been missing since recovering from Tommy John surgery. FB sat on the fringes of triple digits, now sits low-to-mid 90s. CB still has a plus profile. However, lack of FB command has led to hitter laying off pitch.

Burke,Brock

SP | **Texas** | EXP MLB DEBUT: 2019 | H/W: 6-4 180 | FUT: #4 starter | **7C**

Thrws L Age 23
2014 (3) HS (CO)

91-94	FB	+++
79-83	SL	++
84-88	CU	+++

Year	Lev	Team	W	L	Sv	IP	K	ERA	WHIP	BF/G	OBA	H%	S%	xERA	Ctl	Dom	Cmd	hr/9	BPV
2019	Rk	AZL Rangers	0	0	0	4	3	0.00	0.50	13.3	151	19	100		0.0	6.8		0.0	140
2019	A	Hickory	0	0	0	5	1	7.20	1.80	23.1	390	41	56	6.53	0.0	1.8		0.0	50
2019	AA	Frisco	3	5	0	45	49	3.19	1.02	19.2	211	29	68	2.08	2.4	9.8	4.1	0.4	129
2019	AAA	Nashville	0	0	0	8	11	7.88	2.25	20.3	347	49	65	7.82	6.8	12.4	1.8	1.1	59
2019	MLB	Texas	0	2	0	26	14	7.56	1.56	19.1	289	29	54	6.10	3.8	4.8	1.3	2.1	3

When things are working, uses FB/CU combination to get through lineups. Delivery is athletic and comes with some crossfire that adds to deception. FB 92-94 with some natural cut. Sells mid-80s CU well with currently more drop than fade. Has thrown both SL and CB in the past; SL main breaking ball currently. Some injury history adds to risk.

Burrows,Beau

SP | **Detroit** | EXP MLB DEBUT: 2020 | H/W: 6-2 215 | FUT: #4 starter | **8D**

Thrws R Age 23
2015 (1) HS (TX)

92-97	FB	++++
76-79	CB	++
84-86	SL	++
	CU	++

Year	Lev	Team	W	L	Sv	IP	K	ERA	WHIP	BF/G	OBA	H%	S%	xERA	Ctl	Dom	Cmd	hr/9	BPV
2017	AA	Erie	6	4	0	76	75	4.73	1.47	21.8	269	35	67	4.16	3.9	8.9	2.3	0.6	72
2018	AA	Erie	10	9	0	134	127	4.10	1.36	21.5	250	31	71	3.82	3.8	8.5	2.3	0.8	70
2019	A+	Lakeland	0	0	0	4	5	0.00	0.75	14.3	81	14	100		4.5	11.3	2.5	0.0	99
2019	AA	Erie	1	0	0	5	3	0.00	0.80	18.1	124	15	100	0.25	3.6	5.4	1.5	0.0	18
2019	AAA	Toledo	2	6	0	65	61	5.53	1.54	18.9	270	31	68	5.35	4.4	8.4	1.9	1.7	50

Starter with an ability to overpower hitters on his fastball alone. Access to plus-plus velocity, complemented by a bullish ability to pound the zone. Command has gradually improved, but remains a project to continue working on. Four-pitch mix will play well higher up, as long as locating improves.

Burrows,Michael

SP | **Pittsburgh** | EXP MLB DEBUT: 2022 | H/W: 6-2 183 | FUT: #4 starter | **7D**

Thrws R Age 20
2018 (11) HS (CT)

90-94	FB	+++
80-82	CB	+++
83-84	CU	+++

Year	Lev	Team	W	L	Sv	IP	K	ERA	WHIP	BF/G	OBA	H%	S%	xERA	Ctl	Dom	Cmd	hr/9	BPV
2018	Rk	GCL Pirates	0	0	0	14	9	0.00	0.71	12.4	132	16	100	0.11	2.6	5.8	2.3	0.0	53
2019	A-	West Virginia	2	3	0	43	43	4.38	1.48	16.9	265	35	69	3.97	4.2	9.0	2.2	0.4	67

Quick-armed SP without projection, but enough pitch mix and savvy to have success. Athletic delivery that he is able to repeat consistently. Gets groundballs with sinking FB that he locates to both sides of plate. CB won't register many Ks, but can be thrown for strikes or inducing weak contact. Best pitch may be CU with good separation from FB.

Cabrera,Edward

SP | **Miami** | EXP MLB DEBUT: 2021 | H/W: 6-4 175 | FUT: #3 starter | **8C**

Thrws R Age 21
2015 FA (DR)

93-96	FB	++++
81-83	CB	++++
88-90	CU	++

Year	Lev	Team	W	L	Sv	IP	K	ERA	WHIP	BF/G	OBA	H%	S%	xERA	Ctl	Dom	Cmd	hr/9	BPV
2016	Rk	GCL Marlins	2	6	0	47	28	4.21	1.36	17.9	289	34	67	3.84	1.9	5.4	2.8	0.2	63
2017	A-	Batavia	1	3	0	35	32	5.37	1.42	11.5	297	38	59	4.14	2.0	8.2	4.0	0.3	110
2018	A	Greensboro	4	8	0	100	93	4.23	1.47	19.5	271	33	74	4.56	3.8	8.4	2.2	1.0	67
2019	A+	Jupiter	5	3	0	58	73	2.02	0.95	19.9	184	28	78	1.35	2.8	11.3	4.1	0.2	146
2019	AA	Jacksonville	4	1	0	38	43	2.59	1.07	18.6	206	25	86	3.11	3.1	10.1	3.3	1.4	118

Tall, hard-throwing 3/4s RHP continued to refine secondaries in solid season. Has calmed his explosive delivery, and now repeats much better. Mid-90s FB has heavy sink and lives in the lower quadrant of the zone. Power CB continues to flash plus and consistency has improved. CU is firm but eliminated tells in delivery. Has room to add bulk.

Cabrera,Genesis

RP | **St. Louis** | EXP MLB DEBUT: 2019 | H/W: 6-2 190 | FUT: Closer | **8D**

Thrws L Age 23
2013 FA (DR)

95-98	FB	++++
83-85	SL	++
86-90	CU	+

Year	Lev	Team	W	L	Sv	IP	K	ERA	WHIP	BF/G	OBA	H%	S%	xERA	Ctl	Dom	Cmd	hr/9	BPV
2018	AA	Springfield	1	3	0	24	21	4.83	1.53	21.0	260	31	71	4.69	4.8	7.8	1.6	1.1	28
2018	AA	Montgomery	7	6	0	113	124	4.13	1.30	22.2	220	29	70	3.34	4.5	9.9	2.2	0.9	73
2018	AAA	Memphis	0	0	0	2	3	0.00	0.50	6.6	0	0	100		4.5	13.5	3.0	0.0	140
2019	AAA	Memphis	5	6	0	99	106	5.91	1.47	21.3	277	33	64	5.43	3.5	9.6	2.7	1.8	96
2019	MLB	St. Louis	0	2	1	20	19	4.93	1.69	7.0	289	36	72	5.29	4.9	8.5	1.7	0.9	38

Flame-thrower struggled at AAA, giving up 20 HR before moving to relief and making his MLB debut. FB sits at 95-98 mph and runs away from LHB. CU is firm but with late fade vs RHB. SL flashes plus, especially against LHB, but is inconsistent and will keep him in relief. Does have swing-and-miss stuff and lefties who hit 99 mph don't grow on trees.

Campbell,Isaiah

SP | **Seattle** | EXP MLB DEBUT: 2022 | H/W: 6-4 225 | FUT: #3 starter | **8D**

Thrws R Age 22
2019 (2) Arkansas

91-94	FB	++++
85-86	SL	+++
76-78	CB	+++
85-88	CU	++

Year	Lev	Team	W	L	Sv	IP	K	ERA	WHIP	BF/G	OBA	H%	S%	xERA	Ctl	Dom	Cmd	hr/9	BPV
2019		Did not pitch - injury																	

Hard-throwing, physical RHP was drafted out of Arkansas last spring. Missed pro debut as SEA rested taxed arm with history of elbow issues. Physical, slight crossfire delivery. Creates downward plane from arm slot. FB sits low-to-mid 90s and can overpower. SL is two-plane breaker and could be above-average. Rounds out aresnal with CB and CU.

Canterino,Matt

SP | **Minnesota** | EXP MLB DEBUT: 2021 | H/W: 6-2 222 | FUT: #4 starter | **7C**

Thrws R Age 22
2019 (2) Rice

90-93	FB	+++
85-87	SL	+++
75-78	CB	+++
82-84	CU	++

Year	Lev	Team	W	L	Sv	IP	K	ERA	WHIP	BF/G	OBA	H%	S%	xERA	Ctl	Dom	Cmd	hr/9	BPV
2019	A	Cedar Rapids	1	1	0	20	25	1.35	0.65	13.9	96	16	77		3.2	11.3	3.6	0.0	135
2019	Rk	GCL Twins	0	0	0	5	6	1.80	0.60	8.6	124	20	67		1.8	10.8	6.0	0.0	164

Command/control has unorthodox high 3/4s delivery. Effort in delivery but stays online with a little crossfire. Four pitches: FB sits in low 90s with solid command and minimal run; SL is an above-average offering at projection with tight break; CB is a eye level changer with enough effectiveness to survive; CU will need to round into form.

Cantillo,Joey — SP — San Diego

EXP MLB DEBUT: 2022 | H/W: 6-4 220 | FUT: #4 starter | 7C

Thrws L Age 20 — 2017 (16) HS (HI)

Velo	Pitch	Grade
88-91	FB	++
70-72	CB	+++
78-81	CU	++++

Year	Lev	Team	W	L	Sv	IP	K	ERA	WHIP	BF/G	OBA	H%	S%	xERA	Ctl	Dom	Cmd	hr/9	BPV
2017	Rk	AZL Padres 2	1	0	0	8	14	4.50	1.38	4.8	181	37	64	2.20	6.8	15.8	2.3	0.0	119
2018	Rk	AZL Padres 2	2	2	0	45	58	2.20	1.00	15.7	206	32	76	1.57	2.4	11.6	4.8	0.0	162
2018	A	Fort Wayne	0	1	0	3	5	11.25	2.19	16.0	307	50	43	5.92	8.4	14.1	1.7	0.0	43
2019	A	Fort Wayne	9	3	0	98	128	1.93	0.87	19.0	173	27	78	1.13	2.5	11.8	4.7	0.3	163
2019	A+	Lake Elsinore	1	1	0	13	16	4.77	1.44	18.7	244	32	71	4.44	4.8	10.9	2.3	1.4	86

Large but athletic teenage LH who garnered MWL-best Dom and OBA en route to Hi-A bump. Thrives off deceptive delivery and feel for plus fading CU for bulk of whiffs. Able to place FB where he wants, and could add a tick of velo to presently 88-91 mph heater. Working on ability to spin CB. High-floor prospect with back-end upside and good ratios.

Carlson,Sam — SP — Seattle

EXP MLB DEBUT: 2023 | H/W: 6-4 195 | FUT: #3 starter | 8E

Thrws R Age 21 — 2017 (2) HS (MN)

Velo	Pitch	Grade
90-94	FB	++++
81-82	SL	+++
	CU	++

Year	Lev	Team	W	L	Sv	IP	K	ERA	WHIP	BF/G	OBA	H%	S%	xERA	Ctl	Dom	Cmd	hr/9	BPV
2017	Rk	AZL Mariners	0	0	0	3	3	3.00	1.33	6.2	321	42	75	4.04	0.0	9.0		0.0	180
2018		Did not pitch - injury																	
2019		Did not pitch - injury																	

Oft-injured mid-rotation SP hasn't been seen since throwing 3 IP in '17.Lost season rehabbing from 2018 Tommy John surgery. Terrific athlete. Has added muscle to frame in absence. Relies heavily on sink of 2-seam FB to get hitters out. SL featured solid two-plane movement as amateur and should be above-average offering. Has a feel for CU.

Carrillo,Gerardo — SP — Los Angeles (N)

EXP MLB DEBUT: 2022 | H/W: 5-10 154 | FUT: Setup reliever | 7D

Thrws R Age 21 — 2016 FA (MX)

Velo	Pitch	Grade
94-97	FB	++++
80-83	CB	++
89-91	SL	++
87-89	CU	+

Year	Lev	Team	W	L	Sv	IP	K	ERA	WHIP	BF/G	OBA	H%	S%	xERA	Ctl	Dom	Cmd	hr/9	BPV
2018	A	Great Lakes	2	1	0	49	37	1.65	1.02	20.9	202	24	87	2.15	2.8	6.8	2.5	0.6	66
2018	Rk	AZL Dodgers	2	0	1	11	13	0.82	0.73	9.8	162	25	88	0.40	1.6	10.6	6.5	0.0	165
2019	A+	Rancho Cuca	5	9	0	86	86	5.44	1.60	16.5	264	35	64	4.16	5.3	9.0	1.7	0.3	36

Short, slender hurler has a plus 95-99 mph FB and an aggressive approach on the mound. Mixes in a CB/CT, both of which flash potential, but are slurvy at times. Needs to work on command in the zone and CU is ineffective. Does throw with some effort and frame is more suited to a relief role.

Castellani,Ryan — SP — Colorado

EXP MLB DEBUT: 2020 | H/W: 6-4 223 | FUT: #4 starter | 7C

Thrws R Age 24 — 2014 (2) HS (AZ)

Velo	Pitch	Grade
91-94	FB	+++
84-87	SL	+++
78-79	CB	+++
84-86	CU	+++

Year	Lev	Team	W	L	Sv	IP	K	ERA	WHIP	BF/G	OBA	H%	S%	xERA	Ctl	Dom	Cmd	hr/9	BPV
2015	A	Asheville	2	7	0	113	94	4.46	1.44	17.8	296	36	68	4.31	2.3	7.5	3.2	0.4	90
2016	A+	Modesto	7	8	0	167	142	3.82	1.23	26.1	249	31	68	3.14	2.7	7.6	2.8	0.4	83
2017	AA	Hartford	9	12	0	157	132	4.81	1.34	24.2	269	32	65	4.14	2.7	7.6	2.8	0.9	81
2018	AA	Hartford	7	9	0	134	91	5.50	1.53	22.4	263	29	65	4.64	4.7	6.1	1.3	1.0	1
2019	AAA	Albuquerque	2	5	0	43	47	8.35	1.95	20.6	308	35	63	8.12	6.3	9.8	1.6	2.9	26

Four-pitch RHP who has mid-rotation upside but lacks ideal command. Low 3/4 slot and fast arm action produce 91-94 mph FB with tailing action. CU separates well off heater with fade and dive and could be above-average pitch; some feel for spin on SL and CB. Relatively low margin for error with fringe control and lack of putaway offering.

Castillo,Starlyn — SP — Philadelphia

EXP MLB DEBUT: 2024 | H/W: 6-0 210 | FUT: #3 starter | 8E

Thrws R Age 18 — 2018 FA (DR)

Velo	Pitch	Grade
92-94	FB	+++
78-80	SL	++
	CU	++

Year	Lev	Team	W	L	Sv	IP	K	ERA	WHIP	BF/G	OBA	H%	S%	xERA	Ctl	Dom	Cmd	hr/9	BPV
2019	Rk	GCL Phillies	0	2	0	9	10	7.91	1.87	8.5	260	36	53	4.46	7.9	9.9	1.3	0.0	-18

Big 2018 international signing known as an advanced arm but not overly physical. FB sits in the low-90s for now and has a slider and change-up. Only got into five games as a 17-year old in the GCL, the Phillies will likely take this one slow if how they've handled other Latin pitchers are any indication.

Castro,Anthony — SP — Detroit

EXP MLB DEBUT: 2021 | H/W: 6-2 190 | FUT: #5 SP/swingman | 7C

Thrws R Age 24 — 2011 FA (VZ)

Velo	Pitch	Grade
92-97	FB	++++
79-82	CB	++
85-87	CU	+

Year	Lev	Team	W	L	Sv	IP	K	ERA	WHIP	BF/G	OBA	H%	S%	xERA	Ctl	Dom	Cmd	hr/9	BPV
2016	Rk	GCL Tigers	3	3	0	50	54	4.30	1.35	19.1	269	37	65	3.30	2.9	9.7	3.4	0.0	115
2017	A	West Michigan	10	6	0	108	95	2.50	1.17	20.5	230	29	79	2.64	2.9	7.9	2.7	0.3	82
2018	A+	Lakeland	9	4	0	116	101	2.94	1.33	21.9	255	31	80	3.65	3.3	7.8	2.3	0.6	69
2018	AA	Erie	0	0	0	10	4	8.10	2.00	16.1	221	22	58	5.20	10.8	3.6	0.3	0.9	-209
2019	AA	Erie	5	3	1	102	116	4.41	1.37	15.8	207	28	69	3.28	5.7	10.2	1.8	0.8	47

A lean Tommy John success story, Castro added 2-3 ticks in velocity to his above-average fastball in 2018, along with more confidence behind his entire offspeed set. Improvements to curveball shape and bottom-dwelling sinker. Attacks the zone, with good work on the corners and added deception.

Cate,Tim — SP — Washington

EXP MLB DEBUT: 2021 | H/W: 6-0 185 | FUT: #5 SP/swingman | 7C

Thrws L Age 22 — 2018 (2) Connecticut

Velo	Pitch	Grade
89-92	FB	+++
77-82	CB	+++
80-82	CU	++

Year	Lev	Team	W	L	Sv	IP	K	ERA	WHIP	BF/G	OBA	H%	S%	xERA	Ctl	Dom	Cmd	hr/9	BPV
2018	NCAA	Connecticut	5	4	0	52	67	2.93	1.32	19.7	254	37	78	3.31	3.3	11.6	3.5	0.3	137
2018	A-	Auburn	2	3	0	31	26	4.65	1.42	14.6	280	35	65	3.92	2.9	7.5	2.6	0.3	75
2018	A	Hagerstown	0	3	0	21	19	5.57	1.38	22.1	280	32	64	5.15	2.6	8.1	3.2	1.7	95
2019	A	Hagerstown	4	5	0	70	73	2.82	1.06	20.9	236	32	72	2.35	1.7	9.4	5.6	0.3	142
2019	A+	Potomac	7	4	0	73	66	3.32	1.23	22.8	256	32	73	3.29	2.3	8.1	3.5	0.5	101

Small-framed lefty with above-average CB and improved FB command conquered two A-ball levels. Throws strikes from compact, repeatable delivery, though FB can be short and CU is a distant third pitch. Breaking ball has depth and clearly his best offering, though he got hit a bit more in High-A and upper levels will be a test.

Choi,Hyun-il — SP — Los Angeles (N)

EXP MLB DEBUT: 2023 | H/W: 6-2 200 | FUT: #4 starter | 7D

Thrws R Age 19 — 2018 FA (KR)

Velo	Pitch	Grade
90-93	FB	++++
83-85	SL	++
80-83	CB	+
82-84	CU	+++

Year	Lev	Team	W	L	Sv	IP	K	ERA	WHIP	BF/G	OBA	H%	S%	xERA	Ctl	Dom	Cmd	hr/9	BPV
2019	Rk	AZL DodgersM	5	1	0	65	71	2.63	1.05	18.0	237	31	79	2.88	1.5	9.8	6.5	0.8	154

Impressed in his state-side debut. Above-average FB already sits in the low 90s with good late life and room for more velo as he matures. Shelved his CB in favor of a more effective SL and a plus mid-80s CU that has good deception and late fade. Repeats mechanics well, pounds the zone, and has a good idea of how to set up hitters.

Clase,Emmanuel — RP — Cleveland

EXP MLB DEBUT: 2019 | H/W: 6-2 206 | FUT: Setup reliever | 8D

Thrws R Age 22 — 2015 FA (DR)

Velo	Pitch	Grade
97-101	FB	+++++
88-90	SL	++++

Year	Lev	Team	W	L	Sv	IP	K	ERA	WHIP	BF/G	OBA	H%	S%	xERA	Ctl	Dom	Cmd	hr/9	BPV
2017	Rk	AZL Padres 2	2	4	0	35	42	5.37	1.76	17.9	287	39	71	5.54	5.6	10.7	1.9	1.0	59
2018	A-	Spokane	1	1	12	28	27	0.64	0.78	4.6	168	23	91	0.63	1.9	8.6	4.5	0.0	122
2019	A+	Down East	2	0	1	7	11	0.00	0.71	4.1	168	31	100	0.41	1.3	14.1	11.0	0.0	238
2019	AA	Frisco	1	2	11	37	39	3.39	1.13	4.5	245	33	68	2.63	1.9	9.4	4.9	0.2	136
2019	MLB	Texas	2	3	1	23	21	2.34	1.13	4.3	235	29	83	3.02	2.3	8.2	3.5	0.8	102

Traded in the Kluber deal, his main feature is otherworldly arm strength, with a FB that regularly hits triple-digits with significant cut. SL is also hard, coming in at 90 with vicious break. Plus, he knows where it's going; he throws both pitches for strikes. Higher-level hitters have made more contact. Impact RP upside.

Colina,Edwar — SP — Minnesota

EXP MLB DEBUT: 2020 | H/W: 5-11 240 | FUT: Middle reliever | 6C

Thrws R Age 22 — 2015 FA (VZ)

Velo	Pitch	Grade
96-98	FB	++++
85-88	SL	++
88-89	CU	++

Year	Lev	Team	W	L	Sv	IP	K	ERA	WHIP	BF/G	OBA	H%	S%	xERA	Ctl	Dom	Cmd	hr/9	BPV
2018	A	Cedar Rapids	7	4	0	98	95	2.48	1.23	20.9	204	27	80	2.52	4.6	8.7	1.9	0.4	51
2018	A+	Fort Myers	0	1	0	11	11	4.05	1.44	23.7	293	37	73	4.64	2.4	8.9	3.7	0.8	113
2019	A+	Fort Myers	4	2	0	61	61	2.35	1.11	24.1	235	31	80	2.65	2.2	9.0	4.1	0.4	120
2019	AA	Pensacola	4	0	0	31	37	2.03	1.16	17.6	194	29	81	1.85	4.4	10.7	2.5	0.0	94
2019	AAA	Rochester	0	0	0	4	4	19.29	2.38	10.9	403	47	11	10.22	4.3	8.6	2.0	2.1	57

Short, high 3/4s max-effort RHP utilized heavy sinking FB to propel from High-A to Triple-A. Stocky frame, maxed out. Sit high 90s with 2-seam FB with heavy arm-side bore. Lacks command but controls down in zone. SL is more like slow CT. Would add effectiveness if thrown harder. CU is stiff and telegraphs pitch within delivery.

Contreras,Roansy — SP — New York (A)

EXP MLB DEBUT: 2022 | H/W: 6-0 175 | FUT: #4 starter | 8D

Thrws R Age 20 — 2016 FA (DR)

Velo	Pitch	Grade
90-93	FB	+++
82-84	CB	+++
85-88	CU	++++

Year	Lev	Team	W	L	Sv	IP	K	ERA	WHIP	BF/G	OBA	H%	S%	xERA	Ctl	Dom	Cmd	hr/9	BPV
2017	Rk	GCL Yankees	4	1	0	31	17	4.33	1.51	16.9	285	32	71	4.50	3.5	4.9	1.4	0.6	13
2018	A	Charleston (Sc)	0	2	0	34	28	3.42	1.20	19.6	231	27	76	3.42	3.2	7.4	2.3	1.1	65
2018	A-	Staten Island	0	0	0	28	32	1.28	0.85	20.7	159	23	87	0.98	2.9	10.2	3.6	0.3	124
2019	A	Charleston (Sc)	12	5	0	132	113	3.34	1.07	21.4	220	27	70	2.59	2.5	7.7	3.1	0.7	90

Athletic, 3/4s RHP with feel for pitching and remaining upside. Repeatable delivery known for commanding FB. FB sits 90-93 MPH with light movement. Hits different quadrants of strike zone to maximize pitch. CU is best secondary with solid arm-side run and sudden fade. CB is slurvy and shows promise. Could be an above-average pitch at projection.

Corry,Seth

SP | **San Francisco** | EXP MLB DEBUT: 2022 | H/W: 6-2 195 | FUT: #3 starter | **8D**

Thrws L Age 21
2017 (3) HS (UT)

Velo	Pitch	Grade
91-94	FB	+++
76-81	CB	++++
82-86	CU	+++

Year	Lev	Team	W	L	Sv	IP	K	ERA	WHIP	BF/G	OBA	H%	S%	xERA	Ctl	Dom	Cmd	hr/9	BPV
2017	Rk	AZL Giants	0	2	0	24	21	5.60	1.49	8.0	171	22	60	2.81	8.2	7.8	1.0	0.4	-63
2018	A-	Salem-Keizer	1	2	0	19	17	5.63	1.51	16.6	205	26	61	3.33	7.0	8.0	1.1	0.5	-28
2018	Rk	AZL Giants O	3	1	0	38	42	2.61	1.45	18.0	262	36	81	3.66	4.0	9.9	2.5	0.2	88
2019	A	Augusta	9	3	0	122	172	1.77	1.07	17.6	175	29	84	1.67	4.3	12.7	3.0	0.3	131

Consistent, durable SP led SAL in ERA and K in first full season. Saw big spike in K rate as he became more consistent with delivery and arm slot. Induces high amount of weak contact with groundballs and has plus CB that he gets hitters to chase. Changes shape and velocity to add to effectiveness. FB is good, not great, and offers running action.

Cox,Austin

SP | **Kansas City** | EXP MLB DEBUT: 2022 | H/W: 6-4 185 | FUT: #4 starter | **7D**

Thrws L Age 23
2018 (5) Mercer

Velo	Pitch	Grade
90-93	FB	+++
82-85	SL	++
78-80	CB	++++
84-85	CU	++

Year	Lev	Team	W	L	Sv	IP	K	ERA	WHIP	BF/G	OBA	H%	S%	xERA	Ctl	Dom	Cmd	hr/9	BPV
2018	Rk	Burlington	1	1	0	33	51	3.81	1.33	15.3	237	40	70	3.02	4.1	13.9	3.4	0.3	157
2018	NCAA	Mercer	7	4	0	87	124	4.54	1.63	22.8	287	44	72	4.71	4.4	12.8	2.9	0.5	129
2019	A+	Wilmington	3	3	0	55	52	2.78	1.25	20.4	254	31	83	3.78	2.6	8.5	3.3	1.0	100
2019	A	Lexington	5	3	0	75	77	2.76	1.08	22.5	218	29	76	2.50	2.6	9.2	3.5	0.6	113

Physically-mature LHP had strong showing in 2019. High 3/4s crossfire delivery with average extension and rough finish. FB sits low 90s with light arm-side movement and solid control. Best secondary is CB, a sharp downer. SL is short with more of a CT break. CU is below-average offering with firmness and not enough velocity separation off FB.

Crawford,Kutter

SP | **Boston** | EXP MLB DEBUT: 2021 | H/W: 6-1 192 | FUT: #4 starter | **7D**

Thrws R Age 24
2017 (16) Florida Gulf Coast

Velo	Pitch	Grade
90-95	FB	+++
89-92	CT	+++
74-80	CB	++
84-86	CU	++

Year	Lev	Team	W	L	Sv	IP	K	ERA	WHIP	BF/G	OBA	H%	S%	xERA	Ctl	Dom	Cmd	hr/9	BPV
2018	A	Greenville	5	4	0	112	120	2.97	1.23	21.6	248	33	77	3.15	2.7	9.6	3.5	0.5	118
2018	A+	Salem	2	3	0	31	37	4.34	1.35	21.6	242	36	64	2.92	4.1	10.7	2.6	0.0	101
2019	A+	Salem	4	5	0	69	77	3.39	1.42	20.9	259	35	77	3.94	3.9	10.0	2.6	0.7	93
2019	AA	Portland	1	3	0	19	23	4.24	1.78	17.6	261	36	78	5.13	7.1	10.8	1.5	0.9	22

Under-the-radar SP who impresses with nifty CT as top offering. Lacks premium, frontline stuff, but effectively mixes four pitches. FB command comes and goes while lack of life can lead to hard-hit balls. CU needs enhancement, though has good separation from FB. CB features good shape and can get Ks.

Cronin,Matt

RP | **Washington** | EXP MLB DEBUT: 2021 | H/W: 6-2 195 | FUT: Setup reliever | **8D**

Thrws L Age 22
2019 (4) Arkansas

Velo	Pitch	Grade
92-94	FB	+++
77-80	CB	++++

Year	Lev	Team	W	L	Sv	IP	K	ERA	WHIP	BF/G	OBA	H%	S%	xERA	Ctl	Dom	Cmd	hr/9	BPV
2019	A	Hagerstown	0	0	1	22	41	0.82	1.00	4.9	151	32	95	1.29	4.5	16.8	3.7	0.4	198

A polished collegiate RP has a two-pitch mix that's not too far from an MLB bullpen. FB sat mid-90s during college but ticked back as a pro. At its best, can use it up in zone. Pairs it with a downer 12-to-6 curveball that comes out of his over-the-top slot. Delivery has effort, which aids in deception but also adversely affects control.

Crouse,Hans

SP | **Texas** | EXP MLB DEBUT: 2022 | H/W: 6-4 180 | FUT: #2 starter | **9C**

Thrws R Age 21
2017 (2) HS (CA)

Velo	Pitch	Grade
92-95	FB	++++
79-82	SL	++++
83-85	CU	+++

Year	Lev	Team	W	L	Sv	IP	K	ERA	WHIP	BF/G	OBA	H%	S%	xERA	Ctl	Dom	Cmd	hr/9	BPV
2017	Rk	AZL Rangers	0	0	0	20	30	0.45	0.70	7.0	110	19	100	0.21	3.2	13.5	4.3	0.5	176
2018	A	Hickory	0	2	0	16	15	2.78	1.60	14.3	283	36	84	4.66	4.4	8.3	1.9	0.6	48
2018	A-	Spokane	5	1	0	38	47	2.37	0.95	17.9	189	28	76	1.70	2.6	11.1	4.3	0.5	148
2019	A	Hickory	6	1	0	87	76	4.44	1.20	18.5	259	30	67	3.97	2.0	7.8	4.0	1.2	106

Tall and well-proportioned starter with rough delivery including nasty head-whack that he somehow makes work. FB sits and holds mid-90s, though can be straight; SL also plus; CU improving. Pitched through bone spurs that were removed in offseason. Fierce competitor; stuff would work out of bullpen, but might also be special as a starter.

Crowe,Wil

SP | **Washington** | EXP MLB DEBUT: 2020 | H/W: 6-2 240 | FUT: #4 starter | **7B**

Thrws R Age 25
2017 (2) South Carolina

Velo	Pitch	Grade
92-94	FB	+++
82-85	SL	++
77-79	CB	++
84-86	CU	+++

Year	Lev	Team	W	L	Sv	IP	K	ERA	WHIP	BF/G	OBA	H%	S%	xERA	Ctl	Dom	Cmd	hr/9	BPV
2018	A-	Auburn	0	0	0	3	1	0.00	1.33	12.5	191	21	100	2.33	6.0	3.0	0.5	0.0	-90
2018	A+	Potomac	11	0	0	87	78	2.69	1.16	21.6	224	28	79	2.83	3.1	8.1	2.6	0.6	79
2018	AA	Harrisburg	0	5	0	26	15	6.21	1.80	24.1	296	32	67	6.17	5.5	5.2	0.9	1.4	-38
2019	AA	Harrisburg	7	6	0	95	89	3.88	1.13	23.4	241	30	67	3.07	2.1	8.4	4.0	0.8	113
2019	AAA	Fresno	0	4	0	54	41	6.17	1.70	24.4	302	35	65	5.80	4.3	6.8	1.6	1.2	24

Has improved slowly but steadily in three minor league seasons; added a tick to his FB which now has average velocity. Sturdy frame but more finesse than power; knows how to pitch and mixes SL/CB/CU to keep batters off balance. CU is best secondary, especially when thrown off the fastball.

Cruz,Yovanny

SP | **Chicago (N)** | EXP MLB DEBUT: 2023 | H/W: 6-1 190 | FUT: #4 starter | **8D**

Thrws R Age 20
2016 FA (DR)

Velo	Pitch	Grade
90-93	FB	+++
	SL	+++
	CU	+++

Year	Lev	Team	W	L	Sv	IP	K	ERA	WHIP	BF/G	OBA	H%	S%	xERA	Ctl	Dom	Cmd	hr/9	BPV
2018	A-	Eugene	1	0	0	5	5	0.00	0.80	18.1	221	31	100	1.28	0.0	9.0		0.0	180
2018	Rk	AZL Cubs 2	4	2	0	44	50	2.86	1.11	17.3	225	32	73	2.30	2.7	10.2	3.8	0.2	130
2019	A-	Eugene	1	2	0	14	21	8.24	1.76	13.0	245	34	55	5.75	7.6	13.3	1.8	1.9	52
2019	Rk	AZL Cubs 2	0	0	0	9	7	4.00	1.56	9.8	216	28	71	3.15	7.0	7.0	1.0	0.0	-45

Dominican RH with back-end SP upside but who struggled mightily in Low-A with control and command. Lives around 90-93 mph with sinking FB; could add more as he fills out his lean, long frame. Both his SL and CU have flashed above-average but will need more reps. Ease of delivery and clean arm action portend future average command.

Dalquist,Andrew

SP | **Chicago (A)** | EXP MLB DEBUT: 2023 | H/W: 6-1 175 | FUT: #4 starter | **7C**

Thrws R Age 19
2019 (3) HS (CA)

Velo	Pitch	Grade
89-92	FB	+++
72-75	CB	+++
	CU	+++

Year	Lev	Team	W	L	Sv	IP	K	ERA	WHIP	BF/G	OBA	H%	S%	xERA	Ctl	Dom	Cmd	hr/9	BPV
2019	Rk	AZL White Sox	0	0	0	3	2	0.00	1.67	4.5	262	32	100	4.03	6.0	6.0	1.0	0.0	-36

With present pitchability and repeatable delivery, he made his pro debut. Features three pitches, all with average-or-better potential. Has advanced command of two FBs. 2-seam over 4-seam at this point in development. Can spin low-70s CB and has feel for CU. Delivery plays up CU potential.

Davidson,Tucker

SP | **Atlanta** | EXP MLB DEBUT: 2020 | H/W: 6-2 215 | FUT: #3 starter | **8D**

Thrws L Age 24
2016 (19) Midland College

Velo	Pitch	Grade
92-95	FB	++++
78-81	CB	++++
84-87	CU	+++

Year	Lev	Team	W	L	Sv	IP	K	ERA	WHIP	BF/G	OBA	H%	S%	xERA	Ctl	Dom	Cmd	hr/9	BPV
2016	Rk	GCL Braves	0	3	0	29	32	1.54	1.23	10.8	280	38	89	3.44	1.2	9.9	8.0	0.3	162
2017	A	Rome	5	4	2	103	101	2.62	1.22	13.5	248	33	79	3.02	2.6	8.8	3.4	0.3	106
2018	A+	Florida	7	10	0	118	99	4.19	1.51	21.3	265	33	71	4.01	4.4	7.5	1.7	0.4	34
2019	AA	Mississippi	7	6	0	110	122	2.04	1.21	21.1	221	31	84	2.68	3.7	10.0	2.7	0.4	98
2019	AAA	Gwinnett	1	1	0	19	12	2.84	1.53	20.6	272	32	79	3.81	4.3	5.7	1.3	0.0	5

Hard-throwing, high 3/4s LHP with present control made solid strides in 2019. Repeats well exclusively out of stretch, creating some RP role concerns. FB is heavy with solid bore and Dom potential. 1-to-6 CB has plus depth and solid break. Both are plus pitches. CU continues to come along with solid fade and separation off his FB.

De La Cruz,Jasseel

SP | **Atlanta** | EXP MLB DEBUT: 2020 | H/W: 6-1 215 | FUT: Setup reliever | **7C**

Thrws R Age 22
2015 FA (DR)

Velo	Pitch	Grade
93-97	FB	++++
88-90	SL	++++
88-91	CU	++

Year	Lev	Team	W	L	Sv	IP	K	ERA	WHIP	BF/G	OBA	H%	S%	xERA	Ctl	Dom	Cmd	hr/9	BPV
2017	Rk	Danville	0	2	0	23	19	5.43	1.55	14.5	276	34	63	4.29	4.3	7.4	1.7	0.4	35
2018	A	Rome	3	4	0	69	65	4.83	1.43	19.6	250	31	67	4.00	4.4	8.5	1.9	0.8	51
2019	A	Rome	0	1	0	18	22	2.50	1.33	18.7	272	38	83	3.75	2.5	11.0	4.4	0.5	149
2019	A+	Florida	3	1	0	28	26	1.93	0.68	24.5	132	18	68		2.3	8.4	3.7	0.0	108
2019	AA	Mississippi	4	7	0	87	73	3.83	1.24	20.8	224	27	70	3.13	3.8	7.6	2.0	0.7	51

Hard-throwing RHP added weight and muscle to frame, which played up high-octane stuff. 3/4 delivery with solid extension; maintains mid-90s and could hit 100 as RP. FB has solid running action and can sneak up on hitters. SL is tight and breaks late; CU is stiff and unprojectable. Can't consistently command pitches.

De La Cruz,Oscar

RP | **Chicago (N)** | EXP MLB DEBUT: 2020 | H/W: 6-4 200 | FUT: Closer | **7B**

Thrws R Age 25
2012 FA (DR)

Velo	Pitch	Grade
90-93	FB	+++
78-81	CB	+++
83-85	CU	++

Year	Lev	Team	W	L	Sv	IP	K	ERA	WHIP	BF/G	OBA	H%	S%	xERA	Ctl	Dom	Cmd	hr/9	BPV
2017	Rk	AZL Cubs	0	0	0	2	1	0.00	0.00	5.6	0	0			0.0	4.5		0.0	99
2017	A+	Myrtle Beach	4	3	0	54	47	3.49	1.25	18.4	265	32	76	3.94	2.2	7.8	3.6	1.0	100
2018	AA	Tennessee	6	7	0	77	73	5.25	1.39	20.3	259	32	63	4.14	3.6	8.5	2.4	0.9	74
2019	A+	Myrtle Beach	1	0	0	15	17	1.20	1.27	20.4	249	36	89	2.80	3.0	10.2	3.4	0.0	121
2019	AA	Tennessee	4	5	2	81	88	4.11	1.16	10.4	221	29	66	3.02	3.2	9.8	3.0	0.9	107

Tall, maxed-out RH transitioned from SP to RP mid-season and saw his stuff tick up in short spurts. FB will touch 97 mph with unique crossfire angle and good 2-seam movement. Likes to use 12-to-6 CB that will flash plus and has some feel for fading CU. Can struggle to maintain release point, but made progress with his move to the bullpen.

De Leon,Jose | SP | Cincinnati | EXP MLB DEBUT: 2016 | H/W: 6-1 220 | FUT: #5 SP/swingman | 6B

Thrws R Age 27	Year	Lev	Team	W	L	Sv	IP	K	ERA	WHIP	BF/G	OBA	H%	S%	xERA	Ctl	Dom	Cmd	hr/9	BPV
2013 (24) Southern	2017	AAA	Durham	0	2	0	12	14	6.75	1.67	17.9	293	40	58	5.13	4.5	10.5	2.3	0.8	86
89-93 FB +++	2017	MLB	Tampa Bay	1	0	0	2	2	12.27	3.18	13.2	392	42	67	13.84	12.3	8.2	0.7	4.1	-166
80-82 SL +++	2019	A+	Charlotte	0	0	0	4	1	4.29	1.67	9.4	252	22	83	5.95	6.4	2.1	0.3	2.1	-117
81-82 CU ++++	2019	AAA	Durham	2	1	1	51	73	3.52	1.33	12.5	221	34	75	3.25	4.8	12.9	2.7	0.7	121
	2019	MLB	Tampa Bay	1	0	0	4	7	2.25	1.50	5.8	210	41	83	2.84	6.8	15.8	2.3	0.0	119

Former top pitching prospect has struggled with injuries throughout career. Hasn't regained plus velocity from 2018 Tommy John surgery. Three pitches; FB sits high-80s-to-low-90s with a solid arm-side bore. CU remains best secondary, achieving late-fade and solid drop. The SL has shown average projection. Without velo increase, a swingman/RP role.

de los Santos,Enyel | SP | Philadelphia | EXP MLB DEBUT: 2018 | H/W: 6-3 170 | FUT: Middle reliever | 7A

Thrws R Age 24	Year	Lev	Team	W	L	Sv	IP	K	ERA	WHIP	BF/G	OBA	H%	S%	xERA	Ctl	Dom	Cmd	hr/9	BPV
2014 FA (DR)	2017	AA	San Antonio	10	6	0	150	138	3.78	1.19	23.2	236	29	69	3.15	2.9	8.3	2.9	0.7	89
92-95 FB +++	2018	AAA	Lehigh Valley	10	5	0	126	110	2.64	1.16	22.9	226	27	81	3.08	3.1	7.8	2.6	0.9	76
83-85 SL +	2018	MLB	Philadelphia	1	0	0	19	15	4.74	1.42	11.5	262	31	68	4.29	3.8	7.1	1.9	0.9	44
80-83 CU +++	2019	AAA	Lehigh Valley	5	7	0	94	83	4.40	1.23	20.1	234	26	70	3.99	3.4	7.9	2.4	1.5	71
	2019	MLB	Philadelphia	0	1	0	11	9	7.36	1.64	9.8	295	29	64	7.49	4.1	7.4	1.8	3.3	40

Tall/lanky FB/CU-centric pitcher who has been reliable rotation member in Triple-A, but doesn't have a breaking ball he can trust to start in majors. Sells CU on good arm speed, but commanding FB has been a challenge and is a pitch-to-contact reliever at this point.

Del Rosario,Yefri | SP | Kansas City | EXP MLB DEBUT: 2023 | H/W: 6-2 180 | FUT: #3 starter | 8E

Thrws R Age 20	Year	Lev	Team	W	L	Sv	IP	K	ERA	WHIP	BF/G	OBA	H%	S%	xERA	Ctl	Dom	Cmd	hr/9	BPV
2016 FA (DR)																				
92-95 FB ++++																				
78-80 CB ++++	2017	Rk	GCL Braves	1	1	0	32	29	3.93	1.46	12.5	290	37	72	4.16	2.8	8.1	2.9	0.3	89
86-87 CU +++	2018	A	Lexington	6	5	0	79	72	3.19	1.24	21.4	236	28	80	3.66	3.3	8.2	2.5	1.1	76
	2019		Did not pitch - injury																	

Projectable mid-rotation SP was held back in extended to preserve injuries then missed season with bicep injury. Raw, high 3/4s crossfire delivery. FB sits low-to-mid 90s with solid, late run. Should pick up a tick or two refining delivery. 11-to-5 CB has solid depth and late drop; could be plus at projection. Has feel for above-average CU.

Denaburg,Martin | SP | Washington | EXP MLB DEBUT: 2023 | H/W: 6-4 195 | FUT: #3 starter | 8E

Thrws R Age 20	Year	Lev	Team	W	L	Sv	IP	K	ERA	WHIP	BF/G	OBA	H%	S%	xERA	Ctl	Dom	Cmd	hr/9	BPV
2018 (1) HS (FL)																				
90-94 FB +++																				
78-80 CB ++																				
CU ++	2018		Did not pitch - injury																	
	2019	Rk	GCL Nationals	1	1	0	20	19	7.61	1.84	13.4	289	37	56	5.24	6.3	8.5	1.4	0.4	2

Injuries continued to cloud his outlook; had minor shoulder surgery after struggling in a 20-IP GCL stint. Supposedly ready for spring, he sports an above average 90-94 FB, complemented by a CB and CU. No offerings are currently outstanding, though he has had little pro experience. Solid frame and good pedigree are reasons to hold out hope.

Diaz,Yennsy | SP | Toronto | EXP MLB DEBUT: 2019 | H/W: 6-1 202 | FUT: #3 starter | 8D

Thrws R Age 23	Year	Lev	Team	W	L	Sv	IP	K	ERA	WHIP	BF/G	OBA	H%	S%	xERA	Ctl	Dom	Cmd	hr/9	BPV
2014 FA (DR)	2017	A	Lansing	5	2	0	77	82	4.79	1.45	20.6	246	31	70	4.35	4.8	9.6	2.0	1.2	61
93-98 FB ++++	2018	A	Lansing	5	1	0	47	42	2.10	1.00	20.0	142	16	84	1.61	4.8	8.0	1.7	0.8	33
78-81 CB +++	2018	A+	Dunedin	5	4	0	99	83	3.54	1.20	22.2	245	30	70	3.04	2.5	7.5	3.0	0.5	85
85-89 CU ++	2019	AA	New Hampshire	11	9	0	144	116	3.75	1.24	22.5	235	28	71	3.28	3.3	7.2	2.2	0.7	59
	2019	MLB	Toronto	0	0	0	0	0	90.00	25.00	5.6	639	64	60	73.51		0.0	0.0	0.0	-4842

Quick-armed SP who reached MLB on basis of lively FB. Doesn't miss many bats, but gets by with deception and movement. CB has improved to above average status, but needs to fine tune CU. Tough on RHH, but LHH give him fits. Hides ball well and delivery can be tough for hitters to pick up. Arm strength could work in bullpen.

Dibrell,Tony | SP | New York (N) | EXP MLB DEBUT: 2021 | H/W: 6-3 190 | FUT: Middle reliever | 6D

Thrws R Age 24	Year	Lev	Team	W	L	Sv	IP	K	ERA	WHIP	BF/G	OBA	H%	S%	xERA	Ctl	Dom	Cmd	hr/9	BPV
2017 (4) Kennesaw St																				
87-90 FB ++	2017	A-	Brooklyn	1	1	0	19	28	5.16	1.41	6.8	260	36	70	5.03	3.8	13.1	3.5	1.9	153
72-75 CB +++	2018	A	Columbia	7	6	0	131	147	3.50	1.27	23.3	233	31	74	3.24	3.7	10.1	2.7	0.7	100
79-81 SL +++	2019	A+	St. Lucie	8	4	0	90	76	2.40	1.21	21.4	223	29	79	2.54	3.6	7.6	2.1	0.2	58
79-81 CU ++	2019	AA	Binghamton	0	8	0	38	37	9.42	1.88	20.0	321	37	52	7.65	4.9	8.7	1.8	2.4	41

Tall, thin RHP lost command of FB, causing down year. Cuts extension short in high 3/4s delivery. 4-pitch pitcher without overwhelming stuff. FB sits on fringes of effectiveness. Minimal movement, can succeed some due to natural downward plane. Both breaking balls are average-or-better offerings. Feel for CU virtually disappeared in 2019.

Dobnak,Randy | SP | Minnesota | EXP MLB DEBUT: 2019 | H/W: 6-1 230 | FUT: #4 starter | 7C

Thrws R Age 25	Year	Lev	Team	W	L	Sv	IP	K	ERA	WHIP	BF/G	OBA	H%	S%	xERA	Ctl	Dom	Cmd	hr/9	BPV
2017 FA (AldersonBroaddus)	2018	A	Cedar Rapids	10	5	0	129	84	3.14	1.26	21.9	275	32	75	3.59	1.7	5.9	3.4	0.4	76
91-94 FB +++	2019	A+	Fort Myers	3	0	0	22	14	0.41	1.00	21.1	224	27	95	1.84	1.6	5.7	3.5	0.0	77
83-85 CB ++++	2019	AA	Pensacola	4	2	0	66	61	2.58	0.97	22.8	237	29	78	2.68	0.8	8.3	10.2	0.8	145
84-86 CU +++	2019	AAA	Rochester	5	2	0	46	34	2.15	1.00	19.5	178	23	76	1.30	3.5	6.7	1.9	0.0	43
	2019	MLB	Minnesota	2	1	1	28	23	1.60	1.14	12.4	254	32	87	2.88	1.6	7.4	4.6	0.3	107

3/4s RHP went from High-A to MLB, even starting game in ALDS. Independent League find for MIN in 2017. Crossfire, repeatable delivery; Three-pitch pitcher. Relies on heavy 2-seam FB as workhorse to get ground balls and to set up plus CB. CB is tight like SL with late downer break. Has arm-side run and late fade on CU.

Dodson,Tanner | RP | Tampa Bay | EXP MLB DEBUT: 2022 | H/W: 6-1 170 | FUT: Setup reliever | 7D

Thrws R Age 22	Year	Lev	Team	W	L	Sv	IP	K	ERA	WHIP	BF/G	OBA	H%	S%	xERA	Ctl	Dom	Cmd	hr/9	BPV
2018 (2) California																				
93-96 FB ++++																				
88-91 SL +++	2018	NCAA	California	2	1	11	40	35	2.48	1.08	8.2	242	30	80	2.88	1.6	7.9	5.0	0.7	117
79-83 CB ++	2018	A-	Hudson Valley	1	0	1	25	25	1.44	0.68	9.7	145	21	76	0.13	1.8	9.0	5.0	0.0	131
	2019	A+	Charlotte	0	1	0	17	15	5.29	2.18	10.6	369	44	77	8.00	4.8	7.9	1.7	1.1	32

Two-way player struggled with injury early and ineffectiveness late. CF as position player. Switch-hitter with a patient approach and some swing path concerns. Scouts like in RP role better. Hits high-90s but sits mid-90s with late-running FB. SL is best secondary pitch, projecting as above-average. CB is more slurve than true breaker.

Doval,Camilo | RP | San Francisco | EXP MLB DEBUT: 2021 | H/W: 6-2 180 | FUT: Setup reliever | 7C

Thrws R Age 22	Year	Lev	Team	W	L	Sv	IP	K	ERA	WHIP	BF/G	OBA	H%	S%	xERA	Ctl	Dom	Cmd	hr/9	BPV
2015 FA (DR)																				
93-98 FB ++++																				
85-87 SL +++	2017	Rk	AZL Giants	1	2	1	32	51	3.93	1.12	7.4	203	37	61	1.82	3.6	14.3	3.9	0.0	177
88-90 CT +++	2018	A	Augusta	0	3	11	53	78	3.06	1.26	4.9	211	35	75	2.61	4.6	13.2	2.9	0.3	133
	2019	A+	San Jose	3	5	0	56	80	3.85	1.34	5.2	206	33	70	2.71	5.5	12.8	2.4	0.3	102

Career RP who was dominant over last 20 games with high K rate and low oppBA. Hard FB plays up due to violent delivery and is aggressive early in count. Complements with hard SL that has chance to become plus. SL features cutting action with velocity. Doesn't change speeds well and is all power. Control is big issue due to inability to repeat slot.

Doxakis,John | SP | Tampa Bay | EXP MLB DEBUT: 2022 | H/W: 6-4 215 | FUT: #4 starter | 7C

Thrws L Age 21	Year	Lev	Team	W	L	Sv	IP	K	ERA	WHIP	BF/G	OBA	H%	S%	xERA	Ctl	Dom	Cmd	hr/9	BPV
2019 (2) Texas A&M																				
89-92 FB +++																				
79-82 SL +++																				
84-85 CU +++	2019	NCAA	Texas A&M	7	4	0	104	115	2.07	1.02	25.0	214	30	81	2.14	2.2	9.9	4.4	0.4	136
	2019	A-	Hudson Valley	0	0	0	32	31	1.96	0.96	10.2	180	25	77	1.22	3.1	8.7	2.8	0.0	91

Tall, lean funky LHP made professional debut in 2019. Low 3/4s delivery with long arm action and solid extension. Funkiness plays up 3-pitch mix. FB has solid arm-side run with natural downward plane. SL is sweepy with two-plane break. Has feel for CU with solid, arm-side run and late fade. It could be an above-average offering at projection.

Doyle,Tommy | RP | Colorado | EXP MLB DEBUT: 2020 | H/W: 6-6 235 | FUT: Middle reliever | 7C

Thrws R Age 23	Year	Lev	Team	W	L	Sv	IP	K	ERA	WHIP	BF/G	OBA	H%	S%	xERA	Ctl	Dom	Cmd	hr/9	BPV
2017 (2) Virginia																				
94-97 FB ++++	2017	NCAA	Virginia	3	1	14	33	38	1.90	1.14	5.7	230	32	86	2.76	2.7	10.3	3.8	0.5	130
83-86 SL +++	2017	Rk	Grand Junction	3	3	3	21	18	5.14	1.86	4.9	329	40	73	6.31	4.3	7.7	1.8	0.9	41
86-88 CU ++	2018	A	Asheville	7	6	18	58	66	2.32	1.10	4.4	241	34	79	2.57	1.9	10.2	5.5	0.3	152
	2019	A+	Lancaster	2	3	19	36	48	3.25	1.03	3.6	191	27	73	2.41	3.3	12.0	3.7	1.0	146

Tall, strong RH who was a bit old for his level in 2019, but posted best SwK among CAL arms. Attacks hitters with plus FB in mid-90s with low-effort, online delivery, which allows him to fill up the zone. SL is best secondary pitch and will also mix in average CU. Difficult to square up due to steep arm angle and has heavy ground-ball lean.

Dugger,Robert

SP | **Miami** | EXP MLB DEBUT: 2019 | H/W: 6-2 180 | FUT: #5 SP/swingman | **6C**

Thrws R Age 24	Year	Lev	Team	W	L	Sv	IP	K	ERA	WHIP	BF/G	OBA	H%	S%	xERA	Ctl	Dom	Cmd	hr/9	BPV
2016 (18) Texas Tech	2018	A+	Jupiter	3	1	0	41	34	2.41	1.14	23.3	257	32	80	3.03	1.5	7.4	4.9	0.4	111
88-91 FB +++	2018	AA	Jacksonville	7	6	0	109	107	3.79	1.25	24.6	245	30	73	3.72	3.0	8.8	3.0	1.1	97
78-80 SL +++	2019	AA	Jacksonville	6	6	0	70	73	3.33	1.11	21.2	224	29	72	2.82	2.7	9.4	3.5	0.8	114
71-74 CB ++	2019	AAA	New Orleans	2	4	0	53	49	7.63	1.71	24.1	331	38	58	7.08	2.9	8.3	2.9	2.0	90
78-80 CU ++	2019	MLB	Miami	0	4	0	34	25	5.81	1.47	20.9	255	28	64	4.92	4.5	6.6	1.5	1.6	16

Command/control RHP struggled missing barrels in MLB debut. Stiff 3/4s, crossfire delivery better suited for RP role. Solid movement on FB, struggled commanding it in debut. Best secondary is SL with a short break. CB is loopy and not an effective pitch. Little confidence in CU.

Dunn,Justin

SP | **Seattle** | EXP MLB DEBUT: 2019 | H/W: 6-2 185 | FUT: #4 starter | **7B**

Thrws R Age 24	Year	Lev	Team	W	L	Sv	IP	K	ERA	WHIP	BF/G	OBA	H%	S%	xERA	Ctl	Dom	Cmd	hr/9	BPV
2016 (1) Boston College	2017	A+	St. Lucie	5	6	0	95	75	5.02	1.57	20.9	274	33	67	4.37	4.5	7.1	1.6	0.5	23
90-94 FB ++++	2018	A+	St. Lucie	2	3	0	45	51	2.39	1.28	20.6	252	35	82	3.26	3.0	10.2	3.4	0.4	120
81-83 SL +++	2018	AA	Binghamton	6	5	0	89	105	4.24	1.37	24.9	253	35	70	3.76	3.7	10.6	2.8	0.7	108
86-89 CU +++	2019	AA	Arkansas	9	5	0	131	158	3.57	1.20	21.1	242	33	73	3.36	2.7	10.8	4.1	0.9	141
	2019	MLB	Seattle	0	0	0	6	5	2.90	1.77	7.1	103	14	82	2.48	13.1	7.3	0.6	0.0	-204

Former college RP made MLB debut as SP in 2019. Scrapped CB and concentrated on refining SL/CU. Repeatable, crossfire 3/4s delivery. FB sits low 90s with solid running action. SL has above-average potential and has improved consistency. CU is fringe average and battles with firmness. Some evaluators like him better as RP.

Dunning,Dane

SP | **Chicago (A)** | EXP MLB DEBUT: 2020 | H/W: 6-4 200 | FUT: #3 starter | **8D**

Thrws R Age 25	Year	Lev	Team	W	L	Sv	IP	K	ERA	WHIP	BF/G	OBA	H%	S%	xERA	Ctl	Dom	Cmd	hr/9	BPV
2016 (1) Florida	2017	A	Kannapolis	2	0	0	26	33	0.35	0.58	22.1	151	24	93		0.7	11.4	16.5	0.0	205
90-93 FB ++++	2017	A+	Winston-Salem	6	8	0	118	135	3.51	1.27	21.9	255	33	77	3.97	2.7	10.3	3.8	1.1	129
83-86 SL ++++	2018	A+	Winston-Salem	1	1	0	24	31	2.61	0.95	22.7	227	33	76	2.42	1.1	11.6	10.3	0.7	196
78-80 CB +++	2018	AA	Birmingham	5	2	0	62	69	2.76	1.29	23.2	246	35	76	2.82	3.3	10.0	3.0	0.0	108
82-83 CU +++	2019		Did not pitch - injury																	

Ground ball specialist was on the verge of MLB debut before March 2019 Tommy John surgery. 3/4s RHP with easy, repeatable delivery. Shows four pitches; best is a low-90s heavy 2-seam FB with late sink. SL is tight with 2-plane break. CB and CU are both workable MLB offerings. CU has above-average projection at maturity.

Dunshee,Parker

SP | **Oakland** | EXP MLB DEBUT: 2020 | H/W: 6-0 215 | FUT: #5 SP/swingman | **7B**

Thrws R Age 25	Year	Lev	Team	W	L	Sv	IP	K	ERA	WHIP	BF/G	OBA	H%	S%	xERA	Ctl	Dom	Cmd	hr/9	BPV
2017 (7) Wake Forest	2017	A-	Vermont	1	0	0	38	45	0.00	0.60	10.9	123	19	100		1.9	10.6	5.6	0.0	158
89-92 FB +++	2018	A+	Stockton	6	2	0	70	82	2.70	1.11	23.0	236	32	80	3.09	2.2	10.5	4.8	0.9	149
83-86 SL ++	2018	AA	Midland	7	4	0	80	81	2.02	0.91	24.9	207	27	81	1.91	1.6	9.1	5.8	0.6	139
78-81 CB +++	2019	AA	Midland	2	2	0	38	34	1.89	0.97	24.0	195	25	81	1.64	2.6	8.1	3.1	0.2	93
83-85 CU +++	2019	AAA	Las Vegas	4	5	1	92	90	5.38	1.34	19.1	249	28	67	4.92	3.6	8.8	2.4	2.1	79

Pitchability RH got hit around a bit in PCL in 2019 but looks about ready to contribute and produce in deeper formats in 2020. Athletic, repeatable delivery; projects for plus command. FB sits in low-90s and CU flashes above-average. CB/SL combo are usable, but not dominant. Not a high ceiling arm, but one with good ratios as a back-end SP.

Duplantier,Jon

SP | **Arizona** | EXP MLB DEBUT: 2019 | H/W: 6-4 225 | FUT: #3 starter | **8C**

Thrws R Age 25	Year	Lev	Team	W	L	Sv	IP	K	ERA	WHIP	BF/G	OBA	H%	S%	xERA	Ctl	Dom	Cmd	hr/9	BPV
2016 (3) Rice	2018	AA	Jackson	5	1	0	67	68	2.69	1.19	19.2	216	28	79	2.71	3.8	9.1	2.4	0.5	81
91-94 FB +++	2019	Rk	AZL DBacks	0	0	0	2	3	18.00	4.00	6.8	470	60	57	18.04	13.5	13.5	1.0	4.5	-104
82-84 SL ++++	2019	A+	Visalia	0	0	0	3	3	0.00	0.67	10.5	191	27	100	0.59	0.0	9.0		0.0	180
77-79 CB +++	2019	AAA	Reno	1	2	0	38	44	5.21	1.55	12.8	224	32	64	3.43	6.6	10.4	1.6	0.2	27
82-85 CU +++	2019	MLB	Arizona	1	1	1	36	34	4.48	1.57	10.6	276	35	71	4.44	4.5	8.5	1.9	0.5	49

Tall, physical RH who spent time on IL with shoulder inflammation; control took a step back and so did his velocity. Can sit 93-95 mph with late life on plus FB, mixes in above-average SL and CU for high Dom ability. Struggles to throw strikes and establish zone at times, but limits hard contact. Could profile as #3 SP or hard-throwing reliever.

Duran,Jhoan

SP | **Minnesota** | EXP MLB DEBUT: 2020 | H/W: 6-5 230 | FUT: #3 starter | **8C**

Thrws R Age 22	Year	Lev	Team	W	L	Sv	IP	K	ERA	WHIP	BF/G	OBA	H%	S%	xERA	Ctl	Dom	Cmd	hr/9	BPV
2015 FA (DR)	2017	A-	Hillsboro	6	3	0	51	36	4.24	1.20	18.6	234	27	66	3.30	3.0	6.4	2.1	0.9	51
95-97 FB ++++	2018	A	Kane County	5	4	0	64	71	4.77	1.51	18.5	276	36	69	4.58	3.9	10.0	2.5	0.8	91
82-85 CB ++++	2018	A	Cedar Rapids	7	5	0	100	115	3.77	1.26	19.5	237	32	71	3.30	3.4	10.3	3.0	0.7	112
91-94 SP +++	2019	A+	Fort Myers	2	9	0	78	95	3.23	1.21	19.6	223	32	74	2.84	3.6	11.0	3.1	0.6	119
CU +	2019	AA	Pensacola	3	3	0	37	41	4.86	1.16	21.0	246	34	56	2.96	2.2	10.0	4.6	0.5	138

Tall, hard-throwing RHP has filled out frame. High 3/4s delivery with limited extension; four-pitch pitcher. FB best low in the zone but lack of extension in delivery makes it seem less overpowering. Spike CB best pitch with solid shape and plus movement. SP has a plus profile but struggles with consistency. CU is a non-factor.

Elledge,Seth

RP | **St. Louis** | EXP MLB DEBUT: 2020 | H/W: 6-3 240 | FUT: Setup reliever | **6B**

Thrws R Age 23	Year	Lev	Team	W	L	Sv	IP	K	ERA	WHIP	BF/G	OBA	H%	S%	xERA	Ctl	Dom	Cmd	hr/9	BPV
2017 (4) Dallas Baptist	2017	A	Clinton	3	0	5	21	35	3.00	0.95	5.3	191	35	68	1.65	2.6	15.0	5.8	0.4	219
93-95 FB +++	2018	A+	Modesto	5	1	9	38	54	1.18	0.87	4.5	143	24	88	0.76	3.5	12.8	3.6	0.2	152
80-83 SL ++	2018	AA	Springfield	3	1	4	16	20	4.44	1.17	5.0	222	28	69	3.77	3.3	11.1	3.3	1.7	128
CU ++	2019	AA	Springfield	3	3	3	33	43	3.81	1.42	5.4	267	38	75	4.19	3.5	11.7	3.3	0.8	133
	2019	AAA	Memphis	3	1	0	34	32	4.75	1.38	6.8	226	28	66	3.54	5.0	8.4	1.7	0.8	35

Acquired in the Tuivailala trade, features a lively 92-95 mph FB with good late sink. SL has tight, late cutter-like action and an improved CU is third offering. Big, durable frame and made 48 appearances in 2019. Sinking action on FB and deceptive delivery result in a career 11.4 Dom, but lack of secondary stuff limits him to a relief role.

Enlow,Blayne

SP | **Minnesota** | EXP MLB DEBUT: 2022 | H/W: 6-3 170 | FUT: #3 starter | **8D**

Thrws R Age 21	Year	Lev	Team	W	L	Sv	IP	K	ERA	WHIP	BF/G	OBA	H%	S%	xERA	Ctl	Dom	Cmd	hr/9	BPV
2017 (3) HS (LA)																				
92-95 FB ++++	2017	Rk	GCL Twins	3	0	0	20	19	1.34	0.70	11.8	150	19	85	0.64	1.8	8.5	4.8	0.4	123
88-90 CT +++	2018	A	Cedar Rapids	3	5	1	94	71	3.26	1.37	19.7	262	32	76	3.64	3.4	6.8	2.0	0.4	50
78-82 CB ++++	2019	A+	Fort Myers	4	4	0	69	51	3.39	1.22	21.5	238	28	73	3.06	3.0	6.6	2.2	0.5	57
85-87 CU ++	2019	A	Cedar Rapids	4	3	0	41	44	4.60	1.39	21.6	266	35	68	4.17	3.3	9.6	2.9	0.9	103

Athletic, high 3/4s RHP refined delivery, posting solid returns. Projectable frame with present strength. Could see velocity pick up with more bulk. Sits low-to-mid 90s with 2-seam FB with plus arm-side action. Mixes in average CT with short break. CB flashes plus with plus breaking action. CU has arm-side run, struggles creating separation off FB.

Escobar,Luis

RP | **Pittsburgh** | EXP MLB DEBUT: 2019 | H/W: 6-1 205 | FUT: Setup reliever | **6C**

Thrws R Age 23	Year	Lev	Team	W	L	Sv	IP	K	ERA	WHIP	BF/G	OBA	H%	S%	xERA	Ctl	Dom	Cmd	hr/9	BPV
2013 FA (CB)	2018	A+	Bradenton	7	6	0	92	85	4.00	1.24	22.0	226	28	70	3.28	3.7	8.3	2.2	0.9	67
93-97 FB ++++	2018	AA	Altoona	4	0	0	35	25	4.60	1.45	21.5	232	26	70	4.04	5.4	6.4	1.2	1.0	-12
81-83 CB ++++	2019	A+	Bradenton	0	0	3	13	15	0.00	0.92	4.9	140	21	100	0.65	4.1	10.3	2.5	0.0	92
83-87 CU ++	2019	AAA	Indianapolis	2	1	1	55	57	4.09	1.56	10.0	258	32	77	4.76	5.2	9.3	1.8	1.1	45
	2019	MLB	Pittsburgh	0	0	0	5	2	8.65	2.69	7.2	405	42	69	10.71	6.9	3.5	0.5	1.7	-107

Dynamic RP who found niche in pen. K rate increased while also maintaining high groundball rate. Tough on LHH despite lack of CU. Owns potent 1-2 combo in FB and CB and both serve as out pitches. FB exhibits lots of life and CB features nasty breaking action. May struggle with command and control at times due to lots of effort in erratic delivery.

Espino,Daniel

SP | **Cleveland** | EXP MLB DEBUT: 2023 | H/W: 6-2 205 | FUT: #2 starter | **9E**

Thrws R Age 19	Year	Lev	Team	W	L	Sv	IP	K	ERA	WHIP	BF/G	OBA	H%	S%	xERA	Ctl	Dom	Cmd	hr/9	BPV
2019 (1) HS (GA)																				
96-98 FB +++++																				
83-85 SL ++++																				
76-77 CB +++	2019	A-	MahoningVal	0	2	0	10	18	6.30	1.40	14.1	242	44	54	3.83	4.5	16.2	3.6	0.9	188
86-89 CU +++	2019	Rk	AZL Indians	0	1	0	13	16	2.05	0.91	8.2	158	22	82	1.46	3.4	10.9	3.2	0.7	122

Hard-throwing, 3/4s RHP regularly hit 100 MPH working as an amateur in spring. Very athletic delivery, although some risk with very long arm action. Generates plus arm speed with ease. FB sits high 90s with late run and solid control. Best seconary offering is plus SL with tight, 2-plane break. Both CB and CU could be above-average pitches.

Espinoza,Anderson

SP | **San Diego** | EXP MLB DEBUT: 2021 | H/W: 6-0 160 | FUT: #2 SP/closer | **9E**

Thrws R Age 22	Year	Lev	Team	W	L	Sv	IP	K	ERA	WHIP	BF/G	OBA	H%	S%	xERA	Ctl	Dom	Cmd	hr/9	BPV
2014 FA (VZ)	2016	A	Greenville	5	8	0	76	72	4.38	1.37	18.7	264	35	66	3.51	3.2	8.5	2.7	0.2	85
93-96 FB ++++	2016	A	Fort Wayne	1	3	0	32	28	4.77	1.43	17.1	296	37	64	4.17	2.2	7.9	3.5	0.3	99
73-77 CB ++++	2017		Did not play - injury																	
80-84 CU ++++	2018		Did not play - injury																	
	2019		Did not play - injury																	

Former big-time int'l prospect underwent second Tommy John surgery in April; has not pitched in a live pro game since 2016. Durability remains a significant issue and he'll have a large mental hurdle to clear in 2020. Last time we saw him, had lively mid-90s FB with plus off-speed stuff. Could ultimately be used from the 'pen.

Ethridge,Will

SP | Colorado | EXP MLB DEBUT: 2022 | H/W: 6-5 240 | FUT: #5 SP/swingman | 7C

Thrws R Age 22
2019 (5) Mississippi

Velo	Pitch	Grade
91-94	FB	+++
81-84	SL	+++
	CU	+++

Year	Lev	Team	W	L	Sv	IP	K	ERA	WHIP	BF/G	OBA	H%	S%	xERA	Ctl	Dom	Cmd	hr/9	BPV
2019	A-	Boise	0	2	0	30	21	3.87	1.16	13.4	254	30	65	2.92	1.8	6.3	3.5	0.3	82

Tall, muscular RH who lacks plus pitch but has well-rounded arsenal and high floor. Sinking FB in low-90s was ground-ball machine in college and both SL and CU project as avg offerings. Limits hard contact efficiently by locating his stuff well and knowing how to sequence. Overall Dom ability may be limited but should eat innings as back-end SP.

Eveld,Tommy

RP | Miami | EXP MLB DEBUT: 2020 | H/W: 6-5 195 | FUT: Setup reliever | 7D

Thrws R Age 26
2016 (9) South Florida

Velo	Pitch	Grade
93-96	FB	++++
87-89	SL	++++
78-81	CB	++
88-90	CU	++

Year	Lev	Team	W	L	Sv	IP	K	ERA	WHIP	BF/G	OBA	H%	S%	xERA	Ctl	Dom	Cmd	hr/9	BPV
2018	A+	Visalia	2	2	12	36	42	1.25	1.00	4.3	222	32	89	2.01	1.7	10.5	6.0	0.2	159
2018	AA	Jacksonville	2	1	4	14	19	0.64	0.79	3.9	151	25	91	0.42	2.6	12.2	4.8	0.0	168
2018	AA	Jackson	1	0	1	4	5	0.00	0.49	4.5	80	13	100		2.2	11.0	5.0	0.0	156
2019	AA	Jacksonville	2	3	11	26	36	2.77	0.88	4.0	206	30	75	2.25	1.4	12.5	9.0	1.0	205
2019	AAA	New Orleans	1	4	1	23	24	7.79	1.60	5.7	269	27	61	7.23	5.1	9.4	1.8	3.5	50

Hard-throwing RHP struggled early in Triple-A before torrid 2nd half in Double-A. Bulldog mentality, attacks hitters. Two plus pitches highlight arsenal. Struggles commanding movement of 93-96 MPH FB. High 80s SL is a tight, 2-plane breaking pitch. Also throws fringe CB and CU.

Faedo,Alex

SP | Detroit | EXP MLB DEBUT: 2020 | H/W: 6-5 230 | FUT: #4 starter | 8D

Thrws R Age 24
2017 (1) Florida

Velo	Pitch	Grade
90-94	FB	+++
81-84	SL	+++
	CU	++

Year	Lev	Team	W	L	Sv	IP	K	ERA	WHIP	BF/G	OBA	H%	S%	xERA	Ctl	Dom	Cmd	hr/9	BPV
2017	NCAA	Florida	9	2	1	123	157	2.26	1.11	24.2	215	32	80	2.24	3.1	11.5	3.7	0.3	142
2018	AA	Erie	3	6	0	60	59	4.95	1.27	20.4	242	26	70	4.84	3.3	8.9	2.7	2.3	88
2018	A+	Lakeland	2	4	0	61	51	3.10	1.02	19.5	222	28	69	2.26	1.9	7.5	3.9	0.4	102
2019	AA	Erie	6	7	0	115	134	3.91	1.12	20.6	243	31	71	3.60	2.0	10.5	5.4	1.3	154

Dominant SEC hurler out of Florida. Collegiate profile cooled during debut, specifically his slider, which stood out in college but backed up in the pros. After unpredictable 2018 campaign, fastball added 2-3 mph in 2019 with slight tightening to arsenal. Noticeable improvements in 2019 season, but still lacks advertised bite.

Fairbanks,Peter

RP | Tampa Bay | EXP MLB DEBUT: 2019 | H/W: 6-6 219 | FUT: Setup reliever | 7C

Thrws R Age 26
2015 (9) Missouri

Velo	Pitch	Grade
95-98	FB	++++
88-91	SL	++++

Year	Lev	Team	W	L	Sv	IP	K	ERA	WHIP	BF/G	OBA	H%	S%	xERA	Ctl	Dom	Cmd	hr/9	BPV
2019	AA	Frisco	1	0	0	7	14	0.00	0.28	3.7	91	25	100		0.0	17.7		0.0	337
2019	AAA	Nashville	0	0	0	6	11	11.80	1.97	4.2	368	59	36	7.76	3.0	16.2	5.5	1.5	230
2019	AAA	Durham	1	2	0	17	30	5.23	1.22	4.3	236	39	61	3.94	3.1	15.7	5.0	1.6	216
2019	MLB	Texas	0	2	0	8	15	9.88	1.83	4.8	257	33	55	8.39	7.7	16.5	2.1	4.4	107
2019	MLB	Tampa Bay	2	1	2	12	13	5.21	1.65	4.2	333	43	68	5.73	2.2	9.7	4.3	0.7	132

Tall, long RHP made MLB debut after struggling to stay healthy since 2017. Started season in High-A and made stops everywhere in between. Two-pitch pitcher. Uses size in uneven delivery well to make up for lacking movement with his four-seam FB. Hard SL is his true out pitch with a 43% whiff rate. Control is a struggle.

Feigl,Brady

SP | Oakland | EXP MLB DEBUT: 2020 | H/W: 6-4 235 | FUT: Middle reliever | 7B

Thrws R Age 24
2018 (5) Mississippi

Velo	Pitch	Grade
91-93	FB	+++
79-83	SL	+++
	CU	++

Year	Lev	Team	W	L	Sv	IP	K	ERA	WHIP	BF/G	OBA	H%	S%	xERA	Ctl	Dom	Cmd	hr/9	BPV
2018	NCAA	Mississippi	8	5	0	91	93	4.05	1.28	23.4	261	34	70	3.76	2.6	9.2	3.6	0.8	114
2018	A	Beloit	0	1	0	6	7	3.00	1.00	7.6	228	29	80	3.27	1.5	10.5	7.0	1.5	167
2018	A-	Vermont	1	1	0	20	27	1.35	0.65	8.7	96	17	77		3.2	12.2	3.9	0.0	152
2019	A+	Stockton	5	11	0	134	119	4.43	1.36	20.8	281	34	68	4.28	2.3	8.0	3.4	0.8	98

Strong, durable RH with a sinker/slider combo that could work well in middle relief. Garnered one of the heaviest GB% leans in pro ball via a low-90s FB with heavy action. SL can show above-average depth but can get slurvy at times; CU a show-me offering. Lives around the zone. Upside of #5 SP with third pitch, but could ramp it up from the 'pen.

Feliz,Ignacio

SP | San Diego | EXP MLB DEBUT: 2023 | H/W: 6-1 180 | FUT: #4 starter | 7D

Thrws R Age 20
2016 FA (DR)

Velo	Pitch	Grade
88-92	FB	++
85-87	CT	+++
	CB	+++
	CU	++

Year	Lev	Team	W	L	Sv	IP	K	ERA	WHIP	BF/G	OBA	H%	S%	xERA	Ctl	Dom	Cmd	hr/9	BPV
2018	Rk	AZL Indians 2	4	2	0	34	36	2.12	0.97	18.4	193	28	76	1.38	2.6	9.5	3.6	0.0	118
2018	Rk	AZL Indians	5	3	0	45	54	3.00	1.07	17.5	211	32	69	1.82	2.8	10.8	3.9	0.0	137
2019	A-	Tri-City	2	4	0	57	55	4.41	1.47	18.8	261	32	73	4.54	4.3	8.7	2.0	1.1	59

Young, athletic RH with some feel for spin and physical projection remaining on lean frame. Works 88-91 mph with fringe FB now, but will have chance to add a few ticks as he matures. Shows good CB with hammer action and some depth. Likes to use CT; CU remains raw. Low mileage arm who will need time, but has attractive qualities.

Feltman,Durbin

RP | Boston | EXP MLB DEBUT: 2020 | H/W: 6-0 205 | FUT: Setup reliever | 7C

Thrws R Age 22
2018 (3) Texas Christian

Velo	Pitch	Grade
94-98	FB	++++
83-87	SL	+++
87-89	CU	+

Year	Lev	Team	W	L	Sv	IP	K	ERA	WHIP	BF/G	OBA	H%	S%	xERA	Ctl	Dom	Cmd	hr/9	BPV
2018	NCAA	Texas Christian	0	1	6	24	43	0.75	0.75	4.8	150	32	89	0.27	2.2	16.1	7.2	0.0	247
2018	A-	Lowell	0	0	0	4	7	0.00	0.00	2.8	0	0			0.0	15.8		0.0	302
2018	A	Greenville	0	1	3	7	14	2.57	1.00	3.8	233	51	71	1.85	1.3	18.0	14.0	0.0	307
2018	A+	Salem	1	0	1	12	15	2.23	1.32	4.6	260	39	81	3.08	3.0	11.2	3.8	0.0	138
2019	AA	Portland	2	3	5	51	54	5.28	1.43	5.0	226	27	66	4.24	5.5	9.5	1.7	1.4	42

Durable RP who is coming on strong and has better stuff than numbers indicate. Spent all year in AA, his first full season as pro. Can be very stingy against RHH (.198 oppBA) with potent FB/SL combo. Owns max-effort delivery that adds some deception. FB features solid late movement, but can overthrow at times. Can hang SL for flyballs.

Feltner,Ryan

SP | Colorado | EXP MLB DEBUT: 2021 | H/W: 6-4 190 | FUT: #4 starter | 7C

Thrws R Age 23
2018 (4) Ohio State

Velo	Pitch	Grade
92-95	FB	+++
76-78	CB	++
82-85	CU	+++

Year	Lev	Team	W	L	Sv	IP	K	ERA	WHIP	BF/G	OBA	H%	S%	xERA	Ctl	Dom	Cmd	hr/9	BPV
2018	NCAA	Ohio State	5	5	0	91	86	4.54	1.57	23.5	278	35	71	4.54	4.3	8.5	2.0	0.6	54
2018	Rk	Grand Junction	0	0	0	30	39	0.89	0.66	11.7	158	25	89	0.47	1.2	11.6	9.8	0.3	195
2019	A	Asheville	9	9	0	119	116	5.07	1.54	20.7	290	36	68	4.93	3.5	8.8	2.5	0.9	82

Athletic RHP who led SAL in ground-ball rate and has ideal starter's frame. Best pitch is plus FB that can touch 97 mph and live in the mid-90s; at times overpowers hitters in the zone. Working on feel for slurvy breaking ball, but repeats arm speed well on promising CU. Will need to dial in command a bit more, but has #4/5 SP potential.

Fernandez,Junior

RP | St. Louis | EXP MLB DEBUT: 2019 | H/W: 6-1 180 | FUT: Closer | 8D

Thrws R Age 23
2014 FA (DR)

Velo	Pitch	Grade
96-98	FB	++++
85-88	SL	++
78-81	CU	+++

Year	Lev	Team	W	L	Sv	IP	K	ERA	WHIP	BF/G	OBA	H%	S%	xERA	Ctl	Dom	Cmd	hr/9	BPV
2018	AA	Springfield	0	0	0	21	17	5.14	1.67	5.9	243	30	68	4.16	6.9	7.3	1.1	0.4	-36
2019	A+	Palm Beach	0	0	4	11	11	1.61	1.43	5.3	202	28	88	2.64	6.4	8.8	1.4	0.0	4
2019	AA	Springfield	1	1	5	29	42	1.55	1.00	6.2	180	31	83	1.27	3.4	13.0	3.8	0.0	160
2019	AAA	Memphis	2	1	2	24	27	1.49	1.16	5.3	200	29	86	1.93	4.1	10.1	2.5	0.0	89
2019	MLB	St. Louis	0	1	0	11	16	5.63	1.34	3.6	222	31	62	4.12	4.8	12.9	2.7	1.6	119

Hard-thrower had a bounceback season after struggling with injuries and control. Plus FB sits and 95-98, topping at 99 with arm-side run. Power SL remains fringe-average with inconsistent shape and depth, but above-average CU plays up due to velocity of FB. Above-average Dom and below-average Cmd hint at both the upside, and the work to do.

File,Dylan

SP | Milwaukee | EXP MLB DEBUT: 2021 | H/W: 6-1 205 | FUT: #4 starter | 7B

Thrws R Age 23
2017 (21) Dixie State

Velo	Pitch	Grade
91-93	FB	+++
77-79	SL	+++
82-84	CU	+++

Year	Lev	Team	W	L	Sv	IP	K	ERA	WHIP	BF/G	OBA	H%	S%	xERA	Ctl	Dom	Cmd	hr/9	BPV
2018	A	Wisconsin	8	10	0	136	114	3.97	1.32	22.6	284	34	73	4.39	1.9	7.5	4.1	1.0	104
2019	AA	Biloxi	9	2	0	80	73	2.81	1.11	22.5	247	31	76	2.92	1.7	8.2	4.9	0.6	120
2019	A+	Carolina	6	4	0	66	63	3.81	1.18	22.0	276	35	68	3.48	1.0	8.6	9.0	0.5	147

Former small-school, late-round draft pick who had full breakout in A+/AA. Posted elite Cmd by way of solid-average three-pitch mix led by a low-90s fastball, average SL and CU. Works ahead in counts often and displays above-average command and execution of pitches. Limited upside sans putaway offering, but will have quality ratios and high floor.

Fitterer,Evan

SP | Miami | EXP MLB DEBUT: 2024 | H/W: 6-3 195 | FUT: #4 starter | 7E

Thrws R Age 19
2019 (5) HS (CA)

Velo	Pitch	Grade
90-93	FB	+++
80-83	CB	++++
	CU	++

Year	Lev	Team	W	L	Sv	IP	K	ERA	WHIP	BF/G	OBA	H%	S%	xERA	Ctl	Dom	Cmd	hr/9	BPV
2019	Rk	GCL Marlins	0	1	0	22	19	2.43	1.44	10.5	242	30	84	3.56	4.9	7.7	1.6	0.4	25

Tall, projectable RHP made 2019 pro debut with room to grow into frame. High 3/4s delivery with solid extension. Three-pitch pitcher. Two-seam FB sits low 90s with solid, late arm-side run. Plays up due to natural downward plane. Flashes plus CB with solid shape and biting action. Has feel for CU.

Fletcher,Aaron — RP — Seattle

EXP MLB DEBUT: 2020 | H/W: 6-0 220 | FUT: Middle reliever | 6C

Thrws L Age 24 — 2018 (14) Houston

- 91-93 FB +++
- 84-86 SL ++++
- CU +

Year	Lev	Team	W	L	Sv	IP	K	ERA	WHIP	BF/G	OBA	H%	S%	xERA	Ctl	Dom	Cmd	hr/9	BPV
2018	A-	Auburn	2	1	0	29	32	2.48	1.14	9.6	268	38	76	2.74	0.9	9.9	10.7	0.0	172
2019	A	Hagerstown	2	3	1	28	28	1.61	0.68	6.5	151	22	74	0.18	1.6	9.0	5.6	0.0	137
2019	A+	Potomac	3	1	0	26	32	1.38	0.88	8.0	170	25	86	1.21	2.8	11.1	4.0	0.3	143
2019	AA	Harrisburg	0	0	0	6	9	4.43	1.48	5.2	289	46	67	3.86	3.0	13.3	4.5	0.0	177
2019	AA	Arkansas	0	0	0	13	15	3.46	1.31	6.0	276	39	71	3.28	2.1	10.4	5.0	0.0	149

Left-handed RP has moved quickly since 2018 draft. Traded mid-season from WAS. Funky 3/4s delivery. FB sits low 90s with solid arm-side run. SL has varying break. Best when a sweeping SL over tighter variation. Potential LOOGY specialist in traditional terms; will find it difficult without pitch to get righties out.

Florez,Santiago — SP — Pittsburgh

EXP MLB DEBUT: 2023 | H/W: 6-5 222 | FUT: #3 starter | 8E

Thrws R Age 19 — 2016 FA (CB)

- 92-95 FB ++++
- 82-84 CB +++
- 84-85 CU +

Year	Lev	Team	W	L	Sv	IP	K	ERA	WHIP	BF/G	OBA	H%	S%	xERA	Ctl	Dom	Cmd	hr/9	BPV
2018	Rk	GCL Pirates	5	2	0	43	35	4.18	1.39	18.2	233	30	67	2.94	4.8	7.3	1.5	0.0	20
2019	Rk	Bristol	2	2	0	41	36	3.50	1.36	17.2	232	28	77	3.65	4.6	7.9	1.7	0.9	36

Large-framed SP with a big fastball to match. More thrower than pitcher as erratic control leaves him pitching behind in counts often. FB should add more velocity as he matures. Good CB with plenty of power and break serves as go-to pitch when ahead. CU will take time to develop, but hope is that it would give him third above average offering.

Flowers,J.C. — SP — Pittsburgh

EXP MLB DEBUT: 2022 | H/W: 6-3 190 | FUT: #4 starter | 7D

Thrws R Age 21 — 2019 (4) Florida St

- 89-93 FB +++
- 85-87 SL ++
- 84-87 CU ++

Year	Lev	Team	W	L	Sv	IP	K	ERA	WHIP	BF/G	OBA	H%	S%	xERA	Ctl	Dom	Cmd	hr/9	BPV
2019	A-	West Virginia	0	2	0	29	24	4.33	1.51	14.0	287	33	77	5.43	3.4	7.4	2.2	1.5	60

Athletic college closer converting to SP. Throws hard and has potential to add more power and shape to SL. Whether he remains SP prospect may depend on development of CU. Seems to have feel for changing speeds, but can slow arm speed. Doesn't miss many bats yet, but could come as he gets stretched out and sequences with more proficiency.

Franklin,Austin — SP — Tampa Bay

EXP MLB DEBUT: 2022 | H/W: 6-3 215 | FUT: Middle reliever | 6C

Thrws R Age 22 — 2016 (3) HS (FL)

- 91-93 FB +++
- 75-78 CB +++
- CU ++

Year	Lev	Team	W	L	Sv	IP	K	ERA	WHIP	BF/G	OBA	H%	S%	xERA	Ctl	Dom	Cmd	hr/9	BPV
2016	Rk	GCL Rays	1	2	1	43	40	2.71	1.07	15.2	198	27	72	1.68	3.3	8.4	2.5	0.0	78
2017	A-	Hudson Valley	4	2	0	69	71	2.21	1.19	21.3	207	28	83	2.58	4.0	9.2	2.3	0.5	75
2018	A	Bowling Green	6	5	0	82	65	3.62	1.32	21.2	250	30	74	3.59	3.4	7.1	2.1	0.7	55
2019		Did not pitch - injury																	

Physically mature RHP missed all of '19 recovering from Tommy John surgery. High 3/4s online delivery with solid extension. Two-seam FB plays up due to delivery, natural sink but has overall flat profile. Struggles getting on top of 12-to-6 CB, which could be an above-average offering at projection. Profiles as RP long term.

Franklin,Kohl — SP — Chicago (N)

EXP MLB DEBUT: 2023 | H/W: 6-4 190 | FUT: #4 starter | 7C

Thrws R Age 20 — 2018 (6) HS (OK)

- 90-94 FB +++
- CB ++
- CU +++

Year	Lev	Team	W	L	Sv	IP	K	ERA	WHIP	BF/G	OBA	H%	S%	xERA	Ctl	Dom	Cmd	hr/9	BPV
2018	Rk	AZL Cubs 2	0	1	0	8	8	6.59	1.34	6.8	178	25	45	2.14	6.6	8.8	1.3	0.0	-2
2019	A	South Bend	0	0	0	3	3	3.00	1.67	13.5	0	0	80	1.34	15.0	9.0	0.6	0.0	-225
2019	A-	Eugene	1	3	0	39	49	2.31	1.15	15.5	220	32	81	2.57	3.2	11.3	3.5	0.5	134

Big, projectable RH whose velocity has ticked up since signing for over-slot value in 2018's sixth round. Can touch 97 mph from high three-quarters arm slot, but sits more comfortably in low 90s now. Shows aptitude for fading CU, but feel for breaking ball will require reps. Stock could rise with strong start 2020 in full-season ball.

Frias,Luis — SP — Arizona

EXP MLB DEBUT: 2022 | H/W: 6-3 180 | FUT: #4 starter | 8D

Thrws R Age 21 — 2015 FA (DR)

- 93-96 FB ++++
- 77-81 CB +++
- 86-87 SL ++
- 85-86 SP +++

Year	Lev	Team	W	L	Sv	IP	K	ERA	WHIP	BF/G	OBA	H%	S%	xERA	Ctl	Dom	Cmd	hr/9	BPV
2018	A-	Hillsboro	0	4	0	25	27	3.21	1.43	15.3	228	32	75	2.95	5.4	9.6	1.8	0.0	47
2018	Rk	AZL DBacks	1	1	0	29	31	2.48	0.97	15.7	172	24	74	1.42	3.4	9.6	2.8	0.3	99
2019	A	Kane County	3	1	0	26	29	4.47	1.30	18.0	229	32	64	2.95	4.1	10.0	2.4	0.3	86
2019	A-	Hillsboro	3	3	0	49	72	2.01	1.08	19.2	206	35	79	1.76	3.1	13.2	4.2	0.0	171

Physical, strong-armed RHP who has explosive arm speed but lacks polish on secondary offerings. Appears bigger than listed height/weight. Plus FB will touch 99 mph and sit mid-90s and overpower hitters at times. CB flashes plus with depth and SP will show hard, diving action but lacks consistency. Routinely misses barrels; still working on control.

Funkhouser,Kyle — SP — Detroit

EXP MLB DEBUT: 2020 | H/W: 6-2 230 | FUT: #4 starter | 8E

Thrws R Age 26 — 2016 (4) Louisville

- 91-96 FB +++
- 82-85 SL ++++
- 78-82 CB ++
- 82-84 CU ++

Year	Lev	Team	W	L	Sv	IP	K	ERA	WHIP	BF/G	OBA	H%	S%	xERA	Ctl	Dom	Cmd	hr/9	BPV
2018	AA	Erie	4	5	0	89	89	3.74	1.43	22.2	260	33	77	4.31	3.9	9.0	2.3	1.0	74
2018	AAA	Toledo	0	2	0	8	7	6.59	2.20	20.6	257	33	67	5.28	11.0	7.7	0.7	0.0	-140
2019	A+	Lakeland	0	0	0	5	4	0.00	0.60	17.1	124	17	100		1.8	7.2	4.0	0.0	99
2019	AA	Erie	3	1	0	23	29	1.94	0.82	21.1	197	28	82	1.74	1.2	11.3	9.7	0.8	189
2019	AAA	Toledo	3	7	0	63	65	8.56	2.11	17.3	307	40	56	6.18	7.7	9.3	1.2	0.4	-23

Imposing, solidly-built starter. Plus fastball boasts late life low in the zone, and he mixes in an above-average hard slider and a curve with good shape. Change-up lacks confidence, but should end up as above-average offering. Has battled consistent injury issues every year since 2017.

Gaddis,Hunter — SP — Cleveland

EXP MLB DEBUT: 2023 | H/W: 6-6 212 | FUT: #4 starter | 7D

Thrws R Age 21 — 2019 (5) Georgia St

- 92-93 FB +++
- 85-87 SL ++++
- 76-78 CB ++
- 82-83 CU +++

Year	Lev	Team	W	L	Sv	IP	K	ERA	WHIP	BF/G	OBA	H%	S%	xERA	Ctl	Dom	Cmd	hr/9	BPV
2019	NCAA	Georgia St	1	7	0	91	112	4.85	1.21	24.4	258	35	62	3.78	2.1	11.1	5.3	1.1	161
2019	A-	MahoningVal	0	1	0	15	27	2.37	0.99	9.6	204	41	73	1.48	2.4	16.0	6.8	0.0	242
2019	Rk	AZL Indians 2	1	2	0	17	26	3.16	0.94	9.2	212	33	71	2.46	1.6	13.7	8.7	1.1	222

Tall, lanky RHP uses size well in 3/4s delivery. Athleticism in profile, which allows him to throw strikes. Adapted well in pro debut. Sits 92-93, touches 96 with FB in spurts. SL is true plus pitch. CU up has solid movement profile and could be above-average offering. CB changes eye levels. Role question marks. May be best suited for RP role.

Gallardo,Richard — SP — Chicago (N)

EXP MLB DEBUT: 2023 | H/W: 6-1 187 | FUT: #4 starter | 8D

Thrws R Age 18 — 2018 FA (VZ)

- 89-93 FB +++
- CB +++
- CU +++

Year	Lev	Team	W	L	Sv	IP	K	ERA	WHIP	BF/G	OBA	H%	S%	xERA	Ctl	Dom	Cmd	hr/9	BPV
2019	A-	Eugene	0	0	0	4	2	2.25	1.00	7.6	151	18	75	1.03	4.5	4.5	1.0	0.0	-23
2019	Rk	AZL Cubs	0	2	0	30	23	4.19	1.46	11.7	274	33	70	3.95	3.6	6.9	1.9	0.3	45

Lean, athletic RH with advanced feel for three-pitch mix and a chance to add velocity with more muscle. Sits 90-92 mph with four-seam FB that is effective above the letters. Shows good feel for CB spin, flashing plus 12-to-6 action at times; still working on CU. Has short, clean arm action and repeatable delivery that requires moderate effort.

Garcia,Bryan — RP — Detroit

EXP MLB DEBUT: 2019 | H/W: 6-1 203 | FUT: Middle reliever | 7B

Thrws R Age 24 — 2016 (6) Miami

- 94-96 FB +++
- 84-88 SL +++
- CU ++

Year	Lev	Team	W	L	Sv	IP	K	ERA	WHIP	BF/G	OBA	H%	S%	xERA	Ctl	Dom	Cmd	hr/9	BPV
2017	AAA	Toledo	1	0	0	13	12	4.12	1.37	3.9	213	27	71	3.28	5.5	8.2	1.5	0.7	18
2019	A+	Lakeland	0	0	1	4	6	4.50	1.25	4.1	210	27	75	4.35	4.5	13.5	3.0	2.3	140
2019	AA	Erie	0	0	1	4	8	2.25	0.25	4.1	81	0		0.46	0.0	18.0		2.3	342
2019	AAA	Toledo	3	0	0	33	33	2.99	1.21	4.3	218	27	81	3.29	3.8	9.0	2.4	1.1	77
2019	MLB	Detroit	0	0	0	6	7	13.06	2.26	4.5	340	43	38	8.04	7.3	10.2	1.4	1.5	5

A fast-tracking reliever who made a successful return from Tommy John surgery in 2018. Aggressive attack-style work that challenges hitters on both sides of the plate. Strong ability to throw strikes with a mix of power slider and a late-sinking fastball. Finished regular season with major league debut in 2019.

Garcia,Deivi — SP — New York (A)

EXP MLB DEBUT: 2020 | H/W: 5-9 163 | FUT: #3 starter | 8C

Thrws R Age 20 — 2015 FA (DR)

- 92-95 FB ++++
- 78-81 CB +++
- 84-87 SL ++++
- 85-87 CU ++

Year	Lev	Team	W	L	Sv	IP	K	ERA	WHIP	BF/G	OBA	H%	S%	xERA	Ctl	Dom	Cmd	hr/9	BPV
2018	A+	Tampa	2	0	0	28	35	1.28	0.96	21.2	193	30	85	1.33	2.6	11.2	4.4	0.0	151
2018	AA	Trenton	1	0	0	5	7	0.00	0.40	16.1	0	0	100		3.6	12.6	3.5	0.0	148
2019	A+	Tampa	0	2	0	17	33	3.14	1.28	17.6	224	47	73	2.44	4.2	17.3	4.1	0.0	216
2019	AA	Trenton	4	4	0	53	87	3.89	1.30	19.9	223	39	69	2.82	4.4	14.7	3.3	0.3	164
2019	AAA	Scranton/WB	1	3	0	40	45	5.40	1.48	15.6	257	31	69	5.13	4.5	10.1	2.3	1.8	79

Short-statured, athletic RHP on verge of MLB debut. High 3/4s delivery with a little cross-fire action. 4-seam FB has late riding action; has been up to 98 MPH. Relies more on SL, a plus pitch with violent break. CB still high spin-rate pitch but break is more predictable than SL. CU still firm and will need refinement to reach ceiling.

Garcia,Luis | SP | Houston

EXP MLB DEBUT: 2021 | H/W: 6-1 216 | FUT: #4 starter | 7C

Thrws R Age 23
2017 FA (VZ)

Velo	Pitch	Grade
90-95	FB	++++
78-79	CB	++
83-85	SL	++
	CU	+++

Year	Lev	Team	W	L	Sv	IP	K	ERA	WHIP	BF/G	OBA	H%	S%	xERA	Ctl	Dom	Cmd	hr/9	BPV
2018	A	Quad Cities	7	2	0	69	70	2.48	1.32	15.0	230	30	83	3.18	4.3	9.1	2.1	0.5	66
2018	A-	Tri City	0	0	0	16	28	0.00	0.93	12.1	134	29	100	0.58	4.5	15.7	3.5	0.0	179
2019	A+	Fayetteville	6	4	0	65	108	3.04	1.18	17.4	190	33	76	2.46	4.7	14.9	3.2	0.7	160
2019	A	Quad Cities	4	0	1	43	60	2.93	0.91	17.8	159	24	71	1.60	3.3	12.6	3.8	0.8	154

Short, stocky SP who posted very high K rate on two levels. A stat lover's sensation. Suceeds against LHH with tumbling CU that has dramatically improved. FB remains best pitch with late action. Short arm action isn't pretty but adds deception to rudimentary delivery. Velocity has increased, but will need to add stamina to pitch deep into games.

Garcia,Rico | SP | San Francisco

EXP MLB DEBUT: 2019 | H/W: 5-11 190 | FUT: #5 SP/swingman | 7C

Thrws R Age 26
2016 (30) Hawaii Pacific

Velo	Pitch	Grade
92-94	FB	+++
72-75	CB	+++
81-84	CU	+++

Year	Lev	Team	W	L	Sv	IP	K	ERA	WHIP	BF/G	OBA	H%	S%	xERA	Ctl	Dom	Cmd	hr/9	BPV
2018	A+	Lancaster	7	7	0	100	101	3.42	1.21	25.2	260	32	76	3.83	2.0	9.1	4.6	1.1	128
2018	AA	Hartford	6	2	0	67	61	2.28	1.10	23.9	222	26	86	3.08	2.7	8.2	3.1	1.1	93
2019	AA	Hartford	8	2	0	68	87	1.85	0.94	19.7	176	26	83	1.59	3.0	11.5	3.8	0.5	143
2019	AAA	Albuquerque	2	4	0	61	51	6.92	1.72	21.3	309	34	64	6.77	4.1	7.5	1.8	2.1	42
2019	MLB	Colorado	0	1	0	6	2	10.50	2.33	15.5	347	29	64	11.29	7.5	3.0	0.4	4.5	-131

Slightly undersized RH who had breakout in AA en route to big league debut. Comes at hitters with solid-average three-pitch mix including low-90s FB, 12-to-6 curveball and CU with average fade and drop. Shows proclivity to throw strikes at above-avg rate, solid-avg SwK ability and mix in some ground balls as a durable #4/5 type SP.

Garcia,Ryan | SP | Texas

EXP MLB DEBUT: 2022 | H/W: 6-0 180 | FUT: #4 starter | 7C

Thrws R Age 22
2019 (2) UCLA

Velo	Pitch	Grade
90-93	FB	+++
83-86	SL	++
74-76	CB	++
82-83	CU	+++

Year	Lev	Team	W	L	Sv	IP	K	ERA	WHIP	BF/G	OBA	H%	S%	xERA	Ctl	Dom	Cmd	hr/9	BPV
2019	A-	Spokane	0	0	0	4	6	2.25	0.75	7.1	151	27	67	0.31	2.3	13.5	6.0	0.0	200
2019	Rk	AZL Rangers	0	0	0	1	2	9.00	2.00	4.8	262	55	50	4.75	9.0	18.0	2.0	0.0	99

Pitcher of the Year in the Pac-12 in 2019, he has a broad and commandable four-pitch mix. No pitch currently plus, though his over-the-top release point provides good sink on low-90s FB and aids in deception of low-80s CU. Also has CB/SL, both both breakers lag behind. Clean delivery from smaller frame; little projection left.

Garrett,Braxton | SP | Miami

EXP MLB DEBUT: 2021 | H/W: 6-3 190 | FUT: #4 starter | 8D

Thrws L Age 22
2016 (1) HS (AL)

Velo	Pitch	Grade
91-93	FB	+++
78-81	CB	++++
85-87	CU	++

Year	Lev	Team	W	L	Sv	IP	K	ERA	WHIP	BF/G	OBA	H%	S%	xERA	Ctl	Dom	Cmd	hr/9	BPV
2017	A	Greensboro	1	0	0	15	16	2.98	1.26	15.4	234	27	88	4.27	3.6	9.5	2.7	1.8	93
2018		Did not pitch - injury																	
2019	A+	Jupiter	6	6	0	105	118	3.34	1.23	21.3	237	31	78	3.60	3.2	10.1	3.2	1.1	114
2019	AA	Jacksonville	0	1	0	1	1	22.50	5.83	10.4	542	63	57	20.71	22.5	7.5	0.3	0.0	-455

Returned after missing almost 2 seasons recovering from Tommy John surgery and posted surprising results. 3/4s LHP with online delivery, he has two MLB-quality offerings. FB hasn't regained velo yet but mixes between 2-seam FB with arm-side run and cut FB. 12-to-6 CB is still best pitch with plus depth and solid break. Has feel for CU.

Gaston,Sandy | SP | Tampa Bay

EXP MLB DEBUT: 2024 | H/W: 6-3 200 | FUT: #3 starter | 8E

Thrws R Age 18
2018 FA (CU)

Velo	Pitch	Grade
90-93	FB	+++
78-80	CB	++++
83-84	CU	++

Year	Lev	Team	W	L	Sv	IP	K	ERA	WHIP	BF/G	OBA	H%	S%	xERA	Ctl	Dom	Cmd	hr/9	BPV
2019	Rk	GCL Rays	1	2	0	27	31	6.00	1.85	11.5	232	33	65	4.37	9.0	10.3	1.1	0.3	-39

Arm-speed, athletic RHP struggled during professional debut. Delivery is a wreck, flies open and lands all over the place. High 3/4s arm slot with plus, whippy arm speed. Delivery creates natural downward plane for FB, which will be mid-90s as frame fills out. Best secondary is 11-to-6 CB; it's tight and shows good depth. CU is work-in-progress.

Gerber,Joey | RP | Seattle

EXP MLB DEBUT: 2020 | H/W: 6-4 215 | FUT: Setup reliever | 7D

Thrws R Age 22
2018 (8) Illinois

Velo	Pitch	Grade
94-97	FB	++++
87-88	SL	++++

Year	Lev	Team	W	L	Sv	IP	K	ERA	WHIP	BF/G	OBA	H%	S%	xERA	Ctl	Dom	Cmd	hr/9	BPV
2018	NCAA	Illinois	1	1	14	28	45	3.19	1.13	4.5	185	33	71	1.94	4.5	14.4	3.2	0.3	156
2018	A-	Everett	1	0	6	14	21	1.93	1.07	4.2	186	33	80	1.50	3.9	13.5	3.5	0.0	157
2018	A	Clinton	0	0	2	11	22	2.41	1.25	5.1	222	48	79	2.34	4.0	17.7	4.4	0.0	228
2019	A+	Modesto	0	2	8	26	39	3.46	1.12	4.1	188	33	66	1.64	4.2	13.5	3.3	0.0	149
2019	AA	Arkansas	1	2	0	22	30	1.62	1.26	4.8	251	37	92	3.56	2.8	12.2	4.3	0.8	160

Hard-throwing, max-effort RHP has become spin rate darling with double-plus FB. Deceptive delivery. Struggles staying aligned but doesn't give hitters good view of pitch until late. FB sits high 90s with late running action. Complements FB well with two-plane breaking SL, a plus pitch. Control may be issue keeping away from ceiling.

German,Frank | SP | New York (A)

EXP MLB DEBUT: 2021 | H/W: 6-2 195 | FUT: #4 starter | 8D

Thrws R Age 22
2018 (4) North Florida

Velo	Pitch	Grade
93-95	FB	++++
82-84	SL	+++
87-88	CU	+++

Year	Lev	Team	W	L	Sv	IP	K	ERA	WHIP	BF/G	OBA	H%	S%	xERA	Ctl	Dom	Cmd	hr/9	BPV
2018	Rk	GCL YankeesW	0	0	0	2	3	0.00	0.00	5.6	0	0			0.0	13.5		0.0	261
2018	A-	Staten Island	1	3	1	28	38	2.24	1.00	10.7	217	35	75	1.70	1.9	12.2	6.3	0.0	185
2019	Rk	GCL YankeesW	0	0	0	1	0	18.00	4.00	6.8	415	41	50	12.62	18.0	0.0	0.0	0.0	-468
2019	Rk	GCL Yankees	0	1	0	4	5	6.75	1.00	7.6	210	24	33	3.74	2.3	11.3	5.0	2.3	160
2019	A+	Tampa	4	4	0	76	82	3.79	1.38	20.0	246	32	76	4.06	4.1	9.7	2.3	1.1	81

Hard-throwing RHP skipped Single-A, pitching well with High-A Tampa. Struggled with health, giving durability concerns more credence. 3/4s, cross-armed delivery with effort. Sits mid-90s with late moving FB. SL is best secondary with solid two-plane break. CU is a workable third pitch with solid fading action.

Gil,Luis | SP | New York (A)

EXP MLB DEBUT: 2022 | H/W: 6-3 176 | FUT: #3 starter | 8D

Thrws R Age 21
2015 FA (DR)

Velo	Pitch	Grade
93-97	FB	++++
81-83	CB	+++
90-92	CU	++

Year	Lev	Team	W	L	Sv	IP	K	ERA	WHIP	BF/G	OBA	H%	S%	xERA	Ctl	Dom	Cmd	hr/9	BPV
2018	A-	Staten Island	0	2	0	6	10	5.81	2.74	17.2	386	57	81	10.07	8.7	14.5	1.7	1.5	44
2018	Rk	Pulaski	2	1	0	39	58	1.38	1.18	15.6	160	28	89	1.70	5.8	13.4	2.3	0.2	103
2019	A+	Tampa	1	0	0	13	11	4.85	1.46	18.6	231	30	63	3.08	5.5	7.6	1.4	0.0	6
2019	A	Charleston (Sc)	4	5	0	83	112	2.39	1.19	19.6	204	33	79	2.14	4.2	12.1	2.9	0.1	122

Lean RHP with easy velocity had breakout season in Single-A. High 3/4 delivery with some longish arm action from a slim body. Control over command long-term; shows three pitches. Best offering clearly 93-97 MPH FB with solid late run. Best secondary is CB, which looks like a sweepy SL at times. CU is firm and doesn't show much fading potential.

Gilbert,Logan | SP | Seattle

EXP MLB DEBUT: 2020 | H/W: 6-6 225 | FUT: #3 starter | 8C

Thrws R Age 22
2018 (1) Stetson

Velo	Pitch	Grade
92-95	FB	++++
75-78	CB	+++
81-84	SL	+++
84-87	CU	+++

Year	Lev	Team	W	L	Sv	IP	K	ERA	WHIP	BF/G	OBA	H%	S%	xERA	Ctl	Dom	Cmd	hr/9	BPV
2019	AA	Arkansas	4	2	0	50	56	2.88	0.98	21.1	194	27	70	1.74	2.7	10.1	3.7	0.4	127
2019	A+	Modesto	5	3	0	62	73	1.74	1.03	19.9	229	32	85	2.35	1.7	10.6	6.1	0.4	161
2019	A	West Virginia	1	0	0	22	36	1.62	0.68	15.5	126	21	85	0.63	2.4	14.6	6.0	0.8	215

Tall, projectable RHP coasted through three levels in first pro season after missing pro debut year due to mono. Showed no ill-effects. Athletic delivery with long arm-action and plus extension. Dominates hitters with mid 90s 4-seam FB with late riding action. Also, mixes 2-seam FB. All secondaries are average-to-above-average pitches at maturity.

Gilliam,Ryley | RP | New York (N)

EXP MLB DEBUT: 2020 | H/W: 5-10 170 | FUT: Setup reliever | 7D

Thrws R Age 23
2018 (5) Clemson

Velo	Pitch	Grade
92-95	FB	++++
77-79	CB	++++

Year	Lev	Team	W	L	Sv	IP	K	ERA	WHIP	BF/G	OBA	H%	S%	xERA	Ctl	Dom	Cmd	hr/9	BPV
2018	NCAA	Clemson	3	3	11	38	54	1.42	1.15	5.6	170	27	90	1.99	5.2	12.8	2.5	0.5	107
2018	A-	Brooklyn	0	1	5	17	31	2.11	1.40	4.2	186	37	87	2.81	6.8	16.3	2.4	0.5	127
2019	A+	St. Lucie	0	0	2	10	16	2.65	0.98	5.5	218	39	70	1.64	1.8	14.1	8.0	0.0	224
2019	AA	Binghamton	3	0	1	18	28	4.45	1.21	6.1	226	38	62	2.79	3.5	13.8	4.0	0.5	174
2019	AAA	Syracuse	2	0	0	9	12	13.85	3.08	5.4	425	54	56	13.20	8.9	11.9	1.3	3.0	-9

Short-statured, athletic hurler moved up to Triple-A in first full season. Max-effort, 3/4s delivery has been scaled back some to achieve better command of offerings. Low-to-mid-90s FB has late run and misses bats, especially when movement is controlled well. Power CB achieves a high spin rate with solid depth and late-breaking action.

Gingery,Steven | SP | St. Louis

EXP MLB DEBUT: 2021 | H/W: 6-1 210 | FUT: #5 SP/swingman | 7D

Thrws L Age 22
2018 (4) Texas Tech

Velo	Pitch	Grade
88-92	FB	++
78-81	CB	++
72-75	CU	++++

Year	Lev	Team	W	L	Sv	IP	K	ERA	WHIP	BF/G	OBA	H%	S%	xERA	Ctl	Dom	Cmd	hr/9	BPV
2019	Rk	GCL Cardinals	0	1	0	0	1	45.00	10.00	2.6	639	177	50	35.26	45.0	45.0	1.0	0.0	-387

Soft-tosser worked his way back from Tommy John surgery. Prior to the injury featured a plus CU with good fade/ sink. Fringe-average FB sits at 88-92 but has good late sink and is located well to both sides. CB gives him a solid 3rd offering. FB/CU combo from LH-side gives him the potential to pitch in the show, but the upside is as a back-end starter.

Gomez,Yoendrys — SP — New York (A)

EXP MLB DEBUT: 2023 | H/W: 6-3 175 | FUT: #4 starter | 7C

Thrws R Age 20
2016 FA (VZ)

Velo	Pitch	Grade
91-94	FB	+++
74-78	CB	+++
87-88	CT	++
84-86	CU	+++

Year	Lev	Team	W	L	Sv	IP	K	ERA	WHIP	BF/G	OBA	H%	S%	xERA	Ctl	Dom	Cmd	hr/9	BPV
2018	Rk	DSL Yankees	1	0	0	9	7	1.00	1.00	17.2	73	10	89	0.27	7.0	7.0	1.0	0.0	-45
2018	Rk	GCL Yankees	3	1	0	38	43	2.36	1.10	15.0	200	29	78	2.00	3.5	10.1	2.9	0.2	105
2019	A	Charleston (Sc)	0	3	0	26	25	6.18	1.41	18.5	275	35	54	4.19	3.1	8.6	2.8	0.7	89
2019	Rk	Pulaski	4	2	0	29	28	2.16	1.23	19.7	240	32	83	2.90	3.1	8.6	2.8	0.3	90

Projectable RHP made full-season debut in 2019. Tall & fall, high-3/4s delivery creates natural downward plane on 4-pitch mix. 91-94 MPH FB has sinking and late-cutting action. Also throws CT as a variation of FB. Has feel for spin with slurvy CB. Has moderate fade and good separation with CU.

Gonsalves,Stephen — SP — New York (N)

EXP MLB DEBUT: 2018 | H/W: 6-5 220 | FUT: #5 SP/swingman | 6B

Thrws L Age 25
2013 (4) HS (CA)

Velo	Pitch	Grade
87-91	FB	++
82-85	SL	++
70-74	CB	+++
79-82	CU	+++

Year	Lev	Team	W	L	Sv	IP	K	ERA	WHIP	BF/G	OBA	H%	S%	xERA	Ctl	Dom	Cmd	hr/9	BPV
2018	AAA	Rochester	9	3	0	100	95	2.97	1.20	21.2	187	24	76	2.40	4.9	8.5	1.7	0.5	38
2018	MLB	Minnesota	2	2	0	24	16	6.69	2.07	16.9	291	33	67	6.15	8.2	6.0	0.7	0.7	-96
2019	Rk	GCL Twins	0	1	0	9	16	2.00	0.67	6.3	191	30	100	2.40	0.0	16.0		2.0	306
2019	AA	Pensacola	0	0	0	2	3	13.50	2.00	4.8	262	27	33	9.02	9.0	13.5	1.5	4.5	18
2019	AAA	Rochester	0	1	0	2	2	4.50	3.00	11.6	151	22	83	6.03	22.5	9.0	0.4	0.0	-428

Pitchability LHP missed most of 2019 with elbow strain; was claimed on waivers from MIN in Nov. Once an HQ100 prospect, has lost stuff and velocity in upper minors. Upright motion with high 3/4s slot. Best offering is 12-to-6 CB with solid depth and late break. Struggled to command FB and CU in 2018 MLB debut.

Gonsolin,Tony — SP — Los Angeles (N)

EXP MLB DEBUT: 2019 | H/W: 6-3 205 | FUT: #4 starter | 8D

Thrws R Age 25
2016 (9) St. Mary's

Velo	Pitch	Grade
93-97	FB	++++
84-86	SP	++++
	CB	+++
	SL	++

Year	Lev	Team	W	L	Sv	IP	K	ERA	WHIP	BF/G	OBA	H%	S%	xERA	Ctl	Dom	Cmd	hr/9	BPV
2018	A+	Rancho Cuca	4	2	0	83	106	2.70	1.18	19.6	235	34	78	2.89	2.8	11.5	4.1	0.5	148
2018	AA	Tulsa	6	0	0	44	49	2.45	1.09	19.2	205	28	80	2.37	3.3	10.0	3.1	0.6	110
2019	AAA	Oklahoma City	2	4	0	41	50	4.38	1.51	13.7	261	36	72	4.39	4.6	10.9	2.4	0.9	91
2019	MLB	Los Angeles	4	2	1	40	37	2.93	1.03	14.0	187	22	76	2.30	3.4	8.3	2.5	0.9	77

Athletic hurler features a high leg kick and attacks hitters from a high 3/4 slot. FB continues to gain velocity and heater now sits at 93-96, topping at 99 in relief. Best offering is a plus splitter that has swing-and-miss action with a CB and SL to keep hitters honest. Hamstring injury limited him to 13 starts at AAA, but shined in MLB debut.

Gore,MacKenzie — SP — San Diego

EXP MLB DEBUT: 2020 | H/W: 6-3 195 | FUT: #1 starter | 9B

Thrws L Age 21
2017 (1) HS (NC)

Velo	Pitch	Grade
91-95	FB	+++
84-86	SL	+++
77-80	CB	+++
78-82	CU	++++

Year	Lev	Team	W	L	Sv	IP	K	ERA	WHIP	BF/G	OBA	H%	S%	xERA	Ctl	Dom	Cmd	hr/9	BPV
2017	Rk	AZL Padres	0	1	0	21	34	1.28	1.00	11.5	190	35	86	1.35	3.0	14.5	4.9	0.0	198
2018	A	Fort Wayne	2	5	0	60	74	4.49	1.31	15.5	264	37	66	3.82	2.7	11.1	4.1	0.7	144
2019	AA	Amarillo	2	1	0	21	25	4.25	1.32	17.6	251	33	72	4.15	3.4	10.6	3.1	1.3	117
2019	A+	Lake Elsinore	7	1	0	79	110	1.02	0.71	18.6	139	22	90	0.53	2.3	12.5	5.5	0.5	182

Athletic, polished LH who has moved quickly and profiles as top-of-the-rotation linchpin. Produces quality ratios with four plus pitches and advanced command and pitchability. FB sits 92-95 mph with angle to plate and snaps off hammer CB and fading CU when needed; also has quality SL. Quite possibly the best arm in the minors right now.

Goss,JJ — SP — Tampa Bay

EXP MLB DEBUT: 2023 | H/W: 6-3 185 | FUT: #4 starter | 8E

Thrws R Age 19
2019 (1) HS (TX)

Velo	Pitch	Grade
90-93	FB	+++
80-83	SL	++++
82-83	CU	+++

Year	Lev	Team	W	L	Sv	IP	K	ERA	WHIP	BF/G	OBA	H%	S%	xERA	Ctl	Dom	Cmd	hr/9	BPV
2019	Rk	GCL Rays	1	3	0	17	16	5.82	1.24	7.7	284	36	50	3.72	1.1	8.5	8.0	0.5	142

Tall, projectable RHP was 36th overall pick in 2019 draft. Repeatable, on-line 3/4s delivery. Advanced command, but hit around some during debut. FB has some late run to it and will pick up velocity as he matures into his frame. SL best offering with solid, tight break. CU flashes average with late fade, but athleticism will play it up.

Graterol,Brusdar — SP — Minnesota

EXP MLB DEBUT: 2019 | H/W: 6-1 265 | FUT: #2 starter | 9D

Thrws R Age 21
2014 FA (VZ)

Velo	Pitch	Grade
96-99	FB	++++
88-90	SL	++++
89-91	CU	+++

Year	Lev	Team	W	L	Sv	IP	K	ERA	WHIP	BF/G	OBA	H%	S%	xERA	Ctl	Dom	Cmd	hr/9	BPV
2018	A+	Fort Myers	5	2	0	60	56	3.14	1.30	22.5	258	34	73	3.01	2.8	8.4	2.9	0.0	92
2019	Rk	GCL Twins	0	0	0	3	4	0.00	0.33	4.7	106	18	100		0.0	12.0		0.0	234
2019	AA	Pensacola	6	0	1	52	50	1.72	1.02	16.7	179	24	84	1.65	3.6	8.6	2.4	0.3	75
2019	AAA	Rochester	1	0	0	5	7	5.29	1.18	5.1	218	29	60	3.81	3.5	12.4	3.5	1.8	145
2019	MLB	Minnesota	1	1	0	9	10	4.89	1.30	3.8	278	36	64	4.22	2.0	9.8	5.0	1.0	141

Physically-mature, electric 3/4s RHP made MLB debut after successful minors campaign. Athleticism missing from delivery, doesn't achieve extension. 2-seam FB sits high-90s with heavy arm-side bore. Will throw 4-seam FB to keep hitters honest. SL is second double-plus pitch with tight, 2-plane movement. CU mimics FB movement but didn't use in MIN.

Gray,Josiah — SP — Los Angeles (N)

EXP MLB DEBUT: 2022 | H/W: 6-1 190 | FUT: #3 starter | 9D

Thrws R Age 22
2018 (2) Le Moyne

Velo	Pitch	Grade
91-96	FB	++++
84-86	SL	+++
88-90	CU	++

Year	Lev	Team	W	L	Sv	IP	K	ERA	WHIP	BF/G	OBA	H%	S%	xERA	Ctl	Dom	Cmd	hr/9	BPV
2018	Rk	Greeneville	2	2	0	52	59	2.59	0.88	16.1	165	24	69	0.99	2.9	10.2	3.5	0.2	122
2019	AA	Tulsa	3	2	0	39	41	2.76	1.13	17.1	230	32	73	2.21	2.5	9.4	3.7	0.0	120
2019	A+	Rancho Cuca	7	0	0	67	80	2.15	0.97	21.2	216	31	79	2.00	1.7	10.7	6.2	0.4	164
2019	A	Great Lakes	1	0	0	23	26	1.95	0.87	17.0	166	25	75	0.80	2.7	10.1	3.7	0.0	127

Plus athlete who played SS in college features a lively 90-95 mph FB that tops at 96 with some arm-side run. Mid-80s SL shows plus action, but is inconsistent. CU is below-average and very much a work in progress. Does pound the zone, can miss bats, and get plenty of weak contact. Will need a 3rd offering to remain a starter.

Green,Josh — SP — Arizona

EXP MLB DEBUT: 2021 | H/W: 6-3 210 | FUT: #5 SP/swingman | 7B

Thrws R Age 24
2018 (14) SE Louisiana

Velo	Pitch	Grade
91-94	FB	+++
	SL	+++
	CB	++
84-86	CU	+++

Year	Lev	Team	W	L	Sv	IP	K	ERA	WHIP	BF/G	OBA	H%	S%	xERA	Ctl	Dom	Cmd	hr/9	BPV
2018	A-	Hillsboro	3	1	11	33	25	1.09	1.21	5.3	250	31	90	2.71	2.5	6.8	2.8	0.0	74
2018	NCAA	SE Louisiana	6	6	0	91	59	3.16	1.13	24.0	253	30	72	2.92	1.6	5.8	3.7	0.4	80
2019	AA	Jackson	2	4	0	48	32	4.30	1.43	25.6	310	36	69	4.50	1.5	6.0	4.0	0.4	85
2019	A+	Visalia	9	1	0	78	69	1.73	1.05	21.6	239	31	83	2.26	1.5	8.0	5.3	0.1	121

Former RP draftee transitioned to full-time SP in 2019 and performed well. Relies on sinking FB around 91-94 mph for ground balls and displays plus control down in zone. CB/SL/CU each showed improvement this spring. Delivery is deceptive with significant crossfire toward plate; tough on RHH. High-floor RHP with back-end SP potential.

Greene,Hunter — SP — Cincinnati

EXP MLB DEBUT: 2022 | H/W: 6-4 215 | FUT: #1 starter | 9D

Thrws R Age 20
2017 (1) HS (CA)

Velo	Pitch	Grade
97-100	FB	+++++
83-85	SL	++++
90-92	CU	++++

Year	Lev	Team	W	L	Sv	IP	K	ERA	WHIP	BF/G	OBA	H%	S%	xERA	Ctl	Dom	Cmd	hr/9	BPV
2017	Rk	Billings	0	1	0	4	6	13.17	2.20	6.9	409	59	33	7.81	2.2	13.2	6.0	0.0	196
2018	A	Dayton	3	7	0	68	89	4.49	1.31	15.6	256	37	66	3.72	3.0	11.8	3.9	0.8	148
2019	A	Did not pitch - injury																	

Athletic, hard-thrower lost all of 2019 in recovery from April Tommy John surgery. When healthy, velocity is generated easily in 3/4s delivery with plus-plus arm speed. High velocity FB is effective despite straightness. Plus extension in delivery, which causes FB to get on hitters even quicker. SL has tight movement and has plus feel for CU.

Groome,Jay — SP — Boston

EXP MLB DEBUT: 2022 | H/W: 6-6 200 | FUT: #2 starter | 9E

Thrws L Age 21
2016 (1) HS (NJ)

Velo	Pitch	Grade
92-96	FB	++++
80-84	CB	++++
82-85	CU	+++

Year	Lev	Team	W	L	Sv	IP	K	ERA	WHIP	BF/G	OBA	H%	S%	xERA	Ctl	Dom	Cmd	hr/9	BPV
2016	A-	Lowell	0	0	0	2	2	4.09	1.82	10.2	0	0	75	1.73	16.4	8.2	0.5	0.0	-277
2017	A-	Lowell	0	2	0	11	14	1.64	0.91	13.7	139	23	80	0.61	4.1	11.5	2.8	0.0	114
2017	A	Greenville	3	7	0	44	58	6.73	1.56	17.6	261	36	57	4.85	5.1	11.8	2.3	1.2	93
2019	Rk	GCL Red Sox	0	0	0	2	3	0.00	1.00	3.8	262	43	100	2.27	0.0	13.5		0.0	261
2019	A-	Lowell	0	0	0	2	3	4.50	2.00	9.6	347	53	75	6.12	4.5	13.5	3.0	0.0	140

Hard-thrower who returned in Aug after Tommy John surgery. Velocity not all way back, but expected to be at full health with plus FB/CB combo. All pitches exhibit power and movement, though CU needs refinement. Uses height well for effective plane to plate. If control/command improves, he could become ace. Just needs innings.

Grove,Michael — SP — Los Angeles (N)

EXP MLB DEBUT: 2022 | H/W: 6-3 200 | FUT: #3 starter | 8E

Thrws R Age 23
2018 (2) West Virginia

Velo	Pitch	Grade
90-94	FB	+++
82-84	SL	+++
77-80	CB	+
	CU	+

Year	Lev	Team	W	L	Sv	IP	K	ERA	WHIP	BF/G	OBA	H%	S%	xERA	Ctl	Dom	Cmd	hr/9	BPV
2019	A+	Rancho Cuca	0	5	0	51	73	6.15	1.56	10.7	297	43	62	5.36	3.3	12.8	3.8	1.2	159

Finally made pro debut with mixed results. Prior to Tommy John surgery FB sat at 93-96, but was more in the 90-94 mph range in his return. Backs up the heater with a potentially plus SL while CB and CU are average at best. Struggled with command at times, but should improve as he regains confidence and form.

Guilbeau,Taylor — RP — Seattle

EXP MLB DEBUT: 2019 | H/W: 6-4 180 | FUT: Middle reliever | 6C

Thrws L Age 26 — 2015 (10) Alabama

Velo	Pitch	Grade
93-96	FB	++++
86-87	SL	++
86-89	CU	+++

Year	Lev	Team	W	L	Sv	IP	K	ERA	WHIP	BF/G	OBA	H%	S%	xERA	Ctl	Dom	Cmd	hr/9	BPV
2018	A+	Potomac	1	0	0	35	35	2.56	1.39	5.3	255	35	80	3.21	3.8	8.9	2.3	0.0	76
2019	AA	Harrisburg	1	2	0	35	44	2.31	1.06	5.0	215	32	78	2.07	2.6	11.3	4.4	0.3	152
2019	AAA	Tacoma	0	0	0	5	5	1.80	1.00	3.8	175	25	80	1.25	3.6	9.0	2.5	0.0	83
2019	AAA	Fresno	2	0	0	8	6	5.49	1.83	5.4	302	37	67	5.01	5.5	6.6	1.2	0.0	-12
2019	MLB	Seattle	0	0	0	12	7	3.72	1.07	2.8	227	23	73	3.48	2.2	5.2	2.3	1.5	51

Low 3/4s LHP made MLB debut after being traded mid-season from WAS. Uses unusual arm angle to create deception. Primarily a 2-pitch RP. Tries to use below-average SL against LHH. FB is true sinker with solid arm-side bore. CU has fading action but struggles with finish his delivery, forcing the ball to stay up. Middle RP ceiling.

Gutierrez,Vladimir — SP — Cincinnati

EXP MLB DEBUT: 2020 | H/W: 6-0 190 | FUT: Middle reliever | 6B

Thrws R Age 24 — 2016 FA (CU)

Velo	Pitch	Grade
90-94	FB	+++
78-82	CB	+++
81-84	CU	+++

Year	Lev	Team	W	L	Sv	IP	K	ERA	WHIP	BF/G	OBA	H%	S%	xERA	Ctl	Dom	Cmd	hr/9	BPV
2017	A+	Daytona	7	8	0	103	94	4.46	1.23	22.0	271	33	65	3.86	1.7	8.2	4.9	0.9	121
2018	AA	Pensacola	9	10	0	147	145	4.35	1.20	21.9	251	31	67	3.72	2.3	8.9	3.8	1.1	115
2019	AAA	Louisville	6	11	0	137	117	6.04	1.40	21.4	272	30	60	5.08	3.2	7.7	2.4	1.7	71

Former top organization pitching prospect continued uneven performances, this time in Triple-A. Improved delivery in 2018 to throw from a more favorable slot. Struggles staying on top of ball, especially FB. CB has solid 12-to-6 downer break when it's on. CU has solid fading action. Stuff/command likely works best in RP role.

Guzman,Jorge — SP — Miami

EXP MLB DEBUT: 2020 | H/W: 6-2 182 | FUT: Closer | 8D

Thrws R Age 24 — 2014 FA (DR)

Velo	Pitch	Grade
96-99	FB	++++
87-89	SL	+++
87-89	CU	++

Year	Lev	Team	W	L	Sv	IP	K	ERA	WHIP	BF/G	OBA	H%	S%	xERA	Ctl	Dom	Cmd	hr/9	BPV
2016	Rk	Greeneville	2	3	0	22		4.86	1.44	15.8	285	42	65	4.12	2.8	11.8	4.1	0.4	153
2016	Rk	GCL Astros	1	1	0	17	25	3.16	0.82	8.9	77	15	57		5.3	13.2	2.5	0.0	113
2017	A-	Staten Island	5	3	0	66	88	2.31	1.04	19.7	215	32	80	2.29	2.4	12.0	4.9	0.5	167
2018	A+	Jupiter	0	9	0	96	101	4.03	1.54	19.9	237	31	74	3.96	6.0	9.5	1.6	0.7	26
2019	AA	Jacksonville	7	11	0	138	127	3.52	1.21	22.3	198	24	73	2.83	4.6	8.3	1.8	0.8	42

Hard-throwing RHP continues to struggle with command despite continued effectiveness. High 3/4s delivery with some effort. Holds high-90s FB velocity with late action. CB has transitioned into a true SL, flashing tight two-plane break. CU is firm and has no feel. Outside shot at starting, but likely a RP.

Haake,Zach — SP — Kansas City

EXP MLB DEBUT: 2022 | H/W: 6-4 186 | FUT: #4 starter | 7C

Thrws R Age 23 — 2018 (6) Kentucky

Velo	Pitch	Grade
94-96	FB	++++
83-85	SL	+++
85-87	CU	+++

Year	Lev	Team	W	L	Sv	IP	K	ERA	WHIP	BF/G	OBA	H%	S%	xERA	Ctl	Dom	Cmd	hr/9	BPV
2018	NCAA	Kentucky	2	4	0	34	36	8.47	1.82	10.5	294	34	57	7.09	5.8	9.5	1.6	2.4	32
2018	Rk	Idaho Falls	0	0	0	5	4	1.73	0.77	9.3	120	16	75	0.12	3.5	6.9	2.0	0.0	49
2018	Rk	AZL Royals	0	0	0	9	10	1.96	0.98	7.0	212	27	88	2.54	2.0	9.8	5.0	1.0	141
2019	Rk	Idaho Falls	0	0	0	4	4	0.00	1.22	16.6	147	21	100	1.51	6.6	8.8	1.3	0.0	-2
2019	A	Lexington	4	6	0	75	90	2.87	1.28	17.1	221	32	77	2.68	4.3	10.8	2.5	0.2	96

Tall, high 3/4 RHP with big velocity potential made full-season debut. Solid build despite big height. Repeatable, online delivery with three pitches. Sits mid-to-high 90s with FB, using height well to create downward plane. SL has quick, sharp bite with above-average potential. Uses CU often, projects as average offering.

Hall,DL — SP — Baltimore

EXP MLB DEBUT: 2021 | H/W: 6-2 195 | FUT: #1 starter | 9C

Thrws L Age 21 — 2017 (1) HS (GA)

Velo	Pitch	Grade
93-96	FB	++++
88-91	CT	+++
80-82	CB	++++
82-84	CU	++++

Year	Lev	Team	W	L	Sv	IP	K	ERA	WHIP	BF/G	OBA	H%	S%	xERA	Ctl	Dom	Cmd	hr/9	BPV
2017	Rk	GCL Orioles	0	0	0	10	12	7.13	1.98	9.7	260	35	63	5.58	8.9	10.7	1.2	0.9	-30
2018	A	Delmarva	2	7	0	94	100	2.10	1.17	17.1	204	27	85	2.54	4.0	9.6	2.4	0.6	82
2019	A+	Frederick	4	5	1	80	116	3.48	1.33	17.5	190	31	73	2.53	6.1	13.0	2.1	0.3	89

Athletic, high-3/4s LHP features three potentially plus pitches. Struggled early, came on late before minor core injury shut down his season. Easy, repeatable delivery generates plus extension. Mid-90s FB has late action, especially tough down. Hard CB has tremendous depth and sharp break; CU features terrific separation and solid fade.

Hanifee,Brenan — SP — Baltimore

EXP MLB DEBUT: 2022 | H/W: 6-5 215 | FUT: Middle reliever | 6C

Thrws R Age 21 — 2016 (4) HS (VA)

Velo	Pitch	Grade
90-93	FB	+++
84-87	SL	+++
85-87	CU	++

Year	Lev	Team	W	L	Sv	IP	K	ERA	WHIP	BF/G	OBA	H%	S%	xERA	Ctl	Dom	Cmd	hr/9	BPV
2017	A-	Aberdeen	7	3	0	68	44	2.77	1.13	22.4	253	30	75	2.80	1.6	5.8	3.7	0.3	80
2018	A	Delmarva	8	6	0	132	85	2.86	1.08	22.4	244	28	75	2.81	1.5	5.8	3.9	0.5	82
2019	A+	Frederick	9	10	0	129	78	4.60	1.42	22.8	257	29	68	4.13	4.0	5.4	1.4	0.8	9

Tall, 3/4s heavy sinker ball pitcher struggled in High-A. Crossfire delivery with solid extension is best suited for relief. Struggles commanding low-90s sinker with heavy downward action created by plane and movement. The SL is a tight, 2-plane breaker with above-average upside. Struggles replicating FB delivery with CU.

Hankins,Ethan — SP — Cleveland

EXP MLB DEBUT: 2023 | H/W: 6-6 200 | FUT: #2 starter | 9D

Thrws R Age 19 — 2018 (1) HS (GA)

Velo	Pitch	Grade
93-96	FB	++++
83-86	SL	+++
72-75	CB	++
85-86	CU	+++

Year	Lev	Team	W	L	Sv	IP	K	ERA	WHIP	BF/G	OBA	H%	S%	xERA	Ctl	Dom	Cmd	hr/9	BPV
2018		Did not pitch																	
2019	A	Lake County	0	3	0	21	28	4.69	1.52	18.3	252	35	72	4.65	5.1	11.9	2.3	1.3	95
2019	A-	MahoningVal	0	0	0	38	43	1.41	1.07	16.5	176	25	88	1.65	4.2	10.1	2.4	0.2	86

Tall, athletic 3/4s hurler alleviated shoulder concerns with dominant short-season run. Repeats and incorporates lower half well in delivery. Peppers zone with mid-90s, late-run FB; it's double-plus with potential of being more. Has feel for potentially plus CU, just inconsistent. SL has tight, two-plane break. Introduced CB to mixed results.

Hansen,Alec — RP — Chicago (A)

EXP MLB DEBUT: 2020 | H/W: 6-7 235 | FUT: Middle reliever | 6C

Thrws R Age 25 — 2016 (2) Oklahoma

Velo	Pitch	Grade
92-95	FB	++++
83-85	CB	++++

Year	Lev	Team	W	L	Sv	IP	K	ERA	WHIP	BF/G	OBA	H%	S%	xERA	Ctl	Dom	Cmd	hr/9	BPV
2017	AA	Birmingham	0	0	0	10	17	4.46	1.78	23.2	345	57	72	5.51	2.7	15.1	5.7	0.0	218
2018	A+	Winston-Salem	0	1	0	15	20	5.92	2.04	14.8	246	38	68	4.70	10.1	11.8	1.2	0.0	-41
2018	AA	Birmingham	0	4	0	35	35	6.65	2.05	19.0	232	30	67	5.28	10.7	8.9	0.8	0.8	-111
2019	A+	Winston-Salem	1	0	0	12	21	2.21	0.66	4.7	28	7	63		5.2	15.5	3.0	0.0	157
2019	AA	Birmingham	1	2	1	39	45	5.51	2.04	6.4	280	37	75	6.26	8.5	10.3	1.2	1.1	-25

Hard-throwing RHP who struggles repeating delivery. Once top prospect, delivery issues continue to plague profile. As RP, has been two-pitch pitcher. FB sit low-to-mid 90s with late run, which is difficult to control. Hard breaking-ball has tight movement and solid depth. Both pitches are plus-offerings and very inconsistent.

Harris,Hogan — SP — Oakland

EXP MLB DEBUT: 2021 | H/W: 6-3 230 | FUT: #5 SP/swingman | 7C

Thrws L Age 23 — 2018 (3) LA-Lafayette

Velo	Pitch	Grade
90-93	FB	+++
78-81	SL	++
75-77	CB	+++
	CU	++

Year	Lev	Team	W	L	Sv	IP	K	ERA	WHIP	BF/G	OBA	H%	S%	xERA	Ctl	Dom	Cmd	hr/9	BPV
2019	A+	Stockton	0	2	0	28	29	2.55	0.99	15.4	185	24	77	1.93	3.2	9.3	2.9	0.6	98
2019	A-	Vermont	1	3	0	26	36	3.12	0.88	12.0	160	24	67	1.42	3.1	12.5	4.0	0.7	158

Four-pitch LH best known for a uber-crossfire delivery and big-bending CB. Was roughly average age for his Hi-A assignment but posted a quality Dom by way of solid command of his low-90s FB and CB. SL and CU lag behind, but usable pitches. Strong frame; should eat innings. Not a high-ceiling arm, but could be a back-end SP.

Harvey,Hunter — SP — Baltimore

EXP MLB DEBUT: 2019 | H/W: 6-3 175 | FUT: Closer | 8D

Thrws R Age 25 — 2013 (1) HS (NC)

Velo	Pitch	Grade
97-99	FB	++++
82-85	CB	++++
89-91	CU	++

Year	Lev	Team	W	L	Sv	IP	K	ERA	WHIP	BF/G	OBA	H%	S%	xERA	Ctl	Dom	Cmd	hr/9	BPV
2017	A	Delmarva	0	1	0	8	14	2.20	0.85	10.0	147	30	71	0.52	3.3	15.4	4.7	0.0	206
2018	AA	Bowie	1	2	0	32	30	5.61	1.40	15.1	285	35	60	4.45	2.5	8.4	3.3	0.8	101
2019	AA	Bowie	2	5	1	59	61	5.19	1.42	17.9	275	32	71	5.57	3.2	9.3	2.9	2.1	99
2019	AAA	Norfolk	1	1	0	16	22	4.44	1.11	5.3	222	32	63	3.08	2.8	12.2	4.4	1.1	163
2019	MLB	Baltimore	1	0	0	6	11	1.48	1.15	3.5	149	24	100	2.65	5.9	16.2	2.8	1.5	151

Oft-injured former top prospect made MLB debut in RP role, pitching effectively. High 3/4s delivery with solid extension; still has big stuff. Double-plus 4-seam FB sits high-90s with late riding action. 12-to-6 CB has tremendous depth and solid break; it's a second swing-and-miss offering. Incorporates fringy CU against LHP.

Hatch,Thomas — SP — Toronto

EXP MLB DEBUT: 2020 | H/W: 6-1 200 | FUT: #4 starter | 7C

Thrws R Age 25 — 2016 (3) Oklahoma St

Velo	Pitch	Grade
91-96	FB	+++
81-83	SL	+++
80-82	CU	+++

Year	Lev	Team	W	L	Sv	IP	K	ERA	WHIP	BF/G	OBA	H%	S%	xERA	Ctl	Dom	Cmd	hr/9	BPV
2017	A+	Myrtle Beach	5	11	0	124	126	4.06	1.42	20.2	265	36	69	3.54	3.6	9.1	2.5	0.1	85
2018	AA	Tennessee	8	6	0	143	117	3.83	1.31	22.8	253	28	74	3.76	3.8	7.4	1.9	1.0	47
2019	AA	New Hampshire	2	3	0	35	34	2.82	0.77	21.0	202	24	73	2.18	0.5	8.7	17.0	1.3	161
2019	AA	Tennessee	4	10	0	100	93	4.59	1.41	20.1	269	33	70	4.56	3.3	8.4	2.5	1.2	79

Repeated AA and was acquired from CHC in late July '19. ERA rose, but peripherals were much improved. Lacks ideal put-away pitch in mix, yet keeps ball down and can induce weak contact. All pitches can flash plus at times, particularly CU that keeps LHH off-guard. Lack of movement on FB makes him susceptible to hard hit balls. Development of SL is key.

Hearn,Taylor

SP | Texas | EXP MLB DEBUT: 2019 | H/W: 6-5 210 | FUT: #3 starter | 8D

Thrws L Age 25
2015 (5) Oklahoma Baptist

Velo	Pitch	Grade
92-95	FB	++++
80-84	SL	+++
82-86	CU	+++

Year	Lev	Team	W	L	Sv	IP	K	ERA	WHIP	BF/G	OBA	H%	S%	xERA	Ctl	Dom	Cmd	hr/9	BPV
2017	A+	Bradenton	4	6	0	87	106	4.13	1.17	19.3	209	29	66	2.83	3.8	11.0	2.9	0.8	112
2018	AA	Frisco	1	2	0	25	33	5.04	1.52	21.7	291	39	73	5.71	3.2	11.9	3.7	1.8	144
2018	AA	Altoona	3	6	0	104	107	3.12	1.09	21.4	204	27	72	2.28	3.3	9.3	2.8	0.5	96
2019	AAA	Nashville	1	3	0	20	26	4.05	1.20	20.1	199	27	71	3.26	4.5	11.7	2.6	1.4	107
2019	MLB	Texas	0	1	0	0	0		70.00	7.3	914	91	43			0.0	0.0	0.0	-9702

Tall and slender lefty with simple upright mechanics and very good low-90s FB. After just four starts in AAA, got emergency call to majors in late April and lasted only eight batters (and one out). Sat out rest of year with elbow injury, though no surgery was required. SL/CU each have average potential, but health questions elevate his risk.

Heasley,Jon

SP | Kansas City | EXP MLB DEBUT: 2022 | H/W: 6-3 215 | FUT: Middle reliever | 6C

Thrws R Age 23
2018 (13) Oklahoma St

Velo	Pitch	Grade
90-93	FB	+++
82-83	SL	+++
	CU	++

Year	Lev	Team	W	L	Sv	IP	K	ERA	WHIP	BF/G	OBA	H%	S%	xERA	Ctl	Dom	Cmd	hr/9	BPV
2018	NCAA	Oklahoma St	4	6	0	80	79	5.96	1.64	23.8	292	38	62	4.88	4.3	8.9	2.1	0.6	53
2018	Rk	Idaho Falls	1	3	0	50	35	5.20	1.41	17.7	280	32	63	4.31	2.9	6.3	2.2	0.7	63
2019	A	Lexington	8	5	0	112	120	3.13	1.13	17.7	227	29	76	3.02	2.7	9.6	3.5	0.9	118

Big bodied RHP cleaned up mechanics and had posted positive results in first full-season. 3/4 cross-fire delivery. 3-pitch pitcher. Sits low-90s with FB. Commands well to both sides of plate. SL is best overall pitch with tight movement profile. CU solid enough for lower minors. Firm feel.

Heatherly,Jacob

SP | Cincinnati | EXP MLB DEBUT: 2022 | H/W: 6-1 215 | FUT: #4 starter | 7C

Thrws L Age 21
2017 (3) HS (AL)

Velo	Pitch	Grade
91-93	FB	++++
75-78	CB	+++
82-84	CU	+++

Year	Lev	Team	W	L	Sv	IP	K	ERA	WHIP	BF/G	OBA	H%	S%	xERA	Ctl	Dom	Cmd	hr/9	BPV
2017	Rk	AZL Reds	2	1	0	30	26	2.98	1.39	14.1	234	28	82	3.78	4.8	7.7	1.6	0.9	29
2017	Rk	Billings	0	1	0	9	5	12.00	2.33	15.5	401	45	43	8.08	4.0	5.0	1.3	0.0	0
2018	Rk	Greeneville	1	5	0	38	49	5.89	1.94	16.5	240	35	69	5.02	9.4	11.5	1.2	0.7	-29
2019	A	Dayton	1	2	0	8	10	8.78	2.20	10.3	342	48	56	6.54	6.6	11.0	1.7	0.0	38

Physically mature, stocky LHP struggled with shoulder soreness and spent almost the entire season on injured list. Cleaned up mechanics in 2018, improving efficiency. Three-pitch pitcher. FB is sneaky quick with solid deception created by arm-slot and strong late-run. CB and CU both are at least average offerings at maturity.

Hendrix,Ryan

RP | Cincinnati | EXP MLB DEBUT: 2020 | H/W: 6-3 185 | FUT: Setup reliever | 7D

Thrws R Age 25
2016 (5) Texas A&M

Velo	Pitch	Grade
94-97	FB	++++
86-88	CB	++++

Year	Lev	Team	W	L	Sv	IP	K	ERA	WHIP	BF/G	OBA	H%	S%	xERA	Ctl	Dom	Cmd	hr/9	BPV
2017	A	Dayton	4	1	6	34	61	2.38	0.85	5.4	165	33	74	1.19	2.6	16.1	6.1	0.5	237
2017	A+	Daytona	1	4	2	27	27	3.64	1.76	5.2	274	33	84	5.66	6.3	8.9	1.4	1.3	9
2018	A+	Daytona	4	4	12	51	79	1.76	1.25	4.7	209	36	87	2.56	4.6	13.9	3.0	0.4	145
2019	Rk	AZL Reds	1	0	0	5	8	0.00	0.20	3.8	66	14	100		0.0	14.4		0.0	277
2019	AA	Chattanooga	3	0	2	19	23	2.36	1.15	4.7	206	31	77	1.97	3.8	10.8	2.9	0.0	111

Max-effort, high 3/4s RHP lost most of the season due to a right elbow strain. 2-pitch pitcher. Relies heavily on over-powering hitters. FB sit mid-to-high 90s with some late run. Complements nicely with hard CB with solid depth and late downer action. The velocity of the CB is tough to keep consistent shape with and will become slurvy at times.

Henriquez,Ronny

SP | Texas | EXP MLB DEBUT: 2022 | H/W: 5-10 155 | FUT: #3 starter | 8C

Thrws R Age 19
2017 FA (DR)

Velo	Pitch	Grade
92-95	FB	++++
81-85	SL	+++
86-89	CU	++

Year	Lev	Team	W	L	Sv	IP	K	ERA	WHIP	BF/G	OBA	H%	S%	xERA	Ctl	Dom	Cmd	hr/9	BPV
2019	A	Hickory	6	6	0	82	99	4.50	1.44	16.6	282	39	69	4.31	3.0	10.9	3.7	0.7	134

Short RHP with athleticism, strong lower half and a whip for an arm. Plus FB tops out at 97, ability to ride it up in zone. SL with moderate break and occasional bite; CU has some splitter action. Mild torso turn and back-leg ball hide aids in deception. Some reliever risk, but mechanics are clean and still room to add strength. Promising.

Henry,Tommy

SP | Arizona | EXP MLB DEBUT: 2022 | H/W: 6-3 205 | FUT: #4 starter | 7C

Thrws L Age 22
2019 (2) Michigan

Velo	Pitch	Grade
89-92	FB	+++
83-85	SL	+++
82-84	CU	+++

Year	Lev	Team	W	L	Sv	IP	K	ERA	WHIP	BF/G	OBA	H%	S%	xERA	Ctl	Dom	Cmd	hr/9	BPV
2019	A-	Hillsboro	0	0	0	3	4	6.00	1.33	4.2	321	47	50	4.01	0.0	12.0		0.0	234

Polished, high-floor LH who had standout junior campaign with Wolverines. Athletic, loose arm action produces avg low-90s FB and blends in above-average fading CU. SL a tick behind his CU, but will be third useable offering for him. Presently above-average control and athleticism project future plus command, perhaps as a back-end SP.

Hentges,Sam

SP | Cleveland | EXP MLB DEBUT: 2021 | H/W: 6-8 245 | FUT: #4 starter | 7D

Thrws L Age 23
2014 (4) HS (MN)

Velo	Pitch	Grade
91-93	FB	+++
88-89	SL	+++
77-79	CB	+++
84-87	CU	+++

Year	Lev	Team	W	L	Sv	IP	K	ERA	WHIP	BF/G	OBA	H%	S%	xERA	Ctl	Dom	Cmd	hr/9	BPV
2017	Rk	AZL Indians	0	3	0	13	18	4.85	1.46	9.3	304	43	71	5.36	2.1	12.5	6.0	1.4	186
2017	A-	MahoningVal	0	1	0	17	23	2.09	0.99	13.1	93	14	81	0.86	6.3	12.0	1.9	0.5	65
2018	A+	Lynchburg	6	6	0	118	122	3.28	1.41	21.7	255	34	76	3.55	4.0	9.3	2.3	0.3	76
2019	AA	Akron	2	13	0	128	126	5.12	1.65	22.1	290	37	69	5.10	4.5	8.8	2.0	0.8	56

Long-limbed, high 3/4s cross-fire LHP struggled with command in 2019. Tall frame and delivery create natural downward plane on pitches. Struggled commanding movement of 2-seam FB, missing mostly to glove-side. Added CT as additional tool against LHH. CB and CU have average pitch profiles. Size could help pitches play up in RP role.

Hernandez,Aaron

SP | Los Angeles (A) | EXP MLB DEBUT: 2021 | H/W: 6-1 170 | FUT: #5 SP/swingman | 8D

Thrws R Age 23
2018 (3) Texas A&M-CC

Velo	Pitch	Grade
91-95	FB	+++
78-81	SL	+++
72-75	CB	+++
80-82	CU	+++

Year	Lev	Team	W	L	Sv	IP	K	ERA	WHIP	BF/G	OBA	H%	S%	xERA	Ctl	Dom	Cmd	hr/9	BPV
2019	A+	Inland Empire	1	4	0	72	81	4.49	1.68	16.2	269	36	74	4.81	5.7	10.1	1.8	0.7	45

Slender, fast-armed RH who profiles as a back-end SP with four-pitch mix. Can run FB up to 97 mph and cruise at 92-95 mph with some sink and run. True ability to spin both SL and CB and both will be effective, while CU has made progress. Lack of command and physicality holds his ceiling down. Could transition to long relief if it doesn't progress.

Hernandez,Carlos

SP | Kansas City | EXP MLB DEBUT: 2022 | H/W: 6-4 175 | FUT: Setup reliever | 7D

Thrws R Age 23
2016 FA (VZ)

Velo	Pitch	Grade
91-95	FB	++++
82-84	SL	+++
84-86	CU	+++

Year	Lev	Team	W	L	Sv	IP	K	ERA	WHIP	BF/G	OBA	H%	S%	xERA	Ctl	Dom	Cmd	hr/9	BPV
2017	Rk	Burlington	1	4	0	62	62	5.51	1.47	22.2	268	34	62	4.39	3.9	9.0	2.3	0.9	74
2018	A	Lexington	6	5	0	79	82	3.30	1.19	21.1	241	31	75	3.26	2.6	9.3	3.6	0.8	115
2019	Rk	Burlington	0	0	0	10	13	9.71	2.25	17.3	277	39	55	6.49	10.6	11.5	1.1	0.9	-61
2019	Rk	AZL Royals	0	2	0	11	12	7.36	1.55	9.6	311	41	50	5.17	2.5	9.8	4.0	0.8	128
2019	A	Lexington	3	3	0	36	43	3.50	1.19	20.6	251	33	76	3.82	2.3	10.8	4.8	1.3	151

Big-bodied, 3/4s RHP missed 3 months with broken rib. Maxed-out physique. Struggles repeating with long arm action. 3-pitch pitcher with all pitches projecting as average-or-better. FB can overpower at higher velocities but settles in well with movement at 91-93 MPH. Has tightened up grip on SL and has improved CU. Command is rough overall.

Hernandez,Daysbel

RP | Atlanta | EXP MLB DEBUT: 2021 | H/W: 5-10 220 | FUT: Middle reliever | 6C

Thrws R Age 23
2017 FA (CU)

Velo	Pitch	Grade
94-97	FB	++++
87-89	SL	+++

Year	Lev	Team	W	L	Sv	IP	K	ERA	WHIP	BF/G	OBA	H%	S%	xERA	Ctl	Dom	Cmd	hr/9	BPV
2018	A+	Florida	1	2	0	13	10	6.82	1.59	7.3	259	29	58	5.07	5.5	6.8	1.3	1.4	-7
2018	A	Rome	1	0	1	24	26	3.36	1.24	7.5	181	26	70	1.92	5.6	9.7	1.7	0.0	42
2019	A+	Florida	5	2	7	52	70	1.72	1.09	5.8	188	29	85	1.91	4.0	12.1	3.0	0.3	128

Hard-throwing 3/4s overpowered High-A hitters. Stiff, crossfire delivery with good extension for size. Max-effort. Two-pitch pitcher. Best pitch is mid-90s FB with natural downward plane and some arm-side run. Struggles with consistency of SL, which is above-average, two-plane breaker. Overall command concerns blurs projection.

Hernandez,Jonathan

SP | Texas | EXP MLB DEBUT: 2019 | H/W: 6-2 175 | FUT: Setup reliever | 8D

Thrws R Age 23
2013 FA (DR)

Velo	Pitch	Grade
94-97	FB	+++++
88-90	SL	++++
88-90	CU	++

Year	Lev	Team	W	L	Sv	IP	K	ERA	WHIP	BF/G	OBA	H%	S%	xERA	Ctl	Dom	Cmd	hr/9	BPV
2017	A+	Down East	3	6	0	65	64	3.46	1.49	20.0	264	35	76	3.85	4.3	8.8	2.1	0.3	62
2018	A+	Down East	4	2	0	57	77	2.21	0.95	21.5	187	27	83	2.10	2.7	12.1	4.5	0.9	164
2018	AA	Frisco	4	4	0	64	57	4.92	1.47	22.9	243	30	67	4.05	5.1	8.0	1.6	0.8	26
2019	AA	Frisco	5	9	0	96	95	5.16	1.44	18.6	270	34	65	4.50	3.6	8.9	2.5	1.0	82
2019	MLB	Texas	2	1	0	16	19	4.44	1.67	8.1	235	29	79	5.19	7.2	10.6	1.5	1.7	13

Unbridled arm strength, as pumps both four-seamers and two-seamers in the upper 90s. Also features hard high-80s SL with downer break that is hard to pick up from crossfire delivery. But mechanics are tough to repeat, front shoulder flies open and adversely affects control. Moved to bullpen in 2019 and ditched CU. Two VG pitches; but extreme risk.

Heuer,Codi
RP | Chicago (A) | EXP MLB DEBUT: 2020 | H/W: 6-5 195 | FUT: Middle reliever | 6C

Thrws R Age 23
2018 (6) Wichita St

- 93-96 FB ++++
- 89-90 CT +++
- 84-85 SL ++
- CU ++

Year	Lev	Team	W	L	Sv	IP	K	ERA	WHIP	BF/G	OBA	H%	S%	xERA	Ctl	Dom	Cmd	hr/9	BPV
2018	NCAA	Wichita St	6	5	0	79	82	4.32	1.37	20.7	241	33	67	3.28	4.2	9.3	2.2	0.3	72
2018	Rk	Great Falls	0	1	0	38	35	4.74	1.66	12.2	314	38	73	5.64	3.3	8.3	2.5	0.9	78
2019	AA	Birmingham	2	3	9	29	22	1.86	1.10	5.2	234	29	81	2.21	2.2	6.8	3.1	0.0	82
2019	A+	Winston-Salem	4	1	2	38	43	2.83	1.10	7.5	240	35	71	2.28	1.9	10.2	5.4	0.0	150

Hard-throwing, cross-fire 3/4s RHP made full-time conversion to RP role and succeeded. Tall with a solid build, creates downward plane. Relies mostly on FB & CT at this point. 2-seam FB is heavy sinker with solid late drop. CT has above-average potential. SL is ahead of CU in development. SL sometimes bleeds into CT movement.

Hill,Adam
SP | Seattle | EXP MLB DEBUT: 2022 | H/W: 6-6 225 | FUT: #5 SP/swingman | 7D

Thrws R Age 23
2018 (4) South Carolina

- 90-94 FB +++
- SL +++
- CU +++

Year	Lev	Team	W	L	Sv	IP	K	ERA	WHIP	BF/G	OBA	H%	S%	xERA	Ctl	Dom	Cmd	hr/9	BPV
2018	NCAA	South Carolina	7	5	0	83	101	4.12	1.33	21.5	190	27	69	2.73	6.0	11.0	1.8	0.5	54
2018	A-	Brooklyn	1	1	0	15	26	2.38	1.52	7.3	273	47	86	4.29	4.2	15.5	3.7	0.6	184
2019	A	Wisconsin	7	9	0	121	109	3.94	1.39	19.6	248	30	74	3.96	4.1	8.1	2.0	0.9	53

Tall, skinny RH acquired via trade last winter. Will sit 91-94 mph with fastball that creates good arm-side movement and occasional sink. SL and CU project to be at least average offerings at next level, the latter a bit more advanced than the former. Long levers and slight crossfire prohibit him from finding zone at times, but has Dom ability.

Hjelle,Sean
SP | San Francisco | EXP MLB DEBUT: 2021 | H/W: 6-11 225 | FUT: #3 starter | 8D

Thrws R Age 22
2018 (2) Kentucky

- 91-94 FB ++++
- 80-83 CB +++
- 81-84 SL +++
- 84-86 CU ++

Year	Lev	Team	W	L	Sv	IP	K	ERA	WHIP	BF/G	OBA	H%	S%	xERA	Ctl	Dom	Cmd	hr/9	BPV
2018	NCAA	Kentucky	7	5	0	99		3.45	1.10	25.9	237	30	68	2.68	2.0	8.3	4.1	0.5	113
2018	A-	Salem-Keizer	0	0	0	21	22	5.12	1.33	7.3	287	35	67	5.10	1.7	9.4	5.5	1.7	141
2019	A	Augusta	1	2	0	40	44	2.69	1.24	18.2	266	35	81	3.61	2.0	9.9	4.9	0.7	141
2019	A+	San Jose	5	5	0	77	74	2.80	1.19	22.1	251	33	76	2.88	2.2	8.6	3.9	0.2	113
2019	AA	Richmond	1	2	0	25	21	6.10	1.87	23.6	349	43	65	6.23	3.2	7.5	2.3	0.4	66

Very tall SP with breakout campaign. Not a flamethrower, but uses height and extension to make FB appear quicker. Spots in lower half of zone for extreme groundball rate. Repeats delivery that enhances two breaking balls. Uses sweeping SL often and can use as chase pitch. CU lags behind other three, but has chance to be plus. Exhibits plus control.

Holloway,Jordan
SP | Miami | EXP MLB DEBUT: 2021 | H/W: 6-6 215 | FUT: Setup reliever | 7D

Thrws R Age 23
2014 (20) HS (CO)

- 94-97 FB ++++
- 80-82 CB ++++
- 90-91 CT ++
- 88-90 CU ++

Year	Lev	Team	W	L	Sv	IP	K	ERA	WHIP	BF/G	OBA	H%	S%	xERA	Ctl	Dom	Cmd	hr/9	BPV
2016	A	Greensboro	2	4	0	30	24	6.26	1.52	16.4	267	27	66	5.96	4.5	7.2	1.6	2.4	26
2017	A	Greensboro	1	2	0	50	50	5.22	1.26	18.5	225	25	64	4.18	4.0	9.0	2.3	1.8	73
2018	Rk	GCL Marlins	0	0	0	2	5	0.00	1.82	3.4	392	77	100	6.43	0.0	20.5		0.0	386
2018	A-	Batavia	0	0	0	5	4	0.00	0.00	7.1	0	0			0.0	7.2		0.0	148
2019	A+	Jupiter	4	11	0	95	93	4.45	1.51	19.6	223	29	70	3.62	6.3	8.8	1.4	0.6	8

Tall, hard-throwing 3/4s RHP stuff returned after 2017 Tommy John surgery. Uses height well in otherwise stiff delivery. Overpowers with heavy FB. Movement profile better in 94-95 range. Can reach back for 100. CB is power downer with a plus profile. CT & CU are show me pitches against LHH at this point with CT ahead of CU in development.

Holmes,Grant
SP | Oakland | EXP MLB DEBUT: 2020 | H/W: 6-1 215 | FUT: #4 starter | 7B

Thrws R Age 24
2014 (1) HS (SC)

- 91-93 FB +++
- 79-83 CB +++
- 83-86 CU +++

Year	Lev	Team	W	L	Sv	IP	K	ERA	WHIP	BF/G	OBA	H%	S%	xERA	Ctl	Dom	Cmd	hr/9	BPV
2016	A+	Rancho Cuca	8	4	1	105	100	4.02	1.39	22.1	258	33	71	3.73	3.7	8.6	2.3	0.5	73
2017	AA	Midland	11	12	0	148	150	4.50	1.42	21.6	263	33	70	4.24	3.7	9.1	2.5	0.9	82
2018	A+	Stockton	0	0	0	6	8	4.50	1.00	11.5	191	25	60	2.81	3.0	12.0	4.0	1.5	153
2019	AA	Midland	6	5	0	81	76	3.33	1.21	14.9	237	29	76	3.45	3.0	8.4	2.8	1.0	89
2019	AAA	Las Vegas	0	0	0	4	5	2.14	1.67	18.8	336	42	100	7.13	2.1	10.7	5.0	2.1	153

Strong RH missed nearly all of 2018 post-Tommy John surgery, but returned and got significantly better as 2019 wore on. Operates in low-90s with sinking two-seam FB. Feel for hard CB is still there, and burgeoning CU made strides oin 2020. Has proclivity for ground balls and has improved strike-throwing ability. Plus makeup and is a competitor.

Holmes,William
SP | Los Angeles (A) | EXP MLB DEBUT: 2023 | H/W: 6-2 185 | FUT: #3 starter | 8D

Thrws R Age 19
2018 (5) HS (MI)

- 93-95 FB +++
- SL +++
- CU +++

Year	Lev	Team	W	L	Sv	IP	K	ERA	WHIP	BF/G	OBA	H%	S%	xERA	Ctl	Dom	Cmd	hr/9	BPV
2019	Rk	AZL Angels	0	2	0	17	25	5.79	1.81	11.3	237	36	69	4.99	8.4	13.2	1.6	1.1	27
2019	Rk	Orem	0	0	0	7	13	3.86	1.14	13.9	168	23	83	3.88	5.1	16.7	3.3	2.6	180

Two-way prospect who shows a bit more promise on the mound. Chiseled, developed frame with little physical projection left. Can run FB up to 97 mph with some late life but has a ways to go with command. Flashes solid SL/CU combo but both require more reps to develop feel for both. Good athlete with a wide range of potential pitching outcomes.

Honeywell,Brent
SP | Tampa Bay | EXP MLB DEBUT: 2021 | H/W: 6-2 195 | FUT: #2 starter | 8D

Thrws R Age 25
2014 (2) Walters St CC

- 92-96 FB ++++
- 87-88 SL +++
- 81-84 CU ++++
- 75-79 SC ++++

Year	Lev	Team	W	L	Sv	IP	K	ERA	WHIP	BF/G	OBA	H%	S%	xERA	Ctl	Dom	Cmd	hr/9	BPV
2015	A+	Charlotte	5	2	0	65	53	3.46	1.11	21.3	237	30	67	2.53	2.1	7.3	3.5	0.3	94
2016	A+	Charlotte	4	1	0	56	64	2.41	0.96	21.2	214	29	80	2.35	1.8	10.3	5.8	0.8	155
2016	AA	Montgomery	3	2	0	59	53	2.28	1.10	23.2	234	29	82	2.78	2.1	8.1	3.8	0.6	106
2017	AA	Montgomery	1	1	0	13	20	2.08	0.62	22.3	98	15	71	0.11	2.8	13.8	5.0	0.7	192
2017	AAA	Durham	12	8	0	123	152	3.65	1.31	21.2	272	38	74	3.97	2.3	11.1	4.9	0.8	157

Five-pitch pitcher didn't return from Tommy John surgery as expected in '19. Pre-injury, sat low-to-mid 90s with 2-seam FB. Best secondary is a late-fading CU that doesn't get enough credit because of true screwball. All of FB, CU & SC are plus pitches; CB and SL are average or less.

Houck,Tanner
SP | Boston | EXP MLB DEBUT: 2020 | H/W: 6-4 210 | FUT: #3 starter | 8D

Thrws R Age 23
2017 (1) Missouri

- 92-96 FB ++++
- 83-87 SL +++
- 79-83 CB ++
- 82-85 CU ++

Year	Lev	Team	W	L	Sv	IP	K	ERA	WHIP	BF/G	OBA	H%	S%	xERA	Ctl	Dom	Cmd	hr/9	BPV
2017	NCAA	Missouri	4	7	0	94	95	3.34	1.08	26.3	227	30	69	2.52	2.3	9.1	4.0	0.5	119
2017	A-	Lowell	0	3	0	22	25	3.67	1.31	9.1	252	36	69	2.96	3.3	10.2	3.1	0.0	113
2018	A+	Salem	7	11	0	119	111	4.24	1.43	22.0	247	31	72	3.98	4.5	8.4	1.9	0.8	47
2019	AA	Portland	8	6	0	82	80	4.27	1.44	20.6	271	35	69	3.95	3.5	8.8	2.5	0.4	81
2019	AAA	Pawtucket	0	0	1	25	27	3.24	1.32	6.5	212	27	80	3.49	5.0	9.7	1.9	1.1	57

Tall, durable SP who has moved quickly despite mediocre results. Pitched out of pen in AAA, but projects as mid-rotation SP. Sinking FB thrown from lower slot; gets plenty of grounders. Has found consistency in crossfire delivery and is very tough on RHH. Nasty SL induces weak contact and gets Ks. May scrap iffy CB, but needs better CU for LHH.

Howard,Brian
SP | Oakland | EXP MLB DEBUT: 2020 | H/W: 6-9 185 | FUT: #5 SP/swingman | 7C

Thrws R Age 24
2017 (8) Texas Christian

- 89-92 FB ++
- 87-89 CT +++
- 76-80 CB +++
- CU ++

Year	Lev	Team	W	L	Sv	IP	K	ERA	WHIP	BF/G	OBA	H%	S%	xERA	Ctl	Dom	Cmd	hr/9	BPV
2017	A-	Vermont	2	1	1	31	29	1.16	0.74	10.1	201	27	83	0.89	0.3	8.4	29.0	0.0	161
2018	A+	Stockton	7	3	0	72	77	2.38	0.93	22.5	207	26	83	2.49	1.8	9.6	5.5	1.1	144
2018	AA	Midland	4	4	0	67	63	3.49	1.31	23.1	256	31	77	3.90	3.1	8.5	2.7	0.9	87
2019	AA	Midland	8	8	0	130	118	3.25	1.35	23.6	272	34	76	3.81	2.7	8.2	3.0	0.5	92
2019	AAA	Las Vegas	0	1	0	14	16	14.04	2.55	18.9	413	50	44	11.23	5.1	10.2	2.0	2.6	64

Statuesque RH racked up nearly 150 innings and posted solid peripherals in his first full tour of AA/AAA. Average four-pitch mix headlined by sharp CT with ability to induce dribblers; can sink his low-90s FB low in the zone with surprising command for his size. SL/CB are avg offerings. Durability, production and command all point to #4/5 SP value.

Howard,Spencer
SP | Philadelphia | EXP MLB DEBUT: 2020 | H/W: 6-2 205 | FUT: #2 starter | 9C

Thrws R Age 23
2017 (2) Cal Poly

- 94-97 FB ++++
- 85-90 SL +++
- 80-83 CU ++++
- 74-79 CB +++

Year	Lev	Team	W	L	Sv	IP	K	ERA	WHIP	BF/G	OBA	H%	S%	xERA	Ctl	Dom	Cmd	hr/9	BPV
2018	A	Lakewood	9	8	0	112	147	3.78	1.26	19.9	242	36	70	3.13	3.2	11.8	3.7	0.5	144
2019	Rk	GCL Phillies W	0	0	0	3	5	0.00	0.67	10.5	106	22	100		3.0	15.0	5.0	0.0	207
2019	Rk	GCL Phillies E	0	0	0	2	3	12.86	1.90	9.9	336	41	33	9.72	4.3	12.9	3.0	4.3	134
2019	A+	Clearwater	2	1	0	35	48	1.29	0.69	17.5	161	26	83	0.52	1.3	12.3	9.6	0.3	205
2019	AA	Reading	1	0	0	30	38	2.38	0.96	19.0	190	28	78	1.86	2.7	11.3	4.2	0.6	149

Took a step forward despite missing 2 months from minor shoulder strain. Advanced four-pitch mix anchored by swing-and-miss FB that sits mid-90s; touches 99. Secondaries have each flashed plus; diving CU most effective in 2019; deep two-plane SL is a fantastic breaker. Could tighten command but nearly ready.

Humphreys,Jordan
SP | New York (N) | EXP MLB DEBUT: 2021 | H/W: 6-2 223 | FUT: #4 starter | 7D

Thrws R Age 23
2015 (18) HS (FL)

- 90-93 FB +++
- 75-78 CB +++
- 82-85 SL ++
- 82-85 CU +++

Year	Lev	Team	W	L	Sv	IP	K	ERA	WHIP	BF/G	OBA	H%	S%	xERA	Ctl	Dom	Cmd	hr/9	BPV
2016	Rk	Kingsport	3	5	0	69	76	3.78	1.16	22.9	250	34	66	2.91	2.0	9.9	5.1	0.4	143
2016	A-	Brooklyn	0	1	0	6	9	1.50	1.33	24.9	293	47	88	3.55	1.5	13.5	9.0	0.0	221
2017	A	Columbia	10	1	0	69	80	1.43	0.72	22.3	174	25	81	0.76	1.2	10.4	8.9	0.3	174
2017	A+	St. Lucie	0	0	0	11	3	4.09	1.82	25.5	354	36	79	6.66	2.5	2.5	1.0	0.8	-4
2019	Rk	GCL Mets	0	0	0	2	2	4.50	1.50	4.3	262	35	67	3.58	4.5	9.0	2.0	0.0	59

Pitchability RHP made return from Tommy John surgery, looking sharp in AFL action. Sturdy frame; 3/4s online delivery with long arm action that contributes to FB command issues and is best suited for RP. 4-pitch pitcher. Nothing sets the world on fire but all pitches should compete in the big leagues. Best when hitting spots with 2-seam FB.

Irvin,Jake | SP | Washington | EXP MLB DEBUT: 2022 | H/W: 6-6 225 | FUT: #4 starter | 7D

Thrws R Age 23
2018 (4) Oklahoma

Velo	Pitch	Grade
89-91	FB	+ + +
77-81	SL	+ +
83-84	CU	+ +

Year	Lev	Team	W	L	Sv	IP	K	ERA	WHIP	BF/G	OBA	H%	S%	xERA	Ctl	Dom	Cmd	hr/9	BPV
2018	NCAA	Oklahoma	6	2	0	95	115	3.41	1.08	23.2	219	30	73	2.93	2.7	10.9	4.1	1.0	142
2018	Rk	GCL Nationals	1	0	0	12	9	1.48	1.07	6.8	225	28	85	2.03	2.2	6.6	3.0	0.0	78
2018	A-	Auburn	0	0	0	8	6	2.25	1.25	8.1	210	27	80	2.30	4.5	6.8	1.5	0.0	18
2019	A	Hagerstown	8	8	0	128	113	3.79	1.25	20.8	252	30	73	3.75	2.7	7.9	3.0	1.0	89

Solidly-built, barrel-chested RHP whose stuff ticked back a bit from his collegiate days at Oklahoma. Delivery has a bit of deception from partial windup, and was able to show decent control in full-season debut. FB 89-91 but was low-90s previously; SL at 77-80 that flashes average. Also throws a mid-80s CU, which he'll need going forward.

Ivey,Tyler | SP | Houston | EXP MLB DEBUT: 2020 | H/W: 6-4 195 | FUT: #4 starter | 7B

Thrws R Age 23
2017 (3) Grayson JC

Velo	Pitch	Grade
90-95	FB	+ + +
78-79	CB	+ + +
84-85	SL	+ + +
82-84	CU	+ +

Year	Lev	Team	W	L	Sv	IP	K	ERA	WHIP	BF/G	OBA	H%	S%	xERA	Ctl	Dom	Cmd	hr/9	BPV
2018	A	Quad Cities	1	3	2	41	53	3.50	1.07	17.8	237	35	67	2.54	1.7	11.6	6.6	0.4	179
2018	A+	Buies Creek	3	3	1	70	82	2.70	1.01	17.9	202	29	74	1.93	2.7	10.5	3.9	0.4	135
2019	Rk	GCL Astros	0	0	0	3	5	0.00	1.00	5.7	0	0	100		9.0	15.0	1.7	0.0	45
2019	A+	Fayetteville	0	0	0	3	2	0.00	0.33	9.5	0	0	100		3.0	6.0	2.0	0.0	45
2019	AA	Corpus Christi	4	0	0	46	61	1.57	0.96	15.8	178	25	92	2.06	3.1	11.9	3.8	1.0	148

Long, lanky SP who missed time mid-year due to injury, but returned late. Numbers look better than stuff. Throws consistent strikes with all pitches and gets good movement to FB and sharp SL. Has lot of effort in delivery and arm action and may not have the durability to remain SP. CB may be best pitch in arsenal with great spin. CU lags behind.

Jackson,Andre | SP | Los Angeles (N) | EXP MLB DEBUT: 2021 | H/W: 6-3 210 | FUT: Setup reliever | 8E

Thrws R Age 23
2017 (12) Utah

Velo	Pitch	Grade
92-95	FB	+ + + +
	CB	+ +
	CT	+
	CU	+ + +

Year	Lev	Team	W	L	Sv	IP	K	ERA	WHIP	BF/G	OBA	H%	S%	xERA	Ctl	Dom	Cmd	hr/9	BPV
2018	Rk	AZL Dodgers	2	0	0	18	31	3.48	1.22	18.3	261	47	68	2.78	2.0	15.4	7.8	0.0	242
2018	A	Great Lakes	1	5	0	49	45	4.39	1.81	16.3	257	32	76	4.81	7.5	8.2	1.1	0.5	-36
2019	A	Great Lakes	4	1	0	48	50	2.25	1.00	18.4	176	25	77	1.43	3.6	9.4	2.6	0.2	90
2019	A+	Rancho Cuca	3	1	0	66	91	3.68	1.50	19.0	247	37	77	3.97	5.2	12.4	2.4	0.7	101

Was a two-way player in college and had a breakout season, dominating at Low and High-A. Athletic frame and lightning quick arm result in a plus mid-90s FB. CU and CB show promise, but need refinement. Relatively new to pitching and needs to refine his mechanics and repeat delivery. Worth watching.

Jameson,Drey | SP | Arizona | EXP MLB DEBUT: 2022 | H/W: 6-0 165 | FUT: Closer | 8D

Thrws R Age 22
2019 (1) Ball St

Velo	Pitch	Grade
92-96	FB	+ + + +
83-85	SL	+ + +
77-80	CB	+ + +
88-90	CU	+ + +

Year	Lev	Team	W	L	Sv	IP	K	ERA	WHIP	BF/G	OBA	H%	S%	xERA	Ctl	Dom	Cmd	hr/9	BPV
2019	A-	Hillsboro	0	0	0	11	12	6.43	2.05	6.8	307	40	68	6.38	7.2	9.6	1.3	0.8	-4

Athletic, slightly undersized RHP with quick arm speed and three above-average pitches. Will touch 97 mph and sit 92-95 mph with control of plus FB, but command will require work. Likes to use SL and CB and has feel for spin. Firm CU that remains raw. Will need to add mass to skinny frame to remain SP. Delivery and Dom ability point to RP future.

Javier,Cristian | SP | Houston | EXP MLB DEBUT: 2021 | H/W: 6-1 204 | FUT: #3 starter | 8D

Thrws R Age 23
2015 FA (DR)

Velo	Pitch	Grade
89-95	FB	+ + +
72-76	CB	+ + +
80-82	SL	+ + + +
83-85	CU	+ +

Year	Lev	Team	W	L	Sv	IP	K	ERA	WHIP	BF/G	OBA	H%	S%	xERA	Ctl	Dom	Cmd	hr/9	BPV
2018	A	Quad Cities	2	2	1	49	80	1.83	1.04	17.2	168	30	85	1.73	4.2	14.7	3.5	0.5	168
2018	A+	Buies Creek	5	4	0	60	66	3.44	1.18	17.2	206	27	74	2.89	4.0	9.9	2.4	0.9	87
2019	A+	Fayetteville	2	0	1	28	40	0.96	1.10	15.8	159	26	93	1.58	5.1	12.8	2.5	0.3	110
2019	AA	Corpus Christi	6	3	3	74	114	2.07	0.95	16.4	129	22	82	1.16	4.7	13.9	2.9	0.6	140
2019	AAA	Round Rock	0	0	0	11	16	1.64	0.82	20.0	139	21	88	1.14	3.3	13.1	4.0	0.8	165

Breakout who led minors in ERA and 6th in K. Pitched on 3 levels and was HOU org pitcher of year. Was nearly impossible to hit (.130 oppBA) due to riding FB and knockout SL. CU took major steps forward and was more consistent in zone. FB command still needs enhanced, but getting better. Can elevate pitches, but needs better control overall.

Jax,Griffin | SP | Minnesota | EXP MLB DEBUT: 2020 | H/W: 6-2 195 | FUT: #5 SP/swingman | 6C

Thrws R Age 25
2016 (3) Air Force

Velo	Pitch	Grade
89-91	FB	+ +
81-83	SL	+ + +
82-84	CU	+ + +

Year	Lev	Team	W	L	Sv	IP	K	ERA	WHIP	BF/G	OBA	H%	S%	xERA	Ctl	Dom	Cmd	hr/9	BPV
2017	Rk	Elizabethton	0	1	0	4	7	4.29	1.43	17.8	336	51	80	6.49	0.0	15.0		2.1	288
2017	A	Cedar Rapids	2	1	0	26	13	2.41	1.00	24.9	205	23	76	1.95	2.4	4.5	1.9	0.3	34
2018	A+	Fort Myers	3	4	0	87	66	3.72	1.24	23.6	274	33	69	3.41	1.5	6.8	4.4	0.3	99
2019	AA	Pensacola	4	5	0	111	84	2.67	1.10	21.8	238	29	76	2.65	1.9	6.8	3.5	0.4	88
2019	AAA	Rochester	1	2	0	16	10	4.50	1.38	22.4	296	33	70	4.85	1.7	5.6	3.3	1.1	74

Athletic, 3/4s RHP known more for command/control than velocity. Lives in lower half of zone with 2-seam FB with moderate arm-side run. Commands FB well. CU best secondary offering with solid late-fade and good deception. SL is a fringe-average offering with loose break.

Jefferies,Daulton | SP | Oakland | EXP MLB DEBUT: 2021 | H/W: 6-0 182 | FUT: #3 starter | 8C

Thrws R Age 24
2016 (1) California

Velo	Pitch	Grade
91-94	FB	+ + +
85-87	CT	+ + +
73-76	CB	+ + +
82-85	CU	+ + + +

Year	Lev	Team	W	L	Sv	IP	K	ERA	WHIP	BF/G	OBA	H%	S%	xERA	Ctl	Dom	Cmd	hr/9	BPV
2016	Rk	AZL Athletics	0	0	0	11	17	2.43	1.17	8.9	260	43	77	2.67	1.6	13.8	8.5	0.0	222
2017	A+	Stockton	0	0	0	7	6	2.57	1.14	13.9	262	34	75	2.69	1.3	7.7	6.0	0.0	122
2018	Rk	AZL Athletics	0	0	0	2	5	0.00	0.50	6.6	151	61	100		0.0	22.5		0.0	423
2019	A+	Stockton	1	0	0	15	21	2.40	0.80	10.9	191	30	73	1.45	1.2	12.6	10.5	0.6	212
2019	AA	Midland	1	2	0	64	72	3.66	1.09	11.9	259	34	70	3.42	1.0	10.1	10.3	1.0	174

Former first-round pick who has dealt with injuries as a pro, but impressed in AA and could be turned loose soon. Best known for a tumbling CU with elite shape and advanced FB command around 92-94 mph. Has developed feel for CT, and CB now looks like a solid-average pitch. Is a well proportioned, quality athlete with superb feel for pitching.

Jennings,Steven | SP | Pittsburgh | EXP MLB DEBUT: 2023 | H/W: 6-2 175 | FUT: #4 starter | 7D

Thrws R Age 21
2017 (2) HS (TN)

Velo	Pitch	Grade
89-92	FB	+ + +
82-86	SL	+ +
75-77	CB	+ +
83-85	CU	+ + +

Year	Lev	Team	W	L	Sv	IP	K	ERA	WHIP	BF/G	OBA	H%	S%	xERA	Ctl	Dom	Cmd	hr/9	BPV
2017	Rk	GCL Pirates	0	2	0	26	13	4.14	1.57	11.5	296	32	74	4.95	3.4	4.5	1.3	0.7	6
2018	Rk	Bristol	3	4	0	65	53	4.84	1.46	21.4	270	33	67	4.26	3.7	7.3	2.0	0.7	49
2019	A	Greensboro	7	12	0	130	115	4.71	1.33	20.0	268	32	66	4.22	2.7	8.0	2.9	1.0	88

Athletic SP who had solid August to give hope. Has deep repertoire and saw walk rate decline while K rate rose slightly. Not a flamethrower and may not have more in tank, but has feel for pitch mixing and using CU to complement harder stuff. Two breaking balls are relatively flat and can be hittable, particularly against LHH (.307 oppBA).

Jensen,Ryan | SP | Chicago (N) | EXP MLB DEBUT: 2022 | H/W: 6-0 180 | FUT: Closer | 8D

Thrws R Age 22
2019 (1) Fresno St

Velo	Pitch	Grade
94-97	FB	+ + + +
82-85	SL	+ + +
	CU	+ +

Year	Lev	Team	W	L	Sv	IP	K	ERA	WHIP	BF/G	OBA	H%	S%	xERA	Ctl	Dom	Cmd	hr/9	BPV
2019	A-	Eugene	0	0	0	12	19	2.25	1.75	9.1	171	32	86	3.05	10.5	14.3	1.4	0.0	-9

Live-armed, first-round RH whose stuff drastically improved in three years at Fresno State. Owns best FB in the system, which will touch 99 mph with often wicked two-seam sink. Still learning feel for SL and CU. Owns plus arm speed, but has long arm action and moving parts in delivery. Dom upside if presently fringe command improves as a pro.

Johnson,Jared | SP | Atlanta | EXP MLB DEBUT: 2024 | H/W: 6-2 225 | FUT: #4 starter | 7E

Thrws R Age 19
2019 (14) HS (MS)

Velo	Pitch	Grade
90-94	FB	+ + + +
80-82	SL	+ + +

Year	Lev	Team	W	L	Sv	IP	K	ERA	WHIP	BF/G	OBA	H%	S%	xERA	Ctl	Dom	Cmd	hr/9	BPV
2019	Rk	GCL Braves	0	0	0	15	12	3.58	1.26	10.3	260	33	68	2.97	2.4	7.2	3.0	0.0	82

Made pro debut after going almost unnoticed in prep ranks. Extremely raw, crossfire 3/4s delivery. FB velocity will vary between starts. Mostly sits 90-92 with FB with good downward plane. SL is a solid pitch with potential to be better than that. Will slow delivery to achieve break. CU wasn't seen. Long-term project.

Johnson,Seth | SP | Tampa Bay | EXP MLB DEBUT: 2023 | H/W: 6-1 200 | FUT: #4 starter | 8D

Thrws R Age 21
2019 (1) Campbell

Velo	Pitch	Grade
91-93	FB	+ + + +
83-86	SL	+ + + +
72-74	CB	+ +
84-88	CU	+ + +

Year	Lev	Team	W	L	Sv	IP	K	ERA	WHIP	BF/G	OBA	H%	S%	xERA	Ctl	Dom	Cmd	hr/9	BPV
2019	Rk	Princeton	0	1	0	7	9	5.14	1.57	7.7	336	48	64	4.87	1.3	11.6	9.0	0.0	192
2019	Rk	GCL Rays	0	0	0	10	7	0.00	0.90	7.4	199	25	100	1.29	1.8	6.3	3.5	0.0	83

Projectable RHP went from Junior College IF to #1 collegiate starter and 40th overall pick in '19 draft. Athletic, 3/4s delivery. Repeats well despite rawness. 4-pitch pitcher with easy velocity. Can hit 97 but sits low-90s with a late-ridding FB. Mid-80s SL is potential plus with solid 2-plane break. CB is loopy and slow and has a feel for a CU.

Johnson,Tyler

SP | **Chicago (A)** | EXP MLB DEBUT: 2020 | H/W: 6-2 205 | FUT: Setup reliever | **6B**

Thrws R Age 24
2017 (5) South Carolina

Velo	Pitch	Grade
94-96	FB	++++
76-79	CB	+++
	CU	++

Year	Lev	Team	W	L	Sv	IP	K	ERA	WHIP	BF/G	OBA	H%	S%	xERA	Ctl	Dom	Cmd	hr/9	BPV
2018	A	Kannapolis	5	0	7	27	46	1.33	0.96	5.1	174	33	88	1.39	3.3	15.3	4.6	0.3	204
2018	A+	Winston-Salem	4	0	7	31	43	1.45	0.81	5.4	179	29	83	1.04	1.7	12.5	7.2	0.3	196
2019	Rk	AZL White Sox	0	0	0	3	5	0.00	1.67	4.5	371	59	100	5.71	0.0	15.0		0.0	288
2019	A+	Winston-Salem	0	1	0	10	15	1.80	1.00	5.5	175	27	89	2.05	3.6	13.5	3.8	0.9	164
2019	AA	Birmingham	2	0	0	18	23	3.48	0.88	5.6	164	20	69	2.21	3.0	11.4	3.8	1.5	143

Hard-throwing RP prospect continues to progress to big leagues. 3/4s RHP with rough delivery. Doesn't use height or long limbs well. FB sits mid-90s with RP plane. Has late boring movement and very effective against RHH. Slow SL with slurve action; average pitch at projection. Flashes CU to LHH but is firm and just a change of pace offering.

Johnston,Kyle

SP | **Toronto** | EXP MLB DEBUT: 2021 | H/W: 6-0 190 | FUT: #4 starter | **7D**

Thrws R Age 23
2017 (6) Texas

Velo	Pitch	Grade
90-95	FB	++++
80-86	SL	+++
86-89	CT	++
82-86	CU	++

Year	Lev	Team	W	L	Sv	IP	K	ERA	WHIP	BF/G	OBA	H%	S%	xERA	Ctl	Dom	Cmd	hr/9	BPV
2017	A-	Auburn	0	2	0	44	32	3.46	1.45	13.5	248	30	76	3.66	4.7	6.5	1.4	0.4	9
2018	A	Hagerstown	2	3	2	55	59	3.43	1.36	12.8	243	33	75	3.43	4.1	9.6	2.4	0.5	81
2018	A+	Potomac	5	2	0	47	37	4.97	1.46	20.2	236	28	66	3.88	5.4	7.1	1.3	0.8	1
2019	A+	Potomac	9	9	0	105	100	4.03	1.23	21.3	237	30	67	3.13	3.2	8.6	2.7	0.6	87
2019	A+	Dunedin	1	3	0	19	13	10.31	1.98	15.4	250	28	44	5.53	9.4	6.1	0.7	0.9	-125

Short, strong SP with two dynamic offerings that could be lethal in short stints. May lack frontline size and stamina, but takes advantage of fast arm. FB exhibits late movement to arm side while hard SL features sharp action. Command has been issue. Tough to hit, but needs to throw consistent strikes to have value. Crude mechanics need attention.

Jones,Damon

SP | **Philadelphia** | EXP MLB DEBUT: 2020 | H/W: 6-5 225 | FUT: #5 SP/swingman | **7C**

Thrws L Age 25
2017 (18) Washington St

Velo	Pitch	Grade
90-96	FB	+++
79-81	SL	++
84-86	CU	++

Year	Lev	Team	W	L	Sv	IP	K	ERA	WHIP	BF/G	OBA	H%	S%	xERA	Ctl	Dom	Cmd	hr/9	BPV
2017	A-	Williamsport	2	3	3	26		4.85	1.65	8.9	239	39	67	3.61	6.9	13.2	1.9	0.0	68
2018	A	Lakewood	10	7	0	113	123	3.42	1.37	20.6	248	33	76	3.57	4.0	9.8	2.5	0.6	87
2019	A+	Clearwater	4	3	0	58	88	1.55	1.07	20.5	188	32	88	1.96	3.7	13.6	3.7	0.5	163
2019	AA	Reading	1	0	0	22	31	0.82	0.82	20.0	127	22	89	0.25	3.7	12.7	3.4	0.0	147
2019	AAA	Lehigh Valley	0	1	0	34	33	6.62	1.56	18.6	220	27	57	4.17	6.9	8.7	1.3	1.1	-11

Big, sturdy LHP had velocity spike into mid-90s early on and blew through two levels in first-half success story. Hit a wall at Triple-A as stuff backed up and walks returned in bunches. Balanced in delivery, though some crossfire affects FB command; at times he lacks overall aggressiveness. Secondaries both below average and limit his ceiling.

Kalich,Kasey

RP | **Atlanta** | EXP MLB DEBUT: 2021 | H/W: 6-3 220 | FUT: Middle reliever | **6C**

Thrws R Age 21
2019 (4) Texas A&M

Velo	Pitch	Grade
93-96	FB	++++
87-89	CT	+++

Year	Lev	Team	W	L	Sv	IP	K	ERA	WHIP	BF/G	OBA	H%	S%	xERA	Ctl	Dom	Cmd	hr/9	BPV
2019	A	Rome	1	1	1	20	22	1.34	0.94	5.8	136	20	84	0.69	4.5	9.8	2.2	0.0	74
2019	Rk	GCL Braves	0	0	0	1	2	0.00	2.00	4.8	262	55	100	4.75	9.0	18.0	2.0	0.0	99

Hard-throwing, big-bodied RHP with stiff, 3/4s crossfire delivery, exclusively out of stretch. FB sits mid-90s with below-average command and some movement. Gets on hitters quickly due to extension within delivery. CT has chance to be MLB swing-and-miss pitch, ala AJ Minter from RH side.

Kaprielian,James

SP | **Oakland** | EXP MLB DEBUT: 2020 | H/W: 6-3 220 | FUT: #3 starter | **8D**

Thrws R Age 26
2015 (1) UCLA

Velo	Pitch	Grade
90-93	FB	+++
84-86	SL	++++
78-81	CB	+++
86-88	CU	+++

Year	Lev	Team	W	L	Sv	IP	K	ERA	WHIP	BF/G	OBA	H%	S%	xERA	Ctl	Dom	Cmd	hr/9	BPV
2017		Did not pitch - injury																	
2018		Did not pitch - injury																	
2019	A+	Stockton	2	2	0	36	43	4.49	1.19	13.2	256	33	68	4.10	2.0	10.7	5.4	1.5	157
2019	AA	Midland	2	1	0	27	26	1.65	0.96	14.7	190	24	88	1.93	2.6	8.6	3.3	0.7	101
2019	AAA	Las Vegas	0	0	0	4	6	2.25	1.50	17.3	347	53	83	4.86	0.0	13.5		0.0	261

Strong, physical RH made his upper-minors debut after missing two years post Tommy John surgery. Has high upside, previously touched 97 mph with lively FB and quality blend of SL/CB/CU. Velocity has wavered through rehab process, and his innings were limited in 2019. Likely turned loose in 2020, he could have value soon.

Karinchak,James

RP | **Cleveland** | EXP MLB DEBUT: 2019 | H/W: 6-3 230 | FUT: Setup reliever | **7C**

Thrws R Age 24
2017 (9) Bryant

Velo	Pitch	Grade
96-98	FB	++++
84-86	CB	++++

Year	Lev	Team	W	L	Sv	IP	K	ERA	WHIP	BF/G	OBA	H%	S%	xERA	Ctl	Dom	Cmd	hr/9	BPV
2018	AA	Akron	0	1	0	10	16	2.67	1.88	4.7	197	32	89	4.51	10.7	14.3	1.3	0.9	-14
2019	Rk	AZL Indians 2	0	0	0	3	8	0.00	0.67	3.5	0	0	100		6.0	24.0	4.0	0.0	288
2019	AA	Akron	0	0	6	10	24	0.00	0.40	3.2	66	32	100		1.8	21.6	12.0	0.0	358
2019	AAA	Columbus	1	1	2	17	42	4.74	1.58	4.4	225	66	72	4.15	6.8	22.1	3.2	1.1	231
2019	MLB	Cleveland	0	0	0	5	8	1.76	0.78	3.7	173	32	75	0.63	1.8	14.1	8.0	0.0	224

Hard-throwing, swing-and-miss inducing high 3/4s RHP piled up strikeouts in route to September MLB debut. Also, piled up walks too. Stiff delivery, doesn't finish from pitch-to-pitch. 4-seam FB overpowers hitters with velocity and late ride. Complements well with hard CB with solid depth and violent break. Control limits projection.

Kasowski,Marshall

RP | **Los Angeles (N)** | EXP MLB DEBUT: 2020 | H/W: 6-3 215 | FUT: Setup reliever | **7D**

Thrws R Age 25
2017 (13) West Texas A&M

Velo	Pitch	Grade
91-97	FB	++++
	CB	+
	CU	+

Year	Lev	Team	W	L	Sv	IP	K	ERA	WHIP	BF/G	OBA	H%	S%	xERA	Ctl	Dom	Cmd	hr/9	BPV
2018	A+	Rancho Cuca	2	0	4	23	44	1.16	0.91	5.4	133	30	90	0.85	4.3	17.1	4.0	0.4	210
2018	AA	Tulsa	0	0	1	13	18	2.77	1.23	5.3	160	21	86	2.94	6.2	12.5	2.0	1.4	74
2019	Rk	AZL DodgersM	0	0	0	1	2	0.00	0.91	4.1	244	48	100	1.77	0.0	16.4		0.0	313
2019	Rk	AZL DodgersL	0	0	0	1	3	0.00	0.00	2.8	0	0			0.0	27.0		0.0	504
2019	AA	Tulsa	4	3	2	29	46	2.47	1.13	4.3	172	31	78	1.79	4.9	14.2	2.9	0.3	140

Strong-armed gunslinger with plus FB that sits at 92-95, topping at 97 mph in relief. Comes at hitters from an over-the-top arm slot creating downhill tilt and deception. CB and CU are average to below offerings, but has posted considerable Doms at every stop. Pitched exclusively in relief.

Kauffman,Karl

SP | **Colorado** | EXP MLB DEBUT: 2022 | H/W: 6-2 200 | FUT: #4 starter | **7C**

Thrws R Age 22
2019 (2) Michigan

Velo	Pitch	Grade
88-92	FB	++
82-83	SL	+++
83-85	CU	+++

Year	Lev	Team	W	L	Sv	IP	K	ERA	WHIP	BF/G	OBA	H%	S%	xERA	Ctl	Dom	Cmd	hr/9	BPV
2019		Did not pich																	

Slender, athletic RHP who was productive two-year starter in Big Ten. Chance for three solid average pitches as back-end SP with low-90s FB with sinking arm-side action. Likes to use CU and will repeat arm speed well; SL will flash late two-plane break. May not be a big-time bat misser, but command improved in college and will have good ratios.

Kay,Anthony

SP | **Toronto** | EXP MLB DEBUT: 2019 | H/W: 6-0 218 | FUT: #3 starter | **8C**

Thrws L Age 25
2016 (1) Connecticut

Velo	Pitch	Grade
92-95	FB	+++
75-79	CB	++++
80-85	CU	+++

Year	Lev	Team	W	L	Sv	IP	K	ERA	WHIP	BF/G	OBA	H%	S%	xERA	Ctl	Dom	Cmd	hr/9	BPV
2018	A+	St. Lucie	3	7	0	53	45	3.90	1.47	22.8	254	32	71	3.56	4.6	7.6	1.7	0.2	32
2019	AA	Binghamton	7	3	0	66	70	1.50	0.92	20.6	169	24	85	1.24	3.1	9.5	3.0	0.3	105
2019	AAA	Syracuse	1	3	0	31	26	6.66	1.64	19.8	313	35	64	6.61	3.2	7.5	2.4	2.0	67
2019	AAA	Buffalo	2	2	0	36	39	2.50	1.53	22.4	245	32	87	4.12	5.5	9.8	1.8	0.8	45
2019	MLB	Toronto	1	0	0	14	13	5.79	1.43	19.8	275	36	55	3.59	3.2	8.4	2.6	0.0	82

Aggressive SP with solid three-pitch mix who reached MLB in breakout season. Has feel for changing speeds and has the vicious break in CB to rack up Ks. All pitches tumble downward, particularly CU with average command. When he throws strikes, he's very good. When command falls short, he can be hit hard. Should have mid-rotation SP future.

Keller,Mitch

SP | **Pittsburgh** | EXP MLB DEBUT: 2019 | H/W: 6-2 210 | FUT: #2 starter | **9C**

Thrws R Age 24
2014 (2) HS (IA)

Velo	Pitch	Grade
93-98	FB	++++
81-83	CB	++++
85-89	CU	+++

Year	Lev	Team	W	L	Sv	IP	K	ERA	WHIP	BF/G	OBA	H%	S%	xERA	Ctl	Dom	Cmd	hr/9	BPV
2018	A+	Bradenton	0	0	0	4	2	2.25	2.00	19.3	383	43	88	6.87	2.3	4.5	2.0	0.0	38
2018	AA	Altoona	9	2	0	86	76	2.72	1.12	24.2	209	26	79	2.63	3.3	8.0	2.4	0.7	71
2018	AAA	Indianapolis	3	2	0	52	57	4.84	1.55	22.8	287	38	68	4.54	3.8	9.8	2.6	0.5	93
2019	AAA	Indianapolis	7	5	0	103	123	3.58	1.25	22.1	244	34	73	3.43	3.1	10.7	3.5	0.8	129
2019	MLB	Pittsburgh	1	5	0	48	65	7.13	1.83	20.3	347	48	61	6.77	3.0	12.2	4.1	1.1	156

Still considered prospect despite 11 GS with PIT. 4th in IL in K and misses bats due to power stuff. Both FB and CB are out pitches, though will need to pitch ahead in count for sustained success. Loses command when arm slot varies and needs to throw breaking ball for strikes. Pitches have good life and could still realize potential as top starter.

Kelly,Antoine

SP | **Milwaukee** | EXP MLB DEBUT: 2023 | H/W: 6-6 205 | FUT: Closer | **9E**

Thrws L Age 20
2019 (2) Wabash Valley CC

Velo	Pitch	Grade
95-97	FB	++++
84-86	SL	++
	CU	++

Year	Lev	Team	W	L	Sv	IP	K	ERA	WHIP	BF/G	OBA	H%	S%	xERA	Ctl	Dom	Cmd	hr/9	BPV
2019	A	Wisconsin	0	1	0	3	4	18.00	3.00	17.5	371	40	43	14.74	12.0	12.0	1.0	6.0	-90
2019	Rk	AZL BrewersB	0	0	0	28	41	1.28	0.92	11.7	209	35	85	1.40	1.6	13.1	8.2	0.0	210

Tall, projectable LH who exemplifies thrower rather than pitcher at present. Will reach back for 99 mph on fastball and sit mid-90s with ease from crossfire delivery. Secondary offerings remain raw but displays good control of SL and CU. Chance to add more mass for added velo. Posted near 40% K-rate in AZL debut. An arm one can dream on.

Kelly,Levi — SP — Arizona
EXP MLB DEBUT: 2022 | H/W: 6-4 205 | FUT: #3 starter | 8D
Thrws R · Age 20 · 2018 (8) HS (FL)

90-94 FB +++	
80-82 SL ++++	
CU +++	

Year	Lev	Team	W	L	Sv	IP	K	ERA	WHIP	BF/G	OBA	H%	S%	xERA	Ctl	Dom	Cmd	hr/9	BPV
2018	Rk	AZL DBacks	0	0	0	6	6	0.00	0.83	5.5	151	22	100	0.57	3.0	9.0	3.0	0.0	99
2019	A	Kane County	5	1	0	100	126	2.16	1.11	17.9	203	30	81	2.16	3.5	11.3	3.2	0.4	127

Hard-throwing RHP who had an exceptional year in full-season MWL debut. Relies primarily on FB-SL combo to miss bats at a healthy rate, the former touching 96-97 mph and the latter owning sharp, two-plane action. CU a work in progress. Simplified his delivery and projects to have average command. Strong, ideal build with #3/4 SP upside.

Kilome,Franklyn — SP — New York (N)
EXP MLB DEBUT: 2020 | H/W: 6-6 175 | FUT: Setup reliever | 7D
Thrws R · Age 24 · 2013 FA (DR)

92-96 FB +++	
82-86 SL +++	
82-85 CU ++	

Year	Lev	Team	W	L	Sv	IP	K	ERA	WHIP	BF/G	OBA	H%	S%	xERA	Ctl	Dom	Cmd	hr/9	BPV
2017	A+	Clearwater	6	4	0	97	83	2.60	1.37	21.4	260	32	82	3.67	3.4	7.7	2.2	0.5	64
2017	AA	Reading	1	3	0	29	20	3.70	1.37	24.5	233	27	74	3.47	4.6	6.2	1.3	0.6	4
2018	AA	Reading	4	6	0	102	83	4.24	1.44	22.9	250	30	71	3.87	4.5	7.3	1.6	0.6	28
2018	AA	Binghamton	4	9	0	140	125	4.18	1.34	22.4	243	30	69	3.55	3.9	8.0	2.0	0.6	57
2019		Did not pitch - injury																	

Big body, 3/4s RHP missed all of 2019 recovering from Tommy John surgery. A SP in the minors, quirky arm action has caused issues developing off-speed stuff and likely moves profile to RP. Easy velocity with plus FB; commands pitch well. SL is best secondary and lacks consistency. CU is a distant 3rd pitch.

King,John — SP — Texas
EXP MLB DEBUT: 2022 | H/W: 6-2 215 | FUT: #5 SP/swingman | 7C
Thrws L · Age 25 · 2017 (10) Houston

91-94 FB +++	
SL ++	
CB ++	
CU ++	

Year	Lev	Team	W	L	Sv	IP	K	ERA	WHIP	BF/G	OBA	H%	S%	xERA	Ctl	Dom	Cmd	hr/9	BPV
2018	Rk	AZL Rangers	0	0	0	1	1	7.50	3.33	7.4	470	56	75	12.19	7.5	7.5	1.0	0.0	-50
2018	A-	Spokane	0	0	0	3	2	6.00	1.67	13.5	371	44	60	5.80	0.0	6.0		0.0	126
2019	A	Hickory	1	2	0	26	29	3.45	1.26	21.3	296	40	72	3.79	0.7	10.0	14.5	0.3	179
2019	A+	Down East	2	4	0	71	62	2.03	0.99	19.3	228	28	82	2.32	1.4	7.9	5.6	0.5	122

Groundball machine with pinpoint control, receives accolades for competitiveness and work ethic after coming back from Tommy John surgery as a senior-sign. Four-pitch mix, none of secondaries average yet, but gets outs and fared well in first full-season assignments. Will continue to be tested up the ladder.

King,Michael — SP — New York (A)
EXP MLB DEBUT: 2019 | H/W: 6-3 210 | FUT: #4 starter | 8D
Thrws R · Age 24 · 2016 (12) Boston College

90-93 FB ++++	
82-84 SL +++	
81-83 CB +++	
84-86 CU +++	

Year	Lev	Team	W	L	Sv	IP	K	ERA	WHIP	BF/G	OBA	H%	S%	xERA	Ctl	Dom	Cmd	hr/9	BPV
2019	Rk	GCL YankeesW	0	0	0	5	8	5.19	0.96	6.6	170	31	40	1.05	3.5	13.8	4.0	0.0	174
2019	A-	Staten Island	0	0	0	4	0	0.00	1.00	15.3	262	26	100	2.41	0.0	0.0		0.0	18
2019	AA	Trenton	0	1	0	12	8	10.33	1.80	18.8	368	42	38	6.76	1.5	5.9	4.0	0.7	84
2019	AAA	Scranton/WB	3	1	0	23	28	4.27	1.12	22.9	234	31	65	3.33	2.3	10.9	4.7	1.2	151
2019	MLB	NY Yankees	0	0	0	2	1	0.00	1.00	7.6	262	30	100	2.36	0.0	4.5		0.0	99

High 3/4s sinker ball pitcher made surprise September debut in MLB. On-line delivery with a long arm-circle, relying on lower half for strength. Sits 90-93 MPH with bowling ball 2-seam FB, suffocating loft. SL & CB blend into each other. SL is slurvy with solid 2-plane break. CU projects with solid separation off FB.

Kirby,George — SP — Seattle
EXP MLB DEBUT: 2021 | H/W: 6-4 201 | FUT: #3 starter | 8D
Thrws R · Age 22 · 2019 (1) Elon

90-94 FB ++++	
82-85 SL +++	
77-79 CB +++	
83-85 CU +++	

Year	Lev	Team	W	L	Sv	IP	K	ERA	WHIP	BF/G	OBA	H%	S%	xERA	Ctl	Dom	Cmd	hr/9	BPV
2019	NCAA	Elon	8	2	0	88	107	2.76	0.90	23.4	227	33	68	1.87	0.6	10.9	17.8	0.3	198
2019	A-	Everett	0	0	0	23	25	2.35	1.04	9.9	270	37	78	2.90	0.0	9.8		0.4	194

Polished-high floor RHP with ceiling left. Repeatable, athletic 3/4s crossfire delivery. Creates natural downward plane from slot. Has advanced command of low-90s FB with solid late run. Breaking pitches lack consistency and blend into each other. The SL looks the better of the two. Above-average CU.

Kloffenstein,Adam — SP — Toronto
EXP MLB DEBUT: 2023 | H/W: 6-5 243 | FUT: #2 starter | 8D
Thrws R · Age 19 · 2018 (3) HS (TX)

91-95 FB ++++	
81-84 SL +++	
75-79 CB +++	
81-84 CU ++	

Year	Lev	Team	W	L	Sv	IP	K	ERA	WHIP	BF/G	OBA	H%	S%	xERA	Ctl	Dom	Cmd	hr/9	BPV
2019	A-	Vancouver	4	4	0	64	64	2.25	1.09	19.3	206	27	82	2.37	3.2	9.0	2.8	0.6	93

Large, durable SP who finished 2nd in NWL in ERA. Can be lethal with 3 above-average-to-plus offerings. Repeats delivery well for age and pitches with confidence. Lots of development time left, but gets groundballs and Ks. Could add velocity which would add effectiveness to sinking FB. Has advanced feel for spin and can cut FB.

Knight,Blaine — SP — Baltimore
EXP MLB DEBUT: 2022 | H/W: 6-3 165 | FUT: Setup reliever | 7E
Thrws R · Age 23 · 2018 (3) Arkansas

91-93 FB ++++	
83-84 SL ++	
74-77 CB +++	
81-84 CU ++	

Year	Lev	Team	W	L	Sv	IP	K	ERA	WHIP	BF/G	OBA	H%	S%	xERA	Ctl	Dom	Cmd	hr/9	BPV
2018	NCAA	Arkansas	14	0	0	112	102	2.81	1.08	23.0	233	27	83	3.50	2.0	8.2	4.1	1.4	111
2018	A-	Aberdeen	0	1	0	10	8	2.67	1.58	11.1	313	37	87	5.41	2.7	7.1	2.7	0.9	74
2019	A+	Frederick	1	12	0	83	56	6.17	1.54	20.1	275	31	60	4.90	4.2	6.1	1.4	1.1	13
2019	A	Delmarva	3	0	0	26	33	0.69	0.57	17.8	130	20	93		1.4	11.3	8.3	0.3	185

Tall, thin 3/4s RHP was dismal in High-A last season. Crossfire, upright delivery doesn't get appropriate extension and isn't consistent. 4-pitch pitcher who needs to corral movement of 2-seam fastball with natural downward plane and moderate arm-side run. Best secondary is a slurvy CB, which would improve with better depth. SL is workable.

Kochanowicz,Jack — SP — Los Angeles (A)
EXP MLB DEBUT: 2023 | H/W: 6-6 220 | FUT: #3 starter | 8D
Thrws R · Age 19 · 2019 (3) HS (PA)

89-93 FB +++	
75-78 CB +++	
CU +++	

Year	Lev	Team	W	L	Sv	IP	K	ERA	WHIP	BF/G	OBA	H%	S%	xERA	Ctl	Dom	Cmd	hr/9	BPV
2019		Did not pitch																	

Long-limbed, projectable RH has yet to make his debut. Chance for three plus pitches at maturity, currently sporting a low-90s FB that has good angle to the plate. Ability to spin two-plane CB that could be legit out pitch. CU feel is advanced for his age, but will need more reps. Will need to add more strength, but could be a popup arm next year.

Kopech,Michael — SP — Chicago (A)
EXP MLB DEBUT: 2018 | H/W: 6-3 205 | FUT: #1 starter | 9C
Thrws R · Age 23 · 2014 (1) HS (TX)

96-99 FB +++++	
87-90 SL ++++	
81-83 CB ++	
88-91 CU +++	

Year	Lev	Team	W	L	Sv	IP	K	ERA	WHIP	BF/G	OBA	H%	S%	xERA	Ctl	Dom	Cmd	hr/9	BPV
2016	A+	Salem	4	1	0	52	82	2.25	1.04	18.2	146	27	77	1.14	5.0	14.2	2.8	0.2	138
2017	AA	Birmingham	8	7	0	119	155	2.87	1.15	21.5	187	28	76	2.15	4.5	11.7	2.6	0.5	106
2017	AAA	Charlotte	1	1	0	15	17	3.00	1.33	20.8	262	37	75	3.14	3.0	10.2	3.4	0.0	121
2018	AAA	Charlotte	7	7	0	126	170	3.71	1.28	21.5	221	33	72	3.06	4.3	12.1	2.8	0.6	121
2018	MLB	Chi White Sox	1	1	0	14	15	5.11	1.56	15.4	335	39	78	7.23	1.3	9.6	7.5	2.6	156

Hard-throwing, athletic 3/4 RHP missed 2019 recovering from Tommy John surgery. Made return during Instructional League and dominant velocity was in tact. High-octane FB has late run. 80-grade pitch prior to TJS. SL also double-plus with tight, 2-plane movement. Fading CU continues to improve. CB an eye-level-changing pitch.

Kowar,Jackson — SP — Kansas City
EXP MLB DEBUT: 2021 | H/W: 6-5 180 | FUT: #3 starter | 8B
Thrws R · Age 23 · 2018 (1) Florida

93-95 FB ++++	
76-78 CB +++	
83-85 CU ++++	

Year	Lev	Team	W	L	Sv	IP	K	ERA	WHIP	BF/G	OBA	H%	S%	xERA	Ctl	Dom	Cmd	hr/9	BPV
2018	NCAA	Florida	10	5	0	112	115	3.05	1.28	25.6	242	31	79	3.52	3.5	9.2	2.7	0.8	91
2018	A	Lexington	0	1	0	26	22	3.45	1.19	11.6	205	25	72	2.73	4.1	7.6	1.8	0.7	43
2018	AA	NW Arkansas	2	7	0	74	78	3.52	1.27	23.0	259	33	76	3.86	2.6	9.5	3.7	1.0	120
2019	A+	Wilmington	5	3	0	74	66	3.53	1.22	23.0	246	31	71	3.11	2.7	8.0	3.0	0.5	90

Long, lean 3/4s RHP made significant strides with breaking pitch. Easy, repeatable crossfire delivery creating natural downward plane, playing up FB. Sits low-to-mid 90s, touching 97. Struggles commanding to glove-side. Double-plus CU is best pitch with excellent late drop/fade. MPH separation is unreal off FB. Flashed quality CB with tight spin.

Kranick,Max — SP — Pittsburgh
EXP MLB DEBUT: 2021 | H/W: 6-3 175 | FUT: #4 starter | 7C
Thrws R · Age 22 · 2016 (11) HS (PA)

90-95 FB +++	
81-84 SL ++	
81-85 CU +++	

Year	Lev	Team	W	L	Sv	IP	K	ERA	WHIP	BF/G	OBA	H%	S%	xERA	Ctl	Dom	Cmd	hr/9	BPV
2016	Rk	GCL Pirates	1	2	0	33	21	2.45	1.06	14.3	249	29	76	2.58	1.1	5.7	5.3	0.3	91
2017	Rk	GCL Pirates	0	0	0	9	11	0.00	1.31	16.8	259	32	100	3.08	3.0	6.6	2.3	0.0	58
2017	Rk	Bristol	1	0	0	11	9	2.41	1.07	21.8	240	28	82	2.98	1.6	7.2	4.5	0.8	105
2018	A	West Virginia	4	5	1	78	77	3.81	1.15	18.2	247	31	69	3.26	2.1	8.9	4.3	0.8	121
2019	A+	Bradenton	6	7	0	109	78	3.79	1.19	21.9	245	28	71	3.45	2.5	6.4	2.6	0.9	67

Underrated SP who ended season early due to innings limit. K rate fell. but focus on command and developing CU. Needs to develop fringy breaking ball and will mix in a power slurve at times. Has clean, quick delivery that makes FB look quicker. Can spot it low in zone or blow it by upstairs. CU made great strides and is true weapon against LHH.

Kremer,Dean

SP | **Baltimore** | EXP MLB DEBUT: 2020 | H/W: 6-3 180 | FUT: #4 starter | **7B**

Thrws R Age 24
2016 (14) UNLV

Velo	Pitch	Grade
89-93	FB	+++
83-86	SL	+++
72-74	CB	+++
84	CU	++

Year	Lev	Team	W	L	Sv	IP	K	ERA	WHIP	BF/G	OBA	H%	S%	xERA	Ctl	Dom	Cmd	hr/9	BPV
2018	AA	Tulsa	1	0	0	7	11	0.00	0.86	25.7	132	26	100	0.39	3.9	14.1	3.7	0.0	168
2018	AA	Bowie	4	2	0	45	53	2.59	1.22	22.8	230	32	81	3.00	3.4	10.6	3.1	0.6	117
2019	A+	Frederick	0	0	0	9	14	0.00	1.09	18.0	188	33	100	1.56	3.9	13.7	3.5	0.0	159
2019	AA	Bowie	9	4	0	84	87	2.99	1.24	22.8	240	30	80	3.52	3.1	9.3	3.0	1.0	102
2019	AAA	Norfolk	0	2	0	19	21	8.95	1.78	22.0	358	46	47	6.67	1.9	9.9	5.3	0.9	145

High, 3/4s RHP with solid presence and 5 fringe-average-or-better offerings. Repeatable, easy delivery achieves above-average extension, which helps FB play up. 4-seam FB has late ride. Complements well with CT to LHH. 12-to-6 CB is best secondary with above-average potential. SL is sweepy and CU is decent offering.

Kuhnel,Joel

RP | **Cincinnati** | EXP MLB DEBUT: 2019 | H/W: 6-5 260 | FUT: Middle reliever | **6C**

Thrws R Age 25
2016 (11) Texas-Arlington

Velo	Pitch	Grade
94-97	FB	++++
85-87	SL	+++
89-90	CU	+

Year	Lev	Team	W	L	Sv	IP	K	ERA	WHIP	BF/G	OBA	H%	S%	xERA	Ctl	Dom	Cmd	hr/9	BPV
2017	A	Dayton	2	4	11	64	54	4.36	1.38	5.6	302	36	70	4.65	1.4	7.6	5.4	0.8	117
2018	A+	Daytona	1	4	17	53	56	3.05	1.22	4.9	265	36	75	3.24	1.9	9.5	5.1	0.3	139
2019	AA	Chattanooga	3	2	10	35	30	2.30	0.97	5.3	208	23	86	2.75	2.0	7.7	3.8	1.3	101
2019	AAA	Louisville	2	1	4	18	20	2.00	1.17	4.5	204	28	85	2.46	4.0	10.0	2.5	0.5	90
2019	MLB	Cincinnati	1	0	0	9	9	4.89	1.41	3.5	236	29	67	3.93	4.9	8.8	1.8	1.0	44

Hard-throwing RP accelerated through upper divisions to make MLB debut. Relies heavily on mixing FB variations. 2-seam FB is a sinking FB, which is more of a contact initiator compared to his 4-seam FB, with plus late-riding action. Mixes SL about 40% of the time. It's an above-average pitch. Will flash CU to keep LHH honest.

Lakins,Travis

RP | **Boston** | EXP MLB DEBUT: 2019 | H/W: 6-1 180 | FUT: Setup reliever | **6B**

Thrws R Age 25
2015 (6) Ohio State

Velo	Pitch	Grade
91-96	FB	+++
87-89	CT	++++
78-82	CB	+++
84-86	CU	++

Year	Lev	Team	W	L	Sv	IP	K	ERA	WHIP	BF/G	OBA	H%	S%	xERA	Ctl	Dom	Cmd	hr/9	BPV
2017	AA	Portland	0	4	0	30		6.28	1.83	17.5	286	33	64	5.34	6.3	5.7	0.9	0.6	-49
2018	AA	Portland	2	2	1	38	42	2.61	1.05	5.7	201	27	78	2.34	3.1	9.9	3.2	0.7	114
2018	AAA	Pawtucket	1	0	2	16	15	1.68	0.99	6.1	195	27	81	1.46	2.8	8.4	3.0	0.0	93
2019	AAA	Pawtucket	3	4	6	45	42	4.60	1.53	4.9	266	33	71	4.48	4.6	8.4	1.8	0.8	45
2019	MLB	Boston	0	1	0	23	18	3.90	1.43	6.1	261	32	72	3.77	3.9	7.0	1.8	0.4	39

Converted to RP in 2018, has bounced back and forth between AAA and BOS. Durable arm with plus CT that registers Ks against hitters from both sides. Owns athletic delivery that he repeats well. FB can be too straight while fading CU lacks consistency in depth. CB has moments of plus action, though CT remains his go-to pitch.

Lambert,Jimmy

SP | **Chicago (A)** | EXP MLB DEBUT: 2021 | H/W: 6-2 190 | FUT: #4 starter | **7C**

Thrws R Age 25
2016 (5) Fresno St

Velo	Pitch	Grade
91-94	FB	+++
82-84	SL	++
74-76	CB	+++
80-84	CU	+++

Year	Lev	Team	W	L	Sv	IP	K	ERA	WHIP	BF/G	OBA	H%	S%	xERA	Ctl	Dom	Cmd	hr/9	BPV
2017	A	Kannapolis	7	2	0	74	43	2.19	1.19	24.7	270	31	80	3.05	1.3	5.2	3.9	0.1	76
2017	A+	Winston-Salem	5	4	0	76	59	5.45	1.51	23.5	286	33	66	5.09	3.4	7.0	2.0	1.2	51
2018	A+	Winston-Salem	5	7	0	70	80	3.97	1.11	21.2	224	31	64	2.69	2.7	10.3	3.8	0.6	130
2018	AA	Birmingham	3	1	0	25	30	2.88	1.04	19.3	221	31	75	2.54	2.2	10.8	5.0	0.7	154
2019	AA	Birmingham	3	4	0	59	70	4.57	1.51	23.2	271	35	76	5.28	4.1	10.7	2.6	1.7	99

Four-pitch, strike-throwing RHP struggled with forearm soreness last year, resulting in June Tommy John surgery. Remade self prior to 2018 campaign. Added bulk, which improved velocity. Commands 4-seam FB. Sequences well off of pitch with 11-to-5 CB and fading CU. SL has become more like a CT and doesn't rely on it often. Likely back-end SP.

Lange,Alex

SP | **Detroit** | EXP MLB DEBUT: 2020 | H/W: 6-3 197 | FUT: #4 starter | **7B**

Thrws R Age 24
2017 (1) Louisiana St

Velo	Pitch	Grade
91-94	FB	+++
81-84	CB	+++
82-85	CU	++

Year	Lev	Team	W	L	Sv	IP	K	ERA	WHIP	BF/G	OBA	H%	S%	xERA	Ctl	Dom	Cmd	hr/9	BPV
2017	A-	Eugene	0	1	0	9	13	4.95	1.32	9.4	260	42	58	3.05	3.0	12.9	4.3	0.0	169
2018	A+	Myrtle Beach	6	8	0	120	101	3.75	1.18	20.9	235	29	68	2.86	2.8	7.6	2.7	0.4	77
2019	A+	Myrtle Beach	1	9	0	47	51	7.44	1.78	19.7	303	40	56	5.60	5.0	9.7	2.0	0.8	59
2019	AA	Tennessee	2	3	0	39	28	3.92	1.41	23.6	247	28	75	4.04	4.4	6.5	1.5	0.9	16
2019	AA	Erie	2	1	0	15	15	3.55	1.38	7.1	233	32	71	2.89	4.7	8.9	1.9	0.0	50

Sturdy, confident mid-rotation innings-eater. Low-90s fastball locates well to both sides. Best offering is a power curve that complements an improving changeup. Pounds the zone, despite low velocity. Location is there, but lack of bite for a starter is a concern.

Lawrence,Justin

RP | **Colorado** | EXP MLB DEBUT: 2020 | H/W: 6-3 218 | FUT: Closer | **9E**

Thrws R Age 25
2015 (12) Daytona JC

Velo	Pitch	Grade
95-99	FB	+++++
84-86	SL	+++
87-91	SP	++

Year	Lev	Team	W	L	Sv	IP	K	ERA	WHIP	BF/G	OBA	H%	S%	xERA	Ctl	Dom	Cmd	hr/9	BPV
2016	A	Asheville	2	5	0	36	23	7.23	1.72	6.3	320	36	57	5.97	3.5	5.7	1.6	1.0	27
2017	A	Asheville	0	2	6	16	20	1.68	0.87	3.7	180	26	85	1.48	2.2	11.2	5.0	0.6	159
2018	A+	Lancaster	0	2	11	54	62	2.66	1.16	3.9	191	27	77	2.14	4.5	10.3	2.3	0.3	82
2019	AA	Hartford	0	4	0	26	26	8.93	2.10	4.3	321	42	54	6.30	6.9	8.9	1.3	0.3	-7
2019	AAA	Albuquerque	1	1	0	10	6	8.91	2.08	6.2	296	29	61	8.08	8.0	5.3	0.7	2.7	-102

High-octane sidearm RH with elite velocity and some deception, but control backed up on him in 2019. FB will touch 99 mph with bowling-ball action required for ground balls and whiffs. Feel for SL and SP remains raw. Has elite arm speed but exceptionally long arm action in back limits his ability to spot his pitches and repeat consistently.

Lawson,Reggie

SP | **San Diego** | EXP MLB DEBUT: 2020 | H/W: 6-4 205 | FUT: #4 starter | **7B**

Thrws R Age 22
2016 (2) HS (CA)

Velo	Pitch	Grade
92-95	FB	+++
74-78	CB	++++
85-88	CU	+++

Year	Lev	Team	W	L	Sv	IP	K	ERA	WHIP	BF/G	OBA	H%	S%	xERA	Ctl	Dom	Cmd	hr/9	BPV
2016	Rk	AZL Padres	0	0	0	8	7	8.78	1.83	7.6	342	43	47	5.65	3.3	7.7	2.3	0.0	67
2017	A	Fort Wayne	4	6	0	73	89	5.30	1.37	18.0	240	33	62	3.86	4.3	11.0	2.5	1.0	99
2018	A+	Lake Elsinore	8	5	0	117	117	4.69	1.55	21.3	283	36	71	4.78	3.9	9.0	2.3	0.8	74
2019	AA	Amarillo	3	1	0	27	36	5.29	1.51	19.6	267	37	68	4.89	4.3	11.9	2.8	1.3	116

Athletic RHP who opened eyes in short AFL stint after missing bulk of 2019 with injuries. Short, powerful arm action produces 93-95 mph FB (t96) and flashes of plus CB that can miss bats vs. L/R. Has made strides with CU, which should be a usable pitch in MLB. Looked better this fall with control, and has Dom upside, but command will require work.

Lewis,Jimmy

SP | **Los Angeles (N)** | EXP MLB DEBUT: 2024 | H/W: 6-6 200 | FUT: #3 starter | **8D**

Thrws R Age 19
2019 (2) FA (TX)

Velo	Pitch	Grade
91-95	FB	++++
75-78	CB	+++
	CU	+

Year	Lev	Team	W	L	Sv	IP	K	ERA	WHIP	BF/G	OBA	H%	S%	xERA	Ctl	Dom	Cmd	hr/9	BPV
2019		Did not pitch																	

Projectable HS RHP signed an over-slot deal. FB sits at 91-95 mph and should add more as he fills out his tall frame. Shows an early ability to spin a breaking ball and CB has plus potential. Some feel for a CU, but didn't need it much in HS. Attacks hitters from a high 3/4 arm slot that results in downhill action/sink and CB has nice 11-to-5 action.

Liberatore,Matthew

SP | **St. Louis** | EXP MLB DEBUT: 2022 | H/W: 6-5 200 | FUT: #3 starter | **8C**

Thrws L Age 20
2018 (1) HS (AZ)

Velo	Pitch	Grade
92-94	FB	++++
76-79	CB	++++
80-82	SL	++
84-87	CU	+++

Year	Lev	Team	W	L	Sv	IP	K	ERA	WHIP	BF/G	OBA	H%	S%	xERA	Ctl	Dom	Cmd	hr/9	BPV
2018	Rk	GCL Rays	1	2	0	27	32	0.99	0.99	13.0	173	26	89	1.19	3.6	10.6	2.9	0.0	110
2018	Rk	Princeton	1	0	0	5	5	3.60	1.40	21.1	262	35	71	3.32	3.6	9.0	2.5	0.0	83
2019	A	Bowling Green	6	2	0	78	76	3.11	1.29	20.1	241	32	75	3.00	3.6	8.8	2.5	0.2	79

Polished, athletic LHP had successful full-season debut. Improved staying tight with high 3/4s delivery. 4-pitch pitcher who uses height to create downward plane on his pitches. FB sits 92-94 with slight run and little margin for error. 1-to-7 CB is his best pitch and projects to be a plus. CU is also future MLB pitch. SL lags behind. Traded from TAM to STL in January.

Linares,Resly

SP | **Tampa Bay** | EXP MLB DEBUT: 2022 | H/W: 6-2 170 | FUT: #5 SP/swingman | **7E**

Thrws L Age 22
2014 FA (DR)

Velo	Pitch	Grade
87-91	FB	++
73-77	CB	+++
79-82	CU	+++

Year	Lev	Team	W	L	Sv	IP	K	ERA	WHIP	BF/G	OBA	H%	S%	xERA	Ctl	Dom	Cmd	hr/9	BPV
2016	Rk	Princeton	2	3	0	32	30	5.34	1.50	17.3	307	36	69	5.83	2.3	8.4	3.8	1.7	109
2017	A-	Hudson Valley	3	3	0	61	60	2.36	0.97	17.8	173	23	75	1.42	3.4	8.8	2.6	0.3	86
2018	A	Bowling Green	7	3	0	84	97	3.21	1.12	19.5	225	31	73	2.72	2.7	10.4	3.9	0.6	133
2019	A+	Charlotte	0	0	0	4	2	6.43	2.86	11.9	336	38	75	8.18	12.9	4.3	0.3	0.0	-252

Paper-thin pitchability LHP missed most of 2019 with a left forearm strain. Throws from 3/4s to low 3/4s arm slot with deceptive arm angles. 2-seam FB has solid arm-side run with it increasing at his lower slot. Throws slurve, which is like a slow variation of a CB/SL hybrid. Maintains arm speed with CU. It has late fading action.

Lindow,Ethan

SP | **Philadelphia** | EXP MLB DEBUT: 2022 | H/W: 6-3 180 | FUT: #4 starter | **7C**

Thrws L Age 21
2017 (5) HS (GA)

Velo	Pitch	Grade
88-90	FB	+++
70-71	CB	+++
83-85	CT	++
79-81	CU	++

Year	Lev	Team	W	L	Sv	IP	K	ERA	WHIP	BF/G	OBA	H%	S%	xERA	Ctl	Dom	Cmd	hr/9	BPV
2017	Rk	GCL Phillies	2	2	0	27	34	4.63	1.40	14.3	253	36	67	3.80	4.0	11.3	2.8	0.7	113
2018	A-	Williamsport	3	2	0	70	63	2.19	1.10	21.1	227	29	80	2.36	2.4	8.1	3.3	0.3	98
2019	A+	Clearwater	0	2	0	16	16	1.69	1.19	21.4	274	37	84	2.95	1.1	9.0	8.0	0.0	150
2019	A	Lakewood	5	2	2	94	103	2.68	0.99	15.6	216	30	73	2.04	1.9	9.8	5.2	0.4	144

Lanky strike-throwing LHP won the Phillies minor league pitcher of the year award with a 2.52 ERA across two A-ball levels at age 20. A control/command guy, can throw each of FB, CB, CT and CU in the zone and mixes/matches to create weak contact. Needs precision to get by, as FB currently barely scrapes 90. Quintessential 'crafty lefty'.

Little,Brendon — SP — Chicago (N)
EXP MLB DEBUT: 2021 | H/W: 6-1 195 | FUT: Middle reliever | 6B

Thrws L Age 23
2017 (1) State Coll of FL

Velo	Pitch	Grade
89-92	FB	++
75-77	CB	+++
80-83	CU	++

Year	Lev	Team	W	L	Sv	IP	K	ERA	WHIP	BF/G	OBA	H%	S%	xERA	Ctl	Dom	Cmd	hr/9	BPV
2017	A-	Eugene	0	2	0	16	12	9.50	1.86	12.6	316	36	46	6.37	5.0	6.7	1.3	1.1	3
2018	A	South Bend	5	11	0	101	90	5.16	1.47	19.7	271	33	65	4.32	3.8	8.0	2.1	0.7	59
2019	Rk	AZL Cubs	0	0	0	7	9	3.80	1.13	14.0	167	15	83	3.83	5.1	11.4	2.3	2.5	86
2019	A	South Bend	0	1	0	28	25	1.92	1.10	18.4	185	25	81	1.63	4.2	8.0	1.9	0.0	50
2019	A+	Myrtle Beach	2	1	0	19	23	6.09	1.56	21.0	279	38	61	4.84	4.2	10.8	2.6	0.9	98

First-round pick from 2017 missed some time last spring due to lat injury; pitched at three levels after. Best pitch is an above-average CB that has 1-to-7 shape and late break when it's on. Velo has backed up on him as a pro, now living around 89-92 mph. CU remains raw. Medium frame with some strength. Will need to throw more strikes to remain SP.

Llovera,Mauricio — SP — Philadelphia
EXP MLB DEBUT: 2020 | H/W: 5-11 200 | FUT: Setup reliever | 8C

Thrws R Age 23
2015 FA (VZ)

Velo	Pitch	Grade
92-95	FB	++++
82-84	SL	+++
84-86	SP	+++

Year	Lev	Team	W	L	Sv	IP	K	ERA	WHIP	BF/G	OBA	H%	S%	xERA	Ctl	Dom	Cmd	hr/9	BPV
2016	Rk	GCL Phillies	7	1	0	53	56	1.87	0.96	18.2	207	29	78	1.51	2.0	9.5	4.7	0.0	134
2017	A	Lakewood	2	4	0	86	94	3.35	1.33	11.9	250	35	73	3.17	3.5	9.8	2.8	0.2	102
2018	A+	Clearwater	8	7	0	121	137	3.72	1.11	20.7	227	30	70	3.09	2.5	10.2	4.0	1.0	133
2019	AA	Reading	3	4	0	65	72	4.56	1.35	19.4	246	32	68	3.89	3.9	10.0	2.6	1.0	93

Short pitcher with strong lower half missed two months with elbow soreness. But comfortably sits mid-90s with FB that can touch 98. SL also flashes plus and had success adding a splitter as well. The three-pitch mix is good enough to start, though many feel he's trending towards an impact relief role. A worthy follow.

Locey,Tony — RP — St. Louis
EXP MLB DEBUT: 2022 | H/W: 6-3 239 | FUT: Setup reliever | 6C

Thrws R Age 21
2019 (3) Georgia

Velo	Pitch	Grade
92-95	FB	++++
83-85	SL	+++
	CB	++
	CU	++

Year	Lev	Team	W	L	Sv	IP	K	ERA	WHIP	BF/G	OBA	H%	S%	xERA	Ctl	Dom	Cmd	hr/9	BPV
2019	A	Peoria	1	2	0	15	28	6.00	1.67	6.7	262	49	63	4.48	6.0	16.8	2.8	0.6	158
2019	Rk	GCL Cardinals	0	0	0	2	3	0.00	1.50	4.3	151	27	100	2.20	9.0	13.5	1.5	0.0	18

Thick, big-bodied hurler struggled with command in his pro debut. FB sits at 92-95, topping out at 98 mph in relief. Mid-80 power SL flashes plus at times, but loses shape and needs to be thrown for strikes. Below average CU and CB make starting unlikely, but has the stuff and mentality to be an effective late inning reliever.

Lockett,Walker — SP — New York (N)
EXP MLB DEBUT: 2018 | H/W: 6-5 225 | FUT: Middle reliever | 6C

Thrws R Age 25
2012 (4) HS (FL)

Velo	Pitch	Grade
91-94	FB	++
78-81	CB	+++
85-87	CU	+++

Year	Lev	Team	W	L	Sv	IP	K	ERA	WHIP	BF/G	OBA	H%	S%	xERA	Ctl	Dom	Cmd	hr/9	BPV
2018	AAA	El Paso	5	9	0	133	118	4.73	1.34	24.1	279	33	67	4.49	2.2	8.0	3.6	1.1	101
2018	MLB	San Diego	0	3	0	15	12	9.60	2.13	18.6	342	37	57	8.68	6.0	7.2	1.2	2.4	-14
2019	A+	St. Lucie	1	0	0	7	6	5.14	1.14	13.9	288	34	57	4.28	0.0	7.7		1.3	157
2019	AAA	Syracuse	3	3	0	59	39	3.66	1.46	22.9	311	35	77	4.94	1.7	5.9	3.5	0.8	80
2019	MLB	NY Mets	1	1	0	22	16	8.51	1.76	11.3	345	37	55	7.83	2.4	6.5	2.7	2.4	69

Athletic, high 3/4s RHP filled depth role for MLB club. Repeats cross-fire delivery well. FB hit hard in MLB action. It lacks movement and has minimal shape without much velocity. Spins off a solid CB, which could play up in RP role. CU has late fading action and achieves some separation off FB. Could work as 3-pitch middle reliever.

Lodolo,Nick — SP — Cincinnati
EXP MLB DEBUT: 2021 | H/W: 6-6 202 | FUT: #3 starter | 8B

Thrws L Age 22
2019 (1) Texas Christian

Velo	Pitch	Grade
90-94	FB	+++
82-84	SL	++++
88-89	CU	+++

Year	Lev	Team	W	L	Sv	IP	K	ERA	WHIP	BF/G	OBA	H%	S%	xERA	Ctl	Dom	Cmd	hr/9	BPV
2019	NCAA	Texas Christian	6	5	0	98	125	2.48	0.95	24.6	207	30	78	2.15	1.9	11.5	6.0	0.7	173
2019	Rk	Billings	0	1	0	11	21	2.43	1.08	7.2	277	52	82	3.42	0.0	17.0		0.8	324
2019	A	Dayton	0	0	0	7	9	2.57	0.86	12.9	233	36	67	1.55	0.0	11.6		0.0	226

Tall/polished, was first pitcher taken in 2019 draft; floor over ceiling projection. Repeats tall-and-fall 3/4s delivery with slight crossfire action. FB effectiveness benefits from natural downward plane, slight running action and command, especially to glove-side. Plus SL can vary shape between 11-to-5 CB and sweeping SL. CU has late fade/drop.

Lowther,Zac — SP — Baltimore
EXP MLB DEBUT: 2020 | H/W: 6-2 235 | FUT: #4 starter | 7D

Thrws L Age 23
2017 (2) Xavier

Velo	Pitch	Grade
89-92	FB	+++
75-76	CB	++
82-84	CU	+++

Year	Lev	Team	W	L	Sv	IP	K	ERA	WHIP	BF/G	OBA	H%	S%	xERA	Ctl	Dom	Cmd	hr/9	BPV
2017	A-	Aberdeen	2	2	0	54	75	1.66	0.85	16.5	187	30	80	1.12	1.8	12.5	6.8	0.2	193
2018	A	Delmarva	3	1	0	31	51	1.16	0.68	18.1	121	22	89	0.36	2.6	14.8	5.7	0.6	214
2018	A+	Frederick	5	3	0	92	100	2.54	1.08	21.2	222	30	79	2.55	2.5	9.8	3.8	0.6	125
2019	AA	Bowie	13	7	0	148	154	2.55	1.11	22.4	196	26	78	2.23	3.8	9.4	2.4	0.5	83

High-3/4s, pitchability LHP was difficult to square up relying heavily on FB/CU mix. Hides ball well in repeatable delivery. FB is thrown with a natural downward tilt and will move, depending on location. It's best riding towards RHH. Best secondary is CU with solid arm-side late fade. Throws 12-to-6 CB, mostly to change eye levels.

Luzardo,Jesus — SP — Oakland
EXP MLB DEBUT: 2019 | H/W: 6-0 209 | FUT: #2 starter | 9B

Thrws L Age 22
2016 (3) HS (FL)

Velo	Pitch	Grade
92-97	FB	++++
80-83	CB	++++
83-86	CU	++++

Year	Lev	Team	W	L	Sv	IP	K	ERA	WHIP	BF/G	OBA	H%	S%	xERA	Ctl	Dom	Cmd	hr/9	BPV
2018	AAA	Nashville	1	1	0	16	18	7.31	2.00	19.3	357	46	63	7.37	3.9	10.1	2.6	1.1	94
2019	Rk	AZL A's Green	0	0	0	2	5	0.00	0.50	6.6	151	61	100		0.0	22.5		0.0	423
2019	A+	Stockton	1	0	0	10	18	0.90	0.60	11.4	175	33	100	1.02	0.0	16.2		0.9	310
2019	AAA	Las Vegas	1	1	0	31	34	3.19	1.19	17.8	249	33	76	3.44	2.3	9.9	4.3	0.9	133
2019	MLB	Oakland	0	0	2	12	16	1.50	0.67	7.0	129	18	86	0.60	2.3	12.0	5.3	0.8	173

Young, advanced LH has been quick riser through system and made debut from bullpen in 2019. At his best, flaunts three plus pitches and a FB that can touch 100 mph in short stints. Low, repeatable arm angle produces hard two-plan CB and fading CU that misses bats. A quality athlete who likes to compete, the sky is his limit as a front-end SP.

Lynch,Daniel — SP — Kansas City
EXP MLB DEBUT: 2021 | H/W: 6-6 190 | FUT: #1 starter | 9C

Thrws L Age 23
2018 (1) Virginia

Velo	Pitch	Grade
92-96	FB	++++
83-86	SL	++++
77-78	CB	++
81-84	CU	+++

Year	Lev	Team	W	L	Sv	IP	K	ERA	WHIP	BF/G	OBA	H%	S%	xERA	Ctl	Dom	Cmd	hr/9	BPV
2018	Rk	Burlington	0	0	0	11	14	1.62	0.99	14.1	223	34	82	1.77	1.6	11.4	7.0	0.0	179
2018	A	Lexington	5	1	0	40	47	1.58	1.03	17.1	237	34	85	2.24	1.4	10.6	7.8	0.2	172
2019	Rk	Burlington	1	0	0	9	7	4.00	1.78	20.7	339	39	80	6.42	3.0	7.0	2.3	1.0	63
2019	Rk	AZL Royals	0	0	0	9	12	1.00	1.00	11.5	191	31	89	1.40	3.0	12.0	4.0	0.0	153
2019	A+	Wilmington	5	2	0	78	77	3.11	1.27	21.3	257	33	76	3.35	2.7	8.9	3.3	0.5	106

Tall, lean potential SP1 came back from mid-season injury with improved velocity and movement. Repeatable, 3/4s delivery with solid extension. 4-pitch pitcher. FB bumped up to mid 90s with late run, especially up. SL is double-plus pitch with tight, 2-plane break. CU has late fade and great separation off FB. Introduced CB to mixed results.

MacGregor,Travis — SP — Pittsburgh
EXP MLB DEBUT: 2022 | H/W: 6-3 180 | FUT: #3 starter | 8E

Thrws R Age 22
2016 (2) HS (FL)

Velo	Pitch	Grade
89-94	FB	+++
80-82	CB	++
82-84	CU	++

Year	Lev	Team	W	L	Sv	IP	K	ERA	WHIP	BF/G	OBA	H%	S%	xERA	Ctl	Dom	Cmd	hr/9	BPV
2016	Rk	GCL Pirates	1	1	0	31	19	3.17	1.25	14.1	248	29	74	3.06	2.9	5.5	1.9	0.3	39
2017	Rk	Bristol	1	4	0	41	32	7.88	1.97	16.4	345	41	58	6.68	4.4	7.0	1.6	0.7	26
2018	Rk	GCL Pirates	0	0	0	7	6	2.57	1.00	13.4	233	27	83	3.16	1.3	7.7	6.0	1.3	122
2018	A	West Virginia	1	4	0	63	74	3.28	1.25	17.1	246	33	78	3.65	3.0	10.5	3.5	1.0	127

Tall SP who did not pitch in 2019 after in 2018 Tommy John surgery. Has potential to be high K guy if FB velocity returns and increases. Showed improved FB command prior to surgery and uses high arm slot effectively. Rest of pitch mix needs time to develop. Lacks touch and feel for CU, though CB shows flashes of being consistently average.

Madero,Luis — SP — Los Angeles (A)
EXP MLB DEBUT: 2021 | H/W: 6-3 185 | FUT: #5 SP/swingman | 7C

Thrws R Age 22
2013 FA (VZ)

Velo	Pitch	Grade
90-93	FB	+++
85-87	CT	+++
	CB	+++
	CU	++

Year	Lev	Team	W	L	Sv	IP	K	ERA	WHIP	BF/G	OBA	H%	S%	xERA	Ctl	Dom	Cmd	hr/9	BPV
2017	A	Burlington	1	2	0	26	18	7.90	1.95	20.8	362	41	58	7.30	3.1	6.2	2.0	1.0	46
2018	A	Burlington	2	7	0	61	49	4.27	1.37	18.3	286	34	70	4.31	2.2	7.2	3.3	0.7	88
2018	A+	Inland Empire	2	1	0	44	46	2.45	1.20	19.7	248	33	82	3.21	2.4	9.4	3.8	0.6	121
2019	A+	Inland Empire	1	0	0	16	23	1.13	1.38	16.8	250	40	91	3.05	3.9	12.9	3.3	0.0	145
2019	AA	Mobile	5	11	0	89	75	5.75	1.58	19.6	317	38	65	5.66	2.4	7.6	3.1	1.1	89

Loose, athletic RH has solid three-pitch mix and Dom continues to trend upward. FB sits in low-90s and will have a chance to add more velo as he strengthens up. Big CB is the focal point of his arsenal with plus potential, also mixing in a CT and CU that are average. Throws strikes, but stuff can be hittable in the zone. Back-end SP profile.

Malone,Brennan — SP — Arizona
EXP MLB DEBUT: 2023 | H/W: 6-4 205 | FUT: #3 starter | 9E

Thrws R Age 19
2019 (1) HS (FL)

Velo	Pitch	Grade
93-96	FB	++++
80-82	SL	+++
74-76	CB	+++
	CU	++

Year	Lev	Team	W	L	Sv	IP	K	ERA	WHIP	BF/G	OBA	H%	S%	xERA	Ctl	Dom	Cmd	hr/9	BPV
2019	Rk	AZL DBacks	1	2	0	7	7	5.14	1.29	4.8	168	24	56	1.90	6.4	9.0	1.4	0.0	6
2019	A-	Hillsboro	0	0	0	1	1	0.00	0.00	2.8	0	0			0.0	9.0		0.0	180

Strong, projectable RHP taken in 1st round of 2019 draft. Chance for four above-average pitches, headlined by plus 92-95 mph FB of which he has solid command. Leans heavily on plus SL with two strikes and has some feel for CB spin. CU will require work but flashes average. Generally around the plate but command will need polishing up.

Manning,Matt — SP — Detroit

EXP MLB DEBUT: 2020 | H/W: 6-6 215 | FUT: #3 starter | 8B

Thrws R Age 22
2016 (1) HS (CA)

Velo	Pitch	Grade
92-97	FB	++++
74-76	CB	+++
82-85	CU	+++

Year	Lev	Team	W	L	Sv	IP	K	ERA	WHIP	BF/G	OBA	H%	S%	xERA	Ctl	Dom	Cmd	hr/9	BPV
2017	A	West Michigan	2	0	0	17	26	5.76	1.45	14.7	224	38	56	2.92	5.8	13.6	2.4	0.0	107
2018	A	West Michigan	3	3	0	55	76	3.42	1.36	21.0	232	36	75	3.25	4.6	12.4	2.7	0.5	118
2018	A+	Lakeland	4	4	0	51	65	2.99	1.00	21.7	182	26	72	1.96	3.3	11.4	3.4	0.7	134
2018	AA	Erie	0	1	0	10	13	4.41	1.47	21.9	277	41	67	3.68	3.5	11.5	3.3	0.0	129
2019	AA	Erie	11	5	0	133	148	2.57	0.98	21.1	198	27	75	1.91	2.6	10.0	3.9	0.5	129

Athletic, mid-rotation starter poised to be an MLB impact arm. Works long arms and legs to produce impressive extension towards attacking the strike zone. Curve is a developing out-pitch and ahead of above-average changeup. Fastball is a lively easy plus offering that plays well in front of his offspeed mix.

Manoah,Alek — SP — Toronto

EXP MLB DEBUT: 2021 | H/W: 6-6 260 | FUT: #3 starter | 8C

Thrws R Age 22
2019 (1) West Virginia

Velo	Pitch	Grade
93-97	FB	++++
84-88	SL	+++
82-85	CU	++

Year	Lev	Team	W	L	Sv	IP	K	ERA	WHIP	BF/G	OBA	H%	S%	xERA	Ctl	Dom	Cmd	hr/9	BPV
2019	A-	Vancouver	0	1	0	17	27	2.65	1.06	11.0	213	36	76	2.28	2.6	14.3	5.4	0.5	204

Large-framed SP who has stuff and tenacity to advance thru minors quickly. Works off hard, plus FB that misses bats due to vicious, late sink. Command could improve and should with more innings. Repeats delivery which adds to potential improvement of CU. Hard SL has plus potential and could give him two devastating swing-and-miss offerings.

Marquez,Brailyn — SP — Chicago (N)

EXP MLB DEBUT: 2022 | H/W: 6-4 185 | FUT: #3 starter | 9E

Thrws L Age 21
2015 FA (DR)

Velo	Pitch	Grade
93-96	FB	++++
79-82	CB	+++
87-88	CU	++

Year	Lev	Team	W	L	Sv	IP	K	ERA	WHIP	BF/G	OBA	H%	S%	xERA	Ctl	Dom	Cmd	hr/9	BPV
2017	Rk	AZL Cubs	2	1	0	44		5.52	1.41	16.9	287	39	59	4.27	2.5	10.6	4.3	0.6	143
2018	A-	Eugene	1	4	0	47	52	3.24	1.27	19.3	257	34	78	3.82	2.7	9.9	3.7	1.0	124
2018	A	South Bend	0	0	0	7	7	2.57	1.29	14.4	262	35	78	3.04	2.6	9.0	3.5	0.0	111
2019	A	South Bend	5	4	0	77	102	3.62	1.39	19.1	227	34	74	3.25	5.0	11.9	2.4	0.5	97
2019	A+	Myrtle Beach	4	1	0	26	26	1.72	1.07	20.3	222	30	85	2.30	2.4	9.0	3.7	0.3	114

High-ceiling LH who comes with risk but also premium velocity. Will touch 102 mph and sit 94-96 with crossfire delivery and some angle to the plate, making him difficult to barrel up. CB can be slurvy and CU will require work; feel for secondaries isn't quite there yet. Low effort and short, unique arm action allow him to stay around the zone.

Marsh,Alec — SP — Kansas City

EXP MLB DEBUT: 2023 | H/W: 6-2 220 | FUT: #4 starter | 7D

Thrws R Age 21
2019 (2) Arizona St

Velo	Pitch	Grade
90-93	FB	++++
81-84	SL	+++
73-78	CB	++
83-86	CU	+++

Year	Lev	Team	W	L	Sv	IP	K	ERA	WHIP	BF/G	OBA	H%	S%	xERA	Ctl	Dom	Cmd	hr/9	BPV
2019	NCAA	Arizona St	9	4	0	101	99	3.47	1.26	24.2	242	30	76	3.62	3.2	8.8	2.8	1.0	90
2019	Rk	Idaho Falls	0	1	0	33	38	4.08	1.03	9.8	243	31	66	3.40	1.1	10.3	9.5	1.4	175

Physically mature, high 3/4s RHP made pro debut. Repeatable, crossfire delivery with solid extension, using legs to power velocity with four pitches. Four-seam FB is plus pitch with late rising action; two-seamer pitches to bats. SL has above-average profile while CB is more of a eye-level changer. Has feel for average CU.

Martin,Corbin — SP — Arizona

EXP MLB DEBUT: 2019 | H/W: 6-2 200 | FUT: Setup reliever | 8C

Thrws R Age 24
2017 (2) Texas A&M

Velo	Pitch	Grade
93-95	FB	++++
84-86	SL	+++
79-82	CB	+++
86-88	CU	++

Year	Lev	Team	W	L	Sv	IP	K	ERA	WHIP	BF/G	OBA	H%	S%	xERA	Ctl	Dom	Cmd	hr/9	BPV
2017	A-	Tri City	0	1	1	27	38	2.65	1.03	13.1	207	33	74	1.96	2.6	12.6	4.8	0.3	173
2018	A+	Buies Creek	2	0	1	19	26	0.00	0.58	16.1	69	13	100		3.3	12.3	3.7	0.0	150
2018	AA	Corpus Christi	7	2	0	103	96	2.97	1.09	19.2	224	28	74	2.63	2.4	8.4	3.4	0.6	103
2019	AAA	Round Rock	2	1	0	37	45	3.15	1.37	17.3	240	34	78	3.40	4.4	10.9	2.5	0.5	97
2019	MLB	Houston	1	1	0	19	19	5.65	1.83	17.8	299	30	85	8.50	5.7	9.0	1.6	3.8	26

High-velocity SP prospect who made shaky MLB debut mid-year and ultimately required Tommy John surgery. Touches 97 mph with plus FB and sits 93-95; can elevate but command is well below-average. SL is plus offering with huge swing-and-miss ability. Feel for CU not quite there yet. Innate ability to miss barrels but control is major question mark.

Mata,Bryan — SP — Boston

EXP MLB DEBUT: 2021 | H/W: 6-3 160 | FUT: #3 starter | 8D

Thrws R Age 20
2016 FA (VZ)

Velo	Pitch	Grade
93-98	FB	++++
78-80	CB	+++
86-89	SL	+++
84-86	CU	++

Year	Lev	Team	W	L	Sv	IP	K	ERA	WHIP	BF/G	OBA	H%	S%	xERA	Ctl	Dom	Cmd	hr/9	BPV
2017	A	Greenville	5	6	0	77	74	3.74	1.31	18.7	257	33	70	3.36	3.0	8.6	2.8	0.4	92
2018	A+	Salem	6	3	0	72	61	3.50	1.61	18.8	222	29	77	3.47	7.3	7.6	1.1	0.1	-41
2019	AA	Portland	4	6	0	53	59	5.08	1.47	20.7	265	35	67	4.47	4.1	10.0	2.5	1.0	88
2019	A+	Salem	3	1	0	51	52	1.76	1.10	20.0	209	29	84	2.04	3.2	9.2	2.9	0.2	97

Improving SP with significant upside predicated on outstanding FB and potential for two plus breaking balls. All pitches thrown with velocity, though SL behind CB at present. Uses two-seam FB to get very high amount of groundballs as well as K. Command should improve with more polished mechanics. Development of CU will dictate upside.

May,Dustin — SP — Los Angeles (N)

EXP MLB DEBUT: 2019 | H/W: 6-6 180 | FUT: #1 starter | 9C

Thrws R Age 22
2016 (3) HS (TX)

Velo	Pitch	Grade
94-98	FB	++++
90-93	CT	++++
80-83	CB	++++
84-87	CU	++

Year	Lev	Team	W	L	Sv	IP	K	ERA	WHIP	BF/G	OBA	H%	S%	xERA	Ctl	Dom	Cmd	hr/9	BPV
2018	A+	Rancho Cuca	7	3	0	98	94	3.30	1.10	22.6	248	31	73	3.16	1.6	8.6	5.5	0.8	131
2018	AA	Tulsa	2	2	0	34	28	3.70	1.14	22.5	219	28	64	2.14	3.2	7.4	2.3	0.0	66
2019	AA	Tulsa	3	5	0	79	86	3.75	1.15	20.9	241	33	67	2.95	2.3	9.8	4.3	0.6	133
2019	AAA	Oklahoma City	3	0	0	27	24	2.32	1.11	21.3	216	29	77	2.00	3.0	8.0	2.7	0.0	81
2019	MLB	Los Angeles	2	3	0	34	32	3.68	1.11	9.6	255	32	67	3.00	1.3	8.4	6.4	0.5	134

Has emerged as one of the top pitching prospects in baseball. Comes after hitters with a plus four-pitch mix highlighted by a 94-98 mph sinking FB. Backs up the heat with a plus CT, CB, and improved CU. Features a high leg kick that generates plus arm speed and misses bats with both a high spin rate on breaking balls and sink on his two-seamer.

McAvene,Michael — SP — Chicago (N)

EXP MLB DEBUT: 2022 | H/W: 6-3 210 | FUT: Setup reliever | 8D

Thrws R Age 22
2019 (3) Louisville

Velo	Pitch	Grade
93-96	FB	++++
81-83	SL	+++

Year	Lev	Team	W	L	Sv	IP	K	ERA	WHIP	BF/G	OBA	H%	S%	xERA	Ctl	Dom	Cmd	hr/9	BPV
2019	A-	Eugene	0	0	0	12	20	1.48	0.74	7.2	127	26	78	0.03	3.0	14.8	5.0	0.0	204

Low-mileage RH who was drafted as college closer but was SP in his debut. Flashed upper-90s heat on plus FB while at Louisville and good feel for spinning his breaking ball. Will need time to develop trust in his CU. Is several years removed from Tommy John surgery so durability could be a question mark, but the FB/SL combo could work from bullpen.

McClanahan,Shane — SP — Tampa Bay

EXP MLB DEBUT: 2021 | H/W: 6-1 200 | FUT: #3 starter | 8C

Thrws L Age 22
2018 (1) South Florida

Velo	Pitch	Grade
92-96	FB	++++
81-83	SL	++++
85-87	CU	++

Year	Lev	Team	W	L	Sv	IP	K	ERA	WHIP	BF/G	OBA	H%	S%	xERA	Ctl	Dom	Cmd	hr/9	BPV
2018	Rk	Princeton	0	0	0	4	7	0.00	0.75	7.1	151	32	100	0.29	2.3	15.8	7.0	0.0	241
2018	Rk	GCL Rays	0	0	0	3	6	0.00	0.33	4.7	106	29	100		0.0	18.0		0.0	342
2019	A	Bowling Green	4	4	0	53	74	3.40	1.30	19.9	203	32	74	2.77	5.3	12.6	2.4	0.5	102
2019	A+	Charlotte	6	1	0	49	59	1.47	0.84	19.9	192	29	83	1.18	1.5	10.8	7.4	0.2	173
2019	AA	Montgomery	1	1	0	18	21	8.45	1.99	21.8	370	47	58	7.94	3.0	10.4	3.5	1.5	125

Lean, power-throwing LHP made full-season debut, pitching way up 3 levels to Double-A. Low 3/4s athletic delivery, struggles rushing through progression. Sits low-to-mid 90s with late-running FB; can reach back for 97-100 too. Power SL also has double-plus potential and does great job tunneling with FB. CU is improving but likely fringe-average.

McDonald,Trevor — SP — San Francisco

EXP MLB DEBUT: 2024 | H/W: 6-2 180 | FUT: #3 starter | 8E

Thrws R Age 19
2019 (11) HS (MS)

Velo	Pitch	Grade
91-94	FB	+++
75-78	CB	++
80-82	SL	++
81-84	CU	++

Year	Lev	Team	W	L	Sv	IP	K	ERA	WHIP	BF/G	OBA	H%	S%	xERA	Ctl	Dom	Cmd	hr/9	BPV
2019	Rk	AZL Giants B	0	0	0	4	8	2.25	1.00	5.1	151	38	75	0.90	4.5	18.0	4.0	0.0	221

Big bonus despite 11th round selection. Far from SF, but offers potential due to crude arm action that should be revised. Should continue to add velocity as he smooths out delivery. Shows good feel for spin with both CB and SL. CU remains distant 4th pitch. Command and control are OK for age. Very interesting prospect to watch develop.

McKay,Brendan — SP — Tampa Bay

EXP MLB DEBUT: 2019 | H/W: 6-2 212 | FUT: #3 starter | 8A

Thrws L Age 24
2017 (1) Louisville

Velo	Pitch	Grade
91-94	FB	+++
79-83	CB	+++
88-90	CT	+++
85-87	CU	+++

Year	Lev	Team	W	L	Sv	IP	K	ERA	WHIP	BF/G	OBA	H%	S%	xERA	Ctl	Dom	Cmd	hr/9	BPV
2018	A	Bowling Green	2	0	0	24	40	1.12	0.41	13.0	105	20	78		0.7	14.9	20.0	0.4	266
2018	A+	Charlotte	3	2	0	47	54	3.24	1.19	17.2	253	35	72	3.01	2.1	10.3	4.9	0.4	147
2019	AA	Montgomery	3	0	0	41	62	1.31	0.83	18.8	177	30	88	1.20	2.0	13.5	6.9	0.4	209
2019	AAA	Durham	3	0	0	32	40	0.84	0.81	16.6	159	24	92	0.84	2.5	11.3	4.4	0.3	152
2019	MLB	Tampa Bay	2	4	0	49	56	5.14	1.41	15.9	277	35	67	4.93	2.9	10.3	3.5	1.5	124

Two-way performer made MLB debut on strength of his pitching ability. All pitches are above-average offerings but he struggled putting away MLB hitters. Sequences and tunnels pitches well with athletic, high 3/4s delivery. Commands all four pitches well. FB, CT & CU close to maturity. CB has chance to be swing-and-miss pitch with added depth.

McKenzie,Triston — SP — Cleveland — EXP MLB DEBUT: 2021 — H/W: 6-5 165 — FUT: #3 starter — 8D

Thrws R Age 22
2015 (1) HS (FL)

Velo	Pitch	Grade
91-93	FB	++++
77-79	CB	++++
83-85	CU	+++

Year	Lev	Team	W	L	Sv	IP	K	ERA	WHIP	BF/G	OBA	H%	S%	xERA	Ctl	Dom	Cmd	hr/9	BPV
2016	A-	MahoningVal	4	3	0	49	55	0.55	0.96	20.6	183	26	98	1.56	2.9	10.1	3.4	0.4	120
2016	A	Lake County	2	2	0	34	49	3.18	0.97	21.5	220	35	68	2.15	1.6	13.0	8.2	0.5	209
2017	A+	Lynchburg	12	6	0	143	186	3.46	1.05	22.1	207	30	70	2.53	2.8	11.7	4.1	0.9	152
2018	AA	Akron	7	4	0	90	87	2.69	1.01	21.6	199	25	77	2.29	2.8	8.7	3.1	0.8	99
2019		Did not play - injury																	

Tall, rail-thin high 3/4s RHP missed all of 2019 with upper back and shoulder strain. Athletic delivery and does solid job repeating. Has struggled gaining mass and with injuries. FB sits low 90s with solid run and natural downward action. CB is a true downer with great shape and solid break; it's a true out-pitch. Has good feel for late-fading CU.

Medina,Adonis — SP — Philadelphia — EXP MLB DEBUT: 2021 — H/W: 6-1 185 — FUT: #4 starter — 8C

Thrws R Age 23
2014 FA (DR)

Velo	Pitch	Grade
91-94	FB	+++
79-83	SL	++++
85-87	CU	++

Year	Lev	Team	W	L	Sv	IP	K	ERA	WHIP	BF/G	OBA	H%	S%	xERA	Ctl	Dom	Cmd	hr/9	BPV
2015	Rk	GCL Phillies	3	2	0	45	35	2.99	1.20	18.1	248	31	74	2.84	2.4	7.0	2.9	0.2	79
2016	A-	Williamsport	5	3	0	64	34	2.94	1.11	19.4	206	22	76	2.57	3.4	4.8	1.4	0.7	13
2017	A	Lakewood	4	9	0	119	133	3.02	1.19	21.7	235	32	76	2.92	2.9	10.0	3.4	0.5	119
2018	A+	Clearwater	10	4	0	111	123	4.13	1.25	20.6	247	33	69	3.58	2.9	10.0	3.4	0.9	119
2019	AA	Reading	7	7	0	105	82	4.96	1.37	20.0	258	30	65	4.09	3.5	7.0	2.0	0.9	50

Inconsistency plagued him all year in his first taste of the upper levels. FB lost a tick of velocity; SL flattened out; CU was too firm and not a weapon. Still mixed in some good starts, but had awful second half and lefties pounded him, so questions of stamina via his slight frame resurfaced. 2020 will be big year in deciding his future role.

Medina,Luis — SP — New York (A) — EXP MLB DEBUT: 2022 — H/W: 6-1 175 — FUT: #2 starter — 9E

Thrws R Age 20
2015 FA (DR)

Velo	Pitch	Grade
96-99	FB	+++++
82-84	CB	++++
88-92	CU	+++

Year	Lev	Team	W	L	Sv	IP	K	ERA	WHIP	BF/G	OBA	H%	S%	xERA	Ctl	Dom	Cmd	hr/9	BPV
2017	Rk	Pulaski	1	1	0	23	22	5.09	1.22	15.5	178	23	56	2.20	5.5	8.6	1.6	0.4	25
2018	Rk	Pulaski	1	3	0	36	47	6.25	2.17	15.0	240	35	71	5.64	11.5	11.8	1.0	0.8	-81
2019	A+	Tampa	0	0	0	10	12	0.88	0.98	19.4	196	29	90	1.42	2.6	10.6	4.0	0.0	137
2019	A	Charleston (Sc)	1	8	0	93	115	6.00	1.65	20.8	247	34	63	4.54	6.5	11.1	1.7	0.9	43

Athletic RHP harnessed control down the stretch, setting up explosive finish to season. High 3/4s on-line delivery. High-velocity FB has sick 2-seam life and is unfair to hitters. A plus CB is hard and sometimes mimics SL two-plane movement. Overthrows CU at times, which firms up. Could be a breakout performer.

Mejia,Jean Carlos — SP — Cleveland — EXP MLB DEBUT: 2021 — H/W: 6-4 240 — FUT: #3 starter — 8E

Thrws R Age 23
2013 FA (DR)

Velo	Pitch	Grade
90-94	FB	++++
82-83	SL	++++
86-88	CU	+++

Year	Lev	Team	W	L	Sv	IP	K	ERA	WHIP	BF/G	OBA	H%	S%	xERA	Ctl	Dom	Cmd	hr/9	BPV
2017	Rk	AZL Indians	1	0	6	14	19	3.19	1.28	5.8	246	39	72	2.77	3.2	12.1	3.8	0.0	150
2017	A-	MahoningVal	1	0	3	22	31	0.00	0.50	6.7	87	16	100		2.0	12.6	6.2	0.0	189
2018	A	Lake County	4	8	0	92	97	3.13	1.13	21.4	245	33	71	2.68	2.0	9.5	4.9	0.3	136
2018	A+	Lynchburg	0	1	0	6	3	6.00	1.00	22.9	228	26	33	1.92	1.5	4.5	3.0	0.0	59
2019	A+	Lynchburg	3	1	0	33	36	4.09	1.12	16.3	231	33	59	2.21	2.5	9.8	4.0	0.0	128

Tall, powerful RHP struggled with hip injury that required June surgery. Heavy 2-seam FB is workhorse pitch. Lives in the lower half of zone and relies on both plane and movement to induce ground balls and strikeouts. Plus 2-plane SL has long, sweepy break that will miss RH bats. CU has solid arm-side run and late fade. Average pitch at projection.

Menez,Conner — SP — San Francisco — EXP MLB DEBUT: 2019 — H/W: 6-3 205 — FUT: #4 starter — 7D

Thrws L Age 24
2016 (14) Master's College

Velo	Pitch	Grade
89-93	FB	+++
82-84	SL	+++
80-81	CB	+++
83-85	CU	++

Year	Lev	Team	W	L	Sv	IP	K	ERA	WHIP	BF/G	OBA	H%	S%	xERA	Ctl	Dom	Cmd	hr/9	BPV
2018	AA	Richmond	6	4	0	74	92	4.38	1.45	21.0	259	38	67	3.50	4.1	11.2	2.7	0.1	108
2018	AAA	Sacramento	1	1	0	11	9	3.27	1.00	21.0	162	21	64	1.12	4.1	7.4	1.8	0.0	40
2019	AA	Richmond	3	3	0	59	70	2.74	0.96	20.4	181	25	75	1.92	3.0	10.6	3.5	0.8	127
2019	AAA	Sacramento	3	1	0	61	84	4.86	1.47	21.9	258	35	73	5.09	4.4	12.4	2.8	1.8	121
2019	MLB	SF Giants	0	1	0	17	22	5.29	1.47	9.1	213	26	71	4.84	6.4	11.6	1.8	2.1	56

Breakout SP who reached majors after dominating AA. K rate has increased over last two seasons as extension in delivery makes FB quicker than it appears. Uses four pitches to deceive hitters and keep off guard. Lacks putaway pitch, but sequences well and changes speeds. FB has good spin rate and SL can be nasty at times. Fits back-end profile.

Miller,Erik — SP — Philadelphia — EXP MLB DEBUT: 2022 — H/W: 6-5 240 — FUT: #4 starter — 8D

Thrws L Age 22
2019 (4) Stanford

Velo	Pitch	Grade
90-94	FB	+++
80-84	SL	++
80-83	CU	++

Year	Lev	Team	W	L	Sv	IP	K	ERA	WHIP	BF/G	OBA	H%	S%	xERA	Ctl	Dom	Cmd	hr/9	BPV
2019	Rk	GCL PhilliesW	0	0	0	3	6	3.00	1.33	6.2	191	45	75	2.18	6.0	18.0	3.0	0.0	180
2019	A-	Williamsport	0	0	0	20	29	0.90	1.00	12.7	187	32	90	1.35	3.2	13.1	4.1	0.0	168
2019	A	Lakewood	1	0	0	13	17	2.08	1.23	17.6	214	34	81	2.26	4.2	11.8	2.8	0.0	118

Large-framed lefty battled inconsistency at Stanford, but improved in his draft year and blew through three MiLB stops in 2019 (52K/15 BB in 36 IP). FB is 90-94; can occasionally reach back for more. Breaking ball is a 80-84 slurve; CU 80-83 and improving. Some bullpen risk due to past control problems, but stuff is promising.

Miller,Tyson — SP — Chicago (N) — EXP MLB DEBUT: 2020 — H/W: 6-4 215 — FUT: #5 SP/swingman — 7C

Thrws R Age 24
2016 (4) California Baptist

Velo	Pitch	Grade
90-93	FB	++
83-86	SL	++
82-86	CU	++

Year	Lev	Team	W	L	Sv	IP	K	ERA	WHIP	BF/G	OBA	H%	S%	xERA	Ctl	Dom	Cmd	hr/9	BPV
2016	A-	Eugene	1	1	0	22	14	4.05	1.35	15.4	293	31	77	5.21	1.6	5.7	3.5	1.6	76
2017	A	South Bend	6	7	0	120	99	4.49	1.33	17.8	265	32	67	3.91	2.8	7.4	2.6	0.7	75
2018	A+	Myrtle Beach	9	9	0	127	126	3.54	1.09	21.6	225	28	70	2.87	2.5	8.9	3.6	0.9	112
2019	AA	Tennessee	4	3	0	88	80	2.56	1.00	22.4	220	28	77	2.36	1.8	8.2	4.4	0.6	116
2019	AAA	Iowa	3	5	0	48	43	7.66	1.80	20.3	313	35	62	7.40	4.7	8.0	1.7	2.4	36

Breakout RH from 2018 struggled mightily after mid-year callup to PCL. Chance for solid-average, three-pitch mix including 90-93 mph FB with which he can cut or sink. SL will flash good two-plane break. CU remains raw and it shows with weak splits vLHH. Has back-end SP upside with tall, durable build if he can develop feel for CU.

Mills,Wyatt — RP — Seattle — EXP MLB DEBUT: 2020 — H/W: 6-3 175 — FUT: Setup reliever — 7D

Thrws R Age 25
2017 (3) Gonzaga

Velo	Pitch	Grade
91-93	FB	++++
84-85	SL	+++

Year	Lev	Team	W	L	Sv	IP	K	ERA	WHIP	BF/G	OBA	H%	S%	xERA	Ctl	Dom	Cmd	hr/9	BPV
2017	A-	Everett	0	1	2	7	11	2.57	0.86	3.7	132	26	67	0.39	3.9	14.1	3.7	0.0	168
2017	A	Clinton	0	1	4	13	18	1.37	0.84	4.4	119	21	82	0.24	4.1	12.4	3.0	0.0	129
2018	A+	Modesto	6	0	11	42	49	1.92	0.90	4.5	196	29	78	1.43	1.9	10.5	5.4	0.2	155
2018	AA	Arkansas	0	2	0	10	10	10.59	2.16	5.6	385	49	45	7.26	3.5	8.8	2.5	0.0	82
2019	AA	Arkansas	4	2	8	52	66	4.31	1.15	5.1	226	34	60	2.52	2.9	11.4	3.9	0.3	144

Low 3/4s to sidearm right-handed RP had solid season despite weak ERA. Pitches play up due to delivery and variation of lower slots. Manipulates between heavy sinker and 4-seam FB with riding action. SL is more than typical sidearm Frisbee pitch. Both FB and SL are plus pitches.

Misiewicz,Anthony — SP — Seattle — EXP MLB DEBUT: 2020 — H/W: 6-1 190 — FUT: #5 SP/swingman — 6C

Thrws L Age 25
2015 (18) Michigan St

Velo	Pitch	Grade
88-91	FB	++
78-80	CB	+++
86-88	CT	+++
81-84	CU	++

Year	Lev	Team	W	L	Sv	IP	K	ERA	WHIP	BF/G	OBA	H%	S%	xERA	Ctl	Dom	Cmd	hr/9	BPV
2017	AA	Arkansas	3	3	0	41	32	4.38	1.24	23.8	257	30	66	3.69	2.4	7.0	2.9	0.9	79
2018	Rk	AZL Mariners	0	0	0	5	4	0.00	0.40	8.1	124	17	100		0.0	7.2		0.0	148
2018	AA	Arkansas	3	12	0	98	91	5.51	1.65	20.9	325	39	69	6.12	2.7	8.4	3.1	1.3	97
2019	AA	Arkansas	1	2	0	35	36	2.56	1.22	20.3	266	36	77	2.93	1.8	9.2	5.1	0.0	135
2019	AAA	Tacoma	8	6	0	95	89	5.39	1.29	20.6	261	30	62	4.56	2.6	8.4	3.2	1.6	98

Command/control LHP has struggled against upper minors competition. Repeats high 3/4s crossfire delivery well. Stuff isn't optimal but mixes well enough to get by. 4-pitch pitcher. Best pitches are CB with solid depth and CT with late break. FB sits high-80s mostly with late arm-side run. CU is lesser than other offerings.

Mize,Casey — SP — Detroit — EXP MLB DEBUT: 2020 — H/W: 6-3 220 — FUT: #3 starter — 8B

Thrws R Age 22
2018 (1) Auburn

Velo	Pitch	Grade
93-96	FB	++++
89-91	SL	++++
86-89	SP	++++

Year	Lev	Team	W	L	Sv	IP	K	ERA	WHIP	BF/G	OBA	H%	S%	xERA	Ctl	Dom	Cmd	hr/9	BPV
2018	NCAA	Auburn	10	6	0	114	156	3.31	0.88	24.8	207	31	64	2.01	1.3	12.3	9.8	0.8	205
2018	Rk	GCL TigersW	0	0	0	2	4	0.00	0.50	6.6	0	0	100		4.5	18.0	4.0	0.0	221
2018	A+	Lakeland	0	1	0	11	10	4.82	1.34	11.6	292	34	69	5.12	1.6	8.0	5.0	1.6	119
2019	A+	Lakeland	2	0	0	30	30	0.89	0.53	16.9	114	17	81		1.5	8.9	6.0	0.0	139
2019	AA	Erie	6	3	0	78	76	3.22	1.11	20.5	238	31	72	2.83	2.1	8.7	4.2	0.6	120

Well-proportioned, front-end collegiate starter with sensational command and the best splitter of his draft class. Able to pound the strike zone with a deceptively fluid delivery and a three-pitch mix grading plus or better across the board. Lively fastball complements vicious mid-to-high 80s splitter and slider. Ability to locate sets him apart.

Morales,Francisco — SP — Philadelphia — EXP MLB DEBUT: 2022 — H/W: 6-4 185 — FUT: #3 starter — 9C

Thrws R Age 20
2016 FA (VZ)

Velo	Pitch	Grade
94-96	FB	++++
85-89	SL	++++
83-85	CU	++

Year	Lev	Team	W	L	Sv	IP	K	ERA	WHIP	BF/G	OBA	H%	S%	xERA	Ctl	Dom	Cmd	hr/9	BPV
2017	Rk	GCL Phillies	3	2	0	41	44	3.07	1.31	17.0	227	31	75	2.85	4.4	9.6	2.2	0.2	73
2018	A-	Williamsport	4	5	0	56	68	5.29	1.55	18.9	254	35	67	4.49	5.3	10.9	2.1	1.0	71
2019	A	Lakewood	1	8	1	96	129	3.84	1.33	14.8	232	34	73	3.43	4.3	12.1	2.8	0.7	119

Big, strong and young hurler had success in first full-season assignment. Piggy-backing kept his innings <100, but FB velo ticked up, giving him two plus pitches. Viscous break to high-80s SL, but CU and control still below average. Has time to clean up both, but they hold keys to rotation vs. reliever future.

Morejon,Adrian
SP | **San Diego** | EXP MLB DEBUT: 2019 | H/W: 6-0 175 | FUT: #3 starter | **8B**

Thrws L Age 21
2016 FA (CU)

Velo	Pitch	Grade
93-96	FB	++++
79-82	CB	+++
86-88	CU	++++

Year	Lev	Team	W	L	Sv	IP	K	ERA	WHIP	BF/G	OBA	H%	S%	xERA	Ctl	Dom	Cmd	hr/9	BPV
2017	A	Fort Wayne	1	2	0	27	23	4.30	1.51	19.6	267	33	72	4.31	4.3	7.6	1.8	0.7	39
2018	Rk	AZL Padres	0	1	0	2	4	8.18	2.27	11.2	446	69	60	8.83	0.0	16.4		0.0	313
2018	A+	Lake Elsinore	4	4	0	62	70	3.33	1.25	19.5	235	31	76	3.41	3.5	10.1	2.9	0.9	107
2019	AA	Amarillo	0	4	0	36	44	4.25	1.22	9.1	222	31	66	3.04	3.8	11.0	2.9	0.8	115
2019	MLB	San Diego	0	0	0	8	9	10.13	2.25	8.1	399	51	53	8.83	3.4	10.1	3.0	1.1	109

Young, promising LH made his MLB debut but landed on IL with shoulder tweak; has struggled staying healthy as a pro. Features good velocity at 94-96 mph (t98) and will drop in a plus fading CU for whiffs, though still ironing out feel for his breaking ball. Strong, athletic build and repeats delivery well. Dom, GB% both above average.

Morel,Yohanse
SP | **Kansas City** | EXP MLB DEBUT: 2023 | H/W: 6-0 170 | FUT: Setup reliever | **7E**

Thrws R Age 19
2017 FA (DR)

Velo	Pitch	Grade
92-95	FB	++++
82-83	SL	+++
86-87	CU	+++

Year	Lev	Team	W	L	Sv	IP	K	ERA	WHIP	BF/G	OBA	H%	S%	xERA	Ctl	Dom	Cmd	hr/9	BPV
2018	Rk	AZL Royals	1	2	0	43	47	3.75	1.30	14.8	247	34	69	3.05	3.3	9.8	2.9	0.2	104
2018	Rk	DSL Nationals	0	0	0	3	5	8.71	2.26	15.7	407	62	57	7.91	2.9	14.5	5.0	0.0	201
2019	A	Lexington	2	6	1	52	57	6.05	1.63	16.6	303	39	64	5.64	3.6	9.8	2.7	1.2	97

Hard-throwing, physical 3/4 RHP struggled in 18-year-old season. A recent convert to pitching, he improved his delivery and did a solid job creating downward plane. 3-pitch pitcher; best is a low-to-mid-90s 2-seam FB with excellent late bore. SL has slurvy profile and could be better with tight grip. CU has solid pitch profile but telegraphs.

Moss,Scott
SP | **Cleveland** | EXP MLB DEBUT: 2020 | H/W: 6-6 225 | FUT: #4 starter | **7D**

Thrws L Age 25
2016 (4) Florida

Velo	Pitch	Grade
90-92	FB	+++
75-78	CB	+++
80-83	CU	+++

Year	Lev	Team	W	L	Sv	IP	K	ERA	WHIP	BF/G	OBA	H%	S%	xERA	Ctl	Dom	Cmd	hr/9	BPV
2017	A	Dayton	13	6	0	135		3.46	1.20	20.9	230	31	73	3.07	3.2	10.4	3.3	0.7	119
2018	A+	Daytona	15	4	0	132	112	3.68	1.33	21.9	266	32	75	4.06	2.8	7.6	2.7	0.9	80
2019	AA	Chattanooga	6	5	0	102	123	3.44	1.38	21.4	226	32	76	3.37	5.0	10.9	2.2	0.6	78
2019	AA	Akron	2	0	0	10	13	0.00	0.80	18.1	96	16	100		4.5	11.7	2.6	0.0	107
2019	AAA	Columbus	2	1	0	18	23	1.98	1.10	17.8	190	28	84	2.10	4.0	11.4	2.9	0.5	116

High 3/4s LHP was acquired in mid-season trade with CIN. Easy, crossfire delivery creates natural downward plane. Sits low 90s with FB, relying on hitting spots and some run to stay above water. An above-average offering at maturity, CB is a 12-to-6 downer with plus shape and moderate break. CU improved as season wore on with solid fade/deception.

Muller,Kyle
SP | **Atlanta** | EXP MLB DEBUT: 2020 | H/W: 6-6 225 | FUT: #4 starter | **8D**

Thrws L Age 22
2016 (2) HS (TX)

Velo	Pitch	Grade
92-95	FB	++++
79-82	CB	+++
84-86	CU	+++

Year	Lev	Team	W	L	Sv	IP	K	ERA	WHIP	BF/G	OBA	H%	S%	xERA	Ctl	Dom	Cmd	hr/9	BPV
2017	Rk	Danville	1	1	0	47	49	4.19	1.29	17.6	244	31	70	3.71	3.4	9.3	2.7	1.0	94
2018	A	Rome	3	0	0	30	23	2.40	1.07	19.4	221	25	83	2.82	2.4	6.9	2.9	0.9	77
2018	A+	Florida	4	2	0	80	79	3.25	1.40	24.2	261	35	75	3.52	3.6	8.9	2.5	0.2	81
2018	AA	Mississippi	4	1	0	29	27	3.10	0.97	22.0	212	26	72	2.47	1.9	8.4	4.5	0.9	119
2019	AA	Mississippi	7	6	0	111	120	3.16	1.34	21.0	205	28	76	2.82	5.5	9.7	1.8	0.4	44

Big-bodied, hard-throwing LHP continues to struggle with command and consistency. High 3/4s delivery with solid extension. Creates downward plane staying tall and falling in delivery. FB plays up due to delivery and sink. Can hit 98-99 MPH in short bursts. CB turning into more slurve than true downer. CU shows solid late fade and drop.

Munoz,Anderson
SP | **New York (A)** | EXP MLB DEBUT: 2023 | H/W: 5-8 158 | FUT: #4 starter | **7E**

Thrws R Age 21
2017 FA (VZ)

Velo	Pitch	Grade
92-95	FB	++++
88-90	SL	++
83-85	CU	++

Year	Lev	Team	W	L	Sv	IP	K	ERA	WHIP	BF/G	OBA	H%	S%	xERA	Ctl	Dom	Cmd	hr/9	BPV
2018	Rk	GCL Yankees	1	5	0	36	38	5.24	1.77	15.1	272	35	72	5.33	6.5	9.5	1.5	1.0	14
2019	A	Charleston (Sc)	1	1	0	22	31	6.14	1.55	16.0	244	37	59	4.18	5.7	12.7	2.2	0.8	92
2019	A-	Staten Island	7	2	0	62	63	2.61	1.11	18.8	208	29	75	2.04	3.3	9.1	2.7	0.1	92

Short-statured RHP with plus arm speed and repeatable 3/4 delivery pitched well in short-season NYPL. Best pitch is low-to-mid 90s FB with solid, late run. SL is work-in-progress. Mostly, a one-plane breaking pitch but flashes occasional two-plane break. CU is firm with solid seperation but will fly out in delivery, telegraphing the pitch.

Munoz,Andres
RP | **San Diego** | EXP MLB DEBUT: 2019 | H/W: 6-2 165 | FUT: Closer | **9E**

Thrws R Age 21
2015 FA (DR)

Velo	Pitch	Grade
97-101	FB	+++++
86-88	SL	++++

Year	Lev	Team	W	L	Sv	IP	K	ERA	WHIP	BF/G	OBA	H%	S%	xERA	Ctl	Dom	Cmd	hr/9	BPV
2018	A-	Tri-City	0	0	0	5	9	0.00	0.38	3.3	0	0	100		3.5	15.6	4.5	0.0	205
2018	AA	San Antonio	2	1	7	19	19	0.95	1.16	3.8	170	24	91	1.60	5.2	9.0	1.7	0.0	39
2019	AA	Amarillo	0	2	4	16	34	2.22	1.23	4.1	165	41	84	2.15	6.1	18.9	3.1	0.6	193
2019	AAA	El Paso	3	2	2	19	24	3.79	1.21	4.0	230	31	75	3.74	3.3	11.4	3.4	1.4	133
2019	MLB	San Diego	1	1	1	23	30	3.91	1.17	4.2	198	29	68	2.65	4.3	11.7	2.7	0.8	113

Athletic, hard-throwing RHP who made debut from bullpen and flashed elite SwK ability. Short, powerful arm action produces upper-90s heat with arm-side movement; capable of touching 103 mph. Tight SL shows ability to miss bats and produce grounders. Still has a ways to go with command, but at 20 years old, there's elite upside here.

Murphy,Chris
SP | **Boston** | EXP MLB DEBUT: 2022 | H/W: 6-1 175 | FUT: #4 starter | **7D**

Thrws L Age 21
2019 (6) San Diego

Velo	Pitch	Grade
89-94	FB	+++
74-76	CB	+++
81-84	SL	++
80-83	CU	+++

Year	Lev	Team	W	L	Sv	IP	K	ERA	WHIP	BF/G	OBA	H%	S%	xERA	Ctl	Dom	Cmd	hr/9	BPV
2019	NCAA	San Diego	4	3	1	64	87	3.51	1.36	20.6	196	30	74	2.75	6.0	12.2	2.0	0.4	75
2019	A-	Lowell	0	1	0	33	34	1.09	0.91	12.3	198	27	90	1.52	1.9	9.2	4.9	0.3	133

Athletic SP with terrific pro debut upon signing. Lacks premium stuff and velocity, but succeeds with pitch location and deception. Fits more at back-end of rotation and could eventually move to pen. Relies on FB and can rear back for few more mph. Sets up offspeed stuff well, including solid-average CU. Added more power to decent CB.

Murphy,Patrick
SP | **Toronto** | EXP MLB DEBUT: 2020 | H/W: 6-4 220 | FUT: #4 starter | **7C**

Thrws R Age 24
2013 (3) HS (AZ)

Velo	Pitch	Grade
92-98	FB	++++
77-82	CB	+++
86-88	CU	++

Year	Lev	Team	W	L	Sv	IP	K	ERA	WHIP	BF/G	OBA	H%	S%	xERA	Ctl	Dom	Cmd	hr/9	BPV
2017	A	Lansing	4	3	0	88	57	2.96	1.36	24.6	259	30	79	3.70	3.4	5.8	1.7	0.5	32
2017	A+	Dunedin	0	1	0	9	5	7.00	1.89	21.2	356	41	59	6.07	3.0	5.0	1.7	0.0	27
2018	A+	Dunedin	10	5	0	146	135	2.65	1.20	22.6	234	30	78	2.76	3.1	8.3	2.7	0.3	84
2018	AA	New Hampshire	0	0	0	6	6	3.00	1.17	23.9	191	27	71	1.85	4.5	9.0	2.0	0.0	59
2019	AA	New Hampshire	4	7	0	84	86	4.71	1.21	18.8	240	31	61	3.27	2.9	9.2	3.2	0.8	106

Tall, strong SP who has overcome health issues to increase velocity and K rate. Owns fast delivery which offers hint of deception and throws on steep downhill plane. Heavy FB among tops in org and is difficult to make hard contact against. Throws consistent strikes and likely better than numbers indicate. Arm action leads to solid pitch movement.

Murray,Joey
SP | **Toronto** | EXP MLB DEBUT: 2021 | H/W: 6-2 195 | FUT: #5 SP/swingman | **7D**

Thrws R Age 23
2018 (8) Kent St

Velo	Pitch	Grade
88-93	FB	+++
76-77	CB	++
82-84	SL	+++
81-84	CU	++

Year	Lev	Team	W	L	Sv	IP	K	ERA	WHIP	BF/G	OBA	H%	S%	xERA	Ctl	Dom	Cmd	hr/9	BPV
2018	NCAA	Kent St	9	2	0	95	141	2.46	0.99	22.7	167	29	73	1.18	3.8	13.3	3.5	0.1	156
2018	A-	Vancouver	1	1	0	25	39	1.79	1.15	7.7	211	36	86	2.33	3.6	13.9	3.9	0.4	172
2019	A	Lansing	3	1	0	30	40	3.87	1.32	20.9	247	36	73	3.75	3.6	11.9	3.3	0.9	136
2019	A+	Dunedin	5	2	1	63	77	1.71	0.94	19.7	184	27	84	1.57	2.7	11.0	4.1	0.4	143
2019	AA	New Hampshire	2	4	0	43	52	3.54	1.27	19.6	233	32	75	3.39	3.8	10.8	2.9	0.8	112

Intriguing SP who found success at three levels in first full season as pro. Posted plus K rate, but more predicated on deception and pitch location than natural stuff. Pitches up in zone, but may not have premium velo to withstand at upper levels. Uses two breaking balls with SL the better of two. Good feel for pitching and changes speeds adeptly.

Naughton,Packy
SP | **Cincinnati** | EXP MLB DEBUT: 2020 | H/W: 6-2 195 | FUT: #5 SP/swingman | **6B**

Thrws L Age 23
2017 (9) Virginia Tech

Velo	Pitch	Grade
88-90	FB	++
81-83	SL	+++
78-80	CU	+++

Year	Lev	Team	W	L	Sv	IP	K	ERA	WHIP	BF/G	OBA	H%	S%	xERA	Ctl	Dom	Cmd	hr/9	BPV
2017	NCAA	Virginia Tech	2	6	0	57	63	6.29	1.91	15.9	329	43	66	6.34	4.7	9.9	2.1	0.8	69
2017	Rk	Billings	3	3	0	60	63	3.15	1.30	17.7	255	33	78	3.68	3.0	9.5	3.2	0.8	107
2018	A	Dayton	5	10	0	154	137	4.03	1.31	22.7	279	34	70	4.01	2.0	8.0	4.0	0.7	108
2019	A+	Daytona	5	2	0	51	50	2.64	1.14	22.5	254	33	77	2.88	1.6	8.8	5.6	0.4	134
2019	AA	Chattanooga	6	10	0	105	81	3.68	1.28	22.7	269	32	72	3.79	2.2	6.9	3.1	0.7	83

Deceptive, jerky LHP continues to exceed expectations despite less-than-premium stuff. Long-arm action, varying slots with inconsistent rhythm in delivery throws hitters off. FB sits high 80s mostly with slight arm-side run and advanced command. SL is sweepy and projects average. CU is above-average offering. Really sells FB arm speed.

Neidert,Nick
SP | **Miami** | EXP MLB DEBUT: 2020 | H/W: 6-1 202 | FUT: #4 starter | **7B**

Thrws R Age 23
2015 (2) HS (GA)

Velo	Pitch	Grade
89-92	FB	+++
83-85	SL	+++
81-84	CU	+++

Year	Lev	Team	W	L	Sv	IP	K	ERA	WHIP	BF/G	OBA	H%	S%	xERA	Ctl	Dom	Cmd	hr/9	BPV
2017	AA	Arkansas	1	3	0	23	13	6.62	1.65	17.2	336	36	62	6.58	1.9	5.1	2.6	1.6	57
2018	AA	Jacksonville	12	7	0	152	154	3.25	1.14	23.2	249	31	76	3.43	1.8	9.1	5.0	1.0	132
2019	Rk	GCL Marlins	0	0	0	3	3	0.00	0.94	6.0	181	25	100	1.17	2.8	8.4	3.0	0.0	94
2019	A+	Jupiter	0	1	0	9	6	4.95	1.54	19.8	280	31	69	4.89	4.0	5.9	1.5	1.0	18
2019	AAA	New Orleans	3	4	0	41	37	5.05	1.63	20.3	280	34	70	5.01	4.8	8.1	1.7	0.9	34

Cross-body 3/4 RHP struggled with command/control after knee surgery. Regained form in AFL, walking only 2 batters in 22.1 IP. Stuff doesn't pop, but is solid all-around. 2-seam FB relies on good arm-side movement. Will mix 4-seam FB in for additional look. SL improved to an above-average breaker. CU is also above average.

Nelson,Nick

SP	New York (A)	EXP MLB DEBUT: 2020	H/W: 6-1 195	FUT: Setup reliever	7C

Thrws R Age 24 — 2016 (4) Gulf Coast CC

Velo	Pitch	Grade
92-95	FB	++++
78-80	CB	++++
87-89	SP	++

Year	Lev	Team	W	L	Sv	IP	K	ERA	WHIP	BF/G	OBA	H%	S%	xERA	Ctl	Dom	Cmd	hr/9	BPV
2018	A+	Tampa	7	5	0	88	99	3.37	1.32	20.2	217	31	72	2.62	4.8	10.1	2.1	0.1	70
2018	AA	Trenton	0	0	0	8	10	5.49	2.32	14.0	302	41	78	7.23	9.9	11.0	1.1	1.1	-51
2019	A+	Tampa	0	0	0	3	7	0.00	1.56	14.0	307	66	100	4.29	2.8	19.7	7.0	0.0	296
2019	AA	Trenton	7	2	0	65	83	2.35	1.28	20.5	208	30	84	2.81	4.8	11.5	2.4	0.6	94
2019	AAA	Scranton/WB	1	1	0	21	24	4.71	1.29	21.6	252	34	64	3.70	3.0	10.3	3.4	0.9	122

Physically mature, high 3/4s RHP likely fits long-term RP role. Uses size well in delivery. 92-95 MPH FB gets on hitter quickly. Likely finds more velocity in RP role. 11-to-5 CB is best secondary with good shape and solid break. Telegraphs splitter by slowing delivery but achieves good break.

Nelson,Ryne

RP	Arizona	EXP MLB DEBUT: 2022	H/W: 6-3 184	FUT: Setup reliever	8D

Thrws R Age 22 — 2019 (2) Oregon

Velo	Pitch	Grade
93-96	FB	+++
84-87	SL	+++
	CB	++
	CU	++

Year	Lev	Team	W	L	Sv	IP	K	ERA	WHIP	BF/G	OBA	H%	S%	xERA	Ctl	Dom	Cmd	hr/9	BPV
2019	A-	Hillsboro	0	1	0	18	26	2.97	1.37	7.6	226	36	79	3.22	4.9	12.9	2.6	0.5	116

Long, athletic reliever with high-octane stuff in short stints. Possesses clean, fast arm action and plus FB that will touch 99 mph and sit mid-90s with ease, though lack of movement makes pitch more hittable. Slurvy breaking ball shows potential to miss bats and CU will flash average. Will need to find the zone more, but has late-inning RP upside.

Newsome,Ljay

SP	Seattle	EXP MLB DEBUT: 2020	H/W: 5-11 210	FUT: #5 SP/swingman	6C

Thrws R Age 23 — 2015 (26) HS (MD)

Velo	Pitch	Grade
89-93	FB	+++
77-79	SL	+++
83-84	CU	++

Year	Lev	Team	W	L	Sv	IP	K	ERA	WHIP	BF/G	OBA	H%	S%	xERA	Ctl	Dom	Cmd	hr/9	BPV
2018	A+	Modesto	6	10	0	138		4.88	1.32	22.0	302	35	68	5.18	0.8	8.0	9.5	1.6	139
2018	AAA	Tacoma	0	0	0	5	2	5.40	0.80	18.1	175	20	25	0.80	1.8	3.6	2.0	0.0	34
2019	A+	Modesto	6	6	0	100	124	3.77	1.14	22.0	271	37	70	3.70	0.8	11.1	13.8	1.0	197
2019	AA	Arkansas	3	4	0	48	35	2.80	1.00	20.4	232	27	75	2.63	1.3	6.5	5.0	0.7	100
2019	AAA	Tacoma	0	0	0	5	10	6.92	1.15	20.7	254	46	40	4.14	1.7	17.3	10.0	1.7	283

Pitchability RHP with elite control added velocity after off-season work outside of the org. FB sat mid-to-high 80s previously, now sits in the 90s. FB has solid run and exceptional control. SL is best secondary with sharp break. CU is below average but plays up due to command.

Nix,Jacob

SP	San Diego	EXP MLB DEBUT: 2020	H/W: 6-4 220	FUT: #5 SP/swingman	6A

Thrws R Age 24 — 2015 (3) HS (FL)

Velo	Pitch	Grade
90-93	FB	+++
74-77	CB	+++
80-83	CU	+++

Year	Lev	Team	W	L	Sv	IP	K	ERA	WHIP	BF/G	OBA	H%	S%	xERA	Ctl	Dom	Cmd	hr/9	BPV
2018	AAA	El Paso	1	0	0	6	3	0.00	0.83	21.9	228	26	100	1.50	0.0	4.5		0.0	99
2018	MLB	San Diego	2	5	0	42	21	7.05	1.54	20.4	305	31	56	5.96	2.8	4.5	1.6	1.7	24
2019	Rk	AZL Padres	0	0	0	4	6	2.14	1.90	9.9	336	51	88	5.69	4.3	12.9	3.0	0.0	134
2019	A+	Lake Elsinore	0	2	0	8	11	3.29	1.59	18.1	302	43	83	5.37	3.3	12.1	3.7	1.1	146
2019	AAA	El Paso	1	0	0	11	12	0.82	0.73	19.5	184	24	100	1.42	0.8	9.8	12.0	0.8	173

Big, strong RHP who missed time in 2019 with UCL tear in his pitching elbow. Ideally profiles as long relief arm with pitch-to-contact style due to lack of a plus offering. Operates with low-90s FB and blends in big-bending CB; average CU shows most potential for missing bats. Fills up the zone and works ahead in the count. Low ceiling arm.

Norwood,James

RP	Chicago (N)	EXP MLB DEBUT: 2018	H/W: 6-2 215	FUT: Setup reliever	7B

Thrws R Age 26 — 2014 (7) Saint Louis

Velo	Pitch	Grade
95-99	FB	++++
85-87	SL	+++
87-89	SP	+++

Year	Lev	Team	W	L	Sv	IP	K	ERA	WHIP	BF/G	OBA	H%	S%	xERA	Ctl	Dom	Cmd	hr/9	BPV
2018	AA	Tennessee	1	2	2	32	36	2.52	1.15	5.1	216	30	80	2.61	3.4	10.1	3.0	0.6	109
2018	AAA	Iowa	1	1	0	17	21	2.62	1.34	4.8	185	27	82	2.68	6.3	11.0	1.8	0.5	46
2018	MLB	Chi Cubs	0	1	0	11	10	4.09	1.73	4.5	311	40	74	4.88	4.1	8.2	2.0	0.0	55
2019	AAA	Iowa	3	2	6	57	81	4.25	1.24	5.2	199	28	71	3.42	4.9	12.7	2.6	1.4	116
2019	MLB	Chi Cubs	0	1	0	9	11	2.97	1.87	4.7	260	35	88	5.38	7.9	10.9	1.4	1.0	0

Hard-throwing RHP with some of the best velo in the system. Will touch 99 mph with running action to plus-plus FB and blends in fringe (but usable) SP and SL combo to keep hitters honest. Strong, durable build. Delivery requires moderate effort and may not have exceptional command. High-leverage upside if he can execute more consistently.

Nunez,Dedniel

SP	New York (N)	EXP MLB DEBUT: 2021	H/W: 6-2 180	FUT: Middle reliever	6C

Thrws R Age 23 — 2016 FA (DR)

Velo	Pitch	Grade
90-93	FB	+++
81-84	SL	+++
80-82	CU	++

Year	Lev	Team	W	L	Sv	IP	K	ERA	WHIP	BF/G	OBA	H%	S%	xERA	Ctl	Dom	Cmd	hr/9	BPV
2017	Rk	GCL Mets	1	3	0	44	46	5.29	1.52	19.2	290	38	64	4.59	3.3	9.4	2.9	0.6	99
2018	Rk	Kingsport	4	1	1	40	36	3.82	1.35	15.2	252	32	71	3.48	3.6	8.1	2.3	0.4	66
2019	A+	St. Lucie	2	3	0	57	61	4.56	1.38	20.0	268	36	66	3.80	3.1	9.6	3.1	0.5	106
2019	A	Columbia	3	1	0	22	33	4.07	0.77	19.8	183	29	47	1.48	1.2	13.4	11.0	0.8	227

3/4s RHP with online delivery looks more like future RP than SP. Delivery is bulky and fits best in relief. 3-pitch pitcher. Low 90s FB has late arm-side bore. Plays up at higher velocity; could be a plus offering in RP role. Calls breaking pitch a CB but looks more like a SL with tight, 2-plane break. It has above-average potential. No feel for CU.

O'Brien,Riley

SP	Tampa Bay	EXP MLB DEBUT: 2021	H/W: 6-4 170	FUT: Setup reliever	7C

Thrws R Age 25 — 2017 (8) Coll. of Idaho

Velo	Pitch	Grade
91-94	FB	++++
	CB	+++
87-88	CU	++

Year	Lev	Team	W	L	Sv	IP	K	ERA	WHIP	BF/G	OBA	H%	S%	xERA	Ctl	Dom	Cmd	hr/9	BPV
2017	Rk	Princeton	1	0	0	41	40	2.20	1.10	14.6	195	26	80	1.93	3.7	8.8	2.4	0.2	75
2018	A	Bowling Green	4	1	0	48	66	2.06	0.91	12.0	145	22	80	1.21	3.9	12.3	3.1	0.6	134
2018	A+	Charlotte	4	3	0	40	37	3.60	1.43	17.0	242	32	73	3.34	4.7	8.3	1.8	0.2	40
2019	A+	Charlotte	2	0	0	34	35	1.59	1.03	21.8	173	23	88	1.79	4.0	9.3	2.3	0.5	78
2019	AA	Montgomery	5	6	0	68	72	3.96	1.25	19.8	226	30	68	2.95	3.8	9.5	2.5	0.5	86

Tall, projectable RHP enjoyed breakout season split between High-A & Double-A. Has developed into tall frame while adding MPH to FB. Sits Low-to-mid 90s, reaching 96, with good plane on FB. CB is a solid secondary pitch but may not have enough depth to work as SP in MLB. CU has improved but still a work-in-progress.

Ogle,Braeden

RP	Pittsburgh	EXP MLB DEBUT: 2021	H/W: 6-2 170	FUT: Middle reliever	6B

Thrws L Age 22 — 2016 (4) HS (FL)

Velo	Pitch	Grade
93-97	FB	+++
82-86	SL	+++
	CU	++

Year	Lev	Team	W	L	Sv	IP	K	ERA	WHIP	BF/G	OBA	H%	S%	xERA	Ctl	Dom	Cmd	hr/9	BPV
2016	Rk	GCL Pirates	0	2	0	27	20	2.65	1.07	13.2	190	22	78	2.23	3.6	6.6	1.8	0.7	39
2017	Rk	Bristol	2	3	0	43	35	3.14	1.30	17.7	248	31	75	3.11	3.3	7.3	2.2	0.2	59
2018	A	West Virginia	2	0	0	17	21	2.65	1.53	18.5	250	36	84	3.97	5.3	11.1	2.1	0.5	75
2019	A	Greensboro	1	2	4	31	34	3.75	1.22	6.3	241	29	78	4.21	2.9	9.8	3.4	1.7	117
2019	A+	Bradenton	2	1	0	11	10	3.24	0.99	6.0	204	25	70	2.32	2.4	8.1	3.3	0.8	98

Converted to RP full time and could become solid situational lefty. Has two solid offerings in FB and sharp SL. FB exhibits sufficient armside run and looks quicker due to fast arm action. SL thrown with power and depth and serves as out pitch. Tends to overthrow, leaving FB flat. Has history of health issues, but has good chance as RP.

Olivarez,Helcris

SP	Colorado	EXP MLB DEBUT: 2023	H/W: 6-2 192	FUT: #4 starter	8E

Thrws L Age 19 — 2016 FA (DR)

Velo	Pitch	Grade
92-95	FB	+++
	CB	+++
	CU	++

Year	Lev	Team	W	L	Sv	IP	K	ERA	WHIP	BF/G	OBA	H%	S%	xERA	Ctl	Dom	Cmd	hr/9	BPV
2018	Rk	DSL Rockies	4	1	0	35	36	2.81	1.34	16.3	201	28	78	2.63	5.6	9.2	1.6	0.3	32
2018	Rk	DSL Colorado	2	0	0	19	24	1.42	0.79	17.1	170	27	80	0.64	1.9	11.4	6.0	0.0	171
2019	Rk	Grand Junction	3	4	0	46	61	4.87	1.54	18.3	265	35	74	5.33	4.7	11.9	2.5	1.8	106

Young, projectable LH who lacks polish but has back-end rotation upside. Sans much effort, will touch 97 mph and sit 92-95 with plus FB and blend in flashes of solid CB and CU. Chance to add even more velo with strength to lower half. Struggles to repeat delivery and will require reps to refine his sequencing. Will be tested in full-season ball.

Oritz,Luis

SP	Baltimore	EXP MLB DEBUT: 2018	H/W: 6-3 230	FUT: Middle reliever	6B

Thrws R Age 24 — 2014 (1) HS (CA)

Velo	Pitch	Grade
91-95	FB	++++
85-88	SL	+++
80-81	CB	++
83-85	CU	++

Year	Lev	Team	W	L	Sv	IP	K	ERA	WHIP	BF/G	OBA	H%	S%	xERA	Ctl	Dom	Cmd	hr/9	BPV
2018	AAA	Norfolk	2	1	0	31	21	3.75	1.35	21.7	279	31	76	4.54	2.3	6.1	2.6	1.2	65
2018	MLB	Baltimore	0	1	0	2	0	17.14	4.76	8.0	542	54	60	18.08	12.9	0.0	0.0	0.0	-329
2019	Rk	GCL Orioles	0	0	0	1	3	0.00	0.00	2.8	0	0			0.0	27.0		0.0	504
2019	AAA	Norfolk	3	7	0	66	47	6.40	1.63	21.0	292	31	66	6.30	4.2	6.4	1.5	2.0	19
2019	MLB	Baltimore	0	1	0	3	3	11.61	2.90	17.7	314	26	71	13.34	14.5	8.7	0.6	5.8	-217

Husky, crossfire 3/4s RHP struggled in Triple-A and MLB, leading to outright assignment off 40-man. 5-pitch pitcher, utilizing 2 variations of FB. 2-seam with true sink plus variety with 4-seam way behind. SL is best when tight and not slurvy. Other secondaries lag behind. FB/SL RP upside.

Ortiz,Robinson

SP	Los Angeles (N)	EXP MLB DEBUT: 2023	H/W: 6-0 180	FUT: #4 starter	7D

Thrws L Age 20 — 2017 FA (DR)

Velo	Pitch	Grade
92-94	FB	+++
	CB	++
	CU	++

Year	Lev	Team	W	L	Sv	IP	K	ERA	WHIP	BF/G	OBA	H%	S%	xERA	Ctl	Dom	Cmd	hr/9	BPV
2018	Rk	AZL Dodgers	2	2	0	32	42	4.21	1.21	11.8	230	34	65	2.93	3.4	11.8	3.5	0.6	139
2019	A	Great Lakes	4	5	0	86	74	4.60	1.31	18.7	231	27	67	3.69	4.2	7.7	1.9	1.0	44

Short lefty made his full-season debut as a 19-year-old in the MWL. FB sits at 92-94 with good late life. CU and CB both flash above-average to plus, but needs refinement. Command was am issue in 2019 and will need to find the zone and miss bats more frequently to remain a starter.

Otto,Glenn — SP — New York (A)

Thrws R Age 24 | 2017 (5) Rice | EXP MLB DEBUT: 2021 | H/W: 6-3 240 | FUT: Middle reliever | 6C

Year	Lev	Team	W	L	Sv	IP	K	ERA	WHIP	BF/G	OBA	H%	S%	xERA	Ctl	Dom	Cmd	hr/9	BPV
2017	A-	Staten Island	3	0	0	17	25	1.59	1.00	9.3	200	34	82	1.49	2.6	13.2	5.0	0.0	185
2018	A	Charleston (Sc)	1	1	0	10	8	3.56	1.49	21.7	219	25	79	3.84	6.2	7.1	1.1	0.9	-22
2019	Rk	GCL YankeesW	0	0	0	4	5	2.25	1.00	7.6	81	14	75	0.30	6.8	11.3	1.7	0.0	38
2019	Rk	GCL Yankees	0	0	0	1	1	9.00	1.00	3.8	262	35	0	2.32	0.0	9.0		0.0	180
2019	A+	Tampa	3	3	0	56	68	3.21	1.55	17.5	254	37	78	3.74	5.3	10.9	2.1	0.2	71

- 93-95 FB +++
- 79-81 CB +++
- 88-89 CT ++
- 86-88 CU ++

Crossfire 3/4 RHP used height and size well in delivery to overpower lower minors hitters. Nothing in arsenal screams SP. FB is best when it is sinking on the edges of the bottom of the zone. CB has 10-to-4 break. The break is sharp but doesn't project as a swing-and-miss offering. Has struggled mastering CU. Hopes developing CT neutralizes LHH threat.

Oviedo,Johan — SP — St. Louis

Thrws R Age 22 | 2016 FA (CU) | EXP MLB DEBUT: 2022 | H/W: 6-6 210 | FUT: #3 starter | 8D

Year	Lev	Team	W	L	Sv	IP	K	ERA	WHIP	BF/G	OBA	H%	S%	xERA	Ctl	Dom	Cmd	hr/9	BPV
2017	Rk	Johnson City	2	1	0	27	31	4.96	1.47	19.5	223	32	63	2.98	6.0	10.3	1.7	0.0	42
2017	A-	State College	2	2	0	47	39	4.59	1.51	25.5	285	35	69	4.48	3.4	7.5	2.2	0.6	59
2018	A	Peoria	10	10	1	121	118	4.23	1.54	21.2	240	31	72	3.82	5.9	8.8	1.5	0.4	17
2019	A+	Palm Beach	5	0	0	33	35	1.63	1.23	22.4	236	32	88	2.82	3.3	9.5	2.9	0.3	101
2019	AA	Springfield	7	8	0	113	128	5.65	1.63	21.9	274	37	65	4.72	5.1	10.2	2.0	0.7	64

- 92-95 FB ++++
- CB +++
- CU ++

Cuban RHP is more of a thrower than a finished product. FB topped at 97 mph in the past, but sits at 92-95 mph now. Inconsistent mechanics results in sub-par command. CB flashes can be plus at times, but lacks consistent depth. Also lacks feel for CU and will need to show improvement to remain a starter, but the upside is significant.

Oviedo,Luis — SP — Cleveland

Thrws R Age 20 | 2015 FA (VZ) | EXP MLB DEBUT: 2022 | H/W: 6-4 170 | FUT: #3 starter | 8E

Year	Lev	Team	W	L	Sv	IP	K	ERA	WHIP	BF/G	OBA	H%	S%	xERA	Ctl	Dom	Cmd	hr/9	BPV
2017	Rk	AZL Indians	4	2	0	51	70	7.21	1.64	16.3	300	45	52	4.79	3.9	12.3	3.2	0.4	135
2018	A	Lake County	1	0	0	9	6	3.00	1.33	18.7	165	21	75	2.01	7.0	6.0	0.9	0.0	-63
2018	A-	MahoningVal	4	2	0	48	61	1.88	0.92	19.9	201	29	83	1.84	1.9	11.4	6.1	0.6	173
2019	A	Lake County	6	6	0	87	72	5.38	1.38	19.2	246	30	60	3.66	4.1	7.4	1.8	0.6	40

- 88-93 FB ++++
- 80-82 SL +++
- 74-75 CB +++
- 82-83 CU +++

Tall, hard-throwing RHP struggled maintaining velocity throughout 2019. Pitched with back issue most of season, which affected velocity and stuff. FB as high as 95 and as low as 86. 2-seam FB with heavy bore when it is right. Three quality off-speed pitches; nothing plus but SL could get there. Each serves purpose keeping hitters off-balance.

Pallante,Andre — SP — St. Louis

Thrws R Age 21 | 2019 (4) UC-Irvine | EXP MLB DEBUT: 2022 | H/W: 6-0 203 | FUT: #4 starter | 7D

Year	Lev	Team	W	L	Sv	IP	K	ERA	WHIP	BF/G	OBA	H%	S%	xERA	Ctl	Dom	Cmd	hr/9	BPV
2019	A-	State College	1	0	0	35	38	2.81	1.08	12.5	214	29	75	2.37	2.8	9.7	3.5	0.5	117

- 91-94 FB +++
- 82-84 SL +++
- 72-74 CB ++
- 80-84 CU ++

UC Irvine ace is undersized but has a solid four-pitch mix. FB sits at 91-94 with good late sink and run. Above-average low-80s SL, fringe CU, and below-average CB round out the arsenal. Mechanics are not pretty and he comes at hitters from a high 3/4 arm slot to get downhill action with some deception and he does repeat his delivery consistently.

Palumbo,Joe — SP — Texas

Thrws L Age 25 | 2013 (30) HS (NY) | EXP MLB DEBUT: 2019 | H/W: 6-1 168 | FUT: #4 starter | 7B

Year	Lev	Team	W	L	Sv	IP	K	ERA	WHIP	BF/G	OBA	H%	S%	xERA	Ctl	Dom	Cmd	hr/9	BPV
2018	A+	Down East	1	4	0	27	34	2.67	1.11	17.7	240	33	81	3.22	2.0	11.3	5.7	1.0	168
2018	AA	Frisco	1	0	0	9	10	1.98	0.99	17.3	190	28	78	1.37	3.0	9.9	3.3	0.0	116
2019	AA	Frisco	0	0	0	53	69	3.21	1.28	19.8	223	32	78	3.28	4.2	11.7	2.8	0.8	114
2019	AAA	Nashville	3	0	0	27	39	2.67	0.85	16.5	146	20	79	1.78	3.3	13.0	3.9	1.3	162
2019	MLB	Texas	0	3	0	16	21	9.44	1.79	10.7	315	36	55	8.72	4.4	11.7	2.6	3.9	108

- 92-95 FB +++
- 75-79 CB ++++
- 84-87 CU ++

Successful first full year back from Tommy John surgery included MLB debut that wasn't so successful. But still an impressive three-pitch mix that he can mostly command and get strikeouts. Can run FB up to mid-90s; CB has depth and is his best pitch, and mid-80s CU keeps RHH honest. Will strive for more consistency in 2020.

Pardinho,Eric — SP — Toronto

Thrws R Age 19 | 2017 FA (BR) | EXP MLB DEBUT: 2022 | H/W: 5-10 155 | FUT: #2 starter | 8C

Year	Lev	Team	W	L	Sv	IP	K	ERA	WHIP	BF/G	OBA	H%	S%	xERA	Ctl	Dom	Cmd	hr/9	BPV
2018	Rk	Bluefield	4	3	0	50	64	2.88	1.06	17.6	208	29	77	2.60	2.9	11.5	4.0	0.9	148
2019	A	Lansing	1	1	0	33	30	2.44	1.27	19.4	236	31	80	2.91	3.5	8.1	2.3	0.3	69
2019	Rk	GCL Blue Jays	1	0	0	4	5	0.00	1.00	15.3	81	14	100	0.30	6.8	11.3	1.7	0.0	38

- 92-95 FB +++
- 79-83 CB ++++
- 82-85 SL ++
- 83-85 CU ++

Short SP with tantalizing upside. Will need time to develop body and pitch mix, but flashes frontline stuff. Began 2019 in June due to elbow soreness, but no major concerns. Possesses easy, clean delivery with fast arm. Has potential for three plus offerings, highlighted by FB and knockout CB. Velocity on upswing and CU improved with each outing.

Paredes,Enoli — SP — Houston

Thrws R Age 24 | 2014 FA (DR) | EXP MLB DEBUT: 2021 | H/W: 5-11 168 | FUT: Setup reliever | 7D

Year	Lev	Team	W	L	Sv	IP	K	ERA	WHIP	BF/G	OBA	H%	S%	xERA	Ctl	Dom	Cmd	hr/9	BPV
2017	A	Quad Cities	1	3	0	38	33	2.13	0.89	17.7	163	19	81	1.53	3.1	7.8	2.5	0.7	75
2018	A	Quad Cities	2	3	2	55	71	1.47	0.98	13.1	152	25	83	0.93	4.2	11.6	2.7	0.0	112
2018	A+	Buies Creek	4	1	0	13	19	1.37	0.69	5.7	140	22	88	0.69	2.1	13.1	6.3	0.7	197
2019	A+	Fayetteville	3	1	0	44	59	1.64	0.95	16.6	145	22	87	1.36	4.3	12.1	2.8	0.6	119
2019	AA	Corpus Christi	2	3	1	50	69	3.78	1.00	15.9	171	28	59	1.33	3.8	12.4	3.3	0.2	140

- 92-96 FB ++++
- 81-84 SL ++++
- 83-84 CU ++

Short SP who leverages elite arm and speed to generate plus natural stuff. FB can be electric, thrown with fast arm action and generating late sink. Slower SL gives him 2nd plus pitch in repertoire and can have vicious break. CU lags far behind and can slow arm speed when using. Lacks deception in delivery and struggles with command.

Parkinson,David — SP — Philadelphia

Thrws L Age 24 | 2017 (12) Mississippi | EXP MLB DEBUT: 2021 | H/W: 6-2 210 | FUT: #5 SP/swingman | 7C

Year	Lev	Team	W	L	Sv	IP	K	ERA	WHIP	BF/G	OBA	H%	S%	xERA	Ctl	Dom	Cmd	hr/9	BPV
2017	NCAA	Mississippi	6	3	0	77	76	3.39	1.29	22.6	257	32	79	4.07	2.8	8.9	3.2	1.2	102
2017	A-	Williamsport	1	3	0	32	42	2.52	1.21	11.8	248	36	81	3.16	2.5	11.7	4.7	0.6	161
2018	A	Lakewood	8	1	0	95	115	1.51	1.05	21.7	216	31	88	2.19	2.5	10.9	4.4	0.4	147
2018	A+	Clearwater	3	0	0	29	26	1.24	0.90	21.6	172	22	88	1.26	2.8	8.1	2.9	0.3	88
2019	AA	Reading	10	9	0	119	118	4.08	1.23	21.9	242	31	68	3.33	2.9	8.9	3.0	0.8	99

- 90-93 FB ++
- 78-80 SL ++
- 80-84 CU +++

Control/command lefty with good size who has moved quickly. Doesn't wow with tools but when has his command, could fit that the back of a rotation. FB 90-93; CU best secondary at 80-84 with a chance to be a swing and miss pitch. Lack of reliable breaking ball holding him back from higher rating. Triple-A will be a good challenge.

Parsons,Tommy — SP — St. Louis

Thrws R Age 24 | 2018 FA (Adrian College) | EXP MLB DEBUT: 2020 | H/W: 6-4 185 | FUT: Middle reliever | 6C

Year	Lev	Team	W	L	Sv	IP	K	ERA	WHIP	BF/G	OBA	H%	S%	xERA	Ctl	Dom	Cmd	hr/9	BPV
2018	Rk	Johnson City	5	1	1	57	43	3.00	1.21	17.7	268	31	81	4.00	1.6	6.8	4.3	1.1	98
2019	A	Peoria	4	0	0	35	26	0.26	0.54	23.5	124	15	100		1.3	6.7	5.2	0.3	104
2019	A+	Palm Beach	3	2	0	42	39	2.14	1.14	23.8	257	33	81	2.81	1.5	8.3	5.6	0.2	128
2019	AA	Springfield	4	6	0	83	77	5.31	1.25	24.2	280	29	71	5.85	1.4	8.3	5.9	2.8	130
2019	AAA	Memphis	0	1	0	5	6	9.00	1.80	23.1	332	38	57	8.76	3.6	10.8	3.0	3.6	115

- 89-93 FB ++
- CB ++
- SL ++
- CU ++++

After a standout Division 3 college career, he is on the verge of his MLB debut. Extreme strike-thrower lacks top-shelf stuff and instead relies on moving the ball around and pounding the zone. FB sits at 89-93 mph with good arm-side run. Plus CU has good late fade and sink and 12-6 CB and SL give him a solid four-pitch mix.

Patino,Luis — SP — San Diego

Thrws R Age 20 | 2016 FA (CB) | EXP MLB DEBUT: 2021 | H/W: 6-0 192 | FUT: #2 SP/closer | 9D

Year	Lev	Team	W	L	Sv	IP	K	ERA	WHIP	BF/G	OBA	H%	S%	xERA	Ctl	Dom	Cmd	hr/9	BPV
2017	Rk	AZL Padres	2	1	0	40	43	2.48	1.20	17.9	221	30	80	2.70	3.6	9.7	2.7	0.5	95
2018	A	Fort Wayne	6	3	0	83	98	2.17	1.07	19.0	217	32	78	2.00	2.6	10.6	4.1	0.1	139
2019	AA	Amarillo	0	0	0	7	10	1.25	1.67	16.2	283	44	92	4.26	5.0	12.5	2.5	0.0	108
2019	A+	Lake Elsinore	6	8	0	87	113	2.69	1.09	18.9	199	30	76	2.12	3.5	11.7	3.3	0.4	133

- 94-97 FB ++++
- 87-89 SL ++++
- 77-80 CB +++
- 85-88 CU ++

Shorter, live-armed RH who was youngest pitcher to reach AA in 2019. Lives in mid-90s with explosive FB that will touch 98 mph in short stints. Shows nice feel for hard SL and will flash plus CB. Will need to make gains with CU, but has athleticism and makeup to do so. Bulldog mentality on mound; Dom continues to tick upward as he advances.

Patterson,Jack — RP — Chicago (N)

Thrws L Age 24 | 2018 (32) Bryant | EXP MLB DEBUT: 2021 | H/W: 6-0 210 | FUT: #5 SP/swingman | 7C

Year	Lev	Team	W	L	Sv	IP	K	ERA	WHIP	BF/G	OBA	H%	S%	xERA	Ctl	Dom	Cmd	hr/9	BPV
2018	Rk	AZL Cubs	0	0	0	3	3	0.00	0.63	3.7	100	14	100		2.8	8.4	3.0	0.0	94
2018	A-	Eugene	0	0	0	5	6	3.60	1.60	22.1	299	43	75	4.34	3.6	10.8	3.0	0.0	115
2019	A	South Bend	5	1	1	42	47	2.35	1.12	10.4	196	29	77	1.77	3.8	10.0	2.6	0.0	95
2019	A+	Myrtle Beach	2	0	0	23	24	0.00	0.69	16.3	109	16	100		3.1	9.3	3.0	0.0	102
2019	AA	Tennessee	1	0	0	13	9	2.73	1.29	18.1	228	26	81	3.27	4.1	6.1	1.5	0.7	18

- 92-93 FB +++
- 80-82 SL +++
- CB ++
- CU +++

Late round, small school draft pick from 2018 who scooted up three levels last summer. Specializes in elite ground-ball rate from low-90s sinker that is difficult to elevate when located below the knees. Has CB, SL and CU that project to be fringe to average offerings. Chance to be a back-end starter with good ratios but limited upside.

Pearson,Nate — SP — Toronto
EXP MLB DEBUT: 2020 | H/W: 6-6 245 | FUT: #1 starter | 9C

Thrws R Age 23			Year	Lev	Team	W	L	Sv	IP	K	ERA	WHIP	BF/G	OBA	H%	S%	xERA	Ctl	Dom	Cmd	hr/9	BPV
2017 (1) JC of Cent FL			2017	A-	Vancouver	0	0	0	19	24	0.95	0.58	9.2	101	17	82		2.4	11.4	4.8	0.0	159
96-100	FB	+++++	2018	A+	Dunedin	0	1	0	1	1	15.00	4.17	8.4	596	63	75	25.77	0.0	7.5		7.5	153
86-90	SL	++++	2019	A+	Dunedin	3	0	0	21	35	0.86	0.62	12.0	144	25	100	0.71	1.3	15.0	11.7	0.9	253
75-79	CB	+++	2019	AA	New Hampshire	1	4	0	62	69	2.60	1.00	14.8	189	26	76	1.94	3.0	10.0	3.3	0.6	116
85-87	CU	++	2019	AAA	Buffalo	1	0	0	18	15	3.00	0.83	21.9	191	22	69	1.97	1.5	7.5	5.0	1.0	113

Hulking RHP who could front rotation some day. Everything out of hand is hard. FB may be among best in all of baseball, particularly as command has improved. Complements heater with nasty SL; changes speeds with slower CB; CU shows potential. Has velocity to pitch up in zone. Once command is polished, watch out.

Pepiot,Ryan — SP — Los Angeles (N)
EXP MLB DEBUT: 2022 | H/W: 6-3 215 | FUT: #4 starter | 7D

Thrws R Age 22			Year	Lev	Team	W	L	Sv	IP	K	ERA	WHIP	BF/G	OBA	H%	S%	xERA	Ctl	Dom	Cmd	hr/9	BPV
2019 (3) Butler																						
90-94	FB	+++																				
	SL	++																				
80-83	CB	++	2019	A	Great Lakes	0	0	0	18	21	2.49	1.22	8.1	203	30	77	2.10	4.5	10.4	2.3	0.0	85
	CU	++++	2019	Rk	AZL DodgersM	0	0	0	5	10	0.00	1.20	5.0	124	33	100	1.14	7.2	18.0	2.5	0.0	148

Has an ideal frame and has a nice four-pitch mix. FB sits at 90-94 with late arm-side run and bumps 96 mph. CB and SL can be above-average at times but lack consistency, but late fading CU is plus and should allow him to remain a starter. Will return to Low-A for first full pro season and has the size and stuff to develop into a solid back-end starter.

Perez,Brayan — SP — Seattle
EXP MLB DEBUT: 2023 | H/W: 6-0 170 | FUT: #4 starter | 7E

Thrws L Age 19			Year	Lev	Team	W	L	Sv	IP	K	ERA	WHIP	BF/G	OBA	H%	S%	xERA	Ctl	Dom	Cmd	hr/9	BPV
2017 FA (VZ)																						
86-90	FB	++																				
74-76	CB	+++																				
	CU	+++	2019	A-	Everett	4	1	0	30	29	3.28	1.59	19.0	314	40	80	5.14	2.7	8.6	3.2	0.6	101
			2019	Rk	AZL Mariners	4	1	0	36	33	3.48	1.10	17.8	239	30	68	2.75	2.0	8.2	4.1	0.5	112

Low 3/4s, deceptive LHP made stateside debut in 2019. Command/control SP. Medium frame with room to grow; three-pitch pitcher. Shows advanced feel for high-80s FB. Mixes and matches location and has late running action. CB has a slow, sweepy SL feel from arm-slot; bove-average potential. Has a feel for the CU. Athleticism should play pitch up.

Perez,Cionel — SP — Houston
EXP MLB DEBUT: 2018 | H/W: 5-11 170 | FUT: Setup reliever | 7C

Thrws L Age 23			Year	Lev	Team	W	L	Sv	IP	K	ERA	WHIP	BF/G	OBA	H%	S%	xERA	Ctl	Dom	Cmd	hr/9	BPV
2016 FA (CU)			2018	MLB	Houston	0	0	0	11	12	4.05	1.17	5.5	161	13	80	3.81	5.7	9.7	1.7	2.4	40
93-98	FB	++++	2019	Rk	GCL Astros	0	0	0	5	14	3.46	1.73	7.9	290	90	78	4.41	5.2	24.2	4.7	0.0	314
85-88	SL	++++	2019	A+	Fayetteville	1	0	0	2	1	0.00	1.00	7.6	262	30	100	2.36	0.0	4.5		0.0	99
84-86	CU	++	2019	AAA	Round Rock	2	1	0	47	43	5.36	1.64	16.1	286	34	69	5.35	4.6	8.2	1.8	1.1	42
			2019	MLB	Houston	1	1	0	9	7	10.00	1.44	7.7	302	30	30	6.87	2.0	7.0	3.5	3.0	90

Slightly built LHP who has pitched in majors last two years. Has dynamic, electric FB that he can blow by hitters. Stingy against LHH by working inside and knocking out with hard SL. Lacks feel for CU and may need to keep RHH off guard. Control comes and goes and may fit best long-term in pen. Has ingredients to be solid, but needs polish.

Perez,Franklin — SP — Detroit
EXP MLB DEBUT: 2021 | H/W: 6-3 197 | FUT: #3 starter | 8E

Thrws R Age 22			Year	Lev	Team	W	L	Sv	IP	K	ERA	WHIP	BF/G	OBA	H%	S%	xERA	Ctl	Dom	Cmd	hr/9	BPV
2014 FA (VZ)			2017	A+	Buies Creek	4	2	2	54	53	2.99	1.00	17.2	199	25	72	2.15	2.7	8.8	3.3	0.7	105
91-95	FB	++++	2017	AA	Corpus Christi	2	1	1	32	25	3.09	1.38	19.2	268	32	79	3.89	3.1	7.0	2.3	0.6	61
81-83	SL	++	2018	Rk	GCL Tigers	0	1	0	8	5	4.50	0.38	8.5	117	15			0.0	5.6		0.0	119
74-77	CB	++++	2018	A+	Lakeland	0	1	0	11	9	8.11	2.07	13.6	324	37	62	7.49	6.5	7.3	1.1	1.6	-26
82-84	CU	++	2019	A+	Lakeland	0	0	0	7	6	2.50	1.67	16.2	256	30	91	5.11	6.3	7.5	1.2	1.3	-16

Has potential to be a future big league impact arm, but constant health issues have plagued him since 2017. At full strength, Perez pounds the zone with a plus fastball. Plus curve creates headaches for hitters on both sides. Change-up and slider project as future plus offerings. Needs a big return in 2020 to stay relevant.

Perez,Hector — SP — Toronto
EXP MLB DEBUT: 2020 | H/W: 6-3 218 | FUT: #4 starter | 7D

Thrws R Age 23			Year	Lev	Team	W	L	Sv	IP	K	ERA	WHIP	BF/G	OBA	H%	S%	xERA	Ctl	Dom	Cmd	hr/9	BPV
2014 FA (DR)			2017	A+	Buies Creek	6	5	2	89	104	3.64	1.53	18.4	215	30	77	3.60	6.8	10.5	1.6	0.6	24
90-97	FB	++++	2018	A+	Buies Creek	3	3	2	72	83	3.86	1.25	17.3	197	27	69	2.69	5.0	10.3	2.1	0.6	70
88-90	SL	+++	2018	AA	New Hampshire	0	1	0	25	32	3.93	1.31	17.3	193	29	69	2.54	5.7	11.4	2.0	0.4	69
75-78	CB	+++	2018	AA	Corpus Christi	0	1	0	16	18	3.33	1.23	16.4	208	30	70	2.21	4.4	10.0	2.3	0.0	78
88-89	SP	++	2019	AA	New Hampshire	7	6	0	121	117	4.61	1.63	20.7	276	35	72	4.72	5.0	8.7	1.7	0.7	40

If not for sub-par control, could be good prospect in any org. Pure stuff is among best in system. Hard, explosive FB features late life while SL can flash plus. Throws SP in lieu of CU and can register Ks. K rate declined in 2019 as advanced hitters dared him to throw strikes. Has tendency to overthrow and lose arm slot. LHH have hit him hard.

Peterson,David — SP — New York (N)
EXP MLB DEBUT: 2020 | H/W: 6-6 240 | FUT: #4 starter | 7C

Thrws L Age 24			Year	Lev	Team	W	L	Sv	IP	K	ERA	WHIP	BF/G	OBA	H%	S%	xERA	Ctl	Dom	Cmd	hr/9	BPV
2017 (1) Oregon			2017	NCAA	Oregon	11	4	0	100	140	2.52	1.03	25.7	238	38	74	2.20	1.3	12.6	9.3	0.2	208
89-92	FB	++	2017	A-	Brooklyn	0	0	0	3	6	2.81	1.56	4.7	307	57	80	4.32	2.8	16.9	6.0	0.0	246
76-79	CB	+++	2018	A	Columbia	1	4	0	59	57	1.83	0.96	24.9	216	29	80	1.78	1.7	8.7	5.2	0.2	129
81-83	SL	+++	2018	A+	St. Lucie	6	6	0	68	58	4.35	1.36	21.9	278	35	65	3.59	2.5	7.7	3.1	0.1	88
81-84	CU	+++	2019	AA	Binghamton	3	6	0	116	122	4.19	1.34	20.1	267	35	69	3.90	2.9	9.5	3.3	0.7	111

Big-bodied, pitchability 3/4s LHP is closing in on MLB callup. Repeatable delivery; varies FB grip to achieve arm-side bore, late ride or cut. Keeps hitters off balance without overpowering stuff. Three off-speed pitches: late-fading CU achieves separation; CB changes eye levels; SL is sweepy. No true out pitch.

Phillips,Tyler — SP — Texas
EXP MLB DEBUT: 2021 | H/W: 6-5 191 | FUT: #4 starter | 7C

Thrws R Age 24			Year	Lev	Team	W	L	Sv	IP	K	ERA	WHIP	BF/G	OBA	H%	S%	xERA	Ctl	Dom	Cmd	hr/9	BPV
2015 (16) HS (NJ)			2017	A	Hickory	1	2	0	25	15	6.45	1.47	15.4	283	32	54	4.53	3.2	5.4	1.7	0.7	28
91-94	FB	+++	2018	A	Hickory	11	5	0	128	124	2.67	1.02	22.4	245	32	73	2.41	1.0	8.7	8.9	0.3	148
79-81	CB	++	2018	A+	Down East	1	0	0	5	3	1.80	0.80	18.1	124	15	75	0.25	3.6	5.4	1.5	0.0	18
82-84	CU	+++	2019	A+	Down East	2	2	0	37	28	1.21	0.91	23.2	211	26	88	1.69	1.5	6.8	4.7	0.2	101
			2019	AA	Frisco	7	9	0	93	74	4.74	1.24	21.0	266	30	66	4.34	1.9	7.2	3.7	1.5	95

Tall pitcher with clean delivery and downhill plane but only average FB. Velocity is fine, and throws strikes, but cannot always command it. Trap-door CU is his best pitch; gets both swings and misses and soft contact due to good arm speed. CB is on its way to an average pitch with big break. Found AA hitters a much bigger challenge.

Pilkington,Konnor — SP — Chicago (A)
EXP MLB DEBUT: 2021 | H/W: 6-3 225 | FUT: #5 SP/swingman | 6C

Thrws L Age 22			Year	Lev	Team	W	L	Sv	IP	K	ERA	WHIP	BF/G	OBA	H%	S%	xERA	Ctl	Dom	Cmd	hr/9	BPV
2018 (3) Mississippi St			2018	NCAA	Mississippi St	3	6	0	102	107	4.49	1.36	23.7	269	35	67	3.98	2.9	9.4	3.2	0.7	109
88-91	FB	++	2018	Rk	Great Falls	0	1	0	12	9	5.25	1.50	8.6	293	34	65	4.75	3.0	6.8	2.3	0.8	59
82-84	SL	+++	2018	Rk	AZL White Sox	0	0	0	2	2	18.00	4.00	6.8	554	66	50	16.51	4.5	9.0	2.0	0.0	59
77-79	CB	+++	2019	A	Kannapolis	1	0	0	33	42	1.63	0.79	19.9	138	20	83	0.81	3.0	11.4	3.8	0.5	143
82-84	CU	+++	2019	A+	Winston-Salem	4	9	0	95	96	5.01	1.45	21.4	269	35	65	4.18	3.7	9.1	2.5	0.7	82

High-3/4s pitchability LHP projects as a back-end SP at maturity. Easy, repeatable delivery with some cross-fire. 4-pitch pitcher. Control FB well to corners with average command. Best secondary pitch is 1-to-7 CB with solid shape and depth. Short SL sometimes bleeds into CB but best when SL shape. Has solid arm-side run on CU.

Pina,Robinson — SP — Los Angeles (A)
EXP MLB DEBUT: 2022 | H/W: 6-4 180 | FUT: Setup reliever | 8E

Thrws R Age 21			Year	Lev	Team	W	L	Sv	IP	K	ERA	WHIP	BF/G	OBA	H%	S%	xERA	Ctl	Dom	Cmd	hr/9	BPV
2017 FA (DR)																						
91-94	FB	+++	2018	Rk	DSL Angels	2	0	1	15	26	4.14	1.18	7.6	219	42	61	2.16	3.6	15.4	4.3	0.0	199
80-83	SL	+++	2018	Rk	AZL Angels	1	1	0	14	17	3.19	1.21	9.5	232	35	71	2.42	3.2	10.9	3.4	0.0	127
	SP	++	2018	Rk	Orem	1	1	0	14	18	3.21	1.50	12.1	248	36	80	3.96	5.1	11.6	2.3	0.6	87
			2019	A	Burlington	5	8	1	108	146	3.83	1.35	17.3	218	34	71	3.00	5.1	12.2	2.4	0.4	100

Tall, projectable RH has vacillated between SP/RP as pro but looks like potential setup reliever. Chance to add velo to his solid-avg FB that will top out at 95 mph with some life. Repeats his delivery well, allowing above-average SL to miss bats at a healthy clip, though SP will require reps. Could thrive as two-pitch, late-inning RP with SwK upside.

Pint,Riley — RP — Colorado
EXP MLB DEBUT: 2021 | H/W: 6-5 225 | FUT: #2 starter | 9E

Thrws R Age 22			Year	Lev	Team	W	L	Sv	IP	K	ERA	WHIP	BF/G	OBA	H%	S%	xERA	Ctl	Dom	Cmd	hr/9	BPV
2016 (1) HS (KS)			2016	Rk	Grand Junction	1	5	0	37	36	5.35	1.78	15.5	292	37	69	5.18	5.6	8.8	1.6	0.5	25
97-99	FB	++++	2017	A	Asheville	2	11	0	93	79	5.42	1.67	19.0	268	34	65	4.37	5.7	7.6	1.3	0.3	1
86-88	SL	+++	2018	A-	Boise	0	2	0	8	8	1.13	1.63	11.9	151	22	92	2.56	10.1	9.0	0.9	0.0	-93
80-83	CB	++++	2018	A	Asheville	0	1	0	0	0		40.00	4.3	876	88	25		0.0	0.0	0.0	0.0	-4842
85-88	CU	+++	2019	A	Asheville	0	1	0	17	23	8.90	2.50	4.4	198	32	60	5.26	16.2	12.0	0.7	0.0	-203

Hard-throwing former top-five overall pick who transitioned to the bullpen in 2019. Big, strong frame produces elite FB that will touch 100 mph and buckles knees with plus hammer CB when he's on. Feel for SL spin and CU will flash above-average. Walked 31 in 17.2 IP and control is cumbersome issue at this point, but pure stuff is electric.

Pipkin,Dominic | SP | Philadelphia | EXP MLB DEBUT: 2024 | H/W: 6-4 160 | FUT: #4 starter | 7C

Thrws R Age 20	Year	Lev	Team	W	L	Sv	IP	K	ERA	WHIP	BF/G	OBA	H%	S%	xERA	Ctl	Dom	Cmd	hr/9	BPV
2018 (9) HS (CA)																				
92-95 FB +++																				
78-80 CB ++																				
82-86 SL ++	2018	Rk	GCL Phillies	1	2	0	29	18	3.70	1.20	11.7	247	27	72	3.52	2.5	5.5	2.3	0.9	51
84-87 CU ++	2019	A	Lakewood	3	4	1	71	44	5.18	1.63	13.2	261	30	67	4.40	5.7	5.6	1.0	0.5	-35

Tall and thin, arm-strength RHP who consistently sits low 90s from simple delivery. FB did less damage than velocity would indicate, and rest of CB/SL/CU arsenal all works in progress. Control is a challenge. Room for added strength, but future will depend on throwing strikes and at least one secondary taking a step up.

Plassmeyer,Michael | SP | Tampa Bay | EXP MLB DEBUT: 2021 | H/W: 6-2 197 | FUT: #5 SP/swingman | 6B

Thrws L Age 23	Year	Lev	Team	W	L	Sv	IP	K	ERA	WHIP	BF/G	OBA	H%	S%	xERA	Ctl	Dom	Cmd	hr/9	BPV
2018 (4) Missouri	2018	NCAA	Missouri	5	4	0	91	103	3.06	1.13	25.7	251	34	74	3.04	1.7	10.2	6.1	0.6	156
88-92 FB ++	2018	A-	Everett	0	1	0	24	44	2.25	0.83	6.7	191	39	74	1.29	1.5	16.5	11.0	0.4	275
76-80 CB +++	2019	A	Bowling Green	2	1	0	29	32	1.24	0.96	22.0	204	26	96	2.34	2.2	9.9	4.6	0.9	138
83-84 CU +++	2019	A+	Charlotte	7	2	0	101	76	2.13	1.04	20.5	238	29	81	2.53	1.4	6.8	4.8	0.4	101
	2019	AAA	Durham	0	0	0	1	1	0.00	0.00	2.8	0	0			0.0	9.0		0.0	180

Pitchability LHP enjoyed success at High-A. Simple, 3/4s crossfire delivery; hides ball well. FB is below average velocity but controls movement and commands pitch. CU is the best secondary with late-fading action, an above-average pitch presently. CB is fringy but effective, primarily changing eye levels.

Priester,Quinn | SP | Pittsburgh | EXP MLB DEBUT: 2023 | H/W: 6-3 195 | FUT: #3 starter | 8C

Thrws R Age 19	Year	Lev	Team	W	L	Sv	IP	K	ERA	WHIP	BF/G	OBA	H%	S%	xERA	Ctl	Dom	Cmd	hr/9	BPV
2019 (1) HS (IL)																				
90-95 FB +++																				
77-80 CB +++																				
82-84 CU ++	2019	A-	West Virginia	0	0	0	4	4	4.50	1.75	18.3	210	29	71	3.54	9.0	9.0	1.0	0.0	-63
	2019	Rk	GCL Pirates	1	1	0	32	37	3.07	1.21	16.2	242	34	74	2.83	2.8	10.3	3.7	0.3	129

High-upside SP with fresh arm and projection. Shows advanced command and feel despite lack of mound time. Can add to FB when necessary. Throws with clean arm action which adds to effectiveness of tight CB. Both FB and CB should develop into plus offerings. Will need to focus on CU to combat LHH. Could be huge reward if he develops.

Puk,AJ | SP | Oakland | EXP MLB DEBUT: 2019 | H/W: 6-7 238 | FUT: #2 SP/closer | 9C

Thrws L Age 24	Year	Lev	Team	W	L	Sv	IP	K	ERA	WHIP	BF/G	OBA	H%	S%	xERA	Ctl	Dom	Cmd	hr/9	BPV
2016 (1) Florida	2017	AA	Midland	2	5	0	64	86	4.36	1.39	20.7	262	40	67	3.53	3.5	12.1	3.4	0.3	141
93-96 FB ++++	2019	A+	Stockton	0	0	0	6	9	6.00	1.50	8.6	228	27	71	5.91	6.0	13.5	2.3	3.0	99
87-90 SL ++++	2019	AA	Midland	0	0	0	8	13	4.44	1.48	5.8	283	42	80	5.86	3.3	14.4	4.3	2.2	188
79-83 CB ++	2019	AAA	Las Vegas	4	1	0	11	16	4.91	0.91	4.6	184	21	57	3.39	2.5	13.1	5.3	2.5	187
85-89 CU +++	2019	MLB	Oakland	2	0	0	11	13	3.24	1.35	4.6	242	33	79	3.68	4.1	10.5	2.6	0.8	98

High-octane LH previously drafted sixth overall made his anticipated debut in September. Can reach back for triple digits on elite FB that plays up with extension to plate from tall, muscular frame. Has solid SL/CB/CU combo, with a tight SL being the best of the bunch. Command can come and go at times given his long levers, but has big upside.

Quezada,Johan | RP | Miami | EXP MLB DEBUT: 2021 | H/W: 6-9 255 | FUT: Middle reliever | 6C

Thrws R Age 25	Year	Lev	Team	W	L	Sv	IP	K	ERA	WHIP	BF/G	OBA	H%	S%	xERA	Ctl	Dom	Cmd	hr/9	BPV
2012 FA (DR)	2016	Rk	Elizabethton	2	1	3	30	29	5.08	1.50	6.8	220	29	64	3.31	6.3	8.7	1.4	0.3	5
96-99 FB ++++	2017		Did not pitch - injury																	
84-86 SL +++	2018	Rk	Elizabethton	2	2	2	23	21	2.35	1.30	7.9	217	29	80	2.51	4.7	8.2	1.8	0.0	39
	2018	A	Cedar Rapids	1	1	2	9	10	0.98	0.98	8.7	212	31	89	1.62	2.0	9.8	5.0	0.0	141
	2019	A+	Fort Myers	7	2	2	52	49	3.45	1.50	6.8	254	33	76	3.79	4.8	8.5	1.8	0.3	40

Hard-throwing, RP-only prospect has moved past low minor struggles and injuries. Tall frame, still learning to use height in online high 3/4s delivery. Struggles repeating mechanics of stiff delivery. Sits high-90s with live FB. SL has slurve profile and could be an above-average pitch at projection.

Ramirez,Alexis | SP | Milwaukee | EXP MLB DEBUT: 2022 | H/W: 6-2 170 | FUT: #4 starter | 8E

Thrws R Age 20	Year	Lev	Team	W	L	Sv	IP	K	ERA	WHIP	BF/G	OBA	H%	S%	xERA	Ctl	Dom	Cmd	hr/9	BPV
2018 FA (DR)																				
92-95 FB ++++																				
77-80 CB +++																				
CU ++																				
	2019	Rk	AZL BrewersB	3	3	0	43	50	5.21	1.74	17.9	299	40	70	5.48	4.8	10.4	2.2	0.8	76

Young Dominican RH who was among AZL leaders in Dom and GB%. Plus FB sits 92-95 mph with a chance to add more as he fills out his wiry, athletic frame. Breaking ball is slurvy but shows aptitude for spin; CU remains a work in progress. Still learning how to sequence his pitches, and command will require work.

Ramirez,Manny | SP | Houston | EXP MLB DEBUT: 2022 | H/W: 5-11 170 | FUT: #4 starter | 8E

Thrws R Age 20	Year	Lev	Team	W	L	Sv	IP	K	ERA	WHIP	BF/G	OBA	H%	S%	xERA	Ctl	Dom	Cmd	hr/9	BPV
2017 FA (DR)																				
94-98 FB ++++	2018	A-	Tri City	0	0	0	5	9	0.00	0.98	9.7	65	16	100	0.06	7.1	15.9	2.3	0.0	113
79-82 CB +++	2018	Rk	GCL Astros	1	1	0	34	46	4.76	1.29	14.0	232	37	59	2.63	4.0	12.2	3.1	0.0	130
86-88 CU ++	2019	A	Quad Cities	0	0	0	1	3	27.00	7.00	4.9	262	122	57	17.26	54.0	27.0	0.5	0.0	-954
	2019	A-	Tri City	0	3	0	37	50	4.38	1.84	13.3	212	34	74	3.75	9.7	12.2	1.3	0.0	-26

Short, compact SP who has never allowed HR in career, but can't throw strikes. Delivery can get out of whack as he can overthrow. Arm is electric with incredible speed and snap. Can thrive exclusively with FB in low minors, but needs to enhance all secondary offerings for success as he advances. CB looks good at times, though CU can be too firm.

Rasmussen,Drew | SP | Milwaukee | EXP MLB DEBUT: 2020 | H/W: 6-1 225 | FUT: #3 starter | 8D

Thrws R Age 24	Year	Lev	Team	W	L	Sv	IP	K	ERA	WHIP	BF/G	OBA	H%	S%	xERA	Ctl	Dom	Cmd	hr/9	BPV
2018 (6) Oregon St																				
95-97 FB ++++																				
88-91 SL +++	2019	A	Wisconsin	0	0	0	2	3	0.00	0.50	6.6	151	27	100		0.0	13.5		0.0	261
87-88 CU ++	2019	A+	Carolina	0	0	0	11	16	1.62	0.81	10.1	183	31	78	0.82	1.6	13.0	8.0	0.0	208
	2019	AA	Biloxi	1	3	0	61	77	3.54	1.28	11.4	222	32	73	3.03	4.3	11.4	2.7	0.6	107

Hard-throwing, two-time Tommy John victim who was effective at three levels of the minors in 2019. FB will touch 99 mph and complements it with late-breaking hard SL in the upper 80s. CU will flash average but needs more consistency. Strong, durable frame despite questions about elbow. High SwK/GB profile. Stuff could play up in bullpen role.

Richan,Paul | SP | Detroit | EXP MLB DEBUT: 2021 | H/W: 6-2 200 | FUT: #4 starter | 7C

Thrws R Age 23	Year	Lev	Team	W	L	Sv	IP	K	ERA	WHIP	BF/G	OBA	H%	S%	xERA	Ctl	Dom	Cmd	hr/9	BPV
2018 (2) San Diego																				
90-94 FB +++	2018	NCAA	San Diego	4	6	0	89	101	4.64	1.26	28.0	282	38	62	3.71	1.3	10.2	7.8	0.5	166
80-83 SL +++	2018	A-	Eugene	0	2	0	29	31	2.16	0.82	10.6	187	25	77	1.51	1.5	9.6	6.2	0.6	148
CB ++	2019	A+	Lakeland	2	2	0	30	29	4.17	1.36	25.2	314	40	69	4.55	0.6	8.6	14.5	0.6	157
CU ++	2019	A+	Myrtle Beach	10	5	0	93	86	3.97	1.23	22.1	268	33	70	3.89	1.7	8.3	4.8	1.0	121

Polished starter acquired by Tigers in 2019. Relies on deception over velocity to stay a step ahead. Low-90s heater is complemented by above-average, late-breaking slider. Overall profile is fairly average, but confidence behind his mix should allow him to hold a rotation slot.

Richardson,Lyon | SP | Cincinnati | EXP MLB DEBUT: 2022 | H/W: 6-2 192 | FUT: #4 starter | 8D

Thrws R Age 20	Year	Lev	Team	W	L	Sv	IP	K	ERA	WHIP	BF/G	OBA	H%	S%	xERA	Ctl	Dom	Cmd	hr/9	BPV
2018 (2) HS (FL)																				
91-94 FB +++																				
82-85 SL +++																				
72-75 CB +++	2018	Rk	Greeneville	0	5	0	29	24	7.14	1.83	12.3	312	37	60	6.02	5.0	7.4	1.5	0.9	18
81-84 CU +++	2019	A	Dayton	3	9	0	112	106	4.17	1.42	18.3	285	36	72	4.45	2.6	8.5	3.2	0.8	100

SP who took to full-season pro pitching load in stride with athletic, 3/4s delivery. He improved consistency of arm angle and thus FB plane. FB has minimal run and must rely on increased velocity as frame fills out. Improved secondary pitches across the board. SL is best of bunch but CB and CU not far behind.

Rijo,Luis | SP | Minnesota | EXP MLB DEBUT: 2022 | H/W: 6-1 200 | FUT: #4 starter | 7C

Thrws R Age 21	Year	Lev	Team	W	L	Sv	IP	K	ERA	WHIP	BF/G	OBA	H%	S%	xERA	Ctl	Dom	Cmd	hr/9	BPV
2015 FA (VZ)	2018	Rk	Pulaski	3	1	0	27	26	2.67	1.07	21.0	269	36	72	2.60	0.3	8.7	26.0	0.0	165
93-96 FB ++++	2018	Rk	Elizabethton	5	1	0	48	43	2.06	1.00	18.4	241	31	79	2.21	0.9	8.0	8.6	0.2	138
73-76 CB +++	2018	A-	Staten Island	0	0	0	6	3	3.00	1.67	26.9	321	36	80	4.93	3.0	4.5	1.5	0.0	18
83-86 CU +++	2018	A+	Tampa	1	0	0	6	3	3.00	1.00	22.9	262	30	67	2.36	0.0	4.5		0.0	99
	2019	A	Cedar Rapids	5	8	0	107	99	2.86	1.05	21.8	228	29	73	2.39	1.9	8.3	4.3	0.4	116

3/4s RHP with arm-speed added velocity to his FB. Now sitting mid-90s, FB has some riding action up. Physically mature but strong lower half. Could find a tick or two more. Secondaries are ordinary. CB is eye level changer while CU has become much better but still average pitch at projection.

Rivera,Blake — SP — San Francisco

EXP MLB DEBUT: 2022 | H/W: 6-4 225 | FUT: #4 starter | 7D

Thrws R Age 22 — 2018 (4) Wallace St CC

Velo	Pitch	Grade
93-96	FB	+ + +
81-84	CB	+ + + +
83-88	CU	+ +

Year	Lev	Team	W	L	Sv	IP	K	ERA	WHIP	BF/G	OBA	H%	S%	xERA	Ctl	Dom	Cmd	hr/9	BPV
2018	NCAA	Wallace St CC	10	0	0	67	98	1.75	0.94	19.4	156	27	82	1.11	3.8	13.2	3.5	0.3	153
2018	A-	Salem-Keizer	0	0	0	19	14	6.16	1.63	9.4	272	31	62	4.96	5.2	6.6	1.3	0.9	-3
2019	A	Augusta	4	6	0	73	87	3.95	1.34	19.0	223	32	69	3.00	4.8	10.7	2.2	0.4	81
2019	Rk	AZL Giants O	0	1	0	2	0	18.00	3.00	5.8	415	41	33	10.10	9.0	0.0	0.0	0.0	-225

Tall SP with excellent full-season debut. Allowed very few HR and had exceptional groundball rate. Could by bullpen candidate as he lacks third pitch and could thrive with solid-average FB and CB with premium break. Walks have been an issue as he struggles to locate FB. Power CB is go-to pitch, though can overthrow at times.

Rivera,Jose Alberto — SP — Houston

EXP MLB DEBUT: 2022 | H/W: 6-3 160 | FUT: Setup reliever | 8E

Thrws R Age 23 — 2016 FA (DR)

Velo	Pitch	Grade
93-98	FB	+ + + +
85-88	SL	+ + +
83-87	CU	+

Year	Lev	Team	W	L	Sv	IP	K	ERA	WHIP	BF/G	OBA	H%	S%	xERA	Ctl	Dom	Cmd	hr/9	BPV
2018	A-	Tri City	1	2	0	10	14	4.50	1.70	11.3	242	33	80	5.47	7.2	12.6	1.8	1.8	50
2018	Rk	GCL Astros	1	2	0	39	39	3.23	0.92	14.6	214	27	69	2.38	1.4	9.0	6.5	0.9	143
2019	A	Quad Cities	5	5	1	75	95	3.83	1.29	17.2	223	34	68	2.75	4.3	11.4	2.6	0.2	106

Max-effort SP who may be best served as RP. Throws extremely hard and can blow ball by hitters. Lanky frame and fast arm action could lead to injury concerns, but has been relatively free from ailments. Has promising SL as weapon, but needs consistency. CU shows great promise, but slows arm speed and can aim. Struggles to throw good strikes.

Roberts,Griffin — SP — St. Louis

EXP MLB DEBUT: 2021 | H/W: 6-3 205 | FUT: Setup reliever | 7D

Thrws R Age 23 — 2018 (1) Wake Forest

Velo	Pitch	Grade
90-94	FB	+ + +
82-85	SL	+ + + +
	CU	+ +

Year	Lev	Team	W	L	Sv	IP	K	ERA	WHIP	BF/G	OBA	H%	S%	xERA	Ctl	Dom	Cmd	hr/9	BPV
2018	NCAA	Wake Forest	5	4	0	96	130	3.84	1.21	27.7	223	34	68	2.83	3.6	12.2	3.4	0.6	141
2018	A+	Palm Beach	0	0	0	1	2	0.00	0.00	2.8	0	0			0.0	18.0		0.0	342
2018	Rk	GCL Cardinals	0	1	1	8	11	6.59	1.22	4.7	206	33	40	2.13	4.4	12.1	2.8	0.0	117
2019	A+	Palm Beach	1	7	0	65	36	6.49	1.75	19.9	301	34	60	5.19	4.8	5.0	1.0	0.4	-23

Suspension for a second positive drugs of abuse test (marijuana) cost him 50 games and when he returned the results were hard to watch. At best features a low-90s FB that bumps 96 mph and a plus hard SL that has swing-and-miss action. Some feel for a CU but lacks consistency and command deserted him. A move to relief seems imminent.

Rodriguez,Chris — SP — Los Angeles (A)

EXP MLB DEBUT: 2022 | H/W: 6-2 185 | FUT: #4 starter | 8E

Thrws R Age 21 — 2016 (4) HS (FL)

Velo	Pitch	Grade
93-96	FB	+ + +
81-84	SL	+ + +
77-80	CB	+ +
82-85	CU	+ + +

Year	Lev	Team	W	L	Sv	IP	K	ERA	WHIP	BF/G	OBA	H%	S%	xERA	Ctl	Dom	Cmd	hr/9	BPV
2016	Rk	AZL Angels	0	0	0	11	17	1.62	0.81	5.8	161	30	78	0.57	2.4	13.8	5.7	0.0	200
2017	Rk	Orem	4	1	0	32	32	6.45	1.31	16.6	279	37	46	3.60	2.0	9.0	4.6	0.3	127
2017	A	Burlington	1	2	0	24	24	5.95	1.61	17.9	319	41	61	5.06	2.6	8.9	3.4	0.4	108
2018		Did not play - injury																	
2019	A+	Inland Empire	0	0	0	9	13	0.00	1.10	11.9	190	32	100	1.62	4.0	12.9	3.3	0.0	143

Medium-framed RH has missed time due to injury, but has back-end SP upside if things come together. Owns solid four-pitch blend in mid-90s FB and two-plane SL that is effective vL/R. CB/CU combo is useable and can execute. Delivery has some effort but is generally around the plate and should have solid Dom. High risk, but also a high floor.

Rodriguez,Grayson — SP — Baltimore

EXP MLB DEBUT: 2022 | H/W: 6-5 220 | FUT: #1 starter | 9D

Thrws R Age 20 — 2018 (1) HS (TX)

Velo	Pitch	Grade
92-96	FB	+ + + +
83-85	SL	+ + +
75-78	CB	+ + + +
82-84	CU	+ + +

Year	Lev	Team	W	L	Sv	IP	K	ERA	WHIP	BF/G	OBA	H%	S%	xERA	Ctl	Dom	Cmd	hr/9	BPV
2018	Rk	GCL Orioles	0	2	0	19	20	1.41	1.26	8.7	240	33	88	2.67	3.3	9.4	2.9	0.0	99
2019	A	Delmarva	10	4	0	94	129	2.68	0.99	17.9	177	28	73	1.57	3.4	12.4	3.6	0.4	147

Tall, physical high 3/4s RHP dominated in full-season debut. Tall-and-fall online delivery generates solid extension and power from solid base. Mid-90s FB is heavy due to natural downward plane and arm-side bore. CB is best secondary with solid shape and plus depth. Tight SL also misses bats and has a feel for CU with separation and fade.

Rodriguez,Leonardo — SP — Baltimore

EXP MLB DEBUT: 2023 | H/W: 6-7 215 | FUT: Setup reliever | 7E

Thrws R Age 22 — 2016 FA (DR)

Velo	Pitch	Grade
91-94	FB	+ + + +
83-85	SL	+ + +
86-88	CU	+

Year	Lev	Team	W	L	Sv	IP	K	ERA	WHIP	BF/G	OBA	H%	S%	xERA	Ctl	Dom	Cmd	hr/9	BPV
2018	A-	Aberdeen	0	0	0	2	1	0.00	0.91	8.2	139	16	100	0.69	4.1	4.1	1.0	0.0	-19
2018	Rk	GCL Orioles	1	7	0	47	37	4.39	1.44	16.8	253	31	67	3.50	4.4	7.1	1.6	0.2	27
2019	A-	Aberdeen	2	2	0	71	80	2.66	1.01	19.5	190	26	75	1.91	3.2	10.1	3.2	0.5	115

Tall, long RHP uses height well in delivery to create angles and deception. 3/4s, upright delivery is deliberate and rough but he creates solid extension with the FB getting on hitters quickly. FB has natural downward plane and slight running action. SL tightened up in NY-Penn League and is a legitimate above-average pitch at maturity. CU is flat.

Rodriguez,Osiel — SP — New York (A)

EXP MLB DEBUT: 2024 | H/W: 6-2 210 | FUT: #4 starter | 8E

Thrws R Age 18 — 2018 FA (CU)

Velo	Pitch	Grade
87-91	FB	+ + +
80-82	CB	+ + +
83-85	SL	+ + +
	SP	+ + +

Year	Lev	Team	W	L	Sv	IP	K	ERA	WHIP	BF/G	OBA	H%	S%	xERA	Ctl	Dom	Cmd	hr/9	BPV
2019		Did not pitch in U.S.																	

Cuban RHP made professional debut in Dominican Summer League. Athletic delivery, alternating pitching angles and slots, from high 3/4s to sidearm. Four-pitch pitcher with ability to spin. FB velocity down in DSL from Cuban amateurs. Best current pitch is splitter, with sudden downward movement.

Rodriguez,Yerry — SP — Texas

EXP MLB DEBUT: 2022 | H/W: 6-2 198 | FUT: #3 starter | 8D

Thrws R Age 22 — 2015 FA (DR)

Velo	Pitch	Grade
92-94	FB	+ + +
80-83	CU	+ + +
72-75	CB	+ +

Year	Lev	Team	W	L	Sv	IP	K	ERA	WHIP	BF/G	OBA	H%	S%	xERA	Ctl	Dom	Cmd	hr/9	BPV
2018	A-	Spokane	3	0	0	24	27	1.86	1.12	23.8	244	33	88	3.05	1.9	10.0	5.4	0.7	149
2018	Rk	AZL Rangers	2	2	0	38	55	3.54	1.08	18.6	261	41	65	2.68	0.7	13.0	18.3	0.2	233
2019	A	Hickory	7	3	0	73	85	2.09	0.90	21.0	179	25	80	1.61	2.6	10.5	4.0	0.6	136

Tall, lean starter with good velocity and a knack for throwing strikes. Some effort to his arm-heavy delivery and ball comes out from a lower 3/4s slot. FB 92-94 that garners some swings and misses, 80-83 CU is likely his best pitch. Current CB still a work in progress. Elbow strain kept him out second half of the season and raises his risk.

Rogers,Trevor — SP — Miami

EXP MLB DEBUT: 2021 | H/W: 6-6 185 | FUT: #4 starter | 7C

Thrws L Age 22 — 2017 (1) HS (NM)

Velo	Pitch	Grade
91-93	FB	+ + +
86-88	CT	+ +
82-84	SL	+ + +
86-88	CU	+ +

Year	Lev	Team	W	L	Sv	IP	K	ERA	WHIP	BF/G	OBA	H%	S%	xERA	Ctl	Dom	Cmd	hr/9	BPV
2017	--	Did not pitch																	
2018	A	Greensboro	2	7	0	72	85	5.86	1.57	18.6	297	41	61	4.70	3.4	10.6	3.1	0.5	118
2019	AA	Jacksonville	1	2	0	26	28	4.50	1.31	21.5	254	33	68	3.96	3.1	9.7	3.1	1.0	108
2019	A+	Jupiter	5	8	0	110	122	2.53	1.10	24.0	238	32	79	2.78	2.0	10.0	5.1	0.6	145

Tall, lean 3/4s LHP pitched well in second pro season. Uses height well in easy, repeatable online delivery. Low 90s FB benefits from natural downward plane and late action. Best secondary is slurvy SL that flashes solid-average action. CU and CT lag behind rest of package; will need to sharpen up pitches to reach projection.

Rolison,Ryan — SP — Colorado

EXP MLB DEBUT: 2021 | H/W: 6-2 195 | FUT: #3 starter | 8C

Thrws L Age 22 — 2018 (1) Mississippi

Velo	Pitch	Grade
90-94	FB	+ + +
78-81	CB	+ + + +
80-83	CU	+ + +

Year	Lev	Team	W	L	Sv	IP	K	ERA	WHIP	BF/G	OBA	H%	S%	xERA	Ctl	Dom	Cmd	hr/9	BPV
2018	NCAA	Mississippi	10	4	0	97	120	3.71	1.37	23.9	243	35	73	3.41	4.2	11.1	2.7	0.5	106
2018	Rk	Grand Junction	0	1	0	29	34	1.86	0.79	11.6	155	21	81	1.08	2.5	10.6	4.3	0.6	141
2019	A+	Lancaster	6	7	0	116	118	4.88	1.44	22.5	283	34	72	5.32	2.9	9.1	3.1	1.7	103
2019	A	Asheville	2	1	0	14	14	0.63	0.70	16.7	167	23	90	0.41	1.3	8.9	7.0	0.0	143

Athletic, well-proportioned LH with chance for three plus pitches and plus command. Arsenal is headlined by plus hammer CB with late bite and depth vs. LH/RH. Presently an average FB at 90-94 mph but chance to add more with strength; CU requires more reps but flashes good fading action. Fills up zone and delivery is more on-line to plate as a pro.

Rom,Drew — SP — Baltimore

EXP MLB DEBUT: 2022 | H/W: 6-2 170 | FUT: #5 SP/swingman | 6C

Thrws L Age 20 — 2018 (4) HS (KY)

Velo	Pitch	Grade
89-91	FB	+ + +
80-83	SL	+ +
80-83	CU	+ + +

Year	Lev	Team	W	L	Sv	IP	K	ERA	WHIP	BF/G	OBA	H%	S%	xERA	Ctl	Dom	Cmd	hr/9	BPV
2018	Rk	GCL Orioles	0	2	0	30	28	1.79	0.86	11.1	190	25	80	1.35	1.8	8.3	4.7	0.3	120
2019	A	Delmarva	6	3	1	95	122	2.93	1.22	18.3	236	35	77	2.95	3.1	11.5	3.7	0.5	142

Cross-fire, deceptive 3/4s LHP enjoyed success making jump to full-season ball. 3-pitch pitcher with a solid delivery and pitchability, doesn't overpower. Fairly straight FB, relying on location over stuff. Very sweepy SL isn't going to cut it and will need to refine. Has feel for CU and could be FB/CU dominant lefty.

Romero,JoJo

SP | **Philadelphia** | EXP MLB DEBUT: 2020 | H/W: 5-11 190 | FUT: #4 starter | **7C**

Thrws L Age 23
2016 (4) Yavapai JC

Velo	Pitch	Grade
92-94	FB	+++
81-83	CU	++++
82-84	SL	++
76-79	CB	++

Year	Lev	Team	W	L	Sv	IP	K	ERA	WHIP	BF/G	OBA	H%	S%	xERA	Ctl	Dom	Cmd	hr/9	BPV
2017	A	Lakewood	5	1	0	76	79	2.13	1.08	22.8	221	30	80	2.20	2.5	9.3	3.8	0.2	119
2017	A+	Clearwater	5	2	0	52	49	2.25	1.11	20.5	226	30	80	2.47	2.6	8.5	3.3	0.3	100
2018	AA	Reading	7	6	0	106	100	3.81	1.30	24.3	245	30	74	3.88	3.5	8.5	2.4	1.1	77
2019	AA	Reading	4	4	0	57	52	4.88	1.22	21.0	264	33	59	3.52	1.9	8.2	4.3	0.6	114
2019	AAA	Lehigh Valley	3	5	0	53	40	6.94	1.94	19.5	312	35	65	6.71	5.9	6.8	1.1	1.4	-20

Short lefty with four-pitch mix; not overpowering so the margin is thin. Whether ball or advanced hitters, was a wreck in early-season Triple-A stint; things stabilized a bit back in AA. Went to AFL and had some success out of bullpen; where low-90s FB and plus CU carried the load. Has CB/SL also, but both fringy from a compact delivery.

Romero,Miguel

RP | **Oakland** | EXP MLB DEBUT: 2020 | H/W: 6-0 202 | FUT: Setup reliever | **8D**

Thrws R Age 25
2017 FA (CU)

Velo	Pitch	Grade
94-97	FB	++++
83-86	SL	++++
	CU	++

Year	Lev	Team	W	L	Sv	IP	K	ERA	WHIP	BF/G	OBA	H%	S%	xERA	Ctl	Dom	Cmd	hr/9	BPV
2017	A	Beloit	0	0	0	8	7	2.25	1.00	10.2	210	28	75	1.66	2.3	7.9	3.5	0.0	99
2017	A+	Stockton	3	1	0	18	25	6.96	1.71	10.3	301	41	63	6.52	4.5	12.4	2.8	2.0	121
2018	A+	Stockton	1	2	13	29	33	1.86	0.89	4.9	204	27	87	2.17	1.5	10.2	6.6	0.9	160
2018	AA	Midland	1	1	1	30	33	6.00	1.57	6.0	293	38	63	5.30	3.6	9.9	2.8	1.2	99
2019	AAA	Las Vegas	4	1	3	72	81	3.99	1.40	6.8	242	31	77	4.33	4.5	10.1	2.3	1.4	79

Muscular, hard-throwing RP shows later-inning potential via added velocity and a flashes of a plus breaking ball. Will touch 98 mph with FB that can play down due to its lack of movement. SL has good two-plane depth but feel can come and go at times. Unique CU is distant third pitch. Has athleticism in delivery but still only fringe command.

Romero,Seth

SP | **Washington** | EXP MLB DEBUT: 2022 | H/W: 6-3 240 | FUT: #3 starter | **8E**

Thrws L Age 23
2017 (1) Houston

Velo	Pitch	Grade
91-94	FB	++++
81-83	SL	+++
81-83	CU	+++

Year	Lev	Team	W	L	Sv	IP	K	ERA	WHIP	BF/G	OBA	H%	S%	xERA	Ctl	Dom	Cmd	hr/9	BPV
2017	NCAA	Houston	4	5	0	48	85	3.55	1.37	20.2	253	46	73	3.41	3.7	15.9	4.3	0.4	203
2017	A-	Auburn	0	1	0	20	32	5.40	1.25	13.6	252	44	52	2.76	2.7	14.4	5.3	0.0	204
2018	A	Hagerstown	0	1	0	25	34	3.94	1.12	14.1	220	32	68	3.05	2.9	12.2	4.3	1.1	160
2019		Did not pitch - injury																	

Taken in pieces, the elements are here for at least a mid-rotation starter: A 3-pitch mix that includes a plus FB from the left side and swing-and-miss SL along with useable CU; strong build and good delivery; throws strikes. But off-the-field history and late-2018 Tommy John surgery are significant risks. Pure stuff and package, but lots to prove.

Rondon,Angel

SP | **St. Louis** | EXP MLB DEBUT: 2020 | H/W: 6-2 185 | FUT: #4 starter | **7D**

Thrws R Age 22
2016 FA (DR)

Velo	Pitch	Grade
92-94	FB	+++
	CB	++
	CU	++

Year	Lev	Team	W	L	Sv	IP	K	ERA	WHIP	BF/G	OBA	H%	S%	xERA	Ctl	Dom	Cmd	hr/9	BPV
2017	Rk	GCL Cardinals	3	3	0	47	41	2.67	1.33	17.8	257	32	80	3.46	3.2	7.8	2.4	0.4	71
2018	A-	State College	0	4	0	29	23	3.72	1.24	23.6	262	31	73	3.82	2.2	7.1	3.3	0.9	88
2018	A	Peoria	3	2	0	59	57	2.90	1.12	23.2	228	28	80	3.17	2.6	8.7	3.4	1.1	104
2019	A+	Palm Beach	5	1	0	45	47	2.20	0.96	21.2	170	22	80	1.64	3.4	9.4	2.8	0.6	95
2019	AA	Springfield	6	6	0	115	112	3.21	1.23	23.3	234	29	77	3.33	3.3	8.8	2.7	0.9	87

Converted OF continues to exceed expectations despite less than overpowering stuff. FB sits at 92-94 with good late sink. Backs up the heater with a good but inconsistent CB and a CU that flashes as above-average. Has a loose, athletic frame and could add a tick of velocity. Control comes and goes, but keeps the ball off the barrel.

Rooney,John

SP | **Los Angeles (N)** | EXP MLB DEBUT: 2021 | H/W: 6-5 235 | FUT: #5 SP/swingman | **6B**

Thrws L Age 23
2018 (3) Hofstra

Velo	Pitch	Grade
88-92	FB	++
84-86	SL	+++
82-84	CU	+++

Year	Lev	Team	W	L	Sv	IP	K	ERA	WHIP	BF/G	OBA	H%	S%	xERA	Ctl	Dom	Cmd	hr/9	BPV
2018	NCAA	Hofstra	8	2	0	95	108	1.23	0.82	26.6	160	23	87	0.89	2.6	10.2	4.0	0.3	133
2018	Rk	AZL Dodgers	0	0	0	5	7	0.00	0.60	8.6	124	22	100		1.8	12.6	7.0	0.0	196
2018	A	Great Lakes	0	0	0	15	14	2.40	1.27	10.2	221	30	79	2.46	4.2	8.4	2.0	0.0	56
2019	A	Great Lakes	5	2	0	54	44	2.66	1.27	20.2	224	28	79	2.83	4.2	7.3	1.8	0.3	37
2019	A+	Rancho Cuca	5	2	0	50	45	3.06	1.30	22.9	266	32	80	3.98	2.5	8.1	3.2	0.9	96

Soft-tossing lefty comes after hitters from a low 3/4 arm slot. Continues to put up impressive numbers despite a FB that tops at 92 mph. SL and CU are a tick above-average but not elite. Uses huge frame to get on hitters with solid deception and above-average command. Future is likely in relief.

Rutledge,Jackson

SP | **Washington** | EXP MLB DEBUT: 2022 | H/W: 6-8 250 | FUT: #3 starter | **8D**

Thrws L Age 21
2019 (1) San Jacinto JC

Velo	Pitch	Grade
94-96	FB	++++
85-87	SL	+++
79-81	CB	+++
	CU	++

Year	Lev	Team	W	L	Sv	IP	K	ERA	WHIP	BF/G	OBA	H%	S%	xERA	Ctl	Dom	Cmd	hr/9	BPV
2019	A	Hagerstown	2	0	0	27	31	2.32	0.92	16.9	155	24	72	0.82	3.7	10.3	2.8	0.0	105
2019	A-	Auburn	0	0	0	9	6	3.00	0.78	10.8	136	9	80	2.19	3.0	6.0	2.0	2.0	45
2019	Rk	GCL Nationals	0	0	0	1	2	27.00	5.00	7.8	587	83	40	20.27	9.0	18.0	2.0	0.0	99

Huge and athletic, pumps out mid-90s fastballs with ease. Short arm action and mild torso tilt adds to deception, and though it's not pinpoint, currently controls his arsenal well. 85-87 SL has plus potential, and CB and CU have flashed average. The pitch mix, youth, size and relative polish makes him the top pitching prospect in organization.

Ryan,Joe

SP | **Tampa Bay** | EXP MLB DEBUT: 2020 | H/W: 6-1 185 | FUT: #4 starter | **8D**

Thrws R Age 23
2018 (7) Cal St Stanislaus

Velo	Pitch	Grade
91-94	FB	++++
82-84	CT	++
76-78	CB	++
82-83	CU	+++

Year	Lev	Team	W	L	Sv	IP	K	ERA	WHIP	BF/G	OBA	H%	S%	xERA	Ctl	Dom	Cmd	hr/9	BPV
2018	NCAA	Cal St	8	1	0	98	127	1.65	0.84	25.6	200	30	84	1.60	1.2	11.7	9.8	0.6	196
2018	A-	Hudson Valley	2	1	0	36	51	3.74	1.11	11.8	203	31	68	2.51	3.5	12.7	3.6	0.7	153
2019	A	Bowling Green	2	2	0	27	47	2.98	1.10	17.8	199	36	75	2.33	3.6	15.6	4.3	0.7	200
2019	A+	Charlotte	7	2	0	82	112	1.42	0.72	19.4	169	27	82	0.74	1.3	12.3	9.3	0.3	203
2019	AA	Montgomery	0	0	0	13	24	3.44	1.15	17.3	229	41	77	3.47	2.7	16.5	6.0	1.4	241

Unorthodox 3/4s RHP absolutely dominated High-A & Double-A on explosive FB. Former water polo player, delivers ball from similar slot, creating significant backspin. Low-90s FB plays up due to these characteristics and plus extension in delivery. The FB rises naturally and misses bats. Secondaries lag behind, with CU best for future progression.

Sampen,Caleb

SP | **Tampa Bay** | EXP MLB DEBUT: 2022 | H/W: 6-2 185 | FUT: #5 SP/swingman | **6C**

Thrws R Age 23
2018 (20) Wright St

Velo	Pitch	Grade
89-92	FB	++
87-88	CT	+++
	CB	+++
82-84	CU	+++

Year	Lev	Team	W	L	Sv	IP	K	ERA	WHIP	BF/G	OBA	H%	S%	xERA	Ctl	Dom	Cmd	hr/9	BPV
2018	NCAA	Wright St	5	0	0	47	33	3.26	1.15	17.0	232	29	69	2.32	2.7	6.3	2.4	0.0	59
2018	Rk	Ogden	0	2	0	30	43	5.08	1.33	9.6	268	41	61	3.75	2.7	12.9	4.8	0.6	177
2019	A	Bowling Green	9	4	0	121	104	2.68	1.02	21.1	211	27	73	1.92	2.4	7.7	3.3	0.2	93

Solid, bloodlines RHP pounds zone with 4-pitch mix of fringe-average-to-average stuff. Sequences arsenall, keeping hitters off-balance. Commands fringe FB to all quadrants of the zone. Mixes secondaries well, using CT to battle RHH and CU to battle LHH. CU is best pitch with solid arm-side run and fade. Slurvy CB gets job done.

Sanchez,Cristopher

SP | **Philadelphia** | EXP MLB DEBUT: 2021 | H/W: 6-5 165 | FUT: Setup reliever | **7C**

Thrws L Age 23
2013 FA (DR)

Velo	Pitch	Grade
93-96	FB	++++
83-87	SL	++++
	CU	+

Year	Lev	Team	W	L	Sv	IP	K	ERA	WHIP	BF/G	OBA	H%	S%	xERA	Ctl	Dom	Cmd	hr/9	BPV
2018	Rk	Princeton	3	2	0	43	34	4.60	1.74	19.6	304	36	74	5.42	4.6	7.1	1.5	0.6	22
2018	A-	Hudson Valley	1	0	0	9	11	4.00	1.56	19.7	262	38	71	3.70	5.0	11.0	2.2	0.0	81
2019	A	Bowling Green	3	1	2	40	37	2.02	0.97	13.8	198	25	83	2.08	2.5	8.3	3.4	0.7	101
2019	A+	Charlotte	1	0	0	34	36	1.85	1.21	11.4	226	32	83	2.36	3.4	9.5	2.8	0.0	97
2019	AAA	Durham	0	0	0	1	0	24.55	3.64	7.1	392	39	25	11.22	16.4	0.0	0.0	0.0	-424

Tall LHP added strength and ironed out delivery, finding velocity along the way. Acquired in a trade with TAM in Nov and added to 40-man, went from struggling in rookie ball to High-A performer. FB sits mid-90s with double-plus arm-side movement. Variates between sweepy SL and tight, two-plane breaker. CU is not a factor presently.

Sanchez,Sixto

SP | **Miami** | EXP MLB DEBUT: 2020 | H/W: 6-0 185 | FUT: #1 starter | **9B**

Thrws R Age 21
2015 FA (DR)

Velo	Pitch	Grade
96-99	FB	+++++
88-90	SL	++++
88-92	CU	++++

Year	Lev	Team	W	L	Sv	IP	K	ERA	WHIP	BF/G	OBA	H%	S%	xERA	Ctl	Dom	Cmd	hr/9	BPV
2017	A	Lakewood	5	3	0	67	64	2.41	0.82	18.8	196	26	69	1.16	1.2	8.6	7.1	0.1	140
2017	A+	Clearwater	0	4	0	27	20	4.63	1.32	22.5	260	31	63	3.45	3.0	6.6	2.2	0.3	57
2018	A+	Clearwater	4	3	0	46	45	2.53	1.08	22.5	230	31	76	2.29	2.1	8.8	4.1	0.2	118
2019	A+	Jupiter	0	2	0	11	6	4.91	1.45	23.5	311	34	67	4.99	1.6	4.9	3.0	0.8	62
2019	AA	Jacksonville	8	4	0	103	97	2.53	1.03	22.0	230	30	76	2.39	1.7	8.5	5.1	0.4	126

Short-statured, powerful RHP added bulk to frame, alleviating prior durability concerns. Mechanically sound, 3/4s cross-fire delivery. Sits high 90s both 2-seam and 4-seam FB. Hard to square up but doesn't miss many bats, pitching more to contact. SL and CU both plus pitches. SL gets more swings and misses but CU neutralizes LHH. Plus athlete, too.

Sandlin,Nick

RP | **Cleveland** | EXP MLB DEBUT: 2020 | H/W: 5-11 175 | FUT: Middle reliever | **6A**

Thrws R Age 23
2018 (2) Southern Miss

Velo	Pitch	Grade
90-93	FB	+++
83-86	SL	++++
	CU	+

Year	Lev	Team	W	L	Sv	IP	K	ERA	WHIP	BF/G	OBA	H%	S%	xERA	Ctl	Dom	Cmd	hr/9	BPV
2018	A	Lake County	0	0	1	10	15	1.78	0.89	3.7	240	40	78	1.71	0.0	13.4		0.0	259
2018	A+	Lynchburg	1	0	4	6	10	1.48	0.66	3.0	104	22	75		3.0	14.8	5.0	0.0	204
2018	AA	Akron	1	0	0	4	7	10.98	2.20	4.1	409	64	44	7.79	2.2	15.4	7.0	0.0	235
2019	AA	Akron	0	0	2	17	27	1.58	1.23	4.6	212	34	95	3.19	4.2	14.2	3.4	1.1	160
2019	AAA	Columbus	1	0	0	9	11	4.00	1.33	4.2	165	17	80	3.84	7.0	11.0	1.6	2.0	27

2018 2nd round pick on cusp of MLB debut. Sidearm RHP, exclusively RP now after starting in college. FB sits low-90s with excellent run and solid sink. Tunnels well with Double-plus SL. A sweeping offering is death on RHH. Will show CU against LHH but isn't enough to keep honest. Middle RP floor/ceiling.

Sandoval,Patrick — SP — Los Angeles (A)

EXP MLB DEBUT: 2019 | H/W: 6-3 190 | FUT: #4 starter | 7B

Thrws L Age 23
2015 (11) HS (CA)

Velo	Pitch	Grade
90-93	FB	+++
86-88	SL	+++
76-79	CB	+++
82-85	CU	+++

Year	Lev	Team	W	L	Sv	IP	K	ERA	WHIP	BF/G	OBA	H%	S%	xERA	Ctl	Dom	Cmd	hr/9	BPV
2018	A+	Buies Creek	2	0	1	23	26	2.74	0.70	16.2	156	22	60	0.63	1.6	10.2	6.5	0.4	159
2018	AA	Mobile	1	0	0	19	27	1.41	1.04	18.5	181	31	85	1.39	3.8	12.7	3.4	0.0	145
2019	AA	Mobile	0	3	0	20	32	3.60	1.05	15.5	199	35	65	2.01	3.2	14.4	4.6	0.5	192
2019	AAA	Salt Lake	4	4	0	60	66	6.44	1.98	19.2	331	43	68	6.82	5.2	9.9	1.9	1.0	54
2019	MLB	Los Angeles	0	4	0	39	42	5.06	1.38	16.4	241	30	67	4.29	4.4	9.7	2.2	1.4	74

Four-pitch LH posted elite Dom in upper minors and made a solid debut in 2019's final two months. Operates in low-90s with FB and CB will flash plus. CU garnered quality SwK and hard, mid-80s SL looks like it could be a fourth solid offering with which he can get LH/RH out. Can struggle to find the zone consistently, but is high-floor SP prospect.

Sands,Cole — SP — Minnesota

EXP MLB DEBUT: 2021 | H/W: 6-3 215 | FUT: #4 starter | 7D

Thrws R Age 22
2018 (5) Florida St

Velo	Pitch	Grade
89-93	FB	++
75-77	CB	+++
82-84	CU	+++

Year	Lev	Team	W	L	Sv	IP	K	ERA	WHIP	BF/G	OBA	H%	S%	xERA	Ctl	Dom	Cmd	hr/9	BPV
2019	AA	Pensacola	0	0	0	4	6	4.50	1.25	16.3	262	43	60	2.90	2.3	13.5	6.0	0.0	200
2019	A+	Fort Myers	5	2	0	52	53	2.25	0.83	21.1	197	25	77	1.71	1.2	9.2	7.6	0.7	150
2019	A	Cedar Rapids	2	1	0	41	49	3.07	1.27	21.0	261	38	73	2.96	2.4	10.7	4.5	0.0	146

Athletic, 3/4s RHP returned to health after some arm troubles in '18. Pitched in 3 levels. Repeatable, cross-fire delivery. 3-pitch pitcher. FB sits low 90s with run but isn't a bat misser. Best pitch is late-fading CU with solid arm-side running action. CB is a big 11-to-5 breaker with above-average potential.

Santana,Dennis — SP — Los Angeles (N)

EXP MLB DEBUT: 2018 | H/W: 6-2 190 | FUT: Closer | 8E

Thrws R Age 23
2014 FA (DR)

Velo	Pitch	Grade
93-96	FB	++++
84-85	SL	+++
81-83	CU	+

Year	Lev	Team	W	L	Sv	IP	K	ERA	WHIP	BF/G	OBA	H%	S%	xERA	Ctl	Dom	Cmd	hr/9	BPV
2018	AA	Tulsa	0	2	0	38		2.59	1.05	18.5	194	29	78	2.22	3.3	12.0	3.6	0.7	145
2018	AAA	Oklahoma City	1	1	0	11	14	2.45	1.09	21.5	244	37	75	2.28	1.6	11.5	7.0	0.0	180
2018	MLB	LA Dodgers	1	0	0	3	4	14.06	2.19	16.0	399	54	29	7.61	2.8	11.3	4.0	0.0	145
2019	AAA	Oklahoma City	5	9	0	93	105	6.96	1.76	15.8	297	38	62	6.19	5.1	10.2	2.0	1.5	62
2019	MLB	Los Angeles	0	0	0	5	6	7.20	2.00	8.0	299	38	67	7.04	7.2	10.8	1.5	1.8	18

Hard-thrower has an electric arm, but durability and struggles with command cloud future. Comes at hitters with a plus mid-90s FB that tops at 98. Mid-80s SL has swing-and-miss action while below-average CU needs refinement. Cross-body delivery gives FB arm-side run and sink, but 2019 was a slog as he fell behind too often.

Santillan,Tony — SP — Cincinnati

EXP MLB DEBUT: 2020 | H/W: 6-3 240 | FUT: #4 starter | 7C

Thrws R Age 22
2015 (2) HS (TX)

Velo	Pitch	Grade
92-95	FB	++++
87-90	SL	++++
81-83	CB	+
89-92	CU	++

Year	Lev	Team	W	L	Sv	IP	K	ERA	WHIP	BF/G	OBA	H%	S%	xERA	Ctl	Dom	Cmd	hr/9	BPV
2016	A	Dayton	2	3	0	30	38	6.88	1.69	19.4	241	34	58	4.61	7.2	11.4	1.6	0.9	29
2017	A	Dayton	9	8	0	128	128	3.38	1.25	20.8	224	29	74	3.04	3.9	9.0	2.3	0.6	74
2018	A+	Daytona	6	4	0	86	73	2.71	1.19	23.1	250	31	79	3.15	2.3	7.6	3.3	0.5	93
2018	AA	Pensacola	4	3	0	62	61	3.62	1.30	23.3	271	33	77	4.30	2.3	8.8	3.8	1.2	115
2019	AA	Chattanooga	2	8	0	102	92	4.85	1.61	21.5	276	34	70	4.72	4.8	8.1	1.7	0.7	35

Big-bodied, overpowering RHP struggled with command and delivery consistency throughout 2019. Mostly three pitches, but flirted with true CB early on. High 3/4s crossfire delivery and deceptively athletic. FB has natural heavy arm-side bore. SL is more like a slurve with 11-to-4 shape. CU is heavy but struggles repeating delivery.

Santos,Gregory — SP — San Francisco

EXP MLB DEBUT: 2022 | H/W: 6-2 190 | FUT: #2 starter | 8E

Thrws R Age 20
2015 FA (DR)

Velo	Pitch	Grade
92-97	FB	++++
82-86	SL	+++
84-87	CU	+

Year	Lev	Team	W	L	Sv	IP	K	ERA	WHIP	BF/G	OBA	H%	S%	xERA	Ctl	Dom	Cmd	hr/9	BPV
2018	A-	Salem-Keizer	2	5	0	49	46	4.57	1.61	18.1	316	40	71	5.16	2.7	8.4	3.1	0.5	95
2019	A	Augusta	1	5	0	34	26	2.89	1.26	17.4	261	30	82	3.96	2.4	6.8	2.9	1.1	77

High-upside SP who ended season in July due to shoulder. Don't let low K rate deceive you. Has tantalizing FB/SL combo that can be downright vicious. Struggles with LHH and needs to develop CU or bullpen may be in future. Holds velocity and hard SL can wipe out batters. Solid control due to clean delivery and arm action.

Santos,Junior — SP — New York (N)

EXP MLB DEBUT: 2023 | H/W: 6-8 218 | FUT: #4 starter | 7E

Thrws R Age 18
2017 FA (DR)

Velo	Pitch	Grade
93-97	FB	++++
82-86	SL	++
	CU	+

Year	Lev	Team	W	L	Sv	IP	K	ERA	WHIP	BF/G	OBA	H%	S%	xERA	Ctl	Dom	Cmd	hr/9	BPV
2018	Rk	DSL Mets	1	1	0	45	36	2.80	0.91	15.3	216	27	68	1.71	1.2	7.2	6.0	0.2	115
2018	Rk	GCL Mets	0	0	0	5	3	0.00	0.80	6.0	221	26	100	1.32	0.0	5.4		0.0	115
2019	Rk	Kingsport	0	5	0	40	36	5.15	1.77	13.2	289	35	72	5.48	5.6	8.1	1.4	0.9	12

Tall, powerful high 3/4s RHP struggled with command in advanced assignment to Appy Lg. Big frame. Stiff delivery that achieves plus extension. FB is electric with late-riding action. With added power in frame, should throw 100 someday. SL is sloppy offering and has no feel for CU. May be better suited for CB. Heavy RP risk.

Santos,Victor — SP — Philadelphia

EXP MLB DEBUT: 2023 | H/W: 6-1 191 | FUT: #4 starter | 7D

Thrws R Age 19
2016 FA (DR)

Velo	Pitch	Grade
90-92	FB	+++
78-81	SL	++
78-81	CU	+++

Year	Lev	Team	W	L	Sv	IP	K	ERA	WHIP	BF/G	OBA	H%	S%	xERA	Ctl	Dom	Cmd	hr/9	BPV
2018	Rk	GCL Phillies	6	1	0	59	65	3.05	1.13	21.2	274	37	75	3.39	0.6	9.9	16.3	0.6	180
2019	A	Lakewood	5	10	0	105	89	4.02	1.18	15.6	263	31	68	3.69	1.5	7.6	4.9	0.9	114

Broad-bodied strike thrower with easy, simple mechanics. FB just 88-91, but has movement; especially 88-90 mph two-seamer that runs in on RHH. SL in progress, will back-door it to LHH; CU shows fade. Advanced pitch mixer and keeps hitters off balance. Still a teenager, will need to keep tabs on his body, but a touch more velo would go a long way.

Sauer,Matt — SP — New York (A)

EXP MLB DEBUT: 2023 | H/W: 6-4 195 | FUT: #4 starter | 8E

Thrws R Age 21
2017 (2) HS (CA)

Velo	Pitch	Grade
91-94	FB	++++
78-79	CB	+++
85-87	CU	+++

Year	Lev	Team	W	L	Sv	IP	K	ERA	WHIP	BF/G	OBA	H%	S%	xERA	Ctl	Dom	Cmd	hr/9	BPV
2017	Rk	GCL Yankees	0	2	0	11	12	5.63	1.88	8.8	292	40	67	4.94	6.4	9.6	1.5	0.0	18
2018	A-	Staten Island	3	6	0	67	45	3.90	1.16	20.5	241	28	65	2.86	2.4	6.0	2.5	0.4	62
2019	A	Charleston (Sc)	0	1	0	8	8	2.20	1.46	17.6	206	28	83	2.77	6.6	8.8	1.3	0.0	-2

Max-effort 3/4s RHP made full-season debut but missed most of season due to April Tommy John surgery. When healthy, struggles to repeat delivery, effecting control. Sits 91-94 MPH with late-running FB. High-70s CB has a 11-to-5 movement and solid shape/break. Has feel for CU, throwing with same conviction as FB. It has solid arm-side run.

Sawyer,Dalton — SP — Oakland

EXP MLB DEBUT: 2021 | H/W: 6-5 210 | FUT: Middle reliever | 7D

Thrws L Age 26
2016 (9) Minnesota

Velo	Pitch	Grade
89-91	FB	++
	SL	+++
	CU	+++

Year	Lev	Team	W	L	Sv	IP	K	ERA	WHIP	BF/G	OBA	H%	S%	xERA	Ctl	Dom	Cmd	hr/9	BPV
2017	A	Beloit	4	3	1	56	64	2.25	0.98	17.7	177	25	79	1.67	3.4	10.3	3.0	0.5	112
2017	A+	Stockton	5	5	0	66	74	3.68	1.32	21.0	265	33	80	4.68	2.7	10.1	3.7	1.6	126
2017	AAA	Nashville	0	1	0	8	2	12.07	2.20	20.6	342	30	47	9.72	6.6	2.2	0.3	3.3	-120
2018		Did not pitch - injury																	
2019		Did not pitch - injury																	

Lanky, low-angle lefty who underwent Tommy John surgery and hasn't pitched competitively since 2017. Last we saw him, presented an average three-pitch mix of FB/SL/CU and velocity around 88-91 mph. Now 26, major questions revolve around his health and ability to be a starter long-term. We should have our answer early in 2020.

Schaller,Reid — SP — Washington

EXP MLB DEBUT: 2022 | H/W: 6-3 210 | FUT: Setup reliever | 7C

Thrws R Age 23
2018 (3) Vanderbilt

Velo	Pitch	Grade
91-94	FB	+++
84-86	SL	++
	CU	+

Year	Lev	Team	W	L	Sv	IP	K	ERA	WHIP	BF/G	OBA	H%	S%	xERA	Ctl	Dom	Cmd	hr/9	BPV
2018	A-	Auburn	2	2	0	29	16	5.90	1.34	17.3	268	31	51	3.32	2.8	5.0	1.8	0.0	32
2018	Rk	GCL Nationals	0	1	0	11	16	1.61	1.07	8.7	222	34	91	2.69	2.4	12.9	5.3	0.8	184
2019	A	Hagerstown	4	3	0	52	47	3.29	1.21	17.5	206	25	76	2.96	4.3	8.1	1.9	0.9	48

Second year of a SP role on a short-season club, but all things point to a reliever long-term. Low-90s FB that might tick up in relief due to strong build. Some deception in delivery; and command is only fringe average. SL is mid-80s with potential but CU is rarely used. Somewhat of a project, and a bit old for his level so far.

Schmidt,Clarke — SP — New York (A)

EXP MLB DEBUT: 2020 | H/W: 6-1 200 | FUT: #2 starter | 9D

Thrws R Age 24
2017 (1) South Carolina

Velo	Pitch	Grade
93-96	FB	++++
81-82	CB	++++
86-88	CU	++++

Year	Lev	Team	W	L	Sv	IP	K	ERA	WHIP	BF/G	OBA	H%	S%	xERA	Ctl	Dom	Cmd	hr/9	BPV
2018	Rk	GCL Yankees	0	2	0	7	12	7.50	1.39	10.1	283	46	44	4.71	2.5	15.0	6.0	1.3	221
2018	A-	Staten Island	0	1	0	8	10	1.11	0.74	14.4	149	24	83	0.30	2.2	11.1	5.0	0.0	158
2019	Rk	GCL Yankees	0	0	0	8	14	3.33	1.11	10.6	208	36	75	2.89	3.3	15.6	4.7	1.1	208
2019	A+	Tampa	4	5	0	63	69	3.85	1.32	20.1	249	34	69	3.20	3.4	9.8	2.9	0.3	103
2019	AA	Trenton	2	0	0	19	19	2.37	0.79	22.9	207	27	71	1.53	0.5	9.0	19.0	0.5	167

Hard-thrower moved further away from Tommy John surgery and posted solid results. Smooth, athletic delivery. Will vary arm slot but tunnels his pitches from each slot well. Mid-90s FB has solid late sink and will show plus run from a 3/4 angle. CB is hard and looks like a SL at times. CH bottoms out and could be a double-plus pitch at projection.

Seabold,Connor — SP — Philadelphia

EXP MLB DEBUT: 2020 | H/W: 6-2 190 | FUT: #4 starter | 7C

Thrws R Age 24
2017 (3) Cal St Fullerton
91-93 FB +++
82-85 SL +++
82-84 CU ++

Year	Lev	Team	W	L	Sv	IP	K	ERA	WHIP	BF/G	OBA	H%	S%	xERA	Ctl	Dom	Cmd	hr/9	BPV
2018	AA	Reading	1	4	0	58	64	4.95	1.27	21.6	251	31	66	4.30	2.9	9.9	3.4	1.5	117
2019	Rk	GCL PhilliesW	0	0	0	5	10	0.00	0.20	7.6	66	20	100		0.0	18.0		0.0	342
2019	Rk	GCL Phillies	0	1	0	2	2	12.86	2.86	11.9	503	60	50	11.93	0.0	8.6		0.0	172
2019	A+	Clearwater	1	0	0	9	10	1.00	0.56	15.2	136	16	100	0.65	1.0	10.0	10.0	1.0	171
2019	AA	Reading	3	1	0	40	36	2.25	1.13	22.5	237	30	81	2.73	2.3	8.1	3.6	0.5	103

Oblique strain kept him out for several months, but returned with a smoother delivery and finished with a flourish in AFL. Nothing pops, but combo of low-90s FB, SL that can flash plus and CU he keeps down is cemented by solid command. Will work inside with FB, though it lacks plane, and doesn't really have a separator pitch.

Sedlock,Cody — SP — Baltimore

EXP MLB DEBUT: 2020 | H/W: 6-3 190 | FUT: Middle reliever | 6C

Thrws R Age 24
2016 (1) Illinois
90-93 FB +++
75-78 CB ++
83-86 SL +++
CU ++

Year	Lev	Team	W	L	Sv	IP	K	ERA	WHIP	BF/G	OBA	H%	S%	xERA	Ctl	Dom	Cmd	hr/9	BPV
2018	Rk	GCL Orioles	0	0	0	9	10	0.98	0.98	7.0	162	24	89	1.04	3.9	9.8	2.5	0.0	88
2018	A-	Aberdeen	0	1	0	7	5	2.57	1.14	13.9	233	29	75	2.32	2.6	6.4	2.5	0.0	64
2018	A+	Frederick	0	2	0	20	13	8.06	1.94	15.9	323	35	58	6.89	5.4	5.8	1.1	1.3	-22
2019	A+	Frederick	4	1	0	61	66	2.36	1.05	18.2	181	24	80	1.99	3.8	9.7	2.5	0.6	90
2019	AA	Bowie	1	2	1	34	34	3.71	1.47	16.2	238	30	77	3.94	5.3	9.0	1.7	0.8	37

Former 1st round pick returned to health in 2019 after several seasons of various arm issues. High 3/4s delivery with long arm action and significant drag cause long term durability concerns. A 4-pitch pitcher, doesn't feature a true out pitch as a starter. With a velocity bump in a RP role, FB and SL would play as near plus-pitches.

Sharp,Sterling — SP — Miami

EXP MLB DEBUT: 2020 | H/W: 6-3 170 | FUT: #5 SP/swingman | 7C

Thrws R Age 24
2016 (22) Drury
88-90 FB +++
81-82 SL ++
75-79 CB ++
80-82 CU ++

Year	Lev	Team	W	L	Sv	IP	K	ERA	WHIP	BF/G	OBA	H%	S%	xERA	Ctl	Dom	Cmd	hr/9	BPV
2018	A+	Potomac	5	3	0	79		3.18	1.30	23.3	269	32	76	3.62	2.4	6.6	2.8	0.5	72
2018	AA	Harrisburg	6	3	0	68	47	4.35	1.44	22.3	272	31	71	4.34	3.4	6.2	1.8	0.8	37
2019	Rk	GCL Nationals	0	0	0	2	2	0.00	0.50	6.6	151	22	100		0.0	9.0		0.0	180
2019	A-	Auburn	0	1	0	7	5	1.29	0.71	12.4	168	21	80	0.48	1.3	6.4	5.0	0.0	99
2019	AA	Harrisburg	5	3	0	49	45	4.02	1.42	23.2	288	37	70	3.93	2.6	8.2	3.2	0.2	97

Oblique injury cut short season at Double-A, then was taken in Rule 5 draft. Slim sinkerballer who barely touches 90 mph, also mixes in SL/CB/CU, all of which are fringe-average. Some funk to delivery, gets a ton of grounders, excellent athlete. If AA Dom repeats, could have some sneaky back-end-of-the-rotation upside.

Shawaryn,Mike — SP — Boston

EXP MLB DEBUT: 2019 | H/W: 6-2 200 | FUT: Middle reliever | 6B

Thrws R Age 25
2016 (5) Maryland
88-93 FB +++
83-88 SL ++++
82-84 CU ++

Year	Lev	Team	W	L	Sv	IP	K	ERA	WHIP	BF/G	OBA	H%	S%	xERA	Ctl	Dom	Cmd	hr/9	BPV
2017	A+	Salem	5	5	0	81	91	3.77	1.31	20.9	237	31	75	3.79	3.9	10.1	2.6	1.1	95
2018	AA	Portland	6	8	0	112	99	3.29	1.13	23.3	240	30	72	2.90	2.2	7.9	3.7	0.6	102
2018	AAA	Pawtucket	3	2	0	36	33	3.98	1.13	20.4	227	26	71	3.60	2.7	8.2	3.0	1.5	92
2019	AAA	Pawtucket	1	2	0	89	76	4.54	1.40	14.5	232	26	71	4.18	4.9	7.7	1.6	1.3	23
2019	MLB	Boston	0	0	0	20	29	9.85	1.94	6.8	314	43	50	7.53	5.8	13.0	2.2	2.2	95

Big, physical swingman who pitched in multiple roles in 2019 and struggled. Career SP prior to year. Fared better as SP with sinking, running FB and plus SL. Shows average command on FB and SL features severe cutting action. SL is most effective pitch, though hasn't thrown for as many strikes. Poor CU may keep him in pen long-term.

Sheffield,Jordan — RP — Los Angeles (N)

EXP MLB DEBUT: 2020 | H/W: 5-10 190 | FUT: Setup reliever | 8E

Thrws R Age 24
2016 (1) Vanderbilt
94-96 FB ++++
79-83 CB +++
86-89 CU ++

Year	Lev	Team	W	L	Sv	IP	K	ERA	WHIP	BF/G	OBA	H%	S%	xERA	Ctl	Dom	Cmd	hr/9	BPV
2017	A+	Rancho Cuca	0	2	0	18	18	8.00	2.11	17.8	312	39	61	6.79	7.5	9.0	1.2	1.0	-23
2018	Rk	AZL Dodgers	0	0	0	3	4	0.00	1.00	3.8	106	18	100	0.52	6.0	12.0	2.0	0.0	72
2018	A+	Rancho Cuca	1	3	0	34	40	6.88	1.74	11.1	289	36	65	6.53	5.3	10.6	2.0	2.1	66
2019	A+	Rancho Cuca	2	2	7	17	26	2.63	0.99	4.3	111	15	80	1.52	5.8	13.7	2.4	1.1	108
2019	AA	Tulsa	2	3	6	37	48	3.63	1.56	4.8	199	29	78	3.58	7.7	11.6	1.5	0.7	18

High-octane 1st rounder had a bounce-back season of sorts. FB sits at 94-96, topping at 99 mph when working in relief. FB lacks command within the zone while plus power CB has swing-and-miss action but remains inconsistent. CU can be a weapon vs LH batters. Limited opponents to a .168 BAA while posting a 12.1 Dom, but 7.0 Ctl.

Sheffield,Justus — SP — Seattle

EXP MLB DEBUT: 2018 | H/W: 6-0 200 | FUT: Setup reliever | 7C

Thrws L Age 23
2014 (1) HS (TN)
91-94 FB ++++
83-85 SL ++++
87-89 CU +++

Year	Lev	Team	W	L	Sv	IP	K	ERA	WHIP	BF/G	OBA	H%	S%	xERA	Ctl	Dom	Cmd	hr/9	BPV
2018	AAA	Scranton/WB	6	4	0	88	84	2.56	1.16	17.5	210	28	78	2.34	3.7	8.6	2.3	0.3	73
2018	MLB	NY Yankees	0	0	0	2	0	12.27	3.18	4.4	392	33	67	13.92	12.3	0.0	0.0	4.1	-313
2019	AA	Arkansas	5	3	0	78	85	2.19	1.03	25.0	220	30	80	2.26	2.1	9.8	4.7	0.5	138
2019	AAA	Tacoma	2	6	0	55	48	6.87	1.82	19.6	276	30	66	6.43	6.7	7.9	1.2	2.0	-22
2019	MLB	Seattle	0	1	0	36	37	5.50	1.72	20.4	302	38	70	5.90	4.5	9.3	2.1	1.3	63

Short-statured, athletic LHP with SP repertoire continues to struggle with control. Athletic, 3/4s crossfire delivery with plus extension. 3-pitch pitcher. Struggles to command FB with late run. SL is best offering. Tight with 2-plane break. CU fades well with good FB seperation.

Shortridge,Aaron — SP — Pittsburgh

EXP MLB DEBUT: 2021 | H/W: 6-3 196 | FUT: #4 starter | 7C

Thrws R Age 22
2018 (4) California
89-93 FB +++
83-86 SL ++
82-84 CU +++

Year	Lev	Team	W	L	Sv	IP	K	ERA	WHIP	BF/G	OBA	H%	S%	xERA	Ctl	Dom	Cmd	hr/9	BPV
2018	NCAA	California	5	3	2	91	74	2.77	1.13	21.2	258	31	77	3.16	1.4	7.3	5.3	0.6	112
2018	A-	West Virginia	1	1	0	30	38	2.69	1.13	14.9	241	36	76	2.63	2.1	11.4	5.4	0.3	166
2019	A+	Bradenton	9	5	0	135	104	3.26	1.14	22.3	253	29	74	3.38	1.7	6.9	4.2	0.9	98

Outstanding athlete who bypassed Low-A. K rate doesn't stand out as he lacks true swing-and-miss offering, but works with plus control and command. Fairly low ceiling due to pitch-to-contact ways, but can live off lively FB low in zone. SL is fringy and can be loose. Repeats delivery and can sequence pitches against hitters from both sides.

Shugart,Chase — SP — Boston

EXP MLB DEBUT: 2021 | H/W: 5-10 180 | FUT: #4 starter | 7D

Thrws R Age 23
2018 (12) Texas
92-95 FB +++
77-79 CB +++
82-84 SL +++
CU +

Year	Lev	Team	W	L	Sv	IP	K	ERA	WHIP	BF/G	OBA	H%	S%	xERA	Ctl	Dom	Cmd	hr/9	BPV
2018	NCAA	Texas	6	3	2	95	69	4.64	1.38	19.0	251	29	67	3.96	3.9	6.5	1.7	0.9	31
2018	A-	Lowell	0	0	0	3	3	0.00	0.00	8.5	0	0			0.0	9.0		0.0	180
2018	Rk	GCL Red Sox	0	1	0	5	6	1.80	1.00	6.4	221	33	80	1.77	1.8	10.8	6.0	0.0	164
2019	A	Greenville	6	4	0	89	73	2.83	1.26	22.7	261	32	78	3.35	2.3	7.4	3.2	0.4	88

Suspended at beginning of season for drug of abuse and returned with successful campaign. Small stature hinders upside as he throws from flat plane. However, has three effective offerings in FB and two breakers. Throws to both sides of plate well and mixes in SL and CB with varying velocities. Doesn't have true dominant pitch in arsenal.

Sikkema,T.J. — SP — New York (A)

EXP MLB DEBUT: 2022 | H/W: 6-0 221 | FUT: #4 starter | 7C

Thrws L Age 21
2019 (1) Missouri
88-92 FB ++
83-85 SL +++
77-79 CB +++
81-83 CU +++

Year	Lev	Team	W	L	Sv	IP	K	ERA	WHIP	BF/G	OBA	H%	S%	xERA	Ctl	Dom	Cmd	hr/9	BPV
2019	A-	Staten Island	0	0	0	10	13	0.88	0.69	8.9	173	28	86	0.41	0.9	11.5	13.0	0.0	201

Physically-mature crafty LHP with bulldog mentality on mound. Variates between over-the-top and 3/4s arm-slot. Mostly 3/4s as a SP. 88-92 MPH FB has solid arm-side run. Works to all 4 quadrants of zone. Best secondary is his late-fading CU. Two-plane SL is effective, just not a swing-and-miss offering. CB has solid depth.

Singer,Brady — SP — Kansas City

EXP MLB DEBUT: 2021 | H/W: 6-5 210 | FUT: #4 starter | 7B

Thrws R Age 23
2018 (1) Florida
91-94 FB ++++
82-85 SL ++++
84-86 CU ++

Year	Lev	Team	W	L	Sv	IP	K	ERA	WHIP	BF/G	OBA	H%	S%	xERA	Ctl	Dom	Cmd	hr/9	BPV
2018		Did not pitch																	
2019	A+	Wilmington	5	2	0	57	53	1.89	1.12	22.5	240	32	83	2.48	2.0	8.3	4.1	0.2	113
2019	AA	NW Arkansas	7	3	0	90	85	3.49	1.24	22.9	253	32	74	3.56	2.6	8.5	3.3	0.8	101

Athletic, low 3/4s RHP with present command/control lacks 3rd pitch needed to be effective mid-rotation SP. Arm angle creates unorthodox slot for hitters and plays up FB/SL. High GB% tendency due to movement/profile of 2-seam FB. SL has tight, two-plane break and is a swing-and-miss offering. Tunnels both pitches well. CU is firm and ineffective.

Skubal,Tarik — SP — Detroit

EXP MLB DEBUT: 2020 | H/W: 6-3 215 | FUT: #3 starter | 8C

Thrws L Age 23
2018 (9) Seattle
92-97 FB ++++
81-83 CB +++
86-89 SL +++
82-85 CU +++

Year	Lev	Team	W	L	Sv	IP	K	ERA	WHIP	BF/G	OBA	H%	S%	xERA	Ctl	Dom	Cmd	hr/9	BPV
2018	Rk	GCL TigersW	1	0	0	3	5	0.00	1.00	5.7	191	37	100	1.37	3.0	15.0	5.0	0.0	207
2018	A-	Connecticut	0	0	1	12	17	0.75	0.83	11.0	191	32	90	0.97	1.5	12.8	8.5	0.0	207
2018	A	West Michigan	2	0	1	7	11	0.00	0.85	8.7	200	36	100	1.09	1.3	13.9	11.0	0.0	235
2019	A+	Lakeland	4	5	0	80	97	2.58	1.01	20.5	215	31	76	2.25	2.1	10.9	5.1	0.6	157
2019	AA	Erie	2	3	0	42	82	2.14	1.02	18.0	174	39	80	1.61	3.8	17.5	4.6	0.4	230

Well-proportioned, front-end collegiate arm with strong command and advanced understanding of his entire four-pitch mix. Able to pound the strike zone with a deceptive ability to play his pitches off one another. Dangerous fastball velocity complements an extremely unpredictable offspeed collection. Ability to mix sets him apart.

Small,Ethan — SP — Milwaukee

EXP MLB DEBUT: 2021 | H/W: 6-3 214 | FUT: #3 starter | 8C

Thrws L Age 23	Year	Lev	Team	W	L	Sv	IP	K	ERA	WHIP	BF/G	OBA	H%	S%	xERA	Ctl	Dom	Cmd	hr/9	BPV
2019 (1) Mississippi St																				
90-93 FB +++																				
74-76 CB +++																				
CU +++	2019	A	Wisconsin	0	2	0	18	31	1.00	0.83	13.2	178	36	87	0.80	2.0	15.5	7.8	0.0	243
	2019	Rk	AZL BrewersG	0	0	0	3	5	0.00	0.00	4.2	0	0			0.0	15.0		0.0	288

Former collegiate SEC standout was taken 28th overall in 2019 draft. Short pro debut included impressive 31:4 K/BB split in the MWL thanks to three above-average pitches and deceptive delivery. Shows command of low-90s FB that plays up with extension to plate. CB and CU both solid-average and shows feel for both. Chance to be a #3/4 SP.

Smeltzer,Devin — SP — Minnesota

EXP MLB DEBUT: 2019 | H/W: 6-3 195 | FUT: #4 starter | 7C

Thrws L Age 24	Year	Lev	Team	W	L	Sv	IP	K	ERA	WHIP	BF/G	OBA	H%	S%	xERA	Ctl	Dom	Cmd	hr/9	BPV
2016 (5) San Jacinto JC	2018	AA	Tulsa	5	5	0	83	67	4.76	1.36	15.1	286	34	66	4.49	2.1	7.2	3.5	1.0	93
88-92 FB +++	2018	AA	Chattanooga	0	0	4	12	16	3.00	1.33	5.0	293	44	75	3.57	1.5	12.0	8.0	0.0	194
82-84 SL ++	2019	AA	Pensacola	3	1	0	30	33	0.60	0.73	21.3	183	27	91	0.66	0.9	9.9	11.0	0.0	172
75-78 CB ++++	2019	AAA	Rochester	1	4	0	74	71	3.64	1.17	19.7	246	28	78	4.14	2.3	8.6	3.7	1.7	111
82-84 CU ++++	2019	MLB	Minnesota	2	2	1	49	38	3.86	1.27	18.2	266	30	76	4.44	2.2	7.0	3.2	1.5	84

RP-turned-SP made 2019 splash in minors before MLB debut. A 3/4s LHP with extreme crossfire delivery, he repeats extremely well. 4-seam FB isn't overpowering. Command and movement (plus spin) key to success. Both CB and CU are plus offerings. Sequences all 3 pitches well and throws each at same slot. SL isn't more than below-average pitch.

Smith,Drew — RP — New York (N)

EXP MLB DEBUT: 2018 | H/W: 6-2 190 | FUT: Setup reliever | 7D

Thrws R Age 26	Year	Lev	Team	W	L	Sv	IP	K	ERA	WHIP	BF/G	OBA	H%	S%	xERA	Ctl	Dom	Cmd	hr/9	BPV
2015 (3) Dallas Baptist	2017	AAA	Durham	0	0	0	1		0.00	1.00	3.8	262	26	100	2.41	0.0	0.0		0.0	18
94-97 FB ++++	2018	AA	Binghamton	0	0	1	4	6	2.20	0.73	7.3	147	26	67	0.24	2.2	13.2	6.0	0.0	196
79-82 CB ++++	2018	AAA	Las Vegas	5	1	2	32	30	2.80	1.18	5.6	223	27	80	3.05	3.4	8.4	2.5	0.8	78
85-86 CU +++	2018	MLB	NY Mets	1	1	0	28	18	3.54	1.43	4.4	301	34	76	4.60	1.9	5.8	3.0	0.6	70
	2019		Did not pitch - injury																	

Hard-throwing RP spent all of '19 recovering from Tommy John surgery. Had promising 2018 MLB debut despite struggling with FB command, though FB/CB showed flashes. FB was too hittable but erased control concerns. Has chance for late-inning RP role but likely ends up as a middle reliever.

Smith,Kevin — SP — New York (N)

EXP MLB DEBUT: 2020 | H/W: 6-5 200 | FUT: #4 starter | 7B

Thrws L Age 22	Year	Lev	Team	W	L	Sv	IP	K	ERA	WHIP	BF/G	OBA	H%	S%	xERA	Ctl	Dom	Cmd	hr/9	BPV
2018 (7) Georgia																				
88-91 FB ++++	2018	A-	Brooklyn	4	1	0	23	28	0.78	0.78	7.0	155	23	94	0.81	2.3	10.9	4.7	0.4	151
80-83 SL ++++	2018	NCAA	Georgia	8	1	0	63	79	3.71	1.27	11.7	236	34	72	3.30	3.6	11.3	3.2	0.7	125
80-83 CU +++	2019	AA	Binghamton	3	2	0	31	28	3.47	1.29	21.3	222	29	72	2.80	4.3	8.1	1.9	0.3	47
	2019	A+	St. Lucie	5	5	0	85	102	3.06	1.26	20.4	257	36	76	3.37	2.5	10.8	4.3	0.5	143

Pitchability LHP with height utilizes unique 3/4s slot to generate plus spin rates. Repeatable, athletic delivery, creates deception through angles and extension. FB is sneaky quick with late-riding action. SL is tight and he can manipulate it, resulting in plus movement utilizing angles and break. CU is effective but not overwhelming.

Solis,Jairo — SP — Houston

EXP MLB DEBUT: 2023 | H/W: 6-2 160 | FUT: #4 starter | 7D

Thrws R Age 20	Year	Lev	Team	W	L	Sv	IP	K	ERA	WHIP	BF/G	OBA	H%	S%	xERA	Ctl	Dom	Cmd	hr/9	BPV
2016 FA (VZ)																				
93-95 FB ++++	2017	Rk	GCL Astros	1	0	0	21	24	3.00	1.24	17.0	243	34	76	3.05	3.0	10.3	3.4	0.4	122
85-88 SL +++	2017	Rk	Greeneville	1	1	0	14	17	1.93	1.29	14.4	233	35	83	2.64	3.9	10.9	2.8	0.0	111
78-82 CB ++	2018	A	Quad Cities	2	5	0	50	51	3.59	1.61	17.1	257	35	76	3.96	5.7	9.1	1.6	0.2	28
82-85 CU +++	2019		Did not pitch - injury																	

Projectable SP missed 2019 due to Tommy John surgery. Should return to full health for 2020. When healthy, owns electric FB that has potential to tick higher. Uses long arms to throw on downward plane and can spot FB low in zone. CB is best secondary offering with ideal late break. Mixes in SL and shows advanced feel for changing speeds.

Solomon,Peter — SP — Houston

EXP MLB DEBUT: 2022 | H/W: 6-4 201 | FUT: #4 starter | 7D

Thrws R Age 23	Year	Lev	Team	W	L	Sv	IP	K	ERA	WHIP	BF/G	OBA	H%	S%	xERA	Ctl	Dom	Cmd	hr/9	BPV
2017 (4) Notre Dame																				
91-96 FB +++	2017	Rk	GCL Astros	0	0	0	1	0	0.00	0.00	2.8	0	0			0.0	0.0		0.0	18
78-82 CB +++	2018	A	Quad Cities	8	1	0	77	88	2.45	1.17	16.2	222	32	78	2.42	3.3	10.3	3.1	0.2	115
84-85 SL +++	2018	A+	Buies Creek	1	0	0	23	26	1.96	0.87	17.0	198	29	75	1.17	1.6	10.2	6.5	0.0	159
83-86 CU ++	2019	A+	Fayetteville	0	0	0	7	14	2.50	1.53	15.7	256	49	90	4.66	5.0	17.5	3.5	1.3	198

Tall SP who ended season in April and underwent Tommy John surgery. Has impressive arsenal, though no pitch categorized as plus. Works off commandable FB that he spots in lower half. Adds in solid-average CB and SL with cutter action. Uses clean arm action in simple delivery, though lacks deception. CU could use enhancement.

Song,Noah — SP — Boston

EXP MLB DEBUT: 2022 | H/W: 6-4 200 | FUT: #3 starter | 8D

Thrws R Age 22	Year	Lev	Team	W	L	Sv	IP	K	ERA	WHIP	BF/G	OBA	H%	S%	xERA	Ctl	Dom	Cmd	hr/9	BPV
2019 (4) Navy																				
92-96 FB ++++																				
77-79 CB +++																				
83-87 SL +++																				
CU ++	2019	A-	Lowell	0	0	0	17	19	1.06	0.88	9.0	173	26	87	0.91	2.6	10.1	3.8	0.0	128

Intriguing SP who led NCAA in K rate in 2019. Likely to have to serve two years of military duty. Owns solid pure stuff that could be as good as any in BOS minors. Has taken drastic step forward with plus FB that features nifty late life. CB and vicious SL both flash plus while CU isn't used often. Exhibits clean arm action and smooth delivery.

Soriano,Jose — SP — Los Angeles (A)

EXP MLB DEBUT: 2022 | H/W: 6-3 168 | FUT: #4 starter | 8D

Thrws R Age 21	Year	Lev	Team	W	L	Sv	IP	K	ERA	WHIP	BF/G	OBA	H%	S%	xERA	Ctl	Dom	Cmd	hr/9	BPV
2016 FA (DR)																				
92-95 FB ++++	2017	Rk	AZL Angels	2	2	0	49	37	2.94	1.16	16.3	237	29	75	2.77	2.6	6.8	2.6	0.4	71
80-84 CB +++	2018	A	Burlington	1	6	0	46	42	4.49	1.50	14.2	207	27	68	3.06	6.8	8.2	1.2	0.2	-19
83-85 CU ++	2019	Rk	AZL Angels	0	1	0	4	8	2.14	1.90	6.6	297	57	88	5.02	6.4	17.1	2.7	0.0	153
	2019	A	Burlington	5	6	0	77	84	2.56	1.31	18.7	196	26	82	2.80	5.6	9.8	1.8	0.6	43

Long, lean Dominican RH who posted good numbers in MWL but upside could be capped by poor command. Can register 98 mph and sit 92-95 with some angle. Feel for CB is advanced and shows swing and miss attributes. CU is raw and needs needs time. Frame is projectable, needs to shore up release point and delivery to reach potential.

Stallings,Garrett — SP — Los Angeles (A)

EXP MLB DEBUT: 2022 | H/W: 6-2 200 | FUT: #5 SP/swingman | 7C

Thrws R Age 22	Year	Lev	Team	W	L	Sv	IP	K	ERA	WHIP	BF/G	OBA	H%	S%	xERA	Ctl	Dom	Cmd	hr/9	BPV
2019 (5) Tennessee																				
88-92 FB ++																				
83-85 SL +++																				
CB +++																				
CU +++	2019		Did not pitch																	

Athletic, medium-framed RH was productive three-year starter in SEC. Survives off command and pitchability and will have a chance to stick as back-end SP. Fringe velocity but spots FB well to all quadrants of the zone. SL has tight two-plane break; CB and CU also grade as solid-average. Not a high-ceiling arm but one that could move quickly.

Stauffer,Adam — SP — Baltimore

EXP MLB DEBUT: 2023 | H/W: 6-7 240 | FUT: Setup reliever | 7E

Thrws R Age 21	Year	Lev	Team	W	L	Sv	IP	K	ERA	WHIP	BF/G	OBA	H%	S%	xERA	Ctl	Dom	Cmd	hr/9	BPV
2017 (19) HS (PA)																				
90-93 FB ++++	2017	Rk	GCL Orioles	2	0	0	3	4	23.23	4.84	4.7	557	70	47	18.73	11.6	11.6	1.0	0.0	-87
74-76 CB ++++	2018	Rk	GCL Orioles	0	2	0	12	6	5.95	1.82	9.4	333	36	67	6.20	3.7	4.5	1.2	0.7	-2
CU ++	2019	A	Delmarva	0	0	0	18	31	0.99	1.04	7.8	135	28	89	0.87	5.4	15.3	2.8	0.0	147
	2019	A-	Aberdeen	2	1	0	25	29	1.08	0.88	18.6	165	24	90	1.15	2.9	10.4	3.6	0.4	128

Tall RHP who utilizes size well in upright, high 3/4s delivery. Delivery is raw and lacks symmetry presently. Mostly two-pitch mix. FB utilizes natural downward plane, deception created by moving parts within delivery and slight, late run. With strength and refinement, could be a high-90s offering. 12-to-6 CB features good downer break.

Staumont,Josh — RP — Kansas City

EXP MLB DEBUT: 2019 | H/W: 6-3 200 | FUT: Setup reliever | 7E

Thrws R Age 26	Year	Lev	Team	W	L	Sv	IP	K	ERA	WHIP	BF/G	OBA	H%	S%	xERA	Ctl	Dom	Cmd	hr/9	BPV
2015 (2) Azusa Pacific	2017	AA	NW Arkansas	3	4	0	48	45	4.48	1.58	21.2	236	31	70	3.78	6.3	8.4	1.3	0.4	-2
94-98 FB ++++	2017	AAA	Omaha	3	8	0	76	93	6.28	1.67	21.3	230	29	65	5.13	7.5	11.0	1.5	1.7	15
81-83 CB ++++	2018	AAA	Omaha	2	5	1	74	103	3.52	1.50	7.8	220	34	77	3.45	6.3	12.5	2.0	0.5	73
	2019	AAA	Omaha	1	5	2	51	74	3.17	1.33	6.6	177	28	78	2.73	6.5	13.0	2.0	0.7	77
	2019	MLB	KC Royals	0	0	0	19	15	3.77	1.62	5.3	281	30	85	5.94	4.7	7.1	1.5	1.9	18

Hard-throwing, former 2nd round pick brought two-plus pitches to MLB debut. Athletic hurler with medium frame. Throws from high 3/4s slot with long arm action. Struggles with FB command and doesn't always stay aligned within delivery. FB is hard and features late action. CB is a plus offering when he stays on top of offering.

Steele,Evan — SP — Kansas City

EXP MLB DEBUT: 2022 | H/W: 6-5 210 | FUT: #4 starter | 7D

Thrws L Age 23 — 2017 (2) Chipola JC

Velo	Pitch	Grade	Year	Lev	Team	W	L	Sv	IP	K	ERA	WHIP	BF/G	OBA	H%	S%	xERA	Ctl	Dom	Cmd	hr/9	BPV
90-93	FB	+++	2017	NCAA	Chipola JC	5	0	0	40	58	2.02	1.15	15.9	210	34	82	2.19	3.6	13.0	3.6	0.2	155
84-85	SL	++	2017	Rk	AZL Royals	0	2	0	8	16	5.63	1.63	7.1	328	58	73	6.91	2.3	18.0	8.0	2.3	281
73-75	CB	++	2018		Did not pitch - injury																	
83-85	CU	+++	2019	A	Lexington	4	3	0	49	56	2.39	1.12	17.6	224	32	79	2.47	2.8	10.3	3.7	0.4	129

'17 draftee returned after missing '18 with shoulder injury to have solid season. 3/4s LHP delivery with solid extension and deception. 4-pitch pitcher, mostly reliant on FB. Commands low-90s FB to both sides with late movement. CU is next best pitch with solid drop and fade. Has struggled with feel for breaking pitch and doesn't show often.

Steele,Justin — SP — Chicago (N)

EXP MLB DEBUT: 2020 | H/W: 6-2 205 | FUT: #5 SP/swingman | 7D

Thrws L Age 24 — 2014 (5) HS (MS)

Velo	Pitch	Grade	Year	Lev	Team	W	L	Sv	IP	K	ERA	WHIP	BF/G	OBA	H%	S%	xERA	Ctl	Dom	Cmd	hr/9	BPV
			2017	A+	Myrtle Beach	6	7	0	98	82	2.93	1.38	20.6	265	33	80	3.87	3.3	7.5	2.3	0.5	64
90-93	FB	+++	2018	Rk	AZL Cubs	0	0	0	18	27	1.49	0.72	12.8	150	25	83	0.69	2.0	13.4	6.8	0.5	206
75-78	CB	+++	2018	A+	Myrtle Beach	2	1	0	18	19	2.49	0.99	17.3	190	27	72	1.40	3.0	9.4	3.2	0.0	108
	CU	++	2018	AA	Tennessee	0	1	0	10	7	3.60	1.10	19.6	221	25	70	2.91	2.7	6.3	2.3	0.9	59
			2019	AA	Tennessee	0	6	0	38	42	5.65	1.70	15.7	295	39	66	5.21	4.7	9.9	2.1	0.7	69

Former Tommy John patient who possesses a high ceiling, but continues to amass injury time. At his best, will touch 95 mph with plus FB, above-average CB with good depth and solid fading CU. Has low-effort delivery and smooth arm action; some crossfire to plate. Control will come and go at times, but has solid SwK foundation to work with.

Stephan,Trevor — SP — New York (A)

EXP MLB DEBUT: 2021 | H/W: 6-5 225 | FUT: Middle reliever | 6C

Thrws R Age 24 — 2017 (3) Arkansas

Velo	Pitch	Grade	Year	Lev	Team	W	L	Sv	IP	K	ERA	WHIP	BF/G	OBA	H%	S%	xERA	Ctl	Dom	Cmd	hr/9	BPV
			2017	A-	Staten Island	1	1	0	32		1.40	0.81	11.7	181	30	81	0.80	1.7	12.1	7.2	0.0	190
88-91	FB	++	2018	A+	Tampa	3	1	0	41	49	1.98	0.78	21.1	166	21	85	1.61	2.0	10.8	5.4	1.1	158
81-83	SL	+++	2018	AA	Trenton	3	8	0	83	91	4.55	1.31	20.2	254	34	64	3.50	3.1	9.9	3.1	0.5	111
84-85	CU	+++	2019	A+	Tampa	2	3	0	33	34	4.07	1.20	16.7	272	36	66	3.48	1.4	9.2	6.8	0.5	147
			2019	AA	Trenton	2	4	0	46	57	5.27	1.63	17.1	282	40	67	4.71	4.7	11.1	2.4	0.6	92

Low 3/4s RHP inched closer to MLB debut. FB sits 88-91 MPH with solid arm-side fade and reliever plane. 81-83 MPH SL has solid 2-plane break and can alternate break by putting additional pressure on the ball. CU is firm but features some arm-side run. There's a chance as SP but in a minimal role.

Stiever,Jonathan — SP — Chicago (A)

EXP MLB DEBUT: 2021 | H/W: 6-2 205 | FUT: #3 starter | 8C

Thrws R Age 22 — 2018 (5) Indiana

Velo	Pitch	Grade	Year	Lev	Team	W	L	Sv	IP	K	ERA	WHIP	BF/G	OBA	H%	S%	xERA	Ctl	Dom	Cmd	hr/9	BPV
94-96	FB	++++	2018	NCAA	Indiana	5	6	0	100	97	3.42	1.26	25.5	250	32	74	3.40	2.9	8.7	3.0	0.6	97
84-86	SL	++++	2018	Rk	Great Falls	0	1	0	28	39	4.18	1.14	8.5	226	33	66	3.07	2.9	12.5	4.3	1.0	166
75-77	CB	++	2019	A+	Winston-Salem	6	4	0	71	77	2.15	0.97	22.4	219	28	84	2.51	1.6	9.8	5.9	0.9	149
81-84	CU	+++	2019	A	Kannapolis	4	6	0	74	77	4.74	1.38	22.2	297	37	68	4.91	1.7	9.4	5.5	1.2	141

Projectable RHP stuff took step forward as season wore on. 3/4s cross-fire delivery with two potentially plus offerings. FB sat 92-94 early and got up to 94-96 range late without losing movement. SL is best secondary with tight, two-plane movement. Has feel for CU but delivery may not allow development. CB is eye-level changing pitch.

Stinson,Graeme — SP — Tampa Bay

EXP MLB DEBUT: 2022 | H/W: 6-5 250 | FUT: Closer | 8E

Thrws L Age 22 — 2019 (4) Duke

Velo	Pitch	Grade	Year	Lev	Team	W	L	Sv	IP	K	ERA	WHIP	BF/G	OBA	H%	S%	xERA	Ctl	Dom	Cmd	hr/9	BPV
93-97	FB	++++																				
83-86	SL	++++																				
	CU	+																				
			2019	Rk	GCL Rays	0	1	0	0	1	45.00	10.00	2.6	780	128	50	48.53	0.0	45.0		0.0	828

Projectable LHP was lights out in RP role than floundered in SP, struggling with a hamstring injury and lost velocity while losing considerable draft capital. In '18, the FB sat upper-90s with wipe out low-80s SL. In 2019, as a SP, struggled mightily to get out of 80s with FB.

Strotman,Drew — SP — Tampa Bay

EXP MLB DEBUT: 2021 | H/W: 6-3 195 | FUT: Setup reliever | 7C

Thrws R Age 23 — 2017 (4) St. Mary's

Velo	Pitch	Grade	Year	Lev	Team	W	L	Sv	IP	K	ERA	WHIP	BF/G	OBA	H%	S%	xERA	Ctl	Dom	Cmd	hr/9	BPV
			2017	NCAA	St. Mary's (CA)	6	1	1	67	75	4.57	1.45	15.9	279	39	66	3.80	3.2	10.1	3.1	0.1	112
93-96	FB	++++	2017	A-	Hudson Valley	2	3	0	50	42	1.79	0.76	16.3	170	23	74	0.60	1.6	7.5	4.7	0.0	110
85-86	SL	+++	2018	A	Bowling Green	3	0	0	46	43	3.52	1.26	20.9	236	32	69	2.63	3.5	8.4	2.4	0.0	74
	CU	++	2019	Rk	GCL Rays	0	1	0	8	11	3.38	1.50	8.6	285	44	75	3.87	3.4	12.4	3.7	0.0	150
			2019	A+	Charlotte	0	2	0	16	13	5.06	1.81	14.8	307	35	77	6.63	5.1	7.3	1.4	1.7	13

Hard-throwing, athletic RHP struggled with command returning from Tommy John surgery. High 3/4s delivery. Uses size well, creating good extension. FB was up to 97-98 in AFL but sits in the mid-90s with some late running action. Struggled getting on top of CB but has shown making of above-average pitch previous to TJS. Doesn't finish CU.

Supak,Trey — SP — Milwaukee

EXP MLB DEBUT: 2020 | H/W: 6-5 240 | FUT: #4 starter | 7A

Thrws R Age 23 — 2014 (2) HS (TX)

Velo	Pitch	Grade	Year	Lev	Team	W	L	Sv	IP	K	ERA	WHIP	BF/G	OBA	H%	S%	xERA	Ctl	Dom	Cmd	hr/9	BPV
			2017	A+	Carolina	3	4	1	72	57	4.62	1.29	19.8	242	27	69	4.21	3.5	7.1	2.0	1.5	52
90-92	FB	+++	2018	A+	Carolina	2	1	0	51	48	1.76	1.04	21.9	205	27	84	2.02	2.8	8.5	3.0	0.4	94
86-87	CT	+++	2018	AA	Biloxi	6	6	0	86	75	2.92	1.18	21.6	233	29	76	2.81	2.9	7.8	2.7	0.4	80
75-77	CB	++	2019	AA	Biloxi	11	4	0	122	91	2.21	0.88	22.6	196	24	76	1.61	1.7	6.7	4.0	0.4	93
84-86	CU	+++	2019	AAA	San Antonio	1	2	0	30	27	9.30	1.67	19.2	326	38	43	6.67	2.7	8.1	3.0	1.8	91

Tall, hulking RH who had stellar year in upper minors. Features well-rounded but not elite four-pitch mix including low-90s FB that will touch 95, fading CU and sharp SL/CT hybrid for weak contact. Blends in CB, but is fringe offering. Deliberate, calculated delivery allows him to stay online and pound the zone whilst racking up innings.

Szapucki,Thomas — SP — New York (N)

EXP MLB DEBUT: 2021 | H/W: 6-2 181 | FUT: #4 starter | 7C

Thrws L Age 23 — 2015 (5) HS (FL)

Velo	Pitch	Grade	Year	Lev	Team	W	L	Sv	IP	K	ERA	WHIP	BF/G	OBA	H%	S%	xERA	Ctl	Dom	Cmd	hr/9	BPV
			2017	A	Columbia	1	2	0	29	27	2.79	1.17	19.3	227	30	74	2.30	3.1	8.4	2.7	0.0	85
92-95	FB	++++	2018		Did not pitch - injury																	
78-82	CB	+++	2019	A	Columbia	0	0	0	21	26	2.12	1.13	7.6	190	28	83	2.12	4.2	11.0	2.6	0.4	102
85-86	CU	++	2019	A+	St. Lucie	1	3	0	36	42	3.25	1.33	16.6	245	35	74	3.15	3.8	10.5	2.8	0.3	106
			2019	AA	Binghamton	0	0	0	4	4	0.00	0.75	14.3	151	22	100	0.36	2.3	9.0	4.0	0.0	119

Funky LHP returned after missing 20 months recovering from Tommy John surgery. Pitched well across 3 levels. Throws from a slightly below 3/4s slot, achieving good extension, angles and deception. He relies on delivery to play up straight FB; also throws CB and can adjust speed, angle and break. CU lags behind.

Tabor,Matt — SP — Arizona

EXP MLB DEBUT: 2022 | H/W: 6-2 180 | FUT: #4 starter | 7C

Thrws R Age 21 — 2017 (3) HS (MA)

Velo	Pitch	Grade	Year	Lev	Team	W	L	Sv	IP	K	ERA	WHIP	BF/G	OBA	H%	S%	xERA	Ctl	Dom	Cmd	hr/9	BPV
90-93	FB	+++																				
84-86	SL	+++	2017	Rk	AZL DBacks	0	1	0	4	9	2.14	1.90	5.0	403	74	88	6.89	0.0	19.3		0.0	365
82-84	CU	+++	2018	A-	Hillsboro	2	1	0	60	46	3.29	1.20	17.3	258	31	74	3.34	1.9	6.9	3.5	0.6	89
			2019	A	Kane County	5	4	0	95	101	2.93	1.00	17.3	228	30	72	2.39	1.5	9.6	6.3	0.6	149

Athletic, projectable RHP who posted elite Cmd and solid ratios in full-season debut. Pounds the zone and flashes plus command of low-90s FB; can reach back for 95 mph. Replicates arm speed on fading CU, his best offspeed pitch, though still working on SL feel. Chance to add strength on lean frame for added velo. Back-end SP ceiling.

Tarnok,Freddy — SP — Atlanta

EXP MLB DEBUT: 2022 | H/W: 6-3 185 | FUT: #4 starter | 8E

Thrws R Age 21 — 2017 (3) HS (FL)

Velo	Pitch	Grade	Year	Lev	Team	W	L	Sv	IP	K	ERA	WHIP	BF/G	OBA	H%	S%	xERA	Ctl	Dom	Cmd	hr/9	BPV
89-93	FB	+++	2017	Rk	GCL Braves	0	3	0	14	10	2.57	1.00	6.7	218	27	71	1.77	1.9	6.4	3.3	0.0	82
77-83	CB	+++	2018	A	Rome	5	5	0	77	83	3.97	1.44	12.2	244	33	73	3.72	4.8	9.7	2.0	0.6	63
80-82	CU	++	2019	A+	Florida	3	7	0	98	82	4.87	1.44	22.0	275	34	65	4.14	3.3	7.5	2.3	0.6	64
			2019	Rk	GCL Braves	0	1	0	8	9	3.38	0.50	8.9	117	13	33	0.44	1.1	10.1	9.0	1.1	170

Tall, athletic 3/4s RHP with projectable frame. Struggled in High-A debut with consistency of stuff. Loose in-line delivery with longish arm-action. Solid arm-side run and borderline plus sink from 2-seam FB, but lacks command. CB is a power 11-to-5 offering on best days, can get slurvy. CU has obvious tells, needs refinement.

Tate,Dillon — SP — Baltimore

EXP MLB DEBUT: 2019 | H/W: 6-2 195 | FUT: Setup reliever | 7D

Thrws R Age 25 — 2015 (1) UC-Santa Barbara

Velo	Pitch	Grade	Year	Lev	Team	W	L	Sv	IP	K	ERA	WHIP	BF/G	OBA	H%	S%	xERA	Ctl	Dom	Cmd	hr/9	BPV
			2018	AA	Bowie	7	5	0	123	96	4.17	1.21	22.6	249	29	66	3.38	2.5	7.0	2.8	0.7	77
92-95	FB	++++	2019	A+	Frederick	0	0	0	1	3	7.50	2.50	6.4	470	84	100	16.99	0.0	22.5		7.5	423
83-86	SL	+++	2019	AA	Bowie	2	3	5	33	30	3.52	1.11	7.7	230	27	73	3.22	2.4	8.1	3.3	1.1	99
84-86	CU	+++	2019	AAA	Norfolk	2	0	2	9	7	2.00	0.89	8.3	216	25	86	2.41	1.0	7.0	7.0	1.0	117
			2019	MLB	Baltimore	0	2	0	21	20	6.43	1.29	5.4	233	28	50	3.87	3.9	8.6	2.2	1.3	68

Former 1st round pick made MLB debut in RP role, struggling to put away hitters. Athletic, RP delivery. Features three average-or-better offerings but no swing-and-miss pitch. Workhorse is ground ball inducing 2-seam FB with heavy sink. His best secondary is a CU with solid fade. The tightness of his SL is inconsistent.

Taylor,Blake — RP — Houston

EXP MLB DEBUT: 2020 | H/W: 6-2 220 | FUT: Setup reliever | 7D

Thrws L Age 24

	Year	Lev	Team	W	L	Sv	IP	K	ERA	WHIP	BF/G	OBA	H%	S%	xERA	Ctl	Dom	Cmd	hr/9	BPV
2013 (2) HS (CA)	2018	A+	St. Lucie	1	8	0	75	72	5.63	1.56	19.4	253	33	62	4.06	5.4	8.6	1.6	0.5	28
93-96 FB ++++	2018	AAA	Las Vegas	2	0	0	11	11	4.09	1.82	25.5	262	35	75	4.38	7.4	9.0	1.2	0.0	-19
78-80 CB +++	2019	A+	St. Lucie	2	2	7	27	29	2.66	1.33	5.4	239	33	80	3.14	4.0	9.6	2.4	0.3	84
84-86 SL +++	2019	AA	Binghamton	0	1	3	39	45	1.85	0.95	8.2	185	26	83	1.65	2.8	10.4	3.8	0.5	130
	2019	AAA	Syracuse	0	0	0	0	0	0.00	0.00	0.3	0								18

Big-bodied, failed SP prospect made successful conversion to RP role in '19. Uses XXL frame to hide ball within high 3/4s delivery. FB bumped up to 93-96 in shorter spurts, leading to AFL domination. Above-average CB is 1-to-7 break with solid shape. SL can get sweepy at times but solid offering. Added to 40-man in Nov.

Taylor,Curtis — RP — Toronto

EXP MLB DEBUT: 2020 | H/W: 6-6 230 | FUT: Setup reliever | 6B

Thrws R Age 24

	Year	Lev	Team	W	L	Sv	IP	K	ERA	WHIP	BF/G	OBA	H%	S%	xERA	Ctl	Dom	Cmd	hr/9	BPV
2016 (4) British Columbia																				
92-96 FB +++	2017	A	Kane County	3	4	0	62	68	3.33	1.26	19.5	239	32	74	3.19	3.3	9.9	3.0	0.6	105
85-87 SL +++	2018	A+	Charlotte	3	0	2	17	23	3.16	1.23	8.7	261	40	71	2.84	2.1	12.1	5.8	0.0	179
82-85 CU +	2018	AA	Montgomery	3	4	6	60	74	2.39	1.00	7.7	167	23	81	1.97	3.9	11.1	2.8	0.9	112
	2019	AA	Montgomery	0	3	7	17	16	3.14	1.10	4.5	224	30	68	2.09	2.6	8.4	3.2	0.0	98

Large-framed RP ended season in May due to elbow injury. Has spent most of career in pen where stuff plays up. Throws hard with average command at best. Can be imposing in short stints and features interesting FB/SL combo. Exhibited decent control in career and will need better location to succeed in majors. Not much upside due to lack of plus stuff.

Teng,Kai-Wei — SP — San Francisco

EXP MLB DEBUT: 2022 | H/W: 6-4 260 | FUT: #5 SP/swingman | 7E

Thrws R Age 21

	Year	Lev	Team	W	L	Sv	IP	K	ERA	WHIP	BF/G	OBA	H%	S%	xERA	Ctl	Dom	Cmd	hr/9	BPV
2017 FA (TW)																				
89-93 FB +++																				
77-78 CB ++	2018	Rk	GCL Twins	3	3	0	42	47	3.63	1.21	17.0	232	33	67	2.44	3.2	10.0	3.1	0.0	112
81-82 SL ++	2019	A	Augusta	3	0	0	29	39	1.55	0.79	21.0	164	27	78	0.57	2.2	12.1	5.6	0.0	177
80-83 CU +++	2019	A	Cedar Rapids	4	0	0	50	49	1.61	1.08	21.7	220	30	85	2.14	2.5	8.8	3.5	0.2	108

Durable SP was excellent in full-season debut. Exhibits outstanding control and is able to get ahead of hitters by spotting FB low in zone. High groundball rate as his FB has late dropping action. Mixes 4 pitches with CU possibly being best one. Repeats arm speed and can be deceptive. Both breaking balls need polish as slot not conducive to CB.

Then,Juan — SP — Seattle

EXP MLB DEBUT: 2023 | H/W: 6-1 155 | FUT: #4 starter | 7C

Thrws R Age 20

	Year	Lev	Team	W	L	Sv	IP	K	ERA	WHIP	BF/G	OBA	H%	S%	xERA	Ctl	Dom	Cmd	hr/9	BPV
2016 FA (DR)																				
92-95 FB ++++	2018	Rk	GCL Yankees	0	3	0	50	42	2.70	0.98	17.3	212	27	72	1.98	2.0	7.6	3.8	0.4	101
81-83 SL ++	2019	A	West Virginia	1	2	0	16	14	2.25	0.69	18.7	134	16	70	0.57	2.3	7.9	3.5	0.6	99
83-85 CU +++	2019	A-	Everett	0	3	0	30	32	3.59	1.10	16.8	220	30	66	2.30	2.7	9.6	3.6	0.3	118
	2019	Rk	AZL Mariners	0	0	0	2	2	0.00	1.00	7.6	262	35	100	2.32	0.0	9.0		0.0	180

Projectable RHP was traded during '17-'18 off-season to NYY and then traded back to SEA in June deal. Projectable frame. Easy 3/4s, online delivery. Sits low-to-mid 90s with late-running FB. Best secondary is advanced CU with solid fade and arm-side run. SL currently lags behind; needs to tighten up. Chance at SP role.

Thomas,Tahnaj — SP — Pittsburgh

EXP MLB DEBUT: 2023 | H/W: 6-4 190 | FUT: #3 starter | 8D

Thrws R Age 20

	Year	Lev	Team	W	L	Sv	IP	K	ERA	WHIP	BF/G	OBA	H%	S%	xERA	Ctl	Dom	Cmd	hr/9	BPV
2016 FA (BM)																				
92-96 FB ++++																				
81-84 SL +++	2017	Rk	AZL Indians	0	3	0	33	29	6.00	1.82	11.8	273	33	68	5.57	6.8	7.9	1.2	1.1	-24
85-87 CU ++	2018	Rk	AZL Indians	0	0	0	19	27	4.69	1.20	9.6	194	29	62	2.80	4.7	12.7	2.7	0.9	119
	2019	Rk	Bristol	2	3	0	48	59	3.18	1.12	15.8	228	31	76	3.04	2.6	11.0	4.2	0.9	146

Raw, athletic SP who hasn't appeared above Rookie ball. Control dramatically improved in 2019 as he spotted FB better to both sides of plate. Can pitch up in zone due to velocity with more in tank. K% has been solid as SL has gotten more consistent and will occasionally mix in CB for slower, loopy pitch. Lack of CU negates top prospect status.

Thompson,Mason — SP — San Diego

EXP MLB DEBUT: 2021 | H/W: 6-7 223 | FUT: #4 starter | 8D

Thrws R Age 22

	Year	Lev	Team	W	L	Sv	IP	K	ERA	WHIP	BF/G	OBA	H%	S%	xERA	Ctl	Dom	Cmd	hr/9	BPV
2016 (3) HS (TX)	2017	A	Fort Wayne	2	4	0	27	28	4.67	1.30	15.9	232	30	64	3.29	4.0	9.3	2.3	0.7	78
92-95 FB +++	2018	A	Fort Wayne	6	8	0	93	97	4.94	1.42	17.9	266	34	65	4.15	3.6	9.4	2.6	0.8	90
85-86 SL ++	2019	Rk	AZL Padres 2	0	0	0	4	3	6.75	2.25	10.1	347	38	75	8.93	6.8	6.8	1.0	2.3	-43
71-74 CB +++	2019	Rk	AZL Padres	0	0	0	1	0	0.00	0.00	2.8	0	0			0.0	0.0		0.0	18
80-84 CU +++	2019	A+	Lake Elsinore	0	5	0	22	22	7.74	1.86	14.8	261	32	58	5.61	7.7	9.0	1.2	1.2	-30

High-upside 3rd round pick from 2016 has yet to reach AA due to litany of injuries. Despite setbacks, has chance for four solid-average pitches including 93-95 mph FB that will touch 97. Still learning feel for CB and CU; added SL. Overall control and command remain sticking points in his development. Has back-end SP upside with a big, strong frame.

Thompson,Matthew — SP — Chicago (A)

EXP MLB DEBUT: 2023 | H/W: 6-3 195 | FUT: #4 starter | 7E

Thrws R Age 19

	Year	Lev	Team	W	L	Sv	IP	K	ERA	WHIP	BF/G	OBA	H%	S%	xERA	Ctl	Dom	Cmd	hr/9	BPV
2019 (2) HS (TX)																				
87-91 FB +++																				
83-84 SL ++++																				
72-75 CB ++																				
	2019	Rk	AZL White Sox	0	0	0	2	2	0.00	1.00	3.8	262	35	100	2.32	0.0	9.0		0.0	180

Oozes athleticism from tall frame and has ability to spin ball despite raw delivery. Good physique to add muscle to. 3-pitch pitcher. FB has ordinary profile but should add velocity by maturity. SL has plus 2-plane profile. CB is behind other pitches. Will need to develop CU for SP role.

Thompson,Riley — SP — Chicago (N)

EXP MLB DEBUT: 2022 | H/W: 6-3 205 | FUT: #4 starter | 8E

Thrws R Age 23

	Year	Lev	Team	W	L	Sv	IP	K	ERA	WHIP	BF/G	OBA	H%	S%	xERA	Ctl	Dom	Cmd	hr/9	BPV
2018 (11) Louisville																				
91-94 FB +++																				
CB ++++	2018	A-	Eugene	0	2	0	25	25	2.87	1.31	11.5	253	33	78	3.33	3.2	9.0	2.8	0.4	92
CU ++	2018	NCAA	Louisville	1	3	0	33	35	6.82	1.76	13.7	262	36	58	4.48	6.8	9.5	1.4	0.3	6
	2019	A	South Bend	8	6	0	94	87	3.06	1.23	18.1	243	30	79	3.47	3.0	8.3	2.8	0.9	88

Medium-framed RH with arm strength and feel for a plus breaking ball. Has shown flashes of 99 mph in college, but FB now hovers around 91-94 mph. 12-to-6 downer CB buckles knees, overhead action and misses bats below the knees. CU has potential to be average. Comes with Tommy John and some shoulder woe history, but has high upside.

Thompson,Zack — SP — St. Louis

EXP MLB DEBUT: 2022 | H/W: 6-2 225 | FUT: #3 starter | 8C

Thrws L Age 22

	Year	Lev	Team	W	L	Sv	IP	K	ERA	WHIP	BF/G	OBA	H%	S%	xERA	Ctl	Dom	Cmd	hr/9	BPV
2019 (1) Kentucky																				
91-94 FB +++																				
84-85 SL +++																				
74-77 CB +++	2019	A+	Palm Beach	0	0	0	13	19	4.12	1.53	5.2	302	47	70	4.19	2.7	13.1	4.8	0.0	179
83-85 CU ++	2019	Rk	GCL Cardinals	0	0	0	2	4	0.00	1.50	4.3	347	65	100	4.81	0.0	18.0		0.0	342

Strong-bodied lefty with checkered medical record has avoided surgery so far. Four-pitch mix highlighted by a low-90s FB that tops at 97 mph. Mid-80 CT/SL has plus spin rates but is inconsistent and gets slurvy. Upper-70s CB is also above average. Mechanics are not pristine, but he repeats them well and maintains a consistent release.

Thorpe,Lewis — SP — Minnesota

EXP MLB DEBUT: 2019 | H/W: 6-1 218 | FUT: #4 starter | 7C

Thrws L Age 24

	Year	Lev	Team	W	L	Sv	IP	K	ERA	WHIP	BF/G	OBA	H%	S%	xERA	Ctl	Dom	Cmd	hr/9	BPV
2012 FA (AU)	2017	AA	Chattanooga	1	0	0	6	7	6.00	1.17	23.9	228	23	60	5.10	3.0	10.5	3.5	3.0	126
89-93 FB ++	2018	AA	Chattanooga	8	4	0	108	131	3.58	1.25	20.0	256	35	75	3.87	2.5	10.9	4.4	1.1	147
83-86 SL +++	2018	AAA	Rochester	0	3	0	21	26	3.40	1.23	21.4	251	33	78	3.91	2.5	11.0	4.3	1.3	148
73-74 CB ++	2019	AAA	Rochester	5	4	0	96	119	4.59	1.21	19.4	251	34	65	3.82	2.3	11.1	4.8	1.2	155
83-85 CU ++++	2019	MLB	Minnesota	3	2	0	27	31	6.29	1.76	10.4	331	43	64	6.22	3.3	10.3	3.1	1.0	113

Command/control LHP had command escape during MLB debut. High 3/4s, cross-fire delivery. Repeates well and creates good extension with deception. 4-pitch pitcher. 4-seam FB plays up due to extension despite limited movement. Has two swing-and-miss secondaries. CU has arm-side run and plus fade; SL has sweepy, horizontal movement.

Torres,Lenny — SP — Cleveland

EXP MLB DEBUT: 2023 | H/W: 6-1 190 | FUT: #3 starter | 8E

Thrws R Age 19

	Year	Lev	Team	W	L	Sv	IP	K	ERA	WHIP	BF/G	OBA	H%	S%	xERA	Ctl	Dom	Cmd	hr/9	BPV
2018 (1) HS (NY)																				
93-95 FB ++++																				
85-86 SL ++++																				
84-86 CU +++	2018		Did not play - injury																	
	2019		Did not play - injury																	

Hard-thrower missed all of 2019 after Tommy John surgery. Solid, athletic body with room to grow. Made improvements in delivery in instructs which calmed some RP concerns. 3-pitch pitcher. FB sits mid-90s with excellent run. SL is a tight, sharp breaker with plus potential. Has a feel for CU with significant drop with tells in delivery.

Tyler,Robert

RP | Colorado | EXP MLB DEBUT: 2020 | H/W: 6-4 226 | FUT: Setup reliever | 8D

Thrws R Age 24	Year	Lev	Team	W	L	Sv	IP	K	ERA	WHIP	BF/G	OBA	H%	S%	xERA	Ctl	Dom	Cmd	hr/9	BPV
2016 (1) Georgia	2016	A-	Boise	0	2	0	7	5	6.43	2.57	7.5	92	12	72	4.40	20.6	6.4	0.3	0.0	-422
95-97 FB ++++	2017		Did not play - injury																	
82-84 CB ++	2018	A	Asheville	4	2	8	38	52	4.02	1.15	4.5	256	37	69	3.71	1.7	12.3	7.4	1.2	194
85-87 CU +++	2018	A+	Lancaster	0	1	0	9	5	9.89	2.42	4.0	398	42	60	10.09	4.9	4.9	1.0	2.0	-27
	2019	A+	Lancaster	1	0	1	28	36	8.30	1.99	4.8	312	42	58	6.71	6.4	11.5	1.8	1.3	52

Power-armed RH who will touch 100 mph and put away hitters with a plus CU with fade and drop when he's on. Transition to bullpen in 2018 highlighted his upside as reliever, but then command and control took a step back. Has natural Dom/GB% ability you look for in a high-leverage reliever. Now 24 at Hi-A, there are some question marks.

Uceta,Edwin

SP | Los Angeles (N) | EXP MLB DEBUT: 2021 | H/W: 6-0 155 | FUT: #4 starter | 7D

Thrws R Age 22	Year	Lev	Team	W	L	Sv	IP	K	ERA	WHIP	BF/G	OBA	H%	S%	xERA	Ctl	Dom	Cmd	hr/9	BPV
2016 FA (DR)	2017	Rk	Ogden	2	3	0	56	62	6.59	1.38	16.8	285	36	52	4.79	2.3	10.0	4.4	1.3	137
90-93 FB +++	2018	A	Great Lakes	5	6	0	99	103	3.27	1.19	19.9	245	32	75	3.34	2.4	9.3	3.8	0.8	120
78-80 CB ++	2018	A+	Rancho Cuca	0	0	0	20	28	7.13	1.44	17.2	230	26	59	5.89	5.3	12.5	2.3	3.1	98
78-82 SL ++	2019	A+	Rancho Cuca	4	0	0	50	65	2.16	1.26	20.4	250	35	89	3.79	2.9	11.7	4.1	1.1	151
83-85 CU ++++	2019	AA	Tulsa	7	2	0	73	76	3.21	1.30	18.8	231	31	77	3.25	4.1	9.4	2.3	0.6	77

Pojectable hurler continues to dominate despite the lack of overpowering stuff. Three-pitch mix keeps hitters off-balance. FB sits at 90-93 mph but misses bats due to late life. Backs up the FB with an above-average CU that dives in on RHB while CB is average but inconsistent. Low 3/4 arm slot and crossfire action raise concerns about durability.

Uelmen,Erich

SP | Chicago (N) | EXP MLB DEBUT: 2021 | H/W: 6-2 185 | FUT: Middle reliever | 6B

Thrws R Age 23	Year	Lev	Team	W	L	Sv	IP	K	ERA	WHIP	BF/G	OBA	H%	S%	xERA	Ctl	Dom	Cmd	hr/9	BPV
2017 (4) Cal Poly	2017	A-	Eugene	0	2	0	17		2.09	1.57	10.8	271	39	92	4.83	4.7	12.0	2.6	1.0	107
90-93 FB +++	2018	A	South Bend	5	5	0	56	58	3.53	1.23	20.7	254	35	68	2.79	2.4	9.3	3.9	0.0	121
SL ++	2018	A+	Myrtle Beach	3	3	0	33	24	4.36	1.61	14.6	290	34	74	5.04	4.1	6.5	1.6	0.8	25
CU +++	2019	A+	Myrtle Beach	5	3	0	62	50	3.05	1.19	22.6	243	29	76	3.11	2.6	7.3	2.8	0.6	78
	2019	AA	Tennessee	0	3	0	29	26	7.76	1.79	22.3	288	33	57	6.15	5.9	8.1	1.4	1.6	4

Funky, low-arm-angle RHP who likes to use his heavy, low-90s sinker to generate ground balls at a high clip. Replicates arm speed well on solid-avg CU; fringy SL produces more gradual break. Has been groomed as SP but has yet to amass 100 IP in a season as a pro. Arm action and quality FB-CU combo could be used as a middle reliever.

Urquidy,Jose

SP | Houston | EXP MLB DEBUT: 2019 | H/W: 6-0 180 | FUT: #4 starter | 7C

Thrws R Age 24	Year	Lev	Team	W	L	Sv	IP	K	ERA	WHIP	BF/G	OBA	H%	S%	xERA	Ctl	Dom	Cmd	hr/9	BPV
2015 FA (MX)	2018	A-	Tri City	0	0	0	11	10	2.43	1.53	12.1	324	41	82	4.60	1.6	8.1	5.0	0.0	120
90-95 FB +++	2018	A+	Buies Creek	2	2	0	46	38	2.35	1.04	19.7	236	29	78	2.46	1.6	7.4	4.8	0.4	110
77-79 CB ++	2019	AA	Corpus Christi	2	2	0	33	40	4.09	1.00	18.0	231	33	58	2.41	1.4	10.9	8.0	0.5	178
83-86 CU ++++	2019	AAA	Round Rock	5	3	0	70	94	4.63	1.19	21.6	253	33	69	4.45	2.1	12.1	5.9	1.9	180
	2019	MLB	Houston	2	1	0	41	40	3.95	1.10	17.8	247	30	69	3.61	1.5	8.8	5.7	1.3	135

Swingman who reached HOU in first full season above A+. Despite lack of size, can dominate with FB and CU. Lacks premium velocity, but doesn't need it as he gets good movement and solid location. Fading CU comes out of hand similarly to FB and tough to pick up. Registers Ks with both pitches. CB is average at best and can be a tad slow.

Vallimont,Chris

SP | Minnesota | EXP MLB DEBUT: 2021 | H/W: 6-5 220 | FUT: #4 starter | 7C

Thrws R Age 23	Year	Lev	Team	W	L	Sv	IP	K	ERA	WHIP	BF/G	OBA	H%	S%	xERA	Ctl	Dom	Cmd	hr/9	BPV
2018 (5) Mercyhurst	2018	NCAA	Mercyhurst	10	3	1	80	147	2.58	0.82	19.5	150	32	68	0.78	2.9	16.5	5.7	0.3	236
93-96 FB ++++	2018	A-	Batavia	0	2	0	29	20	6.21	1.59	10.6	220	24	60	4.15	7.1	6.2	0.9	0.9	-63
74-76 CB +++	2019	A	Clinton	4	4	0	69	80	3.00	1.07	20.7	198	28	73	2.16	3.4	10.4	3.1	0.5	114
87-89 SL ++	2019	A+	Jupiter	2	3	0	36	42	3.50	1.17	23.9	234	32	72	3.06	2.8	10.5	3.8	0.8	133
87-90 CU +++	2019	A+	Fort Myers	2	2	0	22	28	3.67	0.86	20.3	194	30	53	1.08	1.6	11.4	7.0	0.0	179

Big-bodied, tall high 3/4s RHP was acquired from MIA mid-season. Had breakout season. Saw FB pick up velocity back to college levels. Commands FB well, playing up profile. Sequences 3 pitches well of FB. CB 12-to-6 downer with solid depth. Has solid fading action on CU. SL acts more like ineffective CT most of the time. Candidate for RP role.

Vanasco,Ricky

SP | Texas | EXP MLB DEBUT: 2022 | H/W: 6-3 180 | FUT: #3 starter | 8D

Thrws R Age 21	Year	Lev	Team	W	L	Sv	IP	K	ERA	WHIP	BF/G	OBA	H%	S%	xERA	Ctl	Dom	Cmd	hr/9	BPV
2017 (15) HS (FL)																				
93-96 FB +++																				
80-83 CB ++	2018	Rk	AZL Rangers	3	3	0	24	25	4.46	1.57	15.2	268	36	70	4.19	4.8	9.3	1.9	0.4	55
87-89 CU +++	2019	A	Hickory	0	0	0	10	16	1.76	0.78	18.4	148	28	75	0.37	2.6	14.1	5.3	0.0	201
	2019	A-	Spokane	3	1	0	39	59	1.85	1.15	17.2	173	29	86	2.00	5.1	13.6	2.7	0.5	126

Tall, projectable body that starts upright, then get extended and ball comes out quick. FB sits in mid-90s and comes on downhill plane; ate up short-season and Low-A hitters (combined 75 K in 50 IP). High-80s CU is best secondary, with good drop and separation. CB shows promise also, and has the arm slot for it. #3 starter stuff; needs reps.

Vargas,Carlos

SP | Cleveland | EXP MLB DEBUT: 2023 | H/W: 6-3 180 | FUT: Setup reliever | 7D

Thrws R Age 20	Year	Lev	Team	W	L	Sv	IP	K	ERA	WHIP	BF/G	OBA	H%	S%	xERA	Ctl	Dom	Cmd	hr/9	BPV
2016 FA (DR)																				
92-95 FB ++++																				
87-89 SL ++++																				
86-87 CU +	2018	Rk	AZL Indians 2	1	2	0	34	41	3.96	1.67	15.3	255	36	76	4.40	6.3	10.8	1.7	0.5	42
	2019	A-	MahoningVal	6	4	0	77	71	4.55	1.26	21.0	251	32	62	3.26	2.8	8.3	3.0	0.5	91

Hard-throwing, raw 3/4s RHP struggled repeating delivery and command but still turned in solid Low-A performance. Jerky leg lift in crossfire delivery, likely suited best for RP role. Mid-90s FB touches high 90s with solid arm-side break and little command. SL is a tight, 2-plane breaker with more downward action than horizontal break. CU is poor.

Vargas,Emilio

SP | Arizona | EXP MLB DEBUT: 2020 | H/W: 6-3 200 | FUT: #5 SP/swingman | 7D

Thrws R Age 23	Year	Lev	Team	W	L	Sv	IP	K	ERA	WHIP	BF/G	OBA	H%	S%	xERA	Ctl	Dom	Cmd	hr/9	BPV
2013 FA (DR)	2017	A	Kane County	5	7	1	100	98	4.04	1.28	19.6	231	29	69	3.29	3.9	8.8	2.3	0.7	72
89-91 FB ++	2018	A+	Visalia	8	5	0	108	140	2.50	1.23	21.9	232	34	82	3.03	3.4	11.7	3.4	0.6	136
77-80 SL +++	2018	AA	Jackson	1	3	0	35	30	4.09	1.11	23.0	238	27	70	3.73	2.0	7.7	3.8	1.5	101
80-83 CU +++	2019	Rk	AZL DBacks	0	2	0	10	12	4.46	1.09	13.2	240	33	60	3.07	1.8	10.7	6.0	0.9	162
	2019	AA	Jackson	5	3	0	85	70	3.80	1.14	19.8	235	27	70	3.32	2.4	7.4	3.0	1.1	86

Seasoned RHP prospect who spent time on IL in 2019 with biceps tendinitis. At his best, will show three solid-average offerings including a low-90s FB and feel for a two-plane breaking SL with above-average potential. CU has made progress but projects as fringe-avg offering. Future role of long-relief type with FB-SL combo.

Varland,Gus

SP | Oakland | EXP MLB DEBUT: 2021 | H/W: 6-1 205 | FUT: Middle reliever | 7C

Thrws R Age 23	Year	Lev	Team	W	L	Sv	IP	K	ERA	WHIP	BF/G	OBA	H%	S%	xERA	Ctl	Dom	Cmd	hr/9	BPV
2018 (14) Concordia																				
92-94 FB +++	2018	A	Beloit	0	0	0	19	28	0.94	0.58	13.0	129	21	90	0.10	1.4	13.2	9.3	0.5	217
82-84 SL +++	2018	A-	Vermont	0	1	0	17	22	1.05	1.05	9.5	224	35	89	1.91	2.1	11.5	5.5	0.0	169
84-86 CU ++	2018	Rk	AZL Athletics	0	0	0	1	0	0.00	2.00	4.8	262	26	100	4.93	9.0	0.0	0.0	0.0	-225
	2019	A+	Stockton	2	1	0	26	27	2.41	1.19	20.9	238	30	86	3.44	2.8	9.3	3.4	1.0	111

Medium-framed RH with solid three-pitch mix underwent Tommy John surgery last summer. Owns a high-spin FB that can touch 96 mph and can miss barrels when elevated. SL has average two-plane break and bite; CU projects to be at least a usable third pitch. Pounds the zone and should have good ratios as a swingman-type profile.

Vizcaino,Alexander

SP | New York (A) | EXP MLB DEBUT: 2022 | H/W: 6-2 160 | FUT: #4 starter | 8D

Thrws R Age 22	Year	Lev	Team	W	L	Sv	IP	K	ERA	WHIP	BF/G	OBA	H%	S%	xERA	Ctl	Dom	Cmd	hr/9	BPV
2016 FA (DR)	2017	Rk	Pulaski	3	5	0	51	49	5.81	1.80	19.7	324	39	71	6.76	4.1	8.6	2.1	1.6	64
93-96 FB ++++	2018	Rk	Pulaski	3	3	0	54	55	4.50	1.30	20.2	243	30	68	3.91	3.5	9.2	2.6	1.2	89
83-86 SL ++	2018	A	Charleston (Sc)	0	1	0	4	2	13.50	2.50	21.3	415	39	50	13.03	4.5	4.5	1.0	4.5	-23
89-91 CU ++++	2019	A	Charleston (Sc)	5	5	0	87	101	4.44	1.23	22.1	245	34	63	3.24	2.8	10.4	3.7	0.6	130
	2019	A+	Tampa	1	1	0	27	27	4.32	1.62	24.1	302	39	74	5.09	3.7	9.0	2.5	0.7	81

Slim, 3/4s RHP with athletic delivery emerged after FB velocity increased coming out of spring training. Mid-90s FB has some action. However, he must be fine with pitch, locating to corners. Best secondary is a potentially double-plus CU with sudden drop and good velocity separation. SL is sharp but inconsistent.

Vodnik,Victor

RP | Atlanta | EXP MLB DEBUT: 2023 | H/W: 6-0 200 | FUT: Closer | 8E

Thrws R Age 20	Year	Lev	Team	W	L	Sv	IP	K	ERA	WHIP	BF/G	OBA	H%	S%	xERA	Ctl	Dom	Cmd	hr/9	BPV
2018 (14) HS (CA)																				
90-95 FB ++++																				
80-83 CB +++																				
84-86 SL ++++	2018	Rk	GCL Braves	1	1	0	4	9	10.71	2.14	5.2	403	71	50	9.51	2.1	19.3	9.0	2.1	307
87 CU ++	2019	A	Rome	1	3	3	67	69	2.95	1.18	11.7	225	31	73	2.41	3.2	9.3	2.9	0.1	98

Hard-throwing, short statured RHP worked full-season debut with 4-pitch mix. 3/4s in-line delivery, quick arm with abrupt finish. FB ranged 89-97, depending on role. FB has late riding action, especially up. Best secondary is a short SL with excellent two-plane movement. Added hard CB to mix, which has solid depth, changing eye levels. CU is flat.

Wahl,Bobby
SP | Milwaukee | EXP MLB DEBUT: 2017 | H/W: 6-2 210 | FUT: Setup reliever | 7B

Thrws R Age 28		Year	Lev	Team	W	L	Sv	IP	K	ERA	WHIP	BF/G	OBA	H%	S%	xERA	Ctl	Dom	Cmd	hr/9	BPV
2013 (5) Mississippi		2017	MLB	Oakland	0	0	0	7	8	5.00	1.67	4.6	283	39	67	4.28	5.0	10.0	2.0	0.0	63
94-97 FB	++++	2018	AAA	Nashville	3	2	11	39	65	2.30	0.87	4.3	133	25	75	0.85	3.9	14.9	3.8	0.5	181
89-91 CT	++	2018	AAA	Las Vegas	4	2	12	45	73	2.20	0.87	4.4	136	25	76	0.82	3.8	14.6	3.8	0.4	178
82-84 CB	+++	2018	MLB	NY Mets	0	1	0	5	7	10.59	2.55	3.9	385	49	64	11.53	7.1	12.4	1.8	3.5	50
89-90 CU	++	2019		Did not pitch - injury																	

Older, hard-throwing RH prospect who missed all of 2019 with knee injury. Will touch upper-90s with plus FB and drop in hammer CB for high-volume swing-and-miss ability. Blends in CT and has upside of third plus offering. Health remains a big question mark moving forward, but has potential for high-leverage RP in near future.

Wallace,Jacob
RP | Colorado | EXP MLB DEBUT: 2021 | H/W: 6-1 190 | FUT: Setup reliever | 8D

Thrws R Age 21		Year	Lev	Team	W	L	Sv	IP	K	ERA	WHIP	BF/G	OBA	H%	S%	xERA	Ctl	Dom	Cmd	hr/9	BPV
2019 (3) Connecticut																					
94-96 FB	++++																				
83-86 SL	+++																				
		2019	NCAA	Connecticut	2	0	7	19	27	0.47	0.58	5.9	130	23	91		1.4	12.8	9.0	0.0	210
		2019	A-	Boise	0	0	12	21	29	1.29	0.86	3.5	132	21	88	0.81	3.9	12.4	3.2	0.4	138

High-effort college RH with late-inning upside and two plus offerings. Plus-plus FB jumps on hitters with late riding action and will touch 98 mph. SL will flash good length and ability to rack up whiffs against same-handed batters. More control than command right now, but his ability to fill up the zone improved in three years at UConn.

Walston,Blake
SP | Arizona | EXP MLB DEBUT: 2023 | H/W: 6-5 175 | FUT: #4 starter | 8E

Thrws L Age 18		Year	Lev	Team	W	L	Sv	IP	K	ERA	WHIP	BF/G	OBA	H%	S%	xERA	Ctl	Dom	Cmd	hr/9	BPV
2019 (1) HS (NC)																					
89-92 FB	+++																				
72-75 CB	++++																				
CU	+++	2019	Rk	AZL DBacks	0	0	0	5	11	1.80	0.40	5.4	124	39	50		0.0	19.8		0.0	374
		2019	A-	Hillsboro	0	0	0	6	6	3.00	1.33	8.3	262	35	75	3.16	3.0	9.0	3.0	0.0	99

Tall, high-waisted LHP taken 26th overall in 2019 draft. Arsenal revolves around 88-91 mph FB with which he fills up the zone and complements with plus CB with late action and depth when he's on. CU is useable but will require work. Requires extensive physical projection but could develop into back-end SP with good ratios.

Ward,Thad
SP | Boston | EXP MLB DEBUT: 2021 | H/W: 6-3 182 | FUT: #4 starter | 7C

Thrws R Age 23		Year	Lev	Team	W	L	Sv	IP	K	ERA	WHIP	BF/G	OBA	H%	S%	xERA	Ctl	Dom	Cmd	hr/9	BPV
2018 (5) Central Florida																					
91-95 FB	+++	2018	NCAA	Central Florida	5	4	2	63	84	3.28	1.14	11.4	205	32	69	2.06	3.7	12.0	3.2	0.1	134
81-85 SL	+++	2018	A-	Lowell	0	3	0	31	27	3.77	1.45	12.0	274	34	74	4.18	3.5	7.8	2.3	0.6	65
84-87 CT	++	2019	A+	Salem	3	3	0	54	70	2.33	1.30	18.5	200	29	85	2.88	5.3	11.7	2.2	0.7	84
82-84 CU	+	2019	A	Greenville	5	2	0	72	87	2.00	1.05	21.5	201	30	81	1.89	3.1	10.9	3.5	0.2	129

Pitcher of Year in org with solid campaign between two levels in first full season. K rate rose dramatically and showed consistency with powerful arsenal. SL is best pitch and uses for strikes or chase. Can cut FB at times and keep ball on ground. Led org in Ks, though will need to improve CU to combat LHH. Offers good size and some projection.

Warren,Art
RP | Seattle | EXP MLB DEBUT: 2019 | H/W: 6-3 230 | FUT: Setup reliever | 7D

Thrws R Age 27		Year	Lev	Team	W	L	Sv	IP	K	ERA	WHIP	BF/G	OBA	H%	S%	xERA	Ctl	Dom	Cmd	hr/9	BPV
2015 (23) Ashland																					
94-96 FB	++++	2017	A+	Modesto	3	1	8	64	67	3.08	1.29	6.1	243	32	78	3.45	3.5	9.4	2.7	0.7	92
85-87 SL	+++	2018	AA	Arkansas	1	2	2	15	22	1.78	1.58	4.8	189	32	88	2.83	8.3	13.0	1.6	0.0	29
78-81 CB	+++	2019	AA	Arkansas	2	1	15	31	41	1.73	1.15	4.3	207	32	86	2.25	3.8	11.8	3.2	0.3	130
		2019	MLB	Seattle	1	0	0	5	5	0.00	0.78	3.1	122	18	100	0.16	3.5	8.8	2.5	0.0	82

Hard-throwing 3/4s RHP has struggled in career with injuries. Healthy in '19, made MLB debut. High-octane 4-seam FB. Fairly straight, needs to control pitch to corners and down. SL played well in big leagues with above-average break. CB is an effective 3rd pitch, which was seldom used in debut.

Weathers,Ryan
SP | San Diego | EXP MLB DEBUT: 2022 | H/W: 6-1 230 | FUT: #3 starter | 8C

Thrws L Age 20		Year	Lev	Team	W	L	Sv	IP	K	ERA	WHIP	BF/G	OBA	H%	S%	xERA	Ctl	Dom	Cmd	hr/9	BPV
2018 (1) HS (TN)																					
90-94 FB	+++																				
76-79 CB	+++	2018	A	Fort Wayne	0	1	0	9	9	3.00	1.33	12.5	302	40	75	3.75	1.0	9.0	9.0	0.0	153
80-84 CU	+++	2018	Rk	AZL Padres 2	0	2	0	9	9	3.96	1.21	9.2	238	26	78	4.38	3.0	8.9	3.0	2.0	98
		2019	A	Fort Wayne	3	7	0	96	90	3.84	1.24	17.7	272	34	69	3.59	1.7	8.4	5.0	0.6	124

Advanced three-pitch southpaw who posted quality ratios in introduction to full-season MWL bats. Shows three above-average offerings of which he has solid command. FB sits in low-90s with armside movement. Repeats delivery well, allowing CU to play up, while CB shows 1/7 depth. Good athlete with feel for pitching; difficult to square up.

Webb,Braden
SP | Milwaukee | EXP MLB DEBUT: 2020 | H/W: 6-3 200 | FUT: Setup reliever | 8D

Thrws R Age 24		Year	Lev	Team	W	L	Sv	IP	K	ERA	WHIP	BF/G	OBA	H%	S%	xERA	Ctl	Dom	Cmd	hr/9	BPV
2016 (3) South Carolina		2018	AA	Biloxi	1	0	0	20	24	1.80	1.15	19.9	187	29	83	1.75	4.5	10.8	2.4	0.0	91
92-95 FB	+++	2019	Rk	Rocky Mountain	0	1	0	4	4	6.43	1.90	9.9	297	34	71	7.12	6.4	8.6	1.3	2.1	-1
75-78 CB	++++	2019	Rk	AZL BrewersG	0	1	0	8	13	2.25	0.75	5.7	42	9	67		5.6	14.6	2.6	0.0	129
85-88 CU	+++	2019	A+	Carolina	1	2	0	36	31	3.48	1.33	18.8	184	23	74	2.65	6.2	7.7	1.2	0.5	-11
		2019	AA	Biloxi	1	4	0	15	13	9.00	2.00	12.1	262	31	54	5.98	9.0	7.8	0.9	1.2	-85

Tall, strong RHP who missed time on IL with minor injuries in 2019. Has been groomed as SP, but arguably projects better as a high-leverage RP with upper-90s FB and elite hammer CB. CU also shows utility to neutralize LHB. Command and control remain somewhat major question marks, but has some upside as late-inning RP.

Webb,Logan
SP | San Francisco | EXP MLB DEBUT: 2019 | H/W: 6-2 220 | FUT: #3 starter | 8C

Thrws R Age 23		Year	Lev	Team	W	L	Sv	IP	K	ERA	WHIP	BF/G	OBA	H%	S%	xERA	Ctl	Dom	Cmd	hr/9	BPV
2014 (4) HS (CA)		2019	Rk	AZL Giants O	0	0	0	5	6	1.80	1.20	20.1	299	43	83	3.33	0.0	10.8		0.0	212
92-96 FB	++++	2019	A	Augusta	1	0	0	10	9	0.90	0.70	17.6	124	17	86		2.7	8.1	3.0	0.0	91
82-85 SL	++++	2019	AA	Richmond	1	4	0	41	47	2.19	1.29	21.1	261	36	84	3.44	2.6	10.3	3.9	0.4	132
83-87 CU	++	2019	AAA	Sacramento	0	0	0	7	7	1.29	1.00	26.7	262	35	86	2.32	0.0	9.0		0.0	180
		2019	MLB	SF Giants	2	3	0	39	37	5.28	1.48	21.1	285	35	66	4.93	3.2	8.5	2.6	1.1	84

Big SP who reached SF on basis of heavy FB among best in org despite average velocity. Pitches off FB with precision to any area of zone. Induces weak contact and can get Ks with FB. Wipeout SL is 2nd plus pitch. Has fast arm action that makes it play up and features lethal break. Good separation between FB and CU. Injury history to keep an eye on.

Weigel,Patrick
SP | Atlanta | EXP MLB DEBUT: 2020 | H/W: 6-6 240 | FUT: Setup reliever | 7B

Thrws R Age 25		Year	Lev	Team	W	L	Sv	IP	K	ERA	WHIP	BF/G	OBA	H%	S%	xERA	Ctl	Dom	Cmd	hr/9	BPV
2015 (7) Houston		2017	AA	Mississippi	3	0	0	37	38	2.91	1.16	21.1	234	31	76	2.80	2.7	9.2	3.5	0.5	112
92-95 FB	++++	2017	AAA	Gwinnett	3	2	0	41	30	5.27	1.44	21.8	266	30	65	4.54	3.7	6.6	1.8	1.1	36
83-86 SL	+++	2018	Rk	GCL Braves	0	0	0	4	6	0.00	0.50	3.3	151	27	100		0.0	13.5		0.0	261
76-78 CB	+++	2019	AA	Mississippi	0	1	0	15	16	1.78	1.12	8.6	157	23	82	1.35	5.3	9.5	1.8	0.0	45
84-85 CU	++	2019	AAA	Gwinnett	6	1	0	63	55	3.00	1.17	12.0	191	21	82	3.08	4.6	7.8	1.7	1.3	36

Big-bodied RHP continued to move past '18 Tommy John surgery but has yet to debut. Repeats 3/4s delivery and is best suited for RP role due to effort. Sits low-to-mid 90s as SP but peaked to mid-90s as RP with the same late biting action. CB is above-average offering, which could play up in RP role. SL is solid and CU is passable.

Wells,Alex
SP | Baltimore | EXP MLB DEBUT: 2020 | H/W: 6-1 190 | FUT: #5 SP/swingman | 6C

Thrws L Age 23		Year	Lev	Team	W	L	Sv	IP	K	ERA	WHIP	BF/G	OBA	H%	S%	xERA	Ctl	Dom	Cmd	hr/9	BPV
2015 FA (AU)																					
86-89 FB	++	2016	A-	Aberdeen	4	5	0	62	50	2.17	0.92	17.9	215	27	75	1.65	1.3	7.2	5.6	0.1	113
78-81 SL	++	2017	A	Delmarva	11	5	0	140	113	2.38	0.91	20.9	230	27	81	2.67	0.6	7.3	11.3	1.0	131
71-74 CB	+++	2018	A+	Frederick	7	8	0	135	101	3.47	1.30	23.2	272	31	79	4.41	2.2	6.7	3.1	1.3	80
81-84 CU	+++	2019	AA	Bowie	8	6	0	137	105	2.95	1.07	22.2	241	29	74	2.86	1.6	6.9	4.4	0.7	100

Extreme crossfire, High 3/4s command/control LHP pitched well in Double-A. 4-pitch pitcher with very fringy tool upside. Repeats delivery well and commands late-running FB to the edges of the zone. Best secondary is CU with solid fading action. SL is a one-dimensional offering and CB does well changing levels.

Wentz,Joey
SP | Detroit | EXP MLB DEBUT: 2020 | H/W: 6-5 210 | FUT: #3 starter | 8D

Thrws L Age 22		Year	Lev	Team	W	L	Sv	IP	K	ERA	WHIP	BF/G	OBA	H%	S%	xERA	Ctl	Dom	Cmd	hr/9	BPV
2016 (1) HS (KS)		2016	Rk	Danville	1	4	0	32	35	5.06	1.59	17.7	256	36	65	3.72	5.6	9.8	1.8	0.0	43
89-93 FB	+++	2017	A	Rome	8	3	0	131	152	2.61	1.11	19.8	211	30	76	2.17	3.2	10.4	3.3	0.3	120
74-77 CB	+++	2018	A+	Florida	3	4	0	67	53	2.28	1.09	16.4	206	25	80	2.23	3.2	7.1	2.2	0.4	59
80-83 CU	+++	2019	AA	Mississippi	5	8	0	103	100	4.72	1.31	21.3	237	29	66	3.83	3.9	8.7	2.2	1.1	69
		2019	AA	Erie	2	0	0	25	37	2.14	0.95	19.0	220	33	86	2.61	1.4	13.2	9.3	1.1	217

Tall, well-proportioned southpaw who works from a high-3/4 slot. Scouts had concern of repeatability following injury. Traded to Tigers in 2019. Strongest offering is above-average changeup with late fade followed by well-shaped 12-6 curve. Low-90s fastball is a deception-first piece that projects as future plus offering.

White, Mitchell — SP — Los Angeles (N)

EXP MLB DEBUT: 2020 H/W: 6-3 210 FUT: #3 starter **7C**

Thrws R Age 25

			Year	Lev	Team	W	L	Sv	IP	K	ERA	WHIP	BF/G	OBA	H%	S%	xERA	Ctl	Dom	Cmd	hr/9	BPV
2016 (2) Santa Clara			2017	A+	Rancho Cuca	2	1	0	38	49	3.77	1.10	16.6	194	31	62	1.69	3.8	11.5	3.1	0.0	124
92-95	FB	++++	2017	AA	Tulsa	1	1	0	28	31	2.57	1.07	15.6	177	24	79	2.05	4.2	10.0	2.4	0.6	85
86-88	SL	+++	2018	AA	Tulsa	6	7	0	105	88	4.54	1.41	20.2	278	33	70	4.55	2.9	7.5	2.6	1.0	75
75-78	CB	+++	2019	AA	Tulsa	1	0	0	30	37	2.10	0.83	15.7	175	24	82	1.66	2.1	11.1	5.3	0.9	161
	CU	+	2019	AAA	Oklahoma City	3	6	0	63	68	6.55	1.53	17.2	291	35	61	5.81	3.4	9.7	2.8	1.9	100

Ideal frame, but a string of injuries has limited him to 281 IP since 2016. When healthy features a plus 92-95 mph FB that tops at 97 with late sink down in the zone. SL flashes plus at times and CB is above-average. Working on a CU to attack LHB with mixed results. Started the year strong, but imploded when moved up to AAA.

White, Owen — SP — Texas

EXP MLB DEBUT: 2024 H/W: 6-3 170 FUT: #3 starter **8E**

Thrws R Age 20

			Year	Lev	Team
2018 (2) HS (NC)					
91-93	FB	+++			
77-81	CB	+++	2018		Did not pitch
83-85	CU	++	2019		Did not pitch - injury

Has not yet pitched a pro inning, as Tommy John surgery ended his 2019 before it started and did not pitch in 2018 after his 2nd-round selection. Before the draft, showcased short arm action, excellent athleticism, and solid three-pitch mix, from a strong starter's frame. He'll be brought along slowly for now.

Whitley, Forrest — SP — Houston

EXP MLB DEBUT: 2020 H/W: 6-7 195 FUT: #1 starter **9B**

Thrws R Age 22

			Year	Lev	Team	W	L	Sv	IP	K	ERA	WHIP	BF/G	OBA	H%	S%	xERA	Ctl	Dom	Cmd	hr/9	BPV
2016 (1) HS (TX)			2018	AA	Corpus Christi	0	2	0	26		3.79	1.00	12.5	169	25	63	1.80	3.8	11.7	3.1	0.7	127
94-99	FB	+++++	2019	Rk	GCL Astros	0	2	0	4	10	8.78	2.68	11.3	147	56	64	5.07	19.8	22.0	1.1	0.0	-120
81-84	CB	+++	2019	A+	Fayetteville	1	0	0	8	11	2.22	0.62	13.9	149	25	60		1.1	12.2	11.0	0.0	208
85-87	SL	+++	2019	AA	Corpus Christi	2	2	0	22	36	5.68	1.67	16.6	223	38	66	4.20	7.7	14.6	1.9	0.8	73
83-85	CU	+++++	2019	AAA	Round Rock	0	3	0	24	29	12.32	2.07	14.7	340	40	41	9.37	5.6	10.8	1.9	3.4	62

Premium prospect who didn't live up to billing. Still has all ingredients to be ace for years to come. Missed time due to fatigue but showed flashes of double-plus stuff when on, which wasn't often. FB and CU both among top offerings in minors. FB thrown with great angle and high slot. Repeats athletic delivery well and uses nasty CU at will.

Whitlock, Garrett — SP — New York (A)

EXP MLB DEBUT: 2020 H/W: 6-5 190 FUT: Setup reliever **7D**

Thrws R Age 23

			Year	Lev	Team	W	L	Sv	IP	K	ERA	WHIP	BF/G	OBA	H%	S%	xERA	Ctl	Dom	Cmd	hr/9	BPV
2017 (18) Alabama-Birmingh			2017	Rk	GCL Yankees	0	0	0	8	14	1.10	0.49	9.0	147	30	75		0.0	15.4		0.0	295
91-94	FB	+++	2018	A	Charleston (Sc)	2	2	0	40	44	1.13	0.75	20.4	169	24	86	0.76	1.6	9.9	6.3	0.2	154
85-88	SL	++++	2018	A+	Tampa	5	3	0	70	74	2.44	1.24	20.3	233	32	80	2.78	3.5	9.5	2.7	0.3	96
84-85	CU	++	2018	AA	Trenton	1	0	0	10	4	0.88	1.67	22.9	258	29	94	4.00	6.2	3.5	0.6	0.0	-85
			2019	AA	Trenton	3	3	0	70	57	3.08	1.30	20.6	270	33	77	3.68	2.3	7.3	3.2	0.5	87

Tall, crossfire low 3/4s RHP inched closer to MLB. Doesn't use height well in delivery. Low 3/4s slot is close to bleeding into sidearm slot. Natural arm-side movement with 2-seam FB. Velocity may play up in RP role. SL is best secondary. Sharp, sometimes sweepy. CU is firm with good separation but telegraphs pitch. Potential 2-pitch setup man.

Widener, Taylor — SP — Arizona

EXP MLB DEBUT: 2020 H/W: 6-0 195 FUT: #4 starter **7B**

Thrws R Age 25

			Year	Lev	Team	W	L	Sv	IP	K	ERA	WHIP	BF/G	OBA	H%	S%	xERA	Ctl	Dom	Cmd	hr/9	BPV
2016 (12) South Carolina			2016	A-	Staten Island	2	0	1	15	25	0.00	0.40	8.1	45	10	100		2.4	14.9	6.3	0.0	222
91-93	FB	+++	2016	A	Charleston (Sc)	1	0	3	23	34	0.78	0.78	11.8	188	30	100	1.54	1.2	13.3	11.3	0.8	226
84-87	SL	+++	2017	A+	Tampa	7	8	0	119	129	3.40	1.15	17.5	206	28	70	2.33	3.8	9.7	2.6	0.4	91
81-84	CU	+++	2018	AA	Jackson	5	8	0	137	176	2.76	1.04	20.3	204	29	77	2.38	2.8	11.6	4.1	0.8	150
			2019	AAA	Reno	6	7	0	100	109	8.10	1.74	19.8	320	39	56	6.99	3.7	9.8	2.7	2.1	95

Strong, high-floor SP prospect whose control backed up on him in the hitter-friendly PCL. At his best, shows four above-average pitches including FB around 91-93 mph, two-plane SL and fading CU. Generally around zone but can miss up a lot, leading to lots of fly balls. SwK profile remains in tact and should be Dom source as back-end SP.

Williams, Devin — RP — Milwaukee

EXP MLB DEBUT: 2019 H/W: 6-3 165 FUT: Closer **8C**

Thrws R Age 25

			Year	Lev	Team	W	L	Sv	IP	K	ERA	WHIP	BF/G	OBA	H%	S%	xERA	Ctl	Dom	Cmd	hr/9	BPV
2013 (2) HS (MO)			2016	A+	Brevard County	1	2	0	25	20	4.32	1.56	21.9	277	33	73	4.63	4.3	7.2	1.7	0.7	31
95-98	FB	++++	2018	A+	Carolina	0	3	0	34	35	5.82	1.82	11.3	294	38	67	5.35	5.8	9.3	1.6	0.5	28
89-91	SL	+++	2019	AA	Biloxi	7	2	4	53	76	2.37	1.19	6.9	185	30	82	2.27	4.9	12.9	2.6	0.5	117
84-86	CU	+++	2019	AAA	San Antonio	0	0	0	3	6	0.00	0.94	4.0	181	40	100	1.08	2.8	16.9	6.0	0.0	246
			2019	MLB	Milwaukee	0	0	0	13	14	4.09	1.82	4.7	326	41	82	6.62	4.1	9.5	2.3	1.4	79

Former 2nd round pick made his MLB debut in September out of the bullpen. Will touch 99 mph with lively plus-plus fastball and sharp, hard SL in low 90s in short stints. Command and control haven't developed as was once projected, but ability to miss bats and rack up Dom is exciting.

Williams, Garrett — SP — Los Angeles (A)

EXP MLB DEBUT: 2020 H/W: 6-3 195 FUT: #4 starter **7D**

Thrws L Age 25

			Year	Lev	Team	W	L	Sv	IP	K	ERA	WHIP	BF/G	OBA	H%	S%	xERA	Ctl	Dom	Cmd	hr/9	BPV
2016 (7) Oklahoma St			2016	A-	Salem-Keizer	1	2	0	25	22	5.74	1.67	16.1	283	36	63	4.67	5.0	7.9	1.6	0.4	24
90-94	FB	+++	2017	A	Augusta	4	3	0	64	58	2.25	1.31	22.0	246	33	81	2.90	3.5	8.2	2.3	0.0	70
81-84	CB	++++	2017	A+	San Jose	2	2	0	33	38	2.45	1.15	21.8	231	31	83	3.05	2.7	10.4	3.8	0.8	131
82-85	CU	+	2018	AA	Richmond	3	9	1	81	73	6.10	1.93	11.7	295	37	68	5.79	6.8	8.1	1.2	0.7	-19
			2019	AA	Richmond	7	8	0	110	108	3.60	1.35	15.8	221	29	73	3.14	5.0	8.8	1.8	0.5	42

Repeated AA and showed improvement with K rate and control. Also posted better oppBA. Extreme groundballer who uses low 3/4 slot to pitch in bottom half of zone. FB features running action that is tough to elevate. CB can be nasty when consistent as it has power and depth. Slows arm on below average CU and could move to pen without improvement.

Williams, Kendall — SP — Toronto

EXP MLB DEBUT: 2024 H/W: 6-6 205 FUT: #3 starter **8E**

Thrws R Age 19

			Year	Lev	Team	W	L	Sv	IP	K	ERA	WHIP	BF/G	OBA	H%	S%	xERA	Ctl	Dom	Cmd	hr/9	BPV
2019 (2) HS (FL)																						
90-93	FB	+++																				
74-76	CB	+++																				
81-82	SL	++																				
82-84	CU	++	2019	Rk	GCL Blue Jays	0	0	0	16	19	1.13	0.81	9.7	117	19	85	0.17	3.9	10.7	2.7	0.0	104

Projectable SP with great size and room to grow. Throws from high angle and can be tough to pick up FB out of hand. Velocity not plus yet, but could succeed without. Uses four pitches in repertoire and shows nice feel for craft. Possesses good command for age and could get better with more polished arm action. May spend few years in rookie ball.

Williamson, Brandon — SP — Seattle

EXP MLB DEBUT: 2023 H/W: 6-6 210 FUT: #3 starter **8E**

Thrws L Age 22

			Year	Lev	Team	W	L	Sv	IP	K	ERA	WHIP	BF/G	OBA	H%	S%	xERA	Ctl	Dom	Cmd	hr/9	BPV
2019 (2) Texas Christian																						
89-93	FB	+++																				
80-82	SL	+++																				
74-76	CB	+++	2019	NCAA	Texas Christian	4	5	0	77	89	4.20	1.53	21.0	274	37	73	4.36	4.2	10.4	2.5	0.6	92
82-83	CU	++	2019	A-	Everett	0	0	0	15	25	2.38	0.93	5.7	174	34	71	1.00	3.0	14.9	5.0	0.0	206

Tall lefty was solid in pro debut, over-matching low-A hitters. 3/4s, cross-fire delivery naturally creates downward plane. FB has solid profile and projects to be above-average with consistent velocity. Both the CB and SL are distinct offerings, with SL playing closer to average. CU is work-in-progress.

Wilson, Bryse — SP — Atlanta

EXP MLB DEBUT: 2018 H/W: 6-1 225 FUT: Setup reliever **7B**

Thrws R Age 22

			Year	Lev	Team	W	L	Sv	IP	K	ERA	WHIP	BF/G	OBA	H%	S%	xERA	Ctl	Dom	Cmd	hr/9	BPV
2016 (4) HS (NC)			2018	AA	Mississippi	3	5	0	77	89	3.97	1.34	21.3	262	37	69	3.48	3.0	10.4	3.4	0.4	123
92-95	FB	++++	2018	AAA	Gwinnett	3	0	0	22	28	5.32	1.05	17.0	244	29	59	4.47	1.2	11.5	9.3	2.5	191
86-87	SL	++	2018	MLB	Atlanta	1	0	0	7	6	6.43	2.00	11.2	288	37	64	5.23	7.7	7.7	1.0	0.0	-51
78-81	CB	++	2019	AAA	Gwinnett	10	7	0	121	118	3.42	1.21	23.2	260	33	75	3.65	1.9	8.8	4.5	0.9	124
84-87	CU	+++	2019	MLB	Atlanta	1	1	0	20	16	7.20	1.80	15.4	316	34	65	7.26	4.5	7.2	1.6	2.3	26

Hard-throwing, FB heavy 3/4s RHP struggled in 20-inning '19 MLB stint. Throws two variations of FB, both with late movement and solid command. Doesn't have a secondary pitch to get hitters out with. SL is one-plane breaker while CB is slurvy in nature; both are below-average offerings. CU has solid arm-side run.

Winn, Cole — SP — Texas

EXP MLB DEBUT: 2023 H/W: 6-2 190 FUT: #3 starter **8C**

Thrws R Age 20

			Year	Lev	Team	W	L	Sv	IP	K	ERA	WHIP	BF/G	OBA	H%	S%	xERA	Ctl	Dom	Cmd	hr/9	BPV
2018 (1) HS (CA)																						
91-94	FB	+++																				
76-79	CB	++++																				
81-85	SL	++	2018		Did not play																	
84-86	CU	+++	2019	A	Hickory	4	4	0	68	65	4.49	1.44	16.1	235	30	69	3.68	5.1	8.6	1.7	0.7	33

A top prep arm from 2018, started slow but markedly improved in Jul/Aug. Athletic and repeatable delivery of four pitches; command improved throughout. FB 91-94 and had up-in-the-zone life at times; high-70s CB current plus with depth and bite; mid-80s CU could easily get to average. SL a 4th—but usable—pitch. Arsenal/physicality is impressive.

Wolf,Josh — SP — New York (N)

EXP MLB DEBUT: 2023 | H/W: 6-3 170 | FUT: #3 starter | 8D

Thrws R Age 19
2019 (2) HS (TX)

Velo	Pitch	Grade
91-94	FB	++++
78-81	CB	++++
	CU	++

Year	Lev	Team	W	L	Sv	IP	K	ERA	WHIP	BF/G	OBA	H%	S%	xERA	Ctl	Dom	Cmd	hr/9	BPV
2019	Rk	GCL Mets	0	1	0	8	12	3.38	1.25	6.5	285	46	70	3.23	1.1	13.5	12.0	0.0	231

Athletic, high 3/4s RHP repeats delivery well with plus arm speed. 2-seam FB sits 91-94 MPH with very late arm-side bore and advanced command. Sharp CB adds second potentially plus offering, capable of generating swings and misses. Doesn't throw CU much, but will need to develop it to reach ceiling.

Wong,Jake — SP — San Francisco

EXP MLB DEBUT: 2021 | H/W: 6-2 215 | FUT: #3 starter | 8D

Thrws R Age 23
2018 (3) Grand Canyon

Velo	Pitch	Grade
92-95	FB	++++
78-80	CB	+++
82-84	CU	++

Year	Lev	Team	W	L	Sv	IP	K	ERA	WHIP	BF/G	OBA	H%	S%	xERA	Ctl	Dom	Cmd	hr/9	BPV
2018	NCAA	Grand Canyon	9	3	0	89	88	2.83	1.31	24.6	259	34	79	3.45	2.9	8.9	3.0	0.4	99
2018	A-	Salem-Keizer	0	2	0	27	27	2.32	1.25	10.0	268	35	82	3.36	2.0	9.0	4.5	0.3	126
2019	A	Augusta	2	1	0	40	34	2.01	0.92	18.8	187	23	80	1.61	2.5	7.6	3.1	0.4	89
2019	A+	San Jose	3	2	0	72	67	4.99	1.39	20.2	272	34	64	4.14	3.0	8.4	2.8	0.7	88

Durable, groundball SP with excellent control and command. Promoted to A+ in May during first full season as pro. Has clean delivery and arm action that produces movement to all pitches. FB can touch high 90s at times, but best in 92-94 range due to heavy action. CB has potential to be plus offering, but can telegraph pitch by lowering slot.

Woodford,Jake — SP — St. Louis

EXP MLB DEBUT: 2020 | H/W: 6-4 220 | FUT: #4 starter | 7D

Thrws R Age 23
2015 (1) HS (FL)

Velo	Pitch	Grade
90-93	FB	+++
81-83	CT	++
83-85	CU	++
	SL	++

Year	Lev	Team	W	L	Sv	IP	K	ERA	WHIP	BF/G	OBA	H%	S%	xERA	Ctl	Dom	Cmd	hr/9	BPV
2016	A	Peoria	5	5	0	108		3.33	1.30	21.2	254	30	75	3.54	3.1	6.8	2.2	0.6	58
2017	A+	Palm Beach	7	6	0	119	72	3.10	1.40	21.9	276	31	79	4.07	2.9	5.4	1.8	0.5	36
2018	AA	Springfield	3	8	0	81	56	5.22	1.59	22.3	292	32	71	5.62	3.9	6.2	1.6	1.4	25
2018	AAA	Memphis	5	5	0	64	45	4.50	1.42	22.6	262	30	69	4.07	3.8	6.3	1.7	0.7	29
2019	AAA	Memphis	9	8	0	151	131	4.17	1.32	24.1	225	26	73	3.88	4.5	7.8	1.7	1.3	38

Former 1st rounder lacks top of the rotation stuff. FB sits at 90-93, topping at 95 with some late sink which results in weak contact and lots of GB outs. Secondary offerings include a CT, SL, and CU - all of which grade out as just average. Dom and Ctl trending in the wrong direction and now profiles as a back-end starter.

Woods-Richardson,Sime — SP — Toronto

EXP MLB DEBUT: 2022 | H/W: 6-3 210 | FUT: #3 starter | 8D

Thrws R Age 19
2018 (2) HS (TX)

Velo	Pitch	Grade
91-95	FB	++++
81-85	SL	++
80-81	CB	+++
82-86	CU	++

Year	Lev	Team	W	L	Sv	IP	K	ERA	WHIP	BF/G	OBA	H%	S%	xERA	Ctl	Dom	Cmd	hr/9	BPV
2018	Rk	Kingsport	0	0	0	6	11	4.50	1.00	11.5	262	46	60	3.65	0.0	16.5		1.5	315
2018	Rk	GCL Mets	1	0	1	11	15	0.00	1.17	8.9	223	36	100	2.21	3.2	12.2	3.8	0.0	149
2019	A+	Dunedin	3	2	0	28	29	2.56	0.89	17.4	185	25	71	1.38	2.2	9.3	4.1	0.3	125
2019	A	Columbia	3	8	0	78	97	4.26	1.22	15.8	262	37	64	3.38	2.0	11.2	5.7	0.6	166

Athletic, live-armed SP who owns immense upside with tantalizing pitch mix. Pitches effectively to all quadrants of strike zone and rarely beats himself. Could stand to improve command of breaking balls, but that is nit-picking. CU needs attention, but throws with same arm speed as FB. Needs time to develop stamina and durability.

Wright,Kyle — SP — Atlanta

EXP MLB DEBUT: 2018 | H/W: 6-4 200 | FUT: #3 starter | 8C

Thrws R Age 24
2017 (1) Vanderbilt

Velo	Pitch	Grade
93-96	FB	+++
86-88	SL	++++
80-82	CB	+++
86-86	CU	+++

Year	Lev	Team	W	L	Sv	IP	K	ERA	WHIP	BF/G	OBA	H%	S%	xERA	Ctl	Dom	Cmd	hr/9	BPV
2018	AA	Mississippi	6	8	0	109	105	3.71	1.34	22.7	251	32	72	3.49	3.5	8.7	2.4	0.5	78
2018	AAA	Gwinnett	2	1	0	28	28	2.55	0.82	14.6	159	20	71	1.21	2.6	8.9	3.5	0.6	110
2018	MLB	Atlanta	0	0	0	6	5	4.50	1.67	6.7	191	14	88	5.95	9.0	7.5	0.8	3.0	-90
2019	AAA	Gwinnett	11	4	0	112	116	4.17	1.27	21.8	253	32	70	3.84	2.8	9.3	3.3	1.0	110
2019	MLB	Atlanta	0	3	0	19	18	8.91	1.93	13.0	307	36	55	7.08	6.1	8.4	1.4	1.9	5

Tall, athletic RHP struggled mightily during small MLB sample, mostly with FB ineffectiveness. Needs to command flat FB to edges of zone to set up secondary pitches. Best pitch is a tight, 2-plane plus SL. His CB profile is more slurve than CB, as they bleed together. Has feel for solid mid-80s CU with separation and more run than FB.

Yajure,Michael — SP — New York (A)

EXP MLB DEBUT: 2021 | H/W: 6-1 175 | FUT: #4 starter | 8D

Thrws R Age 21
2015 FA (VZ)

Velo	Pitch	Grade
92-94	FB	++++
81-82	CB	+++
86-88	CT	++
87-88	CU	++++

Year	Lev	Team	W	L	Sv	IP	K	ERA	WHIP	BF/G	OBA	H%	S%	xERA	Ctl	Dom	Cmd	hr/9	BPV
2018	A	Charleston (Sc)	4	3	0	64	56	3.93	1.23	18.6	261	33	67	3.29	2.1	7.9	3.7	0.4	103
2019	A+	Tampa	8	6	0	127	122	2.26	1.08	22.6	235	31	80	2.51	2.0	8.6	4.4	0.4	120
2019	AA	Trenton	1	0	0	11	11	0.82	1.00	21.0	225	31	91	1.83	1.6	9.0	5.5	0.0	136

Emerging SP prospect who continued to make strides with sequencing and finding more velocity. Athletic, crossfire high-3/4s delivery. Hides ball well in delivery. FB up to 97 but sits low-to-mid 90s. Average movement. Best secondary is late-fading CU Good separation and late sink. CB is solid but doesn't have much upside.

Yan,Hector — SP — Los Angeles (A)

EXP MLB DEBUT: 2022 | H/W: 5-11 180 | FUT: #4 starter | 8E

Thrws L Age 20
2015 FA (DR)

Velo	Pitch	Grade
92-95	FB	+++
	CB	+++
	CU	++

Year	Lev	Team	W	L	Sv	IP	K	ERA	WHIP	BF/G	OBA	H%	S%	xERA	Ctl	Dom	Cmd	hr/9	BPV
2017	Rk	AZL Angels	0	1	1	16	21	5.03	1.30	6.6	180	29	57	2.05	6.1	11.7	1.9	0.0	63
2018	Rk	Orem	0	4	0	29	29	4.62	1.68	13.1	260	33	74	4.88	6.2	8.9	1.5	0.9	12
2019	A	Burlington	4	5	1	109	148	3.39	1.16	16.7	194	30	70	2.21	4.3	12.2	2.8	0.4	122

Three-pitch lefty whose stuff took a palpable step forward in MWL, garnering elite Dom and making some control gains. Though FB sits 92-95 mph, it plays up even more due to major crossfire delivery and he could have more velo in the tank. CB flashes good depth; CU will require reps. Could be scooted to bullpen, where FB-CB combo could work nicely.

Ynoa,Huscar — SP — Atlanta

EXP MLB DEBUT: 2019 | H/W: 6-3 175 | FUT: Setup reliever | 7D

Thrws R Age 21
2014 FA (DR)

Velo	Pitch	Grade
96-98	FB	++++
86-88	CB	++++
90-91	CU	++

Year	Lev	Team	W	L	Sv	IP	K	ERA	WHIP	BF/G	OBA	H%	S%	xERA	Ctl	Dom	Cmd	hr/9	BPV
2018	A+	Florida	1	4	0	24	31	8.18	1.86	18.9	326	46	52	5.77	4.5	11.5	2.6	0.4	105
2019	A+	Florida	0	1	0	11	16	3.27	1.45	15.7	244	40	75	3.18	4.9	13.1	2.7	0.0	121
2019	AA	Mississippi	1	2	1	13	15	5.45	1.67	9.9	314	40	70	6.03	3.4	10.2	3.0	1.4	110
2019	AAA	Gwinnett	3	5	0	72	79	5.36	1.58	18.7	282	35	71	5.69	4.2	9.8	2.3	1.7	81
2019	MLB	Atlanta	0	0	0	3	3	18.00	2.33	7.7	415	48	17	11.15	3.0	9.0	3.0	3.0	99

Hard-throwing RHP made surprise MLB debut in 2019 while pitching at 3 different minor league levels. Inconsistent cross-fire delivery screams RP role. Lacks command of high-90s FB with late run. Best pitch is a hard downer CB, which sits mid-to-high 80s and can be confused for a SL, it's that hard. CU is firm and mostly a show me pitch.

Zeferjahn,Ryan — SP — Boston

EXP MLB DEBUT: 2022 | H/W: 6-5 225 | FUT: #4 starter | 7C

Thrws R Age 22
2019 (3) Kansas

Velo	Pitch	Grade
92-96	FB	+++
83-87	SL	+++
82-83	CU	+++

Year	Lev	Team	W	L	Sv	IP	K	ERA	WHIP	BF/G	OBA	H%	S%	xERA	Ctl	Dom	Cmd	hr/9	BPV
2019	NCAA	Kansas	5	2	0	88	107	3.98	1.18	23.5	195	27	67	2.58	4.5	10.9	2.4	0.7	93
2019	A-	Lowell	0	2	0	22	31	4.50	1.64	8.2	279	41	74	4.89	4.9	12.7	2.6	0.8	114

Tall, live-armed SP who has chance to advance quickly, particularly if moved to pen. Command and control lag behind, but pure stuff can be wicked. FB lacks movement at times, but can add and subtract from velocity. Has solid secondaries in hard SL and fading CU with late movement. Needs to smooth out mechanics and find consistent slot.

Zeuch,T.J. — SP — Toronto

EXP MLB DEBUT: 2019 | H/W: 6-7 225 | FUT: #5 SP/swingman | 6A

Thrws R Age 24
2016 (1) Pittsburgh

Velo	Pitch	Grade
90-94	FB	++++
76-78	CB	+++
82-85	SL	++
83-85	CU	+

Year	Lev	Team	W	L	Sv	IP	K	ERA	WHIP	BF/G	OBA	H%	S%	xERA	Ctl	Dom	Cmd	hr/9	BPV
2018	A+	Dunedin	3	3	0	36	24	3.49	1.19	24.1	250	28	74	3.61	2.2	6.0	2.7	1.0	65
2018	AA	New Hampshire	9	5	0	120	81	3.08	1.26	23.3	262	31	76	3.49	2.3	6.1	2.6	0.5	65
2019	A+	Dunedin	0	0	0	8	12	4.39	1.10	16.1	232	39	56	2.13	2.2	13.2	6.0	0.0	196
2019	AAA	Buffalo	4	3	0	78	39	3.69	1.31	24.8	241	26	73	3.51	3.7	4.5	1.2	0.7	-1
2019	MLB	Toronto	1	2	0	22	20	4.86	1.49	19.1	260	32	68	4.29	4.5	8.1	1.8	0.8	44

Tall groundballer who pitches off devastating sinker. Throws on downhill plane and induces weak contact with plus FB. Throws strikes, though won't compete for K crowns. Outside of FB, no pitch stands out. CB can show average spin, but SL can be too firm. Fringy CU hasn't been effective against LHH. Very durable arm.

Zimmerman,Bruce — SP — Baltimore

EXP MLB DEBUT: 2020 | H/W: 6-2 215 | FUT: #5 SP/swingman | 6B

Thrws L Age 25
2017 (5) Mount Olive

Velo	Pitch	Grade
88-91	FB	++
82-85	SL	+++
71-75	CB	++
80-83	CU	+++

Year	Lev	Team	W	L	Sv	IP	K	ERA	WHIP	BF/G	OBA	H%	S%	xERA	Ctl	Dom	Cmd	hr/9	BPV
2018	A	Rome	7	3	0	84	99	2.78	1.09	23.5	238	33	76	2.71	1.9	10.6	5.5	0.5	157
2018	AA	Mississippi	2	1	0	28	26	3.19	1.56	20.6	239	29	83	4.33	6.1	8.3	1.4	1.0	4
2018	AA	Bowie	2	3	0	21	16	5.12	1.52	18.3	296	35	67	4.93	3.0	6.8	2.3	0.9	60
2019	AA	Bowie	5	3	0	101	101	2.58	1.21	22.6	236	30	82	3.25	3.0	9.0	3.0	0.8	98
2019	AAA	Norfolk	2	3	0	38	33	4.95	1.62	24.2	290	35	69	4.96	4.2	7.8	1.8	0.7	43

Pitchability 3/4s LHP inched closer to MLB by keeping Double-A hitters off balance. Creates deception with delivery, playing high 80s FB up. Commands FB well to 4 quadrants of zone. Best pitch is an above-average 2-plane SL. CU is a workable pitch, inducing light contact. Loopy CB just changes eye levels. Fringe MLB on stuff but lots of guile.

MAJOR LEAGUE EQUIVALENTS

In his 1985 *Baseball Abstract,* Bill James introduced the concept of major league equivalencies. His assertion was that, with the proper adjustments, a minor leaguer's statistics could be converted to an equivalent major league level performance with a great deal of accuracy.

Because of wide variations in the level of play among different minor leagues, it is difficult to get a true reading on a player's potential. For instance, a .300 batting average achieved in the high-offense Pacific Coast League is not nearly as much of an accomplishment as a similar level in the Eastern League. MLEs normalize these types of variances, for all statistical categories.

The actual MLEs are not projections. They represent how a player's previous performance might look at the major league level. However, the MLE stat line can be used in forecasting future performance in just the same way as a major league stat line would.

The model we use contains a few variations to James' version and updates all of the minor league and ballpark factors. In addition, we designed a module to convert pitching statistics, which is something James did not originally do.

Do MLEs really work?

Used correctly, MLEs are excellent indicators of potential. But just like we cannot take traditional major league statistics at face value, the same goes for MLEs. The underlying measures of base skill—batting eye ratios, pitching command ratios, etc.—are far more accurate in evaluating future talent than raw home runs, batting averages or ERAs.

The charts we present here also provide the unique perspective of looking at up to five years' worth of data. Ironically, the longer the history, the less likely the player is a legitimate prospect—he should have made it to the majors before compiling a long history in AA and/or AAA ball. Of course, the shorter trends are more difficult to read despite them often belonging to players with higher ceilings. But even here we can find small indications of players improving their skills, or struggling, as they rise through more difficult levels of competition. Since players—especially those with any talent—are promoted rapidly through major league systems, a two or three-year scan is often all we get to spot any trends.

Here are some things to look for as you scan these charts:

Target players who...

* spent a full year in AA and then a full year in AAA
* had consistent playing time from one year to the next
* improved their base skills as they were promoted

Raise the warning flag for players who...

* were stuck at a level for multiple seasons, or regressed
* displayed marked changes in playing time from one year to the next
* showed large drops in BPIs from one year to the next

Players are listed on the charts if they spent at least part of 2015-2019 in Triple-A or Double-A and had at least 100 AB or 30 IP within those two levels. Each is listed with the organization with which they finished the season.

Only statistics accumulated in Triple-A and Double-A ball are included (players who split a season are indicated as a/a); Single-A stats are excluded.

Each player's actual AB and IP totals are used as the base for the conversion. However, it is more useful to compare performances using common levels, so rely on the ratios and sabermetric gauges. Complete explanations of these formulas appear in the Glossary.

BATTER	B	Yr	Age	Pos	Lvl	Tm	AB	R	H	D	T	HR	RBI	BB	K	SB	CS	BA	OB	Slg	OPS	bb%	ct%	Eye	PX	SX	RC/G	BPV
Adams,Riley	R	19	23	C	aa	TOR	287	44	72	16	2	11	37	30	113	3	1	252	323	431	754	10%	61%	0.27	155	140	4.73	22.9
Adell,Jo	R	18	19	CF	aa	LAA	63	13	14	6	0	2	6	5	23	2	0	225	285	402	687	8%	63%	0.23	146	109	3.09	20
		19	20	RF	a/a	LAA	280	40	72	23	0	7	25	23	92	6	0	257	315	415	730	8%	67%	0.25	141	116	4.61	28.9
Adolfo,Micker	R	19	23	DH	aa	CHW	78	5	15	7	0	0	9	14	40	0	3	192	313	276	589	15%	48%	0.34	129	10	2.29	-83.6
Alcantara,Sergio	B	18	22	SS	aa	DET	441	45	111	17	3	1	31	35	98	7	5	252	307	310	617	7%	78%	0.36	41	84	2.63	-14
		19	23	SS	aa	DET	324	44	77	10	0	2	26	45	74	7	6	237	329	285	614	12%	77%	0.61	39	80	3.01	-20
Alemais,Stephen	R	18	23	2B	aa	PIT	402	47	102	15	3	1	29	37	73	13	10	254	316	313	629	8%	82%	0.51	39	101	2.70	8
		19	24	SS	aa	PIT	45	4	11	0	0	0	2	1	10	2	0	250	266	250	516	2%	79%	0.10	0	82	2.47	-50.5
Alford,Anthony	R	17	23	CF	a/a	TOR	257	38	76	15	0	5	22	33	52	16	3	297	376	412	789	11%	80%	0.63	73	93	5.04	31
		18	24	CF	aaa	TOR	375	45	83	22	1	4	29	26	123	15	8	222	272	319	591	6%	67%	0.21	79	104	2.23	-22
		19	25	RF	aaa	TOR	282	38	65	15	2	6	30	25	107	18	9	232	295	365	660	8%	62%	0.24	119	178	3.38	10.6
Allen,Austin	L	18	24	C	aa	SD	451	49	115	28	0	17	46	31	112	0	3	254	302	432	733	6%	75%	0.27	113	20	3.69	11
		19	25	C	aaa	SD	270	35	71	22	0	13	45	15	67	0	0	262	301	491	791	5%	75%	0.23	167	48	5.10	60.8
Arauz,Jonathan	S	19	21	2B	aa	HOU	108	11	24	3	2	3	12	9	21	1	1	225	285	358	643	8%	81%	0.44	79	129	3.25	38.7
Arozarena,Randy	R	17	22	LF	aa	STL	163	30	38	10	1	3	8	24	35	7	3	236	332	352	684	13%	78%	0.67	73	115	3.14	34
		18	23	LF	a/a	STL	358	49	85	18	0	9	38	26	92	20	9	237	288	361	649	7%	74%	0.28	83	104	2.91	10
		19	24	CF	a/a	STL	343	52	103	22	3	12	43	29	80	14	14	299	354	480	834	8%	77%	0.36	127	135	5.47	62.4
Avelino,Abiatal	R	17	22	2B	a/a	NYY	291	38	71	12	4	3	32	18	47	7	1	245	288	345	634	6%	84%	0.38	55	121	2.79	29
		18	23	SS	a/a	SF	477	53	119	12	8	10	53	25	113	21	7	249	287	366	653	5%	76%	0.22	66	139	3.05	12
		19	24	SS	aaa	SF	473	55	118	22	7	8	49	18	93	13	6	249	277	377	654	4%	80%	0.20	85	190	3.48	57.3
Azocar,Jose	R	19	23	RF	aa	DET	504	62	139	20	4	10	55	20	137	10	3	276	303	389	692	4%	73%	0.14	84	149	4.14	14.2
Banks,Nick	L	19	25	RF	aa	WAS	156	17	42	11	2	1	19	14	46	6	0	269	328	381	709	8%	70%	0.30	99	164	4.59	24.3
Bannon,Rylan	R	18	22	2B	aa	BAL	98	12	17	5	0	2	8	17	25	0	0	177	297	279	576	15%	74%	0.66	72	31	2.10	-5
		19	23	3B	a/a	BAL	470	54	112	28	3	10	50	43	92	7	6	239	303	373	676	8%	80%	0.47	95	107	3.67	43.1
Barrera,Luis	L	18	23	CF	aa	OAK	131	19	39	7	4	0	14	7	20	10	3	295	331	408	739	5%	85%	0.35	65	160	3.63	52
		19	24	CF	aa	OAK	224	30	66	8	10	3	20	10	54	8	8	294	324	466	790	4%	76%	0.19	106	165	4.85	50.1
Barrera,Tres	R	19	25	C	aa	WAS	357	39	83	23	0	8	42	33	77	1	2	233	297	360	657	8%	78%	0.42	96	44	3.48	17.1
Bart,Joey	R	19	23	C	aa	SF	79	9	24	4	1	3	11	7	22	0	2	302	358	505	863	8%	72%	0.31	143	97	5.91	43.6
Basabe,Luis	B	18	22	CF	aa	CHW	231	39	55	8	3	6	25	30	84	9	4	239	325	378	703	11%	64%	0.35	98	138	3.44	-1
		19	23	CF	aa	CHW	256	31	60	11	1	3	30	28	95	9	4	234	310	322	632	10%	63%	0.30	81	129	3.28	-30.1
Beer,Seth	L	19	23	1B	aa	ARI	322	45	83	15	0	16	65	31	89	0	1	258	324	450	774	9%	72%	0.35	136	42	4.94	24.1
Bishop,Braden	R	17	24	CF	aa	SEA	125	15	37	8	1	1	9	13	18	5	1	295	360	390	750	9%	86%	0.71	59	94	4.26	39
		18	25	CF	aa	SEA	345	55	82	17	0	6	26	30	83	4	2	238	299	343	641	8%	76%	0.36	70	78	2.92	1
		19	26	CF	aaa	SEA	185	20	40	12	0	6	22	16	56	1	2	217	280	373	653	8%	70%	0.29	125	52	3.24	8.7
Blanco,Dairon	R	19	26	CF	aa	KC	427	56	102	19	13	5	41	32	153	28	15	239	291	381	672	7%	64%	0.21	112	200	3.46	19.6
Blankenhorn,Travis	L	19	23	2B	aa	MIN	388	46	103	18	2	17	47	16	99	10	0	266	295	450	745	4%	75%	0.17	126	148	4.76	54.6
Bohm,Alec	R	19	23	3B	aa	PHI	238	34	60	10	1	14	38	25	44	2	2	252	323	478	801	10%	82%	0.57	136	80	5.11	73.3
Bolt,Skye	B	18	24	CF	aa	OAK	285	32	63	16	3	7	29	20	84	8	1	220	272	370	642	7%	71%	0.24	102	119	2.71	15
		19	25	RF	aaa	OAK	305	43	68	17	2	8	46	27	110	5	6	224	288	370	658	8%	64%	0.25	124	147	3.29	13.3
Bradley,Bobby	L	17	21	1B	aa	CLE	467	55	112	26	2	20	75	48	116	3	3	241	311	434	744	9%	75%	0.41	114	58	3.77	29
		18	22	1B	a/a	CLE	483	50	102	27	3	23	69	47	158	1	0	212	282	423	705	9%	67%	0.30	142	60	3.24	20
		19	23	1B	aaa	CLE	402	54	98	22	0	28	62	39	168	0	0	244	311	510	821	9%	58%	0.23	228	34	5.35	40
Brujan,Vidal	S	19	21	2B	aa	TAM	207	27	53	8	4	3	24	20	39	22	8	256	321	377	698	9%	81%	0.51	77	202	4.02	61
Cameron,Daz	R	18	21	CF	a/a	DET	257	35	66	15	7	4	36	23	69	12	6	259	321	420	741	8%	73%	0.34	103	142	3.34	36
		19	22	CF	aaa	DET	448	60	91	21	7	12	38	53	156	15	9	204	288	358	646	11%	65%	0.34	122	182	3.19	28
Cancel,Gabriel	R	19	23	2B	aa	KC	464	63	107	30	0	15	63	31	152	13	2	232	280	393	673	6%	67%	0.20	135	131	3.71	29
Capel,Conner	L	19	22	LF	a/a	STL	371	36	82	15	1	9	39	19	96	8	4	222	260	337	597	5%	74%	0.20	85	103	2.80	7.01
Carlson,Dylan	B	19	21	CF	a/a	STL	489	80	130	26	6	21	57	47	123	17	9	265	330	470	800	9%	75%	0.38	139	180	5.20	77.8
Carpio,Luis	R	19	22	2B	aa	NYM	243	28	60	14	0	3	22	28	56	2	6	245	324	338	661	10%	77%	0.51	75	40	3.35	-4.45
Castro,Willi	B	18	21	SS	a/a	DET	497	59	124	28	4	8	48	30	117	16	5	250	292	372	664	6%	77%	0.25	80	120	2.99	19
		19	22	SS	aaa	DET	465	66	135	28	9	10	55	32	113	15	4	290	335	451	786	6%	76%	0.28	114	196	5.42	65.2
Chatham,C.J.	R	19	25	SS	a/a	BOS	436	42	121	32	1	4	39	18	95	6	1	278	306	382	688	4%	78%	0.19	87	105	4.16	25.3
Clemens,Kody	L	19	23	2B	aa	DET	47	5	8	2	0	1	4	6	19	0	0	163	252	267	519	11%	60%	0.30	96	50	2.05	-51.8
Clement,Ernie	R	18	22	SS	aa	CLE	65	8	15	5	1	0	4	3	7	1	1	238	268	340	608	4%	89%	0.35	68	103	2.03	49
		19	23	SS	a/a	CLE	405	43	103	16	2	1	24	25	37	15	11	254	297	311	608	6%	91%	0.68	40	125	2.97	45.2
Collins,Zack	L	17	22	C	aa	CHW	34	7	8	2	0	2	5	11	12	0	0	229	421	465	887	25%	64%	0.93	159	25	5.67	44
		18	23	C	aa	CHW	418	54	91	22	1	15	63	97	178	5	0	218	366	382	748	19%	58%	0.55	134	69	3.95	-2
		19	24	C	aaa	CHW	294	44	71	16	1	16	58	48	115	0	0	243	350	464	813	14%	61%	0.42	185	68	5.46	28.1
Contreras,William	R	19	22	C	aa	ATL	191	26	48	9	0	3	19	16	41	0	0	253	311	351	662	8%	79%	0.39	74	65	3.72	6.45
Craig,Will	R	18	24	1B	aa	PIT	480	60	105	27	2	16	84	35	140	5	3	219	271	384	656	7%	71%	0.25	110	86	2.77	13
		19	25	1B	aaa	PIT	494	55	106	21	0	17	62	35	163	2	3	214	267	361	628	7%	67%	0.22	115	48	3.04	-13
Cron,Kevin	R	17	24	1B	aa	ARI	515	62	134	33	0	21	75	46	150	1	0	259	320	448	768	8%	71%	0.30	122	35	4.23	10
		18	25	3B	aaa	ARI	392	35	92	22	1	12	59	22	121	1	0	235	276	389	665	5%	69%	0.18	108	39	3.04	-13
		19	26	1B	aaa	ARI	305	49	77	15	1	22	63	38	95	1	2	251	334	525	859	11%	69%	0.40	195	66	5.79	66.4
Cronenworth,Jake	L	17	23	SS	aa	TAM	158	13	40	5	0	1	17	17	22	1	1	255	326	304	630	10%	86%	0.76	31	31	2.96	0
		18	24	SS	a/a	TAM	443	66	97	18	3	3	43	37	88	18	3	219	279	296	574	8%	80%	0.42	49	140	2.32	19
		19	25	SS	aaa	TAM	344	60	97	22	3	8	36	40	77	10	6	283	358	433	791	10%	78%	0.53	107	167	5.34	61.5
Crook,Narciso	R	18	23	LF	aa	CIN	161	16	42	5	1	2	19	16	47	3	4	261	327	343	670	9%	71%	0.34	54	87	3.09	-27
		19	24	LF	a/a	CIN	346	42	88	20	7	10	35	21	121	9	3	254	297	435	732	6%	65%	0.18	145	176	4.36	41.9
Cruz,Oneil	L	19	21	SS	aa	PIT	119	14	32	8	3	1	17	15	36	3	1	269	349	409	759	11%	70%	0.42	114	151	4.98	32
Cumberland,Brett	S	18	23	C	aa	BAL	60	5	9	0	0	2	5	4	18	0	0	145	194	265	460	6%	70%	0.20	66	25	1.54	-47
		19	24	C	aa	BAL	125	19	28	7	0	4	18	21	37	0	0	225	336	371	707	14%	71%	0.57	115	55	4.10	7.36
Dalbec,Bobby	R	18	23	3B	aa	BOS	111	11	27	8	1	4	19	5	49	0	0	240	269	447	716	4%	56%	0.09	176	56	3.26	-9
		19	24	3B	a/a	BOS	472	59	106	20	2	22	63	61	149	5	7	224	313	416	728	11%	68%	0.41	140	84	4.08	26.5
Davis,Jaylin	R	18	24	RF	aa	MIN	240	23	58	12	2	5	27	16	76	4	2	243	291	368	659	6%	69%	0.21	90	83	2.93	-15
		19	25	RF	a/a	SF	468	80	124	24	1	25	80	56	157	9	5	265	344	482	825	11%	67%	0.36	166	113	5.64	47.3
Dawson,Ronnie	L	18	23	CF	aa	HOU	114	16	30	5	1	6	13	5	38	5	3	264	297	474	771	4%	67%	0.14	139	120	3.95	25
		19	24	CF	a/a	HOU	426	55	73	17	1	13	41	38	176	10	11	172	240	312	552	8%	59%	0.22	125	123	2.09	-15

BATTER	B	Yr	Age	Pos	Lvl	Tm	AB	R	H	D	T	HR	RBI	BB	K	SB	CS	BA	OB	Slg	OPS	bb%	ct%	Eye	PX	SX	RC/G	BPV
Daza,Yonathan	R	18	24	CF	aa	COL	219	21	63	17	2	3	23	6	25	3	6	289	307	435	742	2%	89%	0.22	86	82	3.37	55
		19	25	CF	aaa	COL	387	43	122	28	4	8	31	16	58	8	11	316	344	467	811	4%	85%	0.28	102	107	5.45	65.3
Deichmann,Greg	L	19	24	RF	aa	OAK	301	36	58	9	2	9	31	29	115	16	6	194	264	323	587	9%	62%	0.25	106	169	2.69	-3.93
Diaz,Lewin	L	19	23	1B	aa	MIA	241	30	58	21	1	14	43	21	56	0	1	240	301	506	807	8%	77%	0.37	186	69	5.01	89.7
Diaz,Yusniel	R	17	21	RF	aa	LA	108	13	33	8	0	3	11	8	32	2	5	309	357	456	813	7%	70%	0.25	104	49	4.19	-5
		18	22	RF	aa	BAL	354	45	90	13	3	9	34	45	71	9	14	253	338	386	724	11%	80%	0.63	75	87	3.38	30
		19	23	RF	aa	BAL	286	41	70	17	3	11	49	30	71	0	3	243	314	436	750	9%	75%	0.42	134	102	4.40	52.6
Downs,Jeter	R	19	21	SS	aa	LA	48	13	15	2	0	5	10	5	11	1	0	319	386	655	1	10%	77%	0.48	206	114	9.61	122
Dubon,Mauricio	R	17	23	SS	a/a	MIL	492	61	121	26	0	8	47	32	86	31	17	247	293	346	639	6%	83%	0.37	61	100	2.78	23
		18	24	SS	aaa	MIL	108	12	31	8	1	3	12	1	23	4	4	283	292	460	752	1%	79%	0.06	109	119	3.40	43
		19	25	SS	aaa	SF	503	64	129	23	1	13	44	22	78	8	9	257	288	385	672	4%	85%	0.28	83	88	3.55	42.3
Duran,Jarren	L	19	23	CF	aa	BOS	320	37	79	12	5	1	17	20	87	25	9	247	291	323	614	6%	73%	0.23	59	207	3.19	12.5
Erceg,Lucas	L	18	23	3B	aa	MIL	463	48	109	21	1	13	47	34	91	3	1	236	288	369	657	7%	80%	0.37	78	58	3.08	17
		19	24	3B	aaa	MIL	357	41	67	15	1	12	39	33	119	1	2	187	256	332	588	8%	67%	0.28	114	78	2.60	-4.62
Estevez,Omar	R	19	21	2B	aa	LA	299	31	81	23	0	6	33	27	76	0	2	272	333	408	740	8%	74%	0.35	112	25	4.61	8.33
Fairchild,Stuart	R	19	23	CF	aa	CIN	153	22	39	11	1	4	15	18	27	3	2	257	334	421	755	10%	83%	0.67	114	113	4.65	69.8
Fox,Lucius	B	18	21	SS	aa	TAM	104	12	21	3	1	1	8	7	23	5	2	201	251	266	517	6%	78%	0.31	40	123	1.82	-3
		19	22	SS	a/a	TAM	407	59	83	14	9	3	30	54	117	35	12	205	298	301	598	12%	71%	0.46	70	220	2.93	22.3
Fraley,Jake	L	19	24	CF	a/a	SEA	382	57	100	23	4	16	67	29	106	18	8	262	313	469	783	7%	72%	0.27	150	177	4.90	74.7
Friedl,TJ	L	19	24	RF	aa	CIN	226	33	49	10	4	5	25	26	59	11	4	216	298	356	654	10%	74%	0.45	99	200	3.41	50
Fuentes,Josh	R	17	24	3B	aa	COL	414	39	124	27	7	13	58	19	92	6	5	299	330	498	828	4%	78%	0.21	115	97	4.59	43
		18	25	3B	aaa	COL	551	58	155	34	10	10	59	13	113	2	6	281	298	432	729	2%	80%	0.12	91	88	3.36	24
		19	26	3B	aaa	COL	402	41	85	20	2	12	40	16	132	1	1	213	242	359	602	4%	67%	0.12	118	92	2.78	1.63
Garcia,Aramis	R	17	24	C	aa	SF	78	10	20	11	0	0	7	8	24	0	0	257	328	398	726	10%	70%	0.35	128	34	2.89	12
		18	25	C	a/a	SF	339	31	65	13	1	7	28	17	102	0	1	192	230	295	525	5%	70%	0.16	71	50	1.80	-37
		19	26	C	aaa	SF	332	40	74	18	2	10	42	26	133	0	2	224	281	380	660	7%	60%	0.20	139	84	3.39	-10.3
Garcia,Luis	L	19	19	SS	aa	WAS	525	68	141	23	4	4	31	17	86	11	5	268	292	350	642	3%	84%	0.20	58	159	3.52	39.7
Garcia,Robel	B	19	26	3B	a/a	CHC	338	52	83	15	2	22	64	36	140	3	5	246	318	494	813	10%	58%	0.25	208	102	5.07	44.8
Gimenez,Andres	L	18	20	SS	aa	NYM	137	16	34	8	1	0	14	8	24	9	3	250	291	321	612	5%	82%	0.33	52	120	2.52	20
		19	21	SS	aa	NYM	432	54	102	20	4	9	37	24	114	28	16	235	276	363	639	5%	74%	0.21	94	181	3.06	36
Gonzalez,Luis	L	19	24	CF	aa	CHW	473	61	109	16	4	9	57	45	101	16	10	231	298	340	638	9%	79%	0.44	73	145	3.23	29.6
Gonzalez,Oscar	R	19	21	LF	aa	CLE	96	7	18	5	0	1	9	3	18	0	0	187	211	272	482	3%	81%	0.16	66	45	1.80	3.03
Gordon,Nick	L	17	22	SS	aa	MIN	519	74	136	28	8	8	61	48	135	12	7	262	325	394	719	8%	74%	0.35	83	123	3.41	18
		18	23	SS	a/a	MIN	544	53	125	21	6	6	42	28	116	17	5	230	268	325	594	5%	79%	0.25	58	122	2.38	10
		19	24	SS	aaa	MIN	292	41	79	27	3	3	33	15	71	12	4	271	307	417	723	5%	76%	0.21	120	175	4.39	63.1
Grullon,Deivy	R	17	21	C	aa	PHI	83	9	17	3	0	4	11	4	21	0	0	210	249	377	626	5%	75%	0.20	94	24	2.77	-8
		18	22	C	aa	PHI	326	28	79	12	1	18	47	14	93	0	0	244	276	454	730	4%	71%	0.15	127	17	3.84	3
		19	23	C	aaa	PHI	407	44	101	20	0	19	61	36	157	1	0	249	310	438	747	8%	61%	0.23	159	42	4.61	-1.14
Haase,Eric	R	17	25	C	a/a	CLE	339	47	79	17	3	22	48	37	121	3	2	232	307	495	802	10%	64%	0.30	169	90	4.29	41
		18	26	C	aaa	CLE	433	40	88	22	2	15	53	23	167	2	1	203	244	368	612	5%	61%	0.14	125	66	2.39	-22
		19	27	C	aaa	CLE	350	51	67	11	2	22	46	33	169	1	1	191	260	421	681	9%	52%	0.19	210	120	3.40	24.9
Haggerty,Sam	B	18	24	3B	a/a	CLE	297	37	65	21	3	3	31	48	92	21	8	219	327	343	670	14%	69%	0.52	95	136	2.79	22
		19	25	2B	a/a	NYM	289	42	65	10	4	3	19	39	107	20	5	226	317	317	634	12%	63%	0.36	77	213	3.47	-7.4
Harris,Trey	R	19	23	RF	aa	ATL	146	16	41	7	3	2	13	4	34	1	2	283	303	412	714	3%	76%	0.12	90	136	4.18	29.9
Harrison,Monte	R	18	23	CF	aa	MIA	521	73	109	17	2	15	41	38	244	24	10	209	264	338	602	7%	53%	0.16	109	133	2.48	-44
		19	24	CF	aaa	MIA	215	36	51	6	2	7	21	22	84	18	2	239	310	381	691	9%	61%	0.27	114	215	4.23	14.4
Hayes,Ke'Bryan	R	19	22	3B	aaa	PIT	427	54	105	29	2	8	45	37	94	10	1	245	304	376	681	8%	78%	0.39	100	145	3.96	48.5
Hays,Austin	R	17	22	CF	aa	BAL	261	33	75	10	1	14	46	12	52	1	1	286	317	494	811	4%	80%	0.23	107	57	4.97	33
		18	23	RF	aa	BAL	273	25	57	10	1	10	32	9	64	4	3	209	234	363	597	3%	77%	0.14	89	83	2.30	11
		19	24	CF	a/a	BAL	296	43	67	18	1	11	32	13	79	8	6	226	260	407	667	4%	73%	0.17	132	133	3.27	51.1
Heim,Jonah	B	18	23	C	aa	OAK	137	12	22	4	0	1	9	8	24	0	0	157	202	199	401	5%	83%	0.32	28	42	1.06	-22
		19	24	C	a/a	OAK	287	34	78	19	0	7	43	28	51	0	1	270	335	408	744	9%	82%	0.55	99	36	4.71	32.6
Hermosillo,Michael	R	17	22	CF	a/a	LAA	393	50	90	17	2	7	35	38	115	25	12	229	297	337	634	9%	71%	0.33	71	117	2.73	-6
		18	23	CF	aaa	LAA	273	27	57	11	2	8	29	18	102	6	6	209	259	349	608	6%	63%	0.18	101	102	2.31	-24
		19	24	CF	aaa	LAA	259	32	49	6	1	10	27	16	105	4	5	188	236	340	576	6%	60%	0.16	123	126	2.34	-13.3
Hilliard,Sam	L	18	24	RF	aa	COL	435	45	108	21	3	8	31	33	157	18	15	247	300	364	664	7%	64%	0.21	89	105	2.79	-25
		19	25	RF	aaa	COL	500	70	113	26	6	25	64	35	179	14	6	227	277	451	728	7%	64%	0.19	176	191	4.04	66.8
Hoerner,Nico	R	19	22	SS	aa	CHC	268	35	74	16	3	3	21	20	33	7	4	275	326	388	714	7%	88%	0.62	76	155	4.33	70.6
India,Jonathan	R	19	23	3B	aa	CIN	111	22	28	3	0	3	13	21	30	4	0	252	369	358	726	16%	73%	0.68	74	114	4.72	2.55
Isabel,Ibandel	R	19	24	1B	aa	CIN	334	45	75	11	1	25	60	24	180	0	0	225	277	489	766	7%	46%	0.13	270	77	4.45	37.1
Jackson,Alex	R	17	22	C	aa	ATL	110	12	25	2	0	5	20	10	36	0	0	232	298	379	677	9%	67%	0.29	90	19	3.53	-36
		18	23	C	a/a	ATL	333	36	61	22	2	7	35	26	130	0	0	185	243	325	568	7%	61%	0.20	116	66	1.87	-27
		19	24	C	aaa	ATL	306	44	61	8	0	22	55	17	130	1	0	201	242	446	688	5%	58%	0.13	200	82	3.45	26.8
Jeffers,Ryan	R	19	22	C	aa	MIN	87	12	24	5	0	4	8	8	20	0	0	279	343	467	810	9%	77%	0.42	129	46	5.67	39.8
Jenista,Greyson	L	19	23	LF	aa	ATL	222	19	54	4	1	5	28	28	78	2	4	244	330	340	670	11%	65%	0.36	72	60	3.56	-50.3
Jones,Jahmai	R	18	21	2B	aa	LAA	184	29	41	9	3	2	18	21	56	10	1	223	301	333	635	10%	70%	0.37	77	161	2.72	10
		19	22	2B	aa	LAA	482	62	105	21	2	5	47	48	120	8	12	218	288	301	590	9%	75%	0.40	65	103	2.61	-2.04
Jones,Nolan	L	19	21	3B	aa	CLE	178	31	45	10	2	8	21	30	66	2	0	252	360	460	820	14%	63%	0.46	171	147	5.71	49.4
Jones,Taylor	R	18	25	1B	a/a	HOU	452	46	105	26	1	14	61	45	147	2	0	232	302	390	692	9%	67%	0.31	113	54	3.30	-3
		19	26	1B	aaa	HOU	447	58	100	21	0	15	56	46	139	0	1	225	296	373	669	9%	69%	0.33	115	46	3.59	-4.56
Kelenic,Jarred	L	19	20	CF	aa	SEA	83	12	21	4	1	6	18	8	18	3	0	255	324	556	880	9%	78%	0.46	185	144	6.40	117
Kieboom,Carter	R	18	21	SS	aa	WAS	248	31	61	15	1	4	20	19	63	3	1	247	300	366	665	7%	75%	0.30	83	77	3.04	4
		19	22	SS	aaa	WAS	412	61	113	22	2	13	61	52	110	4	2	274	356	431	787	11%	73%	0.48	115	111	5.35	33.7
Kirilloff,Alex	L	19	22	RF	aa	MIN	375	44	103	18	2	8	40	27	79	7	6	276	324	402	726	7%	79%	0.34	88	100	4.36	29
Knizner,Andrew	R	17	22	C	aa	STL	182	24	56	13	0	3	20	12	28	0	1	305	349	430	780	6%	85%	0.44	76	35	4.52	24
		18	23	C	a/a	STL	335	32	92	16	0	5	35	20	53	0	0	273	315	366	681	6%	84%	0.39	58	23	3.53	3
		19	24	C	aaa	STL	246	32	58	9	0	9	26	18	41	2	0	235	288	379	666	7%	83%	0.44	88	80	3.66	40

BATTER	B	Yr	Age	Pos	Lvl	Tm	AB	R	H	D	T	HR	RBI	BB	K	SB	CS	BA	OB	Slg	OPS	bb%	ct%	Eye	PX	SX	RC/G	BPV
Kramer,Kevin	L	17	24	2B	aa	PIT	202	27	55	16	3	5	24	15	54	6	2	273	323	452	775	7%	73%	0.28	116	124	3.92	40
		18	25	2B	aaa	PIT	476	57	127	30	2	11	46	29	144	10	6	266	309	408	717	6%	70%	0.20	102	91	3.53	2
		19	26	2B	aaa	PIT	393	38	87	27	1	7	42	34	132	3	6	221	282	348	630	8%	66%	0.25	115	62	3.04	-10.5
Larnach,Trevor	L	19	22	RF	aa	MIN	156	24	45	4	0	7	21	21	52	0	0	286	369	439	808	12%	67%	0.39	112	48	5.79	-14.4
Lee,Khalil	L	18	20	CF	aa	KC	102	13	24	5	0	2	9	9	28	2	2	234	299	332	631	8%	72%	0.33	72	64	2.64	-16
		19	21	RF	aa	KC	470	69	122	22	3	7	48	61	157	49	13	259	344	363	707	12%	67%	0.39	89	189	4.47	8.98
Lewis,Kyle	R	18	23	CF	aa	SEA	132	15	25	7	0	3	16	14	37	1	0	190	268	318	586	10%	72%	0.38	88	49	2.27	-7
		19	24	LF	aa	SEA	457	60	112	23	2	11	61	55	177	3	2	245	327	375	702	11%	61%	0.31	117	102	4.10	-15.4
Lewis,Royce	R	19	20	SS	aa	MIN	134	17	31	9	1	2	13	11	33	6	2	233	289	360	649	7%	75%	0.32	102	154	3.43	41.2
Leyba,Domingo	B	17	22	SS	aa	ARI	58	9	15	4	0	2	8	4	6	0	0	263	313	423	736	7%	89%	0.66	87	44	3.84	54
		18	23	2B	aa	ARI	320	35	76	16	2	4	25	29	51	4	2	239	302	334	635	8%	84%	0.57	58	80	2.76	25
		19	24	SS	aaa	ARI	457	53	108	28	3	11	48	21	91	0	2	237	270	386	656	4%	80%	0.23	104	89	3.40	41.9
Longhi,Nick	R	17	22	1B	aa	CIN	256	30	69	16	0	8	42	17	49	0	1	269	316	428	743	6%	81%	0.36	93	28	3.95	21
		18	23	LF	a/a	CIN	266	24	59	13	0	2	30	13	74	1	0	220	256	289	545	5%	72%	0.17	55	45	2.03	-42
		19	24	1B	aaa	CIN	389	43	99	26	3	11	43	26	121	0	1	255	302	420	722	6%	69%	0.22	133	80	4.29	18.3
Lowe,Josh	L	19	21	CF	aa	TAM	448	68	108	21	4	17	61	59	147	29	10	241	329	419	748	12%	67%	0.40	136	184	4.61	48.1
Lux,Gavin	L	18	21	SS	aa	LA	105	17	30	4	1	3	7	10	23	2	2	287	352	424	776	9%	79%	0.47	79	79	4.46	21
		19	22	SS	a/a	LA	458	82	144	23	5	22	63	48	115	8	6	314	379	531	911	10%	75%	0.42	146	150	7.29	75.4
Madrigal,Nick	R	19	22	2B	a/a	CHW	282	51	89	16	3	2	25	24	11	16	10	314	369	408	777	8%	96%	2.17	59	166	5.25	94.6
Marsh,Brandon	L	19	22	CF	aa	LAA	360	45	101	20	1	7	40	45	101	17	5	281	361	404	766	11%	72%	0.44	98	125	5.20	18.2
Martin,Jason	L	17	22	LF	aa	HOU	300	33	76	22	3	10	32	16	93	6	6	253	292	445	737	5%	69%	0.18	130	98	3.25	21
		18	23	CF	a/a	PIT	468	57	115	16	7	10	45	37	121	10	13	246	301	375	676	7%	74%	0.30	78	108	2.90	8
		19	24	CF	aaa	PIT	370	38	85	23	4	6	40	24	86	7	7	231	277	364	641	6%	77%	0.27	99	135	3.16	39.3
Mateo,Jorge	R	17	22	SS	aa	OAK	257	42	70	13	9	6	38	19	68	20	11	272	323	461	783	7%	74%	0.28	108	162	3.59	45
		18	23	SS	aaa	OAK	470	40	98	15	15	2	36	23	149	20	11	209	245	320	565	5%	68%	0.15	70	141	1.72	-18
		19	24	SS	aaa	OAK	532	72	133	26	12	13	60	22	166	18	13	249	279	418	697	4%	69%	0.13	125	192	3.69	44.5
Matijevic,J.J.	L	19	24	1B	aa	HOU	281	36	61	18	1	8	31	24	111	7	0	216	277	372	649	8%	60%	0.21	145	148	3.47	15.4
Maton,Nick	L	19	22	2B	aa	PHI	62	5	12	3	0	2	5	8	16	1	1	197	291	341	632	12%	74%	0.52	103	36	3.00	5.96
Mazeika,Patrick	L	17	24	DH	aa	NYM	21	3	6	5	0	0	5	2	7	0	0	300	365	517	882	9%	66%	0.30	208	33	3.99	60
		18	25	C	aa	NYM	295	25	56	10	0	7	30	31	42	0	0	188	266	291	558	10%	86%	0.74	57	18	2.15	15
		19	26	C	aa	NYM	413	46	86	21	1	14	63	34	109	1	0	209	270	368	637	8%	74%	0.31	115	79	3.21	23.3
McCarthy,Joe	L	17	23	1B	aa	TAM	454	66	115	27	6	6	48	79	109	17	6	254	365	379	744	15%	76%	0.73	80	122	3.73	37
		18	24	LF	aaa	TAM	160	26	37	11	1	7	21	21	51	3	1	233	322	435	757	12%	68%	0.41	142	89	3.79	37
		19	25	RF	aaa	SF	227	26	35	8	2	4	21	29	94	1	0	156	250	266	516	11%	58%	0.30	99	136	2.02	-31.2
McCoy,Mason	R	19	24	SS	aa	BAL	429	54	104	11	5	2	28	33	91	9	3	242	296	307	603	7%	79%	0.36	44	179	3.06	17.3
McGuire,Reese	L	17	22	C	aa	TOR	115	17	31	5	1	6	17	14	21	2	1	266	345	470	815	11%	82%	0.68	105	82	4.83	61
		18	23	C	aaa	TOR	322	27	70	9	2	6	33	29	83	3	2	218	283	315	597	8%	74%	0.35	60	61	2.50	-18
		19	24	C	aaa	TOR	243	25	55	12	1	4	24	21	49	3	0	225	286	332	618	8%	80%	0.42	77	112	3.19	27.9
McKay,Brendan	L	19	24	DH	a/a	TAM	145	16	25	3	0	4	16	15	60	1	1	174	251	283	534	9%	59%	0.25	93	65	2.14	-57.4
McKenna,Ryan	R	18	21	CF	aa	BAL	213	27	45	7	1	3	12	22	59	3	1	213	287	293	580	9%	72%	0.38	54	94	2.33	-18
		19	22	CF	aa	BAL	488	74	107	24	5	9	50	56	126	23	12	218	298	341	639	10%	74%	0.44	90	186	3.22	39.7
Mendick,Danny	R	17	24	SS	aa	CHW	147	13	27	5	0	3	19	17	31	1	2	182	266	274	540	10%	79%	0.54	54	38	1.89	-7
		18	25	SS	aa	CHW	453	55	100	22	0	13	53	53	106	18	11	220	301	357	659	10%	77%	0.50	86	79	2.92	22
		19	26	2B	aaa	CHW	477	57	109	21	1	14	48	49	118	14	10	229	301	361	662	9%	75%	0.42	94	93	3.44	18.6
Mesa,Victor Victor	R	19	23	CF	aa	MIA	107	9	18	2	0	0	3	3	17	3	0	171	196	189	385	3%	84%	0.19	16	114	1.24	-7.21
Miller,Brian	L	18	23	LF	aa	MIA	262	25	62	7	2	0	12	16	44	18	8	235	279	274	553	6%	83%	0.35	26	116	2.20	1
		19	24	LF	aa	MIA	449	55	113	23	5	2	41	40	90	23	10	251	312	336	647	8%	80%	0.44	64	176	3.51	37.1
Miller,Jalen	R	19	23	2B	aa	SF	491	53	101	18	3	9	46	48	112	27	14	207	277	311	588	9%	77%	0.43	73	147	2.66	25
Miller,Owen	R	19	23	SS	aa	SD	507	65	132	26	2	10	58	40	94	4	6	261	315	380	696	7%	81%	0.42	83	91	4.00	32.4
Moniak,Mickey	L	19	21	CF	aa	PHI	465	58	112	26	12	11	62	30	125	14	3	241	288	421	708	6%	73%	0.24	126	199	4.10	66
Montero,Elehuris	R	19	21	3B	aa	STL	224	20	38	7	0	6	15	12	77	0	1	170	210	278	489	5%	65%	0.15	88	47	1.75	-41.9
Mountcastle,Ryan	R	17	20	3B	aa	BAL	153	16	28	8	0	3	13	3	39	0	0	181	196	283	479	2%	74%	0.07	68	49	1.42	-28
		18	21	3B	aa	BAL	394	49	105	16	3	11	46	20	84	2	0	267	302	406	708	5%	79%	0.24	81	77	3.71	15
		19	22	1B	aaa	BAL	520	66	146	30	1	22	68	20	139	2	1	281	307	466	773	4%	73%	0.14	134	72	5.04	33.9
Murphy,Sean	R	17	23	C	aa	OAK	191	20	35	6	0	3	18	16	36	0	0	183	248	261	509	8%	81%	0.46	47	34	1.76	-10
		18	24	C	a/a	OAK	265	42	66	23	2	6	34	20	55	2	0	248	301	416	717	7%	79%	0.36	110	101	3.26	52
		19	25	C	aaa	OAK	120	19	31	5	1	7	23	11	37	0	1	256	320	489	808	9%	70%	0.31	164	104	5.14	54.8
Neuse,Sheldon	R	17	23	3B	aa	OAK	67	7	22	4	0	0	5	5	23	0	0	335	379	390	769	7%	66%	0.21	53	24	4.86	-71
		18	24	3B	aaa	OAK	499	38	114	23	3	4	43	25	191	3	1	228	264	307	572	5%	62%	0.13	69	74	2.18	-64
		19	25	3B	aaa	OAK	498	75	132	28	2	19	77	42	156	2	4	265	322	442	764	8%	69%	0.27	138	91	4.81	25.8
Nevin,Tyler	R	19	22	1B	aa	COL	466	61	126	30	3	14	62	66	88	6	2	271	362	439	801	12%	81%	0.76	114	111	5.55	64.8
Ockimey,Josh	L	17	22	1B	aa	BOS	103	10	27	8	0	2	9	14	34	0	0	261	350	403	753	12%	67%	0.41	107	14	3.97	-17
		18	23	1B	a/a	BOS	404	44	93	21	2	16	58	56	157	1	1	229	323	408	732	12%	61%	0.35	136	46	3.68	-7
		19	24	1B	aaa	BOS	377	53	71	18	2	20	47	66	149	0	2	188	309	402	711	15%	60%	0.44	177	75	3.81	22.8
Oliva,Jared	R	19	24	CF	aa	PIT	447	65	117	24	5	5	39	39	111	32	11	262	322	374	696	8%	75%	0.35	85	204	4.14	43.2
Olivares,Edward	R	19	23	RF	aa	SD	488	73	124	23	2	14	66	37	108	30	11	254	307	397	704	7%	78%	0.35	98	158	4.09	50.8
Pache,Cristian	R	18	20	CF	aa	ATL	104	9	27	3	1	1	7	4	29	0	2	256	287	329	616	4%	72%	0.16	49	66	2.54	-41
		19	21	CF	a/a	ATL	487	62	133	36	8	11	60	41	126	8	12	273	330	448	779	8%	74%	0.33	131	138	4.79	56.7
Padlo,Kevin	R	19	23	3B	a/a	TAM	351	57	83	27	1	18	55	62	135	11	4	236	350	471	821	15%	61%	0.46	206	121	5.43	63.7
Paredes,Isaac	R	18	19	3B	aa	DET	131	18	41	9	0	3	20	17	22	1	0	311	389	441	830	11%	83%	0.77	82	42	5.43	36
		19	20	3B	aa	DET	478	64	137	24	1	13	67	56	60	5	3	286	360	424	785	10%	87%	0.93	86	86	5.40	59.2
Peters,DJ	R	18	23	CF	aa	LA	491	59	99	20	2	22	45	32	219	1	2	201	250	383	633	6%	55%	0.15	146	62	2.62	-29
		19	24	CF	a/a	LA	457	56	97	18	1	19	64	45	194	2	1	213	284	378	662	9%	57%	0.23	146	86	3.46	-13.5
Peterson,Dustin	R	17	23	LF	aaa	ATL	314	30	65	10	1	1	26	25	92	1	2	207	265	250	515	7%	71%	0.27	34	51	1.78	-59
		18	24	LF	aaa	ATL	406	37	96	21	0	9	44	23	107	2	0	237	278	354	632	5%	74%	0.21	81	49	2.84	-14
		19	25	1B	aaa	DET	301	26	76	12	0	9	41	11	86	1	1	253	280	385	664	4%	71%	0.13	97	34	3.62	-14.6
Potts,Hudson	R	18	20	3B	aa	SD	78	4	11	0	0	2	4	9	35	1	0	142	229	207	435	10%	55%	0.25	45	31	1.45	-112
		19	21	3B	aa	SD	409	49	86	22	1	13	52	29	136	3	1	209	261	363	623	7%	67%	0.21	125	101	3.04	10.3

BATTER	B	Yr	Age	Pos	Lvl	Tm	AB	R	H	D	T	HR	RBI	BB	K	SB	CS	BA	OB	Slg	OPS	bb%	ct%	Eye	PX	SX	RC/G	BPV
Quinn,Heath	R	19	24	RF	aa	SF	97	6	19	4	1	2	8	13	38	0	0	194	292	306	598	12%	61%	0.35	98	90	2.83	-34.8
Quiroz,Esteban	L	18	26	2B	aa	BOS	87	14	22	5	0	5	18	9	22	1	1	256	327	480	807	10%	75%	0.43	134	53	4.55	44
		19	27	2B	aaa	SD	306	41	62	19	0	11	42	34	101	2	1	203	282	378	660	10%	67%	0.33	143	75	3.38	19.1
Raleigh,Cal	S	19	23	C	aa	SEA	145	16	32	6	0	7	16	14	53	0	0	217	287	403	690	9%	63%	0.26	147	33	3.76	-5.8
Raley,Luke	L	18	24	1B	aa	MIN	484	62	118	17	6	16	54	28	150	3	0	244	284	404	688	5%	69%	0.18	101	111	3.32	3
		19	25	RF	aaa	MIN	126	23	34	6	0	6	17	6	47	3	0	267	299	448	746	4%	63%	0.12	148	135	4.80	20.2
Ramos,Heliot	R	19	20	CF	aa	SF	95	13	23	6	1	3	15	10	33	2	3	244	318	416	734	10%	65%	0.31	145	148	3.99	34.5
Ramos,Roberto	L	18	24	1B	aa	COL	199	20	43	9	0	13	27	21	78	2	1	216	290	453	743	9%	61%	0.27	169	31	3.81	9
		19	25	1B	aaa	COL	431	50	114	25	0	21	68	40	156	0	1	264	327	470	796	8%	64%	0.25	168	22	5.26	10.1
Ray,Corey	L	18	24	CF	aa	MIL	532	77	121	31	6	26	67	54	198	33	8	227	297	457	754	9%	63%	0.27	164	155	3.77	49
		19	25	CF	a/a	MIL	247	24	44	10	0	6	18	22	120	5	3	177	245	294	539	8%	51%	0.19	125	76	2.16	-58.7
Read,Raudy	R	17	24	C	aa	WAS	411	36	95	22	1	13	50	22	89	2	0	232	271	386	658	5%	78%	0.25	91	43	2.99	11
		18	25	C	a/a	WAS	197	13	48	10	1	2	21	10	43	0	0	244	279	345	624	5%	78%	0.22	66	40	2.65	-12
		19	26	C	aaa	WAS	306	37	70	14	2	15	43	12	69	1	1	227	257	430	687	4%	77%	0.17	132	103	3.58	57.7
Reed,Buddy	S	18	23	CF	aa	SD	179	18	28	6	0	1	13	10	71	15	3	158	202	206	409	5%	61%	0.14	46	130	1.19	-69
		19	24	CF	aa	SD	381	41	76	14	2	11	42	36	140	19	9	200	268	329	597	9%	63%	0.25	106	135	2.72	-8.16
Rios,Edwin	L	17	23	1B	a/a	LA	475	58	131	32	0	20	75	27	126	1	2	276	315	473	787	5%	73%	0.21	122	31	4.42	13
		18	24	3B	aaa	LA	309	35	80	22	0	8	42	17	129	0	1	260	298	407	705	5%	58%	0.13	130	32	3.38	-41
		19	25	3B	aaa	LA	393	51	86	19	1	22	64	25	183	1	2	220	266	445	711	6%	53%	0.14	212	82	3.78	20.1
Robert,Luis	R	19	22	CF	a/a	CHW	428	79	123	24	7	23	61	21	121	25	9	288	322	535	857	5%	72%	0.18	172	225	5.98	103
Rodgers,Brendan	R	17	21	SS	aa	COL	150	17	39	5	0	6	15	7	34	0	2	263	295	412	707	4%	77%	0.20	83	33	3.62	-5
		18	22	SS	a/a	COL	426	39	107	26	2	14	49	23	93	9	3	250	289	416	705	5%	78%	0.25	102	84	3.39	32
		19	23	2B	aaa	COL	143	23	45	10	1	7	14	10	29	0	0	315	358	535	894	6%	80%	0.33	145	100	7.14	78
Rodriguez,Alfredo	R	18	24	SS	aa	CIN	26	3	4	0	0	0	0	2	8	0	0	170	221	170	390	6%	69%	0.21	0	59	1.15	-92
		19	25	SS	aa	CIN	486	47	114	20	2	1	29	26	91	14	10	235	274	289	563	5%	81%	0.28	44	113	2.50	6.09
Rodriguez,Julio	R	19	22	C	aa	STL	45	2	9	1	0	1	6	2	16	0	0	201	229	275	503	4%	65%	0.10	59	3	2.00	-81.8
Rogers,Jake	R	18	23	C	aa	DET	352	47	69	14	1	14	46	33	118	6	1	197	266	362	628	9%	66%	0.28	111	95	2.72	2
		19	24	C	a/a	DET	252	41	59	12	2	13	46	32	84	0	0	232	319	449	768	11%	67%	0.38	162	122	4.75	48.3
Rooker,Brent	R	18	24	1B	aa	MIN	503	56	113	28	3	18	62	43	164	5	1	224	285	398	683	8%	67%	0.26	121	85	3.10	10
		19	25	LF	aaa	MIN	228	33	57	15	0	11	38	28	107	2	0	248	332	464	795	11%	53%	0.27	214	71	5.26	20.3
Rortvedt,Ben	L	19	22	C	aa	MIN	197	18	46	8	0	5	18	21	53	0	0	232	307	344	651	10%	73%	0.40	84	28	3.50	-17.4
Ruiz,Keibert	S	18	20	C	aa	LA	377	35	90	13	0	10	37	20	36	0	1	240	278	351	629	5%	90%	0.55	58	24	2.91	27
		19	21	C	a/a	LA	314	32	74	8	0	5	28	24	24	0	0	236	289	312	601	7%	92%	0.97	45	47	3.01	31.8
Rutherford,Blake	L	19	22	RF	aa	CHW	438	50	113	16	3	7	49	37	129	9	2	258	316	359	675	8%	71%	0.29	77	142	3.93	-0.08
Sanchez,Ali	R	19	22	C	a/a	NYM	326	30	76	15	0	1	30	26	72	1	1	234	291	289	580	7%	78%	0.36	49	52	2.77	-20.4
Sanchez,Jesus	L	18	21	RF	aa	TAM	98	12	19	7	0	1	10	10	24	1	1	191	263	290	553	9%	76%	0.40	76	65	1.75	3
		19	22	RF	a/a	MIA	415	49	102	13	2	12	63	39	109	5	4	245	310	369	680	9%	74%	0.36	86	100	3.77	8.15
Santana,Cristian	R	19	22	3B	aa	LA	399	41	113	21	1	9	52	9	97	0	0	282	297	409	706	2%	76%	0.09	95	53	4.32	4.86
Santana,Luis	R	19	20	2B	aa	HOU	57	5	12	2	0	0	2	6	10	0	0	215	285	247	533	9%	83%	0.58	29	40	2.29	-18.3
Shaw,Chris	L	17	24	LF	a/a	SF	469	50	120	32	1	17	68	33	151	0	0	257	306	438	744	7%	68%	0.22	124	30	3.84	-6
		18	25	LF	aaa	SF	394	38	81	17	2	14	46	15	170	0	0	204	233	363	596	4%	57%	0.09	127	53	2.32	-46
		19	26	LF	a/a	SF	442	64	111	25	3	19	78	33	128	2	2	251	303	452	756	7%	71%	0.26	147	110	4.58	47.2
Sheets,Gavin	L	19	23	1B	aa	CHW	464	55	119	17	1	17	82	53	110	3	1	256	332	404	736	10%	76%	0.48	99	79	4.59	22.3
Shewmake,Braden	L	19	22	SS	aa	ATL	46	8	10	0	0	0	1	4	11	2	0	224	291	224	515	9%	76%	0.38	0	133	2.39	-44.2
Short,Zack	R	18	23	SS	aa	CHC	436	58	89	25	2	15	50	73	149	7	3	205	319	372	690	14%	66%	0.49	121	83	3.11	15
		19	24	SS	a/a	CHC	197	25	40	11	2	5	19	26	76	2	2	203	297	354	651	12%	62%	0.35	134	131	3.25	8.06
Siri,Jose	R	18	23	CF	aa	CIN	253	36	53	7	7	11	29	21	102	12	5	211	271	426	697	8%	59%	0.20	147	151	2.92	18
		19	24	CF	a/a	CIN	468	48	100	17	2	10	46	38	195	22	9	214	273	326	599	7%	58%	0.19	103	140	2.85	-29.8
Smith,Kevin	R	19	23	SS	aa	TOR	430	47	88	23	2	18	58	27	162	11	6	205	252	395	647	6%	62%	0.17	159	120	3.06	24.8
Solak,Nick	R	17	22	2B	aa	NYY	119	15	33	8	1	2	9	10	26	1	1	275	330	416	746	8%	78%	0.37	89	75	3.77	23
		18	23	2B	aa	TAM	478	77	120	15	2	16	65	58	131	18	7	250	331	389	720	11%	73%	0.44	85	112	3.92	15
		19	24	2B	aaa	TEX	419	58	107	17	1	21	54	34	114	4	2	256	312	453	765	8%	73%	0.30	135	89	4.79	38.9
Sosa,Edmundo	R	18	22	SS	a/a	STL	452	51	108	27	1	9	46	17	101	5	4	238	265	359	625	4%	78%	0.17	81	69	2.56	5
		19	23	SS	aaa	STL	453	56	115	16	3	13	49	13	106	2	3	254	275	390	665	3%	77%	0.12	90	106	3.56	21.2
Stephenson,Tyler	R	19	23	C	aa	CIN	312	42	83	18	1	6	40	35	70	0	0	266	339	387	726	10%	78%	0.50	91	71	4.55	18.9
Stubbs,Garrett	L	17	24	C	a/a	HOU	340	34	65	15	0	3	27	31	71	8	0	191	258	261	519	8%	79%	0.43	47	86	1.87	-1
		18	25	C	aaa	HOU	297	41	72	15	3	3	26	23	64	4	0	244	299	346	645	7%	78%	0.36	66	115	2.83	17
		19	26	C	aaa	HOU	204	22	37	8	0	5	15	16	47	8	2	183	242	293	535	7%	77%	0.34	78	111	2.24	17.4
Taveras,Leody	B	19	21	CF	aa	TEX	264	30	72	12	5	3	29	22	60	10	8	273	330	391	721	8%	77%	0.38	82	157	4.18	35.9
Taylor,Tyrone	R	17	23	LF	aa	MIL	85	15	20	6	1	1	6	8	20	2	1	241	305	372	677	9%	77%	0.40	85	122	2.85	31
		18	24	CF	aaa	MIL	446	48	102	19	6	14	52	18	87	8	5	228	257	394	651	4%	80%	0.20	92	114	2.70	39
		19	25	RF	aaa	MIL	334	32	76	17	1	11	43	21	102	4	0	226	272	381	653	6%	70%	0.20	120	96	3.47	15
Thompson-Williams,Do	L	19	24	CF	aa	SEA	432	45	94	22	3	12	40	35	176	15	2	218	276	368	645	7%	59%	0.20	136	172	3.41	10.2
Trammell,Taylor	L	19	22	LF	aa	SD	436	53	93	11	3	8	37	59	130	17	9	214	308	310	618	12%	70%	0.45	70	149	3.06	-3.35
Varsho,Daulton	L	19	23	C	aa	ARI	396	80	114	23	6	16	55	41	68	20	5	289	355	502	857	9%	83%	0.60	132	215	6.39	116
Walls,Taylor	S	19	23	SS	aa	TAM	211	40	53	14	5	5	19	25	59	14	10	252	332	445	777	11%	72%	0.43	142	206	4.49	79.1
Walsh,Jared	L	17	24	1B	aa	LAA	69	7	14	3	0	3	8	3	34	1	0	210	240	367	607	4%	51%	0.08	133	50	2.59	-64
		18	25	1B	a/a	LAA	327	41	72	20	0	11	44	25	126	1	0	221	277	388	665	7%	62%	0.20	131	46	2.97	-19
		19	26	1B	aaa	LAA	382	54	94	22	0	24	52	36	145	0	0	247	312	494	806	9%	62%	0.25	203	45	5.22	37.6
Walton,Donnie	L	18	24	2B	aa	SEA	208	18	42	12	1	1	18	17	41	2	1	200	261	276	536	8%	81%	0.42	55	71	1.76	4
		19	25	SS	aa	SEA	480	69	132	20	3	11	48	61	86	10	14	275	357	394	751	11%	82%	0.71	78	97	4.55	35.5
Waters,Drew	S	19	21	LF	a/a	ATL	527	79	161	40	8	6	51	38	169	16	6	306	352	449	801	7%	68%	0.22	124	192	5.73	41.5
Welker,Colton	R	19	22	3B	aa	COL	353	37	96	26	1	11	53	33	66	2	1	272	333	448	782	8%	81%	0.49	122	76	5.21	59.4
White,Eli	R	18	24	2B	aa	OAK	504	63	134	27	7	6	43	47	130	14	10	266	328	386	715	9%	74%	0.36	80	118	3.34	15
		19	25	SS	aaa	TEX	438	45	97	18	5	11	31	32	152	10	6	221	274	355	629	7%	65%	0.21	106	153	3.10	5.04
White,Evan	R	19	23	1B	aa	SEA	365	61	103	12	2	18	55	29	105	2	0	281	334	474	808	7%	71%	0.28	132	125	5.66	41.6
Williams,Justin	L	17	22	RF	aa	TAM	366	47	100	19	2	12	64	33	78	5	2	274	335	437	771	8%	79%	0.43	93	85	4.36	33

PITCHER	Th	Yr	Age	LvL	Org	W	L	G	Sv	IP	H	ER	HR	BB	K	ERA	WHIP	BF/G	OBA	bb/9	k/9	Cmd	hr/9	H%	S%	BPV
Abbott, Cory	R	19	24	aa	CHC	8	8	26	0	148	142	70	19	60	138	4.26	1.36	23.9	000	3.6	8.4	2.3	1.2	30%	62%	70
Abreu, Albert	R	19	24	aa	NYY	5	8	23	0	98	128	64	13	60	76	5.83	1.91	20.2	000	5.5	7.0	1.3	1.2	36%	64%	-4
Adon, Melvin	R	19	25	a/a	SF	2	7	48	14	56	68	40	3	38	61	6.48	1.89	5.5	000	6.1	9.8	1.6	0.5	40%	61%	30
Akin, Keegan	L	18	23	aa	BAL	14	7	25	0	139	128	57	18	57	117	3.68	1.32	23.1	245	3.7	7.5	2.1	1.2	28%	77%	59
		19	24	aaa	BAL	6	7	25	0	113	127	71	12	63	105	5.66	1.68	20.3	000	5.0	8.4	1.7	0.9	35%	60%	34
Alcala, Jorge	R	18	23	aa	MIN	2	7	14	1	62	69	36	6	31	48	5.14	1.60	19.6	281	4.5	7.0	1.6	0.8	33%	68%	49
		19	24	a/a	MIN	6	7	31	0	113	147	92	15	43	94	7.34	1.67	16.4	000	3.4	7.5	2.2	1.2	37%	47%	62
Allen, Logan	L	18	21	a/a	SD	14	6	25	0	150	116	44	10	47	134	2.62	1.09	23.5	215	2.8	8.0	2.9	0.6	27%	78%	102
		19	22	aaa	CLE	5	4	18	0	80	107	66	17	35	70	7.39	1.79	20.5	000	4.0	7.9	2.0	1.9	37%	48%	52
Alzolay, Adbert	R	17	22	aa	CHC	0	3	7	0	33	32	14	0	13	26	3.92	1.37	19.5	257	3.5	7.3	2.1	0.0	33%	68%	91
		18	23	aaa	CHC	2	4	8	0	41	47	23	4	13	23	5.06	1.47	22.1	290	2.8	5.0	1.8	0.9	32%	66%	37
		19	24	aaa	CHC	2	4	15	0	66	64	41	11	34	75	5.57	1.47	18.9	000	4.6	10.3	2.2	1.6	32%	52%	79
Anderson, Ian	R	18	20	aa	ATL	2	1	4	0	20	16	6	0	9	21	2.87	1.24	20.4	222	3.9	9.5	2.4	0.0	31%	74%	118
		19	21	a/a	ATL	8	7	26	0	137	130	73	16	69	147	4.77	1.45	22.5	000	4.5	9.6	2.1	1.0	32%	60%	70
Andrews, Clayton	L	19	23	aa	MIL	3	0	17	0	32	25	15	5	18	29	4.10	1.34	7.9	000	5.0	8.1	1.6	1.3	25%	62%	29
Antone, Tejay	R	19	26	a/a	CIN	11	12	27	0	149	198	91	15	62	112	5.47	1.74	25.2	000	3.7	6.7	1.8	0.9	37%	63%	39
Armenteros, Rogelio	R	16	22	aa	HOU	2	0	3	0	18	19	5	1	4	12	2.23	1.24	24.8	267	1.9	5.7	3.0	0.6	31%	84%	82
		17	23	a/a	HOU	10	4	24	1	124	98	29	8	35	130	2.14	1.07	20.1	219	2.6	9.4	3.7	0.6	29%	83%	129
		18	24	aaa	HOU	8	1	22	0	118	111	48	14	43	112	3.66	1.31	22.1	250	3.3	8.6	2.6	1.1	31%	76%	79
Baez, Michel	R	18	22	aa	SD	0	3	4	0	19	25	18	4	12	18	8.33	1.92	22.6	315	5.6	8.7	1.6	1.9	37%	58%	19
		19	23	aa	SD	3	2	15	1	27	26	8	1	12	32	2.52	1.39	7.6	000	3.9	10.6	2.8	0.4	36%	79%	105
Bahr, Jason	R	19	24	TEX		4	3	12	0	64	56	35	3	30	54	4.93	1.34	22.2	000	4.2	7.6	1.8	0.4	30%	58%	42
Bailey, Brandon	R	18	24	aa	HOU	1	0	5	1	26	25	14	6	9	19	4.88	1.32	21.7	255	3.2	6.6	2.1	2.1	26%	72%	24
		19	25	a/a	HOU	4	5	22	0	94	94	51	17	47	85	4.87	1.50	18.5	000	4.5	8.1	1.8	1.6	30%	59%	43
Banda, Anthony	L	16	23	a/a	ARI	10	6	26	0	150	165	58	11	55	129	3.49	1.47	24.7	281	3.3	7.7	2.3	0.7	34%	77%	74
		17	24	aaa	ARI	8	7	22	0	122	136	77	15	48	96	5.70	1.51	24.0	284	3.6	7.1	2.0	1.1	33%	63%	49
		18	25	aaa	TAM	4	3	8	0	42	52	22	3	19	42	4.67	1.70	23.7	306	4.1	9.0	2.2	0.7	39%	73%	72
Baumann, Michael	R	19	24	aa	BAL	6	2	13	1	70	57	25	3	23	52	3.26	1.14	21.3	000	3.0	6.7	2.2	0.3	27%	67%	58
Bazardo, Eduard	R	19	24	aa	BOS	4	1	21	0	33	35	15	3	14	28	4.01	1.48	6.8	000	3.9	7.7	2.0	0.7	33%	68%	51
Beasley, Jeremy	R	18	23	aa	LAA	3	3	10	0	45	38	15	4	14	32	3.03	1.15	17.9	229	2.8	6.4	2.3	0.7	26%	76%	74
		19	24	a/a	LAA	7	7	26	0	125	143	66	15	47	97	4.76	1.51	20.9	000	3.4	7.0	2.1	1.1	33%	62%	52
Bettinger, Alec	R	19	24	aa	MIL	5	7	26	0	147	165	93	21	42	134	5.68	1.41	23.9	000	2.6	8.2	3.2	1.3	34%	50%	96
Bielak, Brandon	R	18	22	aa	HOU	2	5	11	0	62	60	20	5	22	50	2.88	1.32	23.4	256	3.2	7.2	2.3	0.7	31%	80%	74
		19	23	a/a	HOU	11	4	23	0	123	115	71	15	51	103	5.22	1.35	22.3	000	3.8	7.5	2.0	1.1	29%	53%	52
Bolanos, Ronald	R	19	23	aa	SD	8	5	15	0	78	84	45	7	32	74	5.21	1.47	22.4	000	3.6	8.5	2.3	0.9	34%	58%	73
Bolton, Cody	R	19	21	aa	PIT	2	3	9	0	40	46	37	7	17	28	8.29	1.57	19.5	000	3.9	6.3	1.6	1.6	31%	34%	25
Bowden, Ben	L	19	25	a/a	COL	1	3	48	21	53	47	28	7	27	61	4.67	1.38	4.7	000	4.5	10.3	2.3	1.2	31%	58%	82
Braymer, Ben	L	19	25	a/a	WAS	4	10	26	0	139	171	95	32	60	94	6.14	1.66	24.0	000	3.9	6.1	1.6	2.1	32%	53%	22
Brown, Zack	R	18	24	aa	MIL	9	1	22	0	127	122	50	12	40	98	3.52	1.27	23.7	253	2.9	6.9	2.4	0.8	30%	75%	72
		19	25	aaa	MIL	3	7	25	0	118	160	88	18	66	82	6.69	1.91	22.4	000	5.0	6.2	1.2	1.4	36%	58%	-5
Burdi, Zack	R	16	21	a/a	CHW	2	0	42	2	64	35	25	4	42	83	3.56	1.20	6.1	164	5.8	11.7	2.0	0.6	24%	71%	116
		17	22	aaa	CHW	0	4	29	7	33	33	17	2	18	46	4.64	1.53	5.0	262	4.8	12.4	2.6	0.6	39%	69%	113
		19	24	aa	CHW	0	3	17	3	21	31	21	7	15	20	9.01	2.17	6.2	000	6.2	8.7	1.4	3.1	38%	45%	6
Burke, Brock	L	18	22	aa	TAM	6	1	9	0	56	44	14	2	14	64	2.28	1.03	24.0	218	2.2	10.3	4.6	0.3	31%	78%	161
		19	23	a/a	TEX	3	5	11	0	54	55	30	4	19	49	5.04	1.37	20.6	000	3.1	8.1	2.6	0.6	33%	57%	80
Burrows, Beau	R	17	21	aa	DET	6	4	15	0	76	90	48	5	33	63	5.70	1.61	22.5	294	3.9	7.5	1.9	0.6	36%	64%	62
		18	22	aa	DET	10	9	26	0	134	145	75	14	56	105	5.06	1.50	22.3	278	3.8	7.1	1.9	0.9	33%	67%	54
		19	23	a/a	DET	3	6	16	0	71	87	56	16	36	52	7.06	1.72	20.2	000	4.5	6.6	1.5	2.0	32%	48%	14
Cabrera, Edward	R	19	21	aa	MIA	4	1	8	0	40	36	17	8	15	38	3.78	1.26	20.5	000	3.3	8.5	2.6	1.7	27%	61%	82
Cabrera, Genesis	L	17	21	aa	TAM	5	4	12	0	65	85	31	6	27	46	4.36	1.74	24.6	318	3.8	6.4	1.7	0.9	37%	76%	39
		18	22	a/a	STL	8	9	27	0	141	122	69	13	65	125	4.41	1.33	21.7	235	4.2	8.0	1.9	0.8	29%	68%	72
		19	23	aaa	STL	5	6	20	0	99	121	75	20	37	88	6.82	1.60	21.9	000	3.4	8.0	2.4	1.8	34%	46%	70
Castellani, Ryan	R	17	21	aa	COL	9	12	27	0	157	207	127	24	52	106	7.29	1.65	26.1	319	3.0	6.1	2.0	1.4	35%	56%	28
		18	22	aa	COL	7	9	26	0	135	167	116	21	77	74	7.76	1.81	24.1	305	5.2	4.9	1.0	1.4	32%	57%	1
		19	23	aaa	COL	2	5	10	0	44	59	43	15	29	38	8.84	1.99	21.2	000	5.9	7.7	1.3	3.1	34%	40%	-3
Castro, Anthony	R	19	24	aa	DET	5	3	27	1	103	98	76	13	72	92	6.59	1.65	17.1	000	6.3	8.1	1.3	1.1	30%	52%	-6
Clase, Emmanuel	R	19	21	aa	TEX	1	2	33	11	39	42	20	1	9	33	4.66	1.31	4.9	000	2.1	7.5	3.6	0.3	34%	59%	97
Colina, Edwar	R	19	22	a/a	MIN	4	0	9	0	37	35	21	1	18	35	5.13	1.41	17.5	000	4.3	8.4	2.0	0.3	32%	59%	53
Crawford, Kutter	R	19	23	aa	BOS	1	3	5	0	20	24	13	3	16	19	5.83	1.99	19.4	000	7.2	8.5	1.2	1.1	36%	65%	-24
Crowe, Wil	R	18	24	aa	WAS	0	5	5	0	27	37	23	5	16	12	7.53	1.97	26.0	325	5.5	4.1	0.7	1.5	33%	63%	-16
		19	25	a/a	WAS	7	10	26	0	150	188	106	19	52	106	6.33	1.60	25.5	000	3.1	6.3	2.0	1.1	35%	52%	48
Davidson, Tucker	L	19	23	a/a	ATL	8	7	25	0	131	137	46	6	59	111	3.12	1.50	22.6	000	4.0	7.6	1.9	0.4	34%	76%	46
De La Cruz, Jasseel	R	19	22	aa	ATL	4	7	17	0	87	95	61	10	42	62	6.30	1.57	22.5	000	4.4	6.4	1.5	1.0	32%	52%	15

PITCHER	Th	Yr	Age	LvL	Org	W	L	G	Sv	IP	H	ER	HR	BB	K	ERA	WHIP	BF/G	OBA	bb/9	k/9	Cmd	hr/9	H%	S%	BPV
De La Cruz, Oscar	R	18	23	aa	CHC	6	7	16	0	78	90	57	9	33	62	6.56	1.57	21.5	289	3.8	7.1	1.9	1.1	34%	58%	47
		19	24	aa	CHC	4	5	31	2	82	82	53	10	34	73	5.81	1.41	11.2	000	3.7	8.0	2.2	1.1	31%	50%	63
De Leon, Jose	R	15	23	aa	LA	2	6	16	0	77	71	39	13	28	91	4.54	1.30	19.7	248	3.3	10.6	3.2	1.6	32%	71%	90
		16	24	aaa	LA	7	1	16	0	86	71	33	10	19	93	3.45	1.04	20.8	227	1.9	9.7	5.0	1.1	29%	71%	141
		19	27	aaa	TAM	2	1	17	1	52	51	26	5	30	60	4.48	1.56		000	5.2	10.3	2.0	0.8	35%	66%	63
Diaz, Yennsy	R	19	23	aa	TOR	11	9	26	0	145	160	89	16	59	98	5.51	1.50	24.1	000	3.6	6.1	1.7	1.0	32%	56%	29
Dibrell, Tony	R	19	24	aa	NYM	0	8	9	0	40	64	57	13	23	32	12.73	2.19	22.4	000	5.3	7.2	1.4	2.8	39%	25%	6
Dobnak, Randy	R	19	24	a/a	MIN	9	4	20	0	114	107	41	8	26	77	3.26	1.17	22.8	000	2.1	6.1	3.0	0.6	29%	67%	72
Dugger, Robert	R	18	23	aa	MIA	7	6	18	0	110	113	54	13	36	92	4.39	1.36	25.6	267	3.0	7.6	2.5	1.0	32%	70%	69
		19	24	a/a	MIA	8	10	23	0	126	167	103	21	43	102	7.31	1.66	24.6	000	3.0	7.3	2.4	1.5	36%	46%	67
Dunn, Justin	R	18	23	aa	NYM	6	5	15	0	91	95	47	7	38	92	4.67	1.45	26.0	269	3.7	9.0	2.4	0.7	35%	68%	86
		19	24	aa	SEA	9	5	25	0	133	154	79	18	45	138	5.34	1.50	23.0	000	3.0	9.3	3.1	1.2	36%	56%	103
Dunning, Dane	R	18	24	aa	CHW	5	2	11	0	62	72	27	0	26	59	3.87	1.58	24.8	290	3.8	8.6	2.2	0.0	38%	73%	95
Dunshee, Parker	R	18	23	aa	OAK	7	4	12	0	82	66	21	5	13	67	2.25	0.97	26.0	222	1.5	7.4	5.0	0.5	27%	79%	144
		19	24	a/a	OAK	6	7	26	1	130	131	77	23	49	103	5.32	1.38	21.0	000	3.4	7.1	2.1	1.6	29%	51%	55
Duplantier, Jon	R	18	24	aa	ARI	5	1	14	0	67	61	24	4	29	56	3.27	1.34	19.9	244	3.9	7.6	1.9	0.5	30%	76%	76
		19	25	aaa	ARI	1	2	13	0	38	32	21	1	26	35	4.98	1.55	12.8	000	6.3	8.4	1.3	0.2	31%	64%	0
Duran, Jhoan	R	19	21	aa	MIN	3	3	7	0	37	41	27	3	10	35	6.68	1.37	22.1	000	2.3	8.5	3.7	0.6	36%	43%	109
Elledge, Seth	R	18	22	aa	STL	3	1	13	4	18	14	8	3	5	17	4.14	1.06	5.4	212	2.7	8.4	3.1	1.3	24%	66%	88
		19	23	a/a	STL	6	4	47	3	69	71	38	6	31	62	4.95	1.47	6.3	000	4.0	8.1	2.0	0.8	33%	60%	54
Escobar, Luis	R	18	22	aa	PIT	4	0	7	0	37	34	22	4	21	21	5.26	1.48	22.9	246	5.1	5.1	1.0	1.0	26%	66%	27
		19	23	aaa	PIT	2	1	24	1	55	63	31	7	33	47	5.10	1.75	10.5	000	5.4	7.7	1.4	1.2	34%	65%	9
Eveld, Tommy	R	19	26	a/a	MIA	3	7	42	12	50	57	42	15	20	48	7.58	1.54	5.2	000	3.6	8.6	2.4	2.6	31%	32%	77
Faedo, Alex	R	18	23	aa	DET	3	6	12	0	60	64	42	17	22	48	6.24	1.43	21.3	273	3.4	7.2	2.1	2.6	28%	65%	10
		19	24	aa	DET	6	7	22	0	116	136	76	24	28	107	5.86	1.41	22.3	000	2.1	8.3	3.9	1.8	34%	46%	109
Fairbanks, Peter	R	19	26	a/a	TAM	2	2	29	0	32	34	25	5	9	46	6.88	1.34	4.6	000	2.5	12.9	5.1	1.3	40%	36%	181
Feltman, Durbin	R	19	22	aa	BOS	2	3	43	5	52	52	43	10	33	45	7.35	1.62	5.4	000	5.6	7.8	1.4	1.7	29%	43%	7
Fernandez, Junior	R	18	21	aa	STL	0	0	16	0	21	20	12	1	14	15	5.33	1.64	5.9	252	6.2	6.2	1.0	0.4	30%	66%	52
		19	22	a/a	STL	3	2	36	7	54	39	10	0	21	58	1.74	1.11	5.9	000	3.5	9.7	2.8	0.0	29%	83%	99
File, Dylan	R	19	23	aa	MIL	9	2	14	0	82	99	41	8	18	64	4.45	1.42	24.9	000	1.9	7.0	3.6	0.9	35%	63%	91
Fletcher, Aaron	L	19	23	aa	SEA	0	0	14	0	20	27	12	0	6	21	5.33	1.62	6.4	000	2.5	9.5	3.8	0.0	43%	63%	121
Funkhouser, Kyle	R	18	24	a/a	DET	4	7	19	0	99	118	58	12	52	76	5.22	1.71	23.7	296	4.7	6.9	1.5	1.1	34%	71%	35
		19	25	a/a	DET	6	8	22	0	89	123	95	7	63	73	9.53	2.07	19.9	000	6.3	7.4	1.2	0.7	39%	47%	-19
Garcia, Bryan	R	17	22	a/a	DET	2	1	31	8	32	20	10	2	17	30	2.89	1.15	4.1	182	4.7	8.5	1.8	0.7	23%	77%	88
		19	24	a/a	DET	3	0	34	1	38	34	17	7	15	33	4.04	1.29	4.6	000	3.6	7.7	2.2	1.6	27%	60%	61
Garcia, Deivi	R	19	20	a/a	NYY	5	7	22	0	95	92	57	13	47	119	5.37	1.46	18.5	000	4.4	11.2	2.5	1.2	35%	55%	101
Garcia, Rico	R	18	24	aa	COL	6	2	11	0	67	70	25	12	23	48	3.38	1.38	25.6	269	3.1	6.4	2.1	1.6	29%	83%	36
		19	25	a/a	COL	10	6	26	0	130	148	84	25	57	106	5.82	1.58	22.0	000	3.9	7.4	1.9	1.7	32%	53%	45
Gerber, Joey	R	19	22	aa	SEA	1	2	19	0	24	26	6	3	8	27	2.17	1.41	5.4	000	2.9	10.1	3.1	1.0	37%	81%	122
Gilbert, Logan	R	19	22	aa	SEA	4	2	9	0	50	43	23	3	17	51	4.20	1.19	22.3	000	3.0	9.1	3.1	0.5	31%	59%	102
Gilliam, Ryley	R	19	23	a/a	NYM	5	0	22	1	30	40	29	4	17	36	8.69	1.88	6.5	000	5.0	10.5	2.1	1.3	42%	44%	74
Gonsalves, Stephen	L	16	22	aa	MIN	8	1	13	0	74	49	18	1	36	74	2.19	1.14	22.7	190	4.3	8.9	2.0	0.1	26%	80%	110
		17	23	a/a	MIN	9	5	20	0	110	119	59	15	33	95	4.80	1.39	23.2	278	2.7	7.8	2.8	1.2	33%	68%	70
		18	24	a/a	MIN	12	3	23	0	122	94	50	10	69	97	3.67	1.33	22.0	213	5.1	7.1	1.4	0.7	25%	74%	62
Gonsolin, Tony	R	18	24	aa	LA	6	0	9	0	45	35	13	3	15	41	2.58	1.10	19.7	217	2.9	8.3	2.8	0.6	27%	79%	103
		19	25	aaa	LA	2	4	13	0	42	46	22	4	20	41	4.69	1.56	14.2	000	4.2	8.8	2.1	0.9	35%	64%	64
Gore, MacKenzie	L	19	20	aa	SD	2	1	5	0	23	22	12	3	8	22	4.64	1.31	19.2	000	3.1	8.5	2.8	1.2	31%	56%	88
Graterol, Brusdar	R	19	21	a/a	MIN	7	0	16	1	60	43	17	4	24	49	2.54	1.10	14.8	000	3.6	7.3	2.0	0.5	24%	73%	53
Gray, Josiah	R	19	22	aa	LA	3	2	9	0	40	39	15	0	11	36	3.45	1.23	18.1	000	2.4	8.1	3.4	0.0	33%	69%	99
Green, Josh	R	19	24	aa	ARI	2	4	8	0	49	79	34	3	9	26	6.22	1.79	28.3	000	1.7	4.8	2.8	0.5	40%	60%	59
Guilbeau, Taylor	L	19	26	a/a	SEA	3	2	39	0	50	50	20	1	19	46	3.55	1.36	5.4	000	3.4	8.2	2.5	0.2	34%	71%	75
Gutierrez, Vladimir	R	18	23	aa	CIN	9	10	27	0	147	167	94	24	41	126	5.78	1.41	23.1	287	2.5	7.7	3.1	1.4	33%	61%	66
		19	24	aaa	CIN	7	11	27	0	137	174	120	34	53	103	7.90	1.66	22.7	000	3.5	6.8	1.9	2.2	33%	38%	46
Guzman, Jorge	R	19	23	aa	MIA	7	11	25	0	140	127	86	17	83	109	5.49	1.50	24.2	000	5.3	7.0	1.3	1.1	28%	56%	0
Hansen, Alec	R	18	24	aa	CHW	0	4	9	0	37	38	36	4	48	30	8.81	2.30	21.2	264	11.6	7.2	0.6	1.0	31%	60%	29
		19	25	aa	CHW	1	2	30	1	41	57	37	7	43	38	8.12	2.43	7.2	000	9.3	8.2	0.9	1.6	39%	60%	-86
Harvey, Hunter	R	18	24	aa	BAL	1	2	9	0	33	41	23	3	9	24	6.31	1.51	15.9	306	2.4	6.6	2.7	0.9	35%	58%	61
		19	25	a/a	BAL	3	6	26	1	77	94	56	20	28	65	6.50	1.58	13.1	000	3.3	7.6	2.3	2.4	33%	45%	66
Hatch, Thomas	R	18	24	aa	CHC	8	6	26	0	145	153	79	19	67	97	4.89	1.51	24.2	272	4.1	6.0	1.4	1.2	30%	70%	32
		19	25	aa	TOR	6	13	27	0	136	172	94	26	45	103	6.23	1.59	22.2	000	3.0	6.8	2.3	1.7	34%	51%	60
Hearn, Taylor	L	18	24	aa	TEX	4	8	24	0	129	128	67	14	53	113	4.67	1.40	22.7	260	3.7	7.9	2.1	1.0	31%	68%	66
		19	25	aaa	TEX	1	3	4	0	20	17	11	4	11	20	4.98	1.37	21.0	000	4.9	9.1	1.9	1.6	27%	54%	51
Hendrix, Ryan	R	19	25	aa	CIN	3	0	16	2	20	18	7	0	9	20	3.13	1.34	5.2	000	4.1	8.9	2.1	0.0	32%	74%	66
Hentges, Sam	L	19	23	aa	CLE	2	13	26	0	130	187	106	15	72	107	7.32	1.99	24.1	000	5.0	7.4	1.5	1.0	40%	57%	16

PITCHER	Th	Yr	Age	LvL	Org	W	L	G	Sv	IP	H	ER	HR	BB	K	ERA	WHIP	BF/G	OBA	bb/9	k/9	Cmd	hr/9	H%	S%	BPV
Hernandez, Jonathan	R	18	22	aa	TEX	4	4	12	0	64	68	45	7	39	48	6.33	1.68	24.0	275	5.5	6.7	1.2	1.0	32%	62%	35
		19	23	aa	TEX	5	9	22	0	96	128	82	16	44	77	7.70	1.80	20.1	000	4.2	7.2	1.7	1.5	37%	48%	36
Heuer, Codi	R	19	23	aa	CHW	2	3	22	9	30	32	9	0	8	19	2.67	1.32	5.7	000	2.3	5.7	2.5	0.0	33%	78%	59
Hjelle, Sean	R	19	22	aa	SF	1	2	5	0	26	48	25	1	10	18	8.55	2.21	26.3	000	3.4	6.1	1.8	0.4	45%	56%	35
Holmes, Grant	R	17	21	aa	OAK	11	12	29	0	148	163	83	14	57	126	5.05	1.49	22.0	281	3.5	7.6	2.2	0.8	34%	66%	65
		19	23	a/a	OAK	6	5	23	0	89	88	37	10	28	69	3.73	1.30	16.0	000	2.8	6.9	2.5	1.0	30%	65%	67
Honeywell, Brent	R	16	21	aa	TAM	3	2	10	0	59	57	17	4	14	48	2.62	1.18	23.7	253	2.1	7.2	3.5	0.6	30%	80%	103
		17	22	a/a	TAM	13	9	26	0	137	156	67	13	36	154	4.40	1.41	22.2	288	2.4	10.2	4.2	0.9	38%	70%	121
Houck, Tanner	R	19	23	a/a	BOS	8	6	33	1	109	130	67	8	48	88	5.50	1.63	14.7	000	4.0	7.2	1.8	0.7	36%	61%	41
Howard, Brian	R	18	23	aa	OAK	4	4	12	0	68	73	30	7	22	52	3.93	1.40	23.9	275	2.9	6.9	2.4	0.9	32%	74%	64
		19	24	a/a	OAK	8	9	27	0	145	193	84	11	48	111	5.22	1.66	24.1	000	3.0	6.9	2.3	0.7	38%	63%	62
Howard, Spencer	R	19	23	aa	PHI	1	0	6	0	32	24	11	3	10	34	2.96	1.05	20.8	000	2.7	9.5	3.6	0.8	27%	66%	118
Ivey, Tyler	R	19	23	aa	HOU	4	0	11	0	46	35	12	7	18	53	2.25	1.15	16.6	000	3.4	10.3	3.0	1.3	27%	75%	110
Javier, Cristian	R	19	22	a/a	HOU	6	3	19	3	85	41	23	7	43	115	2.47	1.00	17.1	000	4.6	12.1	2.6	0.7	22%	70%	112
Jax, Griffin	R	19	25	a/a	MIN	5	7	23	0	128	149	58	9	30	75	4.06	1.40	23.5	000	2.1	5.3	2.5	0.6	33%	66%	56
Jefferies, Daulton	R	19	24	aa	OAK	1	2	21	0	64	76	34	8	7	60	4.76	1.31	12.6	000	1.0	8.4	8.1	1.1	36%	55%	141
Johnson, Tyler	R	19	24	aa	CHW	2	0	12	0	19	13	11	4	7	20	5.00	1.04	6.1	000	3.2	9.2	2.9	2.1	20%	31%	98
Jones, Damon	L	19	25	a/a	PHI	1	1	12	0	56	44	35	5	37	55	5.57	1.44	19.9	000	6.0	8.9	1.5	0.8	27%	54%	16
Kaprielian, James	R	19	25	a/a	OAK	2	1	8	0	33	29	7	2	8	26	2.03	1.11	16.3	000	2.2	7.0	3.1	0.4	28%	79%	84
Karinchak, James	R	19	24	a/a	CLE	1	1	27	8	28	20	13	3	17	55	4.02	1.31	4.3	000	5.4	17.5	3.3	0.8	41%	63%	188
Kasowski, Marshall	R	19	24	aa	LA	4	3	27	2	30	21	11	1	16	39	3.19	1.23	4.5	000	4.9	11.6	2.4	0.4	30%	70%	96
Kay, Anthony	L	19	24	a/a	TOR	10	8	26	0	135	140	62	16	61	112	4.15	1.49	22.4	000	4.1	7.4	1.8	1.0	32%	66%	42
Keller, Mitch	R	17	21	aa	PIT	2	2	6	0	35	29	16	2	11	38	4.05	1.18	23.1	232	3.0	9.8	3.3	0.6	31%	65%	119
		18	22	a/a	PIT	12	4	24	0	139	138	63	10	53	111	4.10	1.38	24.3	261	3.4	7.2	2.1	0.7	31%	71%	70
		19	23	aaa	PIT	7	5	19	0	105	110	51	10	36	101	4.38	1.39	23.3	000	3.1	8.6	2.8	0.8	34%	63%	90
King, Michael	R	18	23	a/a	NYY	10	2	18	0	121	102	31	10	20	92	2.33	1.01	25.7	230	1.5	6.9	4.6	0.7	27%	81%	125
		19	24	aa	NYY	3	2	7	0	39	48	32	5	9	30	7.40	1.44	24.0	000	2.0	6.9	3.5	1.2	35%	37%	88
Kopech, Michael	R	17	21	a/a	CHW	9	8	25	0	134	106	53	7	70	156	3.57	1.31	22.2	218	4.7	10.5	2.2	0.5	31%	73%	107
		18	22	aaa	CHW	7	7	24	0	127	115	62	11	62	151	4.39	1.39	22.3	242	4.4	10.7	2.4	0.7	33%	69%	100
Kowar, Jackson	R	19	23	aa	KC	2	7	13	0	75	90	40	9	23	64	4.83	1.51	25.0	000	2.8	7.7	2.8	1.1	35%	61%	82
Kremer, Dean	R	18	22	aa	BAL	5	2	9	0	53	45	14	3	19	54	2.46	1.21	23.8	231	3.3	9.1	2.8	0.6	30%	82%	105
		19	23	a/a	BAL	9	6	19	0	106	124	60	13	35	89	5.06	1.49	24.1	000	2.9	7.5	2.6	1.1	34%	59%	74
Kuhnel, Joel	R	19	24	a/a	CIN	5	3	41	14	55	48	17	8	18	44	2.84	1.19	5.4	000	2.9	7.2	2.5	1.3	26%	70%	68
Lakins, Travis	R	17	23	aa	BOS	0	4	8	0	30	41	27	2	22	16	8.13	2.08	18.6	323	6.6	4.6	0.7	0.7	35%	59%	13
		18	24	a/a	BOS	3	2	36	3	55	47	19	4	19	46	3.11	1.20	6.1	232	3.1	7.5	2.4	0.6	28%	75%	87
		19	25	aaa	BOS	3	4	40	6	45	58	32	5	25	33	6.41	1.84	5.2	000	4.9	6.6	1.3	1.0	36%	59%	4
Lambert, Jimmy	R	18	24	aa	CHW	3	1	5	0	25	25	11	3	7	26	4.04	1.28	20.5	263	2.5	9.2	3.7	1.0	33%	71%	107
		19	25	aa	CHW	3	4	11	0	60	83	47	16	31	59	6.96	1.89	25.8	000	4.7	8.8	1.9	2.5	37%	52%	50
Lange, Alex	R	19	24	aa	DET	4	4	16	0	56	64	35	6	30	34	5.56	1.67	15.8	000	4.8	5.5	1.1	0.9	32%	61%	-12
Lawrence, Justin	R	19	25	a/a	COL	1	5	38	0	39	59	50	6	32	25	11.37	2.32	5.3	000	7.4	5.6	0.8	1.3	38%	42%	-80
Lawson, Reggie	R	19	22	aa	SD	3	1	6	0	29	32	20	4	13	31	6.08	1.56	21.3	000	4.1	9.5	2.3	1.3	35%	52%	77
Llovera, Mauricio	R	19	23	aa	PHI	3	4	14	0	66	72	44	9	30	65	5.96	1.54	20.6	000	4.0	8.8	2.2	1.3	34%	53%	67
Lockett, Walker	R	16	22	a/a	SD	5	3	9	0	53	54	18	4	4	34	3.13	1.09	22.9	266	0.7	5.8	9.0	0.7	30%	74%	204
		17	23	aaa	SD	5	2	10	0	55	70	27	8	12	27	4.39	1.48	23.8	310	1.9	4.5	2.4	1.3	33%	74%	31
		18	24	aaa	SD	5	9	23	0	134	153	69	15	30	100	4.65	1.37	24.4	288	2.0	6.7	3.3	1.0	33%	68%	77
Lowther, Zac	L	19	23	aa	BAL	13	7	26	0	148	126	58	11	69	126	3.53	1.31	23.5	000	4.2	7.7	1.8	0.6	28%	68%	44
Luzardo, Jesus	L	18	21	a/a	OAK	8	4	20	0	96	91	37	7	23	89	3.47	1.19	19.3	251	2.2	8.3	3.8	0.6	32%	72%	116
		19	22	aaa	OAK	1	1	7	0	31	32	12	3	8	29	3.52	1.26	18.1	000	2.2	8.5	3.9	0.8	33%	67%	112
Madero, Luis	R	19	22	aa	LAA	5	11	20	0	91	139	75	14	25	66	7.36	1.80	21.1	000	2.5	6.5	2.6	1.4	39%	50%	67
Manning, Matt	R	19	21	aa	DET	11	5	24	0	135	115	55	9	40	124	3.63	1.15	22.4	000	2.7	8.2	3.1	0.6	29%	63%	95
Martin, Corbin	R	18	23	aa	HOU	7	2	21	0	103	99	43	8	28	82	3.76	1.24	19.9	254	2.5	7.2	2.9	0.7	30%	71%	86
		19	24	aaa	HOU	2	1	9	0	38	37	15	2	18	38	3.48	1.44	18.1	000	4.2	9.0	2.1	0.5	34%	72%	66
Mata, Bryan	R	19	20	aa	BOS	4	6	11	0	55	65	41	7	24	51	6.73	1.62	22.3	000	4.0	8.3	2.1	1.2	35%	50%	60
May, Dustin	R	18	21	aa	LA	2	2	6	0	35	28	14	0	10	25	3.67	1.10	24.8	222	2.7	6.4	2.4	0.0	28%	63%	99
		19	22	a/a	LA	6	5	20	0	108	102	46	5	27	97	3.80	1.19	21.7	000	2.3	8.1	3.6	0.4	32%	63%	103
McClanahan, Shane	L	19	22	aa	TAM	1	1	4	0	19	36	23	4	6	19	10.87	2.24	24.2	000	3.1	9.0	2.9	1.7	48%	41%	97
McKay, Brendan	L	19	24	a/a	TAM	6	0	15	0	75	51	12	3	19	89	1.41	0.94	18.8	000	2.3	10.6	4.6	0.4	28%	82%	146
McKenzie, Triston	R	18	21	aa	CLE	7	4	16	0	92	75	36	10	30	76	3.49	1.13	22.8	224	2.9	7.4	2.6	1.0	26%	73%	80
Medina, Adonis	R	19	23	aa	PHI	7	7	22	0	107	124	77	15	43	74	6.46	1.57	21.4	000	3.6	6.2	1.7	1.3	32%	50%	31
Menez, Conner	L	18	23	a/a	SF	7	5	17	0	85	87	44	1	38	85	4.71	1.47	21.5	267	4.0	9.1	2.3	0.1	36%	65%	101
		19	24	a/a	SF	6	4	23	0	123	120	70	18	55	125	5.08	1.42	22.7	000	4.0	9.1	2.3	1.3	32%	56%	75
Miller, Tyson	R	19	24	a/a	CHC	7	8	26	0	138	163	89	23	48	102	5.81	1.53	23.1	000	3.1	6.6	2.1	1.5	33%	53%	53
Mills, Wyatt	R	19	24	aa	SEA	4	2	41	8	54	56	38	3	20	57	6.31	1.40	5.6	000	3.3	9.5	2.9	0.5	36%	48%	102

PITCHER	Th	Yr	Age	LvL	Org	W	L	G	Sv	IP	H	ER	HR	BB	K	ERA	WHIP	BF/G	OBA	bb/9	k/9	Cmd	hr/9	H%	S%	BPV
Misiewicz, Anthony	L	17	23	aa	TAM	6	4	12	0	70	77	39	8	17	49	4.98	1.35	24.2	282	2.2	6.4	2.9	1.0	32%	64%	69
		18	24	aa	SEA	3	12	21	0	98	154	72	15	30	79	6.57	1.87	21.9	358	2.7	7.3	2.7	1.4	41%	67%	41
		19	25	a/a	SEA	9	8	26	0	134	160	87	20	38	107	5.80	1.47	22.2	000	2.5	7.1	2.8	1.4	34%	51%	78
Mize, Casey	R	19	22	aa	DET	6	3	15	0	80	86	41	7	19	63	4.56	1.31	22.1	000	2.1	7.1	3.3	0.8	33%	59%	87
Morejon, Adrian	L	19	20	aa	SD	0	4	16	0	36	32	20	3	15	39	5.09	1.32	9.3	000	3.7	9.7	2.6	0.8	32%	54%	91
Moss, Scott	L	19	25	a/a	CLE	10	6	26	0	132	127	61	11	80	129	4.17	1.56	22.3	000	5.4	8.8	1.6	0.7	32%	69%	29
Muller, Kyle	L	18	21	aa	ATL	4	1	5	0	29	26	13	4	6	23	4.06	1.10	22.7	241	1.8	7.2	4.0	1.1	28%	67%	100
		19	22	aa	ATL	7	6	22	0	113	108	64	7	78	102	5.11	1.64	23.0	000	6.2	8.1	1.3	0.6	32%	64%	-4
Munoz, Andres	R	18	19	aa	SD	2	1	20	7	19	12	2	0	10	18	1.06	1.17	3.8	181	4.9	8.3	1.7	0.0	25%	90%	105
		19	20	a/a	SD	3	4	35	6	37	26	13	4	17	51	3.06	1.16	4.2	000	4.1	12.4	3.0	0.9	30%	68%	130
Murphy, Patrick	R	19	24	aa	TOR	4	7	18	0	84	98	67	10	31	71	7.13	1.53	20.3	000	3.3	7.6	2.3	1.0	35%	44%	67
Murray, Joey	R	19	23	aa	TOR	2	4	9	0	45	47	25	5	20	44	5.01	1.49	21.6	000	4.0	8.8	2.2	1.1	33%	59%	69
Naughton, Packy	L	19	23	aa	CIN	6	10	19	0	107	133	58	11	29	73	4.85	1.50	24.4	000	2.4	6.1	2.5	0.9	35%	62%	63
Neidert, Nick	R	17	21	aa	SEA	1	3	6	0	23	37	20	4	5	12	7.70	1.79	17.9	360	1.9	4.5	2.4	1.7	38%	58%	11
		18	22	aa	MIA	12	7	26	0	154	158	63	16	31	136	3.67	1.22	24.0	266	1.8	7.9	4.4	1.0	32%	73%	113
		19	23	aaa	MIA	3	4	9	0	41	53	29	4	23	32	6.45	1.86	21.3	000	5.1	6.9	1.4	0.9	37%	59%	6
Nelson, Nick	R	19	24	a/a	NYY	8	3	17	0	86	82	36	8	46	90	3.80	1.49	21.8	000	4.8	9.4	2.0	0.9	33%	70%	58
Newsome, Ljay	R	19	23	a/a	SEA	3	4	10	0	57	54	24	6	8	40	3.69	1.08	22.4	000	1.3	6.3	4.8	0.9	28%	58%	96
Nix, Jacob	R	17	21	aa	SD	1	2	6	0	28	38	23	0	9	19	7.47	1.72	20.9	330	3.0	6.1	2.0	0.0	39%	52%	69
		18	22	a/a	SD	3	3	10	0	60	47	13	3	8	39	1.89	0.92	22.5	216	1.3	5.8	4.6	0.4	25%	81%	131
Norwood, James	R	17	24	aa	CHC	1	4	14	1	19	27	15	1	10	16	7.14	1.98	6.4	340	4.8	7.7	1.6	0.6	41%	62%	50
		18	25	a/a	CHC	2	3	40	2	53	43	17	3	26	46	2.90	1.29	5.5	221	4.4	7.8	1.8	0.6	27%	79%	78
		19	26	aaa	CHC	3	2	45	6	59	50	36	11	35	64	5.47	1.44	5.6	000	5.4	9.8	1.8	1.6	28%	52%	49
O'Brien, Riley	R	19	24	aa	TAM	5	6	14	0	70	71	42	5	33	63	5.44	1.47	21.5	000	4.2	8.0	1.9	0.6	33%	57%	50
Oviedo, Johan	R	19	21	aa	STL	7	8	23	0	113	135	84	9	61	109	6.73	1.74	22.4	000	4.9	8.7	1.8	0.7	38%	55%	43
Paredes, Enoli	R	19	24	aa	HOU	2	3	12	1	50	37	31	1	24	58	5.55	1.22	16.8	000	4.3	10.5	2.5	0.2	30%	48%	92
Parkinson, David	L	19	24	aa	PHI	10	9	22	0	119	132	73	14	42	104	5.53	1.46	23.2	000	3.2	7.8	2.5	1.0	34%	54%	73
Patterson, Jack	L	19	24	aa	CHC	1	0	3	0	15	14	6	1	7	7	3.39	1.37	21.3	000	4.1	4.4	1.1	0.8	26%	71%	-13
Pearson, Nate	R	19	23	a/a	TOR	2	4	19	0	82	66	33	8	26	71	3.65	1.11	17.0	000	2.8	7.8	2.8	0.8	26%	60%	82
Perez, Cionel	L	18	22	a/a	HOU	7	1	20	1	75	63	18	3	26	78	2.18	1.19	15.1	230	3.1	9.3	3.0	0.4	31%	82%	117
		19	23	aaa	HOU	2	1	13	0	47	59	31	6	23	37	5.95	1.74	16.5	000	4.4	7.1	1.6	1.2	35%	59%	26
Perez, Franklin	R	17	20	aa	HOU	2	1	7	1	32	37	13	2	10	23	3.62	1.47	19.6	288	2.9	6.6	2.2	0.6	34%	76%	66
Perez, Hector	R	18	22	aa	TOR	0	2	10	0	43	35	21	1	24	43	4.43	1.37	18.1	223	5.1	8.9	1.8	0.2	30%	65%	94
		19	23	aa	TOR	7	6	26	0	122	166	92	12	74	99	6.77	1.97	22.5	000	5.5	7.3	1.3	0.9	39%	60%	2
Peterson, David	L	19	24	aa	NYM	3	6	24	0	116	150	77	11	41	106	5.96	1.65	21.6	000	3.2	8.2	2.6	0.9	39%	57%	80
Phillips, Tyler	R	19	22	aa	TEX	7	9	18	0	94	119	72	21	23	61	6.86	1.51	22.6	000	2.2	5.9	2.7	2.0	32%	41%	65
Rasmussen, Drew	R	19	24	aa	MIL	1	3	22	0	61	67	40	6	35	66	5.87	1.67	12.5	000	5.2	9.7	1.9	0.9	36%	58%	53
Rogers, Trevor	L	19	22	5	MIA	1	2	5	0	26	32	20	4	10	24	6.99	1.64	23.2	000	3.6	8.5	2.4	1.3	37%	48%	74
Romero, JoJo	L	18	22	aa	PHI	7	6	18	0	108	106	50	15	40	91	4.14	1.35	25.0	258	3.3	7.5	2.3	1.2	30%	73%	61
		19	23	a/a	PHI	7	9	24	0	114	147	89	15	48	83	6.97	1.70	21.6	000	3.8	6.5	1.7	1.2	35%	51%	33
Romero, Miguel	R	18	24	aa	OAK	1	1	22	1	30	40	23	4	12	27	7.01	1.73	6.2	322	3.5	8.0	2.3	1.2	38%	59%	51
		19	25	aaa	OAK	4	1	45	3	74	75	38	11	36	66	4.55	1.50	7.1	000	4.4	8.0	1.8	1.3	31%	63%	43
Rondon, Angel	R	19	22	aa	STL	6	8	20	0	115	113	49	11	41	95	3.85	1.33	23.9	000	3.2	7.4	2.3	0.9	31%	65%	66
Sanchez, Sixto	R	19	21	aa	MIA	8	4	18	0	103	111	45	6	22	85	3.90	1.29	23.5	000	1.9	7.5	4.0	0.5	34%	65%	102
Sandlin, Nick	R	19	22	a/a	CLE	1	0	24	2	27	22	9	5	16	33	3.11	1.39	4.8	000	5.3	10.9	2.0	1.7	28%	71%	70
Sandoval, Patrick	L	18	22	aa	LAA	1	0	4	0	21	14	4	0	8	24	1.58	1.02	20.4	188	3.3	10.1	3.0	0.0	28%	83%	141
		19	23	a/a	LAA	4	7	20	0	81	106	54	9	41	85	6.03	1.81	18.8	000	4.5	9.4	2.1	0.9	40%	61%	65
Santana, Dennis	R	17	21	aa	LA	3	1	7	0	33	35	23	2	20	33	6.25	1.70	21.1	277	5.6	9.1	1.6	0.6	36%	62%	70
		18	22	a/a	LA	1	3	10	0	51	38	15	3	14	57	2.59	1.03	19.7	210	2.5	10.1	4.0	0.5	29%	76%	143
		19	23	aaa	LA	5	9	27	0	94	120	76	16	47	91	7.25	1.77	16.0	000	4.5	8.7	1.9	1.5	37%	50%	51
Santillan, Tony	R	18	21	aa	CIN	4	3	11	0	63	76	32	10	17	55	4.54	1.46	24.6	299	2.4	7.8	3.3	1.4	35%	74%	68
		19	22	aa	CIN	2	8	21	0	103	131	72	11	59	84	6.32	1.84	22.9	000	5.1	7.4	1.4	0.9	37%	60%	12
Schmidt, Clarke	R	19	23	aa	NYY	2	0	3	0	19	17	7	1	1	16	3.21	0.96	23.9	000	0.5	7.7	14.8	0.7	30%	60%	142
Seabold, Connor	R	18	22	aa	PHI	1	4	11	0	60	60	35	11	18	58	5.29	1.30	22.6	261	2.7	8.7	3.2	1.7	30%	64%	71
		19	23	aa	PHI	3	1	7	0	40	42	13	3	11	32	2.98	1.32	23.7	000	2.4	7.3	3.1	0.6	33%	74%	85
Sedlock, Cody	R	19	24	aa	BAL	1	2	9	1	34	38	20	4	22	27	5.22	1.76	17.3	000	5.9	7.2	1.2	1.1	33%	65%	-11
Sharp, Sterling	R	18	23	aa	WAS	6	3	13	0	70	84	41	7	26	39	5.22	1.57	23.7	298	3.4	5.0	1.5	0.9	33%	67%	31
		19	24	aa	WAS	5	3	9	0	51	73	34	1	16	37	5.91	1.74	26.0	000	2.8	6.6	2.3	0.3	40%	62%	61
Sheffield, Jordan	R	19	24	aa	LA	2	3	34	6	39	32	20	4	33	41	4.59	1.64	5.1	000	7.5	9.3	1.2	0.9	29%	67%	-16
Sheffield, Justus	L	17	21	aa	NYY	7	6	17	0	93	115	46	21	35	73	4.43	1.61	24.3	303	3.4	7.0	2.1	2.0	33%	81%	20
		18	22	a/a	NYY	7	6	25	0	116	96	41	5	52	108	3.18	1.28	19.0	227	4.0	8.4	2.1	0.4	29%	75%	91
		19	23	a/a	SEA	7	9	25	0	133	141	76	18	61	118	5.12	1.52	23.1	000	4.1	8.0	1.9	1.2	32%	59%	51
Singer, Brady	R	19	23	aa	KC	7	3	16	0	92	106	49	9	28	70	4.75	1.46	24.7	000	2.8	6.8	2.5	0.9	34%	61%	66
Skubal, Tarik	L	19	23	aa	DET	2	3	9	0	43	32	15	3	20	67	3.09	1.19	19.2	000	4.1	13.9	3.4	0.6	35%	70%	158

PITCHER	Th	Yr	Age	LvL	Org	W	L	G	Sv	IP	H	ER	HR	BB	K	ERA	WHIP	BF/G	OBA	bb/9	k/9	Cmd	hr/9	H%	S%	BPV
Smeltzer, Devin	L	18	23	aa	MIN	5	5	33	4	97	125	59	10	21	68	5.45	1.51	12.7	314	1.9	6.3	3.3	1.0	36%	64%	70
		19	24	a/a	MIN	4	5	20	0	105	108	44	18	24	85	3.78	1.26	21.4	000	2.1	7.2	3.5	1.5	30%	61%	93
Smith, Drew	R	17	24	a/a	NYM	3	2	15	0	20	12	4	1	6	15	1.71	0.89	4.9	176	2.6	6.8	2.6	0.5	21%	84%	100
		18	25	a/a	NYM	5	1	25	3	39	31	11	3	13	30	2.62	1.11	6.2	216	3.0	6.9	2.3	0.6	26%	79%	83
Smith, Kevin	L	19	22	aa	NYM	3	2	6	0	32	30	16	1	16	25	4.59	1.45	22.8	000	4.5	7.1	1.6	0.3	31%	64%	24
Staumont, Josh	R	16	23	aa	KC	2	1	11	0	50	51	23	2	38	60	4.05	1.77	21.0	264	6.9	10.7	1.6	0.4	37%	77%	87
		17	24	a/a	KC	6	12	26	0	125	130	103	18	102	111	7.45	1.86	22.5	270	7.4	8.0	1.1	1.3	32%	60%	34
		18	25	aaa	KC	2	5	41	1	75	72	37	4	55	81	4.45	1.68	8.2	252	6.5	9.7	1.5	0.5	34%	73%	79
Steele, Justin	L	19	24	aa	CHC	0	6	11	0	40	57	34	4	23	35	7.70	1.99	17.6	000	5.2	7.8	1.5	0.9	40%	55%	19
Stephan, Trevor	R	18	23	aa	NYY	3	8	17	0	84	97	56	7	31	79	5.99	1.52	21.5	290	3.3	8.4	2.5	0.8	36%	60%	78
		19	24	aa	NYY	2	4	12	0	47	64	37	4	27	48	7.13	1.92	18.6	000	5.2	9.1	1.8	0.8	41%	57%	43
Supak, Trey	R	18	22	aa	MIL	6	6	16	0	88	90	38	6	30	66	3.87	1.36	23.0	265	3.1	6.7	2.2	0.6	32%	72%	71
		19	23	a/a	MIL	12	6	27	0	154	151	81	15	34	103	4.73	1.20	23.0	000	2.0	6.0	3.0	0.9	29%	52%	72
Tate, Dillon	R	17	23	aa	NYY	1	2	4	0	25	29	13	5	10	15	4.65	1.55	27.3	291	3.6	5.3	1.5	1.7	30%	76%	10
		18	24	aa	BAL	7	5	22	0	124	131	66	12	34	77	4.80	1.33	23.4	273	2.5	5.6	2.3	0.8	31%	64%	57
		19	25	a/a	BAL	4	3	21	7	44	43	20	6	11	29	4.05	1.22	8.5	000	2.2	5.9	2.7	1.3	28%	58%	65
Taylor, Blake	L	19	24	a/a	NYM	0	1	19	3	40	30	10	2	13	39	2.33	1.07	8.2	000	2.9	8.8	3.1	0.5	27%	74%	99
Taylor, Curtis	R	18	23	aa	TAM	3	4	30	6	62	39	19	6	26	66	2.80	1.05	8.0	183	3.8	9.5	2.5	0.9	23%	78%	100
		19	24	aa	TAM	0	3	15	7	19	18	8	0	6	14	3.97	1.21	5.2	000	2.6	6.5	2.5	0.0	30%	64%	64
Thorpe, Lewis	L	18	23	a/a	MIN	8	7	26	0	131	151	67	20	37	129	4.62	1.43	21.5	289	2.6	8.8	3.5	1.4	35%	72%	82
		19	24	aaa	MIN	5	4	20	0	97	111	65	16	27	97	6.00	1.42	20.6	000	2.5	9.0	3.6	1.5	35%	47%	113
Uceta, Edwin	R	19	21	aa	LA	7	2	16	0	73	72	33	6	32	68	4.06	1.43	19.4	000	3.9	8.3	2.1	0.7	32%	66%	62
Uelmen, Erich	R	19	23	aa	CHC	0	3	6	0	29	41	35	6	22	22	10.89	2.16	24.1	000	6.7	6.8	1.0	1.9	37%	38%	-39
Urquidy, Jose	R	19	24	a/a	HOU	7	5	20	0	103	114	65	20	22	113	5.70	1.32	21.3	000	1.9	9.9	5.1	1.8	35%	44%	144
Vargas, Emilio	R	18	22	aa	ARI	1	3	6	0	37	35	19	6	8	26	4.53	1.15	24.6	249	1.9	6.3	3.3	1.4	27%	65%	69
		19	23	aa	ARI	5	3	17	0	87	93	52	13	26	59	5.37	1.37	21.5	000	2.7	6.1	2.2	1.3	30%	51%	54
Wahl, Bobby	R	15	23	aa	OAK	2	0	24	4	32	39	16	2	14	30	4.37	1.61	6.0	298	3.8	8.3	2.2	0.5	38%	72%	77
		16	24	a/a	OAK	1	1	42	14	50	39	16	3	24	50	2.93	1.26	4.9	217	4.3	8.9	2.1	0.6	28%	78%	92
		18	26	aaa	NYM	4	2	38	12	45	21	10	2	18	60	2.10	0.88	4.4	143	3.7	11.9	3.3	0.3	22%	77%	156
Warren, Art	R	18	25	aa	SEA	1	2	14	2	17	12	4	0	15	19	1.91	1.54	5.4	196	7.6	9.8	1.3	0.0	28%	86%	102
		19	26	aa	SEA	2	1	29	15	33	31	10	1	16	34	2.58	1.42	4.9	000	4.2	9.3	2.2	0.4	33%	79%	70
Webb, Braden	R	18	23	aa	MIL	1	0	4	0	20	16	6	0	11	21	2.58	1.37	20.9	224	4.9	9.3	1.9	0.0	31%	79%	106
		19	24	aa	MIL	1	4	6	0	15	20	25	3	18	11	14.93	2.57	13.5	000	10.9	6.7	0.6	1.9	36%	30%	-155
Webb, Logan	R	18	22	aa	SF	1	2	6	0	32	34	16	4	11	22	4.39	1.40	22.7	274	3.1	6.3	2.0	1.0	31%	71%	51
		19	23	a/a	SF	1	4	9	0	49	58	15	2	13	45	2.69	1.45	23.3	000	2.4	8.2	3.5	0.4	37%	79%	102
Weigel, Patrick	R	16	22	aa	ATL	1	2	3	0	21	11	7	2	9	15	3.06	0.96	26.1	160	3.8	6.7	1.8	1.1	17%	74%	68
		17	23	a/a	ATL	6	2	15	0	78	90	48	8	31	60	5.54	1.55	22.8	289	3.6	6.9	1.9	0.9	34%	64%	52
		19	25	a/a	ATL	6	2	28	0	81	66	37	12	47	56	4.07	1.39	12.2	000	5.2	6.3	1.2	1.3	24%	64%	-9
Wells, Alex	L	19	22	aa	BAL	8	6	24	0	138	149	61	13	26	88	3.97	1.26	23.5	000	1.7	5.7	3.4	0.8	31%	62%	76
Wentz, Joey	L	19	22	aa	DET	7	8	25	0	130	138	87	22	52	114	6.02	1.46	22.3	000	3.6	7.9	2.2	1.5	31%	48%	62
Whitley, Forrest	R	18	21	aa	HOU	0	2	8	0	27	17	14	2	11	30	4.48	1.03	13.1	183	3.6	9.9	2.8	0.8	24%	56%	113
		19	22	a/a	HOU	2	5	14	0	49	61	58	13	34	57	10.53	1.93	16.7	000	6.2	10.4	1.7	2.3	37%	30%	37
Whitlock, Garrett	R	19	23	aa	NYY	3	3	14	0	71	89	33	6	20	49	4.12	1.53	22.1	000	2.5	6.2	2.5	0.7	35%	69%	61
Widener, Taylor	R	18	24	aa	ARI	5	8	26	0	138	116	51	12	44	146	3.34	1.16	21.1	229	2.9	9.5	3.3	0.8	30%	74%	111
		19	25	aaa	ARI	6	7	23	0	101	139	86	19	39	88	7.66	1.76	20.1	000	3.4	7.8	2.3	1.7	38%	46%	65
Williams, Devin	R	19	25	a/a	MIL	7	2	34	4	59	45	19	4	33	69	2.94	1.33	7.2	000	5.1	10.4	2.1	0.6	30%	74%	68
Williams, Garrett	L	18	24	aa	SF	3	9	33	1	83	114	69	6	63	61	7.48	2.13	12.5	327	6.9	6.5	1.0	0.6	38%	63%	31
		19	25	aa	SF	8	7	29	0	110	117	68	7	72	86	5.59	1.72	17.2	000	5.9	7.0	1.2	0.6	33%	63%	-14
Wilson, Bryse	R	18	21	a/a	ATL	6	5	20	0	99	111	58	10	28	101	5.27	1.40	20.9	285	2.5	9.2	3.6	0.9	36%	63%	102
		19	22	aaa	ATL	10	7	21	0	121	141	59	13	26	100	4.37	1.38	24.2	000	1.9	7.4	3.8	1.0	35%	62%	99
Woodford, Jake	R	18	22	a/a	STL	8	13	28	0	145	169	84	17	57	85	5.22	1.56	22.7	293	3.5	5.3	1.5	1.0	32%	68%	29
		19	23	aaa	STL	9	8	26	0	153	140	81	22	72	109	4.75	1.38	24.8	000	4.2	6.4	1.5	1.3	27%	57%	19
Wright, Kyle	R	18	23	a/a	ATL	8	9	27	0	140	140	67	9	50	111	4.32	1.35	21.7	261	3.2	7.1	2.2	0.6	31%	68%	74
		19	24	aaa	ATL	11	4	21	0	113	131	69	15	37	94	5.51	1.48	23.2	000	2.9	7.5	2.6	1.2	34%	55%	74
Zeuch, T.J.	R	18	23	aa	TOR	9	5	21	0	120	142	52	8	32	68	3.92	1.45	24.4	296	2.4	5.1	2.1	0.6	33%	73%	53
		19	24	aaa	TOR	4	3	13	0	78	86	43	7	34	32	4.92	1.53	26.1	000	3.9	3.7	1.0	0.8	29%	62%	-21

ORGANIZATION RATINGS/RANKINGS

Each organization is graded on a standard A-F scale in four separate categories, and then after weighing the categories and adding some subjectivity, a final grade and ranking are determined. The four categories are the following:

Hitting: The quality and quantity of hitting prospects, the balance between athleticism, power, speed, and defense, and the quality of player development.

Pitching: The quality and quantity of pitching prospects and the quality of player development.

Top-End Talent: The quality of the top players within the organization. Successful teams are ones that have the most star-quality players. These are the players who are a teams' above average regulars, front-end starters, and closers.

Depth: The depth of both hitting and pitching prospects within the organization.

Overall Grade: The four categories are weighted, with top-end talent being the most important and depth being the least.

TEAM	Hitting	Pitching	Top-End Talent	Depth	Overall
Tampa Bay Rays	A	A	A	A+	A
San Diego Padres	A	A-	A	A	A
Minnesota Twins	A	B	A-	A-	A-
Los Angeles Dodgers	A-	B+	B+	A	A-
Miami Marlins	A-	B	A-	B	B+
San Francisco Giants	A-	C+	A	B+	B+
Seattle Mariners	A	B	A-	C	B
Cleveland Indians	A-	B	B+	C	B
Arizona Diamondbacks	B	C+	B	B+	B
Atlanta Braves	B	B	B	C	B
New York Yankees	C+	A-	B	B	B
Detroit Tigers	B-	B+	B	C	B-
Texas Rangers	B-	C	B	B	B-
Toronto Blue Jays	D	B+	B	C+	B-
Chicago White Sox	B-	C	A-	C-	C+
Baltimore Orioles	B-	C+	B	D	C+
Kansas City Royals	C	B-	B	C	C+
Oakland Athletics	C-	B	B	C-	C+
Pittsburgh Pirates	C+	C	B	C+	C+
St. Louis Cardinals	B	C	C	C+	C+
Cincinnati Reds	C+	B-	C-	B	C+
Houston Astros	C-	C	B	C	C
New York Mets	B	C	B	F	C
Philadelphia Phillies	C	C-	C+	C	C
Los Angeles Angels	B	F	B-	C	C-
Boston Red Sox	D	C-	C-	D	D+
Milwaukee Brewers	D+	D	D	D+	D+
Chicago Cubs	D+	D	D	D+	D
Colorado Rockies	C	D-	D+	D+	D
Washington Nationals	C-	D	C	F	D

This section of the book may be the smallest as far as word count is concerned, but may be the most important, as this is where players' skills and potential are tied together and ranked against their peers. The rankings that follow are divided into long-term potential in the major leagues and shorter-term fantasy value.

ORGANIZATIONAL: Lists the top 15 minor league prospects within each organization in terms of long-range potential in the major leagues.

POSITIONAL: Lists the top 15 prospects, by position, in terms of long-range potential in the major leagues.

TOP POWER: Lists the top 25 prospects that have the potential to hit for power in the major leagues, combining raw power, plate discipline, and at the ability to make their power game-usable.

TOP BA: Lists the top 25 prospects that have the potential to hit for high batting average in the major leagues, combining contact ability, plate discipline, hitting mechanics and strength.

TOP SPEED: Lists the top 25 prospects that have the potential to steal bases in the major leagues, combining raw speed and base-running instincts.

TOP FASTBALL: Lists the top 25 pitchers that have the best fastball, combining velocity and pitch movement.

TOP BREAKING BALL: Lists the top 25 pitchers that have the best breaking ball, combining pitch movement, strikeout potential, and consistency.

2020 TOP FANTASY PROSPECTS: Lists the top 40 minor league prospects likely to have the most value to their respective fantasy teams in 2020, then 35 more players to consider who could get the call and have the skills to produce. Remember that this section addresses 2020 value, not long-term value.

TOP 100 ARCHIVE: Takes a look back at the top 100 lists from the past eight years.

The rankings in this book are the creation of the minor league department at BaseballHQ.com. While several baseball personnel contributed player information to the book, no opinions were solicited or received in comparing players.

TOP PROSPECTS BY ORGANIZATION

AL EAST

BALTIMORE ORIOLES
1. Adley Rutschman, C
2. DL Hall, LHP
3. Grayson Rodriguez, RHP
4. Ryan Mountcastle, 1B/OF
5. Austin Hays, OF
6. Gunnar Henderson, SS
7. Hunter Harvey, RHP
8. Michael Baumann, RHP
9. Adam Hall, SS
10. Yusniel Diaz, OF
11. Ryan McKenna, OF
12. Dean Kremer, RHP
13. Rylan Bannon, 2B/3B/SS
14. Zac Lowther, LHP
15. Keegan Akin, LHP

BOSTON RED SOX
1. Triston Casas, 1B
2. Bobby Dalbec, 1B/3B
3. Jarren Duran, OF
4. Tanner Houck, RHP
5. Jay Groome, LHP
6. Bryan Mata, RHP
7. Noah Song, RHP
8. Gilberto Jimenez, OF
9. Thad Ward, RHP
10. C.J. Chatham, 2B/SS
11. Durbin Feltman, RHP
12. Ryan Zeferjahn, RHP
13. Antoni Flores, 2B/SS
14. Travis Lakins, RHP
15. Matthew Lugo, SS

NEW YORK YANKEES
1. Jasson Dominguez, OF
2. Clarke Schmidt, RHP
3. Deivi Garcia, RHP
4. Luis Medina, RHP
5. Luis Gil, RHP
6. Oswald Peraza, SS
7. Roansy Contreras, RHP
8. Ezequiel Duran, 2B
9. Anthony Volpe, SS
10. Raimfer Salinas, OF
11. Kevin Alcantara, OF
12. Estevan Florial, OF
13. Alexander Vizcaino, RHP
14. Albert Abreu, RHP
15. Michael King, RHP

TAMPA BAY RAYS
1. Wander Franco, SS
2. Brendan McKay, LHP
3. Vidal Brujan, 2B
4. Greg Jones, SS
5. Xavier Edwards, 2B/SS
6. Josh Lowe, OF
7. Shane Baz, RHP
8. Shane McClanahan, LHP
9. Ronaldo Hernandez, C
10. Joe Ryan, RHP
11. Brent Honeywell, RHP
12. Seth Johnson, RHP
13. Randy Arozarena, OF
14. JJ Goss, RHP
15. Lucius Fox, SS

TORONTO BLUE JAYS
1. Nate Pearson, RHP
2. Jordan Groshans, SS
3. Anthony Kay, LHP
4. Alek Manoah, RHP
5. Eric Pardinho, RHP
6. Adam Kloffenstein, RHP
7. Simeon Woods-Richardson, RHP
8. Miguel Hiraldo, 2B/SS
9. Orelvis Martinez, 3B/SS
10. Gabriel Moreno, C
11. Yennsy Diaz, RHP
12. Patrick Murphy, RHP
13. Griffin Conine, OF
14. Kendall Williams, RHP
15. Will Robertson, OF

AL CENTRAL

CHICAGO WHITE SOX
1. Luis Robert, OF
2. Michael Kopech, RHP
3. Andrew Vaughn, 1B
4. Nick Madrigal, SS
5. Jonathan Stiever, RHP
6. Dane Dunning, RHP
7. Andrew Dalquist, RHP
8. Luis Gonzalez, OF
9. Micker Adolfo, OF
10. Jimmy Lambert, RHP
11. Zack Collins, C
12. Yolbert Sanchez, SS
13. Luis Basabe, OF
14. Matthew Thompson, RHP
15. Zack Burdi, RHP

CLEVELAND INDIANS
1. Nolan Jones, 3B
2. George Valera, OF
3. Tyler Freeman, SS
4. Ethan Hankins, RHP
5. Bo Naylor, C
6. Daniel Espino, RHP
7. Aaron Bracho, 2B/SS
8. Brayan Rocchio, 2B/SS
9. Triston McKenzie, RHP
10. Gabriel Rodriguez, SS
11. Daniel Johnson, OF
12. Lenny Torres, RHP
13. Bobby Bradley, 1B
14. Logan Allen, LHP
15. Luis Oviedo, RHP

DETROIT TIGERS
1. Matt Manning, RHP
2. Casey Mize, RHP
3. Riley Greene, OF
4. Isaac Paredes, 3B
5. Tarik Skubal, LHP
6. Alex Faedo, RHP
7. Joey Wentz, LHP
8. Daz Cameron, OF
9. Parker Meadows, OF
10. Willi Castro, SS
11. Jake Rogers, C
12. Anthony Castro, RHP
13. Bryan Garcia, RHP
14. Andre Lipcius, 3B
15. Wenceel Perez, SS

KANSAS CITY ROYALS
1. Bobby Witt Jr., SS
2. Daniel Lynch, LHP
3. Erick Pena, OF
4. Jackson Kowar, RHP
5. Khalil Lee, OF
6. Brady Singer, RHP
7. Kris Bubic, LHP
8. Brady McConnell, SS
9. Zach Haake, RHP
10. Yefri Del Rosario, RHP
11. Jonathan Bowlan, RHP
12. Kyle Isbel, OF
13. Brewer Hicklen, OF
14. Alec Marsh, RHP
15. Carlos Hernandez, RHP

MINNESOTA TWINS
1. Royce Lewis, SS/OF
2. Alex Kirilloff, 1B/OF
3. Trevor Larnach, OF
4. Brusdar Graterol, RHP
5. Jordan Balazovic, RHP
6. Jhoan Duran, RHP
7. Misael Urbina, OF
8. Keoni Cavaco, SS
9. Blayne Enlow, RHP
10. Brent Rooker, 1B/OF
11. Travis Blankenhorn, 2B/OF
12. Gilberto Celestino, OF
13. Ryan Jeffers, C
14. Devin Smeltzer, LHP
15. Randy Dobnak, RHP

AL WEST

HOUSTON ASTROS
1. Forrest Whitley, RHP
2. Bryan Abreu, RHP
3. Abraham Toro, 1B/2B/3B
4. Tyler Ivey, RHP
5. Brandon Bielak, RHP
6. Jose Urquidy, RHP
7. Korey Lee, C
8. Cristian Javier, RHP
9. Freudis Nova, 2B/3B/SS
10. Jordan Brewer, OF
11. Cionel Perez, LHP
12. Hunter Brown, RHP
13. Luis Garcia, RHP
14. Garrett Stubbs, C
15. Grae Kessinger, 2B/3B/SS

LOS ANGELES ANGELS
1. Jo Adell, OF
2. Jordyn Adams, OF
3. Brandon Marsh, OF
4. Jeremiah Jackson, 2B/SS
5. Jahmai Jones, 2B
6. Jose Soriano, RHP
7. D'Shawn Knowles, OF
8. Kyren Paris, SS
9. Chris Rodriguez, RHP
10. Patrick Sandoval, LHP
11. Trent Deveaux, OF
12. Jack Kochanowicz, RHP
13. Aaron Hernandez, RHP
14. Luis Madero, RHP
15. Kevin Maitan, 2B/3B

OAKLAND ATHLETICS
1. Jesus Luzardo, LHP
2. AJ Puk, LHP
3. Robert Puason, SS
4. Sean Murphy, C
5. Daulton Jefferies, RHP
6. Lazaro Armenteros, OF
7. Jorge Mateo, SS
8. Sheldon Neuse, 3B
9. Austin Allen, C
10. Austin Beck, OF
11. Greg Deichmann, OF
12. Logan Davidson, SS
13. Nick Allen, SS
14. James Kaprielian, RHP
15. Grant Holmes, RHP

SEATTLE MARINERS
1. Julio Rodriguez, OF
2. Jarred Kelenic, OF
3. Logan Gilbert, RHP
4. Evan White, 1B
5. Noelvi Marte, SS
6. Jake Fraley, OF
7. Kyle Lewis, OF
8. George Kirby, RHP
9. Justin Dunn, RHP
10. Brandon Williamson, LHP
11. Isaiah Campbell, RHP
12. Cal Raleigh, C
13. Justus Sheffield, LHP
14. Juan Then, RHP
15. Sam Carlson, RHP

TEXAS RANGERS
1. Leody Taveras, OF
2. Josh Jung, 3B
3. Hans Crouse, RHP
4. Sherten Apostel, 3B
5. Sam Huff, C
6. Nick Solak, 2B/OF
7. Maximo Acosta, SS
8. Bayron Lora, OF
9. Cole Winn, RHP
10. Anderson Tejeda, SS
11. Bubba Thompson, OF
12. Joe Palumbo, LHP
13. Ronny Henriquez, RHP
14. Jonathan Ornelas, 2B/SS
15. Ricky Vanasco, RHP

TOP PROSPECTS BY ORGANIZATION

NL EAST

ATLANTA BRAVES
1. Cristian Pache, OF
2. Drew Waters, OF
3. Ian Anderson, RHP
4. Kyle Wright, RHP
5. Tucker Davidson, LHP
6. Kyle Muller, LHP
7. William Contreras, C
8. Shea Langeliers, C
9. Braden Shewmake, SS
10. Bryse Wilson, RHP
11. Patrick Weigel, RHP
12. Jasseel De La Cruz, RHP
13. Freddy Tarnok, RHP
14. Victor Vodnik, RHP
15. Trey Harris, OF

MIAMI MARLINS
1. Sixto Sanchez, RHP
2. JJ Bleday, OF
3. Jazz Chisholm, SS
4. Jesus Sanchez, OF
5. Kameron Misner, OF
6. Edward Cabrera, RHP
7. Monte Harrison, OF
8. Lewin Diaz, 1B
9. Braxton Garrett, LHP
10. Connor Scott, OF
11. Jorge Guzman, RHP
12. Nick Neidert, RHP
13. Jerar Encarnacion, OF
14. Trevor Rogers, LHP
15. Peyton Burdick, OF

NEW YORK METS
1. Ronny Mauricio, SS
2. Francisco Alvarez, C
3. Matt Allan, RHP
4. Brett Baty, 3B
5. Mark Vientos, 3B
6. Andres Gimenez, SS
7. Josh Wolf, RHP
8. Kevin Smith, LHP
9. Thomas Szapucki, LHP
10. David Peterson, LHP
11. Shervyen Newton, 2B/3B/SS
12. Drew Smith, RHP
13. Frankyln Kilome, RHP
14. Jordan Humphreys, RHP
15. Stephen Gonsalves, LHP

PHILADELPHIA PHILLIES
1. Spencer Howard, RHP
2. Alec Bohm, 1B/3B
3. Bryson Stott, SS
4. Francisco Morales, RHP
5. Adonis Medina, RHP
6. Mickey Moniak, OF
7. Johan Rojas, OF
8. Simon Muzziotti, OF
9. Rafael Marchan, C
10. Luis Garcia, 2B/SS
11. Nick Maton, 2B/SS
12. Damon Jones, LHP
13. JoJo Romero, LHP
14. Kendall Simmons, 2B
15. Connor Seabold, RHP

WASHINGTON NATIONALS
1. Carter Kieboom, 2B/SS
2. Luis Garcia, 2B/SS
3. Jackson Rutledge, LHP
4. Wil Crowe, RHP
5. Tim Cate, LHP
6. Drew Mendoza, 1B
7. Jeremy de la Rosa, OF
8. Yasel Antuna, SS
9. Martin Denaburg, RHP
10. Matt Cronin, LHP
11. Seth Romero, LHP
12. Tres Barrera, C
13. Jackson Cluff, SS
14. Viandel Pena, 2B
15. Nick Banks, OF

NL CENTRAL

CHICAGO CUBS
1. Brennen Davis, OF
2. Nico Hoerner, 2B/SS
3. Brailyn Marquez, LHP
4. Miguel Amaya, C
5. Adbert Alzolay, RHP
6. Aramis Ademan, SS
7. Cole Roederer, OF
8. Ryan Jensen, RHP
9. Zack Short, SS
10. Tyson Miller, RHP
11. Chase Strumpf, 2B
12. Cory Abbott, RHP
13. Justin Steele, LHP
14. Riley Thompson, RHP
15. Oscar De La Cruz, RHP

CINCINNATI REDS
1. Hunter Greene, RHP
2. Nick Lodolo, LHP
3. Tyler Stephenson, C
4. Jose Garcia, SS
5. Jonathan India, 3B
6. Mike Siani, OF
7. Lyon Richardson, RHP
8. Stuart Fairchild, OF
9. Rece Hinds, 3B/SS
10. Tony Santillan, RHP
11. Tyler Callihan, 2B/3B
12. Jameson Hannah, OF
13. Mariel Bautista, OF
14. Jose Siri, OF
15. Jacob Heatherly, LHP

MILWAUKEE BREWERS
1. Brice Turang, 2B/SS
2. Mario Feliciano, C
3. Ethan Small, LHP
4. Tristen Lutz, OF
5. Aaron Ashby, LHP
6. Corey Ray, OF
7. Zack Brown, RHP
8. Trey Supak, RHP
9. Carlos Rodriguez, OF
10. Drew Rasmussen, RHP
11. Eduardo Garcia, SS
12. Joe Gray, OF
13. Payton Henry, C
14. Antoine Kelly, LHP
15. Luis Medina, OF

PITTSBURGH PIRATES
1. Mitch Keller, RHP
2. Oneil Cruz, SS
3. Ke'Bryan Hayes, 3B
4. Travis Swaggerty, OF
5. Quinn Priester, RHP
6. Jared Oliva, OF
7. Sammy Siani, OF
8. Cody Bolton, RHP
9. Braxton Ashcraft, RHP
10. Cal Mitchell, OF
11. Lolo Sanchez, OF
12. Ji-Hwan Bae, 2B/SS
13. Tahnaj Thomas, RHP
14. Max Kranick, RHP
15. Will Craig, 1B

ST. LOUIS CARDINALS
1. Dylan Carlson, OF
2. Nolan Gorman, 3B
3. Matthew Liberatore, LHP
4. Andrew Knizner, C
5. Elehuris Montero, 3B
6. Ivan Herrera, C
7. Zack Thompson, LHP
8. Genesis Cabrera, LHP
9. Junior Fernandez, RHP
10. Jhon Torres, OF
11. Justin Williams, OF
12. Johan Oviedo, RHP
13. Angel Rondon, RHP
14. Julio Rodriguez, C
15. Edmundo Sosa, 2B/3B/SS

NL WEST

ARIZONA DIAMONDBACKS
1. Kristian Robinson, OF
2. Daulton Varsho, C
3. Corbin Carroll, OF
4. Alek Thomas, OF
5. Seth Beer, 1B/OF
6. Jon Duplantier, RHP
7. Levi Kelly, RHP
8. Luis Frias, RHP
9. Geraldo Perdomo, SS
10. Matt Tabor, RHP
11. JB Bukauskas, RHP
12. Liover Peguero, SS
13. Taylor Widener, RHP
14. Brennan Malone, RHP
15. Corbin Martin, RHP

COLORADO ROCKIES
1. Brendan Rodgers, 2B/SS
2. Ryan Rolison, LHP
3. Colton Welker, 1B/3B
4. Sam Hilliard, OF
5. Ryan Vilade, 3B/SS
6. Grant Lavigne, 1B
7. Ben Bowden, LHP
8. Terrin Vavra, 2B/SS
9. Michael Toglia, 1B
10. Ryan Castellani, RHP
11. Yonathan Daza, OF
12. Helcris Olivares, LHP
13. Julio Carreras, 3B/SS
14. Aaron Schunk, 3B
15. Riley Pint, RHP

LOS ANGELES DODGERS
1. Gavin Lux, SS
2. Dustin May, RHP
3. Keibert Ruiz, C
4. Kody Hoese, 3B
5. Josiah Gray, RHP
6. Tony Gonsolin, RHP
7. Jeter Downs, 2B/SS
8. Diego Cartaya, C
9. DJ Peters, OF
10. Mitchell White, RHP
11. Michael Busch, 2B
12. Omar Estevez, 2B/SS
13. Davin Mann, 2B/3B/SS
14. Jimmy Lewis, RHP
15. Dennis Santana, RHP

SAN DIEGO PADRES
1. MacKenzie Gore, LHP
2. CJ Abrams, SS
3. Luis Patino, RHP
4. Taylor Trammell, OF
5. Luis Campusano, C
6. Adrian Morejon, LHP
7. Jeisson Rosario, OF
8. Michel Baez, RHP
9. Ryan Weathers, LHP
10. Tucupita Marcano, 2B/3B/SS
11. Edward Olivares, OF
12. Esteury Ruiz, 2B
13. Ronald Bolanos, RHP
14. Hudson Potts, 3B
15. Gabriel Arias, SS

SAN FRANCISCO GIANTS
1. Joey Bart, C
2. Marco Luciano, SS
3. Heliot Ramos, OF
4. Hunter Bishop, OF
5. Logan Webb, RHP
6. Mauricio Dubon, 2B/SS
7. Seth Corry, LHP
8. Sean Hjelle, RHP
9. Jake Wong, RHP
10. Luis Toribio, 3B
11. Alexander Canario, OF
12. Will Wilson, SS
13. Logan Wyatt, 1B
14. Tristan Beck, RHP
15. Melvin Adon, RHP

TOP PROSPECTS BY POSITION

CATCHER
1 Adley Rutschman, BAL
2 Joey Bart, SF
3 Sean Murphy, OAK
4 Keibert Ruiz, LA
5 Daulton Varsho, ARI
6 Luis Campusano, SD
7 Francisco Alvarez, NYM
8 Sam Huff, TEX
9 Bo Naylor, CLE
10 Shea Langeliers, ATL
11 William Contreras, ATL
12 Miguel Amaya, CHC
13 Ronaldo Hernandez, TAM
14 Mario Feliciano, MIL
15 Andrew Knizner, STL

FIRST BASEMEN
1 Andrew Vaughn, CHW
2 Ryan Mountcastle, BAL
3 Evan White, SEA
4 Triston Casas, BOS
5 Lewin Diaz, MIA
6 Seth Beer, ARI
7 Grant Lavigne, COL
8 Kevin Cron, ARI
9 Jared Walsh, LAA
10 Brent Rooker, MIN
11 Michael Toglia, COL
12 Logan Wyatt, SF
13 Will Craig, PIT
14 Tyler Nevin, COL
15 Bobby Bradley, CLE

SECOND BASEMEN
1 Vidal Brujan, TAM
2 Nick Madrigal, CHW
3 Brayan Rocchio, CLE
4 Aaron Bracho, CLE
5 Luis Garcia, WAS
6 Jahmai Jones, LAA
7 Michael Busch, LA
8 Travis Blankenhorn, MIN
9 Terrin Vavra, COL
10 Kendall Simmons, PHI
11 Miguel Hiraldo, TOR
12 Kody Clemens, DET
13 Esteury Ruiz, SD
14 Ezequiel Duran, NYY
15 Viandel Pena, WAS

SHORTSTOP
1 Wander Franco, TAM
2 Gavin Lux, LA
3 Royce Lewis, MIN
4 Carter Kieboom, WAS
5 Bobby Witt, Jr., KC
6 Marco Luciano, SF
7 C.J. Abrams, SD
8 Brendan Rodgers, COL
9 Jazz Chisholm, MIA
10 Oneil Cruz, PIT
11 Jordan Groshans, TOR
12 Ronny Mauricio, NYM
13 Xavier Edwards, TAM
14 Nico Hoerner, CHC
15 Tyler Freeman, CLE

THIRD BASEMEN
1 Alec Bohm, PHI
2 Nolan Gorman, STL
3 Nolan Jones, CLE
4 Ke'Bryan Hayes, PIT
5 Josh Jung, TEX
6 Sherten Apostel, TEX
7 Jonathan India, CIN
8 Abraham Toro, HOU
9 Brett Baty, NYM
10 Isaac Paredes, DET
11 Bobby Dalbec, BOS
12 Mark Vientos, NYM
13 Kody Hoese, LA
14 Sheldon Neuse, OAK
15 Colton Welker, COL

OUTFIELDERS
1 Jo Adell, LAA
2 Luis Robert, CHW
3 Jarred Kelenic, SEA
4 Julio Rodriguez, SEA
5 Dylan Carlson, STL
6 Alex Kirilloff, MIN
7 Cristian Pache, ATL
8 Drew Waters, ATL
9 Kristian Robinson, ARI
10 J.J. Bleday, MIA
11 Heliot Ramos, SF
12 Taylor Trammell, SD
13 Jasson Dominguez, NYY
14 Jesus Sanchez, MIA
15 Hunter Bishop, SF
16 Trevor Larnach, MIN
17 Riley Greene, DET
18 Alek Thomas, ARI
19 Brennen Davis, CHC
20 George Valera, CLE
21 Corbin Carroll, ARI
22 Brandon Marsh, LAA
23 Leody Taveras, TEX
24 Monte Harrison, MIA
25 Jordyn Adams, LAA
26 Josh Lowe, TAM
27 Misael Urbina, MIN
28 Austin Hays, BAL
29 Gilberto Jimenez, BOS
30 Jake Fraley, SEA
31 Erick Pena, KC
32 Khalil Lee, KC
33 Estevan Florial, NYY
34 Alexander Canario, SF
35 Nick Solak, TEX
36 Edward Olivares, SD
37 Travis Swaggerty, PIT
38 Tristen Lutz, MIL
39 Corey Ray, MIL
40 Jarren Duran, BOS
41 Jeisson Rosario, SD
42 Bayron Lora, TEX
43 Mickey Moniak, PHI
44 Randy Arozarena, TAM
45 Jared Oliva, PIT

STARTING PITCHERS
1 MacKenzie Gore, SD
2 Forrest Whitley, HOU
3 Jesus Luzardo, OAK
4 Casey Mize, DET
5 Nate Pearson, TOR
6 Dustin May, LA
7 Michael Kopech, CHW
8 Matt Manning, DET
9 Sixto Sanchez, MIA
10 Brendan McKay, TAM
11 A.J. Puk, OAK
12 Luis Patino, SD
13 Spencer Howard, PHI
14 Mitch Keller, PIT
15 Grayson Rodriguez, BAL

16 Brusdar Graterol, MIN
17 Ian Anderson, ATL
18 Daniel Lynch, KC
19 Matthew Liberatore, STL
20 DL Hall, BAL
21 Hunter Greene, CIN
22 Deivi Garcia, NYY
23 Logan Gilbert, SEA
24 Kyle Wright, ATL
25 Josiah Gray, LA
26 Shane Baz, TAM
27 Nick Lodolo, CIN
28 Hans Crouse, TEX
29 Tarik Skubal, DET
30 Clarke Schmidt, NYY

31 Jordan Balazovic, MIN
32 Ethan Hankins, CLE
33 Brent Honeywell, TAM
34 Brady Singer, KC
35 Adrian Morejon, SD
36 Brailyn Marquez, CHC
37 Jackson Kowar, KC
38 Triston McKenzie, CLE
39 Alek Manoah, TOR
40 Justin Dunn, SEA
41 Edward Cabrera, MIA
42 Anthony Kay, TOR
43 Kyle Muller, ATL
44 Ryan Rolison, COL
45 Ryan Weathers, SD

46 Jhoan Duran, MIN
47 Shane McClanahan, TAM
48 Francisco Morales, PHI
49 Daniel Espino, CLE
50 Simeon Woods-Richardson, TOR
51 George Kirby, SEA
52 Franklin Perez, DET
53 Corbin Martin, ARI
54 Logan Webb, SF
55 Adonis Medina, PHI
56 Jon Duplantier, ARI
57 Daulton Jefferies, OAK
58 Ethan Small, MIL
59 Cole Winn, TEX
60 Eric Pardinho, TOR

61 Quinn Priester, PIT
62 Bryan Abreu, HOU
63 Zack Thompson, STL
64 Trey Supak, MIL
65 Michel Baez, SD
66 Tony Gonsolin, LA
67 Cristian Javier, HOU
68 Braxton Garrett, MIA
69 Bryan Mata, BOS
70 Jackson Rutledge, WAS
71 Seth Corry, SF
72 Adam Kloffenstein, TOR
73 J.J. Goss, TAM
74 Grant Holmes, OAK
75 Nick Neidert, MIA

RELIEF PITCHERS
1 Andres Munoz, SD
2 Ben Bowden, COL
3 Emmanuel Clase, CLE
4 Justin Lawrence, COL
5 Oscar De La Cruz, CHC
6 James Norwood, CHC
7 Melvin Adon, SF
8 James Karinchak, CLE
9 Jorge Alcala, MIN
10 Peter Fairbanks, TAM
11 Junior Fernandez, STL
12 Genesis Cabrera, STL
13 Robert Tyler, COL
14 Ryne Nelson, ARI
15 Camilo Doval, SF

TOP PROSPECTS BY SKILLS

2020 TOP FANTASY IMPACT

TOP POWER

Nolan Gorman, 3B, STL
Jo Adell, OF, LAA
Luis Robert, OF, CHW
Adley Rutschman, C, BAL
Joey Bart, C, SF
Nolan Jones, 3B, CLE
Alec Bohm, 3B, PHI
Wander Franco, SS, TAM
J.J. Bleday, OF, MIA
Dylan Carlson, OF, STL
Ryan Mountcastle, 1B, BAL
Bobby Dalbec, 3B, BOS
Griffin Conine, OF, TOR
Andrew Vaughn, 1B, CHW
Alex Kirilloff, OF, MIN
Jasson Dominguez, OF, NYY
Oneil Cruz, SS, PIT
Kevin Cron, 1B, ARI
Hunter Bishop, OF, SF
Julio Rodriguez, OF, SEA
Monte Harrison, OF, MIA
Triston Casas, 1B, BOS
Sam Hilliard, OF, COL
Heliot Ramos, OF, SF
Seth Beer, 1B, ARI

TOP BA

Wander Franco, SS, TAM
Nick Madrigal, 2B, CHW
Jarred Kelenic, OF, SEA
Andrew Vaughn, 1B, CHW
Vidal Brujan, 2B, TAM
Alex Kirilloff, OF, MIN
Jasson Dominguez, OF, NYY
C.J. Abrams, SS, SD
Jordan Groshans, SS, TOR
Gavin Lux, SS, LAA
Cristian Pache, OF, ATL
Xavier Edwards, SS, TAM
Cobrin Carroll, OF, ARI
Luis Garcia, SS, WAS
Alec Bohm, 3B, PHI
Marco Luciano, SS, SF
Adley Rutschman, C, BAL
Tyler Freeman, SS, CLE
Ke'Bryan Hayes, 3B, PIT
J.J. Bleday, OF, MIA
Brice Turang, SS, MIL
Greg Jones, SS, TAM
Gilberto Jimenez, OF, BOS
Keibert Ruiz, C, LA
Mauricio Dubon, 2B, SF

TOP SPEED

Vidal Brujan, 2B, TAM
Greg Jones, SS, TAM
C.J. Abrams, SS, SD
Jorge Mateo, SS, OAK
Jordyn Adams, OF, LAA
Xavier Edwards, SS, TAM
Lucius Fox, SS, TAM
James Beard, OF, CHW
Royce Lewis, SS, MIN
Jo Adell, OF, LAA
Jarren Duran, OF, BOS
Luis Robert, OF, CHW
Kristian Robinson, OF, ARI
Brennen Davis, OF, CHC
Jasson Dominguez, OF, NYY
Leody Taveras, OF, TEX
Oneil Cruz, SS, PIT
Taylor Trammell, OF, SD
Nick Madrigal, 2B, CHW
Corbin Carroll, OF, ARI
Drew Waters, OF, ATL
Bubba Thompson, OF, TEX
Jared Oliva, OF, PIT
Gilberto Jimenez, OF, BOS
Khalil Lee, OF, KC

TOP FASTBALL

Sixto Sanchez, RHP, MIA
Nate Pearson, RHP, TOR
Forrest Whitley, RHP, HOU
Andres Munoz, RHP, SD
Michael Kopech, RHP, CHW
Hunter Greene, RHP, CIN
Junior Fernandez, RHP, STL
Emmanuel Clase, RHP, CLE
Luis Medina, RHP, NYY
Justin Lawrence, RHP, COL
Riley Pint, RHP, COL
Daniel Espino, RHP, CLE
Jorge Guzman, RHP, MIA
Brusdar Graterol, RHP, MIN
Jonathan Hernandez, RHP, TEX
Mitch Keller, RHP, PIT
Jesus Luzardo, LHP, OAK
Ethan Hankins, RHP, CLE
Luis Patino, RHP, SD
Brailyn Marquez, LHP, CHC
Melvin Adon, RHP, SF
A.J. Puk, LHP, OAK
DL Hall, LHP, BAL
Hunter Harvey, RHP, BAL
Jackson Rutledge, RHP, WAS

TOP BREAKING BALL

Michael Kopech, RHP, CHW
Daniel Lynch, LHP, KC
Brusdar Graterol, RHP, MIN
Shane McClanahan, LHP, TAM
Kyle Wright, RHP, ATL
Hunter Greene, RHP, CIN
MacKenzie Gore, LHP, SD
Spencer Howard, RHP, PHI
A.J. Puk, LHP, OAK
Clarke Schmidt, RHP, NYY
Jesus Luzardo, LHP, OAK
Mitch Keller, RHP, PIT
Matthew Liberatore, LHP, STL

Cole Winn, RHP, TEX
Nate Pearson, RHP, TOR
Luis Patino, RHP, SD
Luis Medina, RHP, NYY
Eric Pardinho, RHP, TOR
DL Hall, LHP, BAL
Grayson Rodriguez, RHP, BAL
Shane Baz, RHP, TAM
Deivi Garcia, RHP, NYY
Jon Duplantier, RHP, ARI
Jackson Rutledge, RHP, WAS
Jhoan Duran, RHP, MIN

THE TOP 40 · RANKED

1 Gavin Lux (2B/SS, LA)
2 Nick Solak (2B/OF, TEX)
3 Nick Madrigal (2B, CHW)
4 Jo Adell (OF, LAA)
5 Mauricio Dubon (SS, SF)
6 Luis Robert (OF, CHW)
7 Austin Hays (OF, BAL)
8 Carter Kieboom (SS, WAS)
9 Willi Castro (SS, DET)
10 Dustin May (RHP, LA)

11 Brendan Rodgers (IF, COL)
12 Kyle Lewis (OF, SEA)
13 Alec Bohm (3B, PHI)
14 Sean Murphy (C, OAK)
15 Jesus Luzardo (LHP, OAK)
16 Dylan Carlson (OF, STL)
17 Cristian Pache (OF, ATL)
18 Nico Hoerner (SS, CHC)
19 Abraham Toro (IF, HOU)
20 Bobby Dalbec (3B, BOS)

21 Jarred Kelenic (OF, SEA)
22 Tony Gonsolin (RHP, LA)
23 AJ Puk (LHP, OAK)
24 Jake Rogers (C, DET)
25 Yusniel Diaz (OF, BAL)
26 Brendan McKay (LHP/DH, TAM)
27 Forrest Whitley (RHP, HOU)
28 Matt Manning (RHP, DET)
29 Michael Kopech (RHP, CHW)
30 Zack Collins (C/1B, CHW)

31 Mitch Keller (RHP, PIT)
32 Isaac Paredes (SS/3B, DET)
33 Ryan Mountcastle (1B, BAL)
34 Sixto Sanchez (RHP, MIA)
35 Brusdar Graterol (RHP, MIN)
36 MacKenzie Gore (LHP, SD)
37 Casey Mize (RHP, DET)
38 Nolan Jones (3B, CLE)
39 Randy Arozarena (OF, TAM)
40 Kyle Wright (RHP, ATL)

THE NEXT 35 · ALPHA ORDER

Ian Anderson (RHP, ATL)
Logan Allen (LHP, CLE)
Seth Beer (1B, ARI)
Bobby Bradley (1B, CLE)
Vidal Brujan (2B, TAM)
Jazz Chisholm (SS, MIA)
Lewin Diaz (1B, MIA)
Justin Dunn (RHP, SEA)
Jon Duplantier (RHP, ARI)
Alex Faedo (RHP, DET)
Wander Franco (SS, TAM)
Delvi Garcia (RHP, NYY)
Logan Gilbert (RHP, SEA)
Andres Gimenez (SS, NYM)
Monte Harrison (OF, MIA)
Ke'Bryan Hayes (3B, PIT)
Brent Honeywell (RHP, TAM)
Alex Kirilloff (OF, MIN)
Andrew Knizner (C, STL)
Jackson Kowar (RHP, KC)
Trevor Larnach (OF, MIN)
Royce Lewis (SS, MIN)
Brandon Marsh (OF, LAA)
Jorge Mateo (2B/SS, OAK)
Adrian Morejon (LHP, SD)
Kyle Muller (LHP, ATL)
Nate Pearson (RHP, TOR)
Keibert Ruiz (C, LA)
Jesus Sanchez (OF, MIA)
Justus Sheffield (LHP, SEA)
Brady Singer (RHP, KC)
Daulton Varsho (C/OF, ARI)
Drew Waters (OF, ATL)
Evan White (1B, SEA)
Bryse Wilson (RHP, ATL)

TOP 100 PROSPECTS ARCHIVE

2019

1. Vladimir Guerrero Jr., (3B, TOR)
2. Eloy Jimenez, (OF, CHW)
3. Fernando Tatis Jr., (SS, SD)
4. Victor Robles, (OF, WAS)
5. Royce Lewis, (SS, MIN)
6. Kyle Tucker, (OF, HOU)
7. Forrest Whitley, (RHP, HOU)
8. Bo Bichette, (SS, TOR)
9. Nick Senzel, (2B, CIN)
10. Alex Kirilloff, (OF, MIN)

11. Jo Adell, (OF, LAA)
12. Wander Franco, (SS, TAM)
13. Jesus Luzardo, (LHP, OAK)
14. Brendan Rodgers, (SS, COL)
15. Michael Kopech, (RHP, CHW)
16. MacKenzie Gore, (LHP, SD)
17. Taylor Trammell, (OF, CIN)
18. Keston Hiura, (2B, MIL)
19. Sixto Sanchez, (RHP, PHI)
20. Casey Mize, (RHP, DET)

21. Dylan Cease, (RHP, CHW)
22. Mike Soroka, (RHP, ATL)
23. Joey Bart, (C, SF)
24. Carter Kieboom, (SS, WAS)
25. Alex Reyes, (RHP, STL)
26. Luis Urias, (2B, SD)
27. Ian Anderson, (RHP, ATL)
28. Brent Honeywell, (RHP, TAM)
29. Mitch Keller, (RHP, PIT)
30. Keibert Ruiz, (C, LA)

31. Peter Alonso, (1B, NYM)
32. Chris Paddack, (RHP, SD)
33. Hunter Greene, (RHP, CIN)
34. A.J. Puk, (LHP, OAK)
35. Austin Riley, (3B, ATL)
36. Kyle Wright, (RHP, ATL)
37. Alex Verdugo, (OF, LA)
38. Luis Robert, (OF, CHW)
39. Jesus Sanchez, (OF, TAM)
40. Nick Madrigal, (SS, CHW)

41. Triston McKenzie, (RHP, CLE)
42. Yordan Alvarez, (OF, HOU)
43. Brendan McKay, (1B/LHP, TAM)
44. Jonathan India, (3B, CIN)
45. Touki Toussaint, (RHP, ATL)
46. Matt Manning, (RHP, DET)
47. Francisco Mejia, (C, SD)
48. Ke'Bryan Hayes, (3B, PIT)
49. Nolan Gorman, (3B, STL)
50. Adrian Morejon, (LHP, SD)

51. Danny Jansen, (C, TOR)
52. Alec Bohm, (3B, PHI)
53. Justus Sheffield, (LHP, SEA)
54. Yusinel Diaz, (OF, BAL)
55. Jarred Kelenic, (OF, SEA)
56. Andres Gimenez, (SS, NYM)
57. Estevan Florial, (OF, NYY)
58. Luis Garcia, (SS/3B, WAS)
59. Jon Duplantier, (RHP, ARI)
60. Luis Patino, (RHP, SD)

61. Leody Taveras, (OF, TEX)
62. Nolan Jones, (3B, CLE)
63. Gavin Lux, (2B, LA)
64. Adonis Medina, (RHP, PHI)
65. Michel Baez, (RHP, SD)
66. Brusdar Graterol, (RHP, MIN)
67. Julio Pablo Martinez, (OF, TEX)
68. Matthew Liberatore, (LHP, TAM)
69. Cristian Pache, (OF, ATL)
70. Dustin May, (RHP, LA)

71. Josh James, (RHP, HOU)
72. Jonathan Loaisiga, (RHP, NYY)
73. Sean Murphy, (C, OAK)
74. Brady Singer, (RHP, KC)
75. Dane Dunning, (RHP, CHW)
76. Khalil Lee, (OF, KC)
77. Ryan Mountcastle, (3B, BAL)
78. Heliot Ramos, (OF, SF)
79. Nate Pearson, (RHP, TOR)
80. Drew Waters, (OF, ATL)

81. Jazz Chisholm, (SS, ARI)
82. Hans Crouse, (RHP, TEX)
83. DL Hall, (LHP, BAL)
84. MJ Melendez, (C, KC)
85. Oneil Cruz, (SS, PIT)
86. Kristian Robinson, (OF, ARI)
87. Ronaldo Hernandez, (C, TAM)
88. Vidal Brujan, (2B, TAM)
89. Colton Welker, (3B, COL)
90. Franklin Perez, (RHP, DET)

91. Travis Swaggerty, (OF, PIT)
92. Daz Cameron, (OF, DET)
93. Griffin Canning, (RHP, LAA)
94. Bryse Wilson, (RHP, ATL)
95. Brandon Marsh, (OF, LAA)
96. Bubba Thompson, (OF, TEX)
97. Logan Allen, (LHP, SD)
98. Justin Dunn , (RHP, SEA)
99. Miguel Amaya, (C, CHC)
100. Dakota Hudson, (RHP, STL)

2018

1. Ronald Acuna (OF, ATL)
2. Victor Robles (OF, WAS)
3. Vladimir Guerrero Jr. (3B, TOR)
4. Eloy Jimenez (OF, CHW)
5. Gleyber Torres (SS, NYY)
6. Brendan Rodgers (SS, COL)
7. Nick Senzel (3B, CIN)
8. Alex Reyes (RHP, STL)
9. Walker Buehler (RHP, LA)
10. Michael Kopech (RHP, CHW)

11. Fernando Tatis Jr. (SS, SD)
12. Kyle Tucker (OF, HOU)
13. Bo Bichette (SS, TOR)
14. Lewis Brinson (OF, MIL)
15. Brent Honeywell (RHP, TAM)
16. MacKenzie Gore (LHP, SD)
17. Forrest Whitley (RHP, HOU)
18. Willy Adames (SS, TAM)
19. Leody Taveras (OF, TEX)
20. Royce Lewis (SS, MIN)

21. Mitch Keller (RHP, PIT)
22. Francisco Mejia (C, CLE)
23. Kyle Wright (RHP, ATL)
24. A.J. Puk (LHP, OAK)
25. Sixto Sanchez (RHP, PHI)
26. Hunter Greene (RHP, CIN)
27. Franklin Barreto (SS, OAK)
28. Juan Soto (OF, WAS)
29. Triston McKenzie (RHP, CLE)
30. Luiz Gohara (LHP, ATL)

31. Alex Verdugo (OF, LA)
32. Franklin Perez (RHP, DET)
33. Luis Robert (OF, CHW)
34. Keston Huira (2B, MIL)
35. Ryan McMahon (1B, COL)
36. Scott Kingery (2B, PHI)
37. Mike Soroka (RHP, ATL)
38. Willie Calhoun (OF/2B, TEX)
39. Kolby Allard (LHP, ATL)
40. Austin Hays (OF, BAL)

41. Jack Flaherty (RHP, STL)
42. J.P. Crawford (SS, PHI)
43. Anthony Alford (OF, TOR)
44. Austin Meadows (OF, PIT)
45. Brendan McKay (1B/LHP, TAM)
46. Luis Urias (2B/SS, SD)
47. Kyle Lewis (OF, SEA)
48. Taylor Trammell (OF, CIN)
49. Yadier Alvarez (RHP, LA)
50. Estevan Florial (OF, NYY)

51. Jay Groome (LHP, BOS)
52. Cal Quantrill (RHP, SD)
53. Nick Gordon (SS, MIN)
54. Jesus Sanchez (OF, TAM)
55. Chance Adams (RHP, NYY)
56. Jorge Mateo (SS, OAK)
57. Ian Anderson (RHP, ATL)
58. Michel Baez (RHP, SD)
59. Alec Hansen (RHP, CHW)
60. Monte Harrison (OF, MIL)

61. Keibert Ruiz (C, LA)
62. Carson Kelly (C, STL)
63. Kevin Maitan (3B, LAA)
64. Riley Pint (RHP, COL)
65. Anderson Espinoza (RHP, SD)
66. Matt Manning (RHP, DET)
67. Austin Beck (OF, OAK)
68. Dylan Cease (RHP, CHW)
69. Jorge Alfaro (C, PHI)
70. Justus Sheffield (LHP, NYY)

71. Blake Rutherford (OF, CHW)
72. Chance Sisco (C, BAL)
73. Ryan Mountcastle (3B, BAL)
74. Corbin Burnes (RHP, MIL)
75. Jake Bauers (OF/1B, TAM)
76. Pavin Smith (1B, ARI)
77. Adonis Medina (RHP, PHI)
78. Jon Duplantier (RHP, ARI)
79. Heliot Ramos (OF, SF)
80. Adrian Morejon (LHP, SD)

81. Dustin Fowler (OF, OAK)
82. Mickey Moniak (OF, PHI)
83. Shane Baz (RHP, PIT)
84. Yusniel Diaz (OF, LA)
85. Jesse Winker (OF, CIN)
86. Stephen Gonsalves (LHP, MIN)
87. Isan Diaz (2B, MIL)
88. Joey Wentz (LHP, ATL)
89. Tyler O'Neill (OF, STL)
90. Alex Faedo (RHP, DET)

91. Jo Adell (OF, LAA)
92. Austin Riley (3B, ATL)
93. Corey Ray (OF, MIL)
94. Brandon Woodruff (RHP, MIL)
95. Mitchell White (RHP, LA)
96. Yordan Alvarez (1B, HOU)
97. Michael Chavis (3B, BOS)
98. Jose De Leon (RHP, TAM)
99. Christian Arroyo (3B, TAM)
100. Chris Shaw (1B, SF)

TOP 100 PROSPECTS ARCHIVE

2017

1. Yoan Moncada (2B, CHW)
2. Andrew Benintendi (OF, BOS)
3. Dansby Swanson (SS, ATL)
4. Alex Reyes (RHP, STL)
5. Lucas Giolito (RHP, CHW)
6. Victor Robles (OF, WAS)
7. J.P. Crawford (SS, PHI)
8. Tyler Glasnow (RHP, PIT)
9. Brendan Rodgers (SS, COL)
10. Austin Meadows (OF, PIT)

11. Gleyber Torres (SS, NYY)
12. Amed Rosario (SS, NYM)
13. Rafael Devers (3B, BOS)
14. Lewis Brinson (OF, MIL)
15. Anderson Espinoza (RHP, SD)
16. Willy Adames (SS, TAM)
17. Eloy Jimenez (OF, CHC)
18. Manuel Margot (OF, SD)
19. Ozzie Albies (2B, ATL)
20. Clint Frazier (OF, NYY)

21. Bradley Zimmer (OF, CLE)
22. Franklin Barreto (SS, OAK)
23. Brent Honeywell (RHP, TAM)
24. Cody Bellinger (1B, LAD)
25. Francis Martes (RHP, HOU)
26. Reynaldo Lopez (RHP, CHW)
27. Jose De Leon (RHP, LAD)
28. Mickey Moniak (OF, PHI)
29. Ian Happ (2B, CHC)
30. Kyle Tucker (OF, HOU)

31. Nick Senzel (3B, CIN)
32. Michael Kopech (RHP, CHW)
33. Aaron Judge (OF, NYY)
34. Josh Bell (1B, PIT)
35. Kyle Lewis (OF, SEA)
36. Hunter Renfroe (OF, SD)
37. Jorge Mateo (SS, NYY)
38. Amir Garrett (LHP, CIN)
39. Corey Ray (OF, MIL)
40. Jeff Hoffman (RHP, COL)

41. Tyler O'Neill (OF, SEA)
42. Josh Hader (LHP, MIL)
43. Kolby Allard (LHP, ATL)
44. Jason Groome (LHP, BOS)
45. Jorge Alfaro (C, PHI)
46. Nick Williams (OF, PHI)
47. Nick Gordon (SS, MIN)
48. Sean Newcomb (LHP, ATL)
49. Alex Verdugo (OF, LAD)
50. Blake Rutherford (OF, NYY)

51. Carson Fulmer (RHP, CHW)
52. Vladimir Guerrero, Jr. (3B, TOR)
53. David Paulino (RHP, HOU)
54. Mitch Keller (RHP, PIT)
55. Riley Pint (RHP, COL)
56. Francisco Mejia (C, CLE)
57. Brady Aiken (LHP, CLE)
58. Yulieski Gurriel (3B, HOU)
59. Braxton Garrett (LHP, MIA)
60. Tyler Jay (LHP, MIN)

61. A.J. Puk (LHP, OAK)
62. Kevin Newman (SS, PIT)
63. Robert Stephenson (RHP, CIN)
64. Sean Reid-Foley (RHP, TOR)
65. Matt Manning (RHP, DET)
66. Anthony Alford (OF, TOR)
67. Jesse Winker (OF, CIN)
68. Dominic Smith (1B, NYM)
69. Raimel Tapia (OF, COL)
70. Zack Collins (C, CHW)

71. James Kaprielian (RHP, NYY)
72. Erick Fedde (RHP, WAS)
73. Luis Ortiz (RHP, MIL)
74. Phil Bickford (RHP, MIL)
75. Jake Bauers (OF, TAM)
76. Justus Sheffield (LHP, NYY)
77. Matt Chapman (3B, OAK)
78. Luke Weaver (RHP, STL)
79. Grant Holmes (RHP, OAK)
80. Bobby Bradley (1B, CLE)

81. Ronald Acuna (OF, ATL)
82. Derek Fisher (OF, HOU)
83. Brett Phillips (OF, MIL)
84. Yadier Alvarez (RHP, LAD)
85. Leody Taveras (OF, TEX)
86. Yohander Mendez (LHP, TEX)
87. Kevin Maitan (SS, ATL)
88. Triston McKenzie (LHP, CLE)
89. Willie Calhoun (2B, LAD)
90. Ryan McMahon (3B, COL)

91. Isan Diaz (2B, MIL)
92. Ian Anderson (RHP, ATL)
93. Trent Clark (OF, MIL)
94. Alex Kirilloff (OF, MIN)
95. Harrison Bader (OF, STL)
96. Tyler Beede (RHP, SF)
97. Richard Urena (SS, TOR)
98. Mike Soroka (RHP, ATL)
99. Dylan Cease (RHP, CHC)
100. Stephen Gonsalves (LHP, MIN)

2016

1. Byron Buxton (OF, MIN)
2. Corey Seager (SS, LAD)
3. Lucas Giolito (RHP, WAS)
4. J.P. Crawford (SS, PHI)
5. Alex Reyes (RHP, STL)
6. Julio Urias (LHP, LAD)
7. Yoan Moncada (2B, BOS)
8. Tyler Glasnow (RHP, PIT)
9. Joey Gallo (3B, TEX)
10. Steven Matz (LHP, NYM)

11. Rafael Devers (3B, BOS)
12. Jose Berrios (RHP, MIN)
13. Orlando Arcia (SS, MIL)
14. Blake Snell (LHP, TAM)
15. Trea Turner (SS, WAS)
16. Bradley Zimmer (OF, CLE)
17. Jose De Leon (RHP, LAD)
18. Brendan Rodgers (SS, COL)
19. Dansby Swanson (SS, ATL)
20. Robert Stephenson (RHP, CIN)

21. Nomar Mazara (OF, TEX)
22. Victor Robles (OF, WAS)
23. Aaron Judge (OF, NYY)
24. Manuel Margot (OF, SD)
25. Clint Frazier (OF, CLE)
26. Lewis Brinson (OF, TEX)
27. Alex Bregman (SS, HOU)
28. Jon Gray (RHP, COL)
29. Ryan McMahon (3B, COL)
30. Austin Meadows (OF, PIT)

31. Nick Williams (OF, PHI)
32. Franklin Barreto (SS, OAK)
33. David Dahl (OF, COL)
34. Brett Phillips (OF, MIL)
35. Gleyber Torres (SS, CHC)
36. Sean Newcomb (LHP, ATL)
37. Carson Fulmer (RHP, CHW)
38. Ozhaino Albies (SS, ATL)
39. Dillon Tate (RHP, TEX)
40. Andrew Benintendi (OF, BOS)

41. Jameson Taillon (RHP, PIT)
42. Raul Mondesi (SS, KC)
43. Archie Bradley (RHP, ARI)
44. Tim Anderson (SS, CHW)
45. Kolby Allard (LHP, ATL)
46. Jake Thompson (RHP, PHI)
47. Dylan Bundy (RHP, BAL)
48. Willy Adames (SS, TAM)
49. Anderson Espinoza (RHP, BOS)
50. Aaron Blair (RHP, ATL)

51. A.J. Reed (1B, HOU)
52. Jeff Hoffman (RHP, COL)
53. Jesse Winker (OF, CIN)
54. Brent Honeywell (RHP, TAM)
55. Josh Bell (1B, PIT)
56. Anthony Alford (OF, TOR)
57. Tyler Kolek (RHP, MIA)
58. Max Kepler (OF, MIN)
59. Hunter Renfroe (OF, SD)
60. Mark Appel (RHP, PHI)

61. Kyle Zimmer (RHP, KC)
62. Jose Peraza (2B, CIN)
63. Kyle Tucker (OF, HOU)
64. Cody Reed (LHP, CIN)
65. Billy McKinney (OF, CHC)
66. Nick Gordon (SS, MIN)
67. Braden Shipley (RHP, ARI)
68. Jorge Lopez (RHP, MIL)
69. Touki Toussaint (RHP, ATL)
70. Hector Olivera (3B, ATL)

71. Derek Fisher (OF, HOU)
72. Jorge Alfaro (C, PHI)
73. Raimel Tapia (OF, COL)
74. Grant Holmes (RHP, LAD)
75. Dominic Smith (1B, NYM)
76. Daz Cameron (OF, HOU)
77. Alex Jackson (OF, SEA)
78. Sean Manaea (LHP, OAK)
79. Amed Rosario (SS, NYM)
80. Reynaldo Lopez (RHP, WAS)

81. Javier Guerra (SS, SD)
82. Hunter Harvey (RHP, BAL)
83. Luis Ortiz (RHP, TEX)
84. Brady Aiken (LHP, CLE)
85. Matt Olson (1B, OAK)
86. Jorge Mateo (SS, NYY)
87. Daniel Robertson (SS, TAM)
88. Taylor Guerrieri (RHP, TAM)
89. Amir Garrett (LHP, CIN)
90. Willson Contreras (C, CHC)

91. Renato Nunez (3B, OAK)
92. Tyler Jay (LHP, MIN)
93. Tyler Stephenson (C, CIN)
94. Christian Arroyo (SS, SF)
95. Josh Naylor (1B, MIA)
96. Brian Johnson (LHP, BOS)
97. Tyler Beede (RHP, SF)
98. Garrett Whitley (OF, TAM)
99. Cody Bellinger (1B, LAD)
100. Michael Fulmer (RHP, DET)

TOP 100 PROSPECTS ARCHIVE

2015

1. Kris Bryant (3B, CHC)
2. Byron Buxton (OF, MIN)
3. Carlos Correa (SS, HOU)
4. Addison Russell (SS, CHC)
5. Corey Seager (SS, LAD)
6. Francisco Lindor (SS, CLE)
7. Joc Pederson (OF, LAD)
8. Miguel Sano (3B, MIN)
9. Lucas Giolito (P, WAS)
10. Joey Gallo (3B, TEX)
11. Dylan Bundy (P, BAL)
12. Jorge Soler (OF, CHC)
13. Archie Bradley (P, ARI)
14. Julio Urias (P, LAD)
15. Jon Gray (P, COL)
16. Daniel Norris (P, TOR)
17. Carlos Rodon (P, CHW)
18. Tyler Glasnow (P, PIT)
19. Noah Syndergaard (P, NYM)
20. Blake Swihart (C, BOS)
21. Aaron Sanchez (P, TOR)
22. Henry Owens (P, BOS)
23. Jameson Taillon (P, PIT)
24. Robert Stephenson (P, CIN)
25. Andrew Heaney (P, LAA)
26. David Dahl (OF, COL)
27. Jose Berrios (P, MIN)
28. Jorge Alfaro (C, TEX)
29. Hunter Harvey (P, BAL)
30. Alex Meyer (P, MIN)
31. Kohl Stewart (P, MIN)
32. J.P. Crawford (SS, PHI)
33. Alex Jackson (OF, SEA)
34. Jesse Winker (OF, CIN)
35. Raul Mondesi (SS, KC)
36. D.J. Peterson (3B, SEA)
37. Austin Meadows (OF, PIT)
38. Josh Bell (OF, PIT)
39. Kyle Crick (P, SF)
40. Luis Severino (P, NYY)
41. Nick Gordon (SS, MIN)
42. Kyle Schwarber (OF, CHC)
43. Aaron Nola (P, PHI)
44. Kyle Zimmer (P, KC)
45. Alex Reyes (P, STL)
46. Braden Shipley (P, ARI)
47. Albert Almora (OF, CHC)
48. Clint Frazier (OF, CLE)
49. Tyler Kolek (P, MIA)
50. Mark Appel (P, HOU)
51. Rusney Castillo (OF, BOS)
52. Sean Manaea (P, KC)
53. A.J. Cole (P, WAS)
54. Matt Wisler (P, SD)
55. Raimel Tapia (OF, COL)
56. C.J. Edwards (P, CHC)
57. Dalton Pompey (OF, TOR)
58. Hunter Renfroe (OF, SD)
59. Hunter Dozier (3B, KC)
60. Brandon Nimmo (OF, NYM)
61. Tim Anderson (SS, CHW)
62. Maikel Franco (3B, PHI)
63. Mike Foltynewicz (P, HOU)
64. Nick Kingham (P, PIT)
65. Eddie Butler (P, COL)
66. Steven Matz (P, NYM)
67. Domingo Santana (OF, HOU)
68. Aaron Judge (OF, NYY)
69. Daniel Robertson (SS, OAK)
70. Stephen Piscotty (OF, STL)
71. Kyle Freeland (P, COL)
72. Kevin Plawecki (C, NYM)
73. Lucas Sims (P, ATL)
74. Yasmany Tomas (OF, ARI)
75. Jose Peraza (2B, ATL)
76. Eduardo Rodriguez (P, BOS)
77. Max Fried (P, ATL)
78. Manuel Margot (OF, BOS)
79. Matt Olson (1B, OAK)
80. Ryan McMahon (3B, COL)
81. Alex Gonzalez (P, TEX)
82. Tyler Beede (P, SF)
83. Alen Hanson (SS, PIT)
84. Grant Holmes (P, LAD)
85. Aaron Blair (P, ARI)
86. Michael Taylor (OF, WAS)
87. Trea Turner (SS, SD/WAS)
88. Christian Bethancourt (C, ATL)
89. Marco Gonzales (P, STL)
90. Michael Conforto (OF, NYM)
91. Sean Newcomb (P, LAA)
92. Alex Colome (P, TAM)
93. Jeff Hoffman (P, TOR)
94. Luke Jackson (P, TEX)
95. Lewis Brinson (OF, TEX)
96. Willy Adames (SS, TAM)
97. Jake Thompson (P, TEX)
98. Nick Williams (OF, TEX)
99. Colin Moran (3B, HOU)
100. Bradley Zimmer (OF, CLE)

2014

1. Byron Buxton (OF, MIN)
2. Oscar Taveras (OF, STL)
3. Xander Bogaerts (SS, BOS)
4. Taijuan Walker (RHP, SEA)
5. Miguel Sano (3B, MIN)
6. Francisco Lindor (SS, CLE)
7. Javier Baez (SS, CHC)
8. Archie Bradley (RHP, ARI)
9. Carlos Correa (SS, HOU)
10. Gregory Polanco (OF, PIT)
11. Addison Russell (SS, OAK)
12. Jameson Taillon (RHP, PIT)
13. Kris Bryant (3B, CHC)
14. Dylan Bundy (RHP, BAL)
15. George Springer (OF, HOU)
16. Nick Castellanos (3B, DET)
17. Noah Syndergaard (RHP, NYM)
18. Kevin Gausman (RHP, BAL)
19. Carlos Martinez (RHP, STL)
20. Robert Stephenson (RHP, CIN)
21. Yordano Ventura (RHP, KC)
22. Jonathan Gray (RHP, COL)
23. Kyle Zimmer (RHP, KC)
24. Albert Almora (OF, CHC)
25. Mark Appel (RHP, HOU)
26. Aaron Sanchez (RHP, TOR)
27. Travis d'Arnaud (C, NYM)
28. Kyle Crick (RHP, SF)
29. Joc Pederson (OF, LA)
30. Alex Meyer (RHP, MIN)
31. Garin Cecchini (3B, BOS)
32. Jorge Soler (OF, CHC)
33. Jonathan Singleton (1B, HOU)
34. Maikel Franco (3B, PHI)
35. Lucas Giolito (RHP, WAS)
36. Eddie Butler (RHP, COL)
37. Andrew Heaney (LHP, MIA)
38. Jackie Bradley (OF, BOS)
39. Taylor Guerrieri (RHP, TAM)
40. Corey Seager (SS, LA)
41. Adalberto Mondesi (SS, KC)
42. Billy Hamilton (OF, CIN)
43. Clint Frazier (OF, CLE)
44. Tyler Glasnow (RHP, PIT)
45. Kolten Wong (2B, STL)
46. Henry Owens (LHP, BOS)
47. Gary Sanchez (C, NYY)
48. Jorge Alfaro (C, TEX)
49. Austin Meadows (OF, PIT)
50. Austin Hedges (C, SD)
51. Alen Hanson (SS, PIT)
52. Marcus Stroman (RHP, TOR)
53. Kohl Stewart (RHP, MIN)
54. Max Fried (LHP, SD)
55. Jake Odorizzi (RHP, TAM)
56. Michael Choice (OF, TEX)
57. C.J. Edwards (RHP, CHC)
58. Trevor Bauer (RHP, CLE)
59. Julio Urias (LHP, LA)
60. Jake Marisnick (OF, MIA)
61. Jesse Biddle (LHP, PHI)
62. Eddie Rosario (2B, MIN)
63. Lucas Sims (RHP, ATL)
64. Lance McCullers (RHP, HOU)
65. A.J. Cole (RHP, WAS)
66. Rougned Odor (2B, TEX)
67. Colin Moran (3B, MIA)
68. Mike Foltynewicz (RHP, HOU)
69. Allen Webster (RHP, BOS)
70. Chris Owings (SS, ARI)
71. Eduardo Rodriguez (LHP, BAL)
72. Miguel Almonte (RHP, KC)
73. Blake Swihart (C, BOS)
74. Jose Abreu (1B, CHW)
75. Zach Lee (RHP, LA)
76. Danny Hultzen (LHP, SEA)
77. Matt Wisler (RHP, SD)
78. Matt Barnes (RHP, BOS)
79. James Paxton (LHP, SEA)
80. Rosell Herrera (SS, COL)
81. Erik Johnson (RHP, CHW)
82. David Dahl (OF, COL)
83. Hak-Ju Lee (SS, TAM)
84. D.J. Peterson (3B, SEA)
85. Luke Jackson (RHP, TEX)
86. Delino DeShields (OF, HOU)
87. Brian Goodwin (OF, WAS)
88. Hunter Dozier (SS, KC)
89. Matt Davidson (3B, CHW)
90. Anthony Ranaudo (RHP, BOS)
91. Jimmy Nelson (RHP, MIL)
92. Bubba Starling (OF, KC)
93. Christian Bethancourt (C, ATL)
94. Courtney Hawkins (OF, CHW)
95. Domingo Santana (OF, HOU)
96. Kaleb Cowart (3B, LAA)
97. Jose Berrios (RHP, MIN)
98. Braden Shipley (RHP, ARI)
99. Justin Nicolino (LHP, MIA)
100. Alex Colome (RHP, TAM)

TOP 100 PROSPECTS ARCHIVE

2013

1. Jurickson Profar (SS, TEX)
2. Dylan Bundy (RHP, BAL)
3. Wil Myers (OF, TAM)
4. Gerrit Cole (RHP, PIT)
5. Oscar Taveras (OF, STL)
6. Taijuan Walker (RHP, SEA)
7. Trevor Bauer (RHP, CLE)
8. Jose Fernandez (RHP, MIA)
9. Travis d'Arnaud (C, NYM)
10. Miguel Sano (3B, MIN)

11. Zack Wheeler (RHP, NYM)
12. Christian Yelich (OF, MIA)
13. Tyler Skaggs (LHP, ARI)
14. Francisco Lindor (SS, CLE)
15. Javier Baez (SS, CHC)
16. Shelby Miller (RHP, STL)
17. Nick Castellanos (OF, DET)
18. Xander Bogaerts (SS, BOS)
19. Jameson Taillon (RHP, PIT)
20. Danny Hultzen (LHP, SEA)

21. Jonathan Singleton (1B, HOU)
22. Mike Zunino (C, SEA)
23. Billy Hamilton (OF, CIN)
24. Anthony Rendon (3B, WAS)
25. Mike Olt (3B, TEX)
26. Byron Buxton (OF, MIN)
27. Nolan Arenado (3B, COL)
28. Carlos Correa (SS, HOU)
29. Archie Bradley (RHP, ARI)
30. Julio Teheran (RHP, ATL)

31. Matt Barnes (RHP, BOS)
32. Gary Sanchez (C, NYY)
33. Jackie Bradley (OF, BOS)
34. Carlos Martinez (RHP, STL)
35. Bubba Starling (OF, KC)
36. Jake Odorizzi (RHP, TAM)
37. Jedd Gyorko (3B, SD)
38. Alen Hanson (SS, PIT)
39. George Springer (OF, HOU)
40. Nick Franklin (2B, SEA)

41. Aaron Sanchez (RHP, TOR)
42. Albert Almora (OF, CHC)
43. Kaleb Cowart (3B, LAA)
44. Taylor Guerrieri (RHP, TAM)
45. Kyle Zimmer (RHP, KC)
46. Noah Syndergaard (RHP, NYM)
47. Kolten Wong (2B, STL)
48. Tyler Austin (OF, NYY)
49. James Paxton (LHP, SEA)
50. Rymer Liriano (OF, SD)

51. Jake Marisnick (OF, MIA)
52. Trevor Story (SS, COL)
53. Kevin Gausman (RHP, BAL)
54. Trevor Rosenthal (RHP, STL)
55. Alex Meyer (RHP, MIN)
56. Jorge Soler (OF, CHC)
57. Matt Davidson (3B, ARI)
58. Brett Jackson (OF, CHC)
59. Michael Choice (OF, OAK)
60. David Dahl (OF, COL)

61. Mason Williams (OF, NYY)
62. Robert Stephenson (RHP, CIN)
63. Chris Archer (RHP, TAM)
64. Oswaldo Arcia (OF, MIN)
65. Zach Lee (RHP, LA)
66. Tony Cingrani (LHP, CIN)
67. Jesse Biddle (LHP, PHI)
68. Gregory Polanco (OF, PIT)
69. Addison Russell (SS, OAK)
70. Robbie Erlin (RHP, SD)

71. Courtney Hawkins (OF, CHW)
72. Brian Goodwin (OF, WAS)
73. Martin Perez (LHP, TEX)
74. Luis Heredia (RHP, PIT)
75. Yasiel Puig (OF, LA)
76. Wilmer Flores (3B, NYM)
77. Justin Nicolino (LHP, MIA)
78. Max Fried (LHP, SD)
79. Adam Eaton (OF, ARI)
80. Gary Brown (OF, SF)

81. Casey Kelly (RHP, SD)
82. Lucas Giolito (RHP, WAS)
83. Wily Peralta (RHP, MIL)
84. Michael Wacha (RHP, STL)
85. Austin Hedges (C, SD)
86. Kyle Gibson (RHP, MIN)
87. Hak-Ju Lee (SS, TAM)
88. Dan Straily (RHP, OAK)
89. Kyle Crick (RHP, SF)
90. Avisail Garcia (OF, DET)

91. Cody Buckel (RHP, TEX)
92. Tyler Thornburg (RHP, MIL)
93. Allen Webster (RHP, BOS)
94. Jarred Cosart (RHP, HOU)
95. Bruce Rondon (RHP, DET)
96. Delino DeShields (2B, HOU)
97. A.J. Cole (RHP, OAK)
98. Manny Banuelos (LHP, NYY)
99. Yordano Ventura (RHP, KC)
100. Trevor May (RHP, MIN)

2012

1. Bryce Harper (OF, WAS)
2. Matt Moore (LHP, TAM)
3. Mike Trout (OF, LAA)
4. Julio Teheran (RHP, ATL)
5. Jesus Montero (C, NYY)
6. Jurickson Profar (SS, TEX)
7. Manny Machado (SS, BAL)
8. Gerrit Cole (RHP, PIT)
9. Devin Mesoraco (C, CIN)
10. Wil Myers (OF, KC)

11. Miguel Sano (3B, MIN)
12. Jacob Turner (RHP, DET)
13. Anthony Rendon (3B, WAS)
14. Trevor Bauer (RHP, ARI)
15. Nolan Arenado (3B , COL)
16. Jameson Taillon (RHP, PIT)
17. Shelby Miller (RHP, STL)
18. Dylan Bundy (RHP, BAL)
19. Brett Jackson (OF, CHC)
20. Drew Pomeranz (LHP, COL)

21. Martin Perez (LHP, TEX)
22. Yonder Alonso (1B, SD)
23. Taijuan Walker (RHP, SEA)
24. Danny Hultzen (LHP, SEA)
25. Gary Brown (OF, SF)
26. Anthony Rizzo (1B, CHC)
27. Bubba Starling (OF, KC)
28. Travis d'Arnaud (C, TOR)
29. Mike Montgomery (LHP, KC)
30. Jake Odorizzi (RHP, KC)

31. Hak-Ju Lee (SS, TAM)
32. Jonathan Singleton (1B, HOU)
33. Garrett Richards (RHP, LAA)
34. Manny Banuelos (LHP, NYY)
35. James Paxton (LHP, SEA)
36. Jarrod Parker (RHP, OAK)
37. Carlos Martinez (RHP, STL)
38. Jake Marisnick (OF, TOR)
39. Yasmani Grandal (C, SD)
40. Trevor May (RHP, PHI)

41. Gary Sanchez (C, NYY)
42. Mike Olt (3B, TEX)
43. Wilin Rosario (C, COL)
44. John Lamb (LHP, KC)
45. Francisco Lindor (SS, CLE)
46. Dellin Betances (RHP, NYY)
47. Michael Choice (OF, OAK)
48. Arodys Vizcaino (RHP, ATL)
49. Trayvon Robinson (OF, SEA)
50. Matt Harvey (RHP, NYM)

51. Will Middlebrooks (3B, BOS)
52. Jedd Gyorko (3B, SD)
53. Randall Delgado (RHP, ATL)
54. Zack Wheeler (RHP, NYM)
55. Zach Lee (RHP, LA)
56. Tyler Skaggs (LHP, ARI)
57. Nick Castellanos (3B, DET)
58. Robbie Erlin (LHP, SD)
59. Christian Yelich (OF, MIA)
60. Anthony Gose (OF, TOR)

61. Addison Reed (RHP, CHW)
62. Javier Baez (SS, CHC)
63. Starling Marte (OF, PIT)
64. Kaleb Cowart (3B, LAA)
65. George Springer (OF, HOU)
66. Jarred Cosart (RHP, HOU)
67. Jean Segura (2B, LAA)
68. Kolten Wong (2B, STL)
69. Nick Franklin (SS, SEA)
70. Alex Torres (RHP, TAM)

71. Rymer Liriano (OF, SD)
72. Josh Bell (OF, PIT)
73. Leonys Martin (OF, TEX)
74. Joe Wieland (RHP, SD)
75. Joe Benson (OF, MIN)
76. Wily Peralta (RHP, MIL)
77. Tim Wheeler (OF, COL)
78. Oscar Taveras (OF, STL)
79. Xander Bogaerts (SS, BOS)
80. Archie Bradley (RHP, ARI)

81. Kyle Gibson (RHP, MIN)
82. Allen Webster (RHP, LA)
83. C.J. Cron (1B, LAA)
84. Grant Green (OF, OAK)
85. Brad Peacock (RHP, OAK)
86. Chris Dwyer (LHP, KC)
87. Billy Hamilton (SS, CIN)
88. A.J. Cole (RHP, OAK)
89. Aaron Hicks (OF, MIN)
90. Noah Syndergaard (RHP, TOR)

91. Tyrell Jenkins (RHP, STL)
92. Anthony Ranaudo (RHP, BOS)
93. Jed Bradley (LHP, MIL)
94. Nathan Eovaldi (RHP, LA)
95. Andrelton Simmons (SS, ATL)
96. Taylor Guerrieri (RHP, TAM)
97. Cheslor Cuthbert (3B, KC)
98. Edward Salcedo (3B, ATL)
99. Domingo Santana, OF, HOU)
100. Jesse Biddle (LHP, PHI)

AVG: Batting Average (see also BA)

BA: Batting Average (see also AVG)

Base Performance Indicator (BPI): A statistical formula that measures an isolated aspect of a player's situation-independent raw skill or a gauge that helps capture the effects of random chance has on a skill. Although there are many such formulas, there are only a few that we are referring to when the term is used in this book. For pitchers, our BPI's are control (bb%), dominance (k/9), command (k/bb), opposition on base average (OOB), ground/line/fly ratios (G/L/F), and expected ERA (xERA). Random chance is measured witih the hit rate (H%) and strand rate (S%).

*Base Performance Value (BPV): A single value that describes a pitcher's overall raw skill level. This is more useful than any traditional statistical gauge to track performance trends and project future statistical output. The BPV formula combines and weights several BPIs:

(Dominance Rate x 6) + (Command ratio x 21) – Opposition HR Rate x 30) – ((Opp. Batting Average - .275) x 200)

The formula combines the individual raw skills of power, command, the ability to keep batters from reaching base, and the ability to prevent long hits, all characteristics that are unaffected by most external team factors. In tandem with a pitcher's strand rate, it provides a complete picture of the elements that contribute to a pitcher's ERA, and therefore serves as an accurate tool to project likely changes in ERA. **BENCHMARKS:** We generally consider a BPV of 50 to be the minimum level required for long-term success. The elite of bullpen aces will have BPV's in the excess of 100 and it is rare for these stoppers to enjoy long-term success with consistent levels under 75.

Batters Faced per Game *(Craig Wright)*

((IP x 2.82) + H + BB) / G

A measure of pitcher usage and one of the leading indicators for potential pitcher burnout.

Batting Average (BA, or AVG)

(H/AB)

Ratio of hits to at-bats, though it is a poor evaluative measure of hitting performance. It neglects the offensive value of the base on balls and assumes that all hits are created equal.

Batting Eye (Eye)

(Walks / Strikeouts)

A measure of a player's strike zone judgment, the raw ability to distinguish between balls and strikes. **BENCHMARKS:** The best hitters have eye ratios over 1.00 (indicating more walks than strikeouts) and are the most likely to be among a league's .300 hitters. At the other end of the scale are ratios

less than 0.50, which represent batters who likely also have lower BAs.

bb%: Walk rate (hitters)

bb/9: Opposition Walks per 9 IP

BF/Gm: Batters Faced Per Game

BPI: Base Performance Indicator

*BPV: Base Performance Value

Cmd: Command ratio

Command Ratio (Cmd)

(Strikeouts / Walks)

This is a measure of a pitcher's raw ability to get the ball over the plate. There is no more fundamental a skill than this, and so it is accurately used as a leading indicator to project future rises and falls in other gauges, such as ERA. Command is one of the best gauges to use to evaluate minor league performance. It is a prime component of a pitcher's base performance value. **BENCHMARKS:** Baseball's upper echelon of command pitchers will have ratios in excess of 3.0. Pitchers with ratios under 1.0 — indicating that they walk more batters than they strike out — have virtually no potential for long term success. If you make no other changes in your approach to drafting a pitching staff, limiting your focus to only pitchers with a command ratio of 2.0 or better will substantially improve your odds of success.

Contact Rate (ct%)

((AB - K) / AB)

Measures a batter's ability to get wood on the ball and hit it into the field of play. **BENCHMARK:** Those batters with the best contact skill will have levels of 90% or better. The hackers of society will have levels of 75% or less.

Control Rate (bb/9), or Opposition Walks per Game

BB Allowed x 9 / IP

Measures how many walks a pitcher allows per game equivalent. **BENCHMARK:** The best pitchers will have bb/9 levels of 3.0 or less.

ct%: Contact rate

Ctl: Control Rate

Dom: Dominance Rate

Dominance Rate (k/9), or Opposition Strikeouts per Game

(K Allowed x 9 / IP)

Measures how many strikeouts a pitcher allows per game equivalent. **BENCHMARK:** The best pitchers will have k/9 levels of 6.0 or higher.

*Expected Earned Run Average (Gill and Reeve)

(.575 x H [per 9 IP]) + (.94 x HR [per 9 IP]) + (.28 x BB [per 9 IP]) - (.01 x K [per 9 IP]) - Normalizing Factor

"xERA represents the expected ERA of the pitcher based on a normal distribution of his statistics. It is not influenced by situation-dependent factors." xERA erases the inequity between starters' and relievers' ERA's, eliminating the effect that a pitcher's success or failure has on another pitcher's ERA.

Similar to other gauges, the accuracy of this formula changes with the level of competition from one season to the next. The normalizing factor allows us to better approximate a pitcher's actual ERA. This value is usually somewhere around 2.77 and varies by league and year. **BENCHMARKS:** In general, xERA's should approximate a pitcher's ERA fairly closely. However, those pitchers who have large variances between the two gauges are candidates for further analysis.

Extra-Base Hit Rate (X/H)

(2B + 3B + HR) / Hits

X/H is a measure of power and can be used along with a player's slugging percentage and isolated power to gauge a player's ability to drive the ball. **BENCHMARKS:** Players with above average power will post X/H of greater than 38% and players with moderate power will post X/H of 30% or greater. Weak hitters with below average power will have a X/H level of less than 20%.

Eye: Batting Eye

h%: Hit rate (batters)

H%: Hits Allowed per Balls in Play (pitchers)

Hit Rate (h% or H%)

(H—HR) / (AB – HR - K)

The percent of balls hit into the field of play that fall for hits.

hr/9: Opposition Home Runs per 9 IP

ISO: Isolated Power

Isolated Power (ISO)

(Slugging Percentage - Batting Average)

Isolated Power is a measurement of power skill. Subtracting a player's BA from his SLG, we are essentially pulling out all the singles and single bases from the formula. What remains are the extra-base hits. ISO is not an absolute measurement as it assumes that two doubles is worth one home run, which certainly is not the case, but is another statistic that is a good measurement of raw power. **BENCHMARKS:** The game's top sluggers will tend to have ISO levels over .200. Weak hitters will be under .100.

k/9: Dominance rate (opposition strikeouts per 9 IP)

Major League Equivalency (Bill James)

A formula that converts a player's minor or foreign league statistics into a comparable performance in the major leagues. These are not projections, but conversions of current performance.

Contains adjustments for the level of play in individual leagues and teams. Works best with Triple-A stats, not quite as well with Double-A stats, and hardly at all with the lower levels. Foreign conversions are still a work in process. James' original formula only addressed batting. Our research has devised conversion formulas for pitchers, however, their best use comes when looking at BPI's, not traditional stats.

MLE: Major League Equivalency

OBP: On Base Percentage (batters)

OBA: Opposition Batting Average (pitchers)

On Base Percentage (OBP)

(H + BB) / (AB + BB)

Addressing one of the two deficiencies in BA, OBP gives value to those events that get batters on base, but are not hits. By adding walks (and often, hit batsmen) into the basic batting average formula, we have a better gauge of a batter's ability to reach base safely. An OBP of .350 can be read as "this batter gets on base 35% of the time."

Why this is a more important gauge than batting average? When a run is scored, there is no distinction made as to how that runner reached base. So, two thirds of the time—about how often a batter comes to the plate with the bases empty—a walk really is as good as a hit. **BENCHMARKS:** We all know what a .300 hitter is, but what represents "good" for OBP? That comparable level would likely be .400, with .275 representing the level of futility.

On Base Plus Slugging Percentage (OPS): A simple sum of the two gauges, it is considered as one of the better evaluators of overall performance. OPS combines the two basic elements of offensive production — the ability to get on base (OBP) and the ability to advance baserunners (SLG). **BENCHMARKS:** The game's top batters will have OPS levels over .900. The worst batters will have levels under .600.

Opposition Batting Average (OBA)

(Hits Allowed / ((IP x 2.82) + Hits Allowed))

A close approximation of the batting average achieved by opposing batters against a particular pitcher. **BENCHMARKS:** The converse of the benchmark for batters, the best pitchers will have levels under .250; the worst pitchers levels over .300.

Opposition Home Runs per Game (hr/9)

(HR Allowed x 9 / IP)

Measures how many home runs a pitcher allows per game equivalent. **BENCHMARK:** The best pitchers will have hr/9 levels of under 1.0.

Opposition On Base Average (OOB)

(Hits Allowed + BB) / ((IP x 2.82) + H + BB)

A close approximation of the on base average achieved by opposing batters against a particular pitcher. **BENCHMARK:** The best pitchers will have levels under .300; the worst pitchers levels over .375.

Opposition Strikeouts per Game: See Dominance Rate.

Opposition Walks per Game: See Control Rate.

OPS: On Base Plus Slugging Percentage

RC: Runs Created

RC/G: Runs Created Per Game

Runs Created *(Bill James)*

(H + BB - CS) x (Total bases + (.55 x SB)) / (AB + BB)

A formula that converts all offensive events into a total of runs scored. As calculated for individual teams, the result approximates a club's actual run total with great accuracy.

Runs Created Per Game *(Bill James)*

Runs Created / ((AB - H + CS) / 25.5)

RC expressed on a per-game basis might be considered the hypothetical ERA compiled against a particular batter. **BENCHMARKS:** Few players surpass the level of a 10.00 RC/G in any given season, but any level over 7.50 can still be considered very good. At the bottom are levels below 3.00.

S%: Strand Rate

Save: There are six events that need to occur in order for a pitcher to post a single save...

1. The starting pitcher and middle relievers must pitch well.
2. The offense must score enough runs.
3. It must be a reasonably close game.
4. The manager must choose to put the pitcher in for a save opportunity.
5. The pitcher must pitch well and hold the lead.
6. The manager must let him finish the game.

Of these six events, only one is within the control of the relief pitcher. As such, projecting saves for a reliever has little to do with skill and a lot to do with opportunity. However, pitchers with excellent skills sets may create opportunity for themselves.

Situation Independent: Describing a statistical gauge that measures performance apart from the context of team, ballpark, or other outside variables. Strikeouts and Walks, inasmuch as they are unaffected by the performance of a batter's surrounding team, are considered situation independent stats.

Conversely, RBIs are situation dependent because individual performance varies greatly by the performance of other batters on the team (you can't drive in runs if there is nobody on base). Similarly, pitching wins are as much a measure of the success of a pitcher as they are a measure of the success of the offense and defense performing behind that pitcher, and are therefore a poor measure of pitching performance alone.

Situation independent gauges are important for us to be able to separate a player's contribution to his team and isolate his performance so that we may judge it on its own merits.

Slg: Slugging Percentage

Slugging Percentage (Slg)

(Singles + (2 x Doubles) + (3 x Triples) + (4 x HR)) / AB

A measure of the total number of bases accumulated per at bat. It is a misnomer; it is not a true measure of a batter's slugging ability because it includes singles. SLG also assumes that each type of hit has proportionately increasing value (i.e. a double is twice as valuable as a single, etc.) which is not true. **BENCHMARKS:** The top batters will have levels over .500. The bottom batters will have levels under .300.

Strand Rate (S%)

(H + BB - ER) / (H + BB - HR)

Measures the percentage of allowed runners a pitcher strands, which incorporates both individual pitcher skill and bullpen effectiveness. **BENCHMARKS:** The most adept at stranding runners will have S% levels over 75%. Once a pitcher's S% starts dropping down below 65%, he's going to have problems with his ERA. Those pitchers with strand rates over 80% will have artificially low ERAs, which will be prone to relapse.

Strikeouts per Game: See Opposition Strikeouts per game.

Walks + Hits per Innings Pitched (WHIP): The number of baserunners a pitcher allows per inning. **BENCHMARKS:** Usually, a WHIP of under 1.20 is considered top level and over 1.50 is indicative of poor performance. Levels under 1.00 — allowing fewer runners than IP — represent extraordinary performance and are rarely maintained over time.

Walk rate (bb%)

(BB / (AB + BB))

A measure of a batter's eye and plate patience. **BENCHMARKS:** The best batters will have levels of over 10%. Those with the least plate patience will have levels of 5% or less.

Walks per Game: See Opposition Walks per Game.

WHIP: Walks + Hits per Innings Pitched

Wins: There are five events that need to occur in order for a pitcher to post a single win...

1. He must pitch well, allowing few runs.
2. The offense must score enough runs.
3. The defense must successfully field all batted balls.
4. The bullpen must hold the lead.
5. The manager must leave the pitcher in for 5 innings, and not remove him if the team is still behind.

X/H: Extra-base Hit Rate

*xERA: Expected ERA

* Asterisked formulas have updated versions in the Baseball Forecaster. *However, those updates include statistics like Ground Ball Rate, Fly Ball Rate or Line Drive Rate, for which we do not have reliable data for minor leaguers. So we use the previous version of those formulas, as listed here, for the players in this book.*

Spring Training just got better.

Introducing...

Join us in St. Petersburg, Florida from **February 28 through March 1, 2020** for two and a half days filled with baseball chatter and events, all aimed at preparing you for the 2020 season!

Modeled after our wildly popular First Pitch Arizona event, First Pitch Florida will feature:

- Interactive sessions on topics like player analysis, breakout picks and injury warning signs
- Gaming strategies for auctions and drafts, including current ADP feedback
- Live drafts where you can complete against your peers
- Tickets to two spring training games—with a group of the friendliest, most passionate fantasy baseball fans around—just like you!

In addition, First Pitch Florida welcomes the granddaddy of expert leagues, USA TODAY's League of Alternative Baseball Reality (LABR)! Attendees will be able to take in both 12-team AL and 12-team NL auctions live and we'll break 'em down afterwards!

Details about specific panels, speakers, program schedule, Grapefruit League games and more will be updated throughout the next several months at the link below. Register NOW!

www.baseballhq.com/first-pitch-florida

*Save the date: **First Pitch Arizona** in Phoenix at the Arizona Fall League • October 8-11, 2020*

Bedtime Without ARTHUR

Jessica Meserve

ANDERSEN PRESS USA

Bella has a bear.
A very special bear called Arthur.

He is as brave as a knight.
He is as strong as ten elephants.

And he does karate.

When Bella sleeps,

Arthur
is
BUSY.

He guards the bed and keeps
away monsters that come

sneaking from the shadows.

Safe in her bed,
Bella dreams
of her favorite things,
like rainbows
and rainforests.

One morning, Arthur was worn out from so much karate.

Bella made him his favorite breakfast of toast and honey, and then tucked him up snug in bed.

That evening, when the
moon had risen full and
white, Bella went to her
room to give
Arthur a slice of
pizza for supper.

Bella pulled
back the quilt
and...

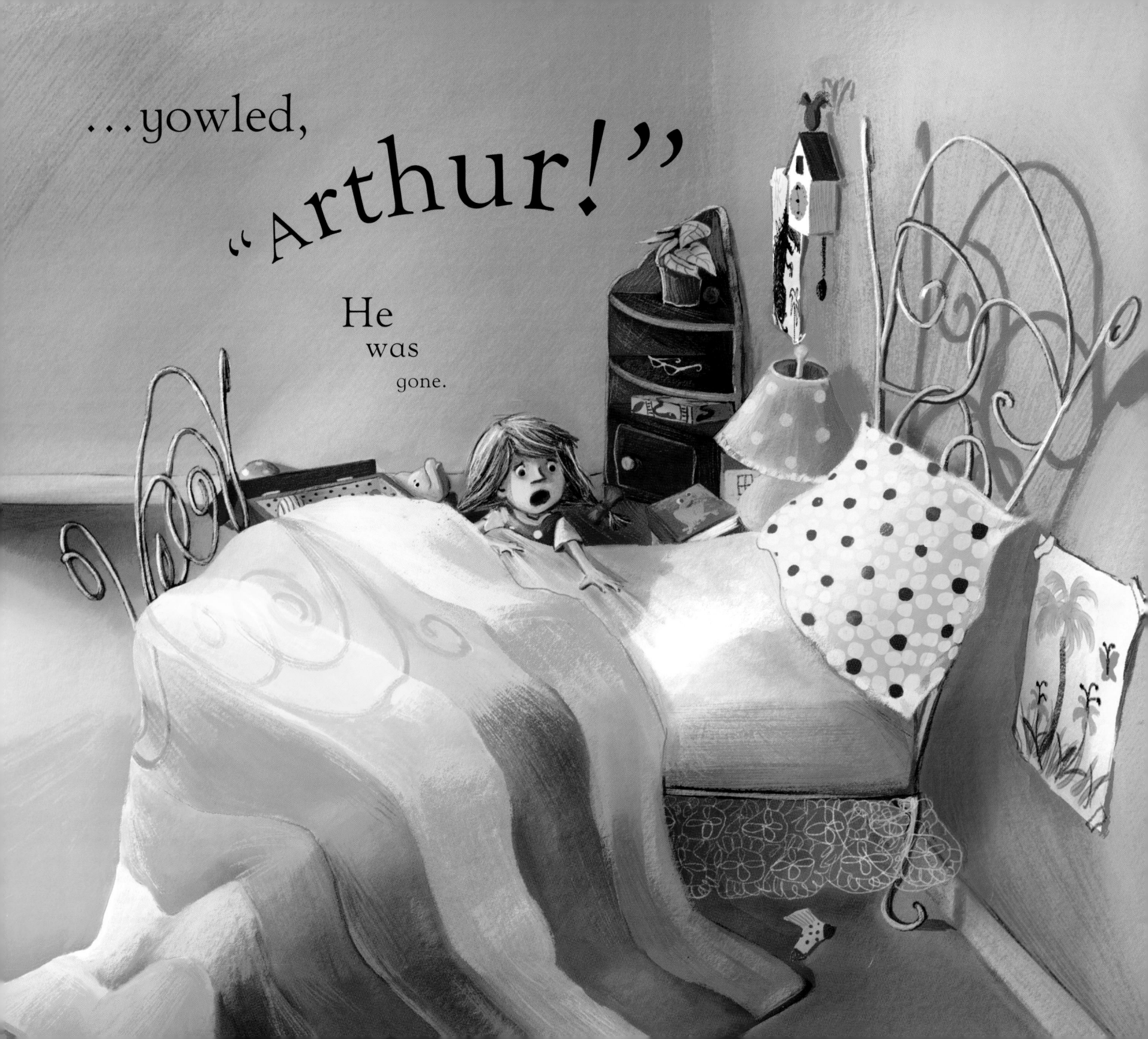

...yowled,

"Arthur!"

He
was
gone.

Bella searched

and searched.

Bella's mom looked upstairs.
Bella's dad looked downstairs.
Bella's brother, Finley,
looked worried.

None of them could find Arthur
ANYWHERE.

Mom said, "We'll find him tomorrow."

Dad said, "He'll turn up."

Finley said, "Sorry."

But Bella didn't believe them.
Her lip trembled as she
climbed into bed.

Bella couldn't sleep.
She was sure there were
MONSTERS
watching and waiting.

Bella squeezed her eyes shut tight.
She fell asleep dreaming of

FIRE-BREATHING DRAGONS,
SLUGS
and grizzly bears.

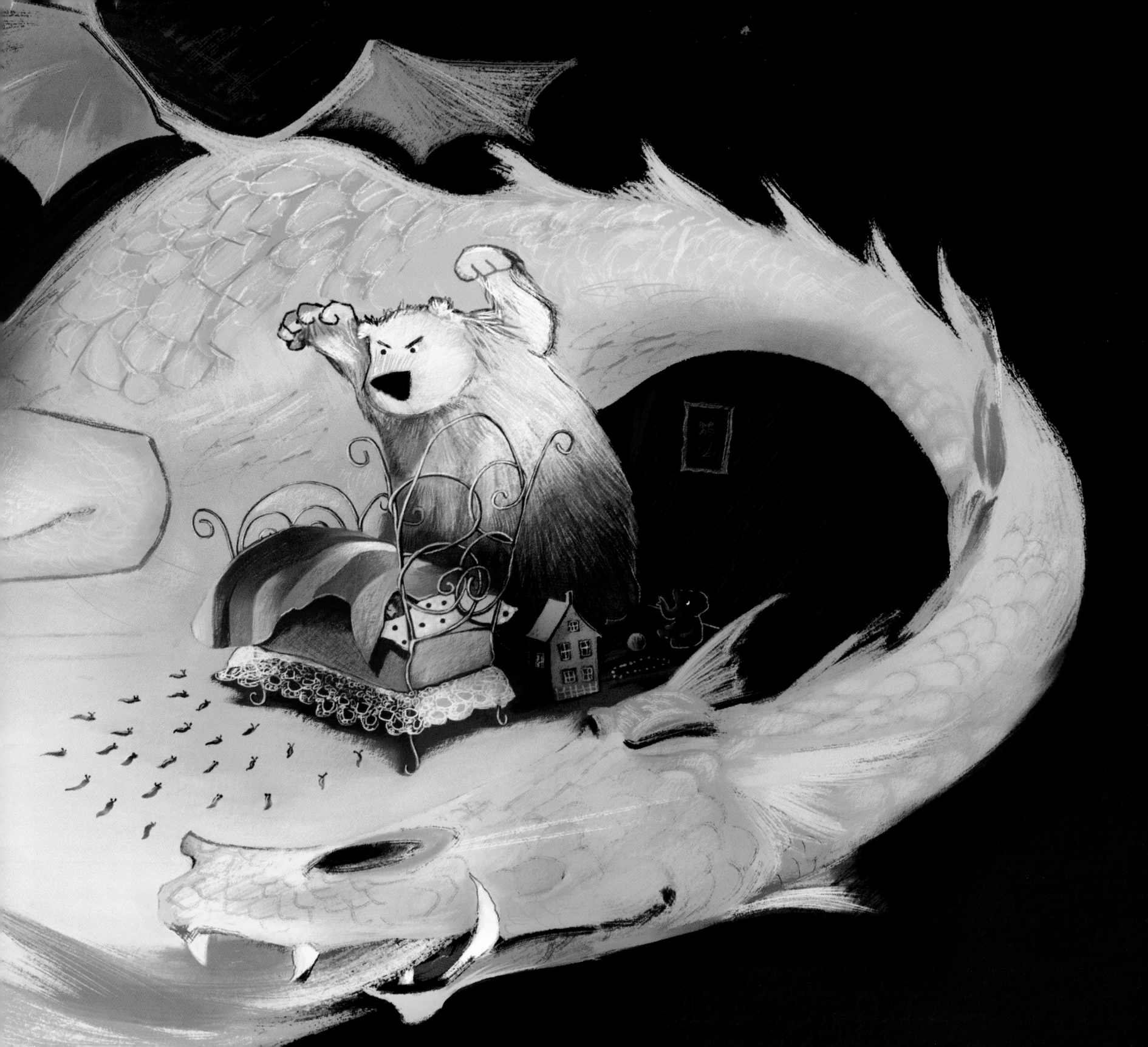

In the morning, Bella was exhausted.

She couldn't juggle.

Even the ice cream didn't cheer her up.

And at bedtime there
was still
no sign
of Arthur.

The wind began to

blow and howl.

Bella woke with a start.

She saw things
looming and
scratching at
the window.

Bella leapt out of bed and ran as fast
as she could across the hallway
into her brother's room.

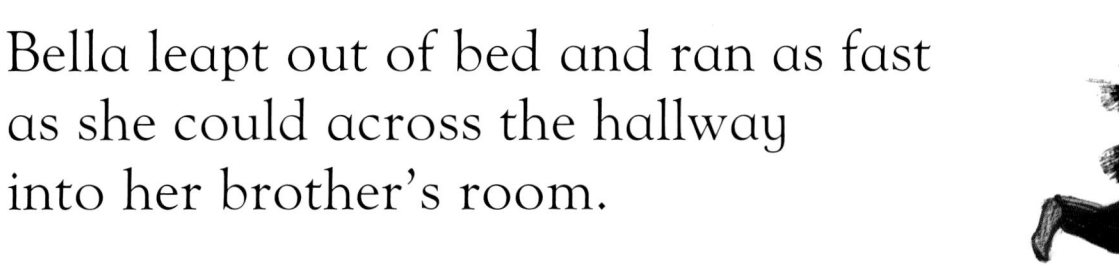

Finley was sound asleep.
Bella began climbing
into his crib.

Peeking from under the blanket, she
saw the tip of a soft, furry nose.

It was Arthur!

Bella was **so** happy to see him . . .

. . . but she was
very angry with her
brother for taking him.

She grabbed Arthur and started back to her room.

Bella realized that Finley needed
Arthur more than she did. Finley
wasn't nearly as strong and brave
as she was.

Bella took Arthur back to
Finley and tucked them
both up in bed.
"Don't be scared, Finley. Arthur
will look after you."

Bella felt braver and
braver with each
step she took back
to her room.

When at last she climbed into bed, Bella felt as brave as a knight. All the monsters shook with fear and fizzled into nothing.

That night Bella slept long and deep and dreamed of all her favorite things.